Frommer's®

Nova Scotia, New Brunswick & Prince Edward Island

With Newfoundland & Labrador

Here's what the critics say about Frommer's:

"Amazingly easy to use. Very portable, very complete."
—*Booklist*

♦

"The only mainstream guide to list specific prices. The Walter Cronkite of guidebooks—with all that implies."
—*Travel & Leisure*

♦

"Complete, concise, and filled with useful information."
—*New York Daily News*

♦

"Hotel information is close to encyclopedic."
—*Des Moines Sunday Register*

♦

"Detailed, accurate and easy to read information for all price ranges."
—*Glamour Magazine*

Other Great Guides for Your Trip:

Frommer's Canada

Frommer's Montréal & Quebec City

Frommer's Vancouver & Victoria

Nova Scotia, New Brunswick & Prince Edward Island

with Newfoundland & Labrador

by Wayne Curtis

IDG Books Worldwide, Inc.
An International Data Group Company
Foster City, CA • Chicago, IL • Indianapolis, IN • New York, NY

ABOUT THE AUTHOR

Wayne Curtis is a freelance writer whose articles have appeared in the *New York Times, House Beautiful, Aqua, Yankee,* and on Discovery Channel Online. He has contributed chapters to the Discovery Channel/Insight Guides series on outdoor adventure, and is the author of *Frommer's Vermont, New Hampshire & Maine* and a co-author of *Frommer's Canada* and *Frommer's New England.* He lives most of the year in eastern Maine, but spends the summer months in a 1985 Volkswagen camper exploring back roads in New England and Atlantic Canada.

IDG BOOKS WORLDWIDE, INC.

An International Data Group Company
919 E. Hillsdale Blvd.
Suite 400
Foster City, CA 94404

Find us online at **www.frommers.com**

ISBN 0-02-863508-6
ISSN 1087-3554

Editor: Margot Weiss
Production Editor: Donna Wright
Design by Michele Laseau
Staff Cartographers: John Decamillis, Roberta Stockwell
Front Cover Photo: Peggy's Cove Lighthouse
Page Creation by Natalie Evans, Angel Perez, Julie Trippetti

SPECIAL SALES

For general information on IDG Books Worldwide's books in the U.S., please call our Consumer Customer Service department at 1-800-762-2974. For reseller information, including discounts, bulk sales, customized editions, and premium sales, please call our Reseller Customer Service department at 1-800-434-3422.

Manufactured in the United States of America

5   4   3   2   1

Contents

List of Maps

AN INVITATION TO THE READER

In researching this book, we discovered many wonderful places—hotels, restaurants, shops, and more. We're sure you'll find others. Please tell us about them, so we can share the information with your fellow travelers in upcoming editions. If you were disappointed with a recommendation, we'd love to know that, too. Please write to:

Frommer's Nova Scotia, New Brunswick & Prince Edward Island, 3rd Edition
IDG Travel
1633 Broadway
New York, NY 10019

AN ADDITIONAL NOTE

Please be advised that travel information is subject to change at any time—and this is especially true of prices. We therefore suggest that you write or call ahead for confirmation when making your travel plans. The author, editors, and publisher cannot be held responsible for the experiences of readers while traveling. Your safety is important to us, however, so we encourage you to stay alert and be aware of your surroundings. Keep a close eye on cameras, purses, and wallets, all favorite targets of thieves and pickpockets.

WHAT THE SYMBOLS MEAN

✪ **Frommer's Favorites**

Our favorite places and experiences—outstanding for quality, value, or both.

The following abbreviations are used for credit cards:

AE	American Express	EURO	Eurocard
CB	Carte Blanche	JCB	Japan Credit Bank
DC	Diners Club	MC	MasterCard
DISC	Discover	V	Visa
ER	EnRoute		

FIND FROMMER'S ONLINE

www.frommers.com offers up-to-the-minute listings on almost 200 cities around the globe—including the latest bargains and candid, personal articles updated daily by Arthur Frommer himself. No other Web site offers such comprehensive and timely coverage of the world of travel.

The Best of the Atlantic Provinces

Planning a trip to Atlantic Canada can present a bewildering array of choices. I've searched Nova Scotia, New Brunswick, Prince Edward Island, and Newfoundland and Labrador for the best places and experiences. Here are some of my personal and opinionated top choices.

1 The Best Active Vacations

- **Sea Kayaking** (Nova Scotia): The twisting, convoluted coastline of this province is custom-made for snooping around by sea kayak. Outfitters are scattered all around the peninsula. For expedition kayaking, contact Coastal Adventures, which leads trips throughout Nova Scotia and beyond. For more easy-going exploration, try Mahone Bay Kayak Adventures southwest of Halifax. See chapter 3.
- **Biking the Cabot Trail** (Nova Scotia): This long and strenuous loop around Cape Breton Highlands National Park is tough on the legs, but you'll come away with a head full of indelible memories. See chapter 3.
- **Exploring Fundy National Park & Vicinity** (New Brunswick): You'll find swimming, hiking, and kayaking at this lovely national park. And don't overlook biking in the hills east of the park, or rappelling and rock climbing at Cape Enrage. See chapter 4.
- **Bicycling Prince Edward Island:** This island province sometimes seems like it was created specifically for bike touring. Villages are reasonably spaced, the hills virtually nonexistent, coastal roads picturesque in the extreme, and a new island-wide bike path offers detours through marshes and quiet woodlands. See chapter 5.
- **Hiking Gros Morne National Park** (Newfoundland): Atlantic Canada's best hiking is found in these rugged hills. You can hike amazing coastal trails, marvel at scenic waterfalls, and stroll alongside landlocked fjords at this exceptional park. See chapter 6.

2 The Best Spots for Observing Nature

- **Digby Neck** (Nova Scotia): Choose from a dozen whale-watch outfitters located along this narrow peninsula of remote fishing villages. Getting to the tip of the peninsula is half the fun—it requires two ferries. See chapter 3.

- **Cape Breton Highlands National Park** (Nova Scotia): The craggy geology of the west coast is impressive, but don't let that overshadow the rest of the park, where you'll find bogs and moose in abundance. See chapter 3.
- **Grand Manan Island** (New Brunswick): This big, geologically intriguing rock off the New Brunswick coast in the western Bay of Fundy is a great base for learning about coastal ecology. Whale tour operators search out the endangered right whale, and dozens of birds roost and pass through. Boat tours from the island will also take you out to see puffins. See chapter 4.
- **Hopewell Rocks** (New Brunswick): The force of Fundy's tremendous tides is the most impressive at Hopewell Rocks, where great rock "sculptures" created by the winds and tides rise from the ocean floor at high tide. See chapter 4.
- **Avalon Peninsula** (Newfoundland): In one busy day you can view a herd of caribou, the largest puffin colony in North America, and an extraordinary gannet colony visible from the mainland cliffs. See chapter 6.

3 The Best Scenic Drives

- **Cape Breton's Cabot Trail** (Nova Scotia): This 280-kilometer (175-mile) loop through the uplands of Cape Breton Highlands National Park is one of the world's great excursions. You'll see Acadian fishing ports, pristine valleys, and some of the most picturesque coastline anywhere. See chapter 3.
- **Along Cobequid Bay** (Nova Scotia): When it comes to scenery, Cobequid Bay (near Truro) is one of the region's better kept secrets. The bay is flanked by two roads: Route 2 runs from Parrsboro to Truro; Route 215 from South Maitland to Brooklyn. Take the time to savor it. See chapter 3.
- **Fundy Trail Parkway** (New Brunswick): East of Saint John, you'll find this 11km parkway winding along the contours of the coast. Get out and stretch your legs at any of the 22 lookouts along the way for fantastic cliffside views. Or if the tides are out, clamber down to one of the stretches of sand nestled between the rocks. See chapter 4.
- **Prince Edward Island National Park:** Much of the north-central shore of PEI is part of the national park, and a quiet park road tracks along the henna-tinted cliffs and grass-covered dunes. There's no single road, but several shorter segments; all are worth a leisurely drive, with frequent stops to explore the beaches and walkways. See chapter 5.
- **Viking Trail** (Newfoundland): Travelers looking to leave the crowds behind needn't look any further. This beautiful drive to Newfoundland's northern tip is wild and solitary, with views of bizarre geology and a wind-raked coast. And you'll end up at one of the world's great historic sites—L'Anse aux Meadows. See chapter 6.

4 The Best Hikes & Rambles

- **Point Pleasant Park** (Nova Scotia): Overlooking the entrance to Halifax's harbor, Point Pleasant Park is a wonderful urban oasis, with wide trails for strolling along the water. You can also crest a wooded rise and visit a stout Martello Tower. See chapter 3.

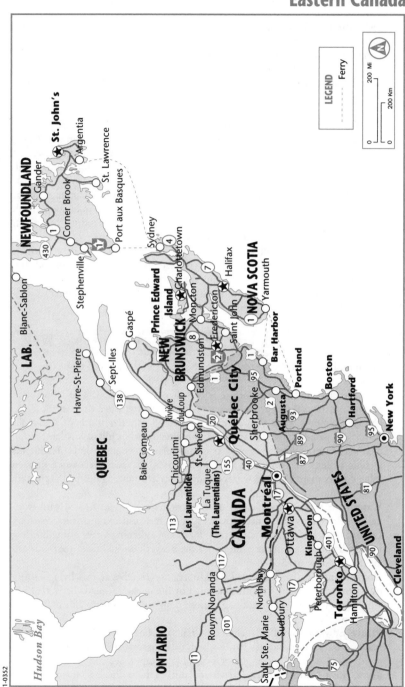

- **Cape Breton Highlands National Park** (Nova Scotia): You'll find bog and woodland walks aplenty at Cape Breton, but the best trails follow rugged cliffs along the open ocean. The Skyline Trail is among the most dramatic pathways in the province. See chapter 3.
- **Grand Manan Island** (New Brunswick): Grand Manan is laced with informal walking trails, through forest and along the ocean's edge. This is a place for exploring; ask around locally for suggestions on the best hikes. See chapter 4.
- **The Confederation Trail** (Prince Edward Island): This 350-kilometer (215-mile) pathway across the island is still being pieced together. But you can already explore 225 kilometers (140 miles) along the old rail line that once stitched the province together. It's best for long-distance biking but superb for a quiet stroll. See chapter 5.
- **Green Gardens Trail** (Gros Morne, Newfoundland): This demanding hike at Gros Morne National Park takes hikers on a 16-kilometer (9.6-mile) loop, much of which follows coastal meadows atop fractured cliffs. Demanding, but worth every step of the way. See chapter 6.
- **North Head Trail** (St John's, Newfoundland): You can walk from downtown St. John's along the harbor, pass through the picturesque Battery neighborhood, and then climb the open bluffs overlooking the Narrows with views out to the open ocean beyond. And where else can you hike from downtown shopping to cliff-side whale watching? See chapter 6.

5 The Best Family Activities

- **Fossil and Mineral Prospecting** (Nova Scotia): On the Bay of Fundy, Parrsboro is a fossil- and mineral-collector's Mecca. You needn't be an expert—a fine, accessible museum and helpful local guides will get you started. The terrain and scenery are the real draw; any finds are icing on the cake. See chapter 3.
- **Upper Clements Park** (Nova Scotia): About 5 minutes south of Annapolis Royal, this wonderfully old-fashioned amusement park is full of low-key amusements and attractions that will especially delight younger kids. Highlights include a flume ride (originally built for Expo '86 in Vancouver) and a wooden roller coaster that twists and winds through trees left standing during the coaster's construction. See chapter 3.
- **Waterfront Walk** (Nova Scotia): Halifax's waterfront walk is filled with wonderful distractions, from the province's finest museum to ships for exploring. Look also for buskers, delightful junk food, and sweeping views of the bustling harbor. If you're here in early August for the Busker Festival, it's all your kids will talk about for years. See chapter 3.
- **King's Landing** (New Brunswick). History comes alive at this living history museum, where young kids are fascinated by life in early Canada between 1790 and 1910. Ask about the weeklong sessions designed to immerse kids in the past. See chapter 4.
- **Prince Edward Island's Beaches:** The red-sand beaches will turn white swim trunks a bit pinkish, but it's hard to beat a day or three splashing around these tepid waters while admiring pastoral island landscapes. See chapter 5.
- **Terra Nova National Park** (Newfoundland): This is the less noted of Newfoundland's two national parks, but the staff has gone the extra mile to make it kid friendly. There's a marine interpretive center with activities for kids, boat tours, hikes just the right length for shorter legs, and campground activities at night. See chapter 6.

6 The Best Places for History

- **Annapolis Royal** (Nova Scotia): The cradle of Canadian civilization is found in this broad green valley, where early French settlers first put down roots. Visit Fort Anne and Port Royal, and walk some of the first streets on the continent. See chapter 3.
- **Maritime Museum of the Atlantic** (Nova Scotia): Nova Scotia's history is the history of the sea, and no place better depicts that vibrant tradition than the sprawling Maritime Museum on Halifax's waterfront. See chapter 3.
- **Louisbourg** (Nova Scotia): This early 18th-century fort and village was part of an elaborate French effort to establish a foothold in the New World. It failed, and the village ultimately fell to ruin. In the 1960s, the Canadian government reconstructed much of it, and now it's one of the most impressive historic sites in the nation. See chapter 3.
- **Village Historique Acadien** (New Brunswick): Around 45 buildings—with the number growing—depict life as it was lived in an Acadian settlement between 1770 and 1890. You'll learn all about the exodus and settlement of the Acadians from costumed guides, who are also adept at skills ranging from letterpress printing to blacksmithing. See chapter 4.
- **Province House National Historic Site** (Prince Edward Island): Canadian history took shape in Charlottetown in 1864, when the idea of joining Britain's North American colonies into an independent confederation was first discussed. Learn about what transpired at this imposing Charlottetown edifice, which has been restored to appear as it did when history was made. See Chapter 5.
- **Bonavista Peninsula** (Newfoundland): Newfoundland might seem like the edge of the earth today, but in past centuries it was the crossroads of European culture as nations scrapped over fishing rights and settlements. You can learn a lot about how the old world viewed the new during a few days exploring this intriguing peninsula. Base yourself in the perfectly preserved village of Trinity, and spend at least a day exploring up to the town of Bonavista, where you can visit the Ryan's Premises National Historic Site and learn why cod was god. See chapter 6.
- **L'Anse aux Meadows National Historic Site** (Newfoundland): This dramatic site on Newfoundland's northern tip celebrates its 1,000th anniversary in 2000—it's been a millennium since the Vikings first landed here and established an encampment. View the intriguing ruins, enter the re-created sod huts, and hear theories about why the colony failed from knowledgeable interpreters. See chapter 6.

7 The Best Picturesque Villages

- **Lunenburg** (Nova Scotia): Settled by German, Swiss, and French colonists, this tidy town not only has a superb location on a hill flanked by two harbors, but boasts some of the most unique and quietly extravagant architecture in the Maritimes. See chapter 3.
- **Victoria** (Prince Edward Island): This wee village west of Charlottetown is surrounded by fields of grain and potatoes, and hasn't changed much in the last 100 years. Try to time your visit to take in an evening show at the town's wonderfully old-fashioned theater. See chapter 5.
- **Trinity** (Newfoundland): Three centuries ago, Trinity was among the most important ports in the new world, when English merchants controlled the flow of goods in and out of the new world. This compact village has also been among

the most aggressive in preserving its past, and the architecture and perfect scale of the village is unmatched in Atlantic Canada. See chapter 6.

- **Twillingate** (Newfoundland): This end-of-the-world village on Newfoundland's north-central shore is located on and around the convoluted harbors and inlets. At the mouth of the harbor, high headlands mark the way for incoming ships; walk out here and scan the watery horizon for whales and icebergs. See chapter 6.

8 The Best Inns

- **Haddon Hall** (Chester, NS; ☎ 902/275-3577): Perched atop an open hill with panoramic views of island-studded Mahone Bay, Haddon Hall's main building dates to 1905. You'll find three rooms in the main house and six others in cottages scattered around the estate. Enjoy dinner on the open porch overlooking the bay. See chapter 3.
- **Gowrie House** (Sydney Mines, NS; ☎ 800/372-1115 or 902/736-0077): The exquisitely decorated Gowrie House is at once resplendent and comfortable, historic and very up-to-date. The smallest guest rooms are more spacious than larger rooms at many other inns. See chapter 3.
- **Kingsbrae Arms** (St. Andrews, NB, ☎ 506/529-1897): This five-star inn manages the trick of being opulent and comfortable at the same time. This shingled manse is lavishly appointed, beautifully landscaped, and well situated for exploring charming St. Andrews. See Chapter 4.
- **Inn at Bay Fortune** (Bay Fortune, PEI; ☎ 902/687-3745, off-season 860/296-1348): This exceptionally attractive shingled compound was most recently owned by actress Colleen Dewhurst, and current innkeeper David Wilmer pulled out all the stops for his renovations. But the real draw here is the dining room, which is noted for the farm-fresh ingredients grown in the extensive gardens on the property. See chapter 5.

9 The Best Bed & Breakfasts

- **Duffus House Inn** (Baddeck, NS; ☎ 902/295-2172 or 902/928-2678): A visit to the Duffus House is like a visit to the grandmother's house everyone wished they had. The inn's two adjacent buildings (constructed in 1820 and 1885) overlook Baddeck's channel and are cozy and tastefully furnished with a well-chosen mix of antiques. See chapter 3.
- **The Manse** (Mahone Bay, NS; ☎ 902/624-1121): There's not a bad room in this four-guest room establishment, built in 1870 and situated on a low hill in the picturesque village of Mahone Bay. Spend the day browsing local shops, and retreat in the evening to the casual luxury of this top-rate lodge. See chapter 3.
- **Shipwright Inn** (Charlottetown, PEI; ☎ 902/368-1905): This in-town, seven-room B&B is within easy walking distance of all the city's attractions yet has a settled and pastoral feel. It's informed by a Victorian sensibility without being over-the-top about it. See chapter 5.
- **Tickle Inn at Cape Onion** (Cape Onion, NF; ☎ 709/452-4321 June–Sept or 709/739-5503 Oct–May): Tickle Inn serves a family-style dinner each night so technically, it isn't a B&B at all, but this tiny and remote home has the cordial bonhomie of a well-run bed and breakfast. Set on a distant cove at the end of a road near Newfoundland's northernmost point (you can see Labrador across the

straits), the Tickle Inn offers a perfect base for visiting L'Anse aux Meadows and walking on the lonesome, windy hills. See chapter 6.

• **At Wit's Inn** (St. John's, NF; ☎ **877/739-7420** or 709/739-742): This centrally located B&B is bright, cheerful, and whimsical. Opened in 1999 by a restaurateur from Toronto, the inn has managed to preserve the best of the historical elements in this century old-home while graciously updating it for modern tastes. See chapter 6.

10 The Best Local Dining

• **Digby Scallops** (Nova Scotia): The productive scallop fleet based in Digby, on Nova Scotia's Bay of Fundy coast, hauls back some of the choicest, most succulent scallops in the world. Sample the fare at local restaurants, or cook up a batch on your own. Simple is better: a light sauté in butter brings out their rich flavor. See chapter 3.

• **Rappie Pie** (Nova Scotia): When traveling between Digby and Yarmouth, watch for shops selling rappie pie—a local Acadian treat made from potatoes plus meat or seafood. See chapter 3.

• **Fresh Lobster** (Nova Scotia and New Brunswick): Wherever you see the wooden lobster traps piled on a wharf, you'll know a fresh lobster meal isn't far away. Among the most productive lobster fisheries are around Shediac, New Brunswick, and all along Nova Scotia's Atlantic coast. Sunny days are ideal for cracking open a crustacean while sitting at a wharfside picnic table, preferably with a locally brewed beer close at hand. See chapters 3 and 4.

• **Prince Edward Island Mussels:** PEI has long been known for its wonderful potatoes, but the farmed mussels do more to thrill the taste buds. You'll see the lines of mussel buoys in inlets and harbors. Order up a mess at an island restaurant to share with your whole table.

• **Newfoundland Berries:** The unforgivingly rocky and boggy soil of this blustery island resists most crops, but produces some of the most delicious berries you can imagine. Look for roadside stands in midsummer, or pick your own blueberries, strawberries, partridgeberries or bakeapples. Many restaurants add berries (on cheesecake, in custard) when they're in season. See chapter 6.

2

Planning a Trip to the Atlantic Provinces

Reading this chapter before you set out can save you money, time, and headaches. Here's where you'll find travel know-how: when to come, the documentation you'll need, and where to get more information. These basics can make the difference between a smooth trip and a bumpy one.

1 Visitor Information

VISITOR INFORMATION It's well worth a toll-free call or postcard in advance of your trip to stock up on the free literature and maps that provincial authorities liberally bestow upon those considering a vacation in their province.

- **Nova Scotia Dept. of Tourism,** P.O. Box 130, Halifax, NS B3J 2M7. ☎ **800/565-0000** in North America; 902/425-5781 outside North America. E-mail nsvisit@fox.nstn.ns.ca.
- **Tourism New Brunswick,** P.O. Box 12345, Fredericton, NB E7M 5C3. ☎ **800/561-0123.** E-mail nbtourism@gov.nb.ca.
- **Tourism PEI,** P.O. Box 940, Charlottetown, PEI C1A 7M5. ☎ **888/734-7529** or 902/368-4444. E-mail tourpei@gov.pe.ca.
- **Newfoundland and Labrador Dept. of Tourism, Culture, & Recreation,** P.O. Box 8730, St. John's, NF A1B 4K2. ☎ **800/563-6353** or 709/729-2830. E-mail info@tourism.gov.nf.ca.

INFORMATION CENTERS All four provinces staff helpful visitor centers at key access points, including the main roadways into the provinces and the major cities. The best-run centers are in Nova Scotia and Prince Edward Island, and have a cordial staff and exceptionally well-stocked brochure racks overflowing with maps, menus, and booklets. These centers provide a surplus of information on local attractions but can also fill you in on what's happening anywhere in the province so you can plan a few days in advance. If the staffers don't have the information you need at their fingertips, they'll make phone calls and track it down for you. New Brunswick's information centers are also helpful, though not as numerous. Newfoundland's visitor centers—with the exception of the modern information centers near the two main ferry terminals—are typically less polished and sophisticated than in the other provinces, but the authorities have been successful in making improvements over the past couple of years. Look in the regional chapters of this guide for addresses and phone numbers of the main visitor centers in each area.

All four provinces publish free, magazine-sized travel guides crammed with routine but often essential information on hotels, inns, campgrounds, and attractions. Nova Scotia's "Doers and Dreamers" guide sets an international standard for high quality information, but the others are all excellent and unfailingly helpful. If you haven't obtained a guide in advance by mail, be sure to request them at the first center you come to when entering a province.

INTERNET RESOURCES   Information on the Web is growing at an explosive rate, with some of the data more reliable than others. Here are a few places to start your search:

- **Nova Scotia:** A tour of "Virtual Nova Scotia," presented by Nova Scotia Economic Development and Tourism, can be found at explore.gov.ns.ca.
- **Nova Scotia Provincial Parks:** The province's Web site provides basic, up-to-date information about the many excellent parks at parks.gov.ns.ca.
- **New Brunswick:** The official tourism site offers a good place to start: www.tourismnbcanada.com.
- **Prince Edward Island:** The official PEI online information center is www.gov.pe.ca/vg/index.asp.
- **Newfoundland & Labrador:** The official Web site is public.gov.nf.ca/tourism.
- **National Parks:** For information about travels in the region's national parks, a good first stop is the Parks Canada official Web site at parkscanada.pch.gc.ca.
- **Outdoor adventures:** The Canadian Recreational Canoeing Association's Web site provides a selection of links to various outfitters based in Atlantic Canada. Look for them at www.crca.ca/links.html.

2 Entry Requirements & Customs

ENTRY REQUIREMENTS   U.S. citizens or permanent residents of the United States, as well as British, Australian, New Zealand, and Irish nationals, need neither a visa nor a passport to enter Canada. Travelers should, however, carry some identifying papers, such as a passport or birth, baptismal, or voter's certificate, to prove one's citizenship; in most cases, a driver's license is all you're asked to provide. Permanent U.S. residents who aren't U.S. citizens must have their Alien Registration Cards. Residents of approximately 60 other countries do not need visas to enter Canada; all others do. Inquire about entry requirements at the nearest Canadian embassy, or consult the Web: cicnet.ci.gc.ca/english/visit/index.html.

A note for teens traveling alone: If you're under 19, it's helpful to have a letter from a parent or guardian stating the purpose of the trip. If customs officers are suspicious when you enter the country, they'll notify immigration officers. A letter will go a long way in proving that you're not running away or up to no good. For more information about immigration, call ☎ **902/426-3155.**

CUSTOMS   Customs regulations allow adult travelers (19 years or older) to bring in duty- and tax-free 1.14 liters (40 oz.) of wine or liquor, or 24 bottles of beer; travelers can also bring in 200 cigarettes or 50 cigars without paying duty or tax. If you're bringing gifts for Canadian friends, you're allowed C$60 (US$40) duty-free. An automated phone service will answer most questions about customs regulations; call ☎ **902/426-2911.**

Regulations regarding firearms are complicated and varied. In short, it's best if you don't bring your gun. If you're traveling for hunting and want to bring your rifle into the country, you should be traveling during hunting season and carry proof of your plans to go hunting (a written confirmation from a guide service or hunting lodge should suffice).

Import Restrictions   Returning **U.S. citizens** who have been away for 48 hours or more are allowed to bring back, once every 30 days, $400 worth of merchandise duty-free. You'll be charged a flat rate of 10% duty on the next $1,000 worth of purchases. Be sure to have your receipts handy. On gifts, the duty-free limit is $100. For more information, contact the **U.S. Customs Service,** 1301 Constitution Ave. (P.O. Box 7407), Washington, DC 20044 (☎ **202/927-6724**) and request the free pamphlet *Know Before You Go.* It's also available on the Web at www.customs.ustreas.gov/travel/kbygo.htm.

U.K. citizens returning from a non-EC country have a customs allowance of: 200 cigarettes; 50 cigars; 250g of smoking tobacco; 2 liters of still table wine; 1 liter of spirits or strong liqueurs (over 22% volume); 2 liters of fortified wine, sparkling wine or other liqueurs; 60cc (ml) perfume; 250cc (ml) of toilet water; and £145 worth of all other goods, including gifts and souvenirs. People under 17 cannot have the tobacco or alcohol allowance. For more information, contact HM Customs & Excise, Passenger Enquiry Point, 2nd Floor Wayfarer House, Great South West Road, Feltham, Middlesex, TW14 8NP (☎ **0181/910-3744;** from outside the U.K. 44/181-910-3744), or consult their Web site at www.open.gov.uk.

The duty-free allowance in **Australia** is A$400 or, for those under 18, A$200. Personal property mailed back from England should be marked "Australian goods returned" to avoid payment of duty. Upon returning to Australia, citizens can bring in 250 cigarettes or 250 grams of loose tobacco, and 1,125ml of alcohol. If you're returning with valuable goods you already own, such as foreign-made cameras, you should file form B263. A helpful brochure, available from Australian consulates or Customs offices, is *Know Before You Go.* For more information, contact **Australian Customs Services,** GPO Box 8, Sydney NSW 2001 (☎ **02/9213-2000**).

The duty-free allowance for **New Zealand** is NZ$700. Citizens over 17 can bring in 200 cigarettes, or 50 cigars, or 250 grams of tobacco (or a mixture of all three if their combined weight doesn't exceed 250 grams); plus 4.5 liters of wine and beer, or 1.125 liters of liquor. New Zealand currency does not carry import or export restrictions. Fill out a certificate of export, listing the valuables you are taking out of the country; that way, you can bring them back without paying duty. Most questions are answered in a free pamphlet available at New Zealand consulates and Customs offices: *New Zealand Customs Guide for Travellers, Notice no. 4.* For more information, contact New Zealand Customs, 50 Anzac Ave., P.O. Box 29, Auckland (☎ **09/359-6655**).

3 Money

CURRENCY   Canadian currency, like U.S. currency, is denominated in dollars and cents. There are some differences. Canada has no $1 bill. It does have a $1 coin (called a "loonie" because it depicts a loon) and a $2 coin (called a "twoonie"). At press time, US$1 was worth approximately C$1.50.

If you're driving into Canada, you needn't worry about stocking up on Canadian dollars before or immediately upon entry into Canada. U.S. currency is widely accepted, especially in border towns, and you'll often see signs at cash registers announcing current exchange rates. These are not always the best rates, however, so it behooves you to visit an ATM (automated teller machine) or cash some traveler's checks as soon as you're able.

ATMs   Obtaining cash is rarely a problem for travelers in Canada. ATMs are widely available in most mid-size towns and cities, and the networks are often compatible with U.S. banks, allowing travelers to use their own ATM or credit cards for cash withdrawals. Your bank will convert the currency at the prevailing rate. For example, if you withdraw $100 from a Canadian bank machine, your bank statement will show a withdrawal of around $70. As of 1999, ATMs in Canada did not charge a transaction fee, as is now commonly done in the United States.

Cirrus (☎ **800/424-7787;** www.mastercard.com/atm/) and **PLUS** (☎ **800/843-7587;** www.visa.com/atms) are the two most popular networks, with PLUS especially well represented in Atlantic Canada. Check the back of your ATM card to see which network your bank belongs to. Be sure to ask about the daily withdrawal limit before you depart, and whether you need a new personal ID number.

TRAVELER'S CHECKS   Traveler's checks are something of an anachronism from the days before the ATM made cash accessible at any time. You might want to bring a few just in case you can't locate a compatible ATM machine. Traveler's checks denominated in U.S. dollars can be cashed at most banks and many hotels and shops. Banks typically charge a transaction fee of around $2.75, so it's best to change several checks at once to avoid paying the fee on each check.

You can get traveler's checks at almost any bank. **American Express** offers denominations of $10, $20, $50, $100, $500, and $1,000. You'll pay a service charge ranging from 1% to 4%. You can also get American Express traveler's checks over the phone by calling ☎ **800/221-7282;** by using this number, Amex gold and platinum cardholders are exempt from the 1% fee. AAA members can obtain checks without a fee at most AAA offices.

Visa offers traveler's checks at Citibank locations nationwide, as well as several other banks. The service charge ranges between 1.5 and 2%; checks come in denominations of $20, $50, $100, $500, and $1,000. **MasterCard** also offers traveler's checks. Call ☎ **800/223-9920** for a location near you.

CREDIT CARDS   Credit cards are invaluable when traveling. They are a safe way to carry money and provide a convenient record of all your expenses. You can also withdraw cash advances from your credit cards at any bank (though you'll start paying hefty interest on the advance the moment you receive the cash, and you won't receive frequent-flyer miles on an airline credit card). At most banks, you don't even need to go to a teller; you can get a cash advance at the ATM if you know your PIN number. If you've forgotten your PIN number or didn't even know you had one, call the phone number on the back of your credit card and ask the bank to send it to you. It usually takes 5 to 7 business days, though some banks will provide the number over the phone if you tell them your mother's maiden name or pass some other security clearance.

THEFT   Almost every credit card company has an emergency 800-number that you can call if your wallet or purse is stolen. They may be able to wire you a cash advance off your credit card immediately, and in many places, they can deliver an emergency credit card in a day or two. The issuing bank's 800-number is usually on the back of the credit card—though of course that doesn't help you much if the card was stolen. The toll-free information directory will provide the number if you dial ☎ **800/555-1212.** Citicorp Visa's U.S. emergency number is ☎ **800/336-8472.** American Express cardholders and traveler's check holders should call ☎ **800/221-7282** for all money emergencies. MasterCard holders should call ☎ **800/307-7309.**

If you opt to carry traveler's checks, be sure to keep a record of their serial numbers, separately from the checks of course, so you're ensured a refund in just such an emergency.

TAXES   There's good news and there's bad news on the tax front. The bad news is that high taxes offset some of the price advantage gained when you convert U.S. to Canadian currency. The good news is that foreign visitors can get back many of their taxes if they're careful about retaining and validating receipts, and filling out forms.

In 1997, three provinces—New Brunswick, Nova Scotia, and Newfoundland—adopted the **Harmonized Sales Tax,** called the HST. This combined the provincial and federal sales into a flat rate of 15%, which is charged on all goods and services. In Prince Edward Island, you'll be charged a Goods and Services Tax of 7%, plus a provincial tax of 10%.

Non-Canadians can apply for a refund of the entire HST (or the GST only in Prince Edward Island) upon leaving the country. But there are a few catches. The refund applies primarily to taxes on accommodations and goods bought for use outside the country. It doesn't apply to meals, beverages, tobacco, transportation, gasoline, or professional services. Beginning in 1999, those leaving Canada by car are required to stop at the border to have their receipts validated by Canadian customs, and officials may check to ensure that the goods claimed are actually leaving the country. This doesn't apply to hotel receipts. Visitors departing by air or boat needn't validate receipts, but must include the used boarding pass or other documentation to prove they left the country.

Requests for **refunds** through the Tax Rebate Program must be accompanied by the original receipts (copies won't do). Refunds can be requested at participating Canadian duty-free shops, or by mail with an application. Rebate forms packaged with an instruction booklet are available at most information centers, or by calling ☎ 902/432-5608. If the application is submitted by mail, refunds are typically sent within 2 or 3 months, with checks issued in U.S. dollars to U.S. citizens.

4 When to Go

CLIMATE   All the Atlantic Provinces lie within the Northern Temperate Zone, which means that they have weather much like neighboring New England in the northeast United States. Spring is damp and cool at the outset, and can be warm and muggy as it eases into summer. Summer's compact high season runs from early July to early September. That's when the great majority of travelers take to the road, enjoying the bright, clear days and warm temperatures. The average high in the southern three provinces is in the upper 70s°F (around 25°C); in Newfoundland, it's more typically in the upper 60s°F (around 20°C). Nights can be cool, even approaching freezing late in the summer.

Be aware that there is no "typical" summer weather in Atlantic Canada. The only thing typical is change, and you're likely to experience balmy, sunny days and howling rainstorms, quite possibly on the same day.

Weather in all four provinces is to a large degree affected by proximity to the ocean. This means frequent fogs, especially on the Fundy Coast of New Brunswick, the Atlantic Coast of Nova Scotia, and Newfoundland's Avalon Peninsula. The ocean also offers an unobstructed corridor for high winds, especially on Prince Edward Island and Newfoundland. Rain is not unusual in summer. Travelers who come well prepared for downpours, both psychologically and equipment-wise, tend to be happier travelers. Note that the ocean also provides some benefits: Prince Edward Island's summer tends to linger into fall thanks to the island's being surrounded by the warm, moderating waters of the Gulf of St. Lawrence.

HOLIDAYS   National holidays are celebrated from the Atlantic to the Pacific to the Arctic Oceans, and for the traveler that means that government offices and banks are closed. (Shops remain open on some but not all national holidays.) These holidays include New Year's Day, Good Friday, Easter Monday, Victoria Day (the third Monday in May, always the week before Memorial Day in the United States), Canada Day (July 1), Labour Day (the first Monday in September, the same as in the United States), Thanksgiving (mid-October, the same as Columbus Day weekend in the United States), Remembrance Day (November 11), Christmas Day (December 25), and Boxing Day (December 26).

Locally observed provincial holidays include a civic holiday (August 2) in Nova Scotia, and New Brunswick Day (the first Monday in August). Newfoundland and Labrador celebrate several holidays, including St. George's Day (April 26), Discovery Day (the third Monday in June), and Orangeman's Day (July 12).

5 The Active Vacation Planner

A growing number of outfitters and entrepreneurs are offering soup-to-nuts trips that take care of all the planning and equipment. That's especially helpful for those arriving by air who are interested in outdoor adventures—it's a bit cumbersome to fly with bikes, canoes, and so forth. In each chapter, we've included a "Great Outdoors" section, which will offer some pointers based on your interests.

Other specialized vacations include learning vacations, during which you can immerse yourself in local culture, and more traditional organized tours, including bus tours.

LEARNING VACATIONS

- **Gaelic College of Art and Culture,** St. Ann's, NS (☎ 902/295-3441). Two-week programs for children and adults specialize in local culture, such as Highland bagpiping, dancing, drumming, and Cape Breton fiddling. More than 100 students attend classes each session; the school is located on Cape Breton near Baddeck.
- **King's Landing,** near Fredericton, NB (☎ 506/363-5090). Children dress up in period costume and learn about how the early Loyalist settlers lived. The programs range from a few hours to a week. Adult programs are also offered.
- **Sunbury Shores Art and Nature Centre,** St. Andrews, NB (☎ 506/529-3386; www.sunburyshores.org). The center offers day- and week-long trips and classes with topics including plant dyes, printmaking, raku pottery, and watercolor and oil painting. The center is located on the water in St. Andrews; lodging can be arranged.
- **Village Historique Acadien,** near Caraquet, NB (☎ 506/726-2600). The life and arts of early Acadian settlers is the focus of this program, held at a re-created historic village.

ADVENTURE TRAVEL

Adventure travel is a growth industry in Atlantic Canada, as it is worldwide. You can request information on adventure outfitters currently leading trips by calling the toll-free provincial information numbers listed at the beginning of this chapter. The free provincial travel guides also list outfitters. Here's a sampling of well-regarded outfitters:

- **Backroads,** Berkeley, California (☎ 800/462-2848 or 510/527-1555; www.backroads.com). One of North America's largest adventure travel companies offers 6-day walking and biking trips through southeast Nova Scotia. Pick according to your budget and inclination: you can stay at luxury inns, or opt for more rustic camping trips.

- **Break Away Adventures,** Happy Valley-Goose Bay, Labrador (☎ **709/896-9343**). Larry Bradley leads multiday canoe and hiking excursions around various parts of Labrador, including a 2-week trip in which you reach base camp by seaplane followed by a 10-hour boat ride.
- **Coastal Adventures,** Tangier, NS (☎ **902/772-2774**). Sea kayak honcho Scott Cunningham and his staff lead trips ranging from 2-day paddles to week-long adventures throughout the Maritimes and Newfoundland.
- **Country Walkers,** Waterbury, VT (☎ **800/464-9255** or 802/244-5661; www.countrywalkers.com). Country Walkers offers van-supported walking trips on Cape Breton Island.
- **Discovery Outripping Company,** Corner Brook, NF (☎ **709/634-6335**). Explore southwest Newfoundland's backcountry on backpacking, canoeing, or heli-hiking trips organized by this guide service.
- **Freewheeling Adventures,** Hubbards, NS (☎ **902/857-3600;** www.freewheeling.ca). This popular outfitter based in Nova Scotia offers guided bike tours throughout its own province, as well as on Prince Edward Island and in Newfoundland.

ORGANIZED TOURS

- **Collette Tours,** Pawtucket, Rhode Island (☎ **800/717-9191** or 410/728-3805) www.collettetours.com. In conjunction with Air Canada, Collette offers tours that range from fly/drive packages to the escorted everything's-done-for-you variety. Request their brochure "Air Canada's Canada" for more information.
- **Cosmos,** Littleton, Colorado (☎ **303/797-2800;** www.globusandcosmos.com). Cosmos bills itself as the leading budget tour operator. Bus tours include an escorted, 12-day tour from Boston through Maine, New Brunswick, Prince Edward Island, and back to Maine for around US$950 per person. Cosmos is affiliated with **Globus,** which offers similar itineraries but more upscale accommodations at a higher price. Call for more information or visit their Web site.
- **Maxxim Vacations,** St. John's, NF (☎ **800/567-6666** or 709/754-6666; www.maxximvacations.com). Newfoundland's largest travel provider has a top-rate reputation and offers a range of trips, including guided and unguided excursions. Call and ask for the extensive and colorful brochure.

6 National & Provincial Parks in Atlantic Canada

If it's the outdoors that attracts you to Atlantic Canada, you should consider planning your trip around visits to the national and provincial parks. Here's a quick overview to aid your planning. More information on each park can be found in the chapters that follow.

NATIONAL PARKS

- **Roosevelt Campobello International Park, New Brunswick:** This unique park—it's the only one in the world jointly managed by two countries—has for a centerpiece the 34-room Roosevelt Cottage, the summer home of U.S. President Franklin D. Roosevelt. Nearby is a 2,800-acre nature preserve with wonderful oceanside hikes.
- **Fundy National Park, New Brunswick:** This wild and wooded park on the Bay of Fundy is an ideal spot to watch the vast tides ebb and flow. There's also good hiking in the rolling hills of the interior.

- **Kouchibouguac National Park, New Brunswick:** Located on the province's northeastern coast, this park is best known for the sandy strands fronting the warm waters of the Gulf of St. Lawrence. This is one of Atlantic Canada's best destinations for family camping trips.
- **Cape Breton Highlands National Park, Nova Scotia:** Dramatic cliffs plunging into the restless ocean and the white-knuckle Cabot Trail driving tour are the main draws of this stunning park in northeast Nova Scotia. But it's also a great destination for hikers, birders, and mountain bikers.
- **Kejimkujik National Park, Nova Scotia:** A canoeist's paradise, this park features miles of water trails along a sprawling network of lakes and ponds. It's best appreciated by backcountry canoeists, but short hiking trails through lush woodlands provide access for more terrestrial souls.
- **Prince Edward Island National Park, Prince Edward Island:** On the north shore of PEI, this park features spectacular sand dunes and red-sand beaches stretching for 25 miles. Green Gables, the house immortalized in *Anne of Green Gables,* is also in the park.
- **Gros Morne National Park, Newfoundland:** Misty rounded mountains, landlocked fjords, geological freaks of nature, and remarkable coastal trails make this park one of the most alluring in Atlantic Canada.
- **Terra Nova National Park, Newfoundland:** A scenic spot along the eastern coast, Terra Nova's dense evergreen forests are webbed with hiking trails that reach remote wilderness campsites. You can also venture to abandoned outport villages by trails or boat shuttle.

THE PROVINCIAL PARKS

Atlantic Canada has dozens of provincial parks, some no more than a few campsites scattered around a field, others more elaborate affairs with organized activities and engaging visitor centers. With few exceptions, the region's parks are well managed and very appealing, well worth stopping at for a few minutes or a few days. Most provincial parks are free to day travelers, with the exception of those in New Brunswick. A few of the more notable parks:

- **Mt. Carleton Provincial Park, New Brunswick:** High, open peaks dot the interior of this wild park, situated in the middle of New Brunswick's commercial woodlands. You can also find good mountain biking along the valleys.
- **Blomidon Provincial Park:** The 13.7 kilometers (8.5 miles) of hiking trails at this rugged coastal park not far from Wolfville offer access to some of the most dramatic coastal terrain in the province.
- **Taylor Head Provincial Park, Nova Scotia:** Located on the little-visited eastern shore, Taylor Head features remote beaches and quiet, misty walks. Come on a weekday and you'll have the place to yourself.
- **Graves Island Provincial Park, Nova Scotia:** Some of the province's best views of islands and inlets are found at the graceful park, which occupies a grassy bluff overlooking Mahone Bay.
- **Green Park Provincial Park, Prince Edward Island:** Estate-like grounds surrounding an extravagant gingerbread mansion are the chief attraction of this elegant park, located on an inlet near the genteel village of Tyne Valley.
- **Cedar Dunes Provincial Park, Prince Edward Island:** A strikingly handsome lighthouse marks this oceanside park on the island's southwest tip, which offers grassy campsites just over the dunes from the Northumberland Strait.

- **LaManche Provincial Park, Newfoundland:** Hike to the remains of an old outport located on a narrow, remote cove. This small park on the Avalon Peninsula also has a hike along a river, and a popular campground.
- **J. T. Cheeseman Provincial Park, Newfoundland:** Located just outside Port aux Basques (the major ferry port), Cheeseman offers access to beaches, a biking and hiking trail on an old railbed, and grassy dunes that are home to the endangered piping plover.

7 Health & Insurance

STAYING HEALTHY If you worry about getting sick away from home, you may want to consider **medical travel insurance** (see the section on travel insurance later in this chapter). In most cases, however, your existing health plan will provide all the coverage you need. Be sure to carry your identification card in your wallet.

If you suffer from a chronic illness, consult your doctor before your departure. For conditions like epilepsy, diabetes, or heart problems, wear a **Medic Alert Identification Tag** (☎ 800/825-3785; www.medicalert.org), which will immediately alert doctors to your condition and give them access to your records through Medic Alert's 24-hour hotline. Membership is $35, plus a $15 annual fee.

Pack prescription medications in your carry-on luggage. Carry written prescriptions in generic, not brand-name form, and dispense all prescription medications from their original labeled vials. Also bring along copies of your prescriptions in case you lose your pills or run out. If you wear contact lenses, pack an extra pair in case you lose one.

If you do get sick, you may want to ask the concierge at your hotel to recommend a local doctor. If you can't find a doctor who can help you right away, try the emergency room at the local hospital. Many emergency rooms have walk-in-clinics for emergency cases that are not life-threatening. You may not get immediate attention, but you won't pay the high price of an emergency room visit.

INSURANCE There are three kinds of travel insurance: trip cancellation, medical, and lost luggage coverage. **Trip cancellation insurance** is a good idea if you have paid a large portion of your vacation expenses up front. The other two types of insurance, however, don't make sense for most travelers. Rule number one: check your existing policies before you buy any additional coverage.

Your existing health insurance should cover you if you get sick while on vacation (though if you belong to an HMO, you should check to see whether you are fully covered when away from home). If you need hospital treatment, most health insurance plans and HMOs will cover out-of-country hospital visits and procedures, at least to some extent. However, most make you pay the bills up front at the time of care, and you'll get a refund after you've returned and filed all the paperwork. Members of **Blue Cross/Blue Shield** can now use their cards at select hospitals in most major cities worldwide (☎ 800/810-BLUE or www.bluecares.com/blue/bluecard/wwn for a list of hospitals). For independent travel health-insurance providers, see below. Your homeowner's insurance should cover stolen luggage. The airlines are responsible for $1,250 on domestic flights if they lose your luggage; if you plan to carry anything more valuable than that, keep it in your carry-on bag.

The differences between travel assistance and insurance are often blurred, but in general the former offers on-the-spot assistance and 24-hour hotlines (mostly oriented toward medical problems), while the latter reimburses you for travel problems (medical, travel, or otherwise) after you have filed the paperwork. The coverage you should consider will depend on how much protection is already contained in your existing health insurance or other policies. Some credit- and charge-card companies may insure you against travel accidents if you buy plane, train, or bus tickets with their cards. Before purchasing additional insurance, read your policies and agreements over carefully. Call your insurers or credit/charge-card companies if you have any questions.

If you do require additional insurance, try one of the companies listed below. But don't pay for more than you need. For example, if you need only trip cancellation insurance, don't purchase coverage for lost or stolen property.

Among the reputable issuers of travel insurance are:

- **Access America,** 6600 W. Broad St., Richmond, VA 23230 (☎ **800/ 284-8300)**
- **Travel Guard International,** 1145 Clark St., Stevens Point, WI 54481 (☎ **800/826-1300)**
- **Travel Insured International,** Inc., P.O. Box 280568, East Hartford, CT 06128 (☎ **800/243-3174)**
- **Columbus Travel Insurance,** 279 High St., Croydon CR0 1QH (☎ **0171/375-0011** in London; www2.columbusdirect.com/columbusdirect)
- **International SOS Assistance,** P.O. Box 11568, Philadelphia, PA 11916 (☎ **800/523-8930** or 215/244-1500), strictly an assistance company
- **Travelex Insurance Services,** P.O. Box 9408, Garden City, NY 11530-9408 (☎ **800/228-9792)**

Medicare only covers U.S. citizens traveling in Mexico and Canada. For Blue Cross/Blue Shield coverage abroad, see above. Companies specializing in accident and medical care include:

- **MEDEX International,** P.O. Box 5375, Timonium, MD 21094-5375 (☎ **888/MEDEX-00** or 410/453-6300; fax 410/453-6301; www.medexassist. com)
- **Travel Assistance International** (Worldwide Assistance Services, Inc.), 1133 15th St. NW, Suite 400, Washington, DC 20005 (☎ **800/821-2828** or 202/828-5894; fax 202/828-5896)
- **The Divers Alert Network** (DAN) (☎ **800/446-2671** or 919/684-2948) insures scuba divers.

CAR RENTER'S INSURANCE   For information on car renter's insurance, see "Getting Around by Car," below.

8 Tips for Travelers with Special Needs

FOR TRAVELERS WITH DISABILITIES   Canada is making tremendous efforts to eliminate barriers to mobility. City pavements feature curb cuts for wheelchair travel, and larger hotels and airports have wheelchair-accessible washrooms. A growing number of restaurants and tourist attractions are now designed for wheelchair accessibility, although much room for improvement remains.

The **Access-Able Travel Source** (www.access-able.com) is a Web site featuring an online database with information about hotels, tour operators, and attractions that can accommodate disabled travelers in the United States and Canada. The offerings for Atlantic Canada are a bit slim at present, but the site is easy to navigate and has good potential for growth.

The **Canadian Paraplegic Association,** 520 Sutherland Dr., Toronto, ON M4G 3V9 (☎ **416/422-5644;** www.canparaplegic.org), offers a range of helpful information of interest to disabled people and may be able to answer your questions.

Those with disabilities headed for Nova Scotia may ask about transportation or recreational facilities by contacting the **Nova Scotia League for Equal Opportunities,** 2786 Agricola St., Suite 208, Halifax, NS B3K 4E1, ☎ **902/455-6942,** fax 902/454-4781, e-mail nsleo@ns.sympatico.ca.

Other resources include the following. *A World of Options,* a 658-page book of resources, covers everything from biking trips to scuba outfitters. It costs $35 ($30 for members) and is available from **Mobility International USA,** P.O. Box 10767, Eugene, OR 97440 (☎ **541/343-1284,** voice and TDD; www.miusa.org). Annual membership for Mobility International is $35.

You can join **The Society for the Advancement of Travel for the Handicapped** (SATH), 347 Fifth Ave., Suite 610, New York, NY 10016 (☎ **212/447-7284;** fax 212-725-8253; www.sath.org) for $45 annually, $30 for seniors and students, to gain access to their vast network of connections in the travel industry.

Travelers with disabilities may also want to consider joining a tour that caters specifically to them. One of the best operators is **Flying Wheels Travel,** 143 West Bridge (P.O. Box 382), Owatonna, MN 55060 (☎ **800/535-6790**). Other reputable specialized tour operators include **Access Adventures** (☎ **716/889-9096**), which offers sports-related vacations; **Accessible Journeys** (☎ **800/TINGLES** or 610/521-0339), for slow walkers and wheelchair travelers; **The Guided Tour, Inc.** (☎ **215/782-1370**); **Wilderness Inquiry** (☎ **800/728-0719** or 612/379-3858); and **Directions Unlimited** (☎ **800/533-5343**).

Vision-impaired travelers should contact the **American Foundation for the Blind,** 11 Penn Plaza, Suite 300, New York, NY 10001 (☎ **800/232-5463**), for information on traveling with seeing-eye dogs.

FOR GAY & LESBIAN TRAVELERS   The **International Gay & Lesbian Travel Association** (IGLTA) (☎ **800/448-8550** or 954/776-2626; fax 954/776-3303; www.iglta.org) links travelers with the appropriate gay-friendly service organization or tour specialist. It offers quarterly newsletters, marketing mailings, and a membership directory that's updated quarterly. Membership often includes gay or lesbian businesses but is open to individuals for $150 yearly, plus a $100 administration fee for new members. Members are kept informed of gay and gay-friendly hoteliers, tour operators, and airline and cruise-line representatives. Contact the IGLTA for a list of its member agencies, who will be tied into IGLTA's information resources.

General gay and lesbian travel agencies include **Family Abroad** (☎ **800/999-5500** or 212/459-1800; gay and lesbian); **Above and Beyond Tours** (☎ **800/397-2681;** mainly gay men); and **Yellowbrick Road** (☎ **800/642-2488;** gay and lesbian).

Out and About, 8 W. 19th St. no. 401, New York, NY 10011 (☎ **800/929-2268** or 212/645-6922), offers guidebooks and a monthly newsletter packed with good information on the global gay and lesbian scene. A year's subscription to the newsletter costs $49. *Our World,* 1104 North Nova Rd., Suite 251, Daytona Beach, FL 32117 (☎ **904/441-5367**), is a slicker monthly magazine promoting and highlighting travel bargains and opportunities. Annual subscription rates are $35 in the U.S., $45 outside the U.S.

FOR SENIORS   Few countries in the world are as attentive to the needs of seniors as Canada. Discounts are extended to people over 60 for everything ranging from public transportation to museum and movie admissions. Even many hotels, tour operators, and restaurants offer discounts, so don't be bashful about inquiring, but always carry some kind of identification that shows your date of birth. (It's always best to inquire before checking in or ordering.) The discount varies widely; in general, the gap between senior prices and regular prices seems to have narrowed in the past few years.

Members of the **American Association of Retired Persons (AARP)**, 601 E St. NW, Washington, DC 20049 (☎ **800/424-3410** or 202/434-2277), get discounts not only on hotels but on airfares and car rentals, too. AARP offers members a wide range of special benefits, including *Modern Maturity* magazine and a monthly newsletter.

The National Council of Senior Citizens, 8403 Colesville Rd., Suite 1200, Silver Spring, MD 20910 (☎ **301/578-8800**), a nonprofit organization, offers a newsletter six times a year (partly devoted to travel tips) and discounts on hotel and auto rentals; annual dues are $13 per person or couple.

Mature Outlook, P.O. Box 9390, Des Moines, IA 50306 (☎ **800/336-6330**), began as a travel organization for people over 50, though it now caters to people of all ages. Members receive discounts on hotels and receive a bimonthly magazine. Annual membership is $19.95, which entitles members to discounts and, often, free coupons for discounted merchandise from Sears.

Grand Circle Travel is also one of the hundreds of travel agencies specializing in vacations for seniors (347 Congress St., Suite 3A, Boston, MA 02210 (☎ **800/221-2610** or 617/350-7500)). Many of these packages, however, are of the tour-bus variety, with free trips thrown in for those who organize groups of 10 or more. Seniors seeking more independent travel should probably consult a regular travel agent. **SAGA International Holidays,** 222 Berkeley St., Boston, MA 02116 (☎ **800/343-0273**), offers inclusive tours and cruises for those 50 and older. SAGA also sponsors the more substantial "Road Scholar Tours" (☎ **800/621-2151**), which are fun-loving but with an educational bent.

If you want something more than the average vacation or guided tour, try **Elderhostel** (☎ **877/426-8056;** www.elderhostel.org) or the University of New Hampshire's **Interhostel** (☎ **800/733-9753**), both variations on the same theme: educational travel for senior citizens. On these escorted tours, the days are packed with seminars, lectures, and field trips, and academic experts lead the sightseeing.

FOR FAMILIES   Several books on the market offer tips to help you travel with kids. *Family Travel* (Lanier Publishing International), *How to Take Great Trips with Your Kids* (The Harvard Common Press), and *Adventuring with Children* (Foghorn Press) are full of good general advice.

Family Travel Times is published six times a year by TWYCH (Travel with Your Children; ☎ **888/822-4388** or 212/477-5524), and includes a weekly call-in service for subscribers. Subscriptions are $40 a year for quarterly editions.

FOR STUDENTS   The best resource for students is the **Council on International Educational Exchange,** or CIEE (www.ciee.org). They can set you up with an ID card (see below), and their travel branch, **Council Travel Service** (☎ **800/226-8624;** www.counciltravel.com), is the biggest student travel agency operation in the world. It can get you discounts on plane tickets, railpasses, and the like. Ask them for a list of CTS offices in major cities so you can keep the discounts flowing (and aid lines open) as you travel.

From CIEE you can obtain the student traveler's best friend, the $18 **International Student Identity Card** (ISIC). It's the only officially acceptable form of student identification, good for cut rates on railpasses, plane tickets, and other discounts. It also provides you with basic health and life insurance and a 24-hour help line. If you're no longer a student but are still under 26 you can get a GO 25 card from the same people, which will get you the insurance and some of the discounts (but not student admission prices in museums).

Campus Travel, 52 Grosvenor Gardens, London SW1W 0AG (☎ **0171/730-3402;** www.campustravel.co.uk), opposite Victoria Station, is Britain's leading specialist in student and youth travel.

9 Getting There

BY PLANE   Airports around Atlantic Canada offer access via scheduled flights. Halifax, Nova Scotia, the region's major air hub, has frequent flights in and out of the region, as well as onward connections to local airports. Other major airports include Saint John, New Brunswick; Charlottetown, Prince Edward Island; and Gander and St. John's, Newfoundland. All offer direct flights to and from airports outside of the region.

The main air carriers serving Atlantic Canada are **Air Canada** and its commuter partner, **Air Nova** (☎ **800/776-3000** in the U.S. or 800/565-3940 in the Maritimes), **Canadian Airlines International** (☎ **800/426-7000**), and **Canada 3000** (☎ **888/226-3000** or 416/259-1118). Other airlines with service to Atlantic Canada include **Icelandair** (☎ **800/223-5500**) and **Business Express** (☎ **800/433-7300**), which is the code-share partner with American, Northwest, and Delta airlines. (At press time both Air Canada and Canadian Airlines were considering mergers with one another as well as with outside airlines.) See the individual "Getting There" sections at the beginning of each chapter for more information.

Tips for Getting the Best Airfares   Passengers within the same airplane cabin rarely pay the same fare for their seats. Passengers who can book their ticket long in advance, who don't mind staying over Saturday night, or who are willing to travel on a Tuesday, Wednesday, or Thursday after 7pm, will pay a fraction of the full fare. Here are a few easy ways to save.

1. Periodically airlines lower prices on their most popular routes. Check your newspaper for advertised discounts or call the airlines directly and ask if any **promotional rates** or special fares are available. If your schedule is flexible, ask if you can secure a cheaper fare by staying an extra day or by flying midweek. Note, however, that the lowest-priced fares are often nonrefundable, require advance purchase of 1 to 3 weeks and a certain length of stay, and carry penalties for changing dates of travel.

2. **Consolidators,** or bucket shops, buy seats in bulk from the airlines and then sell them back to the public at prices below even the airlines' discounted rates. Their small, boxed ads usually run in the Sunday travel section at the bottom of the page. Before you pay, however, ask for a confirmation number and then call the airline itself to confirm your seat. Book your ticket with a different consolidator—there are many to choose from—if the airline can't confirm your reservation. Also be aware that bucket shop tickets are usually nonrefundable or subject to stiff cancellation penalties.

   Council Travel (☎ **800/226-8624;** www.counciltravel.com) and **STA Travel** (☎ **800/781-4040;** www.sta.travel.com) cater to young travelers, but their bargain basement prices are available to people of all ages. **Travel Bargains** (☎ **800/AIR-FARE;** www.1800airfare.com) offers deep discounts on many airlines, with a 4-day advance purchase. Other reliable consolidators include **1-800-FLY-CHEAP** (www.1800flycheap.com); **TFI   Tours   International** (☎ **800-745-8000** or 212/736-1140); and "rebators" like **Travel Avenue** (☎ **800/333-3335** or 312/876-1116) and the **Smart Traveller** (☎ **800/448-3338** in the U.S. or 305/448-3338), which rebate part of their commissions to you.

3. Book a seat on a **charter flight.** Discounted fares have pared the number available, but they can still be found. Most charter operators advertise and sell their seats through travel agents, thus making these local professionals your best source of information for available flights. Before deciding to take a charter flight, however, check the restrictions on the ticket. Summer charters fill up more quickly than others and are almost sure to fly, but if you decide on a charter flight, seriously consider cancellation and baggage insurance.

4. Look into **courier flights.** Companies that hire couriers use your luggage allowance for their business baggage; in return, you get a deeply discounted ticket. Flights are often offered at the last minute, and you may have to arrange a pretrip interview to make sure you're right for the job. **Now Voyager** (☎ 212/431-1616) flies from New York and also offers noncourier discounted fares, so call them even if you don't want to fly as a courier.

5. Join a travel club such as **Moment's Notice** (☎ 718/234-6295) or **Sears Discount Travel Club** (☎ 800/433-9383, or 800/255-1487 to join), which supply unsold tickets at discounted prices. You pay an annual membership fee to get the club's hotline number. Of course, you're limited to what's available, so you have to be flexible.

BY CAR & FERRY

Overland access to Atlantic Canada from the United States is through Maine. The most direct route to New Brunswick is to drive to Bangor (about 4½ hours from Boston), then head east on Route 9 to Calais, Maine (about 2½ hours). Here you can cross into St. Stephen, New Brunswick, and pick up Route 1 to Saint John and beyond. If you don't plan to stop until you hit Moncton or points east of Moncton, a slightly faster alternative is to continue northeastward on the Maine Turnpike to Houlton, then cross the border and pick up the Trans-Canada Highway.

Between early May and late October travelers headed to Nova Scotia can save considerable driving time by taking a ferry. Seasonal ferries to Nova Scotia depart from Portland and Bar Harbor, Maine, and a year-round ferry serves Saint John, New Brunswick.

The Portland to Yarmouth crossing aboard the *Scotia Prince* is approximately 11 hours and costs around US$80 for each adult passenger, US$40 for children, and US$98 for each vehicle. Cabins are available for an additional fare, ranging from about US$32 for a day cabin to US$165 for an overnight suite. Reservations are essential. Call **Prince of Fundy Cruises** at ☎ 800/341-7540 or 207/775-5616. On the Web, head to www.princeoffundy.com.

Bay Ferries (☎ 888/249-7245) operates the Bar Harbor–Yarmouth ferry aboard *The Cat* (short for catamaran), which claims to be the fastest in North America. Since going into service in 1998, the new ship has cut the crossing time from 6 hours to 2¾ hours, zipping along at up to 50 miles per hour. While exhilarating, some passengers complain that the ship is a bit sterile, more like lingering in an airport lounge than taking a boat excursion. There's an open deck on the rear, but I've heard complaints that those trying to enjoy the fresh air find it mingled with exhaust fumes. Summer rates are US$46 adult, US$41 senior, US$23 child (5 to 12), and US$60 for automobile. Off-season and family rates are available. Reservations are vital during the peak summer season.

The year-round ferry from Saint John, New Brunswick, to Digby, Nova Scotia, is 3 hours. Summer fares are C$25 (US$17) for adults, C$12.50 (US$8.35) for children, and C$55 (US$37) per vehicle. Contact **Bay Ferries** (☎ 888/249-7245; www.nfl-bay.com) for schedules and more information.

Cyber Deals for Net Surfers

It's possible to get some great deals on airfare, hotels, and car rentals via the Internet. The Web sites highlighted below are worth checking out, especially since all services are free. Always check the lowest published fare, however, before you shop for flights online.

Frommers (www.frommers.com)   offers detailed information on almost 200 cities around the world, and up-to-the-minute ways to save dramatically on flights, hotels, car reservations, and cruises. The newsletter is updated daily by Arthur Frommer himself to keep you abreast of the latest ways to save, and to publicize new hot spots and best buys.

Microsoft Expedia (www.expedia.com)   The best part of this multi-purpose travel site is the "Fare Tracker": You fill out a form on the screen indicating that you're interested in cheap flights from your hometown, and, once a week, they'll e-mail you the best airfare deals on up to three destinations. The site's "Travel Agent" will steer you to bargains on hotels and car rentals and you can book online.

Travelocity (www.travelocity.com)   This is one of the best travel sites, especially for finding cheap airfares. In addition to its "Personal Fare Watcher," which notifies you via e-mail of the lowest airfares for up to five different destinations, Travelocity will track the three lowest fares for your route. Click on "Last Minute Deals" for the latest travel bargains, including a link to "H.O.T. Coupons" (www.hotcoupons.com), where you can print out electronic coupons for travel in the U.S. and Canada.

E-Savers Programs   Several major airlines offer a free e-mail service known as E-Savers, via which they'll send you their best bargain airfares on a regular basis. Here's the catch: These fares are usually only available if you leave the very next Saturday (or sometimes Friday night) and return on the following Monday or Tuesday.

Rather than checking e-savers for individual airlines, you can save time by heading right for **Smarter Living** (www.smarterliving.com). Sign up for their newsletter service, and every week you'll get a customized e-mail summarizing the discount fares available from your departure city for more than 15 different airlines.

Here's a list of airlines that fly to Canada and their Web sites.

- **Air Canada:** www.aircanada.ca
- **Air Nova:** www.airnova.ca
- **Canadian Airlines International:** www.cdnair.ca/
- **Canada 3000:** www.canada3000.com
- **Business Express:** www.flybex.com
- **Icelandair:** www.icelandair.is

BY BUS

Bus service into and out of the region tends to be slow and cumbersome. To get from New York to Halifax, for instance, you'd have to bus to Montréal (8 to 10 hours), then connect to another bus line to Halifax (18 hours). A late-spring through early-fall alternative from the East Coast of the United States is to bus from New York to Portland, Maine (about 7 hours), take the overnight ferry from Portland to Yarmouth, Nova Scotia (about 11 hours), and then catch the connecting bus onward to Halifax (about 4 hours). It's a bit more expensive, but far more enjoyable.

Greyhound (☎ 800/231-2222) offers service from diverse points around the United States to Montréal, where you can connect to Atlantic Canada–bound buses (☎ 514/842-2281). SMT (☎ 800/567-5151 or 506/859-5060) offers weekly service from Bangor, Maine, to New Brunswick, and daily service within New Brunswick and Prince Edward Island with connections to Nova Scotia. Acadian Lines (☎ 902/453-8912) and DRL Coach Lines (☎ 902/450-1987) offer bus service from Yarmouth to Halifax.

BY TRAIN

Via Rail (☎ 800/561-3949 in the U.S. or 800/561-3952 in the Maritimes) offers train service 6 days a week between Halifax and Montreal, with several stops along the way (see "By Train" in the following section). The entire trip takes between 18 and 21 hours, depending on direction, and costs about C$185 (US$123) each way. (Discounts are available if you purchase at least 1 week in advance.) Sleeping berths and private cabins are available at extra cost. Current fares and schedules are available on the Web at www.viarail.ca.

10 Getting Around

BY CAR & FERRY   Atlantic Canada's road network is extensive and generally well maintained. The Trans-Canada Highway enters the region north of Edmundston, New Brunswick, and continues some 1,800 kilometers (1,050 miles) to St. John's, Newfoundland. Numerous feeder roads connect to the Trans-Canada. American travelers expecting to find six-lane highways with high-speed on- and off-ramps will be in for a surprise. With a few exceptions, the highway system is on a far more intimate scale. Many main arteries—such as the inland route from Yarmouth to Halifax and Route 1 across Newfoundland—are just two lanes, albeit with frequent opportunities for passing.

If you're arriving by plane, the usual suspects offer **car rentals** at major airports. Despite the number of rental outfits, however, it can be difficult to reserve a car during the peak summer season when demand soars. It's best to reserve ahead. Try **Avis** (☎ 800/331-1212), **Budget** (☎ 800/527-0700), **Dollar** (☎ 800/800-4000), **Hertz** (☎ 800/654-3131), or **Tilden** (☎ 800/361-5334).

Saving Money on a Rental Car   Car rental rates vary even more than airline fares. A few key questions could save you hundreds of dollars.

- Are weekend rates lower than weekday rates?
- Is a weekly rate cheaper than the daily rate?
- Does the agency assess a drop-off charge if you don't return the car to the same location where you picked it up?
- Are special promotional rates available?
- Are discounts available for members of AARP, AAA, frequent flyer programs, or trade unions?
- How much tax will be added to the rental bill?
- What is the cost of adding an additional driver's name to the contract?
- How many free miles are included in the price?
- How much does the rental company charge to refill your gas tank if you return with the tank less than full?

Demystifying Renter's Insurance   Before you drive off in a rental car, be sure you're insured. Hasty assumptions about your personal auto insurance or a rental agency's additional coverage could end up costing you tens of thousands of dollars—even if you are involved in an accident that was clearly the fault of another driver.

If you already hold a **private auto insurance** policy, ask if your coverage extends to Canada. Be sure to find out whether your policy covers all persons who will be driving the rental car, how much liability is covered in case an outside party is injured in an accident, and whether the type of vehicle you are renting is included under your contract.

Most **major credit cards** provide some degree of coverage as well—provided they were used to pay for the rental. Terms vary widely, however, so be sure to call your credit card company directly before you rent.

Credit cards **will not cover liability,** or the cost of injury to an outside party and/or damage to an outside party's vehicle. When driving outside the U.S., you may seriously want to consider purchasing additional liability insurance from your rental company. Be sure to check the terms, however: some rental agencies only cover liability if the renter is not at fault; even then, the rental company's obligation varies.

The basic insurance coverage offered by most car rental companies, known as the **Loss/Damage Waiver (LDW)** or **Collision Damage Waiver (CDW),** can cost as much as $20/day. It usually covers the full value of the vehicle with no deductible if an outside party causes an accident or other damage to the rental car. Liability coverage varies according to the company policy. If you are at fault in an accident, however, you will be covered for the full replacement value of the car but not for liability. Most rental companies will require a police report in order to process any claims you file, but your private insurer will not be notified of the accident.

Maps   Excellent **road maps** are available from the provincial tourism authorities (ask at the welcome centers). The maps are free except in Newfoundland, where the province charges C$3.45 (US$2.30) for them. You can usually obtain a free Newfoundland map by calling the visitor information number before your trip and requesting that information on visiting the province be mailed to you; see the phone number above.

Driving Rules   As in most of the United States, drivers may make a right turn at a red light, provided that they first stop fully and confirm that no one is coming from the left. At some intersections, signs prohibit such a turn. Radar detectors are prohibited in all the Atlantic Provinces. Drivers and all passengers are required to wear seat belts.

Gasoline   Some American drivers get rather excited about the price of gasoline when they first cross the border, thinking it to be very cheap. It's not. It's priced by the liter. So it's actually quite a bit more than you'd pay in the United States. If you're headed far north, be aware that Newfoundland gasoline is even more expensive than gasoline in the Maritimes.

Travelers headed to Newfoundland in their own cars will need to take a ferry. Information about ferry schedules and costs is located in the introduction to chapter 6.

BY PLANE   Many smaller airports throughout Atlantic Canada offer connections to the provincial hubs. In New Brunswick, these include Saint Leonard, Bathurst, Fredericton, and Moncton; in Nova Scotia, Yarmouth and Sydney. Contact **Air Canada/Air Nova** (☎ **800/776-3000** in the U.S. or 800/565-3940 in the Maritimes) or **Canadian Airlines International** (☎ **800/426-7000** in the U.S., 800/665-1177 in Maritime Provinces, or 902/427-5500 elsewhere).

Newfoundland and Labrador have a rather extensive system of small airports, which stitch together much of this far-flung province. For more information, contact **Air Labrador** (☎ **800/563-3042** in Newfoundland or 709/896-3387 elsewhere) or **Interprovincial Airlines** (☎ **800/563-2800** in Newfoundland or 709/576-1666 elsewhere).

BY BUS   Decent bus service is offered between major cities and many smaller towns. For service in Nova Scotia, contact **Acadian Lines** (☎ **902/453-8912**) or **MacKenzie Bus Lines** (☎ **902/543-2491**); in New Brunswick call **SMT Ltd** (☎ **506/859-5100**); in Newfoundland try **DRL Coachlines** (☎ **709/738-8090**).

BY TRAIN   Interprovincial rail service is a pale shadow of its former self. Prince Edward Island and Newfoundland lack any rail service at all, as does southern New Brunswick (you can't travel by train any longer to Fredericton or Saint John). **Via Rail** (☎ **800/361-8010**) stops in a handful of towns along its single route between Mont-réal and Halifax. In New Brunswick, stops are Campbellton, Charlo, Jacquet River, Petit Rocher, Bathurst, Miramichi, Rogersville, Moncton, and Sackville. In Nova Scotia, you can stop at Amherst, Springhill Junction, Truro, or Halifax.

11 Tips on Accommodations

TIPS FOR SAVING ON YOUR HOTEL ROOM   The rack rate is the maximum rate that a hotel charges for a room. It's the rate you'd get if you walked in off the street and asked for a room for the night. Hardly anybody pays these prices, however, and there are many ways around them.

- **Check e-mail specials.** Air Canada distributes a weekly e-mail with bargains on airfares for the upcoming weekend (see "Cyber Deals for Net Surfers" above). But they also list good deals on chain hotels, including Delta, Radisson, and Hilton, in cities like Halifax, St. John's, and Saint John. If you check your e-mail just before you leave or while on the road, you may find a weekend bargain waiting. Sign up for the mailing at Air Canada's Web site, www.aircanada.ca.
- **Don't be afraid to bargain.** Ask politely whether a less expensive room is available than the first one mentioned, or whether any special rates apply to you. You may qualify for corporate, student, military, senior citizen, or other discounts.
- **Rely on a qualified professional.** Certain hotels give travel agents discounts in exchange for steering business their way, so if you're shy about bargaining, an agent may be better equipped to negotiate discounts for you.
- **Dial direct.** When booking a room in a chain hotel, call the hotel's local line, as well as the toll-free number, and see where you get the best deal.
- **Watch for coupons and advertised discounts.** Scan ads in your local Sunday travel section, an excellent source for up-to-the-minute hotel deals.
- **Consider a suite.** If you are traveling with your family or another couple, you can pack more people into a suite (which usually comes with a sofa bed), and thereby reduce your per-person rate. Remember that some places charge for extra guests, some don't.
- **Book an efficiency.** A room with a kitchenette allows you to grocery shop and eat some meals in. Especially during long stays with families, you're bound to save money on food this way.
- **Investigate reservation services.** These outfits usually work as consolidators, buying up or reserving rooms in bulk, and then dealing them out to customers at a profit. You're probably better off dealing directly with a hotel, but this is certainly a viable option. Here are a few of the more reputable providers.

Accommodations Express (☎ 800/950-4685; www.accommodationsxpress. com); **Hotel Reservations Network** (☎ 800/96HOTEL; www.180096HOTEL. com); **Quikbook** (☎ 800/789-9887, includes fax on demand service; www. quikbook.com); and **Room Exchange** (☎ 800/846-7000 in the U.S., 800/486-7000 in Canada).

Fast Facts: Atlantic Provinces

American Express   Halifax is the only city in Atlantic Canada with an American Express office. To report lost or stolen American Express traveler's checks, call ☎ **800/221-7282.**

ATM Networks   See "Money," earlier in this chapter.

Automobile Clubs   CAA (the Canadian Automobile Association) extends member benefits (including maps and road service) to AAA cardholders. If you're a member, bring your membership card. For information about membership in CAA, call ☎ **800/268-3750.** For emergency road service, call ☎ **800/222-4357.**

Business Hours   Business hours are generally similar to what you'd find in the United States. Most offices are open from 8 or 9am to 5 or 6pm on Monday to Friday, and are closed on weekends. Boutiques and souvenir shops typically open up around 10am and stay open until 6pm or so, often later during the peak tourist season. Hours vary widely for general merchandise and grocery stores. In general, you can expect early and late hours in the larger cities (24-hour groceries are cropping up), but more limited hours in the smaller towns and villages. Most general merchandise stores are closed on Sundays.

Car Rentals   See "Getting Around," earlier in this chapter.

Climate   See "When to Go," earlier in this chapter.

Currency   See "Money," earlier in this chapter.

Documents   See "Visitor Information & Entry Requirements," earlier in this chapter.

Driving Rules   See "Getting Around," earlier in this chapter.

Drugstores   Chain drugstore and independent pharmacies are located throughout Atlantic Canada. Check the phone book under "pharmacy." Stores in larger cities and towns are likely to be open later than those in more remote villages. One of the larger national chains is Pharmasave, with stores in Nova Scotia, New Brunswick, and Prince Edward Island.

Electricity   Canada uses the same electrical current as the U.S.: 110–115 volts, 60 cycles.

Embassies & Consulates   All embassies are in Ottawa, the national capital. The **Australian High Commission** is at 50 O'Connor St., Suite 710, Ottawa, ON K1P 6L2 (☎ 613/236-0841). The **British High Commission** is at 80 Elgin St., Ottawa, ON K1P 5K7 (☎ 613/237-1530). The **Irish Embassy** is at 130 Albert St., Suite 1105, Ottawa, ON K1P 5G4 (☎ 613/233-6281). The **New Zealand High Commission** is at 99 Bank St., Suite 727, Ottawa, ON K1P 6G3 (☎ 613/238-5991). The **South African High Commission** is at 15 Sussex Dr., Ottawa, ON K1M 1M8 (☎ 613/744-0330). The **U.S. embassy** is at 100 Wellington St., Ottawa, ON K1P 5A1 (☎ 613/238-4470).

In the Maritimes, there's a **U.S. consulate** at 2000 Barrington St., Suite 910, Scotia Square, Halifax, NS B3J 3K1 (☎ **902/429-2485**); the **British Consulate** is at 1 Canal St., Dartmouth, NS (☎ **902/461-1381**).

Emergencies   In life-threatening situations, dial ☎ **911.**

Holidays   See "When to Go," earlier in this chapter.

Information   See "Visitor Information," earlier in this chapter.

Internet Access   Internet access poses no special problems. U.S. residents traveling with their own computers will be able to call their Internet provider in the United States. Some of the larger Internet providers have limited local dial-up numbers in Canada. Those planning a longer stay may find that signing up for a local account is the best route. **Sympatico** is a large and popular provider offering dial-up service throughout Atlantic Canada. For more information visit their Web site at www.sympatico.ca.

Those traveling without a laptop can check e-mail periodically by visiting a cybercafe or copy shop that offers Internet access. These are mostly located in the larger cities; check with the local tourist board. For public access in libraries or other public buildings, log onto cap.ic.gc.ca/cp/capsites/.

Liquor Laws   The legal drinking age is 19 years of age in all provinces. Restaurants that serve alcoholic beverages are said to be "licensed." If you want to tipple with dinner, look for a sign or ask whether the establishment is licensed. Do not drink and drive. Canadian law takes drunken driving seriously.

Mail   Letters (up to 30g) mailed within Canada are C46¢. Letters up to 30g mailed to the United States cost C55¢. For other international destinations, a 20g letter is C95¢. More detailed information on packages and other options is available at www.canadapost.ca.

Maps   Excellent **road maps** are available from the provincial tourism authorities (ask at the welcome centers). For more information, see "Getting Around," earlier in this chapter.

Newspapers & Magazines   Publishers in the major cities of the province—including Halifax, Saint John, Fredericton, Charlottetown, and St. John's—all produce very decent daily newspapers filled with information about goings-on around the town and province. Most also maintain Web sites on the Internet, so you can scout out happenings before your departure. (A handy index of worldwide newspapers is located at www.mediainfo.com.) Canada's two national newspapers—the *Globe and Mail* and the *National Post*—are also widely available in most cities and many larger towns.

U.S. papers such as the *Wall Street Journal* and the *New York Times* can be found in larger cities, but you shouldn't count on it. When available, they often sell out early. Newsmagazines such as *Time* and *Newsweek* are not difficult to find on newsstands.

Pets   Traveling into Canada with your pet dog or cat should pose no difficulties. Be sure to have with you a certificate from your veterinarian certifying that your pet is currently vaccinated against rabies. (Puppies and kittens under 3 months are exempt.)

Police   For police call ☎ **911.**

Safety   The cities of Atlantic Canada are relatively small, well policed, and generally safe. Rowdies and drunks sometimes can be threatening, especially late on weekend nights in boisterous downtown neighborhoods, but serious crime is rather rare in this part of Canada. Nonetheless, whenever you're traveling in an unfamiliar place, stay alert. Be aware of your immediate surroundings.

Taxes   See "Money," earlier in this chapter.

Telephones   Pay phones are located throughout Atlantic Canada and are self-explanatory. Local calls are C25¢. Calls to the United States or elsewhere abroad can be pricey, and you should check in advance whether your calling card works in Canada. (Some do, many don't.) Check at drugstores or convenience stores for prepaid calling cards, which usually offer a better rate than feeding in coins.

The United States and Canada are on the same long-distance system. To make a long-distance call between the United States and Canada (in either direction), simply dial "1" first, then the area code and number. It's no different than calling long distance in the United States.

Time Zone   Most of Atlantic Canada is on Atlantic Standard Time, 1 hour ahead of Eastern Standard Time (as observed in New England and the U.S. East Coast). The exceptions are Newfoundland and southeast Labrador, which are one *half*-hour ahead of Atlantic time.

Tipping   As in the United States, tips provide a significant portion of the income for waiters, bellhops, and chambermaids. It's standard to leave 15% of the pre-sales-tax total for basic service at a restaurant, more if the service is exceptional. Plan to tip around C$1 per bag for assistance at your hotel and C$1 to C$2 per day to your chambermaid.

Toilets   Generally called "washrooms" in Canada, public bathrooms are typically abundant and clean. Many towns have a visitor information center, and most of these have washrooms for visitors. In larger cities, washrooms can be found in public buildings, major hotels, some larger shops, and restaurants.

Nova Scotia 3

Nova Scotia proves cagey to characterize. It generally feels more cultured than wild ... but then you stumble upon those blustery, boggy uplands at Cape Breton Highlands National Park, which seem a good home for Druids and trolls. It's a province full of rolling hills and cultivated farms, especially near the Northumberland Straits on the northern shore ... but then you find the vibrant, edgy, and lively arts and entertainment scene in Halifax, a city that's got more intriguing street life than many cities three times its size. It's a place that earned its name—Nova Scotia is Latin for "New Scotland"—with Highland games and kilts and a touch of a brogue hear and there ... but then suddenly you're amid the enclaves of rich Acadian culture along the coast between Digby and Yarmouth. The place resists characterization at every turn.

This picturesque and historic province is an ideal destination for travelers who are quick to hit the remote control when parked on the couch back home. There's an extravagant variety of landscapes and low-key attractions, and the scene seems to change kaleidoscopically as you travel along the winding roads: from dense forests to bucolic farmlands, from ragged coast to melancholy bogs, and from historic villages to dynamic downtowns. (About the only terrain it doesn't offer is towering mountain peaks.)

Nova Scotia is twice blessed: it's compact enough that you needn't spend all your time in a car. Yet it has fewer than a million residents (and one in three are in and around Halifax), making it unpopulated enough to provide empty places when you're seeking solitude. Even along the more populated shoreline it's possible to find a sense of remoteness, of being surrounded by big space and a profound history. More than once while traveling here, I've had the fleeting sense that I was traveling in New England, but 60 or 70 years ago, well before anyone referred to tourism as an industry.

1 Exploring Nova Scotia

Visitors to Nova Scotia would do well to spend some time poring over a map and this travel guide before leaving home. The hardest chore will be to narrow your options before you set off. Numerous loops and circuits are available, made more complicated by ferry links to the United States, New Brunswick, Prince Edward Island, and Newfoundland. Figuring out where to go and how to get there is the hardest part.

The only people I've ever heard complain about Nova Scotia are those who tried to see it all, and to see it within a week. Such an approach will leave you strung out and exhausted. Instead, prioritize your interests and decide accordingly. Looking for those picture-postcard-perfect scenes of coastal villages? Focus mostly on the south shore. If you're drawn to hiking amid rocky coastal scenery, allow plenty of time at Cape Breton. For more pastoral ocean scenery, head for the Fundy coast. Canoeing? Kejimkujik National Park. Gourmet dining and urban buzz? Factor a few days in Halifax. Above all, schedule plenty of time for simply doing not much of anything. It's the best way to let Nova Scotia's charms unfold at their own unhurried pace.

ESSENTIALS

VISITOR INFORMATION Every traveler to Nova Scotia should have a copy of the massive (350+ page) official tourism guide, which is the province's best effort to put travel-guide writers like me out of business. This comprehensive, colorful, well-organized and free guide lists all hotels, campgrounds, and attractions within the province, with brief descriptions and current prices. (Restaurants are given only limited coverage.)

The guide, entitled *Nova Scotia: Compete Guide For Doers and Dreamers,* is available starting each March by phone (☎ **800/565-0000** in North America or 902/425-5781 outside North America), mail (P.O. Box 130, Halifax, NS B3J 2M7), fax (902/453-8401), and e-mail (nsvisit@fox.nstn.ns.ca). If you wait until you arrive in the province before obtaining a copy, ask for one at the numerous visitor information centers, where you can also request the excellent free road map.

The provincial government administers about a dozen official **Visitor Information Centres** throughout the province, as well as in Portland, Maine, and Wood Islands, PEI. These mostly seasonal centers are amply stocked with brochures and tended by knowledgeable staffers. In addition, virtually every town of any note has a local tourist information center filled with racks of brochures covering the entire province, staffed with local people who know the area. You won't ever be short of information.

In general, the local and provincial visitor information centers are run with cordiality and brisk efficiency. I have yet to come across a single one that wasn't remarkably helpful, although the press of crowds can sometimes require a few minute's wait to get individual attention at the more popular gateways like Amherst and Port Hawksbury on Cape Breton Island. (A special thanks to the folks at the Sheet Harbour visitor center, who gamely tracked down a veterinarian one evening to help me wrestle the 200 porcupine quills out of my dog's snout.)

For general questions about travel in the province, call **Nova Scotia's information hotline** at ☎ **800/565-0000** (North America) or 902/425-5781 (outside North America).

GETTING THERE By Car & Ferry Most travelers reach Nova Scotia overland by car from New Brunswick. Plan on 4 plus hours driving from the U.S. border at Calais, Maine, to Amherst (at the New Brunswick–Nova Scotia border). Incorporating ferries into your itinerary can significantly reduce time behind the wheel. Daily seasonal ferries connect both Portland and Bar Harbor, Maine, to Yarmouth, Nova Scotia, at the peninsula's southwest end.

The **Portland–Yarmouth ferry** is approximately 11 hours and costs around US$80 for each adult passenger, US$40 for children, and US$98 for each vehicle. Cabins are available for an additional fare, ranging from about US$32 for a day cabin to US$165 for an overnight suite. Reservations are essential. Call **Prince of Fundy Cruises** at ☎ **800/341-7540** or 207/775-5616. On the Web, head to www.princeoffundy.com.

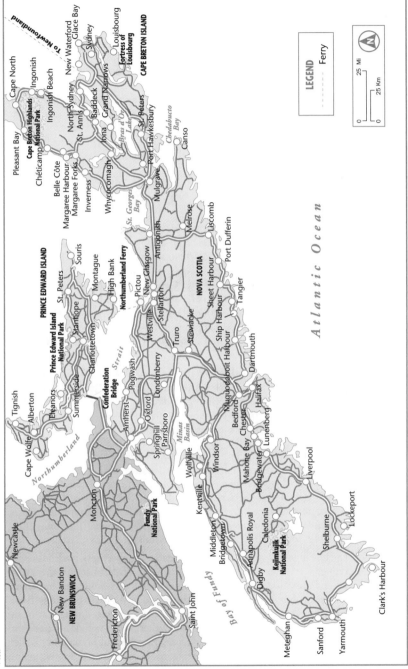

Bay Ferries (☎ 888/249-7245) operates the Bar Harbor–Yarmouth ferry. The Cat (short for catamaran) claims to be the fastest ferry in North America and since going into service in 1998 has cut the crossing time from 6 to 2¾ hours, zipping along at up to 50 miles per hour. Summer season rates are US$46 adult, US$41 senior, US$23 child (5 to 12), and US$60 for automobile. Off-season and family rates are available. Reservations are vital during the peak summer season.

To shorten the slog around the Bay of Fundy, a 3-hour ferry links **Saint John, New Brunswick, and Digby, Nova Scotia.** The ferry sails year-round, with as many as three crossings daily in summer. Summer fares are C$25 (US$17) for adults, C$12.50 (US$8.30) for children, and C$55 (US$37) per vehicle. It's also operated by **Bay Ferries** (☎ 888/249-7245). Schedules and more information on Bay Ferries may be found at www.nfl-bay.com.

For those traveling further afield, ferries also connect Prince Edward Island to Caribou, Nova Scotia, and Newfoundland to North Sydney, Nova Scotia. See chapters 5 and 6 for more detailed information.

By Plane   Halifax is the air hub of the Atlantic Provinces. **Air Canada** provides direct service from New York and Boston, and **Air Nova**, its commuter partner (☎ 800/776-3000 in the U.S. or 800/565-3940 in the Maritimes), serves Sydney and Yarmouth, plus about a dozen other Atlantic Canada destinations. Halifax, Sydney, and Yarmouth are also served by **Canadian Airlines International** (☎ 800/426-7000 in the U.S., 800/665-1177 in the Maritime Provinces, 902/427-5500 locally, and 709/576-0274 in Newfoundland). Routes that involve connections at Montréal or Toronto can turn a short hop into an all-day excursion. (Note that at press time both Air Canada and Canadian Airlines were considering mergers with one another as well as with outside airlines.)

By Train   Via Rail (☎ 800/561-3949 in the U.S. or 800/561-3952 in the Maritimes) offers train service 6 days a week between Halifax and Montréal. The entire trip takes between 18 and 21 hours, depending on direction. The fare is about C$185 (US$123) each way, with discounts for those buying at least 1 week in advance. Sleeping berths and private cabins are available at extra cost.

2 The Great Outdoors

Nova Scotia's official travel guide *(The Doer's and Dreamer's Complete Guide)* has a very helpful "Outdoors" section in the back that lists camping outfitters, bike shops, whale-watching tour operators, and the like. A free brochure that lists adventure outfitters is published by the **Adventure Tourism Association,** 1099 Marginal Rd., Suite 201, Halifax, NS B3H 4P7 (☎ 902/423-4480). Write or call for a copy.

BIKING   The low hills of Nova Scotia and the gentle, largely empty roads make for wonderful cycling. Cape Breton is the most challenging of destinations; the south coast and Bay of Fundy regions yield wonderful ocean views while making fewer demands on cyclists. A number of bike outfitters can aid in your trip planning. **Freewheeling Adventures** (☎ 902/857-3600) offers guided bike tours throughout Nova Scotia, Prince Edward Island, and Newfoundland. Walter Sienko's guide, *Nova Scotia & the Maritimes by Bike: 21 Tours Geared for Discovery,* is helpful in planning a bike excursion. For an Internet introduction to cycling in Nova Scotia and beyond, point your Web browser to www.atl-canadacycling.com.

BIRD WATCHING   More than 400 species of birds have been spotted in Nova Scotia, ranging from odd and exotic birds blown off course in storms to majestic bald eagles, of which some 250 nesting pairs reside in Nova Scotia, mostly on Cape Breton

Island. Many whale-watching tours also offer specialized sea bird–spotting tours, including trips to puffin colonies. More-experienced birders will enjoy checking regularly with the **Nova Scotia Bird Society**'s information line (☎ 902/852-2428), which features up-to-date recorded information about intriguing sightings around the province.

CAMPING   With backcountry options rather limited, Nova Scotia's forte is drive-in camping. The 20 provincial parks with campgrounds are uniformly clean, friendly, well managed, and reasonably priced, and offer some 1,500 campsites among them. For a brochure and map listing all campsites, write to **Nova Scotia Department of Natural Resources, Parks and Recreation Division,** R.R. no. 1, Belmont, NS B0M 1C0; or call ☎ 902/662-3030.

Another free and helpful guide is the Campground Owners Association of Nova Scotia's *Campers Guide,* which includes a directory of private campgrounds that are members of the association. Ask for it at the visitor information centers, or contact the association at ☎ 902/423-4480.

CANOEING   Nova Scotia offers an abundance of accessible canoeing on inland lakes and ponds. The premier destination is **Kejimkujik National Park** in the southern interior, which has 44 backcountry sites accessible by canoe. A number of other fine canoe trails allow paddlers and portagers to venture off for hours or days. General information is available from **Canoe Nova Scotia,** 5516 Spring Garden Rd., Halifax, NS B3J 3G6, ☎ 902/425-5450. Tour maps outlining 22 canoe trips in Annapolis County are available for C$16 (US$11) from **Canoe Annapolis County,** P.O. Box 100, Annapolis Royal, NS B0S 1A0, ☎ 902/532-2334.

FISHING   Saltwater fishing tours are easily arranged on charter boats berthed at many of the province's harbors. Inquire locally at the visitor information centers, or consult the "Boat Tours & Charters" section of the *Doers & Dreamers* guide. No fishing license is needed for those on charters. For saltwater regulations, contact **Department of Fisheries and Oceans,** ☎ 902/426-5952.

Committed freshwater anglers come to Nova Scotia in pursuit of the tragically dwindling Atlantic salmon, which requires a license separate from that for other freshwater fish. **Salmon licenses** must be obtained from a provincial Natural Resources office, provincial campground, or licensed outfitter. Other freshwater species popular with anglers are brown trout, shad, smallmouth bass, rainbow trout, and speckled trout. For a copy of the current fishing regulations, contact the **Department of Natural Resources License Section,** ☎ 902/424-6608.

GOLF   More than 50 golf courses are located throughout Nova Scotia. Among the most memorable: the **Cape Breton Highland Links** (☎ 902/285-2600) in Ingonish, which features a dramatic oceanside setting, and **Bell Bay Golf Club** (☎ 800/565-3077) near Baddeck, which is also wonderfully scenic, and was voted "Best New Canadian Golf Course" by *Golf Digest* in 1998. For one-stop shoppers, **Golf Nova Scotia** (☎ 877/204-4653, www.golfnovascotia.com) represents 18 well-regarded properties around the province and can arrange customized golfing packages at its member courses. A handy directory of Nova Scotia's golf courses (with phone numbers) is published in the "Outdoors" section of *The Doer's and Dreamer's Complete Guide.*

HIKING & WALKING   Serious hikers make tracks for Cape Breton Highlands National Park, which is home to the most dramatic terrain in the province. But you're certainly not limited to here. Trails are found throughout Nova Scotia, although in many cases they're a matter of local knowledge. (Ask at the visitor information centers.) An ambitious and exceptionally attractive 30-kilometer (18-mile) hiking loop is under construction on the Fundy Coast near Parrsboro; for more information, see the "Parrsboro" section, below. Published hiking guides are widely available at local bookstores. Especially helpful are the back-pocket-sized guides published by **Nimbus Publishing of Halifax** (call for a catalog: ☎ **800/646-2879** or 902/455-4286).

SAILING Any area with so much convoluted coastline is clearly inviting to sailors and gunkholers. Tours and charters are available almost everywhere there's a decent-sized harbor. Those with the inclination and skills to venture out on their own can rent 16-foot Wayfarers, or one of several slightly larger boats, by the hour and maneuver among beautiful islands at **Sail Mahone Bay** (☎ **902/624-8864**) on the south shore near Lunenburg. The province's premier sailing experience is an excursion aboard the *Bluenose II,* which is virtually an icon for Atlantic Canada. See the "Lunenburg" section later in this chapter.

SEA KAYAKING Nova Scotia is increasingly attracting the attention of kayakers worldwide. Kayakers traveling on their own should be especially cautious on the Bay of Fundy side, since the massive tides create strong currents that overmatch even the fittest of paddlers. Nearly 40 kayak outfitters (and growing) do business in Nova Scotia, and they offer everything from 1-hour introductory paddles to intensive week-long trips; consult the directory in *Doers and Dreamers.*

Among the more respected outfitters is **Coastal Adventures,** P.O. Box 77, Tangier, NS B0J 3H0, ☎ **902/772-2774.** The company is run by veteran kayaker Scott Cunningham, who leads trips throughout the Maritimes and Newfoundland. For kayaking on the eastern side of Cape Breton, check with **Island Seafari,** 20 Paddys Lane, Louisbourg, NS B0A 1M0, ☎ **902/733-2309.**

WHALE WATCHING If you're on the coast, it's likely you're not far from a whale-watching operation. Around two dozen whale-watching outfits offer trips in search of finback, humpback, pilot, and minke whales, among others. The richest waters for whale watching are found on the Fundy Coast, where the endangered right whale is often seen feeding in summer. Digby Neck has the highest concentration of whale-watching excursions, but you'll find them in many other coves and harbors. Just ask the staff at visitor information centers to direct you to the whales.

3 Minas Basin & Cobequid Bay

If you're not content except off the beaten track, a detour along the Minas Basin and Cobequid Bay will be one of the highlights of your trip. With the exception of Truro, this region is rural and quiet, and full of hidden surprises. You can turn down a dirt road, shut off your car's engine, and not hear much other than the wind and maybe a blackbird or two. You can trek along spectacular hiking trails, or picnic alone on a long stretch of remote and misty coast, literally watching the tides roll in.

There's also a rich history here, but it tends to be hidden and subtle rather than preening and obvious. And don't look for the quaint seaside villages or the surf-washed rocky coast for which Nova Scotia is famous; that will have to wait until Yarmouth and the South Shore. The natural drama here is pegged to the region's profound remoteness and the powerful but silent tides, among the highest in the world.

PARRSBORO

Samuel de Champlain stumbled upon amethyst while exploring Partridge Island in 1604. He and his crew brought the gemstones back to France, where they were cut and polished. They are now part of the French crown jewels.

A few miles away and a few centuries later, another discovery was made near Parrsboro. In 1986 two scientists uncovered one of the world's largest caches of dinosaur fossils—some 100,000 pieces of fossilized bone dating back 200 million years. The trove included skulls, teeth, and bones that belonged to dinosaurs, lizards, sharks, and crocodiles.

Parrsboro's richness in gems and fossils stems from a confluence of two factors: First, it's at the seam where two continents collided back in the days of primeval ooze. (Evidence: The fossils found here are the same as those you'll find in parts of Africa.) And second, the region's shores are exposed to the world's highest tides, which means that constant erosion reveals new geological treasures.

The town is terminally somnolent and has only a handful of tourist amenities, but that only adds to its appeal. Perhaps it's telling that another Parrsboro attraction is **Dave's Sports Museum and Barber Shop** at 49 Main St. You can admire the collection of championship softballs while you get a shave and a trim. The town is striving to capitalize on its renown as a fossil capital (note the dinosaur footprints painted in the sidewalk, and the illuminated dinos on the lampposts). But for now, it's still a well-kept secret, and you're likely to have it to yourself.

ESSENTIALS

GETTING THERE   Parrsboro is reached via Route 2 from either Springhill (46km/27 miles) or Truro (90km/54 miles).

VISITOR INFORMATION   The **Parrsboro Tourist Info Centre** (☎ 902/254-3266) faces the bandstand and small park in the village center. It's open daily in summer from 8:30am to 8:30pm.

EXPLORING THE AREA

ROCK HOUNDING   It's somewhat ironic that in an area that boasts outstanding seacoast landscapes so many people spend their time with eyes glued to the ground. But this is a rock hound's and fossil scavenger's paradise, and you're missing out on the area's unique character if you admire only the landscape.

If you're an experienced rock hound, you know the drill. If you're a novice, you'll want guidance. Start with a trip to the **Fundy Geological Museum** (see below) to get up to speed on the region's unique geology. Then sign up for a guided mineral- or fossil-collecting tour with either the museum or Eldon George.

Another option is to explore with **Dinatours** (☎ 902/254-3700), an outfit that maintains a headquarters and gift shop in a converted lobster boat at the causeway near the museum. Sonja Prell and Randy Corcoran offer various guided collecting tours both by foot and by boat around the Minas Basin. Costs range from C$40 (US$27) per adult (C$20/US$13 for children under 16) for a 6-hour boat trip to the mineral-rich Five Islands, to C$20 (US$13) for a 2½-hour interpretive walking tour. (Some minimums apply on boat tours.)

Fundy Geological Museum. 6 Two Island Rd. ☎ **902/254-3814.** www. fundygeomuseum.com. Admission C$3.50 (US$2.35) adults, C$1.75 (US$1.20) ages 6–17, C$2.75 (US$1.85) seniors, C$8.50 (US$5.65) family. Daily in summer 9:30am–5:30pm; closed Mon in winter.

The modern Fundy Geological Museum (built in 1993) does a fine job of putting the region's complex geology into context. Operated by the Cumberland Geological Society, the museum starts with displays and a video presentation to help you brush up on various epochs and eras (does Jurassic come before or after Triassic?). Then you can view various minerals and fossils on display, and learn what to look for when you head out on your own. There's more than enough to engage curious adults, but it's displayed in a fashion that makes it accessible to most children. Field trips are regularly scheduled to mineral- and fossil-rich areas; ask at the front desk for a schedule.

Parrsboro Rock and Mineral Shop & Museum. 39 Whitehall Rd. ☎ **902/254-2981.** Free admission to shop; donations requested for museum. Closed Christmas–Apr. Mon–Sat 9am–dusk, Sunday by chance. From town, bear right at the war memorial and follow the road toward Ottawa House. Look for the shop on your left, with the dinosaur in front.

Eldon George is a celebrity in rock-collecting circles for his extraordinary finds—including the world's smallest dinosaur footprints (they're about the size of a penny, made by dinosaurs as big as sparrows). His shop sells prospecting gear along with raw and polished stones. You can see the famed tiny footprints, huge amethyst geodes, and other wondrous geological displays at the small museum. George himself is often here, and he is quite congenial and accessible. He and his son also lead guided tours (1 to 3 hours) to collecting areas, with rates starting at C$20 (US$13) per person, under 12 free.

HIKING   Just 3 kilometers (1.8 miles) southwest of town is **Partridge Island,** connected to the mainland by a pebbly causeway. You can park along the beach, then hike out to the high, tree-studded island, which has trails for exploring. You'll get great views of Minas Basin and the stupendous tides. Watch the ground from time to time to ensure you don't trip over amethyst or other rare stones.

After your hike, stop by the **Ottawa House** (☎ 902/254-2376)—that massive white home at the far end of the causeway. Once occupied by Sir Charles Tupper, who briefly served as Canadian prime minister (for just 16 days in 1896), the home was originally built in 1775 and went through various incarnations, serving as a hotel between 1922 and 1979. It's now a historical museum (admission C$1, under 12 free), with rather mundane displays that include knot boards and a "Victorian parlor." My advice: Buy an ice cream cone in the snack shop, and enjoy it while admiring the view from the broad front porch.

Cape Chignecto Provincial Park (about 45km/28 miles west of Parrsboro on Route 209) has been developed over the past couple of years as one of Nova Scotia's premier hiking destinations, giving even the national park at Cape Breton a run for its money. This is by far the largest provincial park (10,500 acres) and is wild and remote, with the highest coastal cliffs on mainland Nova Scotia—as much as 600 feet above tide-raked Advocate Bay and the Bay of Fundy. A hiking trail circuit of about 30 kilometers (18 miles) runs along the cliffs and through the rugged backcountry. You can camp at some 40 sites spread among five locations. Day hikes to secluded beaches are also an option. Camping is C$14 (US$9) per night plus the $2 (US$1.35) day use fee; advance reservations are strongly recommended. For more information, stop by the park's visitor information center on Route 209 in Advocate Harbour, or call ☎ 902/392-2085.

WHERE TO STAY

If you're equipped for camping, one of the province's true gems is **Glooscap Park and Campground** (☎ 902/254-2529), on the coast about 6 kilometers (3.6 miles) from the village. (Look for directional signs in town.) There are 56 sites spread about a tall bluff of grass and forest. A steel staircase leads to the beach, where you can walk for miles along crumbling cliffs and watch the huge tides slosh in and out. (This is a popular area to scout for fossils.) This is a well-run, old-fashioned campground, managed by the town, of the sort that's harder to find these days—you actually park and camp on grassy lawns, not on gravel pads. It's C$10 (US$7) for a tent site; C$15 (US$10) for a trailer site with hookups.

Gillespie House Inn. 358 Main St., Parrsboro, NS B0M 1S0. ☎ **902/254-3196.** 5 units (all share 2 bathrooms). C$50–C$75 (US$33–US$50) double, including continental breakfast. AE, MC, V. Closed Nov–Apr.

This handsome 1890s Victorian farmhouse sits on a shady rise—an easy walk from the village center—and was originally home to prominent shipbuilders and merchants. Innkeepers Lori Lynch and David Beattie offer a pleasant, homey atmosphere with five guest rooms, which share two bathrooms (plans call for creating two rooms with private bathrooms by the summer of 2000). Room 3 is the largest and brightest of the bunch; Room 5 has wonderful maple wainscoting. Public spaces are limited, although there's a small TV room and a first-floor sauna and hot tub. Ask about packages such as the yoga and hiking weekends.

The Maple Inn. 2358 Western Ave. (P.O. Box 457), Parrsboro, NS B0M 1S0. ☎ **902/254-3735.** 9 units (6 with private bathrooms; 3 share 2 bathrooms). C$59–C$99 (US$39–US$66) double, including full breakfast. AE, MC, V.

The Maple Inn, located in a peaceful village setting, is actually two century-old homes joined together. The pair of sturdy, yellow-and-brown buildings served as the town's hospital for 30 years but has been made over in a glossy, country Victorian style with dried flowers and period furniture. It's likely to be considered a bit overly renovated by those who prize historic authenticity; but it's comfortable and cheerful, and many of the rooms are quite spacious. The third-floor suite is perfect for families, with its king canopied bed and spare room with two twin beds (the suite also has the inn's only in-room TV). The three shared-bathroom guest rooms offer especially good value; of these, cozy Room 4 has a sitting area in the bay window.

Riverview Cottages. Route 2 (P.O. Box 71), Parrsboro, NS B0M 1S0. ☎ **902/254-2388.** 19 units. C$38–C$65 (US$25–US$43) double. Credit cards not accepted. Closed Nov 15–Apr 30.

This tidy assortment of simple, rustic cottages is located a mile from the village in a grassy riverside setting dotted with Adirondack chairs. Some of the cabins have been updated (I prefer the older, more rustic ones), 10 have kitchenettes, and a dozen have woodstoves. All guests have access to the free rowboats and canoes.

WHERE TO DINE

A good option for a light meal is **John's Cafe**, 151 Main St. (☎ 902/254-3255). It has a casual attitude and offerings like chili and salads, along with coffee and baked goods. It's open daily from early till late in summer; there's a small patio out back for good weather.

Stowaway Restaurant. 69 Main St., ☎ **902/254-3371**. Main courses C$6–C$13 (US$4–US$9). AE, ER, MC, V. Daily 9am–10pm (until 11pm in July and Aug). CANADIAN.

The downhome Stowaway is a family-style restaurant, which is to say the food is good but not fancy, fresh but not elaborate. They do all their baking on premises, and all meals are homecooked—the fish in the fish and chips is local flounder. The pies are tasty, and a meal here is usually light on the wallet.

PARRSBORO AFTER DARK

Yes, Parrsboro has nightlife, with an attraction that regularly merits glowing reviews in the Halifax newspaper. The **Ship's Company Theater** (☎ 800/565-7469 or 902/254-2003) offers performances throughout the summer aboard the M.V. *Kipawo*, a beached showpiece that's now more artifact than vessel. The setting is inspired, and the acting is of first-rate quality. Performances are staged daily except Monday in summer, with tickets C$18 (US$12) for adults, C$16 (US$11) for seniors and students, and C$11 (US$7) for youths.

TRURO

Truro is the region's commercial hub, with an old-fashioned downtown surrounded by a sprawling mass of strip malls and shopping plazas. The town (pop. 12,000) has served as a traveler's crossroads since 1858, when the rail line between Montréal and Halifax first passed through. (Passenger rail service is still available.) With a convenient location just off the Trans-Canada Highway and a profusion of motels and chain restaurants, Truro still serves the traveler well. It is, however, best regarded as an intermediate stop rather than a destination.

ESSENTIALS

GETTING THERE   Truro is located on Route 102, just south of the junction with Route 104 (the Trans-Canada Highway). Truro is also served by **Via Rail** (☎ 800/361-8010), which connects Moncton to Halifax. The train station is at 104 Esplanade St., next to the downtown Esplanade Mall.

VISITOR INFORMATION   The **Truro Information Centre and Tourist Bureau** (☎ 902/893-2922) is located in a glass-walled pavilion downtown at Victoria Square (corner of Prince and Willow Streets). Open daily from mid-May to early November 8am to 8pm; closed the rest of the year.

EXPLORING TRURO

Aficionados of public spaces—especially of parks that trace their ancestry back to the turn of the century—will enjoy **Victoria Park,** a 1,000-acre retreat flanking a shady gorge not far from the town center. It's well-used by Truro residents, and a bit worn and shabby around the edges. But park your car and stroll past the playing fields and playground, following the brook into the dusky glen. Elaborate arrangements of staircases, boardwalks, and bridges work their way up into the narrowing gorge, which is lined with Norway spruce and hemlock. Local kids are at play here, some swimming in the waterfalls, others intent on triggering rock slides on hapless hikers. Younger children often find the upper reaches of the gorge magical.

The park is open daily from dawn to dusk; admission is free. It's located at Brunswick Street and Park Road. It's a bit tricky to track down; your best bet is to ask for a map and directions at the visitor center.

EXPERIENCING THE TIDAL BORE

Let it be said: The tidal bore has to be one of the more overrated attractions in Nova Scotia. It's quite interesting in theory—a bore is a low wave approximately a meter in height that rolls upstream ahead of the incoming tide, marking the moment the flows of rivers and brooks change direction. Bores are found in England, India, Brazil, and China, but in North America are seen only around the Bay of Fundy, including some rivers in New Brunswick. The bore tends to be especially pronounced around Cobequid Bay, where the tides are greatly amplified (up to 50 feet) thanks to its funnel-like shape.

I'm told the tidal bore can be truly impressive at times, but this has not been my experience. The bore, as seen from the shore, is a curious geographic quirk, nothing more, and offers little to inspire awe or wonder. If you happen to be in the area when the bore is due, by all means swing by and have a look. But I wouldn't rearrange travel plans to view it.

In Truro, visitors are directed to **Tidal Bore Park** along the Salmon River, located on a grassy slope next to a motel and restaurant (take Exit 14 off Route 102). Be forewarned: The site is not all that charming. A busy highway runs along one side of the viewing area, and power lines clutter the horizon. But you get a good view of the bore steadfastly chugging up the muddy river. Ask at the visitor center for tide times, check the local paper, or call **Dial-a-Tide** (☎ **902/426-5494**).

A more heart-thumping way to experience the bore is to incorporate some outdoor adventure into the experience. Several **rafting outfitters** are based south of Truro on the Shubenacadie River, Nova Scotia's largest river. Here you can spend 2 to 4 hours charting the bore's progress aboard motorized Zodiacs (rafts) that follow the wave's progress upstream. You'll typically don rain suits and prowl around the mouth of the river, then follow the bore upstream, crashing through the wave time and again. It's often about 3 feet high, but when the winds and moon work together the wave can crest at 8 feet high.

Tidal Bore Rafting (☎ 888/244-9283 or 902/752-0899) offers half-day adventures on the Shubenacadie River that include a riverside lunch. **Shubenacadie Tidal Bore Park Rafting** (☎ 800/565-7238) has 2- and 4-hour trips; as many as 75 adventurers at a time follow the bore in a herd of noisy Zodiacs. Other options include trips with **Shubenacadie River Adventure Tours** in South Maitland (☎ 888/878-8687 or 902/471-6595) and **Shubenacadie River Runners Ltd.** in Maitland (☎ 800/856-5061 or 902/261-2770). Plan on paying C$40 to C$65 (US$27 to US$43) per person, depending on the length of the tour. Times, of course, vary according to the tide. Call for information.

A Scenic Drive

If you're headed from Truro southwestward along the Fundy coast toward Digby, Route 215 offers a wonderful coastal detour from Maitland to Windsor. This winding, fast, and rather narrow road (not suggested for bicycling) passes through a number of quiet hamlets, some with handsome early buildings. But the chief appeal comes in the sudden vistas of lush green farmland (often accompanied by the redolent smells of cow by-product) and broad views of expansive Minas Basin beyond. At the town of Walton, there's a handsome lighthouse on a rocky bluff with a nearby picnic area just off the main route (it's well marked). This detour runs 93 kilometers (56 miles) from South Maitland to Brooklyn. Few services for tourists are offered along the route, other than a handful of restaurants, B&Bs, and campgrounds. Look for general stores and farm stands if you need a snack.

Where to Stay & Dine

Truro is located at a major fork on the Trans-Canada Highway: you can continue on the Trans-Canada toward Cape Breton, or veer southward toward Halifax (about an hour away). Because of its key location, the town is home to about a dozen serviceable motels and B&Bs. Among the chains are the **Comfort Inn,** 12 Meadow Dr. (☎ 800/228-5150 or 902/893-0330), and **Best Western Glengarry,** 150 Willow St. (☎ 800/567-4276 or 902/893-4311). Rooms at either place are typically in the C$70 to C$90 (US$47 to US$60) range. Rooms often book up early in summer; plan to call in advance for reservations if you're likely to arrive later in the day.

The Palliser Motel & Restaurant. Tidal Bore Rd. (Route 102/Exit 14), Truro, NS B2N 5G6. ☎ **902/893-8951.** Fax 902/895-8475. E-mail: palliser@auracom.com. 42 units. TV. C$47 (US$31) double, including buffet breakfast (discounts in off-season). AE, DC, ER, MC, V.

This vintage 1950s-era motel is arrayed in a horseshoe pattern around a well-tended lawn that slopes down toward the Palliser Restaurant and the viewing area for the tidal bore. Rooms are simple and basic, as are the meals at the restaurant (fried scallops, fried haddock, lobster rolls). The Palliser has the most character of any Truro motel, but I can't foresee circumstances under which anyone would wish to spend more than a night here. The tidal bore is floodlit at night for after-dark viewing.

WOLFVILLE

The trim and tidy Victorian village of Wolfville (pop. 3,500) has a distinctly New England feel to it, in both its handsome architecture and its layout—a small commercial downtown just 6 blocks long is surrounded by shady neighborhoods of elegant homes. And it's not hard to trace that sensibility to its source. The area was largely populated in the wake of the American Revolution by transplanted New Englanders, who forced off the Acadian settlers who had earlier done so much to tame the wilds.

The town's mainstay these days is handsome **Acadia University,** which has nearly as many full-time students as there are residents of Wolfville. The university's presence gives the small village an edgier, more youthful air. Don't miss the university's **Art Gallery at the Beveridge Arts Center** (☎ 902/585-1373), which showcases both contemporary and historic Nova Scotian art.

The town has emerged in recent years as a popular destination for weekending Halifax residents, who come to relax at the many fine inns, wander the leafy streets, and explore the countryside. Also a consistent draw is the **Atlantic Theatre Festival** (☎ 800/337-6661 or 902/542-4242), which has attracted plaudits in the few years it has been presenting shows. Performances are staged throughout the summer season in a comfortable 500-seat theater. Reservations are encouraged; ticket prices are C$21 to C$38 (US$14 to US$25).

EXPLORING WOLFVILLE

Strolling the village is the activity of choice. The towering elms and maples that shade the extravagant Victorian architecture provide the dappled light and rustling sounds for an ideal walk. A good place to start is the **Wolfville Tourist Bureau** at Willow Park (☎ 902/542-7000) on the north edge of the downtown. If you'd prefer to cover more ground, you can rent a mountain or touring bike at **Valley Stove and Cycle,** 232 Main St. (☎ 902/542-7280).

One of the more intriguing sights in town occurs each summer day at dusk, in an unprepossessing park surrounded by a parking lot a block off Main Street. At **Robie Swift Park,** a lone chimney (dating from a long-gone dairy plant) rises straight up like a stumpy finger pointed at the heavens. Around sunset, between 25 and 100 chimney swifts flit about and then descend into the chimney for the night. Alas, the swifts have been declining in number in recent years, ever since some predatory merlins starting nesting nearby. But you'll learn a lot by browsing the informational plaques posted here, where you can read interesting tidbits such as this: No one knew where swifts migrated in winter until 1943, when explorers in the Peruvian jungle found natives wearing necklaces adorned with small aluminum rings. These, it turned out, were tracking bands placed on swifts by North American ornithologists.

HIKING CAPE SPLIT

Several trails through rugged landscapes and intriguing geological formations are on Cape Split, the hook of land that extends far into the Bay of Fundy north of Wolfville.

At **Blomidon Provincial Park** (☎ 902/582-7319), 25 kilometers (15 miles) north of Route 101 (Exit 11), some 13.7 kilometers (8.5 miles) of trail at the park take walkers through forest and along the coast. Among the most dramatic trails is the 6-kilometer (3.7-mile) **Jodrey Trail,** which follows towering cliffs that offer broad views over the Minas Basin.

For a more demanding adventure, head north of Wolfville about 25 minutes on Route 358, and park off the side of the road near the beginning of the **Cape Split**

Trail. This 16-kilometer (10-mile) trail offers some of the more breathtaking vistas in Nova Scotia, cresting oceanside cliffs that approach 400 feet in height. Allow most of a day to truly enjoy this in-and-back excursion. Basic maps and additional information are available from the Wolfville Tourist Bureau (see above).

Grand-Pré National Historic Site. Route 1, Grand-Pré. ☎ **902/542-3631.** Admission C$2.50 (US$1.65) adults, C$2 (US$1.35) seniors, C$1.10 (US75¢) ages 6–16, C$7 (US$4.65) family. Daily 9am–6pm. Closed Nov–mid-May.

Long before roving New Englanders arrived in this region, hardworking Acadians had vastly altered the local landscape. They did this in large part by constructing a series of dikes outfitted with ingenious log valves, which allowed farmers to convert the salt-water marshes to productive farmland. At Grand-Pré, a short drive east of Wolfville and just off Route 1, you can learn about these dikes along with the tragic history of the Acadians, who populated the Minas Basin between 1680 and their expulsion in 1755.

More a memorial park than a living history exhibit, Grand-Pré (which means "great meadow") has superbly tended grounds that are excellent for idling, a picnic lunch, or simple contemplation. Among the handful of buildings on the grounds is a graceful **stone church,** built in 1922 on the presumed site of the original church. Evangeline Bellefontaine, the revered (albeit fictional) heroine of Longfellow's epic poem, was said to have been born here; look for the statue of this tragic heroine in the garden. It was created in 1920 by Canadian sculptor Philippe Hérbert, and the image has been reproduced widely since.

WHERE TO STAY

Gingerbread House Inn. 8 Robie Tufts Dr. (P.O. Box 819), Wolfville, NS B0P 1X0. ☎ **888/542-1458** or 902/542-1458. Fax 902/542-4718. www.gingerbreadhouse.ns.ca. E-mail: hedly@gingerbreadhouse.ns.ca. 6 units. TV. C$69–C$145 (US$46–US$97) double, includes breakfast. Ask about theater packages. MC, V.

The ornate Gingerbread House Inn was originally the carriage house for the building now housing Victoria's Historic Inn (see below). A former owner went woodshop-wild, adding all manner of swirly accouterments and giving the place a convincingly authentic air. The guest rooms are a modern interpretation of the gingerbread style and are generally quite comfortable, although the two rooms in the back are dark and small. The floral Carriage House Suite is the most spacious, and it features luxe touches like a propane fireplace and two-person Jacuzzi. The budget choice is the lovely Terrace Room, which is somewhat minuscule but has a lovely private deck on the second floor under a gracefully arching tree. Breakfasts tend toward the elaborate and are served by candlelight.

✪ **Tattingstone Inn.** 434 Main St. (P.O. Box 98), Wolfville, NS B0P 1X0. ☎ **800/565-7696** or 902/542-7696. Fax 902/542-4427. E-mail: tattingstone@ns.sympatico.ca. 10 units. A/C TV TEL. C$89–C$138 (US$59–US$92) double; suite C$168 (US$112). AE, MC, V. Children 12 and up.

"We sell romance and relaxation," says innkeeper Betsy Harwood. And that pretty well sums it up. This handsome Italianate-Georgian mansion dates back to 1874 and overlooks the village's main artery. The inn is furnished with a mix of reproductions and antiques, and traditional and modern art blend well. The attitude isn't over-the-top Victorian as one might guess by looking at the manse, but decorated with a deft touch that mixes informal country antiques and regal Empire pieces. The rooms in the Carriage House are a bit smaller, but they are still pleasant and showcase fine examples of modern Canadian art.

Dining: The spacious semiformal dining room is rather refined, and diners sup amid white tablecloths and stern Doric columns. Dinner is served nightly in summer from 5:30 to 9:30pm. Ask for a seat on the enclosed porch, which captures the lambent early evening light to good effect. House specialties include the rack of lamb and the chicken served with pear and ginger sauce; the latter uses pears grown on the property. Entrees range in price from C$16 to C$26 (US$11 to US$17).

Amenities: Heated outdoor pool, steam room, tennis court.

Victoria's Historic Inn. 416 Main St., Wolfville, NS B0P 1X0. ☎ **800/556-5744** or 902/542-5744. Fax 902/542-7794. 15 units. A/C TV TEL. C$95–C$175 (US$63–US$117) double, including full breakfast. AE, ER, MC, V.

Victoria's Historic Inn was constructed by apple mogul William Chase in 1893 and is architecturally elaborate. This sturdy Queen Anne–style building features bold pediments and massed pavilions, which have been adorned with balusters and ornate Stick-style trim. Inside, the effect seems a bit as if you'd wandered into one of those stereoscopic views of a Victorian parlor. Whereas the nearby Tattingstone Inn resists theme decor, Victoria's Historic Inn embraces it. There's dense mahogany and cherry woodwork throughout, along with exceptionally intricate ceilings. The deluxe Chase Suite features a large sitting room with a gas fireplace and an oak mantle. The lessexpensive third-floor rooms are smaller and somewhat less historic in flavor.

WHERE TO DINE

Coffee strong enough to make the mummified snap bolt upright is available at **The Coffee Merchant of Wolfville,** 334 Main St. (☎ **902/542-4315**). The shop also has a selection of pastries and sweets.

In addition to these restaurants, the dining rooms mentioned above serve some of the more elegant meals in town, but at a price to match.

Al's Homestyle Deli. 314 Main St. ☎ **902/542-5908.** No reservations. All selections C$2–C$4 (US$1.35–US$2.65). V. Mon–Thurs 9am–6:30pm, Fri–Sun 9am–9pm. DELI.

Randy and Linda Davidson now operate the place, but Al Waddell's popular recipes for sausages live on: choose from Polish, German, hot Italian, and honey garlic sausages. Buy some links to cook later, or order up a quick road meal. You won't find a better cheap lunch: A sausage on a bun with a cup of soup will run you less than C$5 (US$3).

Chez la Vigne. 117 Front St. ☎ **902/542-5077.** Reservations suggested. Lunch C$6–C$11 (US$4–US$7); dinner C$13–C$25 (US$9–US$17). AE, ER, MC, V. Daily 11am–10pm (until 9pm in winter). INTERNATIONAL.

Chez la Vigne is on a quiet side street a few steps off Main Street. The place is informal and comfortable, and the chef maintains the welcome philosophy that everyone should be able to afford a good meal. Dishes range from country simple (paella for two) to rather more complex (rabbit stuffed with herbs and rice). The quality varies, but more often than not, it's very good.

4 Annapolis Royal

Annapolis Royal is arguably Nova Scotia's most historic town—it even bills itself, with justification, as "Canada's birthplace." The nation's first permanent settlement was established at Port Royal, just across the river from the present-day Annapolis Royal, in 1605 by a group of doughty settlers that included Samuel de Champlain. (Champlain called the beautiful Annapolis Basin "one of the finest harbours that I have seen on all these coasts.") The strategic importance of this well-protected harbor was proven in the tumultuous later years, when a series of forts was constructed on the low hills overlooking the water.

Annapolis Royal today is truly a treat to visit. Because the region was largely overlooked by later economic growth (trade and fishing moved to the Atlantic side of the peninsula), it requires little in the way of imagination to see Annapolis Royal as it once was. (The current population is just 700.) The original settlement was rebuilt on the presumed site. Fort Anne overlooks the upper reaches of the basin, much as it did when abandoned in 1854. And the village itself maintains much of its original historic charm, with narrow streets and historic buildings fronting the now-placid waterfront.

Indeed, Annapolis Royal is also considered by many historians to be the birthplace of historic preservation. Starting early in this century, town residents have been unusually active in preserving the character of the place. As testament to their dedication, note that some 150 buildings and homes in town are officially designated heritage sites.

For anyone curious about Canada's early history, Annapolis Royal is one of Nova Scotia's don't-miss destinations.

ESSENTIALS

GETTING THERE   Annapolis is located at Exit 22 of Route 101. It is 206 kilometers (124 miles) from Halifax, and 133 kilometers (80 miles) from Yarmouth.

VISITOR INFORMATION   The **Annapolis District Tourist Bureau** (☎ 902/532-5454) is 1.2 kilometers (0.7 miles) north of the town center (follow Prince Albert Road and look for the Annapolis Royal Tidal Generating Station). It's open daily in summer 8am to 8pm (9am to 5pm in spring and fall).

EXPLORING THE TOWN

Start at the tourist bureau, which is located at the **Annapolis Royal Tidal Generating Station** (☎ 902/532-5454), where the extreme tides have been harnessed to produce electricity. It's the only tidal generator in North America, and the world's largest straight-flow turbine. Learn about the generator at the free exhibit center upstairs from the visitor center.

Before leaving the center, be sure to request a copy of the free "Footprints with Footnotes" walking-tour brochure. The annotated map provides architectural and historic context for a stroll around the downtown and waterfront. Take a moment to note that as you walk down lower St. George Street, you're walking down the oldest street in Canada.

One of the more entertaining ways to learn about local history is to attend the ✪ **Old Burying Ground Walking Tour.** These tours depart Fort Anne at 9:30pm on Tuesday, Thursday, and Sunday during the summer. Visitors are given candle lanterns, then led on a 1-hour tour of the ancient cemetery next to the fort. You'll learn about fads in headstone art and hear tales of the early inhabitants of Annapolis Royal, including the flamboyant mistress of the Duke of Wellington. Tours are C$4 (US$2.65); confirm times and days at Fort Anne National Historic Park (see below).

Children and adults alike adore ✪ **Upper Clements Park** (☎ 888/248-4567 or 902/532-7557) on Route 1, 5 miles south of Annapolis Royal. This is a wonderfully old-fashioned amusement park (you arrive after driving through an old orchard). It's full of low-key amusements and attractions that will especially delight younger kids. Highlights include the flume ride (originally built for Expo '86 in Vancouver) and a wooden roller coaster that twists and winds through trees left standing during the coaster's construction. It's open daily in season 11am to 7pm; admission to the grounds is C$2.30 (US$1.55), children under 5 free. The rate includes admission to the adjacent wild animal park. Unlimited rides are C$10 (US$7) additional per person.

In the evening there's often entertainment in downtown Annapolis Royal at **King's Theatre**, 209 St. George St., ☎ **800/818-8587** or 902/532-5466. Shows range from movies to musical performances to variety shows to touring plays. Stop by or call to find out what's on during your stay.

✪ **Fort Anne National Historic Site.** Entrance on St. George St. ☎ **902/532-2321.** Admission to grounds is free; museum is C$2.75 (US$1.85) adult, C$2.25 (US$1.50) senior, C$1.35 (US90¢) child, C$7 (US$5) family. May 15–Oct 15 9am–6pm; off-season by appointment only (grounds open year-round).

What you'll likely remember most from a visit here are the impressive grassy earthworks that cover some 35 acres of high ground overlooking the confluence of the Annapolis River and Allains Creek. The French built the first fort here around 1643. Since then, dozens of buildings and fortifications have occupied this site. You can visit the 1708 gunpowder magazine (the oldest building of any Canadian National Historic Site), then peruse the museum located in the 1797 British field officer's quarters. The model of the site as it appeared in 1710 is particularly intriguing. If you find all the history a bit tedious, ask a guide for a croquet set and practice your technique on the lush rolling lawns.

A good strategy for visiting is to come during the day to tour the museum and get a feel for the lay of the land. Then return for the evening sunset, long after the bus tours have departed, to walk the Perimeter Trail with its river and valley vistas.

✪ **Historic Gardens.** 441 St. George St. ☎ **902/532-7018.** Admission C$5 (US$3) adult, C$3.50 (US$2) seniors and students, C$11 (US$7) family. Mid-May to mid-Oct daily 8am–dusk; closed remainder of year.

You don't need to be a flower nut to enjoy an hour or two at these exceptional gardens. Created in 1981, the 10-acre grounds are uncommonly beautiful, with a mix of formal and informal gardens dating from varied epochs. Set on a gentle hill, the plantings overlook a beautiful salt marsh (now diked and farmed), and they include a geometric Victorian garden, a knot garden, a rock garden, and a colorful perennial border garden. Rose fanciers should allow plenty of time—some 2,000 rose bushes track the history of rose cultivation from the earliest days through the Victorian era to the present day. A garden cafe (see below) offers an enticing spot for lunch.

North Hills Museum. 5065 Granville Rd., Granville Ferry. ☎ **902/532-2168**, off-season 902/532-7754. Admission by donation. Mon–Sat 9:30am–5:30pm, Sun 1–5:30pm. Closed mid-Oct to May 30.

On the road to Port Royal, the North Hills Museum occupies a tidy, early shingled home (1764) that's filled with a top-rate collection of Georgian furniture, ceramics, and glassware. This compact museum will be of interest primarily to serious antique collectors and history buffs, although even they will be frustrated by the limited access to the opulently furnished rooms (you need to be content mostly with views from roped-off doorways).

✪ **Port Royal National Historic Site.** 10 kilometers (6 miles) south of Route 1, Granville Ferry (turn left shortly after passing the tidal generating station). ☎ **902/532-2321.** Admission C$2.75 (US$1.85) adult, C$2.25 (US$1.50) senior, C$1.35 (US90¢ child, C$8 (US$5.35) family. Daily May 15–Oct 15 9am–6pm.

Canada's first permanent settlement, Port Royal was located on an attractive point with sweeping views of the Annapolis Basin. After the dreadful winter of 1604 spent on an island in the St. Croix River (along the current Maine–New Brunswick border), the survivors moved to this better protected location. Settlers lived here for 8 years in a high style that approached decadent given the harsh surroundings. Many of the handsome, compact French-style farmhouse buildings were designed by Samuel de Champlain to re-create the comfort they might have enjoyed at home.

Although the original settlement was abandoned and eventually destroyed, this 1939 re-creation is convincing in all the details. You'll find a handful of costumed interpreters engaged in traditional handicrafts like woodworking, and they're happy to fill you in on life in the colony during those difficult early years, an "age of innocence" when the French first forged an alliance with local natives. Allow an hour or two to wander and explore.

OUTDOOR PURSUITS

A short drive from Annapolis Royal and Port Royal are the **Delaps Cove Trails,** which provide access to the rugged Fundy coastline. The tricky part is finding the trailhead, as signs tend to vanish. Directions and a brochure are usually available from the visitor information center. Otherwise, head to Delaps Cove from Granville Ferry; veer left on the dirt road that cuts steeply downhill at a rightward bend shortly before the cove. (If you get to Tidal Cove Campground and Cabins, you've gone too far.) Follow this dirt road to the end, where you'll find parking and trail maps.

Two trails lead from an overgrown farm road to the rocky coastline. My advice is to take the **Bohaker Trail** (1.8km/1 mile) first, then decide whether you want to continue on to **Charlie's Trail** (7.2km/4.3 miles). The Bohaker is a lovely loop through woodlands to a short coastline trail. The highlight is a cobblestone cove piled with driftwood, into which a small waterfall tumbles. This is a fine destination for a picnic. The trails are well marked—once you find them.

Herbert Eisengruber, ☎ **902/532-2546**, offers rough and ready **adventure tours** of the backroads hereabouts aboard a suitably road-weary Land Rover. The tours run about 3 hours (depending on the fortitude of the passengers), and are not recommended for anyone with back problems. Children must be 12 or older. The price is C$49 (US$33) per person (C$35/US$23 for teens 12 to 16), which includes lunch or dinner. You can ask about the tours at the Emins' Store at 302 St. George St., where you can also admire Herbert's quirky collection of ancient computers, including Kaypros, PETs, and early Apples.

WHERE TO STAY

The closest campground to Annapolis Royal is on a handsome 22-acre waterfront property across the embayment from the tidal generating station. The privately owned **Dunroamin Campsite** (☎ **902/532-2808**) has full hookups for trailers and RVs, and attractive tenting sites along the water's edge.

For more modern, motel-like accommodations near town, try **Wandlyn Inn–Annapolis Royal** (☎ **902/532-2323**) on Highway 101, Exit 22 (south of town). Doubles are C$70 to C$105 (US$47 to US$70).

Garrison House Inn. 350 St. George St., Annapolis Royal, NS B0S 1A0. ☎ **902/532-5750.** Fax 902/532-5501. www.come.to/garrison. garhed@ns.sympatico.ca. 7 units. C$65–C$95 (US$43–US$63) double, including full breakfast. AE, MC, V. Street parking. Open May–Oct; call in advance for weekends rest of year.

The historic Garrison House sits across from Fort Anne in the town center and has bedded and fed guests since it first opened to accommodate officers at Fort Anne in 1854. Flowers make the inn welcoming, and the rooms are nicely appointed with antiques, some worn, some pristine. There's no air conditioning but fans are provided;

the top floor can still get a bit stuffy on warm days. Room 2 is appealing, with wide pine floors, braided rug, and settee, but it faces the street and at times can be a bit noisy. Room 7 is tucked in the back of the house, away from the hubbub of St. George Street, and it has two skylights to let in a wonderfully dappled light.

Hillsdale House. 519 St. George St. (P.O. Box 148), Annapolis Royal, NS B0S 1A0. ☎ **902/532-2345.** 14 units. C$65–C$95 (US$43–US$63) double, including full breakfast. MC, V. Closed Nov–Apr.

This pale yellow clapboard Italianate home (1849) sits just across the road from the slightly fancier Queen Anne Inn. The first floor features a Georgian-style sitting room with furniture that's both nice to look at and comfortable to sit on. The carpeted guest rooms are handsome if slightly basic, furnished with antiques that aren't overly elaborate. Only the top-floor rooms have air-conditioning. And this might be good news: There's not a single television in the place.

King George Inn. 548 St. George St., Annapolis Royal, NS B0S 1A0. ☎ **888/799-5464** or 902/532-5286. 8 units. TV. C$79–C$145 (US$53–US$97) double, includes breakfast. MC, V. Closed mid-Oct to mid-May.

The handsome King George Inn was built as a sea captain's mansion in 1868, and served a stint as a rectory before becoming an inn. It's befittingly busy and cluttered for its era; guest rooms are furnished entirely with antiques, most of the country Victorian ilk. (Those who prefer clean lines might find a surplus of decor here.) All rooms have queen-sized beds; two family suites have separate bedrooms and a bathroom that's shared between them. The best in the house is Room 7, with a Jacuzzi and a small private deck off the back of the house.

The Moorings. P.O. Box 118, Granville Ferry, NS B0S 1K0. ☎ **902/532-2146.** E-mail: tileston@tartannet.ns.ca. 3 units (2 share 1 bathroom). C$48–C$52 (US$32–US$35) double, including full breakfast. MC, V. Closed Oct 31–Apr 30.

Just across the river from Annapolis Royal is the personable and appealing Moorings, a three-room B&B with great views of the town and Fort Anne across the water. This spot is much less "historic" compared to the high-Victorian inns in Annapolis, but is comfortably decorated with brushed walls and an attractive mix of antique furniture and modern art. Guests have the run of two downstairs parlors, one of which has a television. One guest room has a private bathroom, but this was actually my least favorite. The two others face the water and are brighter and more cheerful. The yellow room is flooded with afternoon light and has a half-bathroom in the room; showers are in the shared bathroom in the hallway.

Queen Anne Inn. 494 St. George St., Annapolis Royal, NS B0S 1A0. ☎ **902/532-7850.** Fax 902/532-2078. www.queenanneinn.ns.ca. E-mail: queenanne@queenanneinn.ns.ca. 10 units. C$85–C$130 (US$57–US$87) double, includes breakfast. MC, V.

This Second Empire mansion, built in 1865, looks like the city hall of a small city. You won't miss it driving into town. Like the Hillsdale House across the street, the Queen Anne (built for the sister of the Hillsdale's owner) has benefitted from a preservation-minded owner, who has restored the Victorian detailing to its former luster. This includes the zebra-striped dining-room floor (alternating planks of oak and maple) and the grand central staircase. The guest rooms are quite elegant, and furnished appropriately to the Victorian era. With their towering elms, the parklike grounds are shady and inviting.

WHERE TO DINE

Fat Pheasant. 200 St. George St. ☎ **902/532-5315.** Reservations suggested on weekends and Mon. Main courses, lunch C$4.50–C$9.50 (US$3–US$6.35, dinner C$12.95–C$19.50 (US$8.65–US$13). V. Daily 11:30am–9pm (usually open until 10pm in summer). ECLECTIC.

The Fat Pheasant offers creative dining on two levels in what used to be the town post office. The decor is a blend of modern and traditional, with eggplant walls, oak antiques, and an unobtrusive pheasant theme. The menu is likewise creative, and the chef manages to surprise even with run-of-the-mill items. Lunches feature a selection of pastas, sandwiches, and omelets. At dinner, you might start with an appetizer of fried Camembert with cranberry chutney or roasted onion and garlic soup. Main courses include lamb chops with a mint-citrus glaze, spicy Creole pork, and seafood pasta.

Garrison House. 350 St. George St. (in the Garrison House Inn). ☎ **902/532-5750.** Reservations recommended in summer. Main courses C$11.50–C$16.95 (US$7.65–US$11.30). AE, MC, V. Daily 5:30–8:30pm. ECLECTIC.

The Garrison House is the most intimate and attractive of the village's restaurants. The three cozy dining rooms in this historic home each have a different feel, some with colonial colors, some contemporary, most with black Windsor chairs and modern piscine art. (My favorite room is the one with the green floors and the humpback whale.) The menu is also tricky to categorize, with starters like an Acadian seafood chowder and carrot vichyssoise with coconut, and entrees ranging from jambalaya to scallops in a Vietnamese curry to a simple pasta with garden vegetables. There's also individual-serving pizzas.

✪ **Newman's.** 218 St. George St. ☎ **902/532-5502.** Reservations recommended. Main courses C$7–C$25 (US$5–US$17). V. July–Aug daily 11:30am–9pm, June and Sept Tues–Sun 11:30am–9pm, May and Oct Tues–Sun 11:30am–2:30pm and 5:30–8:30pm. SEAFOOD.

Newman's is an informal spot located in an oddly out-of-place pink Spanish Revival building on Annapolis Royal's historic waterfront. But don't let that confuse you. Inside, you'll find some of the most carefully prepared food in Nova Scotia, with an eye to fresh produce and meats. The place has been run by the same folks for 20 years, and they haven't let standards slip. It's hard to nail down a specialty—the kitchen does so much so very well. The seafood is especially delectable (grilled Atlantic salmon with tarragon sauce, halibut sautéed with sliced almonds), as are the generous, old-fashioned desserts (bananas with chocolate and whipped cream, homemade strawberry shortcake). Unexpected bonus: The wine list is surprisingly creative.

Secret Garden. 471 St. George St. ☎ **902/532-2200.** Reservations not needed. Lunch C$5–C$14 (US$3–US$9). V. Daily in summer 11:30am–4:30pm, weather permitting. Closed Oct–May. LIGHT FARE.

Located at the edge of the Historic Gardens, the Secret Garden is the ideal location for a light lunch on one of those beguilingly warm days touched with a mild breeze. The best seats are on the patio, which occupies a shady spot under a huge American elm overlooking the knot garden. The selections are tasty and light, with fare like tuna sandwiches and penne in a spicy tomato sauce. It's managed by the same folks who run the Garrison House, and the food quality is similarly high. There's also a children's menu.

5 Kejimkujik National Park

About 46 kilometers (28 miles) southeast of Annapolis Royal is a popular national park that's a world apart from coastal Nova Scotia. Kejimkujik National Park, founded in 1968, is located in the heart of south-central Nova Scotia, and it is to lakes and bogs what the south coast is to fishing villages and fog. Bear and moose are the full-time residents here; park visitors are the transients. The park, which was largely scooped and shaped during the last glacial epoch, is about 20 percent water, which makes it especially popular with canoeists. A few trails also weave through the park but hiking is limited; the longest hike in the park can be done in 2 hours. Bird watchers are also drawn to the park in search of the 205 species that have been seen both here and at the Seaside Adjunct of the park, a 22-square-kilometer (14-square-mile) coastal holding west of Liverpool. Among the more commonly seen species are pileated woodpeckers and loons, and at night you can listen for the raspy call of the barred owl.

ESSENTIALS

GETTING THERE Kejimkujik National Park is approximately midway on Kejimkujik Scenic Drive (Route 8), which extends 115 kilometers (71 miles) between Annapolis Royal and Liverpool. The village of Maitland Bridge (pop. 130) is near the park's entrance. Plan on about 2 hours' drive from Halifax.

VISITOR INFORMATION The park's **visitor center** (☎ **902/682-2772**) is open daily and features slide programs and exhibits about the park's natural history.

FEES Entrance fees are charged from mid-May to the end of October. Daily fees are C$3.25 (US$2.15) for adults, C$2.50 (US$1.65) for seniors, C$1.75 (US$1.15) ages 6 to 16, and C$7.50 (US$5) for families; 4-day passes are available in all categories for the price of 3 days.

EXPLORING THE PARK

The park's 381 square kilometers (237 square miles) of forest, lake, and bog are peaceful and remote. Part of what makes the terrain so appealing is the lack of access by car. One short, forked park road from Route 8 gets you partway into the park. Then you need to continue by foot or canoe. A stop at the visitor center is worthwhile, both for the exhibits on the region's natural history and for a preliminary walk on one of the three short trails. The Beech Grove loop (2.2km/1.4 miles) takes you around a glacial hill called a drumlin. The park has a taped walking tour available for use; ask at the information center.

Canoeing is the optimal means of traversing the park. Bring your own, or rent a canoe at **Jake's Landing** for C$4 (US$3) per hour, or C$20 (US$13) per day. (The same rate applies to rentals of bikes, paddleboats, kayaks, and rowboats.) Canoeists can cobble together wilderness excursions from one lake to the other, some involving slight portaging. Multiday trips are easily arranged to backcountry campsites and are the best way to get to know the park. Canoe route maps are provided at the visitor center. Rangers also lead short guided canoe trips for novices.

The park also has 15 **walking trails,** ranging from short easy strolls to, well, longer easy strolls. (There's no elevation gain to speak of.) The 6-kilometer (4-mile) **Hemlocks and Hardwoods Trail** loops through stately groves of 300-year-old hemlocks; the 3-kilometer (1.8-mile) **Merrymakedge Beach Trail** skirts a lakeshore to end at a beach. A free map that describes the trails is available at the visitor center.

Mountain bikers can explore the old **Fire Tower Road,** a round trip of about 20 kilometers (12 miles). The road becomes increasingly rugged, and ends at a fire tower near an old-growth forest of birch and maple.

CAMPING

Backcountry camping is the park's chief draw. So much in demand are the 44 sites that they actually cost more than the drive-in campsites. Overnighting on a distant lakeshore is the best way to get to know the park; even if you're planning to car camp, I'd argue that it's worth the extra hassle and expense of renting a canoe and paddling off for a night just for the experience.

The canoe-in and hike-in sites are assigned individually, which means you needn't worry about noisy neighbors playing "La Bamba" over and over on their car stereo. Backcountry rangers keep the sites in top shape, and each is stocked with firewood for the night (the wood is included in the campsite fee). Most sites can handle a maximum of six campers. Naturally, there's high demand for the best sites; you're better off here midweek, when fewer weekenders are down from Halifax. You can also reserve backcountry sites up to 60 days in advance for an additional fee of C$4.25 (US$2.85); call the **visitor center** (☎ 902/682-2772). The backcountry camping fee is C$16.25 (US$10.85) per night.

The park's drive-in campground at **Jeremys Bay** offers 329 sites, some of which are quite close to the water's edge. Campground rates are C$14 (US$9) per night. (During the shoulder seasons in spring and fall campsites are C$9.50/US$6.35.) Starting early each May reservations at the drive-in campground may be made for an additional fee of C$7 (US$4.65) by calling ☎ 800/414-6765.

6 Digby to Yarmouth

Two towns serving as gateways to Nova Scotia bracket this 113-kilometer (70-mile) stretch of coast. Whereas the South Shore—the stretch between Yarmouth and Halifax—serves to confirm popular conceptions of Nova Scotia (small fishing villages, shingled homes), the Digby-to-Yarmouth route seems determined to confound them. Look for Acadian enclaves, fishing villages with more corrugated steel than weathered shingle, miles of sandy beaches, and spruce-topped basalt cliffs that seem transplanted from Labrador.

DIGBY

The unassuming port town of Digby (pop. 2,300) is located on the water at Digby Gap—where the Annapolis River finally forces an egress through the North Mountain coastal range. Set at the south end of the broad watery expanse of the Annapolis Basin, Digby is home to the world's largest inshore scallop fleet, which drags the ocean bottom for tasty and succulent Digby scallops. Ferries to Saint John, N.B., sail year-round from a dock a few miles west of downtown.

The town is named after Admiral Sir Robert Digby, who arrived here from New England in 1783. He led a group of loyalists who found relations with their neighbors somewhat strained following the unfortunate outcome of the War of Independence. Today, Digby is an active community where life centers around fishing boats, neighborhoods of wood-frame houses, and no-frills seafood restaurants. It's certainly worth a brief stopover when you're heading to or from the ferry.

ESSENTIALS

GETTING THERE   Digby is Nova Scotia's gateway for those arriving from Saint John, N.B., via ferry. The ferry terminal is on Route 303 west of Digby. If you're arriving by ferry and want to visit the town before pushing on, watch for signs directing you downtown from the bypass. Otherwise, you'll end up on Route 101 before you know it.

From other parts of Nova Scotia, Digby is accessible via Exit 26 off Route 101.

VISITOR INFORMATION   The province maintains a **visitor information center** (☎ 902/245-2201) on Route 303 (on your right shortly after you disembark from the Saint John ferry). There's also the municipal **Visitor Information Centre** (☎ 902/245-5714), located on the harbor at 110 Montague Row. It's open daily mid-June to mid-October from 9am to 8:30pm.

EXPLORING DIGBY

Water Street runs along the water (of course), with views of the scallop fleet from various points. A narrow grassy promenade extends from the visitor information center to the small downtown; parking is usually plentiful.

Near the information center is the **Admiral Digby Museum,** 95 Montague Row (☎ **902/245-6322**). The Georgian home dates to the mid-19th century; inside you'll find a wide-ranging selection of artifacts, ranging from documentary photos of a Mi'kmaq porpoise hunt in the 1930s, to ship models and early Victorian fashions. Also on display are two of the 100 toy stuffed dogs made of old coats by local craftsperson Alma Melanson. Open Tuesday to Sunday 9am to 5pm from June to August; 9am to 5pm Monday to Friday September to mid-October. Open by appointment the rest of the year. Admission by donation.

Learn about the scallop industry at the **Lady Vanessa** fisheries exhibit (34 Water St., ☎ **902/245-4555**). Set in a 98-foot scallop dragger, it features videos and exhibits about the prized local catch. It's open daily 9am to 7pm from June until late September; admission is C$1.75 (US$1.15).

Continue walking northward on Water Street and you'll arrive at **Royal Fundy Fish Market** (☎ **902/245-5411**) at the head of Fisherman's Wharf. You can buy fresh scallops or smoked fish, including locally popular "smoked chicks"—slang for smoked herring. They got their name when early Digby settlers had to settle for these rather than poultry during impoverished Christmas dinners. The market also offers take-out meals, with picnic tables nearby. It's open daily.

To get out on the water, contact **Basin Charters,** Digby Marina (☎ **902/245-8446**), which offers sightseeing and sport fishing excursions daily in summer aboard its 45-foot boat. Prices range from C$20 to C$40 (US$13 to US$27) per person.

About 12 kilometers (7.4 miles) east of Digby is the tidy riverside town of **Bear River** (take Exit 24 off Route 101). Formerly a center for shipbuilding, the town has been discovered by craftspeople and artists who have bought and restored a number of the old homes along the river and high up in the flanking hills. The tiny, attractive downtown, with crafts shops and a couple of restaurants, straddles the river and is linked by a bridge. Note the buildings constructed on stilts above silty waters. Browsing options are rich here if you're at all interested in contemporary crafts; start at the **visitor information center,** ☎ **902/467-3200,** in the windmill at the waterfront park, which can provide information on studios open to the public and area shops.

WHERE TO STAY

Digby is an entryway for those arriving or departing by ferry, and as such it has a number of basic motels. Two within walking distance of the promenade and downtown are the cottage-style efficiency units of **Seawinds Motel,** 90 Montague Row (☎ **902/245-2573**), offering good sea views and charging C$65 to C$75 (US$43 to US$50) double; and the more basic **Siesta Motel,** 81 Montague Row (☎ **902/245-2568**) just across the street, charging C$50 to C$65 (US$33 to US$43) double.

✪ **The Pines.** Shore Rd., P.O. Box 70, Digby, NS B0V 1A0. ☎ **800/667-4637** or 902/245-2511. Fax 902/245-6133. www.gov.ns.ca/resorts. 84 units and 30 cottages. TV TEL. C$135–C$280 (US$90–US$187) double, cottages C$280 (US$187) and up. AE, DC, DISC, ER, MC, V. Closed mid-Oct to mid-May.

The Pines, situated on 300 acres with marvelous views of the Annapolis Basin, is redolent of an earlier era when old money headed to fashionable resorts for an entire summer. Built in 1929 in a Norman château style, the inn today is owned and operated by the province of Nova Scotia, and it should silence those who believe that government can't do anything right. The imposing building of stucco and stone is surrounded by the eponymous pines, which rustle softly in the wind. Throughout, the emphasis is more on comfort than historical verisimilitude, although the gracious lobby features old-world touches like Corinthian capitals, floral couches, and parquet floors. The guest rooms vary slightly as to size and views (ask for a water-view room; there's no extra charge), and all now have ceiling fans, although air-conditioning is said to be on the way. The cottages have one to three bedrooms and most feature wood fireplaces.

Dining: The Annapolis Dining Room is open for all three meals, and the cuisine might best be described as Nova Scotian with a French flair. Look for entrees like roasted pork tenderloin with apples and a cider sauce, or poached char infused with green Chinese tea. Entrees are priced from C$14 to C$27 (US$9 to US$18). Dinner reservations are advised.

Amenities: Concierge, baby-sitting, dry cleaning, laundry, VCR rentals, afternoon tea, turndown service, courtesy car to the ferry, tour desk, pool and fitness center, hiking trails, shuffleboard, bike rentals, two night-lit tennis courts, an 18-hole golf course, a sauna, a children's center, and a shopping arcade.

Thistle Down Country Inn. 98 Montague Row (P.O. Box 508), Digby, NS B0V 1A0. ☎ **800/565-8081** or 902/245-4490. 12 units (1 with private hallway bathroom). C$70–C$115 (US$47–US$77) double, includes breakfast. AE, ER, MC, V. Closed Nov 1–May 1. Pets accepted with prior permission.

This personable inn on the harbor has a dozen rooms evenly divided between the main house (built in 1904) and a two-story motel-style annex in the back. In the older house you get the charm of the oak staircase, banister and trim, the eclectic antiques in the rooms, and a sitting parlor in front. But the bathrooms are small, the views limited, and the front rooms noisy. The more modern units (built in 1996) are larger, more modern; and the two end units (the most expensive) have great views of the basin and hills beyond. The innkeepers—Ed Reid and Lester Bartson—know the region well and are generous with their time in helping guests plan day trips and excursions further afield.

Dining: Dinners in the intimate Edwardian dining room are among the best in Digby, with an emphasis on the local scallops prepared both creatively and simply (entrees C$21/US$14 to C$27/US$18).

WHERE TO DINE

A meal at The Pines (see above) offers a grand setting. Otherwise, the few downtown seafood restaurants are more or less interchangeable, serving up heaps of fried scallops. Of these, the spot with the best harbor view is the **Fundy Restaurant,** 34 Water St. (☎ **902/245-4950**); ask for a seat in the solarium. If you'd like your scallops with a more exotic tang, head to **Kaywin Restaurant,** 51 Water St. (☎ **902/245-5543**), an above-average Chinese-Canadian restaurant that serves scallops stir-fried with vegetables, as well as the more common fried variant.

Red Raven Pub. 100 Water St. ☎ **902/245-5533.** Sandwiches C$3.50–C$7 (US$2.35–US$4.65); main courses C$8–C$16 (US$5–US$11). AE, DISC, MC, V. Tues–Sat 11am–10am, Sun–Mon 11am–9pm. SEAFOOD.

The locally popular hangout Red Raven Pub serves up well-prepared seafood in a pubby atmosphere with a fine harbor view, especially from the upstairs lounge and outdoor deck. You can find the usual suspects on the menu, like sautéed or fried scallops, and fish and chips. Or try the local favorite: creamed lobster on toast. There's also commendable seafood chowder and a great coconut cream pie. Movie trivia extra: Scenes from Stephen King's film *Dolores Claiborne* were filmed here.

DIGBY NECK

Look at a map of Nova Scotia and you'll see the thin strand of Digby Neck extending southwest from Annapolis Basin. You might guess from its appearance on the map that it's a low, scrubby sandspit. You would be wrong. In fact, it's a long, bony finger of high ridges, spongy bogs, dense forest, and expansive ocean views. The last two knuckles of this narrow peninsula are islands, both of which are connected via 10-minute ferries across straits swept with currents as strong as 9 knots.

Although neither the neck nor the islands have much in the way of services for tourists—just one real lodge, a couple of B&Bs, and a few general stores—it's worth the drive if you're a connoisseur of end-of-the-world remoteness. The town of Sandy Cove on the mainland is picture-perfect, with its three prominent church steeples rising from the forest. Both Tiverton on Long Island and Westport on Brier Island are unadorned fishing villages where pickup trucks are held together with Bondo and bailing wire. You get the distinct feeling that life hasn't changed much in the past few decades—or at least since 1960, when the roads were finally paved on Brier Island.

ESSENTIALS

GETTING THERE   Route 217 runs 75 kilometers (45 miles) south from Digby to Brier Island. Two ferries fill in when you run out of mainland. Ferries leave East Ferry on the mainland for Long Island every hour on the half-hour; they depart from Long Island for Brier Island on the hour. Ferries are timed such that you can drive directly from one ferry to the next, provided you don't dawdle. Fares are C$2 per car round-trip on both ferries; fares are collected on the outbound leg only.

VISITOR INFORMATION   A **seasonal information booth** (☎ 902/839-2853) is located at the local historical museum in Tiverton on Long Island. It's allegedly open 9am to 7:30pm in July and August, but hours are more erratic than that. You might be better off collecting information at the Visitor Information Centre in Digby (see above) before you set off.

WHALE WATCHING

In the Bay of Fundy ocean currents mingle and the vigorous tides cause upwelling, which brings a rich assortment of plankton to the surface. That makes it an all-you-can-eat buffet for whales, which feed on these minuscule bits of plant and animal. As the fishing industry has declined, the number of fishermen offering whale-watching tours has boomed. Most of these are down-home operations on converted lobster boats—don't expect the gleaming whale-watch ships with comfy seats and full-service cafeterias that you find in larger cities or on the New England coast.

Declining inshore herring stocks means tours need to head farther out into the bay to find whales than in years past, but you'll almost always have sightings of fin, minke, or humpback whales. Right, sperm, blue, and pilot whales, along with the seldom-seen orcas, have also been spotted over the years. Plan on spending around C$35 to C$45 (US$23 to US$30) for a 3- to 4-hour cruise.

Mariner Cruises (☎ 800/239-2189 or 902/839-2346) in Westport on Brier Island sails aboard the 45-foot *Chad and Sisters Two,* which is equipped with a heated cabin. Both whale- and bird-watching tours are offered. **Pirate's Cove Whale Cruises** (☎ 888/480-0004 or 902/839-2242), located in Tiverton, has been leading offshore cruises since 1990; three tours are offered daily aboard the 34-foot M/V *Todd*. **Petite Passage Whale Watch** (☎ **902/834-2226**) sails out of East Ferry aboard a 37-foot, 20-passenger boat with a partially covered deck.

For a saltier adventure, **Ocean Explorations** (☎ **902/839-2417**) offers tours on rigid-hulled inflatable Zodiacs. The largest boat holds up to a dozen passengers and moves with tremendous speed and dampness through the fast currents and frequent chop around the islands and the open bay. Guests are provided with survival suits for warmth and safety.

HIKING

On Long Island, two short but rewarding woodland hikes take you to open vistas of St. Mary's Bay and the Bay of Fundy.

The trailhead for the half-mile hike to **Balancing Rock** is 4 kilometers (2.5 miles) south of the Tiverton ferry on Route 217; look for the well-marked parking area on the left. The trail crosses through swamp, bog, and forest and is dead straight and flat—until the last 100 yards. That's when you plummet nearly straight down a sheer bluff to the ocean's edge along some 169 steps. At the base a series of boardwalks leads you over the surging ocean to get a dead-on view of the tall column of basalt balancing improbably atop another column. For another short hike, return to the parking lot and drive 3 miles south to the picnic area on the right. From the parking lot atop the hill, a hike of 1 kilometer (0.6 miles) descends gradually through a forest of moss, ferns, and roots to the remote **Fundy shore.** The coastline here is nearly lunar, with the dark rock marbled with thin streaks of quartz. You're likely to have the coast to yourself, since few venture here.

Farther along, **Brier Island** is laced with hiking trails, offering fantastic opportunities for seaside exploration. Pick up one of the maps offered free around the island. A good place to start is the Grand Passage Lighthouse (turn right after disembarking the ferry, and continue until you can't go any farther). Park near the light, and walk through the stunted pines to the open meadows on the western shore, where you can pick up the coastal trail.

BICYCLING

Brier Island offers an ideal destination for mountain bikers. At just 6.5 kilometers (4 miles) long and 2.4 kilometers (1.5 miles) wide, it's the right scale for spending a slow afternoon poking around dirt roads that lead to the two picturesque lighthouses. Brier Island maps are available free at island stores and lodges. If you park your car on the Long Island side and take your bike over on the ferry, you'll save C$2; there's no charge for bikes or pedestrians.

Bike rentals are available at **Back Street Bicycles** in Digby, ☎ **902/245-1989.**

WHERE TO STAY & DINE

Brier Island Lodge. Westport, Brier Island. ☎ **800/662-8355** or 902/839-2300. Fax 902/839-2006. E-mail: brierisl@atcon.com. 23 units. TV. C$60–C$109 (US$49–US$73) double. MC, V.

Built to jump-start local eco-tourism, the Brier Island Lodge has a rustic-modern motif, with log-cabin construction and soaring glass windows overlooking the Grand Passage 130 feet below. The rooms on two floors all have great views, the usual motel amenities (cable TV, private bathrooms), and some unexpected touches (double Jacuzzis in the pricier rooms). There's a well-regarded dining room that serves up traditional favorites, and an airy lounge where local fishermen congregate in the evening to play cards and watch the satellite TV. There's a small but good selection of field guides near the upholstered chairs in the corner of the lounge; hiking trails connect directly from the lodge to the Fundy shore.

ACADIAN COAST

The Acadian Coast runs roughly from Salmon River to St. Bernard. This hardscrabble coast, where the fields were once littered with glacial rocks and boulders, was one of the few areas where Acadians were allowed to resettle after the 1755 expulsion.

Today, you'll find abundant evidence of the robust Acadian culture, from the frequent sightings of the *stella maris* (the Acadian tricolor flag with its prominent star) to the towering churches around which each town seems to cluster. The region is more populous and developed than much of the Nova Scotia coast, and thus lacks somewhat the wild aesthetic that travelers often seek. You'll also find few tourist amenities along this stretch.

ESSENTIALS

GETTING THERE   The Acadian Coast is traversed by Route 1. Speedier Route 101 runs parallel and inland some distance; the Acadian Coast is served by exits 28 to 32.

VISITOR INFORMATION   The **visitor information center** (☎ **902/645-2389**) for the Acadian Coast is in Meteghan Center. It's located in La Vielle Maison, the local history museum. Follow the "?" signs on Route 1. The center is open daily June to August from 9am to 7pm; May and September from 10am to 6pm.

EXPLORING THE ACADIAN COAST

A drive along this seaside route offers a pleasant detour, in both pace and culture. You can drive the whole length, or pick up segments by exiting from Route 101 and heading shoreward. What follows is a selected sampling of attractions along the coast, from north to south:

- **St. Mary's Church,** Church Point. Many of the towns along the Acadian coast are proud of their impressive churches, but none is quite as extraordinary as St. Mary's. You can't miss it; it's adjacent to the campus of Université Sainte-Anne, the sole French-speaking university in Nova Scotia. The imposing, gray-shingled church has the stature of a European cathedral made of stone, but St. Mary's, built 1903 to 1905, is made entirely of wood.

  Outside, it's impressive—the fanciful steeple rises some 185 feet above the parking lot, with some 40 tons of rock hidden within to provide stability in the high winds. Inside, it's even more extraordinary—all bright and airy and deftly adorned. Whole tree trunks serve as columns, although they're covered in plaster to lend a more traditional appearance. A small museum in the rear offers glimpses of church history. Admission by donation.

- **Rappie Pie.** This Acadian dish is a whole-meal pie typically made with beef or chicken. The main ingredient is grated potatoes, from which the moisture has been extracted and replaced with chicken broth. The full and formal name is "pâté à la rapure," but look for signs for "rapure" or "rappie pie" along Route 1 on the Acadian Coast.

- **Rapure Acadienne Ltd.** (☎ **902/769-2172**). At this unassuming shop on Route 1 just south of Church Point, you can pick up a freshly baked beef or chicken rappie pie for C$5 (US$3.35); it costs about a dollar more for a clam pie. Commandeer an outdoor picnic table to enjoy your meal, or take it to the shady campus of Université Sainte-Anne, a few minutes' drive north.

- **La Vielle Maison,** Meteghan. This small historical museum displays artifacts of Acadian life in the 19th century. Look for the scrap of original French wallpaper uncovered during restoration of the summer bedroom. This is also home to the region's visitor information center. Open daily in summer (see visitor center hours, above). Admission is free.
- **Smuggler's Cove,** Meteghan. This small provincial picnic area a few minutes south of town has a set of steps running steeply down to a cobblestone cove. From here, you'll have a view of a tidal cave across the way. Rumrunners were said to have used this cave—about 15 feet high and 60 feet deep—as a hideout during the Prohibition era. Truth or local tourism boosterism? You be the judge. Admission is free.
- **Mavilete Beach,** Mavilete. This beautiful crescent beach has nearly all the ingredients for a pleasant summer afternoon—lots of sand, grassy dunes, changing-stalls, a nearby snack bar with ice cream, views across the water to scenic Cape Mary. All that's lacking is an ocean warm enough to actually swim in. It's seriously frigid here, although the courageous appear to be able to splash around for a time without lapsing into immediate cardiac arrest. The beach, managed as a provincial park, is 1 kilometer (0.6 miles) off Route 1, and the turnoff is well marked; admission is free.
- **Port Maitland Beach,** Port Maitland. Another provincial park beach, Port Maitland Beach is near the breakwater and town wharf. It isn't as scenic or pristine as Mavilete Beach; it's closer to Yarmouth and attracts larger crowds, principally families. Signs direct you to the beach from the village center.

YARMOUTH

The constant lament of Yarmouth restaurateurs and shopkeepers is this: The summer tourists who steadily stream off the incoming ferries rarely linger long enough to appreciate the city before they mash the accelerator and speed off to higher-marquee venues along the coast.

There might be a reason for that. Yarmouth is a pleasant burg that offers some noteworthy historic architecture dating from the golden age of seafaring. But the town's not terribly unique, and thus not high on my list of places I'd choose to spend a few days. It's too big (pop. 7,800) to be charming; too small to generate urban buzz and vitality. It has more of the flavor of a handy pit stop than a destination.

By all means plan to dawdle a few hours while awaiting the ferry (Portland-bound passengers could enjoyably spend the night here before their early morning departure) or to while away an afternoon looping around the coast. Take the time to follow the self-guided walking tour, enjoy a meal, or wander around the newly renovated waterfront, where efforts to coax it back from decrepitude have started to take root.

Then: onward.

ESSENTIALS

GETTING THERE   Yarmouth is at the convergence of two of the province's principal highways, Route 101 and Route 103. It's approximately 300 kilometers (180 miles) from Halifax. Yarmouth is the gateway for two daily ferries (seasonal) connecting to Maine. **Air Nova** serves Yarmouth with infrequent flights; call ☎ 888/247-2262 or 902/742-2450. The airport is located a few minutes' drive east of town on Starrs Road.

VISITOR INFORMATION   The **Yarmouth Visitor Centre** (☎ 902/742-6639 or 902/742-5033) is at 228 Main St., just up the hill from the ferry in a modern, shingled building you simply can't miss. Both the provincial and municipal tourist offices are located here; open May to October daily from 8am to 7pm.

EXPLORING THE AREA

The tourist bureau and the local historical society publish a very informative **walking tour brochure** covering downtown Yarmouth. It's well worth requesting at the visitor information center. The guide offers general tips on what to look for in local architectural styles (how *do* you tell the difference between Georgian and Classic Revival?), as well as brief histories of significant buildings. The whole tour is 4 kilometers (2.5 miles).

The most scenic side trip—and an ideal excursion by bike or car—is to ✪ **Cape Forchu** and the Yarmouth Light. Head west on Main Street (Route 1) for 2.2 kilometers (1.3 miles) from the visitor center, then turn left at the horse statue. The road winds picturesquely out to the cape, past seawalls and working lobster wharves, meadows, and old homes.

When the road finally ends, you'll be at the red-and-white-striped concrete lighthouse that marks the harbor's entrance. (This modern lighthouse dates to the early 1960s, when it replaced a much older octagonal light that succumbed to wind and time.) There's a tiny photographic exhibit on the cape's history in the visitor center in the keeper's house.

Leave enough time to ramble around the dramatic rock-and-grass bluffs—part of Leif Ericson Picnic Park—that surround the lighthouse. Don't miss the short trail out to the point below the light. Bright red picnic tables and benches are scattered about; bring lunch or dinner if the weather is right.

Firefighters Museum of Nova Scotia. 451 Main St. ☎ **902/742-5525.** Admission C$2 (US$1.35) adult, C$4 (US$2.65) family. July and August Mon–Sat 9am–9pm, Sun 10am–5pm; rest of year, closed Sunday, limited hours Mon–Sat.

This two-story museum will appeal mostly to confirmed fire buffs, historians, and impressionable young children. The museum is home to a varied collection of early fire-fighting equipment, with hand-drawn pumpers as the centerpiece of the collection. Also showcased here are uniforms, badges, helmets, and pennants. Look for the photos of notable Nova Scotian fires ("Hot Shots").

Yarmouth County Museum. 22 Collins St. ☎ **902/742-5539.** Admission to museum and Pelton-Fuller House C$4 (US$2.65) adult (C$2.50/US$1.65 museum or house only), C$2 (US$1.35) students, C$1 (US65¢) children, C$8 (US$5.35) family. June to mid-October Mon–Sat 9am–5pm, Sun 2–5pm; mid-Oct to May Tues–Sun 2–5pm. (House open summers only.)

The Yarmouth County Museum consists of three buildings. First, there's the museum itself, with displays of seafaring artifacts, Victorian furniture, paintings, costumes, and examples of early decorative arts. Next door is the Pelton-Fuller House, the Queen Anne–style (ca. 1895) summer home of Primrose and Alfred Fuller. Mr. Fuller, a Nova Scotia native, was best known as the founder of the famed Fuller Brush Co. The home, donated to the museum in 1996, is richly furnished with antiques, much as it was left. And down on the waterfront (90 Water St.) is the Killam Brothers Shipping Office (free admission), where visitors learn about a prominent family of successful entrepreneurs, as well as the ways of 19th century commerce.

WHERE TO STAY

Fifteen kilometers (9 miles) west of town on Route 1 is the **Lake Breeze Campground** (☎ **902/649-2332**), a privately run spot with the appealingly low-key character of a small municipal campground. It has 32 sites, some right on the shores of tiny Lake Darling, and it's well cared for by owners Kim and Todd Allen. It's open mid-May to mid-October.

Yarmouth is home to a number of chain motels. Among them are the **Best Western Mermaid Motel,** 545 Main St. (☎ **800/772-2774** or 902/742-7821), with rates of C$90 to C$100 (US$60 to US$67) double; **Comfort Inn,** 96 Starrs Rd. (☎ **902/742-1119**), at C$70 to C$100 (US$47 to US$67) double; and the **Rodd Grand Hotel,** 417 Main St. (☎ **902/742-2446**), C$80 to C$115 (US$53 to US$77) double.

Churchill Mansion Inn. Route 1 (14.5km/9 miles west of Yarmouth), Yarmouth, NS B5A 4A5. ☎ **902/649-2818.** 10 units. C$40–C$60 (US$27–US$40) double. DISC, MC, V. Closed Nov to mid-May.

Between 1891 and 1920, the Churchill Mansion was occupied just 6 weeks a year, when Aaron Flint Churchill, a Yarmouth native who amassed a shipping fortune in Atlanta, Georgia, returned to Nova Scotia to summer. This extravagant mansion with its garish furnishings, situated on a low bluff overlooking the highway and a lake, was converted to an inn in 1981 by Bob Benson, who is likely to be found on a ladder or with a hammer in hand when you arrive ("It never ends," he sighs).

The home is built on three tiers, echoing Churchill's Savannah mansion, and furnished with flea market antiques and a spooky portrait of Churchill in the hallway. The mansion boasts some original carpeting, lamps, and woodwork, although it can be a little threadbare, flaky, or water-stained in other spots. This is a popular destination among those who like quirky history and don't mind a little mustiness, as well as among kids with lively imaginations. Are there any ghosts? Benson says yes— but they only do good things, never bad.

Harbour's Edge B&B. 12 Vancouver St., Yarmouth NS B5A 2N8. ☎ **902/742-2387.** Fax 902/742-4471. E-mail: harboursedge@klis.com. 3 units (1 with private hallway bathroom). C$86–C$98 (US$57–US$65) double, including full breakfast. MC, V. Head toward Cape Forchu (see above); watch for the inn shortly after turning at the horse statue.

This exceptionally attractive early Victorian home (1864) sits on 2 leafy acres and 250 feet of harbor frontage. You can lounge on the lawn while watching herons and king-fishers below, making it hard to believe you're right in town and only a few minutes from the ferry terminal. Harbour's Edge opened in 1997 after 3 years of intensive restoration (it had previously been abandoned for 5 years). All the rooms are lightly furnished, which nicely highlights the architectural integrity of the design. The guest rooms have high ceilings and handsome spruce floors. The very attractive Audrey Kenney Room is the largest; the Ellen Brown Room is my favorite: it has fine oak furniture and a great view of the harbor, although the private bathroom is down the hall.

Lakelawn Motel. 641 Main St., Yarmouth, NS B5A 1K2. ☎ **902/742-3588.** E-mail: mackie@auracom.com. 31 units. TV. C$49–C$64 (US$33–US$43) double. AE, DC, DISC, ER, MC, V. Closed Nov–Apr.

The clean, well-kept Lakelawn Motel offers basic motel rooms done up in colors that were fashionable some years ago, like harvest orange and brown plaid. It's been a downtown Yarmouth mainstay since the 1950s, when the centerpiece Victorian house (where the office is located) was moved back from the road to make room for the motel wings. Looking for something a bit cozier? The house also has 4 B&B-style guest rooms upstairs, each furnished simply with antiques.

WHERE TO DINE

Harris Quick-N-Tasty. Route 1, Dayton. ☎ **902/742-3467.** No reservations. Sandwiches C$2.95–C$12 (US$2–US$8); main courses C$7–C$18 (US$5–US$12). AE, DC, MC, V. Daily

11am–9pm (until 8pm in winter). Just east of Yarmouth on the north side of Route 1. SEAFOOD.

The name about says it all. This vintage 1960s restaurant has no pretensions (it's the kind of place that still lists cocktails on the menu) and is hugely popular with locals. The Harrises sold the place a few years ago, but current owner Paul Surette is committed to preserving the place as is. The restaurant is adorned with that sort of paneling that was rather *au courant* about 30 years back, and the meals are likewise old-fashioned and generous. The emphasis is on seafood, and you can order your fish either fried or broiled. The "Scarlet O'Harris" lobster club sandwich is notable, as is the seafood casserole.

Queen Molly's Brewpub. 96 Water St. ☎ **902/742-6008.** Reservations not needed. Sandwiches, C$5.95–C$8.75 (US$3.95–US$5.85), entrees C$10.95–C$14.95 (US$7.30–US$9.95). AE, DC, MC, V. Daily 11am–11pm (shorter hours in off-season). BREWPUB.

Yarmouth's first (and Nova Scotia's fourth) brewpub opened in 1997 on the newly spiffed-up waterfront. It occupies an old warehouse dating to the mid-1800s, and you can see the wear and tear of the decades on the battered floor and the stout beams and rafters. The place has been nicely spruced up, and the menu features creative pub fare, with additions including Acadian and Cajun specialties, like rappie pie and jambalaya. The steaks are quite good, as is the beer, especially the best bitter. In summer, there's outdoor seating on a deck with a view of the harbor across the parking lot.

7 South Shore

The Atlantic coast between Yarmouth and Halifax is that quaint, maritime Nova Scotia you see on laminated place mats and calendars. It's all lighthouses and weathered, shingled buildings perched at the rocky edge of the sea, as if tenuously trespassing on the good graces of the sea. If your heart is set on exploring this fabled landscape, be sure to leave enough time to poke in all the nooks and crannies along this stretch of the coast.

As rustic and beautiful as this area is, you might find it a bit stultifying to visit *every* quaint village along the entire coastline—involving about 350 kilometers (210 miles) of twisting road along the water's edge. A more sane strategy would be to sit down with a map and target two or three villages, then stitch together selected coastal drives near the chosen villages with speedier links on Route 103, which runs straight and fast a short distance inland.

It's sensible to allow more time here for one other reason: fog. When the cool waters of the Arctic currents mix with the warm summer air over land, the results are predictable and soupy. The fog certainly adds atmosphere. It also can slow driving to a crawl.

SHELBURNE

Shelburne is a historic town with an unimpeachable pedigree. Settled in 1783 by United Empire Loyalists fleeing New England after the unfortunate outcome of the late war, the town swelled with newcomers and by 1784 was believed to have a population of 10,000—larger than Montréal, Halifax, or Québec. With the decline of boat building and fishing in this century, the town edged into that dim economic twilight familiar to other seaside villages (it now has a population of about 3,000), and the waterfront began to deteriorate, despite valiant preservation efforts.

And then Hollywood came calling, hat in hand. In 1992 the film *Mary Silliman's War* was filmed here. The producers found the waterfront to be a reasonable facsimile of Fairfield, Connecticut, circa 1776. The crew spruced up the town a bit and buried power lines along the waterfront.

Two years later director Roland Joffe arrived to film the spectacularly miscast *Scarlet Letter,* starring Demi Moore, Gary Oldman, and Robert Duvall. The film crew buried more power lines, built some 15 "historic" structures near the waterfront (most demolished after filming), dumped tons of rubble to create dirt lanes (since removed), and generally made the place look like 17th-century Boston.

When the crew departed, it left behind three buildings and an impressive shingled steeple you can see from all over town. Among the "new old" buildings is the waterfront cooperage across from the Cooper's Inn. The original structure, clad in asphalt shingles, was generally considered an eyesore and was torn down, replaced by the faux-17th-century building. Today, barrel makers painstakingly make and sell traditional handcrafted wooden barrels in what amounts to a souvenir of a notable Hollywood flop.

ESSENTIALS

GETTING THERE   Shelburne is 223 kilometers (134 miles) southwest of Halifax on Route 3. It's a short hop from Route 103 via either Exit 25 (southbound) or Exit 26 (northbound).

VISITOR INFORMATION   The **Shelburne Tourist Bureau** (☎ **902/875-4547**) is located in a tidy waterfront building at the corner of King and Dock Streets. It's open daily mid-May to October; hours are 9am to 8pm during peak season, 10am to 6pm off-season.

EXPLORING HISTORIC SHELBURNE

The central **historic district** runs along the waterfront, where you can see legitimately old buildings, Hollywood fakes (see above), and spectacular views of the harbor from small, grassy parks. (Note that some of the remaining *Scarlet Letter* buildings weren't meant to last and might have been demolished by the time you arrive.) A block inland from the water is Shelburne's more commercial stretch, where you can find services that include banks, shops, and a wonderful bakery (see "Where to Dine," below).

Flower fanciers should inquire about the self-guided **garden tours** sponsored by the Shelburne County Garden Club. Some 18 gardens are open to the public. Most of the gardens are indeed quite pleasant, but almost as enjoyable is the chance to meet local gardeners and talk about a shared passion. Ask for a brochure at the tourist bureau.

Shelburne Historic Complex. Dock St. (P.O. Box 39), Shelburne, NS B0T 1W0. ☎ **902/875-3219.** Admission to all 3 museums, C$4 (US$2.65) adult, under 16 free; individual museums C$2 (US$1.35) adult. Daily in summer 9:30am–5:30pm. Closed mid-Oct to May (Dory Shop closes at the end of Sept).

The historic complex is an association of three local museums located within steps of one another. The most engaging is the **Dory Shop,** right on the waterfront. On the first floor you can admire examples of the simple, elegant craft (said to be invented in Shelburne) and view videos about the late Sidney Mahaney, a master builder who worked in this shop from the time he was 17 until he was 96.

Then head upstairs, where all the banging is going on. There you'll meet Sidney's son and grandson, still building the classic boats using traditional methods. "The dory is a simple boat, but there are a lot of things to think about," says the grandson with considerable understatement. While you're there, ask about the difference between a Shelburne dory and a Lunenburg dory.

The Shelburne County Museum features a potpourri of locally significant artifacts from the town's Loyalist past. Most intriguing is the 1740 fire pumper; it was made in

London and imported here in 1783. Behind the museum is the austerely handsome **Ross-Thomson House,** built in 1784 through 1785. The first floor contains a general store as it might have looked in 1784, with bolts of cloth and cast-iron teakettles. Upstairs is a militia room with displays of antique and reproduction weaponry.

WHERE TO STAY

Just across the harbor from Shelburne is **The Islands Provincial Park** (☎ 902/ 875-4304), which offers 64 campsites on 482 acres. Some are right on the water and have great views of the historic village across the way. No hookups for RVs.

✪ **Cooper's Inn.** 36 Dock St., Shelburne, NS B0T 1W0. ☎ **800/688-2011** or 902/ 875-4656. E-mail: coopers@ns.sympatico.ca. 10 units. C$80–C$110 (US$53–US$73) double; C$155 (US$103) suite. Rates include full breakfast. AE, ER, MC, V.

Located facing the harbor in the Dock Street historic area, the impeccably historic Cooper's Inn was originally built by Loyalist merchant George Gracie in 1785. Subsequent additions and updating have been historically sympathetic. The downstairs sitting and dining rooms set the mood nicely, with worn wood floors, muted wall colors (mustard and khaki green), and classical music in the background. The rooms in the main building mostly feature painted wood floors (they're carpeted in the cooper-shop annex), and they are decorated in a comfortably historic-country style. The third-floor suite, added in 1996, features wonderful detailing, two sleeping alcoves, and harbor views. It's worth stretching your budget for. The George Gracie Room has a four-poster bed and water view; the small Roderick Morrison Room has a wonderful clawfoot tub perfect for a late-evening soak.

Dining: The two small, elegant dining rooms serve the best meals in town, with sophisticated dishes like Atlantic salmon with citrus sauce, and beef tenderloin with a port and salsa sauce. The inn has a growing reputation for its scallops sautéed in pinenut butter. Lobster is usually available in one incarnation or another. Dinner is served nightly from 6 to 9pm, and reservations are strongly recommended. Entrees range from C$14 to C$24 (US$9 to US$16).

WHERE TO DINE

For a full dinner out, see Cooper's Inn, above.

Shelburne Pastry. 151 Water St. ☎ **902/875-1168.** Sandwiches C$3.50–C$4.25 (US$2.35–US$2.85); main courses C$7–C$10 (US$5–US$7). V. Mon–Sat 9:30am–7pm. BAKERY/CAFE.

When a family of German chefs set about to open the Shelburne Pastry shop in 1995, the idea was to sell fancy pastries. But everyone who stopped by during the restoration of the Water Street building asked whether they would be selling bread. So they added bread. And today it's among the best you'll taste in the province—especially the delectable Nova Scotian oatmeal brown bread. The simple cafe also offers great pastries (try the pinwheels), as well as sandwiches served on their own bread, and filling meals from a limited menu that includes German bratwurst and chicken cordon bleu. Everything is made from scratch, and everything (except the marked-down day-old goods) is just-baked fresh. You'll find good value for your dollar here.

LUNENBURG

Lunenburg is one of Nova Scotia's most historic and appealing villages, a fact recognized in 1995 when UNESCO declared the old downtown a **World Heritage Site.** The town was first settled in 1753, primarily by German, Swiss, and French colonists. It was laid out on the "model town" plan then in vogue (Savannah, Georgia, and

Philadelphia, Pennsylvania, were also set out along these lines), which meant seven north-south streets intersected by nine east-west streets. Such a plan worked quite well in the coastal plains. Lunenburg, however, is located on a harbor flanked by steep hills, and implementers of the model town plan saw no reason to bend around these. As a result, some of the streets can be exhausting to walk.

About 70 percent of the downtown buildings date from the 18th and 19th centuries, and many of these are possessed of a distinctive style and are painted in bright colors. Looming over all is the architecturally unique Lunenburg Academy, with its exaggerated mansard roof, pointy towers, and extravagant use of ornamental brackets. It sets the tone for the town the way the Citadel does for Halifax. The first two floors are still used as a public school (the top floor was deemed a fire hazard some years ago), and the building is open to the public only on special occasions.

What makes Lunenburg so appealing to visitors is its vibrancy and life. Yes, it's historic, but this is not an ossified village. There's life, including a subtle countercultural tang that dates back to the 1960s. Look and you'll see evidence of the tie-dye-and-organic crowd in the scattering of natural food shops and funky boutiques. A growing number of art galleries, craft shops, and souvenir vendors are moving in, making for rewarding browsing.

ESSENTIALS

GETTING THERE   Lunenburg is 103 kilometers (62 miles) southwest of Halifax on Route 3.

VISITOR INFORMATION   The **Lunenburg Tourist Bureau** (☎ **902/ 634-8100**) is located at the top of Blockhouse Hill Road. It's open daily in summer from 9am to 8pm. It's not in an obvious place, but the brown "?" signs posted around town will lead you there. The staff here is especially good at helping you find a place to spend the night if you've arrived without reservations. You can also call up local information on the Web at www.lunco.com.

EXPLORING LUNENBURG

Leave plenty of time to explore Lunenburg by foot. The excellent **walking tour brochure** outlining the town's architectural heritage went out of print in 1999, but plans called for a newer, expanded version to be available again in 2000. Ask for one at the tourist office on Blockhouse Hill Road.

When exploring, note the architectural influence of later European settlers—especially Germans. Some local folks made their fortunes from the sea; I'd wager that real money was made by carpenters who specialized in ornamental brackets, which elaborately adorn dozens of homes.

Many of the homes also feature a distinctive architectural element that's known as the "Lunenburg bump"—a five-sided dormer and bay window combo installed directly over an extended front door. Other homes feature the more common Scottish dormer. Also look for the double or triple roofs on some projecting dormers, which serve absolutely no function other than to give the home the vague appearance of a wedding cake.

Well worth visiting is **St. John's Anglican Church** at Duke and Cumberland Streets. The original structure was rendered in simple New England meetinghouse style, built in 1754 of oak timbers shipped from Boston. Between 1840 and 1880 the church went through a number of additions and was overlaid with ornamentation and shingles to create a fine example of the "carpenter gothic" style. It's open to the public.

Guided 1½-hour **walking tours** (☎ **902/634-3848**) that include lore about local architecture and legends are hosted daily by Eric Croft, a knowledgeable Lunenburg native who's in possession of a sizeable store of good stories. Tours depart at 10am, 2pm, and 9pm from Bluenose Drive (across from the parking lot for the Atlantic Fisheries Museum); the cost is C$8 (US$5).

Downtown at 194 Montague St. you'll find the pleasantly old-fashioned operations of the **Lunenburg Soap Company** (☎ 902/634-7627), where soap is made the old-fashioned way with natural colorings and the highest-quality ingredients. A Frommer's reader from Pennsylvania puts it thus in a letter: "Fabulous soap, nice store, personable shop owner who will give tours of the soap making process. There's even a 'gentlemen's bench' for the gentlemen to sit and wait while their ladies purchase soap."

Several boat tours operate from the waterfront, most tied up near the Fisheries Museum. **Lunenburg Whale Watching Tours** (☎ 902/527-7175) sails in pursuit of several species of whales, along with seals and seabirds on 3-hour excursions. There are four departures daily, with reservations recommended. The **Harbour Star,** ☎ **902/634-3535,** takes visitors on a mellow, 45-minute tour of Lunenberg's inner harbor (no swells!) in a converted fishing boat. The same folks also offer 1½-hour sailing trips on the *Eastern Star,* a 48-foot wooden ketch, with several sailings daily.

✪ **Fisheries Museum of the Atlantic.** On the waterfront. ☎ **902/634-4794.** Admission C$7 (US$5) adult, C$6 (US$4) seniors, C$2 (US$1.35) children, C$17 (US$11) family. June to mid-Oct daily 9:30am–5:30pm; mid-Oct to May Mon–Fri 8:30am–4:30pm.

The sprawling Fisheries Museum is professionally designed and curated, and it manages to take a topic that some might consider a little, well, dull and make it fun and exciting. You'll find aquarium exhibits on the first floor, including a touch-tank for kids. (Look also for the massive 15-pound lobster, estimated to be 25 to 30 years old.) Detailed dioramas depict the whys and hows of fishing from dories, colonial schooners, and other historic vessels. You'll also learn a whole bunch about the *Bluenose,* a replica of which ties up in Lunenburg when it's not touring elsewhere (see "The Dauntless *Bluenose*" box). Outside, you can tour two other ships—a trawler and a salt-bank schooner—and visit a working boat shop. Allow at least 2 hours to probe all the corners of this engaging waterfront museum.

SHORT ROAD TRIPS FROM LUNENBURG

Blue Rocks is a tiny, picturesque harbor a short drive from Lunenburg. It's every bit as scenic as Peggy's Cove, but without the tour buses. Head out of town on Pelham Street, and keep driving east. Look for signs indicating either "The Point" or "The Lane" and steer in that direction; the winding roadway gets narrower as the homes get more humble. Eventually, you'll reach the tip, where it's just fishing shacks and rocks, with views of spruce- and heath-covered islands offshore. The rocks are said to glow in a blue hue in certain light, hence the name.

If you continue on instead of turning toward "the point," you'll soon come to the enclave of **Stonehurst,** another picturesque cluster of homes gathered around a rocky harbor. The road forks along the way; the route to South Stonehurst is somewhat more scenic. The whole area is ideal for exploring by bicycle, with twisting lanes, great vistas, and limited traffic. (See "Blue Rocks Road B&B," below, for rentals.)

Heading eastward along the other side of Lunenburg Harbor, you'll end up eventually at **The Ovens Natural Park** (☎ 902/766-4621), a privately owned campground and day-use park that sits on a mile of dramatic coastline. You can follow the seaside trail to view the "ovens" (sea caves, actually) for which the park was named. A closer view can be had on a Zodiac boat tour of the caves. The park features a cafe that serves up basic meals and a great view. Entrance fees are C$5.75 (US$3.85) adult, C$3.45 (US$2.30) seniors and children (5 to 13).

The Dauntless *Bluenose*

Take a Canadian dime out of your pocket and have a close look. That graceful schooner on one side? That's the *Bluenose,* Canada's most-recognized and most-storied ship.

The *Bluenose* was built in Lunenburg in 1921 as a fishing schooner. But it wasn't just any schooner. It was an exceptionally *fast* schooner.

U.S. and Canadian fishing fleets had raced informally for years. Starting in 1920 the *Halifax Herald* sponsored the International Fisherman's Trophy, which was captured that first year by Americans sailing out of Massachusetts. Peeved, the Nova Scotians set about taking it back. And did they ever. The *Bluenose* retained the trophy for 18 years running, despite the best efforts of Americans to recapture it. The race was shelved as World War II loomed; in the years after the war, fishing schooners were displaced by long-haul, steel-hulled fishing ships, and the schooners sailed into the footnotes of history. The *Bluenose* was sold in 1942 to labor as a freighter in the West Indies. Four years later it foundered and sank off Haiti.

What made the *Bluenose* so unbeatable? A number of theories exist. Some said it was because of last-minute hull design changes. Some said it was frost "setting" the timbers as the ship was being built. Still others claim it was blessed with an unusually talented captain and crew.

The replica *Bluenose II* was built in 1963 from the same plans as the original, in the same shipyard, and even by some of the same workers. It's been owned by the province since 1971, and it sails throughout Canada and beyond as Nova Scotia's seafaring ambassador. The *Bluenose's* location varies from year to year, and it schedules visits to ports from Labrador to the United States. In midsummer it typically alternates between Lunenburg or Halifax, during which visitors can sign up for 2-hour harbor sailings (C$20 (US$13) adult, C$10 (US$7) children 12 and under). To hear about the ship's schedule, call the ***Bluenose II* Preservation Trust** (☎ **800/763-1963** or 902/634-1963).

WHERE TO STAY

A **municipal campground** is located next to (and managed by) the visitor center on Blockhouse Hill. It has wonderful views and hookups for RVs. Be aware that sites are packed in tightly, but the location is well situated for exploring the town. Ask about pitching your tent on the less crowded far side of the information center, up on the grassy hill next to the fort's earthworks.

Blue Rocks Road B&B. 579 Blue Rocks Rd., Lunenburg, NS B0J 2C0. ☎ **800/818-3426** or 902/634-8033. E-mail: nika@tallships.ca. 3 units (1 private bathroom; 2 others share 1 bathroom). C$55–C$75 (US$37–US$50) double, including full breakfast. V. Closed mid-Oct to mid-May.

Outdoorsy folks who like a place where they can put their feet up will be right at home here. Merrill and Al Heubach offer three guest rooms in their cozy 1879 home, a short drive (or pleasant 20-minute walk) to downtown Lunenburg. It's on the way to scenic Blue Rocks, and Al runs **Lunenburg Bicycle Barn**—a complete bike shop and rental operation (☎ **902/634-3426**)—from an outbuilding behind the house. The handsomely painted floors and pleasant veranda with a view across the marsh to the water beyond make the place instantly relaxing. You'll share the first-floor living areas with the owners, who are very tidy and knowledgeable about the area. The morning coffee is organic and strong.

Boscawen Inn. 150 Cumberland St., Lunenburg, NS B0J 2C0. ☎ **800/354-5009** or 902/634-3325. Fax 902/634-9293. E-mail: boscawen@ns.sympatico.ca. 20 units (1 with private hallway bathroom). C$50–C$120 (US$33–US$80), including full breakfast. AE, ER, MC, V. Pets allowed with prior permission.

This imposing 1888 mansion occupies a prime hillside site just a block from the heart of town. It's almost worth it just to get access to the main-floor deck and its views of the harbor. Most of the rooms are in the main building, which had a newer wing added in 1945. The decor is Victorian, but not aggressively so. Some of the rooms, including two spacious suites, are located in the 1905 MacLachlan House, just below the main house. A few things to know: Room 6 lacks a shower but has a nice tub. Guests on the third floor will need to navigate steep steps. Two rooms have televisions, and in-room phones are available on request.

Dining: The inn's restaurant serves reliable, sometimes imaginative dinners nightly in season from 5:30 to 9pm. Entrees emphasize seafood and might include a mixed seafood platter, Digby scallops, or Cornish game hen. Main courses are C$13 to C$18 (US$9 to US$12). Breakfast is buffet style, with both hot and cold dishes.

Hillcroft Guest House. 53 Montague St. (P.O. Box 1665), Lunenberg, NS B0J 2C0. ☎ **902/634-8031.** 3 units (all share 1 bathroom). C$65 (US$43) double, includes continental breakfast. MC, V. Closed Dec to mid-Apr.

This comfortable, enjoyable spot bills itself as a "guest house" rather than an inn, and that's appropriate. The guest rooms share a single bathroom, and are decidedly small, tucked under slanting eaves. But they're furnished and decorated with a light touch, and the effect is more cozy than claustrophobic. There's also a guest parlor downstairs, and an intimate backyard with luridly painted Adirondack chairs for relaxing. The innkeepers are personable and welcoming, and the first-floor restaurant is among the best in town (see below).

Kaulbach House Historic Inn. 75 Pelham St., Lunenburg, NS B0J 2C0. ☎ **800/568-8818** or 902/634-8818. www.lunco.com/kaulbach. E-mail: kaulbach@istar.ca. 7 units. TV. C$70–C$115 (US$47–US$77) double, including full breakfast. AE, MC, V. Closed mid-Dec to mid-Mar.

The in-town Kaulbach House is decorated appropriately for its elaborate architecture: in high Victorian style, although rendered somewhat less oppressive with un-Victorian colors, like pink and green. The house also reflects the era's prevailing class structure: The nicest room (the tower room) is on top, and features two sitting areas and a great view. The least intriguing rooms are the former servants quarters on street level. It's a unique property in another regard: It's one of the few small Lunenburg inns with all private bathrooms.

Lennox Inn. 69 Fox St. (P.O. Box 254), Lunenberg, NS B0J 2C0. ☎ **902/634-4043.** 6 units. (2 share 1 bathroom.) C$60–C$80 (US$40–US$53) double, including full breakfast. MC, V. Open year-round; by appointment only mid-Oct to April.

In 1991, this strikingly handsome but simple house in a quiet residential area of Lunenberg was condemned and slated for demolition. Robert Cram didn't want to see it go, so he bought it, and spent several years restoring it back to its original 1791 appearance, filling it with antiques and period reproduction furniture. It's more rustic than opulent, but this fine inn should be high on the list for anyone fond of authentically historic houses. In fact, it claims, quite plausibly, to be the oldest unchanged inn in Canada. Three of the four spacious second floor rooms have the original plaster, and all four have the original fireplaces (nonworking). Two new rooms are planned for the third floor in 2000, one with the original wide plank walls. A simple country breakfast is served in the former tavern; be sure to note the ingenious old bar.

WHERE TO DINE

Note that the Boscawen Inn (see above) also serves well-regarded meals.

Hillcroft Café. 53 Montague St. ☎ **902/634-8031.** Reservations recommended. Entrees C$9.95–C$16.95 (US$6.65–US$11.30. MC, V. Daily 5:30–9pm. Closed Nov to mid-April. MIXED INTERNATIONAL.

The cozy Hillcroft, operated on the first floor of the guest house by the same name, is run by two globetrotters, Rafel Albo and Peter Fleischmann. The restaurant is adorned with the gleanings of their trips, lending the place a fun atmosphere and a sort of parlor-game amusement while waiting for dinner ("I bet that's from Bali. Or maybe Thailand.") The menu is equally eclectic, with starters ranging from baba ghannouj and hummus to Greek salad and local favorite clam chowder. Dinner entrees include Thai chicken (with green beans and baby corn in a coconut curry), roasted lamb topped with a mild cheese and green peppercorn sauce, and penne with local scallops and mussels in a Mediterranean sauce. Desserts feature fresh Italian ices, along with apple crisp and a shortbread-crust cheesecake. The kitchen doesn't quite meet the standards of the better small restaurants of Halifax, but it's a good option for a pleasant Lunenburg meal.

Lion Inn. 33 Cornwallis St. ☎ **902/634-8988.** Reservations suggested. Main courses C$13.95–C$20.95 (US$9.30–US$13.95). AE, MC, V. Mon–Sat 6–9pm (open Fri–Sun only Nov–Apr). CONTINENTAL.

The tiny Lion Inn seats just 24 diners in two compact dining rooms in an 1835 home on a Lunenburg side street. The interior is simply appointed with Windsor chairs and pale walls. The reliable menu, which more often than not is prepared with sophistication and flair, often features lamb in summer. Other entrees include baked salmon with a white wine and dill sauce, and peppercorn steak served with a Madeira sauce.

Magnolia's Grill. 128 Montague St. ☎ **902/634-3287.** Reservations not accepted. Main courses C$5–C$12 (US$3–US$8). AE, MC, V. Daily 11:30am–10pm. Closed Nov–Mar. SEAFOOD/ECLECTIC.

This is a bright, cheerful, funky storefront with a checkerboard linoleum floor, lively rock playing in the background, and walls adorned with old Elvis and Beatles iconography. It also serves some of the most delectable food in town. Look for barbecue pork sandwiches, chicken tostadas, and sesame-ginger shrimp stir-fry—or whatever else the kitchen feels like scrawling on the blackboard. The restaurant is especially famed for its fishcakes (served with homemade rhubarb chutney) and, for dessert, Mrs. Zinck's Chocolate Sloppy. No reservations are accepted, so come at off-peak hours or come expecting a wait. Picnic weather? There's also a deli for take-out.

Old Fish Factory Restaurant. 68 Bluenose Dr. (at the Fisheries Museum). ☎ **902/ 634-3333.** Reservations recommended (ask for a window seat). Lunch C$7–C$12 (US$5–US$8), dinner C$13.99–C$29.99 (US$9.35–US$19.99). AE, DC, DISC, ER, MC, V. Daily 11am–9pm (until 9:30pm July and Aug). Closed mid-Oct to early May. SEAFOOD.

The Old Fish Factory Restaurant is—no surprise—located in a huge old fish-processing plant, which it shares with the Fisheries Museum. This large and popular restaurant can swallow whole bus tours at once; come early and angle for a window seat or a spot on the patio. Also no surprise: The specialty is seafood, which tends to involve medleys of varied fish. At lunch you might order a seafood sandwich (made with crab, scallops, and lobster). At dinner, lobster is served four different ways, along with bouillabaisse, snowcrab, and a curried mango seafood pasta. There's steak, lamb, and chicken for more terrestrial tastes.

MAHONE BAY

Mahone Bay, first settled in 1754 by European Protestants, is postcard-perfect Nova Scotia. It's tidy and trim with an eclectic Main Street that snakes along the bay and is lined with inviting shops. This is a town that's remarkably well cared for by its 1,100 residents, a growing number of whom live here and commute to work in Halifax. Architecture buffs will find a range of styles to keep them ogling.

A **visitor information center** (☎ 902/624-6151) is located at 165 Edgewater St., near the three church steeples. It's open daily in summer 9am to 7:30pm.

In late July each year Mahone Bay celebrates the **Wooden Boat Festival** (☎ 902/624-8443), where you can see some of the most beautiful craft on the eastern seaboard put through their paces. Entertainment and workshops are offered as well; admission is free.

EXPLORING THE TOWN

The **Mahone Bay Settlers Museum,** 578 Main St. (☎ 902/624-6263), provides historic context for your explorations (closed Mondays). A good selection of historic decorative arts is on display. Before leaving, be sure to request a copy of "Three Walking Tours of Mahone Bay," a handy brochure that outlines easy historic walks around the compact downtown.

Thanks to the looping waterside routes nearby, this is a popular destination for bikers. And the deep, protected harbor offers superb sea kayaking. If you'd like to give kayaking a go, stop by **Mahone Bay Kayak Adventures** (☎ 902/624-6632) at 618 Main St. They offer everything from half-day introductory classes to a 5-day coastal tour. Among the more popular adventures is the day-long introductory tour, in which paddlers explore the complex shoreline nearby and learn about kayaking in the process. The price is C$85 (US$57) per person, including lunch. Rentals are also available, starting at C$30 (US$20) half day for a single kayak.

Another appealing means of exploring the harbor and islands beyond is aboard the *Spirit,* a 36-passenger sailing ship built in 1998 using traditional means and materials (☎ 902/624-8443). Four sailings daily are offered during the peak summer sailing season from the Mahone Bay town wharf. Cruises are C$20 (US$13) adult, C$10 (US$7) children 6 to 12, under 6 free.

SHOPPING

Mahone Bay serves as a magnet to all manner of creative and crafty types, and Main Street has become a shopping mecca for those who treasure handmade goods. Shops are typically open late spring until Christmas, when Haligonians travel the 55 minutes here for holiday shopping. Among the more interesting options:

Amos Pewterers. 589 Main St. ☎ **902/624-9547.**

Watch pewter come fresh out of the molds at this spacious workshop and gallery located in an 1888 building. The Christmas tree ornament is a popular souvenir.

And Everything Nice. 237 Edgewater St. ☎ **902/624-8463.**

This tasteful shop bills itself as a shop with "fashions for the fully figured woman." Everything here is in plus sizes, with styles by Danskin, Brooke Chapman, and Lady Kates.

Jo-Ann's Market & Café. 9 Edgewater St. ☎ **902/624-6305.**

Gourmet and farm-fresh basic fare are sold at this wonderful food shop, where a bag of carrots serves as a counterweight on the screen door. If you're in the mood for a picnic, this is your destination. The homemade jams, sold to benefit a local museum, are well-priced.

K.R. Thompson. 492 West Main St. ☎ **902/624-9069.**

K.R. Thompson makes sophisticated, softly geometrical pottery in blues and greens reflective of the sea. Her shop-studio is just up from the head of the harbor.

Sensational Chocolates. 605 Main St. ☎ **902/624-8559.**

You'll find handmade Belgian chocolates here, many cast in special shapes with local resonance. You can buy samples for C$1.

Southern Exposure. 567 Main St. ☎ **902/624-6484.**

Here you'll find a selection of funky/chic clothes made mostly of cotton woven by Mayan weavers in the Guatemalan Highlands.

Suttles & Seawinds. 466 Main St. ☎ **902/624-6177.**

Vibrant and distinctive clothing designed and made in Nova Scotia is sold at this stylish boutique. (There are others from Halifax to Toronto, but this is the original.) The adjacent shop is crammed with quilts and resplendent bolts of fabric.

Vintage Vogue. 533 S. Main St. ☎ **902/624-6127.**

Crammed with previously owned vintage and retro fashions, this is the spot to track down that leopard-skin pillbox or chenille bikini you've been yearning for.

WHERE TO STAY

✪ **The Manse.** Orchard St. (P.O. Box 475), Mahone Bay, NS B0J 2E0. ☎ **902/624-1121.** Fax 902/624-1182. 4 units. TV (on request). C$85–C$105 (US$57–US$70) double, including full breakfast. MC, V.

This is one of my favorite places in Nova Scotia. Innkeepers Rose and Allan O'Brien have made a cozy retreat of their 1870 home, tucked off on a side street that's at once removed from and close to the activity in Mahone Bay. All the guest rooms are bright and uncluttered, feature old pine floors, and are tastefully appointed with furniture that's both modern and classic.

I'd be happy in any of the rooms, but if it were available, I'd opt for the Loft, a former hayloft on the second floor of the barn. With its whitewashed barnboard walls, large sitting area, small balcony, queen-sized bed, and CD player, it's hard to imagine not enjoying a few days hidden away here. (*Caveat:* The room can get a bit hot and stuffy in the later afternoon, but almost always cools off by evening.) The rest of the house is equally attractive, and a morning spent with a cup of coffee in one of the over-sized Adirondack chairs on the front deck is a morning well spent indeed.

WHERE TO DINE

Innlet Café. Edgewater St. ☎ **902/624-6363.** Reservations suggested for dinner. Main courses C$12–C$21 (US$8–US$14) (mostly C$13–C$15/US$9–US$10). MC, V. Daily 11:30am–8:30pm. SEAFOOD/GRILL.

Jack and Katherine Sorensen have been serving up great meals here for two decades, and they've styled a menu that's brought back legions of devoted customers. Everything is good, especially the seafood. The menu is all over the place (oven-braised lamb shank to scallop stir-fry), but the smart money hones in on the unadorned seafood. Notable are the "smoked and garlicked mackerel" and the mixed seafood grill. The best seats are on the stone patio, which has a view of the harbor and the famous three-steepled townscape of Mahone Bay. If you end up inside, nothing lost. The clean lines and lack of clutter make it an inviting spot, and the atmosphere is informal and relaxed.

✪ **Mimi's Ocean Grill.** 662 Main St. ☎ **902/624-1342.** Main courses, lunch C$5.95–C$8.95 (US$3.95–US$5.95), dinner C$12–C$17.95 (US$8–US$11.95). AE, MC, V. Summer open daily noon–9pm; limited hours in the off-season. Closed Jan–Mar. ECLECTIC.

Set under an overarching tree in a historic Colonial-style home painted a rich Cherokee red, Mimi's offers some of the region's most wonderful cooking amid a relaxed and informal atmosphere. The whimsical wall paintings put you immediately at ease, and the servers are jovial without overdoing it. The menu changes every 6 weeks or so to reflect available ingredients. For lunch you might opt for the shrimp and lobster roll, or mussel linguine with pesto cream. For dinner, how about the restaurant's famous bayou haddock (with a spicy cornmeal crust), salmon Napoleon, or a grilled steak with wild mushroom butter? If the weather's right, angle for a table on the narrow front porch, where you can enjoy a glimpse of the bay and the ongoing parade of Main Street.

CHESTER

Chester is a short drive off Route 103 and has the feel of an old-money summer colony, perhaps somewhere along the New England coast circa 1920. It was first settled in 1759 by immigrants from New England and Great Britain, and today it has a population of 1,250. The village is noted for its regal homes and quiet streets, along with the picturesque islands offshore. The atmosphere here is uncrowded, untrammeled, lazy, and slow—the way life used to be in summer resorts throughout the world. Change may be on the horizon: actors and authors have discovered the place, and are snapping up waterfront homes in town and on the islands as private retreats, giving a bit of an edge to the lazy feel of the spot.

The **Chester Visitor Information Center** (☎ 902/275-4616) is in the old train station on Route 3 on the south side of town. It's open daily 10am to 5pm in summer.

EXPLORING THE AREA

Like so many other towns in Nova Scotia, Chester is best seen out of your car. But unlike other towns, where the center of gravity seems to be in the commercial district, here the focus is on the graceful, shady residential areas that radiate out from the Lilliputian village.

In your rambles, plan to head down Queen Street to the waterfront, then veer around on South Street, admiring the views out toward the mouth of the harbor. Continue on South Street past the yacht club, past the statue of the veteran (in a kilt), past the sundial in the small square. Then you'll come to a beautiful view of Back Harbour. At the foot of the small park is a curious municipal saltwater pool, filled at high tide. On warmer days, you'll find what appears to be half the town out splashing and shrieking in the bracing water. Bikes and small boats may be rented from **Cap't Evans' Wharf,** ☎ 902/275-2030, on the town's front harbor.

Some creative shops are beginning to find a receptive audience in and around Chester, and right now there's good browsing for new goods and antiques both downtown and in the outlying areas. Among them: **Fiasco,** 54 Queen St., ☎ 902/275-2173, which has an appealing selection of funky and fun home accessories and clothing; and **Christal Design,** 33 Queen St., ☎ **902/275-4580,** where you can shop for jewelry, watch bands, and belts made of fish leather.

For an even slower pace, plan an excursion out to the **Tancook Islands,** a pair of lost-in-time islands with a couple hundred year-round residents. The islands, accessible via a short ferry ride, are good for walking the lanes and trails. There's a small cafe on Big Tancook, but little else to cater to travelers. Several ferry trips are scheduled daily between 6am and 6pm. The ferry ties up on the island, however, so don't count on a last trip back to the mainland. Tickets are C$5 (US$3) round-trip, children under 12 free.

In the evening, the intimate **Chester Playhouse,** 22 Pleasant St. (☎ **800/363-7529** or 902/275-3933), hosts plays, concerts, and other high-quality performances throughout the summer season. Tickets are usually C$16 (US$11) adult. Call for a schedule or reservations.

WHERE TO STAY

Graves Island Provincial Park (☎ **902/275-4425**) is 3 kilometers (1.8 miles) north of the village on Route 3. The 125-acre estate-like park is one of the province's more elegant campgrounds, as befits moneyed Chester. The park has 73 sites, many dotting a high grassy bluff with views out to the spruce-clad islands of Mahone Bay. No hookups are available; the camping fee is C$14 (US$9) per night.

Gray Gables. 19 Graves Island Rd., Chester, NS B0J 1J0. ☎ **902/275-3983**, off-season 813/584-7506. 3 units. C$80–C$95 (US$53–US$63) double, including full breakfast. MC, V.

This spacious, modern Cape-Cod-style home north of the village (on the road to the provincial park) is tidy and trim in a Better Homes and Garden kind of way, with colonial reproduction furniture and great views of the bay from the wraparound porch. There's nothing rustic about it: The three guest rooms each have private bathrooms, and there's a sitting area with a television upstairs. Dutch innkeepers David and Jeanette Tomsett are quite helpful in directing you to activities in the area.

✪ **Haddon Hall.** 67 Haddon Hill Rd., Chester NS B0J 1J0. ☎ **902/275-3577**. Fax 902/275-5159. 9 units. A/C TV TEL. C$150–C$400 (US$100–US$267) double, includes breakfast. MC, V.

If there's no fog, Haddon Hall has the best view of any inn in Atlantic Canada, bar none. Perched atop an open hill with panoramic views of island-studded Mahone Bay, this very distinctive inn dates to 1905. It was built in what might be called "heroic Arts and Crafts" style. You'll recognize the bungalow form of the main house, but it's rendered in an outsized manner. Three stylish guest rooms are located in the main house; the remaining six are scattered in cottages around the property. Four rooms have wood fireplaces, three have Jacuzzis, two have kitchenettes. The styling is eclectic—a woodstove and twig furniture mark the rustic log cabin, spare continental lines are featured in the main house—but everything is united by understated good taste.

Dining: The dining room is open April to mid-October, serving dinner nightly from 5:30 to 8:30pm. Make reservations early, and ask for a table on the front porch with its sweeping vistas. The creative menu might include grilled lamb and papaya, or vegetable strudel with basil and feta. Prix fixe dinners are C$45 (US$30) plus tax and gratuity.

Amenities: The inn has a tennis court and outdoor pool and can arrange for boat tours. Ask about using the free guest bikes or visiting the inn-owned island for picnics or tours.

Mecklenburgh Inn. 78 Queen St., Chester, NS B0J 1J0. ☎ **902/275-4638.** E-mail: frnthrbr@atcon.com. 4 units (all share 2 bathrooms). C$55–C$75 (US$37–US$50) double, including full breakfast. AE, V. Closed Nov 1 to June 1. Children 10 and up.

The wonderfully funky and appealing Mecklenburgh Inn, built around 1890, is located on a low hill in one of Chester's residential neighborhoods. The inn is dominated by broad porches on the first and second floors, which invariably are populated with guests sitting and rocking and watching the town wander by. (Which it does: the post office is just next door.) Innkeeper Suzi Fraser has been running the place with casual bonhomie for 10 years, and she's a great breakfast cook to boot. Rooms are modern Victorian and generally quite bright. What's the catch? The four rooms share two hallway bathrooms, but guests often end up feeling like family, so it's usually not much of a bother.

WHERE TO DINE

Carta. 54 Queen St. (behind Fiasco). ☎ **902/275-5131.** Reservations helpful in summer. Main courses, C$5.95–C$13.95 (US$3.95–US$9.30). Tues–Sun 11:30am–3pm and 5–9pm. Closed late Dec to early April. GLOBAL.

Carta opened in 1999 in an odd sort of mini-mall hidden away in Chester's mini-downtown, but the proprietors have done great and colorful things with their tiny space. They've also concocted an appealing menu that's equally colorful and far-ranging, with offerings like a bento box, fish and chips, and green Thai curry. For more traditional appetites, there are big, meaty hamburgers. It's had to conceive of any craving that won't be satisfied here.

The Gallery Seaside Restaurant. Marriott's Cove (3km/1.8 miles west of village on Route 3). ☎ **902/275-4700.** Reservations advised; ask for a window. Main courses, lunch C$6.50–C$10.95 (US$4.35–US$7.30), dinner C$15.95–C$22.95 (US$10.65–US$15.30). Daily noon–9pm. Closed Nov–Apr. SEAFOOD.

This local institution is tucked off the main road west of town, and sits on the water next to a marina and boatyard. The decor effects the Ye Olde Crusty Mariner look, but it doesn't go overboard into schlock. You'll find everyone from blazer-wearing, gray-haired yachtspeople to casually dressed thirty-somethings who come for the good views and reliable fare. The lunch menu is less oriented toward the sea and specializes in a variety of burgers, including beef, chicken, and haddock burgers. There are also fishcakes and a seafood casserole. Dinner is more elegant, with a number of options listed under "bait," like escargot, calamari, and focaccia (the Gallery has a local reputation for the latter). Main courses include a daily-different fresh catch (prepared as you like it: Cajun, pan-fried, baked, broiled, or poached) and other seafood options such as jambalaya and lobster linguine. Meats include steaks, rack of lamb, and veal; vegetarian dinners are also available.

8 Halifax

During a stop at the sprawling Nova Scotia's visitor center near Amherst, I heard an elderly couple ask an eager young staffer why they should bother to visit Halifax. "It's just a city, isn't it?" they asked.

"Well," the staffer responded brightly, "it's on the second-largest natural harbor in the world, after Sydney, Australia!" And then she seemed at a loss for words.

Oh, dear. I hope that's not the best the tourism folks can come up with. In fact, Halifax is a fun, vibrant, exciting city that's loaded with history but not staid, modern but not slick, big enough to get lost in but not big enough to be intimidating.

Halifax

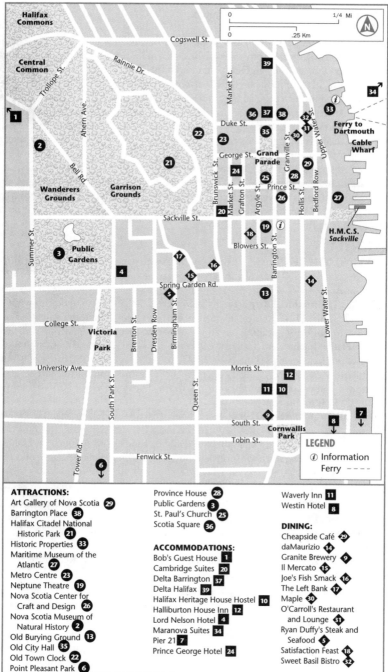

ATTRACTIONS:
Art Gallery of Nova Scotia 29
Barrington Place 38
Halifax Citadel National
  Historic Park 21
Historic Properties 33
Maritime Museum of the
  Atlantic 27
Metro Centre 23
Neptune Theatre 19
Nova Scotia Center for
  Craft and Design 26
Nova Scotia Museum of
  Natural History 2
Old Burying Ground 13
Old City Hall 35
Old Town Clock 22
Point Pleasant Park 6

Province House 28
Public Gardens 3
St. Paul's Church 25
Scotia Square 36

ACCOMMODATIONS:
Bob's Guest House 1
Cambridge Suites 20
Delta Barrington 37
Delta Halifax 39
Halifax Heritage House Hostel 10
Halliburton House Inn 12
Lord Nelson Hotel 4
Maranova Suites 34
Pier 21 7
Prince George Hotel 24

Waverly Inn 11
Westin Hotel 8

DINING:
Cheapside Café 29
daMaurizio 14
Granite Brewery 9
Il Mercato 15
Joe's Fish Smack 16
The Left Bank 17
Maple 30
O'Carroll's Restaurant
  and Lounge 31
Ryan Duffy's Steak and
  Seafood 5
Satisfaction Feast 18
Sweet Basil Bistro 32

LEGEND
ⓘ Information
Ferry - - - -

1-0368

71

Should you bother to visit? By all means.

This unusually pleasing harborside setting, now home to a city of some 115,000 (about three times as many in the greater metro area), first attracted Europeans in 1749, when Col. Edward Cornwallis established a military outpost here. (The site was named after George Montagu Dunk, 2nd Earl of Halifax. Residents tend to agree that it was a great stroke of luck that the city avoided the name Dunk, Nova Scotia.) Halifax plodded along as a colonial backwater for the better part of a century; one historian wrote that it was generally regarded as "a rather degenerate little seaport town."

But Halifax's natural advantages—including that well-protected harbor and its location near major fishing grounds and shipping lanes—eventually allowed it to emerge as a major port and military base. In recent years, the city has grown aggressively (it annexed adjacent suburbs in 1969) and carved out a niche as the vital commercial and financial hub of the Maritimes. The city is also home to a number of colleges and universities, which gives it a youthful, edgy air. Skateboards and bicycles often seem to be the vehicles of choice. In addition to the many attractions, downtown Halifax is home to a number of fine restaurants and hotels.

ESSENTIALS

GETTING THERE   Coming from New Brunswick and the west, the most direct route is via Route 102 from Truro; allow about 2 to 2½ hours from the provincial border at Amherst.

Halifax International Airport is 35 kilometers (21 miles) north of downtown Halifax in Elmsdale. (Take Route 102 to Exit 6.) Nova Scotia's notorious fogs make it advisable to call before heading out to the airport to reconfirm flight times. Airlines serving Halifax include Air Canada, Air Nova, Canadian Airlines International, Air Atlantic, and Icelandair. (See the "Getting There" section of chapter 2 for phone numbers.) **Airbus** (☎ 902/873-2091) offers frequent shuttles from the airport to major downtown hotels daily from 6:30am to 11:15pm. The rate is C$12 (US$8) one-way, C$20 (US$13) round-trip.

Via Rail (☎ 800/361-8010) offers train service 6 days a week between Halifax and Montréal. The entire trip takes between 18 and 21 hours, depending on direction. Stops include Moncton and Campbellton (and bus connections to Québec). Halifax's CN Station, at Barrington and Cornwallis Streets, is within walking distance of downtown attractions.

VISITOR INFORMATION   The **Halifax International Visitor Centre** (☎ 800/565-0000 or 902/490-5946) is located downtown at 1595 Barrington St., at the corner of Barrington and Sackville. It's open daily 8:30am to 7pm in summer (until 6pm in winter), it's huge, and it's staffed with friendly folks who will point you in the right direction or help you make room reservations.

If you're on the waterfront, there's a helpful provincial center at **Red Store Visitor Information Centre** (☎ 902/424-4248) at Historic Properties.

GETTING AROUND   Parking in Halifax can be problematic. Long-term metered spaces are in high demand downtown, and many of the parking lots and garages fill up fast. If you're headed downtown for a brief visit, you can usually find a 2-hour meter. But if you're looking to spend a day, I'd suggest venturing out early to ensure a spot at a parking lot. The city's most extensive parking (fee charged) is available near Sackville Landing. Or try along Lower Water Street, south of the Maritime Museum of the Atlantic, where you can park all day for around C$6 (US$4).

Metro Transit operates buses throughout the city. Route and timetable information is available at the information centers or by phone (☎ 902/490-6600). Bus fare is C$1.65 (US$1.10) adult, C$1.15 (US$75¢) seniors and children.

Between Monday and Saturday throughout the summer **a bright yellow bus** named Fred (☎ **902/423-6658**) cruises a loop through the downtown, passing each stop about every 20 minutes. It's free. Stops include the Maritime Museum, the Grand Parade, and Barrington Place Shops. Request a schedule and map at the visitor center.

EVENTS   The annual **Nova Scotia International Tattoo** (☎ **902/451-1221**) features military and marching bands totaling some 2,000 plus military and civilian performers. This rousing event takes place over the course of a week in early July and is held indoors at the Halifax Metro Center. Tickets are C$12 to C$26 (US$8 to US$17).

The **du Maurier Atlantic Jazz Festival** (☎ **902/492-2225**) has performances ranging from global and avant garde to local and traditional music. Venues include area nightclubs and outdoor stages; prices vary.

In early August expect to see a profusion of street performers ranging from fire-eaters to comic jugglers. They descend on Halifax each summer for the 10-day **International Busker Festival** (☎ **902/429-3910**). Performances take place along the waterfront walkway all day long and are often quite remarkable. Free, with donations requested.

The **Atlantic Film Festival** (☎ **902/422-3456;** www.atlanticfilm.com) offers screenings of more than 150 films in mid-September. The focus is largely on Canadian filmmaking, with an emphasis on independent productions and shorts. Panel discussions with industry players are also part of the festival. Most films cost about C$8 (US$5).

EXPLORING HALIFAX

Halifax is fairly compact and easily reconnoitered on foot or by mass transportation. The major landmark is the Citadel—the stone fortress that looms over downtown from its grassy perch. From the ramparts, you can look into the windows of the tenth floor of downtown skyscrapers. The Citadel is only 9 blocks from the waterfront—albeit 9 sometimes steep blocks—and you can easily roam both areas in 1 day.

A lively neighborhood worth seeking out runs along **Spring Garden Road,** between the Public Gardens and the library (at Grafton Street). You'll find intriguing boutiques, bars, and restaurants along these 6 blocks, set amid a mildly Bohemian street scene. If you have strong legs and a stout constitution, you can start on the waterfront, stroll up and over the Citadel to descend to the Public Gardens, and then return via Spring Garden to downtown, perhaps enjoying a meal or two along the way.

THE WATERFRONT

Halifax's rehabilitated waterfront is at its most inviting and vibrant between Sackville Landing (at the foot of Sackville Street) and the Sheraton Casino, near Purdy Wharf. (You could keep walking, but north of here the waterfront lapses into an agglomeration of charmless modern towers with sidewalk-level vents that assail passersby with unusual odors.) On sunny summer afternoons, the waterfront is bustling with tourists enjoying the harbor, businessfolks playing hooky while sneaking an ice cream cone, and baggy-panted skateboarders striving to stay out of trouble. Plan on about 2 to 3 hours to tour and gawk from end to end.

The city's most extensive parking (fee charged) is available near Sackville Landing, and that's a good place to start a walking tour. Make your first stop the waterfront's crown jewel, the **Maritime Museum of the Atlantic** (see below).

In addition to the other attractions listed below, the waterfront walkway is studded with small diversions, intriguing shops, take-out food emporia, and minor monuments. Think of it as an alfresco scavenger hunt.

Among the treasures, look for **Summit Plaza,** commemorating the historic gathering of world leaders in 1995, when Halifax hosted the G-7 Economic Summit. There's North America's oldest operating **Naval Clock,** which was built in 1767 and chimed at the Halifax Naval Dockyard from 1772 to 1993. You can visit the **Ferry Terminal,** which is hectic during rush hour with commuters coming and going to Dartmouth across the harbor. (It's also a cheap way to enjoy a sweeping city and harbor view.) The passenger-only ferry runs at least every half hour, and the fare is C$1.65 (US$1.10) each way.

The waterfront's **shopping** core is located in and around the 3-block **Historic Properties,** near the Sheraton. These stout buildings of wood and stone are Canada's oldest surviving warehouses and were once the center of the city's booming shipping industry. Today, the historic architecture is stern enough to provide ballast for the somewhat precious boutiques and restaurants they now house. Especially appealing is the granite-and-ironstone **Privateers' Warehouse,** which dates to 1813.

If you're feeling that a pub crawl might be in order, the Historic Properties area is also a good place to wander around after working hours in the early evening. There's a contagious energy that spills out of the handful of public houses, and you'll find a bustling camaraderie and live music.

✪ **Maritime Museum of the Atlantic.** 1675 Lower Water St. ☎ **902/424-7490.** Admission charged June 1–Oct 15: C$4.50 (US$3) adult, C$1 (US65¢) children, C$10 (US$7) family. Free admission Oct 16–May 31. June to mid-Oct Mon–Sat 9:30am–5:30pm (until 8pm Tues), Sun 1–5:30pm. Mid-Oct to May same hours except closed Mon, and at 5pm Wed–Sun.

All visitors to Nova Scotia owe themselves a stop at this standout museum on a prime waterfront location. The exhibits are involving and well executed, and you'll be astounded at how fast 2 hours can fly by. Visitors are greeted by a 10-foot lighthouse lens from 1906, and then proceed through a parade of shipbuilding and sea-going eras. Visit the deckhouse of a coastal steamer (ca. 1940), or learn the colorful history of Samuel Cunard, a Nova Scotia native (born 1787) who founded the Cunard Steam Ship Co. to carry the royal mail and along the way established an ocean dynasty. Another highlight is the exhibit on the tragic Halifax Explosion of 1917, when two warships collided in Halifax harbor not far from the museum, detonating tons of TNT. More than 1,700 people died, and windows were shattered 100 kilometers (60 miles) away.

But perhaps the most poignant exhibit is the lone deck chair from the *Titanic*—150 victims of the *Titanic* disaster are buried in Halifax, where rescue efforts were centered. Also memorable are the Age of Steam exhibit and Queen Victoria's barge.

ON THE WATER

A number of boat tours depart from the Halifax waterfront. You can browse the offerings on **Cable Wharf,** near the foot of George Street, where many tour boats are based. On-the-water adventures range from 1-hour harbor tours (about C$12/US$8) to 5-hour deep-sea fishing trips (about C$40/US$27).

Murphy's on the Water (☎ **902/420-1015**) runs the most extensive tour operation, with three boats and a choice of tours, ranging from a cocktail sailing cruise to whale watching to tours of historic McNab's Island, located near the mouth of the harbor (see below).

The *Christina Lynn* (☎ **902/429-5656**) plies the waters as was done a century ago, on a wooden cargo schooner.

Peggy's Cove Express (☎ **902/422-4200**) operates 4-hour scenic tours from Cable Wharf to the popular fishing village of Peggy's Cove; a walking tour of the town is included as part of the adventure.

A small group of friends traveling together—or a family—can create their own boat tour with the **Harbour Taxsea** (☎ 902/471-3181), which offers charters aboard a modern, 29-foot cabin cruiser. Rates are C$50 (US$33) per hour for the captain and the boat, which can accommodate up to six people.

C.S.S. *Acadia*. On the water, in front of the Maritime Museum, 1675 Lower Water St. ☎ **902/424-7490.** Free admission with museum ticket, or C$1 (can be applied to museum admission). Mon–Sat 9:30am–5:30pm, Sun 1–5pm. Closed mid-Oct to June 1.

This unusually handsome 1913 vessel is part of the Maritime Museum ("our largest artifact"), but it can be viewed independently for a small fee. The *Acadia* was used by the Canadian government to chart the ocean floor for 56 years, until its retirement in 1969. Much of the ship is open for self-guided tours, including the captain's quarters, upper decks, wheelhouse, and oak-paneled chart room. If you want to see more of the ship, ask about the guided half-hour tours (four times daily), which offer access to the engine room and more.

H.M.C.S. *Sackville*. Lower Water St. (near the Maritime Museum). ☎ **902/429-5600.** Free admission. Open early June to early Sept, Mon–Sat 10am–5pm, Sun 1–5pm.

This blue-and-white corvette (a speedy warship smaller than a destroyer) is tied up along a wood-planked wharf behind a small visitor center. There's a short multimedia presentation to provide some background. The ship is outfitted as it was in 1944, and it is now maintained as a memorial to the Canadians who served in World War II.

Pier 21. 1055 Marginal Rd. (on the waterfront behind the Westin Hotel). ☎ **902/425-7770.** C$6 (US$4) adult, C$2.75 (US$1.85) children 14 and under. Daily mid-May to Oct 9am–8pm (last ticket sold at 6:30pm), Nov to mid-May 9am–5pm.

Between 1928 and 1971 more than 1 million immigrants arrived in Canada by disembarking at Pier 21, Canada's version of New York's Ellis Island. In 1999 the pier was restored and reopened, filled with engaging interpretive exhibits, which aid visitors in vividly imagining the confusion and anxiety of the immigration experience. The pier is divided roughly into three sections, which recapture the boarding of the ship amid the cacophony of many languages, the crossing of the Atlantic (a 26-minute multimedia show recaptures the voyage in a ship-like theater), and the dispersal of the recent arrivals throughout Canada via passenger train. For those seeking more in-depth information (one in five Canadians today can trace a link back to Pier 21), there's a reference library and computer resources.

THE CITADEL & DOWNTOWN

Downtown Halifax cascades 9 blocks down a slope between the imposing stone Citadel and the waterfront. There's no fast-and-ready tour route; don't hesitate to follow your own desultory course, alternately ducking down quiet streets and striding along busy arteries. A good spot to regain your bearings periodically is the **Grand Parade,** where military recruits once practiced their drills. It's a lovely urban landscape—a broad terrace carved into the hill, presided over on either end by St. Paul's (see below) and Halifax's City Hall. The sandstone city hall was built between 1887 and 1890, and is exuberantly abristle with the usual Victorian architectural gew-gaws, like a prominent clock tower, dormers, pediments, arched windows, pilasters, and Corinthian columns. Alas, there's not much to see inside. If the weather is nice, the Grand Parade is also a prime spot to bring an alfresco lunch and enjoy some people watching.

✪ **Halifax Citadel National Historic Site.** Citadel Hill. ☎ **902/426-5080.** Admission mid-May to late Oct C$6 (US$4) adult, C$4.50 (US$3) senior, C$3 (US$2) youth (6–16), C$15

(US$10) family. Free the rest of the year. Mid-June to Aug 9am–6pm; Sept to mid-June 9am–5pm. Limited parking at site C$2.75 (US$1.85).

Even if the stalwart stone fort weren't here, it would be worth the uphill trek for the astounding views alone. The panoramic sweep across downtown and the harbor finishes up with vistas out toward the broad Atlantic beyond. At any rate, an ascent makes it obvious why this spot was chosen for the harbor's most formidable defenses: There's simply no sneaking up on the place.

Four forts have occupied the summit since Col. Edward Cornwallis was posted to the colony in 1749. The Citadel has been restored to look much as it did in 1856, when the fourth fort was built out of concern over bellicose Americans. The fort has never been attacked.

The site is impressive to say the least: Sturdy granite walls topped by grassy embankments form a rough star; in the sprawling gravel and cobblestone courtyard you'll find convincingly costumed interpreters in kilts and bearskin hats marching in unison, playing bagpipes, and firing the noon cannon. The former barracks and other chambers are home to exhibits about life at the fort. If you still have questions, stop a soldier, bagpiper, or washerwoman and ask.

The Citadel is the perfect place to launch an exploration of Halifax: It provides a good geographic context for the city and anchors it historically as well. This National Historic Site is the most heavily visited in Canada, and it's not hard to see why.

Art Gallery of Nova Scotia. 1741 Hollis St. (at Cheapside). ☎ **902/424-7542.** Admission C$5 (US$3) adults, C$2 (US$1) students, C$8 (US$5) family. Tues–Fri 10am–6pm, Sat and Sun noon–5pm.

Located in a pair of sandstone buildings between the waterfront and the Grand Parade, the Art Gallery is arguably the premier gallery in the Maritimes, with a focus on local and regional art. You'll also find a selection of other works by Canadian, British, and European artists, with a well-chosen selection of folk and Inuit art. In 1998 the gallery expanded to include the Provincial Building next door, where the entire house (it's tiny) of Nova Scotian folk artist Maud Lewis has been reassembled and is on display. The museum can be comfortably perused in 60 to 90 minutes; consider a lunch break in the attractive Cheapside Cafe (see below).

Province House. Hollis St. (near Prince St.). ☎ **902/424-4661.** Free admission. July and August Mon–Fri 9am–5pm; Sat, Sun, and holidays 10am–4pm. Rest of year Mon–Fri 9am–4pm.

Canada's oldest seat of government, Province House has been home to the Nova Scotian legislature since 1819. This exceptional Georgian building is a superb example of the rigorously symmetrical Palladian style. And like a jewel box, its dour stone exterior hides gems of ornamental detailing and artwork inside; note especially the fine plasterwork, rare for a Canadian building of this era.

Within the building also roost a number of fine stories. My favorite: the headless falcons in several rooms. It's said they were decapitated by an agitated legislator with a free-swinging cane who mistook them for eagles during a period of feverish anti-American sentiment in the 1840s. A well-written free booklet is available when you enter, and provides helpful background about the building's history and architecture. If the legislature is in session, you can obtain a visitor's pass and sit up in the gallery and watch the business of the province take place.

Nova Scotia Centre for Craft and Design. 1683 Barrington St. ☎ **902/424-402.** Free admission. Gallery open Mon–Fri 9am–4pm, Sat 10am–4pm.

The provincial government, with the idea of encouraging and developing craft- and design-based industries across the province, runs this center. Of interest to travelers is the first-floor gallery, where visitors can view oft-changing exhibits of the best of what Nova Scotia craftspeople have produced.

Nova Scotia Museum of Natural History. 1747 Summer St. ☎ **902/424-7353.** C$3.50 (US$2.35) adult, C$3 (US$2) senior, C$1 (US67¢) child, C$8 (US$5) family. June to mid-Oct Mon–Sat 9:30am–5:30pm (until 8pm Wed), Sun 1–5:30pm; mid-Oct to May Tues–Sat 9:30am–5pm (until 8pm Wed), Sun 1–5pm.

Situated on the far side of the Citadel from downtown, this modern, mid-size museum offers a good introduction to the flora and fauna of Nova Scotia. Galleries include geology, botany, mammals, and birds, plus exhibits of archaeology and Mi'kmaq culture. Especially noteworthy is the extensive collection of lifelike ceramic fungus, and the colony of honeybees that freely come and go from their indoor acrylic hive through a tube connected to the outdoors. Allow about 1 hour.

St. Paul's Church. 1749 Argyle St. (on the Grand Parade near Barrington St.). ☎ **902/429-2240.** Daily 9am–4:30pm; Sun services 8, 9:15, and 11am. Free guided tours Tues–Sat in summer.

Forming one end of the Grand Parade, St. Paul's was the first Anglican cathedral established outside of England and is Canada's oldest Protestant place of worship. Part of the building, which dates from 1750, was fabricated in Boston and erected in Halifax with the help of a royal endowment from King George II. A classic white Georgian building, St. Paul's has fine stained-glass windows. A piece of flying debris from the explosion of 1917 (see Maritime Museum of the Atlantic, above) is lodged in the wall over the doors to the nave.

GARDENS & OPEN SPACE

Fairview Lawn Cemetery. Chisholm Ave. off Connaught Ave. ☎ **902/490-4883.** Open daylight hours year-round.

When the *Titanic* went down April 15, 1912, nearly 2,000 people died. Ship captains from Halifax were recruited to help retrieve the corpses (you'll learn about this grim episode at the Maritime Museum). Some 121 victims, mostly crew members, were buried at this quiet cemetery located a short drive north of downtown Halifax. Some of the simple graves have names; others just numbers. Number 227 was J. Dawson, a young crew member who worked in the boiler room. Many teenage girls have convinced themselves that this is Jack Dawson, the fictional character played by Leonardo DiCaprio in the hit movie, and still leave the occasional flower or other token. Interpretive signs highlight some of the stories that survived the tragedy. A brochure with driving directions to this and two other Titanic cemeteries may be found at the Maritime Museum and visitor information centers.

Old Burying Ground. Corner of Spring Garden and Barrington. ☎ **902/429-2240.** Free admission. Open daylight hours mid-May to Nov; closed rest of year.

This was the first burial ground in Halifax, and between 1749 and 1844 some 12,000 people were interred here. (Only 1 in 10 graves is marked with a headstone, however.) You'll find wonderful examples of 18th- and 19th-century gravestone art—especially winged heads and winged skulls. (No rubbings allowed.) Also exceptional is the Welsford-Parker Monument (1855) near the grounds' entrance, which honors Nova Scotians who fought in the Crimean War. This ornate statue features a lion with an unruly Medusa-like mane. The grounds are imbued with a quiet grace a couple of hours before sunset, when the light slants magically through the trees and the traffic seems far away. The cemetery was fully restored in 1991.

Point Pleasant Park. Point Pleasant Dr. (south end of Halifax; head south on South Park St. near Public Gardens and continue on Young). Free admission. Open during daylight hours.

Point Pleasant is one of Canada's finer urban parks, and there's no better place for a walk along the water on a balmy day. This 186-acre park occupies a wooded peninsular point, and it served for years as one of the linchpins in the city's military defense. You'll find the ruins of early forts and a nicely preserved martello tower. Halifax has a 999-year lease from Great Britain for the park, for which it pays 1 shilling—about 10¢—per year. You'll also find a lovely gravel carriage road around the point, a small swimming beach, miles of walking trails, and groves of graceful fir trees. The park is located about 2 kilometers (1.2 miles) south of the Public Gardens. No bikes are allowed on weekends or holidays.

✪ **Public Gardens.** Spring Garden and South Park St. Free admission. Spring to late fall 8am–dusk.

The Public Gardens literally took seed in 1753, when they were founded as a private garden. It was acquired by the Nova Scotia Horticultural Society in 1836, and it assumed its present look in 1875, during the peak of the Victorian era. As such, the garden is one of the nation's Victorian masterpieces, more rare and evocative than any mansard-roofed mansion. You'll find wonderful examples of many of last century's dominant trends in outdoor landscaping, from the "natural" winding walks and ornate fountains to the duck ponds and fussy Victorian bandstand. (Stop by at 2pm on Sundays in summer for a free concert.) There are lots of leafy trees, lush lawns, cranky ducks who have long since lost their fear of humans, and tiny ponds. The overseers have been commendably stingy with memorial statues and plaques. You'll usually find dowagers feeding pigeons, and smartly uniformed guards slowly walking the grounds. Whatever you might think of high Victorian style in furnishings and interiors, the Victorians sure knew how to design gardens that would remain inviting more than a century later.

McNab's Island. Halifax Harbor. ☎ **902/426-5080.** Access via tour boats (see below). Free admission. Open daily during daylight hours.

This island wilderness is located within city limits near the mouth of the harbor, and it's a world apart from downtown Halifax. Once part of the city's military defenses and later the site of a popular amusement park, McNab's hasn't had any permanent residents since 1985. You'll find miles of wooded roads and trails to explore, some 200 species of birds, and great views of the city skyline and Point Pleasant. Fort McNab at the island's south tip dates back to 1888, and it was manned during both world wars in this century. All ships visiting the harbor were required to signal the fort. Those that failed to comply were warned with a shot across the bow.

Murphy's (☎ **902/420-1015**) runs tour boats from Cable Wharf in downtown Halifax daily in summer. A faster (and less expensive) route is to drive to Eastern Passage (south of Dartmouth) and take the **McNab's Island Ferry** (☎ **800/326-4563** or 902/465-4563), charging C$8 (US$5) adult, C$6 (US$4) ages 4 to 15. There's no extra charge for bikes or dogs.

SHOPPING

Halifax has a pleasing mix of shops, from mainstream retailers to offbeat boutiques. There's no central retail district to speak of; shops are scattered throughout downtown. Two indoor malls are located near the Grand Parade—**Scotia Square Mall** and **Barrington Place Shops,** flanking Barrington Street near the intersection of Duke Street. Another downtown mall, the 85-shop **Park Lane Shopping Centre,** is on Spring Garden Road about 1 block from the Public Gardens.

For souvenir shopping, head to the Historic Properties buildings on the waterfront; for idle browsing, try the shops on and around Spring Garden Road between Brunswick Street and South Park Street.

Ambience Home Accents. 5431 Doyle St. ☎ **902/423-9200.**

This home furnishings store features neo-classical and faux-Continental items, most with a funky twist. Look for chairs, wrought iron wall fixtures, lamps, and candle stands.

Art Gallery of Nova Scotia Shop. 1723 Hollis St. ☎ **902/424-4303.**

The museum's gift shops feature limited but choice selections of local crafts, ranging from creative postcards to birdhouses and tabletop sculptures. There's also work by Mi'kmaq artisans.

The Almanac. 2810 Windsor St. ☎ **902/455-1141.**

A classic, old-fashioned antique shop crammed to the eaves with everything from bureaus to barber chairs, the Almanac is a short drive from downtown.

Chilkoot Pass. 5523 Spring Garden Rd. ☎ **902/425-3674.**

This is a good stop for those headed to Cape Breton or other outdoor destinations: you can buy or rent camping equipment, and browse through a selection of outdoor clothing and travel accessories. The staff is often helpful in suggesting day trips from Halifax.

Drala Books & Gifts. 1567 Grafton St. ☎ **902/422-2504.**

This serene shop specializes mostly in Asian imports, including pottery, calligraphy materials, paper screens, chopsticks, and books on Asian design and philosophy.

Furniture and Antiques. 2739 Agricola St. ☎ **902/454-7171.**

Elegant and formal mahogany reproduction Chippendale and Queen Anne pieces, including dining room chairs and highboys, are the specialty at this shop, which is filled with lovely pieces priced less than you might think. Delivery trucks travel to the northeastern United States regularly.

Janet Doble Pottery Studio. 2660 Agricola St. ☎ **902/455-6960.**

Doble's bright and festive pottery is inspired by European majolica; anything purchased here is certain to brighten a drab kitchen.

Micmac Heritage Gallery. 1903 Barrington St. ☎ **902/422-9509.**

Native Canadian crafts and fine arts are the specialty at this shop, which is within Barrington Place mall. Among the goods: quill and split ash baskets, along with leather goods, jewelry, and paintings.

Thornbloom. 5460 Spring Garden Rd. ☎ **902/425-8005.**

This tidy shop in a small indoor mall on Spring Garden features housewares, Umbro kitchen stuff, knives by Henckels, Roots Home linens, and intriguing plaster tile blocks by Vancouver-based Sid Dickens.

Urban Cottage. 1819 Granville St. ☎ **902/423-3010.**

This consignment store in the middle of downtown has an eclectic and sizeable selection of stuff, including furniture, housewares, and collectibles, nicely displayed and generally reasonably priced.

WHERE TO STAY
EXPENSIVE

Cambridge Suites. 1583 Brunswick St., Halifax, NS B3J 3P5. ☎ **888/417-8483** or 902/420-0555. Fax 902/420-9379. www.centennialhotels.com/cambridge. E-mail: reservations@hfx.cambridgesuites.ns.ca. 200 units. A/C MINIBAR TV TEL. C$139–C$240

(US$93–US$160). Children under 18 free with parents. AE, CB, DC, ER, MC, V. Parking C$11 (US$7).

The attractive, modern Cambridge Suites is nicely located near the foot of the Citadel and is well positioned for exploring Halifax. It's perfect for families—40 of the units are two-room suites featuring kitchenettes with microwaves, two phones, coffeemakers, and hair dryers. Expect comfortable, inoffensive decor, and above-average service.

Dining: Dofsky's Grill on the first floor is open for all three meals, which are palatable if not exciting. Look for pasta, blackened haddock, burgers, and jerked chicken (C$8/US$5.33 to C$19/US$12.67).

Amenities: Fitness center with whirlpool, sauna, weights, and exercise bikes; rooftop sundeck with barbecue grill; room service; safe-deposit boxes; concierge; self-service laundry; baby-sitting; dry cleaning; and valet parking.

Delta Barrington. 1875 Barrington St., Halifax, NS B3J 3L6. ☎ **902/429-7410.** Fax 902/420-6524. 202 units. A/C MINIBAR TV TEL. C$115–C$185 (US$77–US$123) double. AE, DC, DISC, ER, JCB, MC, V. Parking C$15/US$10 (valet) and C$12/US$8 (self). Small pets allowed.

Convenience and location form the cornerstones of the Delta Barrington, located just 1 block from the waterfront and 1 block from the Grand Parade, and connected to the Metro Centre and much of the rest of downtown by pedway. It's a modern, large hotel, but one that has been designed and furnished with an eye more to comfort than to flash. The guest rooms are decorated with a contemporary country decor, with pine headboards and country-style reproduction furniture. The king rooms are spacious, furnished with sofas and easy chairs. Some rooms face the pedestrian plaza and have been soundproofed to block the noise from the evening rabble, but these windows don't open (most other rooms have opening windows). The quietest rooms face the courtyard but lack a view.

Dining: McNab's restaurant has a distinguished country-estate atmosphere and is open for three meals daily. Luncheon entrees, under C$10 (US$6.67), feature sandwiches and more intriguing fare like jambalaya, cedar-baked salmon, and three-cheese pasta. For dinner (C$15.95/US$10.65 to C$23.95/US$15.95), look for a rack of lamb with Calvados and green apple cinnamon salsa, and lobster pie.

Amenities: Heated indoor pool, fitness room, sauna, whirlpool, turndown service, concierge, room service, valet parking, safe-deposit boxes, weekend children's programs, baby-sitting, dry cleaning, and laundry.

Delta Halifax. 1990 Barrington St., Halifax, NS B3J 1P2. ☎ **800/268-1133** or 902/425-6700. Fax 902/425-6214. 300 units. A/C MINIBAR TV TEL. C$139–C$189 (US$93–US$126) double. AE, ER, JCB, MC, V. Parking C$12.95 (US$8.65).

The Delta Halifax (formerly the Hotel Halifax, more formerly the Chateau Halifax) is a slick and modern (built in 1972) downtown hotel that offers premium service. It's located just a block off the waterfront, to which it's connected via skyway, but navigating it involves an annoying labyrinth of parking garages and charmless concrete structures. The lobby is streetside; guests take elevators up above a six-floor parking garage to reach their rooms. The hotel is frequented largely by business travelers during the week. Ask for a room in the so-called "resort wing" near the pool, which feels a bit further away from the chatter of downtown and the press of business. A number of rooms have balconies and many have harbor views; ask when you book. Rooms are in two classes: either 300 or 500 square feet, and all are furnished simply and unexceptionally with standard-issue hotel furniture. All feature coffeemakers, hair dryers, and bathrobes.

Dining/Diversions: The Crown Bistrot offers informal continental cuisine, including pan-fried halibut with macadamia nuts, and seared sea scallops with basmati rice. The summertime lobster and steak buffet costs C$24.95 (US$16.65). The Sam Slick Lounge next door is "cigar friendly."

Amenities: Fitness center with indoor pool, sundeck, sauna and whirlpool; concierge; safe-deposit boxes; complimentary coffee; limited room service; shopping arcade; car-rental desk; valet parking; dry cleaning; laundry; and baby-sitting.

Halliburton House Inn. 5184 Morris St., Halifax, NS B3J 1B3. ☎ **902/420-0658.** Fax 902/423-2324. www.halliburton.ns.ca. E-mail: innkeeper@halliburton.ns.ca. 28 units. A/C TV TEL. C$115–C$165 (US$77–US$110) double, including continental breakfast and parking (limited). AE, ER, MC, V.

The Halliburton House is a well-appointed, well-run, and elegant country inn located in the heart of downtown. Named after former resident Sir Brenton Halliburton (Nova Scotia's first chief justice), the inn is spread among three townhouse-style buildings, which are connected via gardens and sundecks in the rear but not internally. The main building was constructed in 1809 and was converted to an inn in 1995, when it was modernized without any loss of its native charm. All guest rooms are subtly furnished with fine antiques, but few are so rare that you'd fret about damaging them. The rooms are rich and masculine in tone, and light on frilly stuff. Among my favorites: Room 113, which is relatively small but has a lovely working fireplace and unique skylighted bathroom. Rooms 102 and 109 are both suites with wet bars and fireplaces. Halliburton is popular with business travelers, but it's also a romantic spot for couples.

Dining: The intimate first-floor dining room, which serves from 5:30 nightly, is dusky and wonderful with a menu that's small and inventive. The chef has a predilection for local game and Atlantic seafood. Look for bison medallions, grilled red deer, and grilled fresh char. The fresh seafood is always reliable. Entrees are priced C$18 to C$27 (US$12 to US$18).

Amenities: Room service, VCRs on request, afternoon refreshments, conference rooms, baby-sitting, dry cleaning.

The Lord Nelson Hotel and Suites. 1515 South Park St., Halifax, NS B3J 2L2. ☎ **800/565-2020** or 902/423-6331. Fax 902/423-7148. 280 units. A/C TV TEL. C$149–C$179 (US$99–US$119) peak season, C$99–C$139 (US$66–US$93) off-peak. Parking C$5.75 (US$3.85) per day. AE, DC, DISC, ER, MC, V.

The Lord Nelson was built in 1928, and was for years the city's preeminent hostelry. It gradually sank in esteem and eventually ended up as a flophouse. In 1998 it was purchased and received a long-overdue top-to-bottom renovation. Today, it's back near the top of the heap as one of the city's better hotels. For starters, it has location: it's right across from the lovely Public Gardens, and abuts lively Spring Garden Road. The standard rooms are furnished with Georgian reproductions and all have hair dryers and coffeemakers; some 40 have kitchenettes, and more than 100 have faxes. (Business-class rooms feature desk chairs, robes, bottled water, and free local phone calls.) The hotel charges a C$15 to C$20 (US$10 to US$13) premium for a room that faces the street or the gardens. It's worth it; the others face into the rather bleak courtyard filled with service equipment.

Dining: The Victoria Arms is a cozy and convincing English-style pub located off the handsome coffered lobby. There's British pub fare like steak and kidney pie, fish and chips, and liver with bacon and onions, along with a daily roast. Pub sandwiches are C$6.95 to C$8.95 (US$4.63 to US$5.97); entrees are C$6.95 to C$14.95 (US$4.63 to US$9.97).

Amenities: Fitness room, sauna, safe-deposit boxes, concierge, free newspaper, limited room service, washer/dryer, baby-sitting, laundry, and dry-cleaning.

✪ **Prince George Hotel.** 1725 Market St., Halifax, NS B3J 3N9. ☎ **800/565-1567** or 902/425-1986. Fax 902/429-6048. www.princegeorgehotel.com. E-mail: reservations@ princegeorgehotel.com. 206 units. A/C MINIBAR TV TEL. C$160–C$220 (US$107–US$147) double, suites from C$250 (US$167). AE, CB, DC, DISC, MC, V. Parking C$11 (US$7).

This contemporary and large downtown hotel features clean and understated styling, with all the underpinnings of elegance, like highly polished wainscotting, plush carpeting, and the discreet use of marble. Expect modern and comfortably appointed hotel rooms, most with balconies. Rooms have a selection of complimentary tea and coffee, coffeemakers, and hair dryers. The hotel is popular among business travelers, but the cordial staff makes individual travelers feel very much at home. The hotel is nicely situated near the Citadel and restaurants and is linked to much of the rest of downtown via underground passageways.

Dining: Georgio's on the first floor features contemporary bistro styling, with a menu to match. Dinners include burgers and pizza (most under C$10/US$6.67), along with more upscale offerings like bouillabaisse, striploin with Asian spices, and scallop stir-fry (C$12.95/US$8.63 to C$17.95/US$11.97).

Amenities: Health club with indoor pool, sauna, and whirlpool. Valet parking, business center, concierge, limited room service, safe-deposit boxes, in-room massages, baby-sitting, dry cleaning, and laundry.

MODERATE

Bobs' Guest House. 2715 Windsor St., Halifax, NS B3K 5E1. ☎ **902/454-4374.** Fax 902/454-2060. www.sjnow.com/bobs. E-mail: bobs@hfx.andara.com. 4 units (3 share 2 bathrooms). C$75–C$95 (US$50–US$63) double, including full breakfast. On-street parking. MC.

Bob Grandfield and Bob Woods (note the correct placement of the apostrophe) have converted their circa 1920 home with blue shingles and a purple door into a comfortable four-room guest home with one room with a private bathroom, and three shared. The welcoming downstairs is extensively decorated with modern Nova Scotian artworks (some mildly alarming) and a baby grand piano (guests are welcome to bang away). The prime room is the spacious third-floor suite with private bathroom. The second floor rooms are relatively cozy, with antiques and high-quality linens and duvets. In the compact backyard there are rose bushes and a hot tub, offering a nice retreat. The guest house is located a few minute's drive from the Citadel and downtown attractions. It's often booked up in summer, so it's best to call well in advance for reservations.

Maranova Suites. 65 King St., Dartmouth, NS B2Y 4C2. ☎ **888/798-5558** or 902/ 463-9520. Fax 902/463-2631. E-mail: maranova@istar.ca. 35 units. A/C TV TEL. C$65–C$110 (US$43–US$73) double. AE, DC, MC, V. Underground parking available.

Located across the harbor from Halifax and a 2-minute walk to frequent ferry service to downtown, the Maranova Suites is one of the better options for travelers on a ginger-ale budget. Housed in a modern concrete building, it features rooms that are large and tidy. All guest rooms have sitting areas, kitchenettes, and balconies. Don't expect anything fancy; the rooms are basic, simple, and clean. Some have wonderful views of the harbor—ask when you book.

Amenities: Coin-operated laundry and dry-cleaning; access to Dartmouth Sportplex can be arranged.

Waverly Inn. 1266 Barrington St., Halifax, NS B3J 1Y5. ☎ **800/565-9346** or 902/ 423-9346. Fax 902/425-0167. www.waverlyinn.com. E-mail: welcome@waverlyinn.com.

32 units. A/C TV TEL. June–Oct C$82–C$155 (US$55–US$103), Nov–May C$75–C$139 (US$50–US$93). Rates include continental breakfast and parking. DC, ER, MC, V.

The Waverly Inn has been adorned in high Victorian style as befits its 1866 provenance. Flamboyant playwright Oscar Wilde was a guest in 1882, and one suspects he had a hand in the decorating scheme. There's walnut trim, red upholstered furniture, and portraits of sourpuss Victorians at every turn. The headboards in the guest rooms are especially elaborate—some look like props from Gothic horror movies. Room 130 has a unique Chinese wedding bed and a Jacuzzi (nine rooms have private Jacuzzis). There's a common deck on which to enjoy sunny afternoons; a first-floor hospitality room stocks complimentary snacks and beverages for guests.

INEXPENSIVE

The **Halifax Heritage House Hostel** (☎ 902/422-3863) is located at 1253 Barrington St., within walking distance of downtown attractions. You'll usually share rooms with other travelers (several private and family rooms are available); there are lockers in each room, shared bathrooms, and a shared, fully equipped kitchen. Rates are C$19 (US$13) per person in dormitories, C$40 (US$27) double for a private room.

A short way from downtown but convenient to bus lines are university dorm rooms open to travelers throughout mid-summer, when school isn't in session. **Dalhousie University** (☎ 902/494-8840) has two-bedroom units in a 33-story tower on Fenwick Street. Rates are C$34 to C$51 (US$23 to US$34) per day (C$4/US$2.65 additional for parking), which includes access to the athletic facility.

WHERE TO DINE

Coffee emporia have cropped up throughout Halifax in the last couple of years, as they have in urban areas everywhere. Among the better spots: **Steve-O-Reno's,** 1536 Brunswick St. (near Spring Garden), ☎ 902/429-3034. You'll have your choice of potent coffee or coffee-like beverages (e.g., chai tea latte), along with fruit smoothies, a limited selection of sandwiches, and a pleasantly relaxed atmosphere.

EXPENSIVE

✪ daMaurizio. 1496 Lower Water St. (in The Brewery). ☎ **902/423-0859.** Reservations highly recommended. Main courses C$20–C$23 (US$13–US$15). AE, ER, MC, V. Mon–Sat 5:30–10pm. ITALIAN.

Halifax's best restaurant does everything right. Located in a cleverly adapted former brewery, the vast space has been divided into a complex of hives with columns and exposed brick that add to the atmosphere and heighten the anticipation of the meal. The decor shuns decorative doodads for clean lines and simple class. Much the same might be said of the menu. You could start with an appetizer of squid quick-cooked with olive oil, tomato, and chiles, or grilled polenta with wild mushrooms. You won't be disappointed if you order from the pasta appetizers—like the open raviolo with lobster and shrimp. The main courses tax even the most decisive of diners: There's veal scaloppine in puff pastry with goose liver paté, rack of lamb with roasted garlic, and veal chops with fresh sage. The kitchen doesn't try to dazzle with creativity but relies instead on the best ingredients and a close eye on perfect preparation.

Maple. 1813 Granville St., ☎ **902/425-9100.** Reservations recommended. Main courses, lunch C$9–C$15 (US$6–US$10), dinner C$20–C$30 (US$13–US$20). AE, DC, ER, MC, V. Mon–Fri 11am–2pm, Mon–Sat 5:30–11pm. NOUVEAU CANADIAN.

Chef-proprietor-TV cooking show host Michael Smith is the Emeril Lagasse of eastern Canada. He started his crusade for an authentic Canadian cuisine while the chef at the well-regarded Inn at Bay Fortune on PEI, and has now carried his campaign off the island with the opening of this splashy new restaurant. The restaurant is located on three levels, with the open kitchen center stage on the middle level. The restaurant was bedeviled with delays in opening, so Frommer's wasn't able to review it by press time, but Smith was anticipating offerings such as saffron oyster broth with chive essence and oyster fritters, potato-crusted monkfish with an onion and leek tart, and roast boar with sage-walnut ravioli.

MODERATE

The Left Bank. 1541 Birmingham St. ☎ **902/492-3049.** Reservations recommended. Main courses, lunch C$5.95–C$11.95 (US$3.95–US$7.95), dinner C$17.95–C$25.95 (US$11.95–US$17.30). AE, DC, ER, MC, V. Daily 11am–3pm and 5:30–10pm (until 11pm Fri and Sat). BISTRO.

The Left Bank is a fashionable spot that's casual without being scruffy—you'll be comfortable in either a tailored suit or jeans. Located in a narrow railroad flat with entrances on either end, The Left Bank has seating outdoors in the summer on a small rear deck, and crisp service that's well above average. Lunches include baked chevre tort and escargot, along with sandwiches, crepes, and pasta. The dinner menu is nicely varied, ranging from veal sweetbreads with oysters to smoked Nova Scotian pheasant with a morel-cream sauce. Other inviting options: deep-dish lobster pie, rack of lamb, and salmon with a mango-coconut cream.

O'Carroll's Restaurant and Lounge. 1860 Upper Water St. ☎ **902/423-4405.** Reservations advised. Main courses, lunch C$6.95–C$11.95 (US$4.65–US$7.95), dinner C$16.95–C$21.95 (US$11.30–US$14.65). AE, MC, V. Daily 11am–2:30pm and 5–10:30pm (weekend hours may vary; call to confirm). SEAFOOD.

O'Carroll's is one of the best options for a fulfilling seafood meal in Halifax. (See Joe's Fish Smack, below, for a less elaborate option.) It's a dusky, Gaelic-influenced spot on Water Street across from Historic Properties. It's fancier than the average fish house, with white tablecloths, potted plants, and stained glass lamps on the tables. The kitchen takes a rather creative slant to seafood, with global offerings like curries and Thai-spiced seafood mingling with more traditional fare like finnan haddie and simply prepared salmon. Non-seafood options include duck, filet mignon, and steak-and-kidney pie. From Wednesday through Saturday there's live Celtic music in the lounge, and you can order off a lighter bar menu until late.

Ryan Duffy's Steak and Seafood. 5640 Spring Garden Rd. ☎ **902/421-1116.** Reservations helpful. Main courses, lunch C$8.95–C$13.95 (US$5.95–US$9.30), dinner C$14.95–C$25.50 (US$9.95–US$17). AE, CB, DC, DISC, ER, MC, V. Dining room: daily 11:30am–2:30pm, Sun–Thurs 5–10pm, Fri–Sat 5–11pm. Grill: Mon–Sat 11:30am–midnight (approx.), Sun 5–11pm. STEAKHOUSE.

Located on the upper level of a small shopping mall on Spring Garden, Ryan Duffy's may at first strike diners as a knockoff of a middle-brow chain, like T.G.I. Friday's. It's not. It's a couple of notches above. The house specialty is steak, for which the place is justly famous. The beef comes from corn-fed Hereford, Black Angus, and Shorthorn, and it is nicely tender. (When the waiter delivered me an oversized steak knife, he said, "You don't really need this, but it's all part of the show.") Steaks are grilled over a natural wood charcoal and can be prepared with garlic, cilantro butter, or other extras upon request. The more expensive cuts, such as the striploin, are trimmed right at the table. If you move away from steak on the menu, expect less consistency—the shrimp cocktail is disappointing; the Caesar salad is wonderful. Americans who are disappointed that they can't order rare steak much anymore owing to liability concerns will like it here—you can even order it "blue-rare."

Sweet Basil Bistro. 1866 Upper Water St. ☎ **902/425-2133.** Reservations recommended. Sandwiches C$7.95–C$12.95 (US$5.30–US$8.65); main courses C$12.95–C$18.95 (US$8.65–US$12.65). AE, DC, ER, MC, V. Daily 11:30am–11pm. UPMARKET PASTA.

If hunger overtakes you while you're snooping around the waterfront's shopping district, this should be your destination. It has the casual feel of a favorite trattoria, but the menu transcends the limited regional offerings that implies. Pastas are well represented (especially good is the squash ravioli with Parmesan and hazelnut sauce), but you'll also find seared scallops with five-spice broth and Asian vegetables, crusted lamb chops with a demi glace, and a selection of stir-fries ("Have it wimpy or volcano!" says the menu). The best name? Slash 'n' Burn, a spicy salmon filet served with a mango-basil sauce.

INEXPENSIVE

Cheapside Café. 1723 Hollis St. (inside the Art Gallery of Nova Scotia). ☎ **902/425-4494.** Sandwiches C$6.95–C$8.95 (US$4.65–US$5.95), other entrees to C$10.95 (US$7.30). MC, V. Sat, Sun, Mon and holidays noon–5pm, Tues–Fri 10am–6pm. CREATIVE SANDWICHES.

The cheerful and lively Cheapside Café is tucked inside the Provincial Building, one of two structures housing the Art Gallery of Nova Scotia. A whole groaning board of sandwiches and other delectables features choices like chicken breast with avocado and mango chutney, roast beef with fried onions, and smoked salmon served with an egg pancake and asparagus. Other fare includes fish cakes, quiche, and poached salmon with sun-dried tomato chutney. For kids, there's peanut butter and jelly and egg salad with carrot sticks. Desserts are delicious—especially notable is the Cheapside Café Torte.

Granite Brewery. 1222 Barrington St. ☎ **902/423-5660.** Reservations usually not needed. Main courses C$6–C$12 (US$4–US$8). AE, DC, MC, V. Mon–Sat 11:30am–12:30am, Sun noon–11pm. BREWPUB.

Eastern Canada's pioneer brewpub—this was the first—is housed in an austere building far down Barrington Street. The starkly handsome 1834 stone building has a medium-fancy dining room upstairs with red tablecloths and captain's chairs. The pubbier downstairs is more boisterous and informal. You can order off the same menu at either spot, and it's what you'd expect at a brewpub. Entrees include steak sandwiches, burgers, and meat loaf. Notable is the "peculiar pork tenderloin," topped with a sauce made with their trademark dark ale.

✪ **Il Mercato.** 5475 Spring Garden Rd. ☎ **902/422-2866.** Reservations not accepted. Main courses C$9–C$15 (US$6–US$10). AE, DC, MC, V. Mon–Sat 11am–11pm. NORTHERN ITALIAN.

Light-colored Tuscan sponged walls and big rustic terra-cotta tiles on the floor set an appropriate mood at this popular spot amid the clamor of Spring Garden. Come early or late or expect to wait a bit (no reservations accepted), but it's worth making the effort. You'll find a great selection of meals at prices that approach bargain level. You can start by selecting antipasti from the deli-counter in the front (you point; the wait-staff will bring them to your table). Pastas run C$9 to C$12 (US$6 to US$8); every entree is less than C$15 (US$10). The focaccias are superb and come with a pleasing salad. The ravioli with roast chicken and wild mushrooms is sublime. Non-Italian entrees include a seafood medley and grilled striploin with wild mushroom sauce. For dessert, repeat the antipasto routine: head to the counter and ogle the luscious offerings under glass, then point and sit, awaiting a fine finale.

✪ **Joe's Fish Smack.** 1520 Queen St. ☎ **902/423-8435.** Main courses C$6.95–C$12.50 (US$4.65–US$8.35. AE, MC, V. Mon–Sat 11am–10pm, Sun 1–8pm. CASUAL/SEAFOOD.

Joe's trademark fish and chips are outstanding—haddock lightly coated with a beer batter, and served with freshly cut fries and a coleslaw that's among the zestiest in the province. There's also chowder and a selection of fish (catfish, tuna, rainbow trout, shark, and more) that can be prepared broiled, pan-fried, baked, poached, or Cajun-style. For the weekend brunch you'll need to arrive with an appetite: the meal includes fish cakes, eggs, hash browns, baked beans, and toast. Joe's opened in the spring of 1999 and quickly attracted a devoted clientele for a simple reason: excellent value for money any time.

Satisfaction Feast. 1581 Grafton St. ☎ **902/422-3540.** Main courses C$5–C$12 (US$3–US$8). AE, DC, MC, V. Mon–Sat 10:30am–10pm (until 9pm Mon–Thurs in winter), Sun 11am–10pm. VEGETARIAN.

Located along the newly cool stretch of Grafton Street, Satisfaction Feast is Halifax's original vegetarian restaurant, and was recently voted one of the top 10 veggie restaurants in Canada by the *Globe and Mail*. It's funky and fun, with a certain spare grace inside and a canopy and sidewalk tables for summer lounging. Entrees include lasagna, bean burritos, pesto pasta, veggie burgers, and a macrobiotic rice casserole. There's also "neatloaf" and tofu-and-rice based "peace burgers" for those who like their food with cute names. The vegan fruit crisp is the dessert to hold out for. Satisfaction Feast also does a brisk business in take-out; consider a hummus-and-pita picnic atop nearby Citadel Hill.

HALIFAX BY NIGHT

For starters, stop by the visitor center or the front desk of your hotel and ask for a copy of *Where Halifax,* a comprehensive monthly guide to the city's entertainment. Among the city's premier venues for shows are the downtown **Halifax Metro Centre,** 5248 Duke St. (☎ 902/451-1202 for recorded information), which hosts sporting events and concerts by the likes of Garth Brooks, Bob Dylan, and Alanis Morissette.

PERFORMING ARTS

Shakespeare by the Sea (☎ 888/759-1516 or 902/422-0295) stages a whole line of Bardic and non-Bardic productions from July through September at several alfresco venues around the city. Most are held at Point Pleasant Park, where the ruins of old forts and buildings are used as the stage settings for delightful performances, with the audience sprawled on the grass, many enjoying picnic dinners. Most shows ask for a suggested donation of C$5 (US$3.33). The more elaborate productions (past shows have included *King Lear* at the Citadel and *Titus Andronicus* at the park's Martello Tower) have limited seating, with tickets ranging from C$25 to C$27 (US$17 to US$18).

The **Neptune Theatre,** 1593 Argyle St. (☎ 902/429-7070), benefitted from a C$13.5 million renovation and now also includes an intimate 200-seat studio theater. Top-notch dramatic productions are offered throughout the year. (The main season runs October to May, with a summer season filling in the gap with eclectic performances.) Mainstage tickets range from C$20 to C$35 (US$13 to US$23).

For a more informal dramatic night out, there's the **Grafton Street Dinner Theater,** 1741 Grafton St. (☎ 902/425-1961), which typically offers light musicals and mysteries with a three-course dinner (choice of prime rib, salmon, or chicken).

CLUB & BAR SCENE

In the evening there's usually lively Maritime music and good beer at the **Lower Deck** (☎ 902/425-1501), one of the popular restaurants in the Historic Properties compound on the waterfront. There's music nightly at 9:30, and late afternoons on Saturdays. Also recommended for live Celtic music and the occasional open mike night is **O'Bryne's Irish Pub,** 1565 Argyle St., ☎ **902/422-0187.**

The young and restless tend to congregate in pubs, in nightclubs, and at street corners along two axes that converge at the public library: **Grafton Street** and **Spring Garden Road.** If you're thirsty, wander the neighborhoods around here, and you're likely to find a spot that could serve as a temporary home for the evening.

A number of popular clubs offer live music around town. Check *The Coast,* Halifax's free weekly newspaper (widely available), for listings of upcoming performances. Among the clubs offering more consistent local rock, ska, and the like are **The Marquee Club,** 2037 Gottigen St., ☎ **902-429-3020,** and **The Attic,** 1741 Grafton St., ☎ **902/423-0909.**

A ROAD TRIP TO PEGGY'S COVE

About 43 kilometers (26 miles) southwest of Halifax is the picturesque fishing village of Peggy's Cove (pop. 120). The village offers a postcard-perfect tableau: an octagonal lighthouse (surely one of the most photographed in the world), tiny fishing shacks, and graceful fishing boats bobbing in the postage-stamp-size harbor. The bonsai-like perfection hasn't gone unnoticed by the big tour operators, however, so it's a rare summer day when you're not sharing the experience with a few hundred of your close, personal, bus-tour friends. The village is home to a handful of B&Bs and boutiques (Wood 'n' Wool, The Christmas Shoppe), but scenic values draw the day-trippers with cameras and lots of film.

9 The Eastern Shore

Heading from Halifax toward Cape Breton Island (or vice versa), you have to choose between two basic routes. If you're burning to get to your destination, take the main roads of Route 102 connecting to Route 104 (the Trans-Canada Highway). If you're in no particular hurry and are most content venturing down narrow lanes, destination unknown, by all means allow a couple of days to wind along the Eastern Shore, mostly along Route 7. Along the way you'll be rewarded with glimpses of a rugged coastline that's wilder and more remote than the coast south of Halifax. Communities tend to be farther apart, less genteel, and those that you come upon have fewer services and fewer tourists. With its rugged terrain and remote locales, this region is a good bet for those drawn to the outdoors and seeking coastal solitude.

Be forewarned that the Eastern Shore isn't always breathtakingly scenic if you limit yourself to the main road. You'll drive through cutover woodlands and past scrappy towns. To get the most out of the Eastern Shore, you should be committed to making periodic detours, the more impetuous the better. Wander down dead-end roads to coastal peninsulas, where you might come upon wild roses blooming madly in the fog, or inland to the persistent forest, home of moose and sudden dusk.

ESSENTIALS

GETTING THERE   Route 107 and Route 7 run along or near the coast from Dartmouth to Stillwater (near Sherbrooke). A patchwork of other routes—including 211, 316, 16, and 344—continues onward along the coast to the causeway to Cape Breton. (It's all pretty obvious on a map.) An excursion along the entire coastal route—from Dartmouth to Cape Breton Island with a detour to Canso—is 422 kilometers (253 miles).

VISITOR INFORMATION   Several tourist information centers are staffed along the route. You'll find the best-stocked and most-helpful centers at **Sheet Harbor** (next to the waterfall, ☎ **902/885-2595;** open daily in summer 9am to 8pm), **Sherbrooke Village** (at the museum, ☎ **902/522-2400;** open daily in summer 9:30am to 5:30pm), and **Canso** (1297 Union St., ☎ **902/366-2170;** open daily in summer 9am to 6pm).

A DRIVING TOUR OF THE EASTERN SHORE

This section assumes travel northeastward from Halifax toward Cape Breton. If you're traveling the opposite direction, hold this book upside down (just kidding).

Between Halifax and Sheet Harbor the route plays hide-and-seek with the coast, touching the water periodically before veering inland. The most scenic areas are around wild and open **Ship Harbor,** as well as **Spry Harbor,** noted for its attractive older homes and islands looming offshore.

At the **Fisherman's Life Museum** (☎ **902/889-2053**) in Jeddore Oyster Ponds you'll get a glimpse of life on the Eastern Shore a century ago. The humble white-shingle-and-green-trim cottage was built by James Myers in the 1850s; early in this century it became of property of his youngest son, Ervin. Ervin and his wife raised a dozen daughters here ("This was quite a popular spot among the young men in the area," reported the laconic guide), and the home and grounds have been restored to look as they might around 1900 or 1920. A walk through the house and barn and down to the fishing dock won't take much more than 20 minutes or so. Open June through mid-September, Monday to Saturday 9:30am to 5:30pm, Sunday 1 to 5:30pm. Admission is free, with donations encouraged. It's located on Route 7 and is well marked.

At the town of Lake Charlotte you opt for a side road that weaves along the coast (look for signs for Clam Harbor). The road alternately follows wooded coves and passes through inland forests; about midway you'll see signs for a turn to **Clam Harbour Beach Provincial Park.** A broad crescent beach attracts sunbathers and swimmers from Halifax and beyond, with lifeguard-supervised swimming on weekends. A picnic area is set amid a spruce grove on a bluff overlooking the beach. No admission charge; gates close at 8pm. Continue on up the coast from the park and you'll re-emerge on Route 7 in Ship Harbour.

Between Ship and Spry Harbors is the town of Tangier, home to **Coastal Adventures** (☎ **902/772-2774**), which specializes in kayak tours. It's run by Scott Cunningham, who literally wrote the book on Nova Scotia kayaking (he's the author of the definitive guide to paddling the coast). This well-run operation is situated on a beautiful island-dotted part of the coast, but it specializes in multiday trips throughout Atlantic Canada. You're best off writing (P.O. Box 77, Tangier, NS B0J 3H0) or calling for a brochure well in advance of your trip.

Northeast of Spry Harbor, watch for signs to **Taylor Head Provincial Park** (no phone). A 3-mile washboard dirt road offers access to several attractive hiking trails, or you can continue to the end. Short trails through a scrubby wood lead to a long and beautiful fine-grained sand beach with views out to evergreen-clad islands. Hearty bathers splash around on weekends, but weekdays it's often empty and wild. Admission is free.

Sheet Harbor (pop. 900) is a pleasant, small town with a campground, a couple of small grocery stores, two motels, and a visitor information center (☎ **902/885-2595**), behind which is a short nature trail and boardwalk that descends along low, rocky cascades. Inland from Sheet Harbor on Route 374 is the **Liscomb Game Sanctuary,** a popular destination for hearty, self-contained explorers equipped with map, compass, canoe, and fishing rod. There are no services to speak of for casual travelers. Continuing eastward from Sheet Harbor, you'll pass through the wee village of **Ecum Secum,** which has little to attract the tourist but is unusually gratifying to say out loud to others in the car.

Adjacent to the well-marked Liscomb Lodge (see below), and just over the main bridge, is the **Liscomb River Trail** system. Trails follow the river both north and south of Route 7. The main hiking trail follows the river upstream for 3 miles, crosses it on a suspension bridge, and then returns on the other side. The Mayflower Point Trail follows the river southward toward the coast, then loops back inland.

Continuing on Route 211 beyond historic Sherbrooke Village (see description below), you'll drive through a wonderful landscape of lakes, ocean inlets, and upland bogs and soon come to the scenic **County Harbor Ferry.** The 12-car cable ferry crosses each direction every half hour; it's a picturesque crossing of a broad river encased by rounded and wooded bluffs. The fare is C$1.75 (US$1.15) per car, which includes driver and passengers. The ferry isn't always running, so it's wise to check at the Canso or Sherbrooke visitor centers before detouring down this way.

Further along (you'll be on Route 316 after the ferry), you'll come to **Tor Bay Provincial Park.** It's 4 kilometers (2.4 miles) off the main road, but well worth the detour on a sunny day. The park features three sandy, crescent beaches backed by grassy dunes and small ponds that are slowly being taken over by bog and spruce forest. The short boardwalk loop is especially picturesque.

Way out on the eastern tip of Nova Scotia's mainland is the end-of-the-world town of **Canso** (pop. 1,200). It's a rough-edged fishing and oil-shipping town, often windswept and foggy. The chief attraction here is **Grassy Island National Historic Site** (☎ **902/366-3136**). First stop by the small interpretive center on the waterfront and ask about the boat schedule. A park-run boat will take you out to the island, which once housed a bustling community of fishermen and traders from New England. (The interpretive center features artifacts recovered from the island.) A trail links several historic sites on this island, which tends to be a bit melancholy whether foggy or not. The boat serves the island from May to mid-August from 10am to 6pm daily. Fares are C$2.50 (US$1.65) adult, C$2 (US$1.35) seniors, and C$1.25 (US85¢) children 6 to 16.

Route 16 between the intersection of Route 316 and Guysborough is an uncommonly **scenic drive.** The road runs high and low along brawny hills, affording soaring views of Chedabucto Bay and grassy hills across the way. Also pleasant, although not quite as distinguished, is Route 344 from Guysborough to the Canso causeway. The road twists, turns, and drops through woodlands with some nice views of the strait. It will make you wish you were riding a large and powerful motorcycle.

✪ **Sherbrooke Village.** Route 7, Sherbrooke. ☎ **902/522-2400.** Admission C$6 (US$4) adult, C$5 (US$3) senior, C$3 (US$2) child, C$18 (US$12) family. Daily 9:30am–5:30pm. Closed mid-Oct to June 1.

About half of the town of Sherbrooke comprises Sherbrooke Village, a historic section surrounded by low fences, water, and fields. (It's managed as part of the Nova Scotia Museum.) You'll have to pay admission to wander around, but the price is well worth it. This is the largest restored village in Nova Scotia, and it's unique in several respects. For one, almost all of the buildings are on their original sites (only two have been moved). Also, many homes are still occupied by local residents, and private homes are interspersed with the buildings open to visitors. The church is still used for services on Sundays, and you can order a meal at the old Sherbrooke Hotel. (The fish cakes and oven-baked beans are good.)

Some 25 buildings have been restored and opened to the public, ranging from a convincing general store to the operating blacksmith shop and post office. Look also for the temperance hall, courthouse, printery, boat-building shop, drugstore, and schoolhouse. These are staffed by genial, costumed interpreters, who can tell you about life in the 1860s. Be sure to ask about the source of the town's early prosperity.

WHERE TO STAY & DINE

Other than a handful of motels and B&Bs, few accommodations are available on the Eastern Shore.

Liscomb Lodge. Route 7, Liscomb Mills, NS B0J 2A0. ☎ **800/665-6343** or 902/779-2307. Fax 902/779-2700. 65 units. TV TEL. C$115–C$125 (US$77–US$83) double, suite C$150 (US$100); inquire about packages. AE, DISC, MC, V. Pets allowed in chalets.

This modern complex, owned and operated by the province, consists of a central lodge and a series of smaller cottages and outbuildings. It's situated in a remote part of the coast, adjacent to hiking trails and a popular boating area at the mouth of the Liscomb River. The lodge bills itself as "the nature lover's resort," and indeed it offers good access to both forest and water. But it's not exactly rustic, with well-tended lawns, bland modern architecture, shuffleboard, a marina, and even an oversized outdoor chessboard. (It's a popular stop for bus tours.) The rooms are modern and motel-like; the cottages and chalets have multiple bedrooms and are good for families.

Dining: The dining room is open to the public and serves resort fare. Especially popular is the salmon cooked on a cedar plank. Some packages include meals, which is recommended given the dearth of other options nearby.

Amenities: In addition to the shuffleboard and such mentioned above, there's an indoor pool and fitness center, a tennis court, room service, and a gift shop.

✪ **Seawind Landing Country Inn.** 1 Wharf Rd., Charlos Cove, NS B0H 1T0. ☎ **800/563-4667.** Fax 902/525-2108. www.seawind.ns.ca. E-mail: jcolvin@auracom.com. 13 units. C$70–C$105 (US$47–US$70). MC, V.

What to do when your boat-building business plummets as the fisheries decline? How about opening an inn? That's what Lorraine and Jim Colvin did, and their 20-acre oceanfront compound is delightful and inviting. Half of the guest rooms are in the 130-year-old main house, which has been tastefully modernized and updated. The others are in a more recent outbuilding—what you lose in historic charm, you make up for in brightness, ocean views, and double Jacuzzis. The innkeepers are especially knowledgeable about local artists (much of the work on display here was produced nearby), and they have compiled an unusually literate and helpful guide to the region for guests to peruse. The property has three private sand beaches, and coastal boat tours and picnic lunches can be easily arranged.

Dining: Full or continental breakfasts are available mornings. The inn also serves dinner nightly (inn guests only), featuring local products prepared in a country-French style. Entrees are priced at C$13 to C$25 (US$9 to US$17).

10 Amherst to Antigonish

The north shore of Nova Scotia—dubbed the Sunrise Trail at visitor information centers and in provincial tourism publications—is chock-full of rolling hills and pastoral landscapes that rarely fail to enchant. Driving along Route 6, you pass through farmlands along the western reaches from Amherst to Pugwash and beyond; around Tatamagouche the landscape at times mirrors that found on the other side of the straits on Prince Edward Island—softly rolling fields of grain punctuated with a well-tended farmhouse and barn, and rust-red soil appearing where the ground cover has been scraped off. Cows will dominate one field, and in the next are those massive bulls-eyes of rolled hay. The Amherst to Pictou drive is especially scenic early or late on a clear day, when the low sun highlights the fields and forests. After Pictou, back on the Trans-Canada Highway, you'll see more forest and hills as you make your way toward Cape Breton Island.

I wouldn't classify any of the towns in this section as final destinations—they're not like Cape Breton Island with its outdoor recreation, or Parrsboro with its fossils. But the drive through these pleasant towns makes for a pleasing detour en route to or from Cape Breton or PEI, and offers a glimpse of life in the slow lane. These villages are also perfectly fine places to spend a night if evening should creep up on you. If you'd like a base to explore the north shore, I'd suggest Pictou, which has several intriguing attractions and the best selection of inns. It's also handy to the PEI ferry.

AMHERST

Amherst is best known for the busy and bustling information center staffed by the province just off the Trans-Canada (see below). But it's a lovely small town perched on a low hill at the edge of the sweeping Amherst Marsh, which demarcates the border between Nova Scotia and New Brunswick. It's worth slowing and taking a detour through town just to appreciate the historic streetscapes.

ESSENTIALS

GETTING THERE Amherst is the first Nova Scotia town you'll come to heading east on the Trans-Canada highway. Amherst is the terminus for both Route 6 (to the north) and Route 2 (to the south). It's about 40 minutes east of Moncton, and a stop on the **Via Rail** (☎ 800/361-8010) train between Montréal and Halifax.

VISITOR INFORMATION The huge **Nova Scotia Visitor Information Center** (☎ 902/667-8429) is on Amherst's western edge, just off Exit 1 of the Trans-Canada Highway. In addition to the usual vast library of brochures and pamphlets, there's an ice cream stand, videos, helpful staff in uniforms, extraordinary views across the usually windy marsh, and often a bagpiper providing the appropriate mood out in front. It's open from May to the end of October. During peak season it's open 8am to 9pm; limited hours during the shoulder seasons. A portion of the center that includes washrooms, vending machines, and phones is open 24 hours a day in summer.

Just east of the provincial visitor center is the **Amherst Visitor Information Center** (☎ 902/667-0696), housed in a handsome 1905 rail car. It's a good bet for more detailed information on activities in the immediate area. It's open late May to early September daily from 10am to 6pm.

EXPLORING AMHERST

Downtown Amherst is compact (just a few blocks, really) but uncommonly attractive in a brick and sandstone way best appreciated by those who were dour Scots in a previous life. A half-dozen or so buildings are rough gems of classical architecture, and are nicely offset by the town's trees, including a few elms that continue to soldier on despite Dutch elm disease. Note especially the elaborately pedimented 1888 courthouse on the corner of Victoria and Church; a short stroll north is the sandstone Amherst First Baptist Church with its pair of prominent turrets. Further north are the stoutly proportioned Doric columns on the 1935 Dominion Public Building, the front of which has apparently attracted the attention of local teens. ("No loitering. No skateboarding.")

Driving east on Route 6 you'll go through a residential area of large and beautiful historic homes dating from the last century and a half that display an eclectic range of architectural styles and materials.

Those seeking more information on Amherst's history can visit the **Cumberland County Museum,** 150 Church St. (☎ **902/667-2561**), located in the 1836 home of R.B. Dickey, one of the Fathers of Canadian Confederation. (Historical trivia: four of the Fathers of Confederation were from Amherst.) The museum is especially strong in documenting details of local industry and labor.

PUGWASH & TATAMAGOUCHE

If you're in the planning phase of your trip, note that it takes roughly the same amount of time—about 2 hours—to drive from Amherst to New Glasgow via the Trans-Canada Highway (which dips southward through Truro) or via Route 6 along the northern shore. On the Trans-Canada the driving is typically steady and fast, but you'll likely glaze over and find yourself punching the radio's scan button for entertainment.

Route 6 has far more visual interest, and you'll speed along sprawling farms, fields of wheat and corn, azure ocean inlets, and verdant coastal marshes. You'll spot the wide straits dotted with sails, with Prince Edward Island in the distance. The landscape changes frequently enough to prevent it from ever growing repetitious. (And you *can* speed along; it's pretty easy to keep up a pace of 50 or 60 miles per hour, slowing down only for the infrequent village or farm vehicle lumbering down the road.) One caveat: Both routes require the same amount of time—assuming you don't stop. But traveling on Route 6 you will stop—to walk on beaches, to order up a mess of French fries and vinegar, or to shop at one of the handful of specialized crafts stores. It's worth the sacrifice in time.

ESSENTIALS

GETTING THERE   Both towns are located on Route 6; you can't miss them from either direction.

VISITOR INFORMATION   The Tatamagouche **Visitor Information Center** (☎ **902/657-3285**) is in the Fraser Culture Center on Main St.

EXPLORING THE REGION

This region is home to a number of picnic parks, as well as local and provincial beaches. Signs along Route 6 point the way; most require a detour of a few miles. Pack a picnic and make an afternoon of it.

Pugwash, which comes from the Mi'kmaq word "Pagweak" meaning deep waters, today has a slightly industrial feel, with its factory and a mid-sized cargo port on the Pugwash River.

Seagull Pewter, Route 6 (☎ **902/243-3850**), is well known throughout the province, and is made in a factory on the east side of Pugwash; look for the retail store (which also stocks antiques) on the other side of town, just west of the Pugwash River bridge on Route 6. It's open 7 days a week year-round.

Look also for the **Caboose Cafe** (12 Durham St., ☎ **902/243-2666**), as you're driving through the village. Located in a cheery red caboose dating from 1917 with a screened deck built alongside for dining, it's a good bet for a snack or lunch. Local beers and wines can be purchased to accompany the fish and chips or lobster. Open daily in summer 9am to 9pm. (*Note:* The restaurant was hit by a freak tornado at press time and it was unclear if it would reopen for business.)

Between Pugwash and Tatamagouche you'll drive through the scenic village Wallace (motto: "A Friendly Place"), where the road winds along the water and you'll discover fine views of the forested shores on the far side of Wallace Bay. East of Wallace watch for the remains of **ancient Acadian dikes** in the marshes, built to reclaim the land for farming (signs point these out).

Near Malagash look for the signs crafted of casks along the road; these direct you to the **Jost Vineyards** (☎ **800/565-4567** or 902/257-2636), which produces wines you may have sipped in Nova Scotia's better restaurants. You can take a free tour of the winery, enjoy a picnic (there's a deli on the premises), or sample the wines produced here and stock up on those that impress you. The vineyard is open Monday to Saturday 9am to 6pm, noon to 6pm on Sunday. Tours are offered twice daily, at noon and 3pm.

Tatamagouche is a pleasant fishing village, and is home to the **Fraser Culture Centre** (Main Street, ☎ 902/657-3285), which strives to preserve the region's cultural heritage through ongoing exhibits, as well as to promote activities that encourage greater involvement in the arts and crafts. It's open daily June through August 9am to 5pm, and is free.

Also in Tatamagouche is the shop of **Sara Bonnyman Pottery** (☎ **902/657-3215**), where you'll find rustic, country-style plates, mugs, and more in a speckled pattern embellished with blueberries and other country motifs. The shop is on Route 246 1 mile from the post office.

WHERE TO STAY

Train Station Inn. 21 Station Rd., Tatamagouche, NS B0K 1V0. ☎ **888/RAILBED** or 902/657-3222. www.trainstation.ns.ca. 10 units. C$69–C$79 (US$46–US$53) in station, C$98–C$139 (US$65–US$93) in railcars; rates include breakfast. AE, DC, ER, MC, V.

This is among the more unique inns in the province. Located down a side street in and around a weedy railyard, the inn offers rooms in the lovely, century-old brick station and in six Canadian National cabooses that have been refurbished as guest rooms. Go for the cabooses, where you don't have to sacrifice comfort to get uniqueness. All have been nicely done over, and vary in style, decor, and layout. Among my favorites: no. 7, which is decorated in a regal Edwardian parlor motif with natural beadboard and striped wallpaper, and has a very excellent bathroom in the rear, just off that area where traveling politicians used to give speeches; and no. 10, one of two later model cars outfitted with hardwood floors, gas woodstove, kitchenette, and private little elevated sitting area (for one). The other, more modern car is no. 11. All cabooses have TVs; inn rooms do not. Rates include a continental breakfast served in the men's waiting room. The reception and gift shop is located in the ladies' waiting room.

PICTOU

Pictou was established as part of a development scheme hatched by speculators from Philadelphia in 1760. Under the terms of their land grant, they needed to place some 250 settlers at the harbor. That was a problem. Few Philadelphians wanted to live there. So the company sent a ship called the *Hector* to Scotland in 1773 to drum up some impoverished souls who might be more amenable to starting life over in North America.

This worked out rather better, and the ship returned with some 200 passengers, mostly Gaelic-speaking Highlanders. The voyage was brutal and full of storms, and the passengers were threatened with starvation. But they eventually arrived at Pictou, and they disembarked wearing tartans and playing bagpipes.

The anniversary of the settlers' arrival is celebrated mid-August each year with the **Hector Festival** (☎ 800/353-5338), when you might spot members of the clans wearing kilts and dining out in high style in memory of their ancestors. Pictou is

Scottish enough that you might find yourself a bit wary that locals will try to slip some haggis into your meal while you're not paying attention.

ESSENTIALS

GETTING THERE   Pictou is located on Route 106, which is just north of Exit 22 off Route 104 (the south branch of the Trans-Canada Highway). The Prince Edward Island ferry is several kilometers north of town at the coast near Caribou. (See the Prince Edward Island chapter for details on the ferry.)

VISITOR INFORMATION   The **Tourist Information Centre** (☎ 902/485-6213) is located just off the rotary at the junction of Route 106 and Route 6. It's open daily 8:30am to 7:30pm mid-May to mid-October.

EXPLORING PICTOU

Pictou is a pleasant and historic harborside town with an abundance of interesting architecture. There's a surfeit of dour sandstone buildings adorned with five-sided dormers, and at times you might think you've wandered down an Edinburgh side street. Water Street is especially attractive, and it offers an above-average selection of boutiques, casual restaurants, and pubs. Look for the headquarters and factory outlet of **Grohmann Knives** (116 Water St., ☎ 902/486-4224). At Grohmann's, located in a 1950s-mod building with a large knife piercing one corner, you'll find a good selection of quality knives (each with a lifetime guarantee) at marked-down prices. It's open daily; free factory tours are offered between 9am and 3pm.

The harbor is well protected and suitable for novices who want to explore by sea kayak or canoe. Check with **Harbourtown Canoe and Kayak** (☎ 902/485-9148), which rents canoes and kayaks from the Hector Visitors Marina on the waterfront at 37 Caladh Ave.

Pictou's one downside is the unsightly and noisome paper mill across the harbor. Even when it's obscured in the fog, you can often tell it's there by the smell.

Hector **Heritage Quay.** 33 Caladh Ave. ☎ **902/485-4371.** Admission C$4 (US$2.65) adult, C$3 (US$2) seniors and teens, C$1 (US65¢) ages 6–12, C$12 (US$8) family. Mid-May to mid-Oct daily 9am–9pm (closes at 6pm in shoulder seasons).

Learn about the hardships endured on the 1773 voyage of the singularly unseaworthy *Hector*—which brought Scottish settlers to the region—at this modern, small museum on the waterfront in downtown Pictou. You'll pass by intriguing exhibits en route to the museum's centerpiece: a full-sized replica of the 110-foot *Hector* under construction at the water's edge. (It's expected to be launched by fall 2000.) Stop by the blacksmith and carpentry shops to get a picture of life in the colonies in the early days.

McCulloch House. Old Haliburton Rd. ☎ **902/485-4563.** Free admission. June to mid-Oct Mon–Sat 9:30am–5:30pm, Sun 1–5:30pm.

Thomas McCulloch was a Scottish minister who was more or less shanghaied by Pictonians on his way to PEI in 1803. Tricked into remaining in town, McCulloch eventually embraced his new home and later emerged as a crusader to improve the education of the ordinary Nova Scotian. Today he's remembered as the father of Nova Scotia's liberalized education system. The home itself is rather modest, but bird watchers will enjoy viewing portions of McCulloch's ornithology collection, which his contemporary and friend John James Audubon declared one of the finest on the continent. The fine gardens also invite a relaxed stroll. The home was closed for renovations in 1999, but was slated to reopen in 2000.

WHERE TO STAY

Auberge Walker Inn. 34 Coleraine St. (P.O. Box 629), Pictou, NS B0K 1H0. ☎ **800/370-5553** or 902/485-1433. Fax 902/85-1222. E-mail: walkerinn@ns.sympatico.ca. 11 units.

TV. C$65–C$82 (US$43–US$55) double, suite C$149 (US$99). AE, MC, V. Parking on street, at rear of building, and in lot 1 block away.

This handsome downtown inn is located in a brick townhouse-style building dating to 1865 and overlooking one of Pictou's more active intersections. The innkeepers have done a commendable job of giving the place a comfortable feel while retaining its historic sensibility. Some rooms (like Room 10 on the third floor) have nice harbor views. A new (1999) first-floor suite has a small kitchen, Jacuzzi, and dark bedroom in the back. All rooms have private bathrooms, but the conversions have come at some sacrifice. (The upstairs rooms have showers only, and one Frommer's reader wrote that his was so small he couldn't bend over to wash his legs.) On the upside: The inn is perfectly situated to enjoy Pictou's restaurants and attractions.

Braeside Inn. 126 Front St., Pictou, NS B0K 1H0. ☎ **800/613-7701** or 902/485-5046. Fax 902/485-1701. E-mail: braeside@north.nsis.com. 18 units. TV TEL. C$65–C$150 (US$43–US$100) double. AE, ER, MC, V. At the end of Water St., make a right on Coleraine St., then left on Front St.

This three-story hotel at the edge of downtown was built in 1938 as an inn, and it has been one of the town's more enduring hostelries. The public rooms are done up in pinks and greens; the TV room has a large herd of wingback chairs and is a good spot to settle in with a book or to catch up on the news before dinner. The guest rooms are all carpeted and comfortable, if a bit small.

Dining: The dining room has hardwood floors and views down a lawn and across the gravel lot to the harbor. Entrees aren't terribly exciting but are well prepared, with selections like prime rib, fresh salmon, and rack of lamb. Prices range from C$19 to C$25 (US$13 to US$17). Dinner reservations suggested.

Consulate Inn. 157 Water St., Pictou, NS B0K 1H0. ☎ **800/424-8283** or 902/485-4554. Fax 902/485-1532. 10 units (1 with private bathroom down hallway). TV. C$54–C$129 (US$36–US$86) double, including continental breakfast. AE, MC, V.

No surprise: This doughty 1810 historic home of sandstone and ivy was originally a consulate. Three guest rooms are upstairs in the main building and share a handsome sitting area; seven larger and more modern rooms are located next door. The decor tends more toward the cute than the elegant, with innkeepers Debbie and Garry Jardine striving to impart a romantic mood to appeal to couples. Two new (1999) rooms are located in a walk-in basement and are a tad claustrophobic, but feature nice touches like Jacuzzis and mood lighting. The PEI ferry is just a 10-minute drive away, and the inn is well situated for exploring Pictou.

Dining: The first-floor restaurant is dim and intimate, with a continental menu that includes sautéed scallops, chicken à l'orange, and steak au poivre (C$13.95/US$9.30 to C$21.95/US$14.63).

✪ **Custom House Inn.** 38 Depot St., Pictou, NS B0K 1H0. ☎ **902/485-4546.** Fax 902/485-2546. E-mail: customhouseinn@ns.sympatico.ca. 8 units. A/C TV TEL. Summer C$79–C$139 (US$53–US$93), off-season C$79–C$109 (US$53–US$73). AE, DC, ER, MC, V.

This hulking brick and sandstone building with heroic arches and dentils was built in 1872 and thoroughly renovated in 1997. The former office building today is home to some of the more spacious and dramatic guest rooms in the province, each with high ceilings (13 feet 6 inches on the first floor), lustrous maple floors, and a certain Spartan grace. The innkeepers have been reserved in their decorating, letting the architectural space speak for itself. Three of the rooms have kitchenettes with refrigerators; all have whirlpool tubs. Many are also adorned with the moody and notable nautical paintings of contemporary local painter Dave Macintosh. Among the best rooms is no. 2F, a bright corner room with kitchenette and water views.

Dining: In the basement is the Old Stone Pub, a wonderfully renovated space with an informal menu (lots of seafood and pasta), 16 beers on tap, and live Celtic music some evenings.

Pictou Lodge Resort. Shore Rd. (P.O. Box 1539), Pictou, NS B0K 1H0. ☎ **800/495-6343** or 902/485-4322. Fax 902/485-4945. E-mail: pictou.lodge@north.nsis.com. 65 units. TV TEL. C$94–C$225 (US$63–US$150) double. AE, DC, DISC, MC, V. Closed mid-Oct to May. Follow Shore Rd. from downtown toward PEI ferry; watch for signs.

The original rustic log lodge and a handful of log outbuildings have gone through a number of owners—including Canadian National Railway—since entrepreneurs built the compound on a far-off grassy bluff overlooking a pristine beach early in this century. It's now owned by Maritime Inns and Resorts (which has four other properties), and has been modestly upgraded and improved. The older log rooms, most of which have kitchenettes, have considerably more character, but some still regard them as a bit dowdy. The newer rooms, alas, have the bland sameness of modern motel rooms everywhere. The lodge is located about 10 minutes' drive from downtown but has a wonderfully remote feel.

Dining: Lunch and dinner are served in the Adirondack-style lodge, with its soaring spaces hammered together with time-burnished logs. Dinner entrees might be termed "creative traditional," and feature dishes such as wild blueberry chicken, seafood linguine, and cedar-planked salmon (C$15/US$10 to C$26/US$17).

Amenities: Outdoor heated pool, free use of recreational boats and bikes, 500 meters of private beach, playground, nature trails, game room, room service.

WHERE TO DINE

For an unhurried, relaxed meal in unstuffy environs, try the **Stone House Cafe** (13 Water St., ☎ **902/465-6885**). There's a decent selection of pizza (including a lobster, scallop, and haddock pizza) and basic meals like smoked pork chops, lasagna, croquettes, and roast chicken. Most entrees are around C$10 to C$15 (US$7 to US$10).

Fougere's. 91 Water St. ☎ **902/485-1575.** Reservations helpful. Main courses, lunch C$5.95–C$13.50 (US$3.95–US$9), dinner C$13.95–C$29.95 (US$9.30–US$19.95; mostly C$14/US$9–C$16/US$11). AE, MC, V. Summer daily 11am–9pm; off-season call first. UPSCALE TRADITIONAL.

Fougere's is situated in a bright, simply furnished dining room right downtown that's as appealing as it is tidy. This local institution was run for years by Ben Fougere; it was taken over by Stefan and Giovanna Sieber in 1998, who have impressed regular diners with their broadly appealing menu and their deftness in the kitchen. The couple moved to Nova Scotia after 12 years in Switzerland, and some Swiss dishes appear from time to time. But the menu is mostly anchored by traditional dishes like surf and turf, seafood casserole, and smoked haddock. Non-seafood dishes include T-bone steak, roast turkey dinner, and jaegerschnitzel.

Piper's Landing. Route 376, Lyons Brook. ☎ **902/485-1200.** Reservations recommended. Main courses, lunch C$5–C$11 (US$3–US$7), dinner C$13–C$23 (US$9–US$15). AE, MC, V. Mon–Sat 11:30am–2:30pm and 4–9pm, Sun 11am–9pm. From the Pictou Rotary take Rt. 376 toward Lyons Brook; it's 3km (1.8 miles) on your left. UPSCALE TRADITIONAL.

This contemporary, attractive dining room on a stretch of residential road outside of Pictou remains a local favorite and your best bet in Antigonish for a sophisticated meal, despite sometimes frustrating service. The interior is sparely decorated and understated. Likewise, the menu looks simple—entrees include grilled beef tenderloin, pork schnitzel, and a filling seafood platter—but you'll be impressed by the flair in preparation. The wine list, alas, is small and tired.

The Name Game ————————————————————————————————

The name Antigonish (pronounced "AN-tee-gun-ish") creates some contention among linguists. In the original native dialect it means either "five-forked rivers of fish" or "place where the branches are torn off by bears gathering beechnuts." There's no consensus.

ANTIGONISH

Antigonish traces its European roots back to the 1650s, when the French arrived, only to be driven off by the Mi'kmaq. The French returned a century later, only to be driven off by Irish Loyalists. These Irish settlers established the first permanent settlement, and today there thrives a handsome town of 5,500 residents with a bustling main street and the respected St. Francis Xavier University, which was founded in 1853.

The town has a bustling commercial center (be prepared for some traffic midsummer) and is a good spot to stock up on groceries or get a bite for lunch. There are several cafes on and around Main Street, and a shop or two that merit browsing. For mild outdoor adventure, drive 9 kilometers (5.6 miles) northeast of town on Route 337 and look for the **Fairmont Ridge Trail.** Here you'll find 12 kilometers (7.4 miles) of hiking that will take you through ravines and into forests with old-growth trees. Nearby is the home base of **Shoreline Adventures** (☎ **902/863-5958**), which offers sea kayaking tours in the Antigonish Harbor area. For self-motivated travelers, sea kayak rentals with instructions on where to go are also available. Advance reservations are requested.

ESSENTIALS

GETTING THERE   Antigonish is on Route 104 (Trans-Canada Highway) 50 kilometers (33 miles) west of the Canso Causeway (the connection to Cape Breton Island).

VISITOR INFORMATION   The **Nova Scotia Tourist Office** (☎ **800/565-0000** or 902/863-4921) is located at 56 West Rd. (Exit 32 on the Trans-Canada Highway). It's open daily from 9am to 8pm.

SPECIAL EVENTS   The **Highland Games** have been staged in mid-July annually since 1861. What started as a community diversion has become an international event—and these are now the oldest continuously played highland games in North America. This is the place for everything Scottish, from piping to dancing to tossing the caber. Contact the **Antigonish Highland Society** (☎ **902/863-4275**) for dates and details. Rooms are scarce during the 3-day games (Friday to Sunday), so if you plan to attend, be sure to book well ahead. You can buy daily tickets or a 3-day pass.

Festival Antigonish (☎ **800/563-7529** or 902/867-3333) features a variety of plays and live performances held on the campus of St. Francis Xavier University from late June to late August. Shows range from locally written productions to Agatha Christie tales and *Rumpelstiltskin.* Tickets for children's productions are under C$5.50 (US$3.65); adult performances are C$18 (US$12).

WHERE TO STAY

Antigonish is conveniently located just off the Trans-Canada Highway and is the last mainland town of any consequence before Cape Breton Island. As such it's home to a number of chain motels, both in town and on the strip outside of town. If nightfall is overtaking you and you're pushing for Cape Breton, I'd suggest overnighting here and pushing onward early the next morning. Port Hastings and Port Hawksbury—the first towns on Cape Breton—also have a slew of chain motels, but both towns tend toward the sprawling and charmless. Antigonish is the better choice for staging an assault on the island, and has better restaurants to boot.

Budget travelers can book a no-frills dorm room at **St. Francis Xavier University** (☎ **902/867-2473**) between mid-May and mid-August. Rooms are simple and share hallway washrooms, but they include all the basics: linen, pillows, towels, and soap. Rates are C$40 (US$27) for two, including tax. All-you-can-eat meals are also available at Morrison Dining Hall; figure about C$5 (US$3) for breakfast, C$10 (US$7) for dinner. If you're looking for a room after business hours, head to the Security Office in the basement of MacKinnon Hall.

At the west edge of town on the Trans-Canada, you'll find the **Chateau Motel,** 112 Post Rd. (☎ **902/863-4842**), which is unexciting, but in a good way. It has 17 rooms and cottages and a Laundromat on the premises. Rates are C$59 to C$94 (US$39 to US$63) for two.

Maritime Inn Antigonish. 158 Main St., Antigonish, NS B2G 2B7. ☎ **888/662-7484** or 902/863-4001. Fax 903/863-2672. 34 units. A/C TV TEL. C$67–C$101 (US$45–US$67) double, C$125 (US$83) suite. AE, DC, DISC, MC, V. Take Exit 33 off the Trans-Canada, follow Church St. to Main St. and turn right.

The basic, modern Maritime Inn Antigonish recently benefitted from new management and renovations. The rooms are comfortable and clean if unexceptional. The best thing about the place? Its location on Antigonish's Main Street, where you can easily walk to the city's best restaurant (Sunshine on Main; see below), and take care of basic shopping needs without getting back in that car you've been caged up in for the past 2 days. A restaurant on the premises—Main Street Cafe—serves three meals daily.

WHERE TO DINE

Lobster Treat. 241 Post Rd. (Route 104), Antigonish. ☎ **902/863-5465.** Main courses, dinner C$9.95–C$26.95 (US$6.65–US$17.95; most everything under C$20/US$13). AE, DC, DISC, ER, MC, V. Closed end-Oct to mid-April. Located west of town on Trans-Canada Highway; look for it on right shortly after limited access highway ends when coming from west. SEAFOOD.

Housed in a red-shingled former schoolhouse (note the original hanging lamps), the Lobster Treat has been doing seafood justice for the past quarter-century. It's not too fancy, and features the usual family restaurant decor (potted plants, mauve carpeting). But the seafood is fresh and well prepared, the service both friendly and professional. The menu ranges from the traditional boiled lobster dinner to surf and turf combos to several spicy seafood concoctions served in curry. You can get haddock just about anywhere in the Maritimes, but here it's in lemon and lime juice and olive oil, and seasoned with oregano before being pan-fried or broiled (your choice). Complete meals for kids are available for under C$5 (US$3.33).

Sunshine on Main Café. 332 Main St., Antigonish. ☎ **902/863-5851.** Reservations suggested. Main courses, lunch C$3.75–C$8 (US$2.50–US$5.35); dinner C$11–C$17 (US$7–US$11). DC, ER, MC, V. Mon–Thurs 7am–9:30pm, Fri 7am–10pm, Sat 8am–10pm, Sun 8am–9:30pm. ECLECTIC.

You'll need to detour a bit off the Trans-Canada Highway and venture downtown, but it's worth it if you're in the mood for simple but creative bistro fare offered at attractive prices. The interior is dominated by a large and lovely wall mural, the other walls painted a cool lemon-sherbet yellow. The creative lunch menu includes a good selection of sandwiches and salads, including a spicy Thai chicken salad. Come evening, the selections expand and get fancier, with an emphasis on pastas (like fettuccine mixed with six varieties of fish, or linguine with roasted veggies and baby clams). There's also a good selection of grilled entrees, ranging from salmon to lamb chops.

11 Cape Breton Island

The isolated and craggy island of Cape Breton—Nova Scotia's northernmost landmass—should be high on the list of don't-miss destinations for travelers, especially those with an adventurous bent. The island's chief draw is Cape Breton Highlands National Park, far north on the island's western lobe. But there's also the historic fort at Louisbourg and scenic Bras d'Or Lake, the inland saltwater lake that nearly cleaves the island in two. Above all, there are the picturesque drives. It's hard to find a road that's not a scenic route in Cape Breton. By turns the vistas are wild and dramatic, then settled and pastoral.

When traveling on the island, be alert to the cultural richness. Just as southern Nova Scotia was largely settled by English Loyalists fleeing the United States after they lost the War of Independence, Cape Breton was principally settled by Highland Scots whose families had come out on the wrong side of rebellions against the Crown. You can still see that heritage in the accents of elders in some of the more remote villages, and in the great popularity of British-style folk music.

You'll often hear references to the ✪ **Cabot Trail** when on the island. This is the official designation for the 300-kilometer (185-mile) roadway around the northwest part of the island, which encompasses the national park. It's named after John Cabot, who many believe first set foot on North American soil near Cape North. (However, many disagree, especially in Newfoundland.)

If you're in a hurry, you'd do well to base yourself in Baddeck, which is centrally located, offers the best accommodations and restaurants, and is well positioned for day excursions to the island's two best attractions: the national park and the reconstructed historic settlement of Louisbourg. The southeastern portion of the island—near Isle Madame and Port Hawkesbury—can be picturesque in parts, but it isn't nearly as inviting as the rest of the island. I'd encourage travelers to focus more on the west and central sections.

One note: I've divided Cape Breton into two sections: Cape Breton Island and Cape Breton Highlands National Park. For information on adventures in the park itself, jump ahead to the next section.

ESSENTIALS

GETTING THERE   Cape Breton is connected to the mainland via the Canso Causeway, an 80-foot-wide, 217-foot-deep, 4,300-foot-long stone causeway built in 1955 with 10 million tons of rock. (You can see a half-mountain, the other half of which was sacrificed for the cause, as you approach the island on the Trans-Canada Highway.) The causeway is 271 kilometers (163 miles) from the New Brunswick border at Amherst, 282 kilometers (169 miles) from Halifax.

VISITOR INFORMATION   Nine tourist information centers dot the island. The best stocked (and a much recommended first stop) is the bustling **Port Hastings Info Centre** (☎ **902/625-4201**), located on your right just after crossing the Canso Causeway. It's open daily 8am to 8:30pm mid-May to mid-October.

MABOU & VICINITY

Mabou (pop. 400) is situated on a deep and protected inlet along the island's picturesque west shore. Scenic drives and bike rides are a dime a dozen hereabouts; few roads fail to yield up opportunities to break out the camera or just lean against your vehicle and enjoy the panorama. The residents are strongly oriented toward music in their activities, unusually so even for musical Cape Breton Island.

Evening entertainment tends to revolve around fiddle playing, square dancing, or a traditional gathering of musicians and storytellers called a *ceilidh* (pronounced *kay-lee*). To find out where things are going on, stop by The Mull (see below) and scope out the bulletin board.

In a handsome valley between Mabou and Inverness is the distinctive post-and-beam **Glenora Distillery** (☎ **800/839-0491** or 902/258-2662). This modern distillery began producing single-malt whiskey in 1990 in charred oak barrels. This includes scotch, which can't technically be called such because it isn't made in Scotland. Production runs take place later in the fall, but tours of the facility are offered throughout the summer. Tours cost C$5 (US$3.33) and last about a half-hour (offered daily 9am to 5pm; closed November to mid-June.) The product has been aged for 10 years, making it eligible for sampling in 2000. Swing by and be among the first to savor this new contribution to local highland lore.

The distillery has an adjoining restaurant and nine-room hotel (see below); traditional music is often scheduled for weekends or evenings in the contemporary pub.

WHERE TO STAY

The **Mabou River Hostel** (19 Mabou Ridge Rd., Mabou, NS B0E 1X0, ☎ **902/945-2356**) is located not far from the river and adjacent to the Mother of Sorrows Pioneer Shrine. Unlike most hostels, this one has no dorm rooms and no bunk beds, but private and semi-private rooms (23 beds in 13 rooms). Rates are C$20 (US$13) per person, including linens and a continental breakfast, with a private room C$5 (US$3) extra.

✪ **Duncreigan Country Inn.** Route 19, Mabou, NS B0E 1X0. ☎ **800/840-2207** or 902/945-2207. Fax 902/945-2206. E-mail: duncreigan@auracom.com. 8 units. TV TEL. C$90–C$140 (US$60–US$93) double, including continental breakfast. AE, MC, V.

The Duncreigan occupies a quiet wooded bluff just across the bridge from the village. Modern and airy (it was built in 1991), the inn manages to meld contemporary and traditional in a most appealing way. Guest rooms are located in the main lodge and an outbuilding (connected via boardwalk), and the landscaping is beginning to mature quite nicely. The rooms are uniformly wonderful, many decorated in soothing dark, burgundy tones, and all have radios and ceiling fans. Many are furnished with Nova Scotian antiques, with headboards creatively designed by a local artisan to match the furnishings. Room 2 has a superb water view, although my favorite is Room 5, with its wood-burning stove, whirlpool, and deck overlooking the estuary. There's no charge to use the inn's bikes or canoe.

Dining: Dinners are served nightly except Mondays between mid-June and mid-October. Entrees might include seafood with basil cream, lemon-peppered pork tenderloin, or scallops with pesto. The prix-fixe 3-course dinner ranges C$23 to C$30 (US$15 to US$20); reservations are requested.

Glenora Inn & Distillery Resort. Route 19, Glenville, NS B0E 1X0. ☎ **800/839-0491** or 902/258-2662. Fax 902/258-3572. 9 units. TV. C$87–C$95 (US$58–US$63); suites to C$115 (US$77). AE, MC, V.

So, when was the last time you spent the night at a distillery? This distiller of single-malt whiskey added nine modern rooms in a building next to the pub, which in turn is located next to the actual distillery. The contemporary but rustic architecture has a pleasant feel to it, but the real attraction is easy access to the pub and restaurant on

the premises, which often features live performers from the area. The distillery has the feel of being in a remote vale in the Scottish highlands. Ask also about the half-dozen modern chalets, located on the hills overlooking the distillery.

Haus Treuburg. 175 Main St. (P.O. Box 92), Port Hood, NS B0E 2W0. ☎ **902/787-2116.** Fax 902/787-3216. www.auracom.com/~treuburg. E-mail: treuburg@auracom.com. 3 units, 3 cottages. TV TEL. C$75–C$95 (US$50–US$63) double, cottages C$110 (US$73). Breakfast C$8.50 (US$5.65) extra. AE, DC, MC, V.

Located a few miles from Mabou in the undistinguished oceanside village of Port Hood, Haus Treuburg is a handsome Queen Anne–style home dating from 1914. The three guest rooms in the main building (one is a suite) are nicely furnished in a spare Scandinavian style. As nice as they are, though, the better deals are the cottages behind the house, each with a private deck, an ocean view, and a gas barbecue. These are usually booked by the week (C$660/US$440), but it can't hurt to ask whether they're open for the night.

Dining: German and Italian specialties are featured in the two downstairs dining rooms. Dinner is served at one seating, and it might include beef Stroganoff with spaetzle, or lobster bordelaise on homemade fettuccine. Four-course meals are C$30 to C$34 (US$20 to US$23) prix fixe. The German "Sunday morning breakfast" is available every morning.

WHERE TO DINE

The Mull. Route 19 (north of village), Mabou. ☎ **902/945-2244.** Reservations accepted for parties of 6 or more. Sandwiches C$4–C$7 (US$3–US$5), main courses C$12–C$16 (US$8–US$11). AE, MC, V. Daily 11am–9pm (closes an hour or two earlier in the off-season). CAFE.

The Mull is a simple country deli that serves simple, well-prepared food. Lunches tend toward items like seafood chowder, fish and chips (both recommended), and deli-style sandwiches. After 5pm, the dinner menu kicks in, with entrees like grilled halibut, T-bone steak, and scallops in a light wine sauce. Don't expect to be wowed by fancy; do expect a satisfying and filling meal.

MARGAREE VALLEY

West of Baddeck and south of Chéticamp, the Margaree Valley region loosely consists of the area from the village of Margaree Valley near the headwaters of the Margaree River, down the river to Margaree Harbor on Cape Breton's west coast. Some seven small communities are clustered in along the valley floor, and it's a world apart from the rugged drama of the surf-battered coast; it's vaguely reminiscent of the farm country of upstate New York. The Cabot Trail gently rises and falls on the shoulders of the gently rounded hills flanking the valley, offering views of the farmed floodplains and glimpses of the river.

The **Margaree River** has been accorded celebrity status in fishing circles—it's widely regarded as one of the most productive Atlantic salmon rivers in North America, and salmon have continued to return to spawn here in recent years, which is unfortunately not the case in many other waterways of Atlantic Canada. The river has been open to fly-fishing only since the 1880s, and in 1991 it was designated a Canadian Heritage River.

Learn about the river's heritage at the **Margaree Salmon Museum** (☎ **902/248-2848**) in Northeast Margaree. The handsome building features a brief video about the life cycle of the salmon, and exhibits include antique rods (including one impressive 18-footer), examples of poaching equipment, and hundreds of hand-tied salmon flies. Museum docents can help you find a guide to try your hand on the water. (Mid-June to mid-July and September and early October are the best times.) The museum is open mid-June to mid-October daily 9am to 5pm. Admission is C$1 adult, C25¢ child.

The whole area is best explored by slow and aimless driving, or better yet, by bike or canoe. (**Margaree River Canoe Rentals,** ☎ **902/235-2658,** based at the Duck Cove Inn in Margaree Harbour, can arrange for a lazy paddle down the river.)

When prowling around, watch for **Cape Breton Clay,** ☎ **902/248-2860,** in the Margaree Valley, northeast of the salmon museum. One of the occupational hazards of being a guidebook writer is the requirement that I look at a lot of pottery, much of it bad and almost all of it claiming to be "unique." This work, by Margaree Valley native Bell Fraser, actually *is* unique. And quite wonderful. Crab, lobster, fish, and ears of corn are worked into her platters and bowls in ways that are both whimsical and elegant. It's worth a stop.

WHERE TO STAY

✪ **Normaway Inn.** P.O. Box 121, Margaree Valley, NS B0E 2C0. ☎ **800/565-9463** or 902/564-5433. Fax 902/248-2600. www.normaway.com. E-mail: normaway@atcon.com. 9 units, 20 cottages. C$85–C$139 (US$57–US$93) double. MC, V. Closed late Oct to May 31. Pets allowed in cottages only.

From the moment you turn down the drive lined with tall Scotch pines, you'll feel you're in another world. And that world is a sort of 1920s Bertie Wooster world, both elegant and rustic at the same time. The lodge is located on some 500 acres, was built in 1928, and has been run by the MacDonald family since the 1940s. While it's the sort of place you might imagine running into gentlemen anglers dressed in tweed, it's not a true fishing resort. It appeals to both families and honeymooners, and is spread out enough to accommodate all.

Nine of the rooms are in the main lodge and have a timeless quality, with a vague 1920s character. I'd opt for one of the three first-floor rooms, which are larger and have corner windows for better ventilation. The cottages are spread around the property an easy walk to the main lodge, and have hardwood floors and a clean, almost Scandinavian quality. The older cottages were built in the 1940s and are a bit smaller. Eight cottages have Jacuzzis, and all but two have woodstoves.

Dining/Diversions: The dining room, decorated in pleasingly simple country farm style, is known for its Atlantic salmon and its lamb, which is raised for the inn about 10 miles away. (Don't fret: The sheep wandering the property are breed stock and won't appear on your dinner plate.) The menu changes nightly, but includes dishes like roast duck with peach and brandy sauce, and pan-fried trout with red onion and orange relish. A three-course dinner is C$29.50 (US$19.65), four courses C$34.50 (US$23). A limited number of outside guests (usually a half-dozen or fewer each night) can dine by advance reservation. The bar specializes in single-malt scotches.

The inn has one tennis court and additional acreage along the river a short drive away that includes five salmon pools. The inn's strong card is evening entertainment, with events ranging from films to live performances, including Acadian music, storytelling, and local fiddling. The famous weekly square dance, held in the inn's barn, attracts up to 350 people, about evenly split between locals and tourists (C$6/US$4).

CHÉTICAMP

The Acadian town of Chéticamp (pop. 1,000) is the western gateway to Cape Breton Highlands National Park and the center for French-speaking culture on Cape Breton. The change is striking as you drive northward from Margaree Harbour—the family names suddenly go from MacDonald to Doucet, and the whole culture and cuisine change.

The town itself consists of an assortment of restaurants, boutiques, and tourist establishments spread along Main Street, which closely hugs the harbor. A winding boardwalk follows the harbor's edge through much of town, and offers a good spot to stretch your legs and get your bearings. (That's Chéticamp Island just across the water; the tall coastal hills of the national park are visible up the coast.) Chéticamp is a good stop for provisioning, topping off the gas tank, and finding shelter.

Chéticamp is noted worldwide for its hooked rugs, a craft perfected by early Acadian settlers. Those curious about the craft should allow time for two stops. **Les Trois Pignons, the Elizabeth LeFort Gallery and Museum,** Main Street (north end of town), ☎ **902/224-2612,** displays 20 of the 300 fine tapestries created by Dr. LeFort, along with a number of other rugs made by local craftspeople. It's open daily 8am to 6pm in July and August; 9am to 5pm spring and fall. Closed November through

April. Admission is C$3.50 (US$2.35) adult, C$3 (US$2) senior, free for ages 12 and under.

In the 1930s artisans formed the **Co-operative Artisanale de Chéticamp,** located at 774 Main St. (☎ **902/224-2170**). A selection of hooked rugs—from the size of a drink coaster on up—are sold here, along with other trinkets and souvenirs. There's often a weaver or other craftsperson at work in the shop. A small museum downstairs (free) chronicles the life and times of the early Acadian settlers and their descendents. Closed late October to May 1.

Several boat tour operators are based in Chéticamp Harbour. **Seaside Whale and Nature Cruises,** ☎ **800/959-4253,** and **Acadian Whale Cruises,** ☎ 877/ 232-2522 or 902/224-1088, both set out in search of whales, seals, and scenery, and both have hydrophones on board for listening to any whales you may encounter.

Capt. Tom Larade, ☎ **800/813-3376,** offers 3½-hour deep-sea fishing excursions aboard the *Danny Lynn.* The price is C$25 (US$17) adult, C$12 (US$8) children 6 to 12, free under 6.

The most pleasing drive or bike ride in the area is out to **Chéticamp Island,** connected to the mainland by road. Look for the turn south of town; the side road is just north of Flora's gift shop on the Cabot Trail.

WHERE TO STAY

A handful of motels service the thousands of travelers who pass through each summer. **Laurie's Motor Inn,** Main Street (☎ **800/959-4253** or 902/224-2400), has more than 50 motel rooms in three buildings well situated right in town, with rates of C$72 to C$125 (US$48 to US$83) double.

Parkview Motel. Cabot Trail, Chéticamp, NS B0E 1H0. ☎ **902/224-3232.** Fax 902/ 224-2596. E-mail: parkview@atcon.com. TV. 17 units. C$65–C$70 (US$43–US$47) double. AE, MC, V. Closed late Oct to late May.

The basic yet comfortable Parkview's best claim is its location—within walking distance of the national park's visitor center, and away from the hubbub of town. Don't expect anything fancy and you won't be disappointed. There's a dining room and lounge in a separate building across the street.

Pilot Whale Lodge. Route 19, Chéticamp, NS B0E 1H0. ☎ **902/224-2592.** Fax 902/ 224-1540. www.pilotwhale.com. E-mail: chalets@pilotwhale.com. 6 cottages. TV. C$119 (US$79) double (each additional guest C$10/US$7; no charge for children 6 and under). AE, MC, V. Closed Nov to mid-May.

These spare, modern cottages (constructed in 1997) each have two bedrooms and full housekeeping facilities, including microwaves. They may have a bit of an antiseptic, condo air, but they are well equipped with TVs and VCRs, gas barbecues, coffeemakers, decks, and woodstoves. The best feature, though, is the grand view northward toward the coastal mountains. (Cottages 1, 2, 4, and 5 have the best vistas.) The lodge added apartments to the walk-out basements beneath two of the cottages in 1999 (C$80/US$53 double), which impinges slightly on the privacy of those both upstairs and down.

WHERE TO DINE

La Boulangerie Aucoin, ☎ **902/224-3220,** has been a staple of Chéticamp life since 1959. Located just off the Cabot Trail between town and the national park (look for signs), the bakery is constantly restocking its shelves with fresh-baked goods; ask what's still warm when you order at the counter. Among the options: croissants, scones, loaves of fresh bread, and berry pies. This is a recommended last stop for snack food before setting off into the park.

For an informal and quick lunch in town, there's **L&M Chéticamp Seafoods, Ltd.,** ☎ **902/224-1551,** located on Main Street just north of the Harbour restaurant. It's a take-out spot with a few picnic tables inside and outside. It's best known for its fish and chips, but also offers hamburgers and chicken fingers. If you're camping in the park, this is also the spot for fresh fish for the grill. Open 8am to 8pm daily from May to mid-September.

Harbour Restaurant and Bar. 15299 Cabot Trail (Main St.). ☎ **902/224-2042.** Reservations recommended in peak season. Light fare C$4.99–C$7.95 (US$3.35–US$5.30), dinner entrees C$12.95–C$16.50 (US$8.65–US$11). A, MC, V. Daily 11am–11pm. Closed late Oct to early May. SEAFOOD.

The Harbour is Chéticamp's sleekest restaurant, located in a easy-to-pass-by building on the waterfront. The water views are excellent, and the food well above average for the region. The light fare menu consists of pub favorites (hamburgers, club sandwich, fish and chips), along with an Acadian specialty or two. The dinner menu favors seafood, with options like an East Coast casserole (scallops, lobster, shrimp, and haddock in a cheese sauce), broiled salmon, and farm-raised Margaree trout, served charbroiled and finished with a tarragon butter.

La Chaloupe. 15283 Cabot Trail (Main St.). ☎ **902/274-3710.** Reservations not necessary. Main courses, lunch C$4.50–C$12.95 (US$3–US$8.65), dinner C$10.95–C$22.95 (US$7.30–US$15.30). AE, DISC, MC, V. Daily 11:30am–10pm. Closed Oct 1–June 1. SEAFOOD/ACADIAN.

This gray shingled cottage on the boardwalk has a fine harbor view, a good selection of deli sandwiches, and a handful of Acadian specialties like meat pie and chowder. Angle for a seat on the outside deck, which offers one of the best spots in town for a lazy lunch or savoring the sunset. The onion rings are crispy and good; the chowder heavily favors potatoes over fish.

Restaurant Acadien. 774 Main St. ☎ **902/224-3207.** Reservations recommended. Breakfast C$3.50–C$5 (US$2.35–US$3.35), lunch C$4.95–C$10.95 (US$3.30–US$7.30), dinner C$4.95–C$16.95 (US$3.30–US$11.30). AE, MC, V. Daily 7am–9pm. Closed late Oct to mid-May. ACADIAN.

This restaurant is attached to a crafts shop on the south side of town and has the uncluttered feel of a cafeteria. The servers wear costumes inspired by traditional Acadian dress, and the menu also draws on local Acadian traditions. Look for fricot, stewed potatoes, and the meat pies for which the region is renown. Also on the menu: blood pudding and butterscotch pie, for the brave and carefree.

PLEASANT BAY

At the north end of the Cabot Trail's exhilarating run along the western cliffs, the road turns inland at the village of **Pleasant Bay.** The attractive, active fishing harbor, protected by a man-made jetty, is about 0.5 kilometers off the Cabot Trail, and sits at the base of rounded, forested mountains that plunge down to the sea.

New for 2000 is a **whale interpretive center,** built on a rise overlooking the harbor. The center, which had just broken ground when I visited at press time, will feature exhibits to help explain why the waters offshore are so rich with marine life. Information on hours and prices was not yet available.

Whale-watch tours have been offered daily since 1974 from the harbor by Capt. Mark Timmons of **Whale and Sea Cruise,** ☎ **888/754-5112** or 902/224-1316. The 2½-hour cruise on the 35-foot *Bay Venture* provides unrivalled glimpses at the rugged coast both north and south, and often a close-up look at whales (almost always pilot whales, frequently finbacks and minkes, occasionally humpbacks). The boat has a hydrophone on board, so you can hear the plaintive whale calls underwater. Trips are C$20 (US$13) per person, and reservations are encouraged.

As you entered town you may have noticed the **folk art** shop near the "Y" in the road. Inside and out you'll find the colorful, whimsical folk art by Reed Timmons (Capt. Mark Timmons' cousin). Reed carves fish, cows, seagulls, and sailors that are rustic and visually arresting.

If you bear right at the "Y" and continue northward, the road wraps around the coastal hills and turns to gravel after 5 kilometers (3 miles). Keep going another 4 kilometers (2.4 miles). Here you'll come to a spectacular coastal hiking trail, which runs to **Pollett's Cove,** about 10 kilometers (6 miles) up the coast. A dozen families once lived here, and two cemeteries remain. The cove and the trail are on private land, but hiking and other quiet recreation are allowed.

CAPE NORTH

Cape North is a much-recommended detour for adventurous travelers hoping to get off the trafficked Cabot Trail. Folks say that Cape North is much like the Cabot Trail used to be 20 or 30 years ago, before the travel magazines started trumpeting its glories and large numbers of tourists started showing up. It's worth the extra driving and backtracking.

Cape North is reached via a turnoff at the northern tip of the Cabot Trail, after you descend into the Aspy Valley. You'll soon come to **Cabot Landing Provincial Park,** where local lore claims that John Cabot first made landfall in North America in 1497. You can debate the issue near the Cabot statue or take a long walk on the lovely 2-mile ocher sand beach fronting Aspy Bay. The views of the remote coast are noteworthy.

The road winds onward to the north; at a prominent fork, you can veer right to Bay St. Lawrence, where you can sign up for a whale-watching trip. Try **Captain Cox's Whale Watch** (☎ **888/346-5556** or 902/383-2981) or **Oshan Whale Cruise** (☎ **877/383-2883** or 902/383-2882). Both offer 2½-hour whale-watch cruises for C$25 (US$17).

Turn left at the fork and you'll continue along a remarkable cliffside road to Meat Cove. The last 3 miles track along a dirt road that runs high on the shoulders of coastal mountains and then drops into shady ravines to cross brooks and rivers. The road ends at Meat Cove, a rough-hewn settlement that's been home to fishermen, mostly named McClellan, for generations.

There's a rustic **private campground** (Meat Cove Camping, ☎ **902/383-2379**) where the 20 campsites have the most dramatic ocean views of any campground in Nova Scotia. Ask owner Kenneth McClellan about the hiking trails in the hills above the campground (day-use fee for noncampers).

The 8-kilometer (5-mile) trip from Bay St. Lawrence to Meat Cove is ideal by **mountain bike** if you've brought one along. This is one of the few places I could pedal my bike and whale-watch simultaneously.

WHERE TO STAY

Four Mile Beach Inn. RR no. 1, Cape North, NS B0C 1G0. ☎ **888/503-5551** or 902/5383-2282, off-season 902/562-3946. E-mail: jcuthbert@ns.sympatico.ca. 6 units. C$65–C$75 (US$43–US$50) double, including full breakfast. MC, V. Closed mid-Oct to early June. Pets in efficiency only.

This handsome new inn (opened in 1998) has quickly became one of my favorites on Cape Breton. Located in an old inn and general store dating from 1898, the inn is run by John Cuthbert and Janet Conner, who have done a superb job fixing the place up, making it feel comfortable and historic yet not cloying. The old general store has been spruced up and stocked with (not-for-sale) items they turned up in the basement and attic; two parlors are perfect for evening reading or card playing; and there's often traditional maritime music piped throughout the downstairs. The breakfast is all you can eat, and tasty. The inn has five rooms plus an efficiency with outside entrance. Two of the rooms share a bathroom, another has a private bathroom across the hall. The best of the lot is no. 2, a snug spot with low eaves and a ceiling fan, and a great bathroom with wainscotting and a tub fit for serious relaxing. The innkeepers have kayaks, canoes, and bikes for rent; you can paddle North Bay after a short stroll down a dirt road through their back yard. This place offers good value for the money.

Markland Coastal Resort. Cabot Trail, Dingwall, NS B0C 1G0. ☎ **800/872-6084** or 902/383-2246. Fax 902/383-2092. www.marklandresort.com. E-mail: markland@ canada.com. 12 units, 13 cottages. TV TEL. C$130 (US$87) double in motel (includes full breakfast), C$165–C$190 (US$110–US$127) double cottages. Discounts off-season and for 5 or more nights. Ask about packages. AE, DC, DISC, ER, MC, V. Closed mid-Oct to mid-May. "Well-behaved pets" allowed.

The Markland may have the best location of any resort on the island. It's sited on 70 acres where a meandering river meets a long sand beach fronting spectacular Aspy Bay. It's hard to imagine a more idyllic spot, especially on clear mornings when the sun illuminates the coastal range to the north. The resort features two kinds of accommodations, both furnished in a uncluttered, not-quite-Scandinavian style. The one and two-bedroom cottages have kitchens and sitting areas, along with porches, most with views of the bay. The motel units are narrow and tend to be a bit dark, and have chairs for sitting on the porch out front. (Expansion plans call for converting the current motel units to efficiencies in the coming 2 years; new motel units will be built as part of the main lodge.) Canoes are available to explore the river, or you can beachcomb just steps from your room.

Dining/Diversions: The dining room offers a nice contrast of modern furniture in a rustic setting with ocean views. Three meals daily are served, including the best dinners in northern Cape Breton (vegetarian meals on request). Dinner entrees include rack of lamb, sautéed scallops, and chicken breast in phyllo, priced at C$18 to C$27 (US$12 to US$18).

Since 1998 the resort has been hosting cultural performances at the Octagon, a performance building on the grounds. Friday nights typically feature Cape Breton music and other traditional tunes; on Sundays, there's a chamber music series.

Amenities: In addition to the beach and canoes, there's a heated outdoor pool, bicycle rental, sundeck, game rooms, self-service Laundromat, and baby-sitting.

WHERE TO DINE

For upscale dining, see the Markland Coastal Resort, above.

Morrison's Restaurant. Cabot Trail, Dingwall. ☎ **902/383-2051.** Reservations not needed. Main courses, lunch C$5.95–C$10.95 (US$3.95–US$7.30), dinner C$10.95–C$16.95 (US$7.30–US$11.30). Open daily 8:30am–9pm. Closed mid-Oct to mid-May. AE, MC, V. SEAFOOD/INFORMAL.

Morrison's is a favorite with locals and travelers, and with good reason. It serves good food at a good price. It's a comfortable, rustic spot, with old wood floors, wood-splint baskets hanging from the ceiling, and moose antlers on the wall. The menu tends toward comfort food, with selections like fettuccine with pesto, and beer-battered haddock (recommended). Other options include braised halibut in a dill cream sauce, and a sinful "Cape Islander"—consisting of scallops and lobster in a velouté sauce sandwiched between halibut and salmon and served with hollandaise. Desserts are traditional: cheesecake, gingerbread, and a tart bumbleberry pie. Bus tours often stop here, and when they do the service can sometimes be aggravating.

WHITE POINT & NEIL'S HARBOR

From South Harbor (near Dingwall) you can drive on the speedy Cabot Trail inland to Ingonish, or stick to the coast on an alternate route that arcs past White Point, continues onward to Neil's Harbor, then links back up with the Cabot Trail. If the weather's agreeable, the coast road is a recommended detour. Initially, the road climbs upward along abrupt and jagged cliffs with sweeping views of Aspy Bay; at White Point, you can veer out to the tip for even more expansive views of this remote section of coast. The road then tracks inland before emerging at **Neil's Harbor,** a postcard-perfect fishing village. On a rocky knob located on the far side of the fishing fleet is a squarish red-and-white lighthouse (now an ice cream parlor). Just beyond that is the **Chowder House,** a low-key, pine-paneled take-out restaurant that specializes in, well, chowder, along with platters of deep-fried seafood and crabcakes (C$4.50/US$3 to C$15.75/US$10.50). There's a grassy area outside the restaurant for picnicking as you admire the panorama of the rocky shoreline shaded with pink-orange rock. It's a popular spot with bus tours. From Neil's Harbor it's just a 2-minute drive back to the Cabot Trail.

INGONISH

This area includes a number of similarly named towns (Ingonish Centre, Ingonish Ferry, South Ingonish Harbor), which together have a population of about 1,300. Like Chéticamp on the peninsula's east side, Ingonish serves as a gateway to the national park and is home to a park visitor information center and a handful of motels and restaurants. Oddly, there's really no critical mass here—the services are spread along a lengthy stretch of the Cabot Trail, and there's never any sense of arrival. You pass a liquor store, some shops, a bank, a post office, and a handful of cottages. Then you're suddenly in the park.

Highlights in the area include a **sandy beach,** good for chilly splashing around (near Keltic Lodge), and a number of shorter hiking trails. (See "Cape Breton Highlands National Park," later in this chapter.) **The Highland Links** golf course (☎ 800/441-1118) is considered one of the best in Nova Scotia, if not all of Atlantic Canada. South of Ingonish the Cabot Trail climbs and descends the hairy 1,000-foot-high promontory of **Cape Smokey,** which explodes into panoramic views from the top. At the highest point, there's a provincial park where you can cool your engine and admire the views. An 11-kilometer (7-mile) hiking trail leads to the tip of the cape along the high bluffs, studded with unforgettable viewpoints along the way.

Sea kayak tours are offered in protected Ingonish Harbor by burly and gregarious raconteur Mike Crimp of **Cape Breton Sea Coast Adventures** (☎ 877/929-2800 or 902/929-2800.). Both full (C$89/US$59 per person) and half-day (C$49/US$33) tours are offered, and both are designed for novices who've never set bottom in a kayak. You'll look for whales, but are more likely to spot bald eagles or blue herons. The landscape hereabouts is dramatic, with Cape Smokey rising powerfully to the south, Middle Head to the north, and marsh grasses serving as home to a mix of shorebirds.

WHERE TO STAY

A number of serviceable cottage courts and motels are located in this area. The **Glenghorm Beach Resort** in Ingonish (☎ 902/286-2049) has 51 units on a spacious property that fronts a sand beach. Some rooms feature painted cinder-block walls, and the decorating is a bit dated, with avocado and gold hues that recall a bygone era. Options include motel rooms and efficiencies, along with cottages. Prices are C$70 to C$120 (US$47 to US$80).

Cape Breton Highlands Bungalows. Cabot Trail, Ingonish, NS B0C 1L0. ☎ **888/469-4816** or 902/285-2000. 25 cottages. TV. C$69 (US$46) double. MC, V. Closed early Oct to June 1.

This attractive cluster of vintage cottages boasts a Cape Breton rarity: it's located on the shore of a freshwater lake rather than the ocean. But the ocean, at Ingonish Beach, is a short walk or paddle away. The green-trimmed white cottages were built in the 1940s and are pleasantly rustic. Two styles are offered: one- and two-room, the latter of which are suitable for families, who make up much of the clientele. All but one cottage have kitchenettes. Numbers 1 through 10 are located in an open grassy area, some with views across the lake to the Keltic Lodge. The rest are tucked away in a grove of birches and hardwoods; no. 11 and no. 12 are nicely sited at the edge of the lake. In the evening, there's a good chance you'll be serenaded by loons.

Castle Rock Country Inn. 39339 Cabot Trail, Ingonish Ferry, NS B0C 1L0. ☎ **888/884-7625** or 902/285-2700. Fax 902/285-2525. E-mail: castlerock@ns.sympatico.ca. 13 units. C$89–C$115 (US$59–US$77); off-season from C$69 (US$46). AE, MC, V.

The recently built Castle Rock Inn sits boldly on a high hill overlooking Ingonish Harbor—a little *too* boldly, say some of the locals, who note that the inn's bulldozers greatly altered the pristine view of the hillside flanking Cape Smokey, and that no landscaping has been added to soften the impact. The inn opened in 1997 and is a squarish two-story lodge clad in wood shingles. The dozen rooms and one suite are surprisingly basic—furnished the way you might expect in a mid-range chain hotel. Rooms facing north have outstanding ocean views (about C$20 [US$13] additional for a view).

Dining: The inn's dining room has—no surprise—stunning water views and features a menu with what might be called "new traditional cuisine." Entrees (C$14.50/US$9.65 to C$26.95/US$17.95) include maple-glazed salmon, mussels with pasta, and cheese crepes with salad.

Keltic Lodge. Middle Head Peninsula, Ingonish Beach, NS B0C 1L0. ☎ **800/565-0444** or 902/285-2880. Fax 902/285-2859. www.gov.ns.ca/resorts. 98 units. TV TEL. C$268–C$283 (US$179–US$189) double, including breakfast and dinner. AE, DC, DISC, ER, MC, V. Closed Oct–Dec and April–May (main lodge closed in winter).

The Keltic Lodge is reached after a series of dramatic flourishes: You pass through a grove of white birches, cross an isthmus atop angular cliffs, and then arrive at the stunning, vaguely Tudor resort that dominates the narrow peninsula. The views are extraordinary. Owned and operated by the province, the resort is comfortable without being slick, nicely worn without being threadbare. Some of the guest rooms are painted in that soothing mint green that was popular in the 1940s; most are furnished rather plainly with run-of-the-mill motel furniture. (You might expect more for the price.) The cottages are set amid birches and have four bedrooms; you can rent just one bedroom and share a common living room with other guests. Be aware that some of the guest rooms are located at the more modern Inn at the Keltic building a couple hundred meters away, which has better views but a more sterile character. A Frommer's reader wrote to lament the inadequate soundproofing in the modern annex, and recommended an upstairs room here to avoid hearing heavy footfalls.

Dining: The management keeps up appearances in the main dining room: no jeans, shorts, or sweat clothes are allowed. The food in the main dining room is among the best on the island; the excellent C$40 (US$27) fixed-price dinner menu (included in room rates) offers several selections, with prime rib and lemon-pepper salmon fillet among the favorites. A less formal option is the new Atlantic Restaurant. It's a 3-minute walk away, housed in a new timberframe building that's airy and bright and has coastal views northward up the coast. The Atlantic is reasonably priced (dinner entrees C$5.50/US$3.65 to C$15.75/US$10.50), and specializes in lighter fare like grilled salmon and pasta.

Amenities: The Highland Links—an adjacent 18-hole golf course—is under separate management but is a major draw (ask about packages). A recent overhaul has boosted the course's reputation among serious duffers, who now come for more than just the ocean views. Also on the grounds: a heated oceanside pool, a game room, laundry service, a guest safe, and a great hiking trail that's worth strolling at least once a day. Tennis courts are nearby, as is a sand beach.

ST. ANN'S

Traveling clockwise around the Cabot Trail, you'll face a choice when you come to the juncture of Route 312. Option 1 is to take the side road to the Englishtown ferry and cross over St. Ann's Harbor in slow but picturesque fashion. The crossing of the fjord-like bay is very scenic, takes just about 2 minutes (when there's no line). The ferry runs around the clock, and the fare is nominal.

In Englishtown, one of Nova Scotia's more unique museums is the **Giant MacAskill Museum,** Route 312 (☎ 902/929-2925). This honors the memory of Angus MacAskill, who lived from 1825 to 1863. He was a big man, standing 7 foot 9 inches, and weighing 425 pounds. At the museum you can see many of his personal effects, including oversized boots, walking stick, and clothing, along with his bed and chair. If you'd care to pay your respects to the man, he's buried at the Englishtown cemetery. The museum is open daily mid-June to mid-September from 9am to 6pm. Admission is C$1.50 (US$1) adults, C$1 (US65¢) seniors and youth, C75¢ (US50¢) under 12.

Your second option is not to cross via ferry, but to stay on the Cabot Trail, heading down the western shore of St. Ann's Harbor. A good launching point for exploring the waters is North River, where kayak guide Angelo Spinazzola offers tours through his **North River Kayak Tours** (☎ 888/865-2925 or 902/929-2628). The full-day tour (C$85/US$57 per person) includes a steamed mussel lunch on a beach; there's also a gold-panning tour. Most every trip includes sightings of a bald eagle or two. Kayaks may also be rented.

In the village of St. Ann's you'll pass **The Gaelic College of Celtic Arts and Crafts,** ☎ 902/295-3411. (It's located 1 kilometer off the Trans-Canada Highway at Exit 11.) The school was founded informally in 1938, when a group of area citizens began offering instruction in Gaelic language in a one-room log cabin. Today, both the campus and the curriculum have expanded significantly, with classes now offered in bagpiping, fiddle, Highland dance, weaving, spinning, and Scottish history.

The 350-acre campus is home to the **Great Hall of Clans,** where visitors can get a quick lesson in Scottish culture. A number of exhibits provide answers to many questions, such as, what *is* the deal with tartan plaid, how did Scotsmen get reputations as fierce warriors, and what do Scotsmen *really* wear under a kilt? (Alas, the question "Is bagpiping really music?" is not addressed.) Robbie Burn's walking stick is on display, and you can buy intriguing clan histories for C$5 (US$3.35) per name. The Hall of Clans is open daily 8:30am to 6pm; admission is C$2.50 (US$1.65), free under 12. A campus crafts shop has shelves full of Gaelic items, including bolts of tartan plaid and tapes of traditional music. Live performances are also offered throughout the summer; call ahead or ask at the crafts shop for a schedule.

WHERE TO STAY

Luckenbooth Bed & Breakfast. R.R. no. 4, Cabot Trail, St. Ann's, NS B0E 1B0. ☎ **877/654-2357** or 902/929-2722. E-mail: luckenbooth@auracom.com. 3 units. Rate C$110–C$120 (US$73–US$80); includes breakfast. MC, V.

Built in 1999, this modern, log-accented B&B has just three bedrooms (all with private bathroom) and is nicely located on 1,000 feet of wooded shore frontage. (There's a trail down to the rocky waters.) Guests have the run of several common areas, including the main living room under a soaring cathedral ceiling, and a yellow-tartan-themed basement room with television. (It's decorated in the clan tartans of proprietors Frances and Wayne McClure; Frances is also a bagpiper.) The guest rooms each have modern furnishings; the best of the lot is no. 3, upstairs with hardwood floors, views of the bay, and a sitting area just outside the door. The other two rooms are in the walk-out basement, and feature cork floors. The inn has a no-shoes-inside policy, and slippers are furnished to guests.

BADDECK

Although Baddeck (pronounced Bah-*deck*) is at a distance from the national park, it's often considered the de facto "capital" of the Cabot Trail. The town offers the widest selection of hotels and accommodations along the whole loop, an assortment of restaurants, and a handful of useful services like grocery stores and Laundromats. Baddeck is also famed as the summer home of revered inventor Alexander Graham Bell, who is memorialized at a national historic site. What's more, Baddeck is compact and easy to reconnoiter by foot, is scenically located on the shores of Bras d'Or Lake, and is within striking distance of the excellent Fortress at Louisbourg. This is the best base for those with limited vacation time and those who plan to drive the Cabot Trail in 1 day (figure on 6 to 8 hours). If, however, your intention is to spend a few days exploring the hiking trails, bold headlands, and remote coves of the national park (which I'd recommend!), you're better off finding a base farther north.

The **Baddeck Welcome Center** (☎ **902/295-1911**) is located just south of the village at the intersection of Route 105 and Route 205. It's open daily in season 8:30am to 8:30pm.

EXPLORING THE TOWN

Baddeck is much like a modern New England village, centered around a small commercial boulevard (Chebucto Street) just off the lake. Ask for a free **walking tour brochure** at the welcome center. A complete tour of the village's architectural highlights won't take much more than 15 or 20 minutes.

Government Wharf (head down Jones Street from the Yellow Cello restaurant) is home to three boat tours, which offer the best way to experience Bras d'Or Lake. **Amoeba Sailing Tours** (☎ **902/295-2481**) offers a mellow cruise on a 50-foot sailboat, from which you'll likely spot bald eagles and other birds, and watch Baddeck's fine lakeshore drift past. Four sailings daily are offered in peak season; the cost is C$15 (US$10) per person. **Fan-A-Sea,** ☎ **902/295-1900,** runs charter fishing trips from Baddeck, and with some luck you may land cod, haddock, or trout. Bait and rods are supplied; the rate is C$35 (US$23) per person per hour. **Loch Bhreagh Boat Tours** (☎ **902/295-2016**) offers motorboat tours that pass Alexander Graham Bell's palatial former estate and other attractions at this end of the lake.

Also available near the wharf are **boat rentals,** ranging from kayaks, canoes, and windsurfers (all at C$8/US$5 per hour) to small motorboats (C$25/US$17 per hour). Call for more information, ☎ **902/295-3318.**

About 200 yards offshore from the downtown wharf is **Kidston Island,** owned by the town. It has a wonderful sand beach with lifeguards and an old lighthouse to explore. The Lion's Club offers frequent pontoon boat shuttles between 10am and 6pm (noon to 6pm on weekends) across St. Patrick's Channel; the crossing is free, but donations are encouraged.

Alexander Graham Bell National Historic Site. Chebucto St., Baddeck. ☎ **902/ 295-2069.** Admission C$4.25 (US$2.85) adult, C$3.25 (US$2.15) senior, C$2.25 (US$1.50) student, C$10.75 (US$7.15) family. Daily June 9am–6pm, July–August 8:30am–7:30pm, Sept to mid-Oct 8:30am–6pm, mid-Oct to May 9am–5pm.

Each summer for much of his life, noted inventor Alexander Graham Bell fled the heat of Washington, D.C., for a hillside retreat high above Bras d'Or Lake. The mansion, which is still owned and occupied by the Bell family, is visible across the harbor from various spots around town. But to learn more about Bell's career and restless mind, you should visit this modern exhibit center, perched on a grassy hillside at the north edge of the village. You'll find extensive exhibits about Bell's invention of the telephone at age 29, as well as considerable information about Bell's less-lauded contraptions, like his ingenious kites, hydrofoils, and airplanes. There's an extensive discovery area, where kids are encouraged to apply their intuition and creativity in solving problems.

WHERE TO STAY

If the places below are booked, try **Auberge Gisele,** 387 Shore Rd. (☎ **800/ 304-0466** or 902/295-2849), a modern 63-room hotel that's popular with bus tours, or the **Cabot Trail Motel,** Route 105 (1.5km/1 mile west of Baddeck), ☎ **902/ 295-2580,** with 40 rooms overlooking the lake and a heated outdoor pool. Doubles run around C$85 to C$100 (US$57 to US$67) at either location.

✪ **Duffus House Inn.** Water St. (P.O. Box 427), Baddeck, NS B0E 1B0. ☎ **902/295-2172.** 7 units (including 3 suites). C$95–C$125 (US$63–US$83) double, suites C$135–C$150 (US$90–US$100). Rates include continental breakfast. V. Closed mid-Oct to mid-May.

A visit to the Duffus House is like a visit to the grandmother's house everyone wished they had. These two adjacent buildings (constructed in 1820 and 1885) overlook the channel and are cozy and very tastefully furnished with a mix of antiques. The Duffus House is located far enough from Baddeck's downtown to keep the commotion at arm's length, yet you can still walk everywhere in a few minutes' time. (The inn also has its own dock, where you can swim or just sit peacefully.) The several cozy common areas are comfortably furnished and offer great places to chat with the other guests, as does the intimate garden. The inn doesn't charge bargain room rates, but delivers fair value for the cost.

Green Highlander Lodge. 525 Chebucto St., Baddeck, NS B0E 1B0. ☎ **902/295-2303.** E-mail: yellow@auracom.com. 3 units. TV. C$90–C$120 (US$60–US$80) double, including full breakfast. AE, MC, V. Closed Dec–May.

The Green Highlander is located atop the Yellow Cello, a popular in-town eatery. The three rooms are nicely decorated in a sort of Abercrombie & Fitch gentleman's fishing camp motif. (Rooms are named after Atlantic salmon flies.) Blue Charm has a private sitting room. Rosie Dawn and Lady Amherst have private decks that look out to Kidston Island. Ask about the moonlight paddle trips, kayak rentals, and the private beach located a mile away.

Inverary Resort. Shore Rd. (P.O. Box 190), Baddeck, NS B0E 1B0. ☎ **800/565-5660** or 902/295-3500. Fax 902/295-3527. www.inveraryresort.com. E-mail: inverary@atcon.com.

144 units. A/C TV TEL. C$95–C$150 (US$63–US$100) double, C$195 (US$130) suites. AE, DC, MC, V. Closed Dec–May.

This sprawling resort, located on 12 lakeside acres within walking distance of town, is a good choice for families with active kids. The slew of activities run the gamut from fishing and paddleboats to nightly bonfires on the beach. Guest rooms and facilities are spread all over the well-maintained grounds, mostly in buildings a dark-chocolate brown with white trim and green roofs. The rooms vary in size and style, but all are quite comfortable, even the snug motel-style units in the cottages, and many are appointed with colonial revival reproductions.

Dining: The resort has two dining rooms: The Lakeside Cafe overlooks the resort's small marina and serves informal fare like penne with pesto and vegetable lasagna (C$10.75/US$7.15 to C$16.95/US$11.30). The more formal Flora's, in the main lodge, has more upscale fare served in a sun-porch setting. Look for mixed grill, broiled halibut, and chicken breast with apple and onion compote (C$15.50/US$10.35 to C$19.95/US$13.30).

Amenities: Indoor pool, hot tub, sauna, three tennis courts, volleyball court, boat tours, boat rentals (canoes, kayaks, paddleboats, surf bikes, Zodiacs), marina, playground, shuffleboard, safe, room service.

Telegraph House. Chebucto Street (P.O. Box 8), Baddeck, NS B0E 1B0. ☎ **902/295-1100.** Fax 902/295-1136. 43 units (4 share 2 bathrooms). TV. C$65–C$92 (US$43–US$61) double. AE, MC, V.

The rooms in this 1861 hotel right on Baddeck's bustling main street are divided between the original inn and two motel units on a rise behind the inn. This is where Alexander Graham Bell stayed when he first visited Baddeck. And not all that much has changed in the main inn—the rooms are still rooming-house small, and decorated eclectically with both antiques and plain, old furniture. Four rooms on the top floor share two bathrooms between them, an arrangement that works well with families. Guests can linger on the front or side porch (there are several sitting nooks) and watch commerce happen on the main drag. I actually prefer the larger if unexciting motel rooms in back. Ask for rooms 22 to 32, which have small sitting decks outside their front doors with glimpses of the lake.

Dining: The dining room serves traditional favorites for both lunch and dinner. Expect shepherd's pie, ham plate, meat loaf, roast turkey, and fish cakes. And big, sloppy, wonderfully nasty desserts.

WHERE TO DINE

Many of Baddeck's larger hotels have dining rooms, where you'll find some of the town's more refined fare. **Auberge Gisele**'s dining room (see above) features continental cuisine, although try to come later in the evening after the bus tours have finished feeding. At the **Inverary Resort** (see above), the aptly named Lakeside Cafe is a popular spot, with a view of the marina and a moderately priced menu with pastas and stir-fries. The resort's main dining room, Flora's, features more creative (and more expensive) fare. At the **Silver Dart Lodge,** Shore Road, ☎ **902/295-2340,** there's informal McCurdy's Dining Room, which has a good reputation for seafood.

Baddeck Lobster Suppers. Ross St. ☎ **902/295-3307.** Reservations accepted for groups of 10 or more. Lobster dinner around C$25 (US$17), lunch items C$3–C$7 (US$2–US$5). Kids' menu available. MC, V. Daily 11:30am–1:30pm and 4–9pm. Closed Nov 1–June 1. SEAFOOD.

Save your appetite for an over-the-top seafood feast at this cavernous, no-frills restaurant. It has the charm of a Legion Hall, but the crowds contentedly and noisily chowing down provide the real atmosphere. The lobster dinner—which virtually everyone orders—includes one steamed crustacean, plus all you-can-eat mussels, chowder, biscuits, dessert, and drinks. Not in the mood for lobster? There's also planked salmon (C$21/US$14).

Yellow Cello. 525 Chebucto St. ☎ **902/295-2303.** Reservations suggested during peak season. Main courses C$5–C$9 (US$3–US$6). MC, V. Daily in season 8am–11pm. PUB FARE.

If you don't set your culinary expectations too high, this is a convivial spot to while away an afternoon or evening. Angle for a seat outdoors under the awning facing Chebucto Street. The menu will be familiar to those who watch a lot of sports on TV: pizza, nachos, chili, lasagna, sandwiches, and the like.

BRAS D'OR LAKE

"Yeah, this is gorgeous, but how much gorgeous can you take?" That was the comment I overheard at a high overlook with a stunning panoramic view of Bras d'Or Lake, the vast inland sea that nearly cleaves Cape Breton Island in two. The man uttered the comment to his family, which then trudged back to their car and set off for the Cape Breton coast.

It was actually a telling comment. With so much beauty around the island's perimeter, the lake hardly gets noticed. This in itself is remarkable. Almost anywhere else in the world, Bras' d'Or Lake (pronounced "*bra'door*") would be a major attraction, ringed by motels, lodges, boat tour operators, and chain restaurants. But today, along the twisting shoreline of this 71-mile long saltwater lake, you'll find ... nothing. Granted, roads circumnavigate the whole lake, but you'll generally find few services for tourists. Is that good or bad? Depends on your outlook.

Bras d'Or is a difficult lake to characterize, since it changes dramatically from one area to the next—near wilderness here, rolling farmland there, a summer home colony at another location. Wherever you go around the lake, watch for the regal silhouettes of bald eagles soaring high above, or that telltale spot of vivid white among the verdant trees indicating a perched eagle. Dozens of pairs of bald eagles nest along the shores or nearby, making this one of the best areas in the Maritimes for eagle sightings.

EXPLORING BRAS D'OR LAKE

What's a good strategy for touring the lake? For starters, I would caution against trying to drive around it in 1 day—or even over 2 days. There's no equivalent to the Cabot Trail around the lake's perimeter. The road serves up breathtaking views from time to time, but for much of the route it's dull and uninteresting, running at a distance from the lakeshore and offering mostly views of scrappy woods. It's better to select one or two portions of the lake, and focus your travels there.

For **scenic drives,** three segments lend themselves nicely to touring by car. One is the quiet shores near Iona and along the St. Andrew's Channel on Route 223. Another is the hump between St. Peters and Dundee, which winds high and low and in recent years has become the area of choice for the summer homes of vacationing Germans. And Route 4 from East Bay to St. Peters, where you'll get the most uninterrupted views of the lake, and best sense of its vast size.

Off-the-beaten-track explorers would do well to roam the road that snakes along western shore backwaters between the towns of Marble Mountain through Orangedale to Estmere. A decent map is essential; you'll cruise over questionable dirt roads and single-lane bridges, see very few people, be rewarded with sudden, unexpected views of coves and inlets. This is a good area to explore by canoe or mountain bike; bring your own or rent in one of the larger towns, because you won't find out-fitters (or any other service providers) around this part of the lake.

Several boat tours are offered from Baddeck (see above). In Johnstown, on the southeastern shores, is **Super Natural Sailing Tours** (☎ **800/903-3371** or 902/535-3371), which operates a 49-passenger catamaran. On-board naturalists help make sense of the lake's complex ecosystem.

On the southeastern shore is the town of St. Peters, where the lake comes within 800 meters of breaking through to the Atlantic Ocean and splitting Cape Breton into two islands. Nature didn't, but humans did when they built **St. Peter's Canal** in 1854. The canal still operates, and if you linger long enough, you may see some impressive pleasure craft making their way up to the lake. The pathway along the canal makes for good strolling.

The village of **Marble Mountain,** on the southwestern shore, offers an intriguing glimpse into history. The town was once a bustling metropolis of sorts. In 1868 a lus-trous seam of marble was located here, and by the early part of this century a full-scale mining operation was in effect, supplying builders worldwide. At it peak, the quarry employed 750, and the town was home to more than 1,000.

Today, it's reverted to a sleepy backwater. The **Marble Mountain Museum and Library** in a former schoolhouse in the village is open daily in summer and provides a glimpse at the former prosperity of the area. Afterwards, drive north of town to the overlook high above the island-dotted lake. On the uphill side, look for the gravel lane across the road that angles upward to the right. It's just a 5- or 10-minute walk up to the quarry, a hulking and melancholy hole encroached upon by thistles and Queen Anne's lace. There's an even better view of the lake from here.

Hot and bothered? You can cool off down at the lake, and in style. The **town beach,** which looks from above to be of white sand, really isn't. It's marble chips from the old quarrying operation. You can scramble down from the overlook, or drive into the vil-lage and make your way to the lakeshore.

Highland Village. Route 223, Iona. ☎ **902/725-2272.** Admission C$5 (US$3.35) adult, C$4 (US$2.65) senior, C$2 (US$1.35) ages 5–18, C$10 (US$6.65) family. Daily 9am–8pm mid-July to mid-August, 9am–6pm June to mid-July and mid-August to mid-Oct. Closed mid-Oct to May 31.

The Highland Village is located near Iona, on a grassy hillside with sweeping views over the lake, easily among the best views anywhere. When you finally turn your back on the panorama, you'll be at a living history museum—a 43-acre village featuring 10 buildings that reflect the region's Gaelic heritage, including historic structures that have been moved here from locations around the island, and exacting replicas. These range from the Black House (ca. 1790), a stone and sod hut of the sort an immigrant would have lived in prior to departing Scotland, to a schoolhouse and general store from the 1920s. Staffers dressed in historical costume will answer any questions you may have about early island life. Ask about Living History Tours (day-long events on Wednesdays that allow visitors to don costumes and immerse themselves in daily life) and candlelight tours after hours (every other Thursday in July and August).

WHERE TO STAY

Highland Heights Inn. Route 223 (P.O. Box 19), Iona, NS B0A 1L0. ☎ **800/660-8122** or 902/725-2360. Fax 902/725-2800. www.highlandheightsinn.com. E-mail: info@highlandheightsinn.com. 32 units. TV. C$79–C$99 (US$53–US$66) double. Ask about multi-night packages. DISC, MC, V.

The Highland Heights is a well-managed motel with clean, well-maintained rooms, but it's different from other well-run motels in one critical way: the views! Every room has a view of the lake. The second-floor rooms cost a bit more (about C$20 on average), but are worth the splurge just for the balconies from which you can monitor the lake's shifting moods. (The second-floor rooms are also a bit bigger and brighter.) All rooms have fans and windows that open.

Dining: The motel's dining room is cheerful and sunny in a 1970s sort of way (the inn was built in 1972), with lake views from the tables along the windows. It's open for three meals daily, and features homestyle cooking. At dinner expect a fairly limited number of entrees, such as poached salmon or peppered beef pasta (C$10.95/US$7.30 to C$17.95/US$11.97). There's an equally limited selection of beers from around the globe.

WHERE TO DINE

Rita's Tea Room. Route 4, Big Pond (about 40km southwest of Sydney). ☎ **902/ 828-2667.** Snacks and sandwiches C$2.50–C$8.95 (US$1.65–US$5.95); tea for 2 C$12.95 (US$8.65). AE, DC, MC, V. Daily 9am–7pm. Closed mid-Oct to June 1. LIGHT FARE.

Singer-songwriter Rita MacNeil grew up in Big Pond, and she never forgot her roots during her rise to fame. She always told audiences to stop by for a cup of tea if they were in the neighborhood. Problem was, they did. So Rita opened a tearoom for her fans, housing it in a converted 1939 schoolhouse. Today it contains a thriving gift shop (offering the music of Rita and others), with a comfortable and homey dining room where you can get baked goods, sandwiches, and soup. The tea for two is perfect on a drizzly Cape Breton day.

SYDNEY

Nova Scotia's third-largest city (pop. 30,000) was northern Nova Scotia's industrial hub for decades, and to this day three out of four Cape Breton Islanders live in and around Sydney. Recent economic trends have not been kind to the area, and once-thriving steel mills and coal mines have not exactly prospered. This gritty port city has been striving to reinvent itself as a tourist destination with the addition of casino gambling and a waterfront boardwalk. Success has been elusive, in part because Cape Breton's other charms offer such tough competition.

Although the commercial downtown is a bit gnarly, the historic residential areas will appeal to architecture and history aficionados. Three early buildings are open to the public in summer and are within easy walking distance of one another. They don't get a lot of traffic: I visited one 20 minutes before closing and found out that only three other visitors had stopped in that day. As a result, the costumed attendants don't display that wearied fatigue so often present in other guides, and their fresh enthusiasm is appealing and infectious.

The Cossit House, 75 Charlotte St. (☎ 902/539-7973), is Sydney's oldest house, built in 1785. It's been lovingly restored and furnished with a fine collection of 18th-century antiques. **The Jost House,** 54 Charlotte St. (☎ 902/539-0366), was built in 1787 and had a number of incarnations in the intervening years, including service as a store. Highlights of the home include an early apothecary. **St. Patrick's Museum,** 87 Esplanade (☎ 902/562-8237), is in Cape Breton's oldest Roman Catholic church, dating to 1828. There's an old burying ground and a collection of local artifacts. Admission to all three buildings is by donation.

PUFFIN TOURS

Thirty minutes west of Sydney (just off the Trans-Canada Highway en route to St. Ann's or Baddeck) is the home port of **Bird Island Boat Tours** (☎ 800/661-6680 or 902/674-2384). On a 2½-hour narrated cruise you'll head out to the Bird Islands, home to a colony of around 300 nesting puffins. You'll get within about 60 feet of the colorful birds (they nest in grassy burrows above rocky cliffs), and you may also see razorbills, guillemots, and the occasional bald eagle. Three tours daily are offered in summer; the fare is C$28 (US$19) adult, C$12.50 (US$8) children 6 to 12; free for children under 5. Reservations are suggested.

AN UNDERGROUND TOUR

Northeast of Sydney is the town of **Glace Bay,** a former coal-mining center. The mines have slipped into a long economic twilight of late, but the province has made lemonade from lemons by inaugurating a surprisingly intriguing **Miners's Museum,** 42 Birkley St. (☎ **902/849-4522**). The museum provides background on the rich geology of the area and offers insight into the region's sometimes rough labor history.

But the highlight of the trip is a 20-minute descent into the mine itself, with damp walls and cool temperatures (it's always 50°F). Retired miners, who can convey what it was like to be working in the mines better than anyone else, lead the tours. One Frommer's reader reported that her two teenage sons were all groans and eye-rolls when she announced their destination, but the two came away in awe of the place.

Admission is C$6.50 (US$4.35) adult, C$3.50 (US$2.35) children for both the museum and the mine tour. Open daily in summer 10am to 6pm; open weekdays in winter 9am to 4pm.

WHERE TO STAY & DINE

✪ Gowrie House. 139 Shore Rd., Sydney Mines, NS B1V 1A6. ☎ **800/372-1115** or 902/736-0077. Fax 902/736-0077. E-mail: gowriehouse@ns.sympatico.ca. 10 units. A/C TV TEL. C$119–C$219 (US$79–US$146) double, including full breakfast. AE, MC, V. Closed Nov–Mar.

This is a standout inn, easily among the best in Nova Scotia. Located across the harbor from Sydney and a few minutes' drive north of the Newfoundland ferry, Gowrie House is at once resplendent and comfortable, historic and very up-to-date. Portions of the gray-shingled house on 10 acres were originally built in 1820, and the building has been expanded tastefully since. The house is exquisitely decorated, with Oriental carpets, Asian ceramics, and stout Regency furniture, along with splashes of modern art. The smallest guest rooms are more spacious than the largest rooms at some other inns. Especially nice is the separate Caretaker's Cottage, lavishly furnished and accompanied by its own small deck and garden. Four rooms are in the more modern Garden House. These are carpeted and airy and have microwaves and refrigerators. All rooms have hair dryers, five have kitchenettes, nine have fireplaces, and three have Jacuzzis. The main problem with the inn? Getting a room. The whole summer season is often booked up by mid-June. Call as far in advance as you can.

Dining: The inn's well-regarded dining room features regional cuisine and local ingredients, such as pork with a rhubarb chutney, or grilled halibut with a mango chutney. The inn is especially noted for its marinated lamb. There's one seating nightly at 7:30pm; the price is C$39 (US$26) per person for four courses. House guests receive a carafe of wine; for outside guests, who should try to reserve a table at least 3 or 4 days in advance, it's BYOB.

LOUISBOURG

In the early 18th century, **✪ Louisbourg on Cape** Breton's remote and windswept easternmost coast was home to an ambitious French fortress and settlement. Despite its brief prosperity and durable construction of rock, it virtually disappeared after the British finally forced the French out (for the second time) in 1760. Through the miracle of archaeology and historic reconstruction, much of the imposing settlement has been re-created, and today Louisbourg is among Canada's most ambitious national historic parks. It's an attraction everyone coming to Cape Breton Island should make an effort to visit.

And a visit does require some effort. The site, 37 kilometers (22 miles) east of Sydney, isn't on the way to anyplace else, and it's an inconvenient detour from Cape Breton Highlands National Park. As such, it's far too easy to justify not going—it's too out of the way, it's not conveniently on a loop, and so on. By employing such excuses you're only cheating yourself. Commit yourself to going, then go. A few hours spent wandering this wondrous rebuilt town, then walking amid ruins and out along the coastal trail, will be one of the highlights of your trip to Atlantic Canada.

EXPLORING THE VILLAGE

The hamlet of Louisbourg—which you'll pass through en route to the historic park—is pleasantly low-key, still scouting for ways to rebound from one devastating economic loss after another, including the cessation of the railway, the decline in boat building, and the loss of the fisheries. Louisbourg is now striving to gear its economy more toward tourism, and you can see the progress year by year.

A short **boardwalk** with interpretive signs fronts the town's tiny waterfront. (You'll get a glimpse of the national historic site across the water.) Nearby is a faux-Elizabethan theater, the **Louisbourg Playhouse** (☎ 902/733-2996). This was originally built near the old town by Disney for filming the movie *Squanto*. After the production wrapped up, Disney donated it to the village, which dismantled it and moved it to a side street near the harbor. Various performances and concerts are staged here throughout the summer.

As you come into town on Route 22 you'll pass the **Sydney and Louisbourg Railway Museum,** ☎ 902/733-2720, which shares the gabled railway depot with the local **visitor information center** (☎ 902/733-2720). The museum commemorates the former railway, which shipped coal from the mines to Louisbourg harbor between 1895 and 1968. You can visit some of the old rolling stock (including an 1881 passenger car), and view the Roundhouse. Open daily mid-May to mid-October; hours in July and August are 8am to 8pm; in spring and fall 9am to 5pm. Admission is free.

Leave enough time during your trip for the detour a couple of miles out to the **Lighthouse Point,** the site of the first Canadian lighthouse. (The current lighthouse is a replacement.) The rocky coastline is dramatic and undeveloped, and it's a perfect spot for a picnic or to just idle away a late afternoon. The road, which is partly gravel, departs from the main road near the visitor information center.

The national park owns some 27 kilometers (17 miles) of coastline north and south of the historic site. Little of it is developed for recreation, but you can a good sense of its beauty on a kayak tour with **Island Seafari,** ☎ 902/733-2309, which leads tours ranging from 4 hours to 2 days. The 4-hour tour includes lunch and costs C$40 (US$27) per person. Rentals are also available, with delivery to area launch sites. (Novices can explore the well-protected harbor on their own with little to fear.)

✪ **Fortress of Louisbourg National Historic Park.** Louisbourg. ☎ **902/733-2280.** Admission June–Sept C$11 (US$7.35) adult, C$8 (US$5.35) senior, C$5.50 (US$3.65) child, C$27.50 (US$18.35) family. Discounts in May and Oct. July and Aug daily 9am–7pm; May, June, Sept, and Oct daily 9:30am–5pm. Costumed interpreters limited in off-season. Closed Nov 1–Apr 30.

The historic French village of Louisbourg has had three lives. The first was early in the 18th century, when the French first colonized this area—aggressively—in a bid to stake their claim in the New World. With the help of creative engineers and strong backs, they built an imposing fortress of stone. Imposing, but not impregnable, as the British were to prove when they captured the fort following the siege of 1745.

The fortress had a second, if short-lived, life after it was returned to the French following negotiations in Europe. War soon broke out again, though, and the British recaptured it in 1758. This time they blew it up for good measure.

The final resurrection came in the 1960s, when the Canadian government decided to rebuild one-fourth of the stone-walled town—virtually creating from whole cloth a settlement out of a handful of grass hummocks and some scattered documents about what once was. (The project also served as an economic lifeline for recently unemployed miners.) The historic park was built to re-create life as it looked in 1744, when this was an important French military capital and seaport.

Visitors today arrive at the site after walking through an interpretive center and boarding a bus for the short ride to the site. (Keeping cars at a distance does much to enhance the historic flavor.) You will wander through the impressive gatehouse—perhaps being challenged by a costumed guard on the lookout for English spies—and then begin wandering the narrow lanes and poking around the faux-historic buildings, some of which contain informative exhibits, others of which are restored and furnished with convincingly worn reproductions. Chicken, geese, and other barnyard animals peck and cluck. Vendors sell freshly baked bread out of wood-fired ovens.

To make the most of your visit, ask about the free guided tours. And don't hesitate to question the costumed interpreters, who are as knowledgeable as they are friendly. Allow at least 4 hours to explore. It's an extraordinary destination, as picturesque as it is historic.

WHERE TO STAY

Cranberry Cove. 12 Wolfe St., Louisbourg, NS B0A 1M0. ☎ **902/733-2171.** Fax 902/ 733-249. www.auracom.com/~crancove. E-mail: crancove@auracom.com. 7 units. TEL. C$85–C$145 (US$57–US$97) double, including continental breakfast. AE, MC, V. Closed mid-Oct to early May.

You won't miss this attractive, in-town inn when en route to the fortress—it's a three-story Victorian farmhouse painted a boisterous cranberry red. Inside it's decorated with a light Victorian motif. The upstairs rooms are carpeted and furnished around themes—Anne's Hideaway is the smallest but has a nice old tub and butterfly collection; Isle Royale is done up in Cape Breton tartan. My favorite room is also the quirkiest: Field and Stream, with a twig headboard, and mounted deer head and pheasant.

Dining: Dinner is served nightly from 5 to 8:30pm in the handsome first-floor dining room, which has a polished wood floor and cherry-wood tables and chairs. Entrees range from charbroiled Atlantic salmon steak with a yogurt dressing to cranberry-marinated breast of chicken, and are priced at C$12 to C$19 (US$8 to US$13).

Louisbourg Harbor Inn. 9 Warren St. (P.O. Box 110), Louisbourg, NS B0A 1M0. ☎ **888/888-8466** or 902/733-3222. E-mail: louisbourg@sprint.ca. 8 units. C$95–C$140 (US$63–US$93) double, including continental breakfast. MC, V. Closed mid-Oct to June 1.

This golden-yellow, century-old clapboard home is conveniently located in the village, a block off the main street and overlooking fishing wharves, the blue waters of the harbor, and, across the way, the Fortress of Louisbourg. The inn's lustrous pine floors have been nicely restored, and all the guest rooms are tidy and attractive, with some fussier than others. The best rooms are on the third floor, requiring a bit of a trek; Room 6 is bright and cheerful, Room 7 is very spacious and boasts an in-room Jacuzzi and a pair of rockers from which to monitor the happenings at the fish pier. A nice touch: All rooms facing the harbor have Jacuzzis. Room 1 and Room 3 also have private balconies.

Dining: Dinner is occasionally available by advance reservations to guests in the first-floor dining room. A three-course meal (entree choices typically includes steak, lobster, or crab) runs C$20 to C$30 (US$13 to US$20), depending on what's being offered.

WHERE TO DINE

Louisbourg has a handful of informal, family-style restaurants, plus upscale dining at Cranberry Cove. My choice for more casual eating out would be **The Grubstake,** at 1274 Main St. (☎ 902/733-2308). The place was founded by a few friends in 1972, and ever since it has embraced the philosophy that food should be fresh and honest. Expect good food at good prices and served with a winning attitude. The seafood is especially tasty.

12 Cape Breton Highlands National Park

Cape Breton Highlands National Park is one of the two crown-jewel national parks in Atlantic Canada (Gros Morne in Newfoundland is the other). Covering some 950 square kilometers (365 square miles) and stretching across a rugged peninsula from the Atlantic to the Gulf of St. Lawrence, the park is famous for its starkly beautiful terrain. It also features one of the most dramatic coastal drives east of Big Sur, California. One of the great pleasures of the park is that it holds something for everyone, from tourists who prefer to sightsee from the comfort of their car, to those who prefer backcountry hiking in the company of bear and moose.

The mountains of Cape Breton are probably unlike those you're familiar with elsewhere. The heart of the park is fundamentally a huge plateau. In the vast interior, you'll find a flat and melancholy landscape of wind-stunted evergreens, bogs, and barrens. This is called the **taiga,** a name that refers to the zone between tundra and the northernmost forest. In this largely untracked area (which is also Nova Scotia's largest remaining wilderness), you might find 150-year-old trees that are only knee-high.

But it's the park's edges that capture the attention. On the western side of the peninsula, the tableland has eroded into the sea, creating a dramatic landscape of ravines and ragged, rust-colored cliffs pounded by the ocean. The **Cabot Trail,** a paved road built in 1939, winds dramatically along the flanks of the mountains, offering extraordinary vistas at every turn. On the park's other coastal flank—the eastern, Atlantic side—the terrain is less dramatic, with a coastal plain interposed between mountains and sea. But the lush green hills still offer a backdrop that's exceptionally picturesque.

Note that this section focuses only on the park proper, which offers no lodging or services other than camping. You will find limited lodging and restaurants in the handful of villages that ring the park. See "Cape Breton Island," above.

ESSENTIALS

GETTING THERE   Access to the park is via the Cabot Trail, one of several tourist routes well marked by provincial authorities. The entire loop is 300 kilometers (185 miles). The distance from the park entrance at Chéticamp to the park entrance at Ingonish is 106 kilometers (65 miles). Although the loop can be done in either direction, I would encourage visitors to drive it in a clockwise direction solely because the visitor center in Chéticamp offers a far more detailed introduction to the park.

VISITOR INFORMATION   Visitor information centers are located at both Chéticamp and Ingonish and are open daily summers from 8am to 7pm. The Chéticamp center has more extensive information about the park, including a 10-minute slide presentation, natural history exhibits, a large-scale relief map, and a very good bookstore specializing in natural and cultural history. The park's main phone number is ☎ **902/224-2306.** In winter, call ☎ 902/285-2691.

FEES   Entrance permits can be purchased either at information centers or at toll houses at the two main park entrances. Permits are required for any activity along the route, even stopping to admire the view. Daily fees are C$3.50 (US$2.35) adult, C$2.50 (US$1.65) senior, C$1.50 (US$1) child (6–16), and C$8 (US$5.35) family; 4-day passes are C$10.50 (US$7) adult, C$7.50 (US$5) senior, C$4.50 (US$3) child, and C$24 (US$16) family.

CAMPING

The park has five drive-in campgrounds. The largest are at **Chéticamp** (on the west side) and **Broad Cove** (on the east), both of which have the commendable policy of never turning campers away. Even if all regular sites are full, they'll find a place for you to pitch a tent or park an RV at an overflow area. All the national park campgrounds are well run and well maintained. Chéticamp and Broad Cove offer three-way hookups for RVs. Rates are C$15 (US$10) for an unserviced site, C$17 (US$11) for electric only, C$21 (US$14) for fully serviced. It costs C$2 more for a site with a fire pit (otherwise you must build fires at picnic areas within the campground). Camp more than 4 days and you get 25% off the daily rate. Remember that you're also required to buy a day-use permit when camping at Cape Breton.

Cape Breton also has two backcountry campsites. ✪ **Fishing Cove** is especially attractive, set on a pristine cove an 8-kilometer (5-mile) hike from the Cabot Trail. Watch for pilot whales at sunset from the cliffs. Lake of Islands, the other backcountry site, is 13 kilometers (8 miles) from the trailhead on a remote lake in the interior; it's accessible by mountain bike. Fees are C$15 (US$10) per night; make arrangements at one of the visitor information centers.

SCENIC DRIVES

Cape Breton Highlands National Park offers basically one drive, and with few lapses it's scenic along the entire route. The most breathtaking stretch is the 44-kilometer (27-mile) jaunt from Chéticamp to Pleasant Bay along the western coast. Double the time you figure you'll need to drive this route, because you'll want to spend time at the pullouts admiring the views and perusing informational signboards. If it's foggy, save yourself the entrance fee and gas money. Without the views, there's little reason to travel and you'd be well advised to wait until the fog lifts. Until then, you could hike in the foggy forest or across the upland bogs, or explore some of the nearby villages in the atmospheric mist.

You'll want to be very confident in your car's brakes before setting out on the Cabot Trail. The road rises and falls with considerable drama, and when cresting some ridges you might feel mildly afflicted with vertigo. Especially stressful on the brakes (when traveling the Cabot Trail clockwise) are the descents to Pleasant Bay, into the Aspy Valley, and off Cape Smokey.

For an excellent detour at the northern apex of the loop, consider a side trip to **Meat Cove** (see the "Cape North" section, page 106).

HIKING

The park has 27 hiking trails departing from the Cabot Trail. Many excursions are quite short and have the feel of a casual stroll rather than a vigorous tromp, but those determined to be challenged will find suitable destinations. All trails are listed with brief descriptions on the reverse side of the map you'll receive when you pay your entry fee.

The ✪ **Skyline Trail** offers all the altitude with none of the climbing. You ascend the tableland from Chéticamp by car, then follow a 7-kilometer (4.3-mile) hiking loop out along dramatic bluffs and through wind-stunted spruce and fir. A spur trail descends to a high, exposed point overlooking the surf; it's capped with blueberry bushes. Moose are often spotted along this trail. Downside: It's a very popular trek and often crowded.

Further along the Cabot Trail, the half-mile-long Bog Trail offers a glimpse of the tableland's unique bogs from a dry boardwalk. Lone Shieling is an easy half-mile loop through a verdant hardwood forest in a lush valley that includes 350-year-old sugar maples. A re-creation of a hut of a Scottish crofter (shepherd) is a feature along this trail.

If you're looking to leave the crowds behind, the Glasgow Lake Lookoff is a relatively gentle 8-kilometer (4.8-mile) round-trip hike that takes you through barrens and scrub forest to a rocky bald overlooking a series of pristine highland lakes with distant views of the ocean. The trail is alternately swampy and rocky, so rugged footwear is advised.

On the eastern shore, a superb hike is out to Middle Head, beyond the Keltic Lodge resort. This dramatic, rocky peninsula thrusts well out into the Atlantic. The trail is wide and relatively flat, you'll cross open meadows with wonderful views north and south. The tip is grassy and open, and it offers a fine spot to scan for whales or watch the waves crash in following a storm. Allow an hour or two for a relaxed excursion out and back.

BIKING

The 292-kilometer (175-mile) **Cabot Trail loop** is the ironman tour for bike trekkers, both arduous and rewarding. The route twists up ravines and plummets back down toward the coast. One breathtaking vista after another unfolds, and the plunging, brake-smoking descent from Mt. MacKenzie to Pleasant Bay will be one you're not likely to forget. Campgrounds and motels are well spaced for a 3- or 4-day excursion. As for disadvantages, the road is uniformly narrow and almost universally without shoulders, and bikers often get the sense that motor-home drivers don't always know where the far side of their rig is located. This can be a bit harrowing.

If you're not inclined to pedal the whole loop, pick and choose. Especially scenic stretches for fit bikers include Chéticamp to Pleasant Bay and back, and the climb and descent from Lone Shieling eastward into the Aspy Valley. See also the "Cape North" section, page 106.

Mountain bikes are allowed on just four trails within the park—check with the visitor center when you arrive for details. The longest backcountry trail is the 13-kilometer (8-mile) route into the Lake of Islands, which doesn't appear on all maps. Ask at one of the two park visitor centers.

New Brunswick 4

Think of New Brunswick as the Rodney Dangerfield of Atlantic Canada—it just gets no respect. Among many Canadians, it has a reputation more for pulp mills, industrial forests, cargo ports, and oil refineries (the huge Irving Oil conglomerate is based here) than for quaint villages and charming byways. As such, travelers tend to view New Brunswick as a place you need to drive through—preferably really fast—en route from Québec or Maine to the rest of Atlantic Canada.

Granted, there's a grain of truth behind the province's reputation. But rest assured, New Brunswick has pockets of wilderness and scenic beauty that are unrivaled anywhere in eastern Canada. You'll find sandy beaches on warm ocean waters that hold their own to anything on Prince Edward Island. Not to mention rocky, surf-pounded headlands that could be in the farthest reaches of Newfoundland. The province's appeal tends to be more hidden than that of other locales. But with a little bit of homework—and by making inquiries at the innovative Day Adventure Centres the province has established—you can quite easily cobble together memorable excursions through an exquisite landscape.

Culturally, New Brunswick is Canada in microcosm. It's split between anglophone and francophone populations (about one-third of the residents speak French). Its heritage is both proudly Acadian and proudly pro-British—in fact, New Brunswick is sometimes called the "Loyalist Province" since so many Loyalists fleeing the United States settled here after the American Revolution.

But the cultural divide is less contentious here than in Québec. Interestingly, French-speaking New Brunswick residents share few cultural roots with French-speaking Québecois. (New Brunswick's French ancestors came mostly from central and western France; Québecois trace their ancestry to Brittany and Normandy.) Acadians celebrate the Feast of the Assumption as their national holiday. In Québec, it's the day of St. Jean Baptiste. With its unusually harmonious detente between two cultures, New Brunswick likes to offer itself as a model for Québec. Québec, in turn, tends to ignore New Brunswick.

1 Exploring New Brunswick

Visitors drawn to rugged beauty should plan to focus on the Fundy Coast with its stupendous tides, rocky cliffs, and boreal landscape.

(The south coast actually feels more remote and northerly than the more densely settled northeast coast.) Those interested in Acadian history or sandy beaches should veer toward the Gulf of St. Lawrence. Those interested in hurrying through the province to get to Prince Edward Island or Nova Scotia . . . well, you should at least detour down through Fundy National Park and visit Cape Enrage and Hopewell Rocks, which number among eastern Canada's more dramatic attractions.

ESSENTIALS

VISITOR INFORMATION   New Brunswick publishes several free annual directories and guides that are helpful in planning a trip to the province, including *Welcome to New Brunswick,* with listings of attractions, accommodations, and campgrounds, and the *Travel Planner,* which includes a catalog of multiday and daylong adventure packages. Write to **Tourism New Brunswick,** P.O. Box 12345, Fredericton, NB E7M 5C3, or call ☎ **800/561-0123** (from North America). On the Web, head to www.gov.nb.ca/tourism.

The province staffs five visitor information centers; most cities and larger towns also have their own municipal information centers. A complete listing of phone numbers for these centers can be found in the *Travel Planner* guide, or look for "?" direction signs on the highway. Phone numbers and addresses for the appropriate visitor information centers are provided in each section of this chapter.

GETTING THERE   The Trans-Canada Highway bisects the province, entering from Québec at St. Jacques. It follows the Saint John River Valley before veering through Moncton and exiting into Nova Scotia at Aulac. The entire distance is about 550 kilometers (330 miles).

The fastest route from New England to southwestern New Brunswick is to take the Maine turnpike to Bangor, then head east on Route 9 to connect to Route 1 into Calais, which is just across the river from St. Stephen, New Brunswick. A more scenic variation is to drive to Campobello Island across the bridge from Lubec, Maine (see the "Passamaquoddy Bay" section, below), then take a ferry to Deer Island, drive the length of the island, and board a second ferry to the mainland. Those headed to Fredericton or Moncton will speed their trip somewhat by following US I-95 to Houlton, then connecting with the Trans-Canada after crossing the border.

By Ferry   Bay Ferries (☎ **888/249-7245**) operates a 3-hour ferry that links Saint John and Digby, Nova Scotia. The ferry sails year-round, with as many as three crossings daily each way in summer. Summer fares are C$25 (US$17) for adults, C$12.50 (US$8.35) for children, and C$55 (US$37) per vehicle. Reservations are advised.

By Air   The province's main airports are at Fredericton (the provincial capital), Saint John, and Moncton, all of which are served by major rental-car companies. These airports are served by **Air Canada** (☎ **800/776-3000** in the U.S., 800/565-3940 in the Maritimes, or 800/563-5151 in Newfoundland) and **Canadian Airlines International** (☎ **800/426-7000** in the U.S. or 800/665-1177 in Canada). (Note that at press time both Air Canada and Canadian Airlines were considering mergers with one another as well as with outside airlines.)

By Train   Via Rail (☎ **800/561-3949** in the U.S., 800/561-3952 in the Maritimes or 506/857-9830) offers train service through the province (en route from Montréal to Halifax) 6 days per week. The train follows a northerly route, with stops in Campbellton, Miramichi, and Moncton.

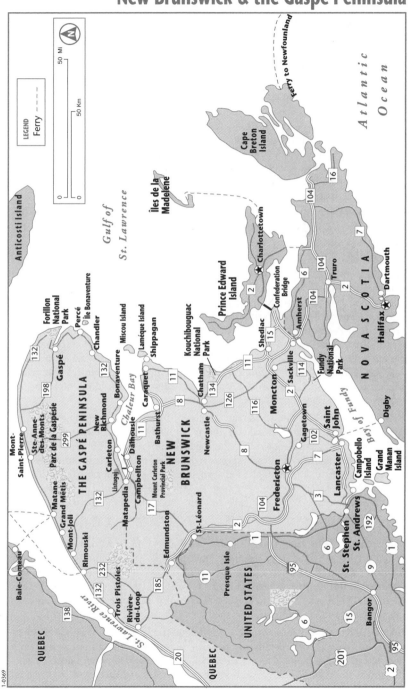

125

2 The Great Outdoors

The province has put together a well-conceived campaign—called **"The New Tide of Adventure"**—to encourage visitors of all budgets to explore its outdoor attractions. The province has funded Day Adventure Centers (well marked from most major roads), where you can stop in, peruse the local adventure options, and then sign up on the spot. The *Travel Planner* also outlines dozens of multiday and day adventures ranging from a C$10 (US$7) guided hike at Fundy National Park to C$389 (US$259) biking packages that include inn accommodations and gourmet dinners. For more information on the program, call ☎ **800/561-1112.**

I'd recommend that readers with an adventurous bent look closely at the outdoor center at **Cape Enrage** (see the "Fundy National Park" section, below), where you can canoe, rappel, rock climb, and kayak in a dramatic coastal setting.

BACKPACKING Among the best destinations for a backcountry tromp are **Mount Carleton Provincial Park** and **Fundy National Park,** both of which maintain backcountry sites. See the appropriate sections below for more information.

BICYCLING The islands and peninsulas of **Passamaquoddy Bay** lend themselves nicely to cruising in the slow lane—especially Campobello, which also has good dirt roads for mountain biking. **Grand Manan** holds appeal for cyclists, although the main road (Route 776) has narrow shoulders and fast cars. Some of the best coastal biking is **around Fundy National Park**—especially the backroads to Cape Enrage, and the **Fundy Trail Parkway,** an 11-kilometer (6.6-mile), multi-use trail that hugs the coast west of the national park. Along the Acadian Coast, **Kouchibouguac National Park** has limited but unusually nice biking trails through mixed terrain (rentals available).

A handy guide is *Biking to Blissville,* by Kent Thompson. It covers 35 rides in the Maritimes, and costs C$14.95 (US$10). Contact Goose Lane Editions, 469 King St., Fredericton, NB E3B 1E5, ☎ **506/450-4251.**

BIRD WATCHING **Grand Manan** is among the province's most noted destinations for birders, located smack on the Atlantic flyway. (Ur-birder John James Audubon lodged here when studying local bird life more than 150 years ago.) Over the course of a year, as many as 275 species are observed on the island, with September typically the best month for sightings. It's not hard to swap information with other birders. On the ferry, look for excitable folks with binoculars and Tilley hats dashing from port to starboard and back. Talk to them. Boat tours from Grand Manan will bring you to Machias Seal Island, with its colonies of puffins, arctic terns, and razorbills.

On **Campobello Island,** the mixed terrain also attracts a good mix of birds, including sharp-shinned hawk, common eider, and black guillemot. Ask for a checklist and map at the visitor center. Shorebird enthusiasts flock to **Shepody Bay National Wildlife Area,** which maintains preserves in the mudflats between Alma (near Fundy National Park) and Hopewell Cape. Also offering excellent birding is the marsh that surrounds **Sackville,** near the Nova Scotia border.

CANOEING New Brunswick has 3,600 kilometers (2,200 miles) of inland waterways, plus lakes and protected bays. Canoeists can find everything from glass-smooth waters to daunting rapids. Novices often enjoy the 3-hour **Voyager Canoe Marine Adventure** (☎ **506/876-2443**) in Kouchibouguac National Park. More experienced canoeists looking for a longer expedition should head to the **St. Croix River** on the U.S. border, where you can embark on a multiday paddle trip and get lost in the woods, spiritually if not in fact.

FISHING   The **Miramichi River** has long attracted anglers both famous and obscure, lured by the wily Atlantic salmon. In some considered opinions, this ranks among the best salmon rivers in the world, although diminished runs have plagued this river in recent years as they have all rivers in the Maritimes. Salmon must be caught on flies, and nonresidents need to hire a guide to go after salmon. For other freshwater species, like bass, and saltwater angling, the restrictions are less onerous. Get up to date on the rules and regulations by requesting copies of two brochures: "Sport Fishing Summary" and "Atlantic Salmon Angling." These are available from **Fish and Wildlife,** P.O. Box 6000, Fredericton, NB E3B 5H1 (☎ **506/453-2440**).

HIKING   The province's highest point is in the center of the woodlands region, at **Mount Carleton Provincial Park.** Several demanding hikes in the park yield glorious views. There's also superb hiking at **Fundy National Park,** with a mix of coastal and woodland hikes on well-marked trails. The multi-use, 11-kilometer (6.6-mile) **Fundy Trail Parkway** has terrific views of the coast and is wheelchair accessible. **Grand Manan** is a good destination for independent-minded hikers who enjoy the challenge of finding the trail as much as the hike itself.

An excellent resource is *A Hiking Guide to New Brunswick,* published by Goose Lane Editions. It's C$14.95 (US$10) and available in bookstores around the province, or directly from the publisher (469 King St., Fredericton, NB E3B 1E5, ☎ **506/450-4251**).

SEA KAYAKING   The huge tides that make kayaking so fascinating along the Bay of Fundy also make it exceptionally dangerous—even the strongest kayakers are no match for a fierce ebb tide if they're in the wrong place. Fortunately, the number of skilled sea-kayaking guides has boomed in recent years.

Among the most extraordinary places to explore is **Hopewell Rocks.** The rocks stand like Brancusi statues on the ocean floor at low tide but offer sea caves and narrow channels to explore at high tide. **Baymount Outdoor Adventures** (☎ **506/734-2660**) offers 90-minute sea kayak tours of Hopewell Rocks for C$35 (US$23) adult, C$30 (US$20) youth. Other kayak outfitters along the Fundy Coast include the **Outdoor Adventure Company** (☎ **800/365-3855** or 506/755-2007) in St. George, **Fresh Air Adventure** (☎ **800/545-0020** or 506/887-2249) in Alma, and **Seascape** (☎ **506/529-4866**) in St. Andrews.

SWIMMING   Parts of New Brunswick offer wonderful ocean swimming. The best beaches are along the **Acadian Coast,** especially near Shediac and in Kouchibouguac National Park. The water is much warmer and the terrain more forgiving along the Gulf of St. Lawrence than the Bay of Fundy.

WHALE WATCHING   The Bay of Fundy is rich with plankton, and therefore rich with whales. Some 15 types of whales can be spotted in the bay, including finback, minke, humpback, the infrequent orca, and the endangered right whale. Whale-watching expeditions sail throughout the summer from Campobello Island, Deer Island, Grand Manan, St. Andrews, and St. George. Any visitor information center can point you in the right direction; the province's travel guide also lists many of the tours, which typically cost around C$40 (US$27) or C$50 (US$33) for 2 to 4 hours of whale watching.

3 Passamaquoddy Bay

The Passamaquoddy Bay region is often the first point of entry for those arriving overland from the United States. The deeply indented bay is wracked with massive tides that produce currents powerful enough to stymie even doughty fishing boats. It's a place of lasting fogs, spruce-clad islands, bald eagles, and widely scattered development. It's also home to a grand old summer colony and a peninsula that boasts two five-star inns and a rambling turn-of-the-century resort.

CAMPOBELLO ISLAND

Campobello is a compact island (about 16km long and 5km wide—or 10 by 3 miles) at the mouth of Passamaquoddy Bay. Among its other distinctions, it's connected by a graceful modern bridge to Lubec, Maine, and is thus easier to get to from the United States than from Canada. To get here from the Canadian mainland without driving through the United States requires two ferries, one of which operates only during the summer.

Campobello has been home to both humble fishermen and wealthy families over the years, and both have coexisted quite nicely. (Locals approved when summer folks built golf courses earlier this century, since it gave them a place to graze their sheep.) Today, the island is a mix of elegant summer homes and less-interesting tract homes of a more recent vintage.

The island offers excellent shoreline **walks** at both Roosevelt Campobello International Park (see below) and **Herring Cove Provincial Park** (☎ **506/752-7010**). The landscapes are extraordinarily diverse. On some trails you'll enjoy a Currier and Ives tableau of white houses and church spires across the channel in Lubec and Eastport; 10 minutes later you'll be walking along a wild, rocky coast pummeled by surging waves. Herring Cove has a mile-long beach that's perfect for a slow stroll in the fog. Camping and golf are also offered at the provincial park.

ESSENTIALS

GETTING THERE   Campobello Island is accessible year-round from the United States. From Route 1 in Whiting, Maine, take Route 189 to Lubec, where a bridge links Lubec with Campobello. In the summer, there's another option. From the Canadian mainland, take the free ferry to Deer Island, drive the length of the island, and then board the small seasonal ferry to Campobello. The ferry is operated by **East Coast Ferries** (☎ **506/747-2159**) and runs from late June to early September. The fare is C$13 (US$9) for car and driver, C$2 (US$1) for each additional passenger, with a maximum of C$18 (US$12) per car.

VISITOR INFORMATION   The **Campobello Welcome Center,** 44 Route 774, Welshpool, NB E5E 1A3 (☎ **506/752-7043**), is on the right just after you cross the bridge from Lubec. It's open from mid-May to mid-October daily from 9am to 7pm (limited hours after Labour Day).

Roosevelt Campobello International Park. Route 774. ☎ **506/752-2922.** Free admission. Daily 10am–6pm. Closed mid-Oct to late May.

Like a number of other affluent Americans, the family of Franklin Delano Roosevelt made an annual trek to the prosperous summer colony at Campobello Island. The island lured folks from the sultry cities with a promise of cool air and a salubrious effect on the circulatory system. ("The extensive forests of balsamic firs seem to affect the atmosphere of this region, causing a quiet of the nervous system and inviting sleep," read an 1890 real-estate brochure.) The future U.S. president came to this island every summer between 1883, the year after he was born, and 1921, when he was stricken with polio. Franklin and his siblings spent those summers exploring the coves and sailing around the bay, and he always recalled his time here fondly. (It was his "beloved island," he said, coining a phrase that gets no rest in local brochures.)

You'll learn much about Roosevelt and his early life at the visitor center, where you can watch a brief film, and during a self-guided tour of the elaborate mansion, covered in cranberry-colored shingles. For a "cottage" this huge, it's surprisingly comfortable and intimate. The park is truly international; run by a commission with representatives from both the U.S. and Canada, it's like none other in the world.

Leave some time to explore farther afield in the 2,800-acre park, which offers scenic coastline and 14 kilometers (8.5 miles) of walking trails. Maps and walk suggestions are available at the visitor center.

WHERE TO STAY & DINE

Lupine Lodge. Welshpool Rd., Campobello, NB E0G 3H0. ☎ **506/752-2555.** 11 units. C$50–C$125 (US$33–US$83) double. MC, V. Closed mid-Oct to mid-June. Pets accepted (C$15/US$10 additional).

In 1915, cousins of the Roosevelts built this handsome compound of log buildings not far from the Roosevelt cottage. A busy road runs between the lodge and the water, but the buildings are located on a slight rise and have the feel of being removed from the traffic. Guest rooms are in two long lodges adjacent to the main building and restaurant. The rooms with bay views cost a bit more but are worth it—they're slightly bigger and better furnished in a log-rustic style. All guests have access to a deck that overlooks the bay.

Dining: The attractive restaurant exudes rustic summer ease with log walls, a stone fireplace, bay views, and mounted moosehead and swordfish. Three meals are served daily. Dinner entrees include favorites like salmon, T-bone, turkey, and steamed lobster, priced at C$10 to C$16 (US$7 to US$11).

The Owen House. 11 Welshpool St., Welshpool, Campobello, NB E5E 1G3. ☎ **506/752-2977.** 9 units (3 share 1 bathroom). C$78 (US$52) double shared bathroom, C$103–C$118 (US$69–US$79) private bathroom. Rates include breakfast. V. Closed mid-Oct to late May. No children under 6 in August.

This three-story clapboard captain's house dates to 1835 and sits on 10 tree-filled acres at the edge of the bay. The first-floor common rooms are nicely decorated in a busy Victorian manner with Persian and braided carpets and mahogany furniture. The guest rooms are a mixed lot, furnished with an eclectic mélange of antique and modern furniture that sometimes blends nicely. Likewise, some rooms are bright and airy and filled with the smell of salty air (Room 1 is the largest, with waterfront views on two sides); others, like Room 5, are tucked under stairs and rather dark. The third-floor rooms share a single bathroom but also have excellent views. A filling breakfast served family style is included in the room rates.

ST. STEPHEN

St. Stephen is the gateway to Canada for many travelers arriving from the United States. It's directly across the tidal St. Croix River from Calais, Maine, and the two towns share a symbiotic relationship—it's a local call across the international border from one town to the other, fire engines from one country will often respond to fires in the other, and during the annual summer parade the bands and floats march right through customs without stopping.

ESSENTIALS

VISITOR INFORMATION The **Provincial Visitor Information Centre** (☎ **506/466-7390**) is open daily 10am to 6pm mid-May to mid-October. It's in the old train station on Milltown Boulevard, about a mile from Canadian customs; turn right after crossing the border (following signs for St. Andrews and Saint John), and watch for the information center at the light where the road turns left.

EXPLORING ST. STEPHEN

St. Stephen is a town in transition. The lumber industry and wood trade that was responsible for the handsome brick and stone buildings that line the main street has by and large dried up. The town now depends on a paper mill and the large Ganong chocolate factory as its economic mainstays. As a regional commercial center, it has a gritty, lived-in feel to it, and not much in the way of stylish boutiques or upscale restaurants.

You can learn about the region's history with a brief stop at the **Charlotte County Museum,** 443 Milltown Blvd., ☎ **506/466-3295.**

The Chocolate Museum. 73 Milltown Blvd. ☎ **506/466-7848.** Admission C$4 (US$2.65) adult, C$3.50 (US$2.35) students, C$2.50 (US$1.65) children under 6, C$10 (US$6.65) family. Summer hours Tues–Sat 8am–8pm, Sun–Mon 1–5pm. Off-season Mon–Thurs 9am–5pm, Fri 9am–8pm, Sat 9am–5pm, Sun 1–5pm.

St. Stephen's claim to fame is that it's the home of the chocolate bar—the first place (1910) where somebody thought to wrap chocolate pieces in foil and sell them individually. At least that's according to local lore. Chocolate is still big around here—not quite like Hershey, Penn., but still a part of the local psyche and economy. The Ganong brothers started selling chocolate from their general store here in 1873, and from this an empire was built, employing some 700 people by the 1930s. Ganong was also the first to package chocolates in heart-shaped boxes for Valentine's Day, and still holds 30% of the Canadian market for heart-box chocolates.

Ganong's modern new plant is on the outskirts of town and isn't open for tours, but in 1999 the nonprofit Chocolate Museum was opened in one of Ganong's early factories, a large brick structure on the town's main street. Here you'll view an 11-minute video about the history of local chocolates, then see the displays and exhibits, including 19th-century chocolate boxes, interactive multimedia displays about the making of candy on iMacs, and games for young children (my favorite: "Guess the Centers"). A highlight of a visit is watching one of the expert hand-dippers make chocolates the old fashioned way; samples are available afterwards.

Want more? Ganong's Chocolatier, an old-fashioned candy shop, is located in the storefront adjacent to the museum. Don't miss the budget bags of factory seconds.

ST. ANDREWS

The lovely village of St. Andrews—or St. Andrews By-The-Sea, as the chamber of commerce likes to call it—traces its roots back to the days of the Loyalists. After the American Revolution, New Englanders who supported the British in the struggle were made to feel unwelcome. They decamped first to Castine, Maine, which they presumed was safely on British soil. It wasn't; the St. Croix River was later determined to be the border between Canada and the United States. Uprooted again, the Loyalists dismantled their houses, loaded the pieces aboard ships, and rebuilt them on the welcoming peninsula of St. Andrews. Some of these saltbox houses still stand today.

This historic community later emerged as a fashionable summer resort in the late 19th century, when many of Canada's affluent and well-connected nabobs built homes and gathered annually here for an active social season. Around this time, the Tudor-style **Algonquin Hotel** was built on a low rise overlooking the town in 1889, and it quickly became the town's social hub and defining landmark.

St. Andrews is beautifully sited at the tip of a long, wedge-shaped peninsula. Thanks to its location off the beaten track, the village hasn't been spoiled much by modern development, and walking the wide, shady streets—especially those around the Algonquin—invokes a more genteel era. Some 250 homes around the village are more than a century old. A number of appealing boutiques and shops are spread along Water Street, which stretches for some distance along the town's shoreline.

ESSENTIALS

GETTING THERE   St. Andrews is located at the apex of Route 127, which dips southward from Route 1 between St. Stephen and St. George. The turnoff is well marked from either direction. **SMT** bus lines, ☎ **800/567-5151** or 506/859-5060, runs one bus daily between St. Andrews and Saint John; the one-way fare is approximately C$15 (US$10).

VISITOR INFORMATION   St. Andrews has two information centers. At the western intersection of Route 1 and Route 127 is the seasonal **St. Andrews Tourist Bureau** (☎ **506/466-4858**), which is staffed by local volunteers. A second facility, the **Welcome Centre** (☎ **506/529-3000**), is located at 46 Reed Ave., on your left as you enter the village. It's in a handsome 1914 home overarched by broad-crowned trees. It's open daily from 9am to 6pm in May and September, to 8pm in July and August. The rest of the year, contact the **Chamber of Commerce** in the same building (☎ **800/563-7397** or 506/529-3555) by writing P.O. Box 89, St. Andrews, NB E0G 2X0; or e-mail them at stachmb@nbnet.nb.ca.

EXPLORING ST. ANDREWS

The chamber of commerce produces two brochures, the *Town Map and Directory* and the *St. Andrews by-the-Sea Historic Guide,* both of which are free and can be found at the two visitor information centers. Also look for *A Guide to Historic St. Andrews,* produced by the St. Andrews Civic Trust. With these in hand you'll be able to launch an informed exploration. To make it even easier, many of the private dwellings in St. Andrews feature plaques with information on their origins. Look in particular for the saltbox-style homes, some of which are thought to be the original Loyalist structures that traveled here by barge.

For a guided tour, contact **Heritage Discovery Tours,** 205 Water St. at Market Wharf, www.caughey.on.ca/hdt (☎ **506/529-4011**). Elaine Bruff's "Magical History Tour" is recommended; prices start at C$15 (US$10) per person for a group of three. Hours are daily from May 15 to October 15, 9am to 4:30pm.

The village's compact and handsome downtown flanks **Water Street,** a lengthy commercial street that parallels the bay. You'll find low, understated commercial architecture, much of it from the turn of the century, that encompasses a gamut of styles. Allow an hour or so for browsing at boutiques and art galleries. There's also a mix of restaurants and inns.

Two blocks inland on King Street, you'll get a dose of local history at the **Ross Memorial Museum** (188 Montague St., ☎ **506/529-5124**). The historic home was built in 1824; in 1945 the home was left to the town by Rev. Henry Phipps Ross and Sarah Juliette Ross, complete with their eclectic and intriguing collection of period furniture, carpets, and paintings. Open late June to mid-October, Tuesday to Saturday 10am to 4:30pm; in July and August it's also open Mondays. Admission is by donation.

Walk up the hill to the head of King Street, and you'll eventually come to the Kingsbrae Horticultural Gardens (see below).

On the west end of Water Street, you'll come to Joe's Point Road at the foot of Harriet Street. The stout wooden **blockhouse** that sits just off the water behind low grass-covered earthworks was built by townspeople during the War of 1812, when the British colonials anticipated a U.S. attack that never came. This structure is all that remains of the scattered fortifications created around town during that war.

Across the street from the blockhouse is the peaceful **Centennial Gardens,** estab-lished in 1967 to mark the centenary of Canadian confederation. The compact, tidy park has views of the bay and makes a pleasant spot for a picnic.

To the east of the blockhouse is the **Niger Reef Tea House,** 1 Joe's Point Rd., ☎ **506/529-8007,** built in 1926 as the chapter house of the Imperial Order of the Daughters of the Empire. Tea was served summer afternoons, with the proceeds going to support the group's charitable endeavors. In 1999, the building was restored by the St. Andrews Civic Trust, with profits going to support the Trust's preservation efforts. Notable are the dreamy, evocative landscape murals on the walls, painted in 1926 by American artist Lucille Douglass. A very limited selection of light meals is served here, along with excellent tea and coffee drinks (including espresso and cappuccino). After-noon tea is served 3 to 5pm (C$8/US$5.33), and includes tea with cakes, sweets, and finger sandwiches. If the weather's right, it's hard to top afternoon tea on the outside deck.

At the other end of Water Street, headed east from downtown, is the open space of **Indian Point** and the Passamaquoddy Ocean Park Campground. The views of the bay are panoramic; somehow it's even dramatic on foggy days, and swimming in these icy waters will earn you bragging rights.

Look for history at your feet when exploring the park's rocky beaches. You'll some-times turn up worn and rounded flint and coral that washed ashore. It's not native, but imported. Early traders sailing here loaded their holds with flint from Dover, Eng-land, and coral from the Caribbean to serve as ballast on the crossing. When they arrived, the ballast was dumped offshore, and today it still churns up from the depths.

For a more protected swimming spot, wander down Acadia Drive, which runs downhill behind the Algonquin Hotel. You'll come to popular **Katy's Cove,** where floating docks form a sort of natural swimming saltwater pool along a lovely inlet. You'll find a snack bar, a playground, and an affable sense of gracious ease here, and it's a fine place for families to while away an afternoon. There's a small fee.

BOAT TOURS

St. Andrews is an excellent spot to launch an exploration of the bay, which is very much alive, biologically speaking. On the water you'll look for whales, porpoises, seals, and bald eagles, no matter which trip you select.

Quoddy Link Marine, ☎ **506/529-2600,** offers whale-watch tours on a 50-foot power catamaran, and the tour includes use of binoculars and seafood snacks. Whale-watch and sunset tours are offered aboard the **Seafox,** ☎ **506/636-0130,** a 40-foot Cape Islander boat with viewing from two decks. Two-hour tours in search of wildlife aboard 24-foot rigid-hull Zodiacs is offered by **Fundy Tide Runners,** ☎ **506/529-4481;** passengers wear flotation suits as they zip around the bay. For a more traditional experience, sign up for a trip aboard the **TallShip Cory,** ☎ **506/529-8116,** which offers 3-hour tours under sail, with music and storytelling on board.

Seascape Kayak Tours, ☎ **506/529-4866,** offers an up-close and personal view of the bay on full- and half-day tours, with lunch provided on full-day trips, and snacks on the half-day (2½-hour) tour. No kayaking experience is needed. The half-day trip runs C$55 (US$37).

Atlantic Salmon Conservation Centre. 24 Chamcook Rd. (4 miles from St. Andrews via Route 127). ☎ **506/529-1384.** Admission C$4 (US$2.65) adults, C$3.50 (US$2.35) stu-dents (college), C$2 (US$1.35) students (K-12). Daily 9am–5pm; closed mid-Sept to mid-May.

The splashy new visitor center of the Atlantic Salmon Federation, sometimes called Salar's World after the main exhibit, opened in 1999 for its first full season and is dedicated to educating the public about the increasingly rare and surprisingly intriguing Atlantic salmon. Located in a bright and airy post and beam facility, the center allows visitors to get oriented through exhibits and presentations and viewing salmon through underwater windows or strolling the outdoor walkways along Chamcook Stream.

Kingsbrae Horticultural Gardens. 220 King St. ☎ **506/529-3335.** Admission C$6 (US$4) adult; C$4 (US$2.65) children, students, and seniors; free under 6. Admission fees are taxed. Daily 9am to dusk. Closed mid-Oct to mid-May.

This 27-acre public garden opened in 1998, using the former grounds of a long-gone estate. The designers incorporated the existing high hedges and trees, and have ambitiously planted open space around the mature plants. The entire project is very promising and as the plantings take root and mature it's certain to become a noted stop for garden lovers. The grounds include almost 2,000 varieties of trees, shrubs, and plants. Among the notable features: a day lily collection, an extensive rose garden, a small maze, a fully functional windmill that circulates water through the two duck ponds, and a children's garden with an elaborate Victorian-mansion playhouse.

With views over the lush lawns to the bay below, the on-site **Garden Cafe** is a pleasant place to stop for lunch. Try the thick, creamy seafood chowder and one of the focaccia bread sandwiches (C$5.75/US$3.85).

○ **Ministers Island Historic Site/Covenhoven.** Route 127 (northeast of St. Andrews), Chamcook. ☎ **506/529-5081** (recorded tour schedule). C$5 (US$3.35) adult, C$2.50 (US$1.65) youth (13–18), under 12 free. Closed mid-October to May 31.

This rugged, 500-plus-acre island is linked to the mainland by a sandbar at low tide, and the 2-hour tours are scheduled around the tides. (Call for upcoming times.) You'll meet your tour guide on the mainland side, then drive your car out convoy-style across the ocean floor to the magical island estate created in 1890 by Sir William Van Horne.

Van Horne was president of the Canadian Pacific Railway, and the person behind the extension of the rail line to St. Andrews. He then built a sandstone mansion (Covenhoven) with some 50 rooms (including 17 bedrooms), a circular bathhouse (where he indulged his passion for landscape painting), and one of Canada's largest and most impressive barns. The estate also features heated greenhouses, which produced grapes and mushrooms, along with peaches that weighed up to 2 pounds each. When Van Horne was home in Montréal, he had fresh dairy products and vegetables shipped daily (by rail, of course) so that he could enjoy fresh produce year-round.

One gathers that the discriminating Van Horne might not have been the most accommodating of bosses. He required that the entire dairy barn, including each cow, be washed down after every milking. And he demanded that a fresh coat of sawdust be spread over the barn floor each night, with the Van Horne coat of arms meticulously stamped in it by the staff.

WHERE TO STAY

St. Andrews offers an abundance of fine B&Bs and inns. Those traveling on a budget should head for the **Picket Fence Motel** (102 Reed Ave., ☎ **506/529-8985**). This trim and tidy motel is near the Algonquin golf course and within walking distance of the village center. Rooms are C$55 to C$65 (US$37 to US$43) in peak season.

The Algonquin. 184 Adolphus St., St. Andrews, NB E0G 2X0. ☎ **800/441-1414** or 506/529-8823. Fax 506/529-7162. 250 units. MINIBAR TV TEL. May–Oct: C$99–C$239 (US$66–US$159) double. Meal package C$45 (US$30) per person per day. Other packages available. Nov–Apr: (limited operations with 51 units) C$85–C$145 (US$57–US$97), including continental breakfast. AE, CB, DC, DISC, ER, MC, V. Pets accepted, first floor only.

The Algonquin's distinguished pedigree dates back to 1889, when it first opened its doors to wealthy vacationers seeking respite from city heat. The original structure was destroyed by fire in 1914, but the surviving annexes were rebuilt in sumptuous Tudor style; in 1993 an architecturally sympathetic addition was built across the road, linked by a gatehouse-inspired bridge.

The red-tile-roofed resort commands one's attention through its sheer size and aristocratic bearing (not to mention through its kilt-wearing, bagpipe-playing staff). The inn is several long blocks from the water's edge, but it perches on the brow of a hill and affords panoramic bay views from the second-floor roof garden and many guest rooms. The rooms were recently redecorated and are comfortable and tasteful; all have coffeemakers and hair dryers. One caveat: The hotel happily markets itself to bus tours and conferences, and if your timing is unfortunate you might feel a bit overwhelmed and small.

Dining: The resort's main dining room is one of the more enjoyable spots in town—it's often bustling (great people-watching) and the kitchen produces some surprisingly creative meals. Informal dining options include The Library (just off the main lobby) and the downstairs lounge. Further afield, the Italian bistro food at the Algonquin Clubhouse on the resort's golf course is well worth the drive—try the seared salmon with cilantro corn salsa served over pasta.

Amenities: The Algonquin's new par 72 golf course (☎ **506/529-7142** for tee times) is scheduled to open in July 2000. Until then, the first 9 "seaside" holes are available for play. Greens fees are C$35 (US$23) for 9 holes and C$50 (US$33) for 18 holes.

Other facilities include two outdoor tennis courts, an outdoor heated pool, bike rentals, a beauty salon, a gift shop, a game room, a squash court, a fitness center, a locker room, saunas, and an indoor whirlpool. The resort also features a shuttle to the Saint John airport (charge), daily children's programs, valet parking, safe-deposit boxes, baby-sitting, laundry, dry cleaning, and massage at the health club.

✪ **Kingsbrae Arms.** 219 King St., St. Andrews, NB E0G 2X0. ☎ **506/529-1897.** Fax 506/529-1197. www.kingsbrae.com. E-mail: kingbrae@nb.aibn.com. 8 units. A/C TV TEL. Off-season midweek C$325–C$475 (US$217–US$317) double, including breakfast; weekends, holidays, and peak season C$475–C$625 (US$317–US$417), including breakfast and dinner. 2-night minimum; 3 nights July and Aug weekends. 5% room service charge additional. MC, V. Children 10 and up. Pets allowed with advance permission.

Kingsbrae Arms, part of the upscale Relais & Chateau network, is a five-star inn informed by an upscale European elegance. Kingsbrae brings to mind a rustic elegance—a bit of Tuscany, perhaps, melded with a genteel London townhouse. Located atop King Street, this intimate inn occupies an 1897 manor house, where the furnishings—from the gracefully worn leather chesterfield to the Delft-tiled fireplace—all seem to have a story to tell. The grand, shingled home, built by prosperous jade merchants, occupies 1 acre, all of which has been well employed. A heated pool sits amid rose gardens at the foot of a lawn, and immediately next door is the 27-acre Kingsbrae Horticultural Gardens (some guest rooms have wonderful views of the gardens; others, a panoramic sweep of the bay). Guests will feel pampered here, with 325-thread-count sheets, plush robes, VCRs, and hair dryers in all rooms, and a complete guest-services suite stocked with complimentary snacks and refreshments. Five rooms have Jacuzzis; all have gas fireplaces.

Dining: Guests enjoy a four-course meal around a stately table in the dining room during peak season. (The dining room is not open to the public.) One meal is offered nightly, and the cuisine is new Canadian. Entrees might include beef tenderloin with buttered noodles or frenched rack of lamb with garlic polenta.

Amenities: The inn can arrange for baby-sitting, dry cleaning, and laundry; an afternoon tea is served. In addition to the heated pool, guests can avail themselves of the Algonquin's facilities (extra charge) a short stroll away.

Salty Towers. 340 Water St., St. Andrews, NB E5B 2R3. ☎ **506/529-4585.** E-mail: steeljm@nbnet.nb.ca. 17 units (12 shared bathrooms). C$45 (US$30) double with shared bathroom, C$65 (US$43) double with private bathroom. V.

Behind this somewhat staid Queen Anne home on Water Street lurks the soul of a wild eccentric. Salty Towers is equal parts turn-of-the-century home, 1940s boarding house, and 1960s commune. Overseen with great affability by artist-naturalist Jamie Steel, this is a world of wondrous clutter—from the early European landscapes with overly wrought gilt frames to exuberant modern pieces. Think Addams-Family meets Timothy Leary.

The guest rooms lack the visual chaos of the public spaces and are nicely done up, furnished with eclectic antiques and old magazines. (Especially nice is Room 2, with hand-sponged walls and a private sitting area surrounded by windows.) The top floor is largely given over to single rooms; these are a bargain at C$30 (US$20) with shared bathroom. Guests have full run of the large if sometimes confused kitchen. Don't be surprised to find musicians strumming on the porch, artists lounging in the living room, and others of uncertain provenance swapping jokes around the stove. If that sounds pretty good to you, this is your place.

☼ The Windsor House. 132 Water St., St. Andrews, NB E0G 2X0. ☎ **888/890-9463** or 506/529-3330. Fax 506/529-4063. 6 units. TV TEL. Summer C$225–C$300 (US$150–US$200), off-season C$150–C$250 (US$100–US$167). AE, DC, ER, MC, V. Restaurant closed Jan–Apr.

Located in the middle of the village on busy Water Street, the lovely Windsor House offers guests a quiet retreat amid lustrous antiques in a top-rate restoration. The three-story home was originally built in 1798 by a ship captain. It's served almost every purpose since then, including stagecoach stop, oil company office, and family home, before reopening its doors as a luxury inn in 1999. The new owners—Jay Remer and Greg Cohane—spent more than 2 years and C$2 million renovating the home, and their attention to detail shows. The rooms are furnished with antiques (no reproductions) far above what one normally expects at an inn; Remer spent 5 years at Sotheby's in New York and knows what he's looking for. All of the rooms are superbly appointed, most with detailed etchings of animals adorning the walls. The best two are the suites on the third floor, with peaceful sitting areas, exposed beams, Asian carpets, handsome armoires, and limited views of the bay. (Both also have clawfoot tubs and glass shower stalls.) The basement features an appealing terracotta-floored billiard room; the first-floor pub is the perfect spot for an early evening libation or after-dinner drink.

WHERE TO DINE

The Gables. 143 Water St. ☎ **506/529-3440.** Reservations not needed. Main courses, breakfast C$3.95–C$6.95 (US$2.65–US$4.65), lunch and dinner C$7.50–C$17.95 (US$5–US$11.95). MC, V. Daily 8am–11pm. Closed Nov to April 15. SEAFOOD/PUB FARE.

This informal eatery is located in a trim home with prominent gables fronting Water Street, but you enter down a narrow alley where sky and water views suddenly blossom through a soaring window from a spacious outside deck. Inside, expect a bright and lively spot with a casual maritime decor; outside there's a plastic-porch-furniture informality. Breakfast is served during peak season, with homemade baked goods and rosemary potatoes. Lunch and dinner options include burgers, steaks, and seafood entrees like breaded haddock and a lobster clubhouse—a chopped lobster salad served with cheese, cucumber, lettuce, and tomato. Margaritas and sangria are available by the pitcher. The view tends to outclass the menu, but those ordering simpler fare will be satisfied.

Lighthouse Restaurant. Patrick St. (drive eastward on Water St. toward Indian Point; look for signs). ☎ **506/529-3082.** Reservations helpful. Lunch C$5.50–C$11 (US$3.65–US$7.35), dinner C$10.50–C$34 (US$7–US$23); most C$16–C$20 (US$10.65–US$13). AE, DC, MC, V. Daily 11:30am–2pm and 5–9pm. Closed mid-Oct to mid-May. SEAFOOD.

Located on the water at the eastern edge of the village, this spot rewards diners with a great view while they enjoy fresh-from-the-boat seafood. It's a bustling, popular place that seems to attract families and those who crave lobster. Look for a good selection of fish and lobster served with little fanfare or pomp. The menu includes sautéed scallops, seafood pasta, and lobster prepared any number of ways. The surf-and-turf specials (including filet mignon and lobster tail for C$34/US$23) are especially popular. Children's meals are offered at both lunch and dinner.

✪ The Windsor House. 132 Water St., ☎ **506/529-3330.** Reservations recommended. Lunch C$9–C$12 (US$6–US$8), dinner of 3 courses C$55 (US$37), 5 courses C$75 (US$50). AE, DC, ER, MC, V. Daily 11:30am–2pm and 6–9pm. Closed Mon–Tues during spring and fall; closed Jan–April. FRENCH/CONTINENTAL.

Guests are seated in one of two intimate dining rooms on the first floor of this historic home (see "Where to Stay" above). The setting is formal, the guests are dressed with a bit more starch than you'll find elsewhere in town, and the service is excellent. Lunches are somewhat less formal and very delectable, and include offerings like spinach and wild mushroom crepes, and smoked salmon with a Brie soufflé and pear chutney. At dinner, you'll choose either a three-course or five-course meal (you can mix and match the minor courses—two appetizers, or maybe save room for a double-barrel dessert). Appetizers include a country paté with toasted pumpkin seeds, and a seafood chowder with lobster, shrimp, and scallops. Main courses include dishes such as rack of lamb, seafood baked in phyllo, and a breast of chicken topped with lobster sauce and truffles. Desserts are equally excellent, ranging from the traditional custard with caramel sauce to lime mousse and rum butter cream sandwiched in a coconut biscuit.

4 Grand Manan Island

Geologically rugged, profoundly peaceable, and indisputably remote, this handsome island of 2,800 year-round residents is a 90-minute ferry ride from Blacks Harbour, southeast of St. George. For adventurous travelers Grand Manan is a much-prized destination and a highlight of their vacation. Yet the island remains a mystifying puzzle for others who fail to be smitten by its rough-edged charm. "Either this is your kind of place, or it isn't," said one island resident. "There's no in between." The only way to find out is to visit.

Grand Manan is a special favorite among serious birders and enthusiasts of novelist Willa Cather. Hiking the island's noted trails, don't be surprised to come across knots of very quiet people peering intently through binoculars. These are the birders. Nearly 300 different species of birds either nest here or stop by the island during their long migrations, and it's a good place to add to one's life list, with birds ranging from bald eagles to puffins (you'll need to sign up for a boat tour for the latter).

Willa Cather kept a cottage here and wrote many of her most beloved books while living on the island. Her fans are as easy to spot as the birders, say locals. In fact, islanders are still talking about a Willa Cather conference some summers ago, when 40 participants wrapped themselves in sheets and danced around a bonfire during the summer solstice. "Cather people, they're a wild breed," one innkeeper intoned gravely to me.

ESSENTIALS

GETTING THERE   Grand Manan is connected to Blacks Harbour on the mainland via frequent ferry service in summer. **Coastal Transport ferries** (☎ **506/662-3724**), each capable of hauling 60 cars, depart from the mainland and the island every 2 hours between 7:30am and 5:30pm during July and August; a ferry makes three to four trips the rest of the year. The round-trip fare is C$8.75 (US$5.85) per passenger (C$4.40/US$2.95 ages 5 to 12), C$26.20 (US$17.45) per car. Boarding the ferry on the mainland is free; tickets are purchased when you leave the island.

No reservations are accepted (although you can buy an advance ticket for the first trip each day off the island); get in line early to secure a spot. A good strategy for departing from Blacks Harbour is to bring a picnic lunch, arrive an hour or two early, put your car in line, and head to the grassy waterfront park adjacent to the wharf. It's an attractive spot; there's even an island to explore at low tide.

VISITOR INFORMATION   The island's **Visitor Information Centre,** P.O. Box 193, Grand Manan, NB E0G 2M0 (☎ **506/662-3442**) is open daily in summer in the town of Grand Harbor. It's beneath the museum, across from the elementary school. If the center is closed, ask around at island stores or inns for one of the free island maps published by the **Grand Manan Tourism Association,** which includes a listing of key island phone numbers.

EXPLORING THE ISLAND

Start your explorations before you arrive. As you come abreast of the island aboard the ferry, head to the starboard side. You'll soon see **Seven Day's Work** in the rocky cliffs of Whale's Cove, where seven layers of hardened lava and sill (intrusive igneous rock) have come together in a sort of geological Dagwood sandwich.

You can begin to open the Japanese puzzle box that is local geology at the **Grand Manan Museum** (☎ **506/662-3524**) in Grand Harbor, one of three villages on the island's eastern shore. The museum's geology exhibit, located in the basement, offers pointers about what to look for as you roam the island. Birders will enjoy the Allan Moses collection upstairs, which features 230 stuffed and mounted birds in glass cases. The museum also has an impressive lighthouse lens from the Gannet Rock Lighthouse, and a collection of stuff that's washed ashore from the frequent shipwrecks. The museum is open mid-June to October from Monday to Saturday 10:30am to 4:30pm, Sunday 1 to 5pm. Admission is C$2 (US$1.35) adult, C$1 (US65¢) seniors and students, and under 12 free.

This relatively flat and compact island is perfect for exploring by **bike;** the only stretches to avoid are some of the faster, less scenic segments of Route 776. All the side roads offer superb biking. Especially nice is the cross-island road (paved) to Dark Harbor, where you'll find a few cabins, dories, and salmon pens. The route is wild and hilly at times but offers a memorable descent to the ocean on the island's west side.

Bike rentals are available at **Adventure High** (☎ **506/662-3563**) in North Head, not far from the ferry. (Day-trippers might consider leaving their car at Blacks Harbour and exploring by bike before returning on the last ferry.) Adventure High also offers **sea kayak tours** of the island's shores for those who prefer a cormorant's-eye view of the impressive cliffs. Bikes rent for C$20 (US$13) per day, C$18 (US$12) for a half-day. Kayak tours run from C$35 (US$23) for a 2-hour sunset tour to C$95 (US$63) for a full-day excursion.

If Grand Manan seems too crowded and hectic (unlikely, that), you can find more solitude at **White Head Island.** Drive to Ingalls Head (follow Ingalls Head Road from Grand Harbor) to catch the half-hour ferry to this rocky island, home to about 200 people. On the island, you can walk along the shore to the lighthouse between Battle Beach and Sandy Cove. The ferry holds 10 cars, is free of charge, and sails up to 10 times daily in summer.

HIKING

Numerous hiking trails lace the island, and they offer a popular diversion throughout the summer. Trails can be found just about everywhere, but most are a matter of local knowledge. Don't hesitate to ask at your inn or the tourist information center, or to ask anyone you might meet on the street. *A Hiking Guide to New Brunswick* (Goose Lane Editions, ☎ 506/450-4251) lists 12 hikes with maps; this handy book is often sold on the ferry.

The most accessible clusters of trails are at the island's northern and southern tips. Head north up Whistle Road to Whistle Beach, and you'll find both the Northwestern Coastal Trail and the Seven Day's Work Trail, both of which track along the rocky shoreline. Near the low lighthouse and towering radio antennae at Southwest Head (follow Route 776 to the end), trails radiate out along cliffs topped with scrappy forest; the views are remarkable when the fog's not in.

WHALE WATCHING & BOAT TOURS

A fine way to experience island ecology is to mosey offshore. Several outfitters offer complete nature tours, providing a nice sampling of the world above and beneath the sea. **Island Coast Boat Tours** (☎ 506/662-8181) sets out for 4- to 5-hour expeditions in search of whales and birds. On an excursion you might see minke, finback, or humpback whales, along with exotic birds like puffins and phalaropes. The cost is C$44 (US$29) adult, C$40 (US$27) seniors, and C$22 (US$15) children. **SeaView Adventures** (☎ 800/586-1922 in Canada or 506/662-3211) offers 3½-hour educational tours with a unique twist: Divers provide a live underwater video feed to an onboard monitor. Prices are C$41 (US$27) adult, C$38 (US$25) seniors, and C$24 (US$16) children. **Sea Watch Tours** (☎ 506/662-8552) runs 5-hour excursions with whales guaranteed aboard a 42-foot vessel with canopy. The rate is C$44 (US$29) adult, and C$10–C$34 (US$7–US$23) per child, depending on age.

WHERE TO STAY

Anchorage Provincial Park (☎ 506/662-7022) has 100 campsites scattered about forest and field. There's a small beach and a hiking trail on the property, and it's well situated for exploring the southern part of the island. It's very popular midsummer; call before you board the ferry to ask about campsite availability. Sites are C$24 (US$16) with hookups for RVs, C$21.50 (US$14) for a tent.

Compass Rose Inn. North Head, Grand Manan, NB E0G 2M0. ☎ 506/662-8570 or 514/458-2607 (Nov–Apr). 7 units. C$79–C$89 (US$53–US$59) double, including full breakfast. MC, V. Closed Nov–Apr.

The shipshape Compass Rose Inn occupies two small but historic homes overlooking the waterfront. All rooms have a water view and are tastefully decorated in a light country style. Among the best rooms: Calico, a corner room with couch and pine floors, and great windows to watch the ferry come and go.

Dining: Breakfast, lunch, and dinner are served in a bright and cheerful dining room overlooking the harbor. Seafood is the specialty. Dishes include coquilles St.

Jacques, sautéed scallops with rosemary, and pork tenderloin with wild blueberry chutney. Open daily for dinner 5:30 to 8pm; entree prices are C$13 to C$19 (US$9 to US$13).

✪ **Inn at Whale Cove Cottages.** Whistle Rd. (P.O. Box 233), North Head, Grand Manan, NB E0G 2M0. ☎ **506/662-3181.** 3 units, 4 cottages. C$85 (US$57) double, including full breakfast; cottages rent by the week only, C$500–C$600 (US$333–US$400). MC, V. Closed Nov–Apr. Pets accepted.

The Inn at Whale Cove is a delightful, family-run compound set in a grassy meadow overlooking a quiet and picturesque cove. The original building is a cozy farmhouse that dates to 1816. It's been restored rustically with a nice selection of simple country antiques. The guest rooms are comfortable (Sally's Attic has a small deck and a large view); the living room has a couple years' worth of good reading and a welcoming fireplace. The cottages are scattered about the property, and they vary from one to four bedrooms. The 10-acre grounds, especially the path down to the quiet coveside beach, are wonderful to explore.

Dining: Innkeeper Laura Buckley received her culinary training in Toronto, and she demonstrates a deft touch with local ingredients. The menu might include bouillabaisse, seafood risotto, salmon in phyllo, or pork tenderloin with a green peppercorn sauce. Dinner is served nightly from 6 to 8:30pm, and entrees are priced from C$11 to C$20 (US$7 to US$13). On Saturday night a full dinner is served with one seating at 7pm.

Shorecrest Lodge. North Head, Grand Manan, NB E0G 2M0. ☎ **506/662-3216.** E-mail: shorcres@nbnet.nb.ca. 10 units (2 with shared bathroom). C$65–C$99 (US$43–US$66) double, including continental breakfast. MC, V. Closed Dec–March.

This century-old inn is a fine place to put your feet up and unwind. Located just a few hundred yards from the ferry, the inn is nicely decorated with a mix of modern furniture and eclectic country antiques. Most of the guest rooms have private bathrooms (a rarity for Grand Manan). The best is Room 8 with burgundy leather chairs and a great harbor view. Kids like the spacious TV room in the back, which also has games and a library that's strong in local natural history.

Dining: The homey country-style dining room has a fireplace and hardwood floors, and a menu that includes local fresh seafood and filet mignon. It's open daily from 5 to 9pm during peak season; hours are limited during the shoulder season. Main courses are priced C$17 to C$25 (US$11 to US$17), with some less expensive specials from time to time.

WHERE TO DINE

Options for dining out aren't exactly extravagant on Grand Manan. The three inns listed above offer appetizing meals and decent value.

In the mood for a dare? Try walking into **North Head Bakery** (☎ 506/662-8862) and walking out without buying anything. *It cannot be done.* This superb bakery has used traditional baking methods and whole grains since it opened in 1990. Breads made daily include a crusty, seven-grain Saint John Valley bread and a delightful egg-and-butter bread. Nor should the chocolate-chip cookies be overlooked. The bakery is on Route 776 on the left when you're heading south from the ferry.

For a ready-made picnic, detour to **Cove Cuisine** at the Inn at Whale Cove (☎ 506/662-3181). Laura Buckley offers a limited but tasty selection of "new traditional" fixin's, like hummus, tabouli, and curried chicken salad to go. The inn is on Whistle Road, which forks off Route 776 near the bakery.

5 Saint John

Centered on a sizeable commercial harbor, Saint John is New Brunswick's largest city, and the center of much of the province's industry. Spread over a low hill, the downtown boasts wonderfully elaborate Victorian flourishes on the rows of commercial buildings. (Be sure to look high along the cornices to appreciate the intricate brickwork.) A handful of impressive mansions lord over side streets, their interiors a forest of intricate wood carving—appropriate for the timber barons who built them.

There's a certain industrial grittiness to Saint John; some find this raw and unappealing, and others find in it a certain ragged raffishness. It all depends on your outlook. Just don't expect a tidy garden city with lots of neat homes. Saint John's got a surfeit of brick architecture in various states of repair, and from throughout the downtown you'll get glimpses of industry: large shipping terminals, oil storage facilities, paper mills, of the sort that was so popular with the Ashcan artists. (A 1978 book on New Brunswick put it diplomatically: "Saint John's heavy industries ensure that the city is not famed for beauty, but the setting is magnificent.")

Don't let this put you off—make the effort to detour from the highway to downtown. And it does take some effort—the traffic engineers have been very mischievous here. When you finally arrive, you'll discover an intriguing place to stroll around for an afternoon while awaiting the ferry to Digby, to grab a delicious bite to eat, or to break up village-hopping with an urban overnight. The streets often bustle with everyone from skateboarders sporting nose rings to impeccably coiffed dowagers shopping at the public market.

One final note: Saint John is always spelled out, just like that. It's never abbreviated as St. John. That's to keep mail aimed for St. John's in Newfoundland from ending up here, and vice versa. Locals will be quick to correct you if you err.

ESSENTIALS

GETTING THERE   Saint John is located on Route 1. It's 107 kilometers (66 miles) from the U.S. border at St. Stephens, and 424 kilometers (265 miles) from Halifax, NS.

Year-round **ferry service** connects Saint John to Digby, NS. See "Exploring New Brunswick" at the beginning of this chapter for information. Saint John's airport has regular flights to Toronto, Halifax, and other Canadian points; contact **Air Canada** (☎ 800/776-3000 in the U.S., 800/565-3940 in the Maritimes, or 506/632-1500) or **Canadian Airlines** (☎ 800/426-7000 in the U.S. or 800/665-1177 in Canada) for more information. Since September 1999 the airport has levied a C$10 (US$7) fee on all departing passengers to finance improvements.

VISITOR INFORMATION   Saint John has three visitor information centers. Arriving from the west, look for a contemporary triangular building just off Route 1 (open mid-May to mid-October), where you'll find a trove of information and brochures (☎ 506/658-2940). A smaller seasonal information center is located inside the observation building overlooking the Reversing Falls on Route 100 (☎ 506/658-2937).

If you've already made your way downtown, look for the **City Centre Tourist Information Centre** (☎ 888/364-4444 or 506/658-2855) inside Market Square, a downtown shopping mall just off the waterfront. Find the info center by entering the square at street level at the corner of St. Patrick and Water Streets. During peak season (mid-June to mid-September) the center is open daily from 9am to 8pm. The rest of the year it's open daily 9:30am to 6pm.

Saint John

Underground Concourse

(i) Visitor Information Center

0 — 1/4 Mi
0 — .25 Km

Accommodations
Earle of Leinster Inn **8**
Parkerhouse Inn & Restaurant **7**
Hilton Saint John **2**

Dining
Beatly and the Beastro **6**
Billy's Seafood Co. **2**
Il Fornello **3**
Incredible Edibles **5**
Taco Pico **4**

EXPLORING SAINT JOHN

If the weather's cooperative, start by wandering around near the waterfront. The Visitor and Convention Bureau has published three **walking tour brochures** that offer plenty of history and architectural trivia. Saint John is noted for the odd and interesting gargoyles and sculpted heads that adorn the brick and stone 19th-century buildings downtown. If you have time for only one tour, I'd opt for "Prince William's Walk," an hour-long, self-guided tour of the impressive commercial buildings. Request the free tour brochures at the Market Square information center.

Try to end your walk at the **Loyalist Burial Ground** (across from King's Square), which is an especially attractive spot to wander while reading the old headstones, or simply to sit and rest your feet. The cemetery dates to 1784 but was recently renovated—note the new beaver fountain, symbolic of the town's hardworking citizens.

If the weather's disagreeable, head indoors. Over the past decade, Saint John has been busy linking its downtown malls and shops with an elaborate network of underground and overhead pedestrian walkways, dubbed **"The Inside Connection."** It's not just for shopping—two major hotels, the provincial museum, the city library, the city market, the sports arena, and the aquatic center are all part of the network.

Canada Games Aquatic Centre. 50 Union St. ☎ **506/658-4715.** Admission C$5 (US$3.35) adults; C$4 (US$2.65) seniors, students, and children; C$15 (US$10) family. Mon–Thurs 6am–10pm, Fri 6am–8pm, Sat 6:30am–6pm, Sun 11am–6pm. Parking next door, C$1 (US 65¢) per hour.

The gleaming and modern Aquatic Centre was built smack downtown in 1985 for the Canada Games. It remains a remarkably popular destination for exercise and recreation, and it's open to the public most hours all week long. Facilities include an eight-lane Olympic-size pool, warm-up and leisure pools, water slides, rope swings, whirlpools, and saunas. Also available: weight and exercise rooms (extra charge).

✪ **Old City Market.** 47 Charlotte St. ☎ **506/658-2820.** Mon–Thurs 7:30am–6pm, Fri 7:30am–7pm, Sat 7:30am–5pm.

Hungry travelers venture here at their peril! This spacious, bustling, and bright marketplace is crammed with vendors hawking meat, fresh seafood, cheeses, flowers, baked goods, and bountiful fresh produce. You can even sample dulse, a snack of dried seaweed from the Bay of Fundy. (One traveler has compared the experience to licking a wharf.) The market was built in 1876, and it has been a center of commerce for the city ever since. Note the construction of the roof—local lore says it resembles an inverted ship because it was made by boat builders who didn't know how to build anything else. And watch for the small, enduring traces of tradition: The handsome iron gates at either end have been in place since 1880, and the loud bell is rung daily by the Deputy Market Clerk, who signals the opening and closing of the market. A number of vendors offer meals to go, and there's a bright seating area in an enclosed terrace on the market's south side.

Loyalist House. 120 Union St. ☎ **506/652-3590.** C$3 (US$2) adult, C$1 (US65¢) children, C$7 (US$4.65) family. Daily 10am–5pm in July and August; Mon–Fri only in May and June. By appt. only mid-Sept to Apr.

A mandatory destination for serious antique buffs, this stately Georgian home was built in 1817 for the Merritt family, who were wealthy Loyalists from Rye, New York. Inside is an extraordinary collection of furniture dating from before 1833, most pieces of which were original to the house and have never left. Especially notable are the extensive holdings of Duncan Phyfe Sheraton furniture and a rare piano-organ combination. Other unusual detailing includes the doors steamed and bent to fit into the curved sweep of the stairway, and the carvings on the wooden chair rails. Tours last 30 to 45 minutes, depending on the number of questions you muster.

✪ **New Brunswick Museum.** Market Square. ☎ **506/643-2360.** Admission C$6 (US$4) adult, C$4.75 (US$3.15) senior, C$3.25 (US$2.15) student and youth ages 4–18, C$13 (US$8.65) families. Mon–Fri 9am–9pm, Sat 10am–6pm, Sun noon–5pm.

The New Brunswick Museum opened in modern, downtown quarters in 1996, and is an excellent stop for anyone in the least curious about the province's natural or cultural history. The collections are displayed on three open floors, and they offer a nice mix of traditional artifacts and quirky objects. (Among the more memorable items is a frightful looking "permanent wave" machine from a 1930s beauty parlor.) The exhaustive exhibits include the complete interior of Sullivan's Bar (where longshoremen used to slake their thirst a few blocks away), a massive section of a ship frame, a wonderful geological exhibit, and even a sporty white Bricklin from a failed New Brunswick automobile manufacturing venture in the mid-1970s. Allow at least 2 hours to enjoy these eclectic and uncommonly well-displayed exhibits.

OUTDOOR PURSUITS

Irving Nature Park. Sand Cove Rd. ☎ **506/632-7777.** Free admission, tours. Open daylight hours; information booth staffed daily May–Oct.

Located along the coast across the Saint John River (take Exit 107 off Route 1 and follow Bleury Street to Sand Cove Road), the Irving Nature Park consists of 600 dramatic coastal acres, where as many as 240 species of birds have been spotted. Soft wood-chipped trails and marsh boardwalks provide access to a lovely forest and wild, salty seascapes. The observation tower on the "Squirrel Trail" gives a fine vantage of the park and its mudflats, where migrating sandpipers devour shrimp for a week to double their weight before flying 4 days nonstop to Surinam. Seals throng the park in mid-June and mid-October and are so thick on the rocks that they've been described as "a great gray noisy carpet." Irving Nature Park can get very busy—there are some 125,000 visitors a year—and Sundays are the most popular. Call beforehand to ask about the excellent tours.

Reversing Falls. Route 100. ☎ **506/658-2937.** Viewing platform free; explanatory film C$1.50 (US$1). Open daylight hours year-round, but best at low or high tide. Call for the tidal schedule.

Just west of downtown is Reversing Falls, located within an impressive, rocky gorge. Owing to the massive tide hereabouts, rapids, low waterfalls, and large, slurping whirlpools flow one way through the gorge during one tide, then reverse during the opposite tide. It's a sometimes dramatic sight in a dramatic location, but few publicity photos or descriptions include one important caveat: The gorge is all but overwhelmed by a huge and often stinky paper mill literally yards upriver. There's also an active train trestle and a busy highway spanning the gorge directly over the falls, which are drowned out by the constant clang and hum of industry and trade. If you don't come expecting wild and brutish nature, you're less likely to be disappointed.

There are several ways of observing this natural spectacle. You can scramble down the wooden steps to a park along the river's edge, or scramble up atop a rooftop viewing platform (free). More sedentary souls can try **The Falls Restaurant** (☎ **506/635-1999**), which is peaceful in that chirpy, elevator-music kind of way. Just remember that you're paying a premium for the view—not the unexciting seafood. My recommendation: If you can't get a table overlooking the falls, take a look out the full-length windows and move on.

Across the river is **Fallsview Park** (turn left on Douglas Avenue, then left again on Fallsview Avenue). Here you'll get a duck's-eye view of the river from this small park directly across from the paper mill.

Departing from a narrow cove at Fallsview Park are the **Reversing Falls Jet Boat Rides** (☎ **506/634-8987**), which offer fun, fast boat trips through the falls at all tides. The always-breezy, sometimes-damp trip takes 20 minutes and costs C$25 (US$17) adult, C$20 (US$13) child, which includes use of a raincoat. Two specially designed boats—one offering a more heart-pounding "thrill ride"—depart several times daily from the park. Reservations are recommended during peak season.

Rockwood Park. Lake Drive South. ☎ **506/658-2829.** Free admission; fees charged for various activities. Interpretation Centre open daily 8am–10pm late May to early Sept.

The footpaths attract walkers and joggers to this 2,200-acre urban preserve of lakes, forest, and rocky hills. But there are also swimming at sandy lake beaches, golf at the 18-hole municipal course (C$24/US$16 greens fees), picnic areas, a campground, and a small zoo with 38 species of exotic animals (including six species of monkeys, all on the endangered species list). Boat rentals at Fisher Lakes include canoes and kayaks (from C$4/US$2.65 per hour.) There's also an aquatic driving range, where duffers practice their swings by hitting floating golf balls into a lake (C$6/US$4 for a large bucket of balls), which are later harvested by boat. The park, located just 5 minutes' drive north of downtown, is especially popular on weekends.

WHERE TO STAY

Budget travelers should head to **Manawagonish Road** for lower-priced motels. Unlike many other motel strips, which tend to be notably unlovely, Manawagonish Road is reasonably attractive. It winds along a high ridge of residential homes west of town, with views out to the Bay of Fundy. It's about a 10-minute drive into downtown.

Among the motels here are the **Fairport Motel** (1360 Manawagonish Rd.; ☎ **800/251-6158** or 506/672-9700), with its home-cooked-meals; the **Seacoast Motel** (1441 Manawagonish Rd.; ☎ **800/541-0277** or 506/635-8700), where the rooms have sweeping views; and the clean, well-lit rooms and cabins at **Balmoral Court Motel** (1284 Manawagonish Rd.; ☎ **888/463-3779** or 506/672-3019). Rates at most Manawagonish motels are approximately C$60 to C$70 (US$40 to US$47) peak season.

In-town camping is available summers at **Rockwood Park** (☎ **506/652-4050**). Some 80 sites are spread across a rocky hill; many overlook downtown, the highway, and a railyard (expect nighttime noise). RVs requesting full hookups are directed to an area resembling a parking lot, but it's quite serviceable. Other sites vary widely in privacy and scenic attributes. Rates range from C$14 (US$9) for a tent site to C$18 (US$12) for hookups. Follow signs to the park from either Exit 111 or Exit 113 off Route 1.

EXPENSIVE

Hilton Saint John. 1 Market Sq., Saint John, NB E2L 4Z6. ☎ **800/561-8282** (in Canada), 800/445-8667 (in the U.S.), or 506/693-8484. Fax 509/657-6610. www.hilton.nb.ca. E-mail: hiltonnb@nbnet.nb.ca. 197 units. A/C MINIBAR TV TEL. Summer to mid-Oct C$99–C$139 (US$66–US$93) double, off-season C$89–C$109 (US$59–US$73). AE, DC, DISC, MC, V. Free parking weekends, otherwise C$12.95 (US$8.65) per day. Pets allowed.

This 12-story waterfront hotel was built in 1984 and has the amenities one would expect from an upscale chain hotel, including coffeemakers and hair dryers in each room. It boasts the best location in Saint John, overlooking the harbor yet just steps from the rest of downtown by street or indoor walkway. Windows in all guest rooms open, a nice touch when the breeze is coming from the sea, but not when it's blowing in from the paper mill to the west. The Hilton is connected to the convention center and attracts major events; ask whether anything's scheduled before you book if you don't want to be overwhelmed by conventioneers.

Dining: The Brigantine Lounge offers light meals from 11:30am to 1am daily. For more refined fare, head to Turn of the Tide, which serves three meals daily in an understated and classical harborside setting. Entrees include creatively prepared steaks, pheasant, and salmon (C$17.95/US$11.95 to C$28.95/US$19.30).

Amenities: Small indoor pool, fitness room, Jacuzzi, sauna, indoor parking, game room, business center, concierge, laundry, baby-sitting, safe-deposit boxes, and 24-hour room service.

Homeport Historic Bed & Breakfast. 80 Douglas Ave., Saint John, NB E2K 1E4. ☎ **888/678-7678** or 506/672-7255. www.homeport.nb.ca. E-mail: stay@homeport.nb.ca. 5 units. A/C TV TEL. C$79–C$125 (US$53–US$83), includes breakfast. AE, MC, V.

This architecturally impressive Italianate home sits high atop a rocky ridge on the north side of Route 1, overlooking downtown and the harbor. Built around 1858, the home opened its doors to guests in 1997, and is one of Saint John's more gracious options for overnighting. (It's the only place in the city to be awarded five stars from Canada Select.) The five rooms are furnished eclectically with furniture gleaned from area auctions and shops; all have individually controlled heat and three have clawfoot tubs. Ask for the Veranda Room; it's spacious, has fine harbor views, and gets superb afternoon sun. (I'm also partial to the pink-tiled bathroom.) The Harbour Master Suite has a small separate sitting room, which is ideal for those traveling with a child. "Come-hungry" breakfasts are served family-style around a long antique table in the formal dining room.

Inn on the Cove. 1371 Sand Cove Rd. (mailing address: P.O. Box 3113, Station B, Saint John, NB E2M 4X7). ☎ **877/257-8080** or 506/672-7799. Fax 506/635-5455. E-mail: inncove@nbnet.nb.ca. 5 units. C$95–C$165 (US$63–US$110) double peak season, C$85–C$145 (US$85–US$97) shoulder season, C$75–C$125 (US$50–US$83) off-season. Rates include full breakfast. MC, V. Children 12 and up. Small dogs allowed in kennels.

Inns like to tout celebrity connections, but the Inn on the Cove has the thinnest link to fame I've yet found: It was built by Alexander Graham Bell's *gardener.* It's in a lovely setting, on a quiet road overlooking the water about 15 minutes' drive from downtown. The Irving Nature Park is next door; guests can hike right from the inn to dramatic Sheldon's Point. The house was once a classic late Victorian, built in 1910. In the 1950s it suffered from "improvements." Architectural preservationists will wince, but the changes did make for bright, spacious rooms that take advantage of the views. Room 3 is the most expensive and has a Jacuzzi with the best bathtub view in the Maritimes. Budget traveler's tip: The least-expensive room—Room 2—has a detached private bathroom down the hall with the same view.

MODERATE

Dufferin Inn. 357 Dufferin Row, Saint John, NB E2M 2J7. ☎ **506/635-5968.** Fax 506/674-2396. E-mail: duffinn@nb.aibn.com. 6 units. C$60–C$100 (US$40–US$67) double, including breakfast. MC, V.

This handsome Queen Anne house, across the harbor from downtown near the Digby ferry, was once home to a former premier of New Brunswick, and it has fine architectural touches like a wood-lined library and splashes of stained glass. The place has a wonderfully settled air, with oak furniture and overstuffed chairs. It's especially handy for anyone planning an early-morning dash to Digby.

Dining: Guests often stay at the inn for access to the excellent dining room, which is open to the public. (Reservations encouraged.) Chef/owner Axel Begner has a deft hand in the kitchen, and he produces fine continental dishes along the lines of filet mignon stuffed with escargot, and Atlantic salmon in potato crust served with a light raspberry sauce. Meals are available à la carte or prix fixe; the better deal is the four-course fixed-price dinner, which runs C$45 to C$52 (US$30 to US$35) per person.

Earle of Leinster Inn. 96 Leinster St., Saint John, NB E2L 1J3. ☎ **506/652-3275.** 7 units. TV TEL. C$55–C$80 (US$37–US$53) double, including continental breakfast. AE, DC, ER, MC, V. Pets allowed.

For more than a decade, Lauree and Stephen Savoie have operated the Earle of Leinster, a handsome Victorian row house in a working-class neighborhood a 5-minute walk from King's Square. It's a welcoming and casual place, nothing fancy, with a kitchen for guests to make themselves at home, and a pool table and TV in the basement. The Fitzgerald and Lord Edward rooms in the main house are the most historic, with high ceilings and regal furniture. Most of the remaining rooms are in the carriage house and are a bit more motel-like, although the second-floor loft is quite spacious. (Some rooms can be musty after a rainy spell.) The bathrooms are all private, but they're also small. Added bonus: there's a free, self-serve washer and dryer, plus VCRs in all rooms and a small library of films to select from.

Parkerhouse Inn & Restaurant. 71 Sydney St., Saint John, NB E2L 2L5. ☎ **888/ 457-2520** or 506/652-5054. Fax 506/636-8076. 9 units. TV TEL. C$79–C$99 (US$53–US$66) double. AE, DC, ER, MC, V. Children 10 and up.

The Parkerhouse is a grand 1890 in-town mansion designed in high Victorian style by a wealthy timber merchant. The attention to architectural detail is above and beyond the usual, from the beveled leaded glass in the front doorway to the exquisite carved staircase of regal mahogany. Much of the downstairs is given over to a restaurant, and there's a bright sitting area fronting the street. Guest rooms are decorated in a light Victorian country style, all have robes and hair dryers, and several feature gas fireplaces. Among the best rooms are no. 5, with its sitting room, wood floors, pine armoire, and wonderful morning light; and no. 3 with maple floors, bay window, old-fashioned shutters, and a handsome birds-eye mahogany bed (alas, the bathroom is small).

Dining: One of Saint John's better restaurants—now called 71 Sydney St.—is located on the ground floor. Angle for a seat in the Victorian solarium with its mosaic floor, although the two other dining rooms are both cozy and romantic. There's also an outside deck for dining in clement weather. Dinner is served daily except Sunday, with entrees along the lines of herb-crusted lamb, striploin with garlic, and roasted Atlantic salmon (C$17.95/US$11.95 to C$22.95/US$15.30). Reservations are encouraged.

WHERE TO DINE

For lunch, don't overlook the **Old City Market,** mentioned above. With a little snooping you can turn up tasty light meals and fresh juices in the market, then enjoy your finds in the alley atrium.

Beatty and the Beastro. 60 Charlotte St. (on King's Square). ☎ **506/652-3888.** Reservations recommended weekends, and when shows are slated at the Imperial Theatre. Main courses, lunch C$5.95–C$8.95 (US$3.95–US$5.95), dinner C$16.95–C$19.95 (US$11.30–US$13.30). AE, DC, ER, MC, V. Mon–Fri 11:30am–3pm; Mon–Sat 5:30–9pm (until 10pm Fri and Sat). BISTRO/CONTINENTAL.

The small, simple, and attractive interior of this large-windowed establishment fronting King's Square features a mild European-moderne look, and is the most handsome eatery in Saint John. The service is cordial and efficient, and the meals are among the best in the city, always good, sometimes excellent. Lunch includes soups, salads, omelets, and elaborate sandwiches. At dinner the restaurant is noted for its lamb, the preparation of which varies nightly according to the chef's desire. When dessert time rolls around, be aware that both the butterscotch pie and the lemon chess pie have large local followings.

Billy's Seafood Co. Fish Market & Oyster Bar. 49–51 Charlotte St. (at City Market). ☎ **506/672-3474.** Reservations suggested. Light meals C$5.95–C$10.95 (US$3.95–US$7.30), dinner entrees C$15.95–C$28.95 (US$10.65–US$19.30). AE, DC, ER, MC, V. Mon–Thurs 11am–10pm, Fri and Sat 11am–11pm, Sun 4–10pm. SEAFOOD.

Billy Grant's restaurant off King's Square boasts a congenial staff, exceptionally fresh seafood (they sell to City Market customers by day), and slightly better prices than the more tourist-oriented waterfront seafood restaurants. The chef knows how to prepare fish without overcooking. This classy but casual restaurant is cozy and comfortable, painted a soothing deep, deep blue, with the likes of Ella Fitzgerald and Dinah Washington crooning in the background. Specialties include Atlantic salmon and the pan-fried rainbow trout. Billy's bouillabaisse is also quite good. Offerings of beef, veal, and pasta fill out the menu for those not in the mood for fish.

Il Fornello. 33 Canterbury St. ☎ **506/648-2377.** Reservations suggested. Lunch C$7–C$15 (US$5–US$10), dinner C$9–C$15 (US$6–US$10), pizza C$6–C$14 (US$4–US$9). AE, DC, ER, MC, V. Mon–Thurs 11:30am–11pm, Fri and Sat 11:30am–midnight, Sun 4–10pm. ITALIAN.

Il Fornello is part of a small chain (most restaurants are in Toronto), and owner Paul Grannan has done a nice job converting an old printing office into a dramatic setting for reliable Italian fare. It's housed in a soaring, two-story space, anchored downstairs by a beautiful bar topped with polished red granite. Guests sit in austerely handsome chairs around lustrous wooden tabletops. You can "build your own" pasta by picking shape and sauce, along with add-ins. The same's true for the wood-fired pizza. Or select from a handful of traditional entrees like veal alla panna or chicken Asiago.

Incredible Edibles. 42 Princess St. ☎ **506/633-7554.** Reservations helpful on weekends. Main courses, lunch C$8.25–C$11.50 (US$5.50–US$7.65), dinner C$10.50–C$23.95 (US$7–US$15.95). Daily 11am–11pm. ECLECTIC.

This is another fine Saint John restaurant with a regrettably cutesy name (see Beatty and the Beastro, above). Located on the first floor of the Brodie Building a block off King St., this relaxed and casual spot has three cozy dining rooms (two nonsmoking), high tin ceilings, mix-and-match seating, and little sand-and-rock Zen gardens on each table to while away the time. The menu is appealingly eclectic. Lunch ranges from omelets to pizza and pad thai. At dinner, there's roasted salmon, prime rib with Yorkshire pudding, and a pineapple curry with prawns and a heap of mussels. Among the more popular dishes: pasta with a white clam sauce. The service is friendly, and the food consistently good.

Taco Pico. 96 Germain St. ☎ **506/633-8492.** Reservations suggested on weekends. Main courses C$7.95–C$16.95 (US$5.30–US$11.30); same menu lunch and dinner. AE, MC, V. Mon–Sat 10am–10pm, closed Sun. LATINO.

This worker-owned cooperative is owned and run by a group of Guatemalans and their friends. It's bright, festive, and just a short stroll off King Street. The restaurant has developed a devoted local following since it opened in 1994, and features a menu that's a notch above the usually dreary Canadian adaptations of Mexican or Latin American fare. Among the most reliably popular dishes are *pepian* (a spicy beef stew with chayote), garlic shrimp, and shrimp taco with potatoes, peppers, and cheese. There's also a good selection of fresh juices.

SAINT JOHN AFTER DARK

The best entertainment destination in town is the **Imperial Theatre** (☎ **506/ 674-4100**) on Kings Square. Not always because of the acts that appear here, but because the performances are in what the *Toronto Globe and Mail* called the "most beautifully restored theatre in Canada." The theater originally opened in 1913 and hosted performances by luminaries like Edgar Bergen, Al Jolson, and Walter Pidgeon (the latter a Saint John native). After being driven out of business by movie houses, then serving a long interim as home to a Pentecostal church, the theater was threatened with demolition in the early 1980s. That's when concerned citizens stepped in, raising funds to ensure that the theater would survive.

The Imperial reopened to much fanfare in 1994, and it has since hosted a wide range of performances from Broadway road shows to local theatrical productions and concerts. Even if nothing is slated during your stay, in the summer a guide is stationed on the premises to give you a tour, during which you can admire the intricate plasterwork and the 9-foot chandelier. Tours are offered Monday to Saturday 10am to 5pm; the cost is C$2.50 (US$1.67) adult, C$1 (US67¢) children 12 and under.

ROAD TRIP TO FUNDY TRAIL PARKWAY

✪ **Fundy Trail Parkway.** ☎ **506/833-2019.** www.fundytrailparkway.com. C$5 (US$3) per car day pass. Open daily 6am–8pm May 14 to Nov 14. Take Route 111 east; the entrance is 10km (6 miles) east of St. Martins (watch for signs). Leashed dogs allowed.

The parkway is an ambitious project that will eventually extend some 50 to 60 kilometers up the coast (it's currently 11 kilometers/6.6 miles) and link up with the Trans Canada Trail. This multi-use trail is nicely integrated with the natural environment, and makes the Fundy Coast accessible without despoiling its beauty. The trail is wide and easy to hike or bike and it has wheelchair-accessible pullouts with spectacular coastal views. Additional hiking trails lead to various beaches, some of which can only be reached at low tide. If you don't have the time or energy to walk, you can drive the paved road that parallels the trail, or catch the shuttle (free with paid admission) that stops at each of the parkway's eight parking lots. To make life even simpler, there are judiciously placed water stations and covered picnic tables at various locations along the way. The interpretive center has some interesting displays and a short film on the logging history of the area.

6 Fredericton

New Brunswick's provincial capital is a compact and historic city of brick and concrete that unfolds lazily along the banks of the wide St. John River. The handsome buildings, broad streets, and wide sidewalks make the place feel more like a big, tidy village than a small city. Keep an eye out for the two icons that mark Fredericton: the stately, stubborn elm trees that have resisted Dutch elm disease and still shade the occasional park and byway, and the Union Jack, which you'll occasionally see fluttering from various buildings, attesting to long-standing historic ties with the Loyalists who shaped the city.

Fredericton

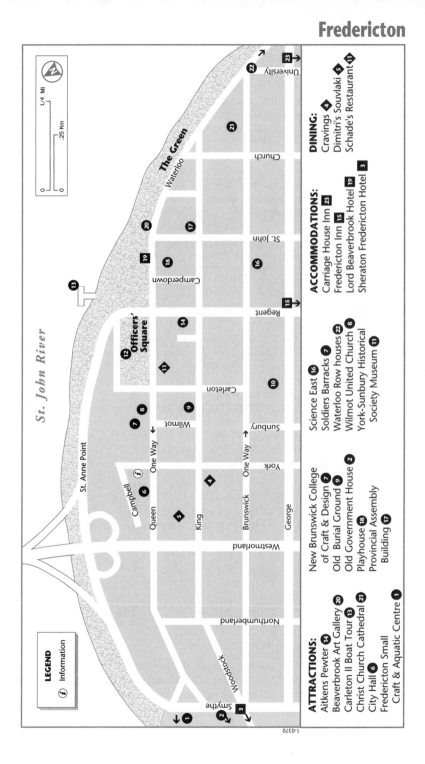

St. John River

The Green

Officers' Square

LEGEND

ⓘ Information

ATTRACTIONS:

Aitkens Pewter ⑭
Beaverbrook Art Gallery ⑳
Carleton II Boat Tour ⑬
Christ Church Cathedral ㉑
City Hall ⑥
Fredericton Small
Craft & Aquatic Centre ①

New Brunswick College
of Craft & Design ⑦
Old Burial Ground ⑨
Old Government House ②
Playhouse ⑱
Provincial Assembly
Building ⑰

Science East ⑯
Soldiers Barracks ⑦
Waterloo Row houses ㉒
Wilmot United Church ⑧
York-Sunbury Historical
Society Museum ⑪

ACCOMMODATIONS:

Carriage House Inn ㉓
Fredericton Inn ⑮
Lord Beaverbrook Hotel ⑲
Sheraton Fredericton Hotel ③

DINING:

Cravings ④
Dimitri's Souvlaki ⑤
Schade's Restaurant ⑪

1-0370

149

For travelers, the city can be seen as divided into three zones: the malls and motels atop the hills and near the link to the Trans-Canada Highway; the impressive, Georgian-style University of New Brunswick on the hillside just south of downtown; and the downtown proper, with its casual blend of modern and historic buildings.

Most visitors focus on downtown. The main artery—where you'll find the majority of the attractions and many restaurants—is Queen Street, which parallels the river between 1 and 2 blocks inland. An ill-considered limited-access four-lane bypass separates much of downtown from the river, but you can still reach the water's edge via the Green or by crossing a pedestrian bridge at the foot of Carleton Street.

Fredericton, with a population of 79,000, is low-key and appealing in a quiet and understated way. There's really no must-see attraction but the collective impact of strolling the streets and visiting several spots adds up to a full sense of history and place. Fredericton's subtle charms won't be everyone's cup of tea. My advice: If eastern Canada's allure for you is the shimmering sea, deep woods, and wide open spaces, you won't miss much by bypassing Fredericton. If your passions include history—especially the history of British settlement in North America—then it's well worth the detour.

ESSENTIALS

GETTING THERE   A major relocation and widening of the Trans-Canada Highway near Fredericton was being planned for 2000, which is likely to result in some inconveniences and confusion until the feeder roadways and signage are sorted out. Look for signs directing you to downtown. From the west, follow Woodstock Road, which tracks along the river to downtown. From Saint John, look for Route 7 to Regent Street, then turn right down the hill.

The **Fredericton Airport** (☎ 506/444-6100) is located 10 minutes southeast of downtown on Route 102 and is served by cab and rental car companies. For flight information, contact **Air Canada** (☎ 800/776-3000 in the U.S., 800/565-3940 in the Maritimes, or 506/632-1500) or **Canadian Airlines** (☎ 800/426-7000 in the U.S. or 800/665-1177 in Canada).

VISITOR INFORMATION   Fredericton was in the throes of rethinking its visitor information centers in late 1999. A new center is likely to open near the relocated Trans-Canada in 2000, and officials were considering moving the longtime downtown information center out of city hall to an as-yet-undetermined location. But Fredericton caters well to travelers, so the new centers are certain to be well-marked; check first at City Hall, 397 Queen St., or call ☎ 506/460-2129 for more information.

When you find a visitor information center, request a **Visitor Parking Pass,** which allows visitors from outside the province to park free at city lots and meters in town for up to 3 days.

You can request travel information in advance by visiting the city's Web site at **www.city.fredericton.nb.ca** or e-mailing tourism@city.fredericton.nb.ca.

EXPLORING FREDERICTON

The free *Fredericton Visitor Guide,* available at the information centers and many hotels around town, contains a well-written and informative walking tour of the downtown. It's worth tracking down before launching an exploration of the city.

City Hall, 397 Queen St., is an elaborate Victorian building with a prominent brick tower and 8-foot clock dial. The second-floor City Council Chamber occupies what was the opera house until the 1940s. Small, folksy tapestries adorn the visitor's gallery and tell the town's history. Learn about these and the rest of the building during the free building tours, which are offered daily from mid-May to mid-October on the hour (on the half hour in French). In the off-season, call ☎ **506/452-9616** to schedule a tour.

Officer's Square, on Queen Street between Carleton and Regent, is now a handsome city park. In 1785, the park was the center of military activity and used for drills, first as part of the British garrison, and later (until 1914) by the Canadian Army. Today, the only soldiers are local actors who put on a show for the tourists. Look also for music and dramatic events staged at the square in the warmer months. The handsome colonnaded stone building facing the parade grounds is the former officer's quarters, now the York-Sunbury Historical Society Museum (see below).

In the center of the square the prominent statue of the robed figure is **Lord Beaverbrook.** That's a name you'll hear a lot of in Fredericton: a street, a museum, and a hotel bear his name. Lord Beaverbrook was Max Aitken, a native of Newcastle, New Brunswick, who amassed a significant fortune as a press baron and through other business endeavors. Although he lived much of his life in Britain (he was made a lord in 1917, taking the name after a stream near Newcastle where he had fished as a young man), he maintained close ties to Canada. He donated an art collection and modern building to house it (the Beaverbrook Art Gallery), along with a modern playhouse, which now is home to Theatre New Brunswick. The playhouse was built in 1964, the same year Lord Beaverbrook died.

Two blocks upriver of Officer's Square is the **Soldier's Barracks,** housed in a similarly grand stone building. Check your watch against the sundial high on the end of the barracks, a replica of the original timepiece. A small exhibit shows the life of the enlisted man in the 18th century. Along the ground floor, local craftspeople sell their wares from small shops carved out of former barracks.

Fredericton is well noted for its distinctive architecture, especially the fine Victorian and Queen Anne residential architecture. Particularly attractive is **Waterloo Row,** a group of privately owned historic homes—some grand, some less so—just downriver of downtown.

An entertaining and enlightening way to learn about the city's history is to sign up for a walking tour with the **Calithumpians** of Fredericton's Outdoor Summer Theatre. Costumed guides offer free tours daily in July and August, pointing out highlights with anecdotes and dramatic tales. Recommended is the evening "Haunted Hike" tour, which runs 3 nights each week. The evening tour is about 2 hours and costs C$12 (US$8) for adults, C$8 (US$5.33) for children; call ☎ **506/457-1975** for more information.

If you happen to be in town on a Saturday, a worthy detour is to the **Boyce Farmers' Market,** ☎ **506/451-1815,** located on George Street, behind the old jail at 668 Brunswick St. The market has been here in one form or another since the late 18th century. The current building was constructed in 1951 and expanded in 1990. More than 200 vendors offer everything fresh, from seasonal vegetables to meats, baked goods, and crafts. The market is adjacent to Science East (see below).

OUTDOOR PURSUITS

Fredericton recently expanded its trail system for walkers and bikers. The centerpiece of the system is **The Green,** a 5-kilometer (3-mile) pathway that follows the river from the Sheraton hotel to near the Princess Margaret Bridge. It's a lovely walk, and you'll pass the Old Government House (see below), downtown, and the open parklands near Waterloo Row.

Connecting with The Green is a well-used pedestrian bridge that crosses an abandoned railroad trestle just east of downtown. From this vantage point you'll get wonderful views of the downtown and river valley. If you continue onward, the **Nash-waak/Marysville Trail** follows an abandoned railbed along the attractive Nashwaak River; after about 4 kilometers (2.5 miles) you can cross the Nashwaak at Bridge Street and loop back to the pedestrian rail-bridge via the **Gibson Trail.**

A number of other trails link up to this expanding network, which comprised about 60 kilometers (37 miles) as of late 1999. A free trail guide brochure is available at the information centers, or contact the New Brunswick Trails Council at ☎ **506/459-1931.**

Bikes may be rented by the hour or the day at the **Fredericton Lighthouse** at the Regent St. Wharf (☎ **506/459-2515**), or at **Radical Edge,** 386 Queen St. (☎ **506/459-3478**). Rentals are around C$25 (US$17) per day.

The *Carleton II* (☎ **506/454-2628**), offers 1-hour excursions on the river aboard a new ship (built 1999–2000) with a capacity of 100 passengers. You'll learn about local history, view the city from the scenic river, and perhaps spot a bald eagle flying along the shoreline. The tours depart several times daily in summer from the wharf near the Fredericton Lighthouse (at the foot of Regent Street). The personable captain is Brad Woodside, a former mayor of Fredericton. Rates are C$7 (US$5) adult, C$4 (US$3) children.

Another option for getting on the water is the **Small Craft Aquatic Center,** on Woodstock Road (behind the Victoria Health Centre and near the Old Government House), ☎ **506/460-2260.** It's open daily from the middle of May to early October, and offers rentals of rowing shells, canoes, and kayaks. Ask also about naturalist-guided tours of the river.

ATTRACTIONS DOWNTOWN

Beaverbrook Art Gallery. 703 Queen St. ☎ **506/458-8545.** Admission C$3 (US$2) adults, C$2 (US$1.35) seniors, C$1 (US65¢) students, children under 6 free. June–Sept Mon–Fri 9am–6pm, Sat and Sun 10am–5pm; Oct–May Tues–Fri 9am–5pm, Sat 10am–5pm, Sun noon–5pm.

This surprisingly fine modern museum overlooks the waterfront and is home to an impressive collection of British paintings, including works by Reynolds, Gainsborough, Constable, and Turner. Antique buffs gravitate to the rooms with period furnishings and early decorative arts. Most everyone finds themselves drawn to Salvador Dali's massive *Santiago El Grande,* and studies for an ill-fated portrait of Winston Churchill. A new curator has brought in more controversial modern art exhibits in the last 2 years; stop by to find out what's currently on display.

Legislative Assembly Building. Queen St. (across from the Beaverbrook Art Gallery). ☎ **506/453-2527.** Free admission. Summer daily 8:45am–7pm; off-season weekdays 9am–4pm.

The Legislative Assembly Building, constructed starting in 1880, boasts an exterior designed in that bulbous, extravagant Second Empire style. But that's just the prelude. Inside, it's even more dressed up and fancy. Entering takes a bit of courage if the doors are closed; they're heavy and intimidating, with slits of beveled glass for peering out. (They're a bit reminiscent of the gates of Oz.) Inside, it's creaky and wooden and comfortable, in contrast to the cold, unyielding stone of many seats of power. In the small rotunda, look for the razor-sharp prints from John James Audubon's elephant folio, on display in a special case.

The assembly chamber nearly takes the breath away, especially when viewed from the heights of the visitor gallery on the upper floors. (You ascend via a graceful wood spiral stairway housed in its own rotunda.) The chamber is ornate and draperied in that fussy Victorian way, which is quite a feat given the vast scale of the room. Note all the regal trappings, including the portrait of the young Queen Elizabeth. This place just feels like a setting for high drama, whether or not it actually delivers when the chamber is in session.

Old Government House. Woodstock Rd. (next to the Sheraton hotel). ☎ **506/453-6440.** Free admission. Tours daily summer to mid-Oct 10am–6pm; tours leave on the hour, with last tour at 5pm. Tours in off-season by appointment only.

The wonderfully severe Government House was built in 1828, when it was created as the official residence of the Lieutenant-Governor, who was the official representative of the British Crown. It was built of locally quarried sandstone in a rigorously classical style, featuring Palladian symmetry, intricate plasterwork, and other haute touches. It served as the official residence until 1890, after which it served variously as a school and home to a detachment of Mounties. Recently spared from the wrecking ball, the home underwent an exhaustive restoration and reopened in 1999. It once again is the official residence of the lieutenant governor, who has an apartment on the third floor and an office on the second floor.

Tours begin in a basement interpretive center, and last about 45 minutes. You'll hike up sweeping staircases and view the extraordinarily high-ceilinged ground-floor reception rooms, and have a chance to peruse art displayed in the second floor art gallery. Guides are loaded with stories and anecdotes. The tour will be of special interest to those who number historic architecture among their passion, and those attracted to the grandeur of bygone days.

Science East. 668 Brunswick St. ☎ **506/457-2340.** C$2 (US$1.35) adult or child, C$6 (US$4) family. Tues–Sat 10am–5pm, Sun 1–4pm. Closed Mon.

Children enjoy a visit at this new (1999) science center for two reasons. First, it's located in the old county jail, a sturdy stone structure built in the 1840s. (It was used as a jail until 1996.) And then there are the great exhibits—some 100 interactive displays including a huge kaleidoscope and a mini-tornado. It's an ideal destination for a family on a chilly or rainy day.

York-Sunbury Historical Society Museum. Off Queen St. near Regent St. ☎ **506/455-6041.** Admission C$2 (US$1.35) adults, C$1 (US65¢) student, C$4 (US$2.65) family. Summer daily 10am–5pm; spring and fall Tues–Sat noon–5pm; closed winter.

This well-done small museum lures visitors with the promise of a stuffed 42-pound frog. It was said to belong to Fred Coleman, who in the late 19th century fed it a nasty concoction of June bugs, cornmeal, buttermilk, and whiskey to give it Rubenesque proportions. After it perished at the hands of some miscreants, the famous frog was displayed at the Burke House Hotel until 1959, when it traveled with little ceremony to the museum. It's displayed on the top floor to ensure that you wander through all the exhibits looking for it—a clever trick on the part of the curator.

Actually, the frog is a disappointment. (Not to mention suspect—it looks like it's made of bad papier mâché.) But the rest of the museum is nicely done. Displays feature the usual artifacts of Life Gone By, but several exhibits rise well above the clutter, including a fine display on Loyalist settlers. Kids will love the claustrophobic re-creation of a German World War II trench on the second floor—and likely will end up talking more about that on the way home than Fred's portly frog.

ATTRACTIONS OUTSIDE OF TOWN

✪ **Kings Landing Historical Settlement.** Exit 259 off the Trans-Canada Highway (Route 2 west). ☎ **506/363-4999** or 506/363-4959 for recorded information. www.

kingslanding.nb.ca. Admission C$10 (US$6.65) adults, C$8 (US$5.35) seniors, C$7.25 (US$4.85) students over 16, C$5.50 (US$3.65) children 6–16, C$25 (US$16.65) family pass. June to mid-Oct daily 10am–5pm.

Kings Landing, on the bank of the St. John River, is 34 kilometers (21 miles) and about 150 years from Fredericton. The authentic re-creation brings to life New Brunswick from 1790 to 1910, with 10 historic houses and nine other buildings relocated here and saved from destruction by the flooding during the Mactaquac hydro project. The aroma of freshly baked bread mixes with the smell of horses and livestock, and the sound of the blacksmith's hammer alternates with that of the church bell. More than 160 costumed "early settlers" chat about their lives.

You could easily spend a day exploring the 150 acres, but if you haven't that much time, focus on the **Hagerman House** (with furniture by Victorian cabinetmaker John Warren Moore), the **Ingraham House** with its fine New Brunswick furniture and formal English garden, the **Morehouse House** (where you'll see a clock Benedict Arnold left behind), and the **Victorian Perley House.** The **Ross Sash and Door Factory** will demonstrate the work and times of a turn-of-the-century manufacturing plant.

Afterward, hitch a ride on the sloven wagon, or relax at the Kings Head Inn, which served up grub and grog to hardy travelers along the St. John River a century or more ago. Today it serves lemonade, chicken pie, and corn chowder, along with other traditional dishes. Lunch prices are C$8 to C$13 (US$5 to US$9), and dinner is C$13 to C$19 (US$9 to US$13).

SHOPPING

Fredericton is home to a growing number of artists and artisans, as well as entrepreneurs who have launched a handful of offbeat shops. It's worth setting aside an hour or two for browsing.

Aitkens Pewter. 65 Regent St. ☎ **800/567-4416** or 506/453-9474.

This well-known shop sells classically designed pewter dishes and mugs based on historic patterns, as well as modern adaptations and jewelry.

By the Light of the Moon. 385 Mazzucca's Lane (off York St. between King and Queen). ☎ **506/455-2828.**

Look for fine handpainted fabrics and crafts done up in quiet, muted patterns and colors. Natural fiber fabrics may be purchased by the yard. Ask about hand-painting workshops.

Critical Mass. 384 Queen St. ☎ **506/452-6773.**

Located in a third-floor walk-up loft across from city hall, this sprawling, cluttered gallery features edgy modern art by both emerging and established artists in the local arts scene.

Cultures Boutique. 383 Mazzucca's Lane (off York St. between King and Queen). ☎ **506/462-3088.**

This is one of a chain of YMCA-run shops that promote alternative trade to benefit craftspeople in the third world. Look for goods from foreign lands as well as North American native cultures, mostly from community-based cooperatives.

Gallery Connexion. Queen St. (behind the Justice Building). ☎ **506/454-1433.**

Expect vibrant modern artwork, much of it experimental and in all sorts of media, at this lively nonprofit gallery run by area artists. Studios are within the same building, and you may have a chance to see the artists at work.

Gallery 78. 796 Queen St. (near the Beaverbrook Art Gallery). ☎ **506/454-5192.**

An exceptionally solid and handsome Queen Anne-style mansion is home to the province's oldest private art gallery. Sunny spaces upstairs and down showcase a range of local art, much of it sold at affordable prices.

Kingfisher Books. 358 Queen St. ☎ **800/577-5133** or 506/458-5531.

This is the kind of small, thoughtful bookshop that the Internet was supposed to put out of business. The shop is also home to a bookstore cat who's a local celebrity.

New Brunswick Fine Craft Centre. 87 Regent St. ☎ **506/450-8989.**

A spare, compact storefront gallery, the center showcases some of the province's finest crafts in juried shows of individual artists.

WHERE TO STAY

A handful of motels and chain hotels are located in the bustling mall zone on the hill above town, mostly along Regent and Prospect Streets. Allow about 10 minutes to drive downtown from here.

Among the classiest of the bunch is the **Fredericton Inn** (1315 Regent St., ☎ **800/561-8777** or 506/455-1430), situated between two malls. It's a soothing-music-and-floral-carpeting kind of place that does a brisk business in the convention trade. But with its indoor pool and classically appointed rooms, it's a comfortable spot for vacation travelers as well. Peak season rates are C$73 to C$129 (US$49 to US$86) and up to C$169 (US$113) for suites.

Also near the malls are the **Comfort Inn,** 255 Prospect St. (☎ **506/453-0800**), at C$78 to C$105 (US$52 to US$70) double; **City Motel,** 1216 Regent St. (☎ **800/268-2858** or 506/459-9900), with rooms for C$70 to C$90 (US$47 to US$60); and the **Country Inn and Suites,** 455 Prospect St. (☎ **506/459-0035**), C$93 to C$106 (US$62 to US$71).

Carriage House Inn. 230 University Ave., Fredericton, NB E3B 4H7. ☎ **800/267-6068** or 506/452-9924. Fax 506/458-0799. E-mail: chinn@nbnet.nb.ca. 11 units (2 with private hall bathrooms). TEL. C$75–C$85 (US$50–US$57) double; includes breakfast. AE, DC, MC, V. "Small, well-trained pets" allowed.

Fredericton's premier bed-and-breakfast is located a short stroll from the riverfront pathway in a quiet residential neighborhood. A former mayor built this imposing three-story Victorian manse in 1875. Inside, it's a bit somber in that heavy Victorian way, with dark wood trim and deep colors, and feels solid enough to resist glaciers. Rooms are eclectically furnished and comfortable without being opulent. Delicious and elaborate breakfasts are served in a sunny room in the rear of the house. There's a friendly Rottweiler named Bailey on the premises.

Dining: Dinner is available at the inn with 48-hour advance notice; ask about the menu when you book. A complete dinner runs around C$25 (US$17) per person.

Lord Beaverbrook Hotel. 659 Queen St., Fredericton, NB E3B 5A6. ☎ **800/561-7666** (Canada and New England only) or 506/455-3371. Fax 506/455-1441. E-mail: lbhotel@nbnet.nb.ca. 165 units. A/C TV TEL. C$95–C$139 (US$63–US$93) double; suites to C$450 (US$300). AE, DC, ER, MC, V.

This stern and hulking 1947 waterfront hotel is severe and boxy in an early deco kind of way, a look that may at first suggest that it houses the Ministry of Dourness. Inside, the mood lightens considerably, with composite stone floors, Georgian pilasters, and chandeliers. The downstairs indoor pool and recreation area are positively whimsical, a sort of tiki-room grotto that kids adore. The guest rooms are nicely appointed with traditional reproduction furniture in dark wood. Standard rooms can be somewhat dim, and most of the windows don't open (ask for a room with opening windows when you book). The suites are spacious and many have excellent river views. The hotel, which was part of the troubled Keddy chain, went into receivership in 1999, but at our last inspection appeared not to be suffering in the least from the turmoil and was still tidy and well-managed. This is the best accommodation for those who want the convenience of a downtown location and who enjoy the solid architectural touches of an old-fashioned hotel. Those looking for a modern polish may be more content at the Sheraton.

Dining: You've got three choices for dining. The Terrace Room is the main dining area, with an indoor gazebo and a seasonal outdoor deck overlooking the river. The menu corrals resort standards, starting with relish trays and puffy white dinner rolls. Main courses, at C$11 to C$17 (US$7 to US$11), range from Oriental shrimp stir-fry to chicken fettuccine Alfredo. The more intimate Governor's Room has higher aspirations, with dinner entrees like duck breast with a raspberry and Grand Marnier coulis, or shrimp Provençal at C$16.95 to C$25.95 (US$11.30 to US$17.30). The River Room lounge is the spot for a beer and a snack.

Amenities: Small indoor pool, a Jacuzzi, and limited fitness equipment; baby-sitting, dry cleaning and laundry, safe-deposit boxes, conference rooms, a business center, and an airport shuttle (fee).

On the Pond. 20 Route 615, Mactaquac, NB E6L 1M2. ☎ **506/363-3420.** www. onthepond.com. 8 units. A/C TV TEL. C$140 (US$93) double, including full breakfast. MC, V. Directions: drive west of Fredericton on Woodstock Rd.; cross the Mactaquac Dam and continue to the Esso station; turn right and look for sign on right.

In 1999, Donna Evans opened On the Pond about 15 minutes west of Fredericton, with the idea of creating a comfortable retreat where guests could be pampered with spa treatments after indulging in soft adventure at the adjacent provincial park and surrounding countryside. The newly built lodge is lovely, constructed in a strong sort of William Morris-inspired style with dark wood trim, slate floors in the entryways, and fieldstone fireplaces. The two downstairs common rooms—one with wood fireplace and one lined with bookshelves—invite lingering and chatting with the other guests. The upstairs guest rooms each feature a queen and a double bed, and are slightly larger than the average hotel room with nice extras like bathrobes and duvets. The lodge is developing a series of packages (golf, spa treatments, outdoor adventures) that makes good use of the Mactaquac area, which isn't wilderness but a rolling river valley of open farms and suburban homes.

Dining: Heart-healthy dinners are served on request if ordered in advance or as part of a package. The cost is approximately C$30 (US$20) for a four-course meal.

Amenities: The lodge features a basement spa, with two massage rooms, an esthetics room (manicures, pedicures, and facials), and a fitness center. (The fitness center wasn't ready for prime time when I visited, but improvements were in the works.) The lodge is on "The Arm"—an impoundment of the St. John River behind the nearby hydroelectric dam—in a marshy setting that's better for bird watching than swimming. Beach swimming is available across the road at the provincial park. The lodge has a small wharf with canoes and kayaks guest may use for free; mountain bikes may be rented. Nearby are a golf course, dog-sledding tours, and King's Landing Historical Settlement.

Sheraton Fredericton Hotel. 225 Woodstock Rd., Fredericton, NB E3B 2H8. ☎ **800/325-3535** or 506/457-7000. Fax 506/457-4000. www.sheraton.com. 223 units. A/C MINIBAR TV TEL. C$92–C$145 (US$61–US$97) double. AE, CB, DC, MC, V.

This modern resort hotel, built in 1992, occupies a prime location along the river about 10 minutes' walk from downtown via the riverfront pathway. Much of summer life revolves around the outdoor pool on the deck overlooking the river, and on Sunday the lobby is surrendered to an over-the-top breakfast buffet. Although decidedly up to date, the interior is done with classical styling and is comfortable and well-appointed. All rooms have hair dryers.

Dining: The lounge is an active and popular spot on many nights, especially weekends. Across the lobby is Bruno's Seafood Cafe, which offers a good alternative to the restaurants downtown. Look also for seasonal and regional specialties, including fiddleheads in early summer. Main courses range from C$7 to C$23 (US$5 to US$15).

Amenities: Fitness room, indoor and outdoor pools, gift shop, and conference facilities.

WHERE TO DINE

A popular local downtown spot for a quick and easy lunch is **Cravings,** 348 King St., ☎ **506/452-7482,** which features generous sandwiches and pita pockets.

Brewbakers. 546 King St. ☎ **506/459-0067.** Reservations recommended on weekends. Main courses, lunch C$7.29–C$8.99 (US$4.85–US$5.99), dinner C$12.99–C$21.99 (US$8.65–US$14.65). AE, CB, DC, ER, MC, V. Daily 11am–11pm (until midnight Fri and Sat). PASTA/PUB FARE.

Brewbakers is a convivial pub, cafe, and restaurant, located on three levels in a cleverly adapted downtown building. It's a bustling and informal spot, creatively cluttered with artifacts and artworks, and does boomtown business during lunch hours and early evenings. The cafe section is quieter, as is the mezzanine dining room above the cafe. The third floor bustles, with an open kitchen and folks lined up for the popular build-your-own pasta buffet. And pasta is the main attraction here, served up with the usual array of sauces. Also good are the personal pizzas, the roasted chicken, the grilled striploin, and the herb-crusted tenderloin. The lunch buffet is one of the better deals in town—bring a large appetite. For a meal on the go, the cafe offers a creative selection of boxed lunches.

Dimitri's Souvlaki. 349 King St. (in Piper's Lane area). ☎ **506/452-8882.** Main courses, C$7.50–C$16.95 (US$5–US$11.30). AE, CB, DC, ER, MC, V. Mon–Sat 11am–11pm. GREEK.

Dimitri's is hard to find, and easy to keep walking past once you've found it. But the generic, chain-restaurant interior with its hide-the-crumbs paisley carpeting belies better-than-average cooking that will appeal especially to budget-conscious diners. You'll get a big plate of food here for not a lot of money. The Greek specialties include moussaka (with and without meat), souvlaki, and dolmades, and all are quite good. (Avoid the mystery-meat donairs.) Deluxe dinner plates are served with delicious potatoes—hearty wedges that are cooked crispy on the outside and remain hot and soft on the inside. The meats are sometimes on the tough side, but most diners will find this a good value.

Schade's Restaurant. 536 Queen St. ☎ **506/450-3340.** Reservations recommended. Main courses, lunch C$3.99–C$7.99 (US$2.65–US$5.35), dinner C$9.95–C$18 (US$6.65–US$12). AE, DC, MC, V. Tues–Fri 11:30am–2pm, 5–9pm; Sat 5–9pm. GERMAN.

This German-owned and -run restaurant features traditional meals from the mid-continent, including a variety of schnitzels (schnitzel specials change daily), beef stroganoff, and beef with broccoli, mushrooms, and spaetzle. The decor at this relaxed storefront restaurant isn't overly fussy (note the attractive tin ceiling), making it an appealing spot for a casual meal over a tall glass of beer. More rarified German specialties (like sauerbraten and schweinehaxe) are offered with advance notice for groups of four or more.

FREDERICTON AFTER DARK

Fredericton's downtown is often lively with university students and young professionals after hours. **Lunar Rouge,** 625 King St., ☎ **506/450-2065,** features over 50 whiskeys and 14 draft beers in a comfortable, pubby atmosphere. Tuesday is nacho night, which lures out the local folks in droves.

Picaroons Brewing Co. and Taproom, 366 Queen St. (☎ **506/454-8277**), on a rooftop in the Pipers Lane area, is reached via a set of steel steps that's easier going up than down, especially after a passel of pints. The open-air deck is a popular spot for sampling the excellent microbrews handcrafted with all-natural malts (the red ale is a personal favorite).

Finally, **Dolan's Pub,** 349 King St. (☎ **506/454-7474**), is your best bet for live Maritime music, which is on tap every Thursday through Saturday. Also on tap is the city's largest selection of microbrews. Don't miss the barrel of free peanuts.

ROAD TRIP TO GAGETOWN

About 55 kilometers (34 miles) southeast of Fredericton is the untroubled, unassuming village of Gagetown. (The village can be visited via a scenic driving detour en route to or from Saint John.) It's been largely unchanged over the years—backed by farm fields on one side and a placid inlet off the St. John River known as Gagetown Creek. The peaceable surroundings and simple vernacular country architecture have attracted the attention of craftspeople and artists, who have settled here and slowly made it a quiet arts colony—quaint and creative, but not annoyingly so. Look for a handful of low-key enterprises, including art galleries, a cafe, a decoy carver, a bookstore, a cider press, a crafts cooperative, and several potters.

Things to do, besides wander around: You can **bird watch** and explore—the region is noted for its avian life, with a wide range of birds enjoying the mixed terrain that includes marsh grass, forest, and field. Some 144 species have been reliably identified in and around Gagetown. Gagetown Island is just offshore (easily accessible by kayak or canoe, which inn guests may borrow; see below). The island is 1,000 acres and features a glacial deposit that rises some 75 feet, the ruins of a stone house that dates back to the early 19th century, and an osprey-viewing platform.

You can visit the **Queens County Museum** (no phone), birthplace of Sir Samuel Leonard Tilley, one of the fathers of confederation. (The 1786 home is located across from the Steamer Stop Inn, and is open to the public in summer.) And you can sign up for an excursion with **Gagetown Boat Tours,** ☎ **506/488-2269,** which offers frequent departures in summer from the wharf below the Steamers Stop Inn. The compact boat can accommodate up to six passengers, who often spot bald eagles while puttering around the quiet waters. Tours runs 1½ to 2 hours, and cost C$20 to C$25 (US$13 to US$17) per adult.

WHERE TO STAY & DINE

Steamer Stop Inn. PO Box 155, Village of Gagetown, NB E0G 1V0. ☎ **506/488-2903.** Fax 506/488-1116. 6 units. C$65–C$95 (US$43–US$63) double, including continental breakfast. AE, MC, V. Closed mid-Oct to May. Pets allowed only if kept in kennel.

Most of the riverside Steamer Stop Inn was built around 1910, with a harmonious addition completed in the 1930s. It's a rustic, homey spot, though the downstairs common rooms are furnished more with an eye to comfort—some modern velour-upholstered, some Victorian—than to attract any design awards. Historic touches add a nice patina, with lots of oak woodwork and old pine paneling. The guest rooms vary in size. Rooms 4 and 5 both face the road; the latter is the smallest, the former the largest and brightest in the inn. Room 3 has nice river views and the original bathroom with hulking old tub; Room 6 is a corner room with a view up the river, a pair of wicker chairs, and a relatively large bathroom in the former linen closet. The inn has two kayaks and a canoe for guests to use; there's also river swimming from the wharf, and a new (1999) outdoor hot tub.

Dining: The inn's dining room is about the only game in town. Dinners are by reservation only, and guests are seated in several pleasant dining areas; request a table on the screened porch if the weather's warm. The well-regarded menu includes favorites like filet mignon, scallops, and halibut, with entrees priced C$18 to C$28 (US$12 to US$19).

7 Fundy National Park

The Fundy Coast between Saint John and Alma is for the most part wild, remote, and unpopulated. It's plumbed by few roads other than the new Fundy Drive (see the Saint John section, above), making it difficult to explore unless you have a boat. The best access to the wild coast is through Fundy National Park, a gem of a destination that's hugely popular with travelers with an outdoor bent. Families often settle in here for a week or so, filling their days with activities in and around the park that include hiking, sea kayaking, biking, and splashing around a seaside pool. Nearby are lovely drives and an innovative adventure center at Cape Enrage. If a muffling fog moves in to smother the coast, head inland for a hike to a waterfall or through lush forest. If it's a day of brilliant sunshine, venture along the rocky shores by foot or boat.

ESSENTIALS

GETTING THERE   Route 114 runs through the center of Fundy National Park. If you're coming from the west, follow the prominent national park signs just east of Sussex. If you're coming from Prince Edward Island or Nova Scotia, head southward on Route 114 from Moncton.

One word of warning for travel from Moncton: Beware the signs at the Route 15 rotary directing you to Fundy National Park. Moncton's traffic czars send tourists on a silly, Mr. Toad's wild ride around the city's outskirts, apparently to avoid downtown traffic; after 16 kilometers (10 miles) of driving you'll end up within sight of the rotary again, just across the river. It's far more sensible to head downtown via Main Street, cross the river on the first steel bridge (you can see it from about everywhere), and then turn left on Route 114.

VISITOR INFORMATION   The park's main **Visitor Centre** (☎ 506/887-6000) is located just inside the Alma (eastern) entrance to the park. The stone building is open daily during peak season 8am to 10pm (with limited hours in the off-season). You can watch a video presentation, peruse a handful of exhibits on wildlife and tides, and shop at the nicely stocked nature bookstore.

The smaller **Wolfe Lake Information Centre** (☎ 506/432-6026) is at the park's western entrance and is open daily in summer, weekdays only in spring.

FEES   Park entry fees are charged from mid-May to mid-October. The fee is C$3.50 (US$2.35) adult, C$2.75 (US$1.85) senior, C$1.75 (US$1.15) children ages 6 to 16, and C$7 (US$4.65) family. Four-day passes are available for the price of 3 days.

EXPLORING FUNDY NATIONAL PARK

Most national park activities are centered around the Alma (east) side of the park, where the park entrance has a cultivated and manicured air, as if part of a landed estate. Here you'll find stone walls, well-tended lawns, and attractive landscaping, along with a golf course, amphitheater, lawn bowling, and tennis.

Also in this area is a **heated saltwater pool,** set near the bay with a sweeping ocean view. There's a lifeguard on duty, and it's a popular destination for families. The pool is open late June to August. The cost is C$2 (US$1.35) adult, C$1.50 (US$1) children, and C$5 (US$3.35) family.

Also unique to the park are two **auto trails**—basically overgrown dirt roads that you can explore with the family car. Hastings Auto Trail is one-way so you needn't worry about oncoming vehicles. It's a good way to see some of the great outdoors without suffering the indignities that often result from actual encounters with nature (rain, bugs, blisters, and so on).

Sea kayaking tours are a way to get a good, close look at the ocean landscape and the tides. **Fresh Air Adventure** (☎ **800/545-0020** or 506/887-2249) in Alma offers tours that range from 2 hours to several days. The half-day tours explore marsh and coastline (C$50/US$33 including lunch); the full-day adventure includes a hot meal and 6 hours of exploring the wild shores (C$90/US$60).

HIKING

The park maintains 104 kilometers (65 miles) of trails for hikers and walkers. These range from a 20-minute loop to a 4-hour trek, and they pass through varied terrain. The trails are arranged such that several can be linked into a 50-kilometer (30-mile) backpacker's loop, dubbed the **Fundy Circuit,** which typically requires 3 nights in the backcountry. Preregistration is required for the overnight trek, so ask at the visitor center.

Among the most accessible hikes is the **Caribou Plain Trail,** a 3.4-kilometer (2-mile) loop that provides a wonderful introduction to the local terrain. You'll hike along a beaver pond, on a boardwalk across a raised peat bog, and through lovely temperate forest. Read the interpretive signs to learn about deadly "flarks," which lurk in bogs and can kill a moose.

The **Third Vault Falls Trail** is a 7.4-kilometer (4.4-mile) in-and-back hike that takes you to the park's highest waterfall, about 45 feet high. The trail is largely a flat stroll through leafy woodlands until you begin a steady descent into a mossy gorge. You round a corner and there you are, suddenly facing the cataract.

All the park's trails are covered in the pullout trail guide you'll find in *Salt & Fir,* the booklet you'll receive when you pay your entry fee.

BIKING

The roads east of Alma offer superb bicycling terrain, at least if you get off busy Route 114. Especially appealing is Route 915 from Riverside-Albert to Alma, along with a detour to Cape Enrage. Along this scenic road you'll pedal through rolling farmland and scattered settlements, past vistas of salt marshes and the wonderfully named Ha Ha Cemetery. The hills are low but can be steep and require a serious grind, so you should be in reasonable shape. Route 915 runs 29 kilometers (17 miles), with the spur to Cape Enrage an additional 6.5 kilometers (4 miles) each way.

Bike rentals have not been available in Alma in recent years, but check with the Alma visitor information center (☎ **506/887-6127**) to see if the situation has changed. Otherwise, bikes may be rented in Saint John or Moncton.

CAMPING

The national park maintains four drive-in campgrounds and 15 backcountry sites. The two main campgrounds are near the Alma entrance. **Headquarters Campground** is within walking distance of Alma, the saltwater pool, and numerous other attractions. Since it overlooks the bay, this campground tends to be cool and subject to fogs. **Chignecto Campground** is higher on the hillside, sunnier, and warmer. You can hike down to Alma on an attractive hiking trail in 1 to 2 hours. Both campgrounds have hookups for RVs, flush toilets, and showers, and sites can be reserved in advance (☎ **800/213-7275** or 506/887-6000).

The **Point Wolfe** and **Wolfe Lake** campgrounds lack RV hookups and are slightly more primitive (Wolfe Lake lacks showers), but they are the preferred destinations for campers seeking a quieter camping experience. Rates at all campgrounds are C$12 to C$19 (US$8 to US$13), depending on services required; Wolfe Lake has pit toilets only and is C$10 (US$7) per night.

Backcountry sites are scattered throughout the park, with only one located directly on the coast (at the confluence of the coast and Goose River). Ask at the visitor centers for more information or to reserve a site (mandatory). Backcountry camping fees are C$3 (US$2) per person per night.

ROAD TRIP TO CAPE ENRAGE

Cape Enrage is a blustery and bold cape that juts impertinently out into Chignecto Bay. It's also home to a wonderful adventure center that could be a model for similar centers worldwide.

✪ **Cape Enrage Adventures** traces its roots back to 1993, when a group of Harrison Trimble High School students in Moncton decided to do something about the decay of the cape's historic lighthouse, which had been abandoned in 1988. They put together a plan to restore the light and keeper's quarters and establish an adventure center. It worked. Today, with the help of experts in kayaking, rock climbing, rappelling, and other rugged sports, a couple dozen high-school students staff and run this program throughout the summer months. The program closes in late August, when the student-managers head back to school.

Part of what makes the program so notable is its flexibility. Day adventures are scheduled throughout the summer, from which you can pick and choose, as if from a menu. These include rappelling workshops, rock-climbing lessons, kayak trips, and canoeing excursions. Prices are C$45 (US$30) per person for a 2-hour rock climbing or rappelling workshop, C$50 (US$33) for a half-day canoe or kayak trip. (Note to parents: This is an ideal spot to drop off restless teens while you indulge in scenic drives or a trip to Hopewell Rocks.)

Families looking to endure outdoor hardships together should inquire about custom adventures. For about C$180 (US$120) per person, the center can organize a 2-night adventure vacation that includes equipment, instruction, food, and lodging. You pick your own activities—maybe a sea kayak trip early one morning, followed by an afternoon of rappelling. It's entirely up to you.

As if running the center didn't keep the students busy enough, they also operate a restaurant (open to the public), called The Keeper's Lunchroom. Light but tasty meals include a notable fish chowder made with fresh haddock from a recipe provided by a local fisherman's wife, served with hot biscuits. A few other selections are offered—like grilled cheese and cheesecake—but the smart money gets the chowder.

For more information about the program, contact Cape Enrage Adventures, ☎ **506/856-6081** (506/887-2273 after May 15); fax 506/856-3480. The program's Web site is located at monctonlife.com/cape_enrage/index.htm.

ROAD TRIP TO THE HOPEWELL ROCKS

There's no better place to witness the extraordinary power of the Fundy tides than at ✪ **Hopewell Rocks** (☎ **506/734-3429**), located about 40 kilometers (24 miles) northeast of Fundy National Park on Route 114. Think of it as a natural sculpture garden. At low tide (the best time to visit), eroded columns as high as 15 meters (50 feet) tower above the ocean floor. They're sometimes called the "flowerpots," on account of the trees and plants that still flourish on their narrowing summits.

You park at the new visitor center and restaurant and wander down to the shore. Signboards fill you in on the natural history. If you're here at the bottom half of the tide, you can descend the steel staircase to the sea floor and admire these wondrous freestanding rock sculptures, chiseled by waves and tides.

The visitor center is a pleasant place to spend some time. It not only has intriguing exhibits (in particular look for the satellite photos of the area, and the time-lapse video of the tides) but the restaurant has terrific views from its floor-to-ceiling windows and serves good, simple food. Salads and various sandwiches (salmon burgers, steak hoagies, lobster rolls, etc.) are satisfying, and the soup of the day, a harvest vegetable bisque, was the perfect antidote to some rather cold, damp weather. There's also a children's menu. Appetizers range from C$3.45 to C$7.50 (US$2.30 to US$5), entrees C$4.99 to C$12.50 (US$3.35 to US$8.35).

The site can be crowded, but that's understandable. If your schedule allows it, come early in the day when the sun is fresh over Nova Scotia across the bay, the dew is still on the ground, and most travelers are still sacked out in bed. The park charges an entry fee of C$4.25 (US$2.85) adult, C$2.25 (US$1.50) children ages 4 to 18, C$10 (US$6.65) family.

If you arrive at the top half of the tide, consider a sea kayak tour around the islands and caves. **Baymount Outdoor Adventures** (☎ **506/734-2660**) runs 90-minute tours daily for C$35 (US$23) adult, C$30 (US$20) youth. (Caving tours at nearby caverns are also offered; inquire for details.)

WHERE TO STAY

Broadleaf Guest Ranch. Hopewell Hill, Fundy, Albert County, E0A-1Z0. (☎ **800/ 226-5405** or 506/882-2349). www.broadleafranch.com. E-mail: broadlef@nbnet.nb.ca. 50 dorm rooms with shared bathroom C$10–C$15 (US$7–US$10). 4 2-bedroom cottages sleep up to 8, C$125 (US$83); C$100 (US$67) with 4-night minimum. 5-bedroom trail lodge sleeps up to 26, C$600 (US$400). V, MC.

The 2-bedroom cottages at this homey, family-operated ranch are a great choice for families or couples traveling together, particularly those with an interest in horses: The ranch offers trail rides of varying duration, cattle checks, and some basic spa packages.

So new they sparkle, the cottages feature full kitchens, a small sitting area with gas stove, TV and VCR, and lovely, sweeping views of the ranch's 1,500 acres and the bay. Bedrooms are furnished with bunkbeds (a single over a double) plus a single bed. You won't mistake these lodgings for a 5-star luxury experience, but staying here is like sinking into a favorite armchair at the end of the day: supremely comforting and satisfying. The same could be said of the hearty, simple home-cooking Broadleaf dishes up in their large, cafeteria-style dining area.

Fundy Park Chalets. Route 114 (P.O. Box 72), Alma, NB E0A 1B0. ☎ **506/887-2808.** 29 cabins. TV. C$50–C$73 (US$33–US$49) double; discounts in spring and fall. MC, V. Closed Oct to mid-May.

These storybook-like cabins are set amid birch and pines just inside the park's eastern entrance and will have immediate appeal to fans of classic motor courts. The steeply gabled white clapboard cabins have interiors that will bring to mind a national park vacation, circa 1950—painted wood floors, pine paneling, metal shower stalls, small kitchenettes. Two beds are located in the main rooms, separated by a hospital-style track curtain that pulls around one bed. What the cabins lack in privacy they more than make up for in convenience and an unironic retro charm. The golf course, playground, tennis courts, lawn bowling, and saltwater pool are all within walking distance.

Parkland Village Inn. Route 114, Alma, NB E0A 1B0. ☎ **506/887-2313.** Fax 506/887-2315. 5 units. TV TEL. C$60–C$65 (US$40–US$43) double. Discounts in off-season. MC, V. Closed mid-Oct to late May.

The Parkland opened the same day as the park in 1948. It's an old-fashioned seaside hotel in the village of Alma, with five two-room suites that have been modernized and thinly furnished in a sort of budget-motel modern style. Some rooms have been set up as two-bedroom units, others with a sitting room and bedroom. All have fine views of the bay. It's not deluxe by any means, but it's handy to the park and offers good value for families.

   Dining: The downstairs dining room specializes in seafood, prepared with little fuss or flair. Prices range from C$8 to C$16 (US$5 to US$11). It's open for breakfast in July and August only.

WHERE TO DINE

Seawinds Dining Room. Route 114 (near park headquarters), Alma, NB E0A 1B0. ☎ **506/887-2098.** Reservations helpful. Sandwiches C$3–C$7 (US$2–US$5), main courses C$9–C$16 (US$6–US$11). MC, V. Daily 8am–9:30pm in summer. Closed Oct–May. PUB FARE/CANADIAN.

Seawinds overlooks the park golf course, and it serves as a de facto clubhouse for hungry duffers. The handsome and open dining room is decorated in rich forest green and mahogany hues, and it has hardwood floors, a flagstone fireplace, and wrought-iron chandeliers. The menu offers enough variations to please most anyone. Lunches include a variety of hamburgers, fish and chips, and bacon and cheese dogs. Dinner is somewhat more refined, with main courses like grilled trout, roast beef, and fried clams.

8 Moncton

Moncton, a city of some 113,500 residents, has been butting heads with Saint John in recent years as it strives to overtake the older port city as the province's economic powerhouse. As such, it's more notable as a regional commercial center than as a vacation destination. Travelers who detour off the Trans-Canada will find a mix of the antique and the modern. Brick buildings with elaborate facades and cornices exist cheek by jowl with boxy office towers of a less ornamental era. Moncton's low and unobtrusive skyline is dominated by an unfortunate concrete tower that houses a cluster of microwave antennae. It looks like a project designed by a former Soviet bureaucrat in a bad mood but serves as a good landmark to keep yourself oriented.

   The residents are also a mix of old and new. Moncton makes the plausible claim that it's at the crossroads of the Maritimes, and it hasn't been bashful about using its geographic advantage to promote itself as a business hub. As such, much of the hotel and restaurant trade caters to people-in-suits, at least on weekdays. But walk along Main Street in the evening or on weekends, and you're likely to spot spiked hair, grunge flannel, skateboards, and other youthful fashion statements from current and lapsed eras. There's life here.

   For families, Moncton offers a good stopover if you're traveling with kids. Magnetic Hill and Crystal Palace both offer entertaining (albeit somewhat pricey) ways to fill an afternoon. The latter is an especially appealing destination for younger kids on rainy days.

ESSENTIALS

GETTING THERE   Moncton is at the crossroads of several major routes through New Brunswick, including Route 2 (the Trans-Canada Highway) and Route 15.

The airport is about 10 minutes from downtown on Route 132 (head northeast on Main Street from Moncton and keep driving). The city is served by daily flights on **Air Canada** (☎ 800/776-3000 in the U.S. or 800/565-3940 in the Maritimes) and **Canadian Airlines International** (☎ 800/426-7000 in the U.S. or 800/665-1177 in Canada).

Via Rail's (☎ 800/561-3949 in the U.S. or 800/561-3952 in the Maritimes) line from Montréal to Halifax stops in Moncton 6 days a week. The rail station is downtown on Main Street, next to Highfield Square.

VISITOR INFORMATION   Moncton's primary **visitor information center** (☎ 506/853-3540) is at Magnetic Hill (Exit 488 off the Trans-Canada Highway). It's located in the wharf village section, and isn't particularly convenient—you're required to walk from the parking lot through the faux "village" of shops and boutiques to reach the center. It's open 8am to 8pm daily in summer; 9am to 5pm in the off-season.

Another visitor information center is downtown at 655 Main St. (☎ 506/853-3590) in the lobby of modern **City Hall.** It's open daily from 8am to 8pm during the peak summer season.

EXPLORING MONCTON

Moncton's downtown can be easily reconnoitered on foot—once you find parking, which can be vexing. (Look for the paid lots a block or so north and south of Main Street.) Downtown Moncton Inc. (☎ 506/857-2991) publishes a nicely designed "Historic Walking Tour" brochure that touches on some of the more locally significant buildings; ask for it at either visitor center.

The most active stretch of Main Street is the few blocks between City Hall (home to the visitor center) and the train underpass. Here you'll find cafes, newsstands, hotels, and restaurants, along with a handful of intriguing shops. Note the sometimes-jarring mix of architectural styles, the earlier examples of which testify to Moncton's historic prosperity as a commercial center.

Exploring by bike offers some wonderful dividends, especially when pedaling along Riverfront Park or through popular 300-acre Centennial Park. A local nonprofit called **Hub City Wheelers** schedules group bike rides nearly every day throughout the summer, and nonmembers are welcome; it's a good way to meet some of the local bikers and find the best routes. Ask at the visitor information center for a brochure with a schedule, or visit the group's Web site: www3.nbnet.nb.ca/jwcarter/hub_city.htm. Bike rentals are available at **Gary's Bicycle Rentals,** 239 Weldon St., Moncton, ☎ 877/858-8754 or 506/855-2394.

Moncton's **Tidal Bore** is a low wave that rolls up the Petitcodiac River at the leading edge of the turning tide. Sadly, the bore has been living up to its name since a dam and causeway were constructed upstream in 1968. Silt has built up in the chocolate-brown river below the causeway, which some say has reduced the height and drama of the bore. The wave, when it comes up around the bend of the river, is rather tiny. (Think of the Stonehenge scene in *Spinal Tap.*) It's more dramatic in winter and fall, I'm told, but in the summer it's not all that impressive.

The bore rolls in twice daily on the tides (at Bore Park it's illuminated at night with banks of floodlights). Check the arrival time in the brochure produced by the tourism authority, or swing by Bore Park on Main Street (across from the Hollins Lincoln-Mercury dealership) and note the time of the next bore on the digital clock. The park has bleachers to sit on and railings to lean against while awaiting the ripple.

Moncton Museum/Free Meeting House. 20 Mountain Rd. (at King St.). ☎ **506/856-4383.** Admission by donation. Mon–Sat 9am–4:30pm, Sun 1–5pm.

A simple way to get a good sense of Moncton's past is to spend 45 minutes or so roaming the Moncton Museum. This handsome, modern museum opened in 1973 (note the clever adaptation of the old City Hall facade), and it displays various artifacts of city life on two floors, including early hotel dishware, fashions, and intriguing, grainy photos of downtown in the early days. Each year the museum also hosts a half dozen or so traveling exhibits on wide-ranging topics. Architecture buffs should inquire at the museum's front desk about visiting the Free Meeting House next door. Constructed in 1821 and restored in 1990, the meeting house has historically served as a gathering point for a wide range of denominations. Inside, it's simplicity itself, with neatly enclosed pews and sunlight streaming in through the windows.

Magnetic Hill. Trans-Canada Highway (Exit 488), Moncton. ☎ **800/217-8111.** Admission: Magnetic Hill C$2 (US$1.35) per car. Magic Mountain Water Park C$20 (US$13) full day age 12 or older, C$14 (US$9) child 4–11. Half-day and evening rates available. Pier Mini Golf C$4.95 (US$3.30) ages 12 and older, C$3.75 (US$2.50) child 4–11. Magnetic Hill Zoo C$6 (US$4) adult, C$5 (US$3.35) youth 12–18 and seniors, C$3.75 (US$2.50) child 4–11. Water park daily 10am–8pm during peak season; until 6pm in shoulder season. Other attractions open varied hours; call for info. AE, MC, V.

Magnetic Hill, located on Moncton's northwest outskirts a few miles from downtown, began as a simple quirk of geography. Cars that stopped at the bottom of a short stretch of downhill started to roll back uphill! Or at least what appeared to be uphill. It's a nifty illusion—not to pull back the curtain, but it works because the slope is on the side of a far larger hill, which tilts the whole countryside and effectively skews one's perspective. Starting in the 1930s, locals capitalized on the phenomenon by opening canteens and gift shops nearby. By the 1950s the hill boasted the largest souvenir shop in the Maritimes.

This mysterious stretch of country road was preserved for posterity when a bypass was built around it, and today you can still experience the mystery. The atmosphere is a bit more glossy than a half-century ago, however. You enter a well-marked drive with magnet-themed road signs and streetlights, pay a C$2 (US$1.33) toll at a gatehouse, and wind around a comically twisting road to wait your turn before being directed to the hill.

Young kids often find the "uphill roll" entertaining—for about 3 yards. Then their attention is riveted by the two amusement complexes that have sprouted in the fields on either side of the road. Attractions within a few hundred yards of the hill include Wharf Village (a collection of souvenir shops and snack bars designed to look like a seaside village), a mini-golf course, a zoo, video arcades, go-kart racing, batting cages, a driving range, a kiddie train, and bumper boats. But the chief attraction is the Magic Mountain Water Park, which features wave pools and numerous slides, including the towering Kamikaze Slide, where daredevils can reach speeds of 40 miles per hour.

Despite—or perhaps because of—the unrepentant cheesiness, Magnetic Hill is actually a great destination for families weary of beaches, hikes, and the dreary natural world. Just be aware that nothing's cheap after you fork over that toonie to roll up the hill; an afternoon here can put a serious hurt on your wallet.

Crystal Palace. At Champlain Place Shopping Centre (Trans-Canada Highway Exit 504-A West), Dieppe. ☎ **877/856-4386** or 506/859-4386. Free admission. Rides are 1 to 4 tickets each (C$1/US65¢ per ticket or 10 for C$8.50/US$5.65). Unlimited ride passes C$21.50 (US$14.35; not including go-karts). Open daily Mon–Sat noon–8pm, Fri and Sat noon–9pm, Sun 10am–8pm.

The indoor amusement park at Crystal Palace will make an otherwise endless rainy day go by quickly. The spacious enclosed park includes a four-screen cinema, shooting arcades, numerous games (ranging from old-fashioned SkeeBall to cutting-edge video games), a medium-size roller coaster, a carousel, a swing ride, laser tag, bumper cars, mini-airplane and mini-semi-truck rides, mini-golf, batting cages, and a virtual-reality ride. From late June to early September, outdoor activities include go-karts and bumper boats. The park will particularly appeal to kids under the age of 12, although teens will likely find a video game to occupy them. To really wear the kids down, you can stay virtually inside the park by booking a room at the adjoining Best Western (see below).

WHERE TO STAY

Several chain hotels have set up shop near Magnetic Hill (Trans-Canada Highway Exit 488). These include **Comfort Inn** at 2495 Mountain Rd. (☎ **800/228-5150** or 506/384-3175); **Country Inn & Suites** at 2475 Mountain Rd. (☎ **800/456-4000** or 506/852-7000); and **Holiday Inn Express,** also just off the exit at 2515 Mountain Rd. (☎ **506/384-1050**). At these clean, convenient hotels, rooms range from C$85 to C$180 (US$57 to US$120).

Best Western Crystal Palace. 499 Paul St., Moncton, NB E1A 6S5. ☎ **800/528-1234** or 506/858-8584. Fax 506/858-5486. 115 units. A/C MINIBAR TV TEL. C$100–C$175 (US$67–US$117) double. Ask about value packages, which include amusement-park passes. AE, DC, DISC, ER, MC, V.

This modern, three-story chain hotel (built in 1990) adjoins the Crystal Palace amusement park and is a short walk from the region's largest mall. As such, it's surrounded by acres of asphalt and has little in the way of native charm. Most rooms are modern but unexceptional—not counting the 12 fantasy suites that go over the top with themes like "Deserted Island" (sleep in a thatched hut) or "Rock 'n' Roll" (sleep in a 1959 replica pink Cadillac bed). Some rooms face the indoor pool; others, the vast parking lot.

   Dining/Diversions: For entertainment there's the amusement park, obviously. Also within the amusement complex is the hotel's restaurant, McGinnis Landing, which offers basic pub fare. Prices are high for what you get at C$12 to C$20 (US$8 to US$13) for main dinner courses; but specials are always available, and the restaurant caters well to younger appetites.

   Amenities: Indoor pool, hot tub, sauna, coffeemakers in rooms, safe, baby-sitting, limited room service, dry cleaning (Monday through Friday), conference rooms.

Delta Beauséjour. 750 Main St., Moncton, NB E1C 1E6. ☎ **800/268-1133** or 506/854-4344. Fax 506/858-0957. 310 units. A/C MINIBAR TV TEL. C$89–C$159 (US$59–US$106) double summer and weekends; higher midweek in off-season. AE, DC, ER, MC, V.

The downtown Delta Beauséjour, constructed in 1972, is boxy, bland, and concrete, and the entrance courtyard is sterile and off-putting in a Cold War Berlin sort of way. But inside, the decor is inviting in a spare, International Modern manner. The property is well maintained, with rooms and public areas recently renovated. The third-floor indoor pool offers year-round swimming. (There's also a pleasant outdoor deck overlooking the distant marshes of the Petitcodiac River.) The hotel is a favorite among business travelers, but in summer and on weekends, leisure travelers largely have it to themselves.

Dining: In addition to the elegant ✪ **Windjammer** (see below), the hotel has a basic cafe/snack bar, a piano bar and lounge, and a rustic, informal restaurant which serves three meals a day.

Amenities: Indoor pool, health club, conference rooms, business center, safe-deposit boxes, turndown service, baby-sitting, dry cleaning, laundry service, washer/dryer, 24-hour room service, valet parking, beauty salon, and shopping arcade.

Victoria Bed & Breakfast. 71 Park St., Moncton, NB E1C 2B2. ☎ **506/389-8296.** 3 units (1 with private bathroom across hall). A/C TV TEL. C$85 (US$57) double, includes breakfast. MC, V.

This vaguely Craftsman-style 1910 home in a reasonably quiet neighborhood across from a church offers three comfortable rooms, all with private bathroom. All rooms are mid-sized, and feature stucco walls, lustrous maple floors, TVs with VCRs, and a relaxed country styling. Room 1 is the best of the bunch: it faces Park Street, is brighter and slightly larger than the other two, and is decorated in dark and soothing tones. Guests often linger in the attractive downstairs common, noodling around on the baby grand piano. For multi-night stays, ask about the corporate suites in a separate building around the corner.

WHERE TO DINE

Boomerang's Steakhouse. 130 Westmoreland St. ☎ **506/857-8325.** Call-ahead seating in lieu of reservations. Hamburgers and grilled sandwiches C$7–C$9 (US$5–US$6); dinners C$12–C$18 (US$8–US$12). AE, DC, DISC, ER, MC, V. Sun–Wed 4–10pm, Thurs–Sat 4–11:30pm. STEAKHOUSE.

Boomerang's is likely to remind diners of the Aussie-themed Outback Steakhouse chain, right down to the oversized knives. But since this is the only Boomerang's (it's not a chain), the service is rather more personal, and the Aussie-whimsical decor is done with a lighter hand. It's a handsome spot with three dining rooms, all quite dim with slatted dividers, drawn shades, and ceiling fans, which create the impression that it's blazingly hot outside. (That's a real trick in February in New Brunswick.) The menu features the usual stuff from the barbie, including grilled chicken breasts and ribs. The steak selection is grand, ranging from an 8-ounce bacon-wrapped tenderloin to a 14-ounce porterhouse. The burgers are also excellent.

✪ **The Windjammer.** 750 Main St. (in the Delta Beauséjour). ☎ **506/854-4344.** Reservations recommended. Main courses C$23–C$35 (US$15–US$23). AE, DC, ER, MC, V. Tues–Sun 5:30–11pm. CONTINENTAL.

Tucked off the lobby of Moncton's best hotel is The Windjammer, an intimate dining room that serves the city's best meals. With its heavy wood and nautical theme, it resembles the private officer's mess of an exclusive ship. The menu is ambitious, and the dining room has garnered an excellent reputation for its seafood dishes, including an appetizer of scallops served with a truffle jus, and entree of pan-fried salmon marinated in molasses and ginger. Despite the seafaring decor, the chef also serves up treats for carnivores, including tournedos of caribou with jus and blueberries, served with a fricassée of wild mushrooms.

EN ROUTE TO KOUCHIBOUGUAC NATIONAL PARK

If you decide to head directly to Kouchibouguac from Moncton, La Dune de Bouctouche makes for a good stop along the way. To reach the dune, take Route 15 east out of Moncton, then go north on Route 11 at its intersection with Shediac. The drive takes about an hour.

This striking, white sand dune stretches an impressive 12 kilometers (7¼ miles) across Bouctouche Bay, and is home to the endangered piping plover, a unique butterfly species, and some rare plants. The sensitive dune area itself can be viewed from a wheelchair-accessible, 2-kilometer boardwalk that snakes along its length. On a sunny day, the sand beach is a lovely spot to while away a couple hours, or even to take a dip in the warm seawater. The visitor center is fairly straightforward in its explanations of the flora and fauna indigenous to the dune; kids will probably be most amused by the larger than life, baby plover puppet that can be removed from its just-hatched "egg." Admission free, boardwalk open year-round in "good weather," visitor center open daily 10am to 8pm, till 5pm off-season.

If you're interested in spending the night in the area, or grabbing a bite to eat, stop by the **Inn by the Dune,** RR no. 1, House no. 589 (☎ 506/743-8182), where the German owner serves up a mean bratwurst and other Bavarian specialties. It's the kind of comfort food that's perfect if you're here on a cold, wet day in fall or winter. The brand-new rooms feature TVs, telephones and private bathrooms; they're pretty and light, but rather cramped. Double with breakfast C$94 (US$63) in season, C$85 (US$57) off-season; open year-round.

9 Sackville

Sackville is an attractive, leafy college town located just south of the Trans-Canada Highway shortly before eastbound travelers start across the Tantramar Marsh into Nova Scotia. Its location at the edge of this vast wetland makes it a popular destination for serious birders, and it's a pleasant way station for travelers looking for an overnight, or just a leg-stretching break during an extended journey east or west.

ESSENTIALS
GETTING THERE   Sackville is located just off the Trans-Canada Highway between Moncton and Amherst, Nova Scotia.

VISITOR INFORMATION   The **Sackville Visitor Information Center,** ☎ **506/364-4967,** is at 6 King St., just off Main Street. It's in an 1855 octagonal home moved from a nearby neighborhood, and is readily visible when heading toward downtown from the highway. The building shares a crafts shop that's operated by a group of local artisans.

EXPLORING SACKVILLE
Sackville's tidy and trim downtown is overshadowed by the large and attractive campus of **Mount Allison University** (☎ 506/364-2269). The university was founded in 1839 and has a top-rate reputation nationally for its undergraduate program; it's especially renowned for its fine arts program, which is the oldest in Canada. The school also holds the distinction of being the first in the nation to grant a bachelor's degree to a woman.

The campus of wide-crowned trees and broad lawns is ideal for a picnic. The **Owens Art Gallery,** off York Street, ☎ 506/364-2574, dates to 1895 (the oldest university art gallery in Canada) and has on display more than 2,000 works by artists from Canada and around the world. It's open daily throughout the summer, and admission is free.

Just off Main Street as you drive from the visitor center toward downtown is the **Swan Pond,** part of the Mount Allison campus. Look for the resident mute swans, pairs of which have been here since the 1950s (the originals were from the Royal

Swanherd, and were registered with the crown). The most recent pair has lived here for a number of years, and has even bred along the pond's shores. (They hatched five goslings in 1994.) The swans are sheltered and fed through the winter; both have been pinioned to disallow flight. The life span of these swans is typically 30 to 35 years.

The **Sackville Waterfowl Park,** located at the edge of downtown, must be one of the more heavily interpreted tracts of wetland in Canada. The small marsh edged by forests and homes is accessible via gravel pathways and boardwalks. A vibrant parade of birds can be spotted here throughout the warm-weather months, including common snipe, northern shoveller, blue-winged teal, common yellowthroat, coot, ring-necked duck, and sora rail. Also look for the osprey nesting platform.

Trails into the marsh can be found at several spots around town, including across from the visitor information center and across from the Swan Pond. The Canadian Wildlife Service, ☎ **506/364-5044,** staffs the **Wetlands Display** at their headquarters, which is adjacent to the park at the end of Waterfowl Lane (on your left when driving on Main Street from the highway toward town). The display includes informative exhibits and a large selection of informational brochures about local wildlife. Guided tours of the center and marsh are also available on request; they last about 45 minutes and cost C\$3 (US\$2) adult, C\$2.50 (US\$1.65) seniors and children 6 to 16, C\$6.25 (US\$4.15) family. Advance reservations for tours are helpful.

WHERE TO STAY & DINE

The new, modern, few-frills **Coastal Inn Sackville,** 15 Wright St. (Exit 541 of the Trans-Canada Highway), ☎ **888/704-7444** or 506/536-0000, is handy to the highway and a 5-minute drive from the campus and the waterfowl park. It was constructed in 1997 and has 50 rooms, each with cable TV, air-conditioning, and continental breakfast. Rates range from C\$50 to C\$90 (US\$33 to US\$60) for two.

Marshland Inn. 55 Bridge St., Sackville, NB E4L 3N8. ☎ **800/561-1266** or 506/536-0170. Fax 506/536-0721. www.marshlands.nb.ca. E-mail: marshlds@nbnet.nb.ca. 8 units. C\$70–C\$89 (US\$47–US\$59) double; C\$125 (US\$83) suite. AE, DC, ER, MC, V.

This imposing white clapboard mansion right in the village was built in 1854, and remains steadfastly old-fashioned ... and I mean that in a good way. Built by a stone merchant, the home has been an inn since 1935 and you'll find creaky floors, original light fixtures, plaster ceiling medallions, and wood. There's even wainscotting in some of the guest bathrooms. In the guest rooms, you'll have the sense they haven't been significantly changed since 1935—they're classy, clean, bright, and unshabby. Room 35 is the most impressive, with a pair of palladian windows, four-poster bed, Victorian furniture, and window seats. Most rooms are appointed with heavy Empire-style furnishings, and several have clawfoot tubs. Some are best suited to solo travelers. (Room 33 has a toilet and shower right in the bedroom, which is old-fashioned in a bad way.) Most rooms have telephones; ask in advance if this is important.

Dining: The clubby dining room with wood paneling and a restored, original William Morris frieze serves three meals daily, and the dinner here is the best in town. The evening menu includes rack of lamb, vegetarian crepes, chicken cordon bleu, and walnut and herb-crusted tenderloin. Entrees are priced C\$11 to C\$25 (US\$7 to US\$17), with most in the C\$15-to-C\$18 (US\$10-to-US\$12) range.

10 Kouchibouguac National Park

Much is made of the fact that this sprawling park has all sorts of ecosystems worth studying, from sandy barrier islands to ancient peat bogs. But that's a little bit like saying Disney World has nice lakes. It causes one's eyes to glaze over, and it entirely misses the point. In fact, this artfully designed national park is a wonderful destination for relaxing biking, hiking, and beach going. If you can, plan to spend a couple of days here doing a whole lot of nothing. The varied ecosystems (which, incidentally, are spectacular) are just an added attraction.

Kouchibouguac is, above all, a place for bikers and families. The park is laced with well-groomed bike trails made of finely crushed cinders that traverse forest and field, and meander along rivers and lagoons. Where bikes aren't permitted (such as on boardwalks and beaches), there are usually clusters of bike racks for locking them up while you continue on foot. If you camp here and bring a bike, there's no need ever to use your car.

Families can easily divide their days to keep kids entertained. Mornings might be spent at the broad and sandy beach, and afternoons biking along the lagoon, crossing a springy bog on a boardwalk, or poking around in a paddleboat.

The only contingent the park might disappoint are gung-ho hikers. This is a place not for serious hiking, but rather for walking and strolling. The pathways are wide and flat and invite a leisurely pace. Most trails are very short—on the order of 1 or 2 kilometers—and seem more like detours than destinations. In fact, approaching the park as a sort of desultory tour with intriguing detours might be the best way to go about a visit here.

Although the park is ideal for campers, day-trippers also find it a worthwhile destination. One tip: Plan to remain here until sunset. The trails tend to empty out, and the dunes, bogs, and boreal forest take on a rich, almost iridescent hue as the sun sinks over the spruce.

Be aware that this is a fair-weather destination. If it's blustery and rainy, there's little to do except take damp and melancholy strolls on the beach. It's best to save a visit here for more cooperative days.

By the way, the ungainly name is a Mi'kmaq Indian word meaning "River of the Long Tides." It's pronounced "*Koosh*-uh-*boog*-oo-*whack*." If you don't get it right, don't worry. Few do.

ESSENTIALS

GETTING THERE   Kouchibouguac National Park is between Moncton and Miramichi. The exit for the park off Route 11 is well marked.

VISITOR INFORMATION   The park is open from mid-May to mid-October. The **Visitors Centre** (☎ 506/876-2443) is just off Route 134, a short drive past the park entrance. It's open from 8am to 8pm during peak season, with shorter hours in the off-season. There's a slide show to introduce you to the park's attractions, and a small collection of field guides to peruse.

FEES   A daily pass is C$3.50 (US$2.35) adult, C$1.75 (US$1.15) children (6 to 16), C$2.75 (US$1.85) senior, and C$7 (US$4.65) family. Four-day passes are also available. A map of the park (helpful) costs C$1 (US65¢) at the information center. You should have permits for everyone in your car when you enter the park. There are no formal checkpoints, only occasional roadblocks during the summer to ensure compliance.

CAMPING

Kouchibouguac is at heart a camper's park, best enjoyed by those who plan to spend at least a night. **South Kouchibouguac,** the main campground, is centrally located and very nicely laid out with 311 sites, most rather large and private. The 46 sites with electricity are nearer the river and somewhat more open. The newest sites (1 to 35) lack grassy areas for pitching a tent, and campers have to pitch tents on gravel pads. It's best to bring a good sleeping pad or ask for another site. Sites are C$16.25 (US$10.85) per night. Reservations are accepted for about half of the campsites; call ☎ **800/414-6765** starting in late April. The remaining sites are doled out first-come-first-served.

Other camping options within the park: Across the river on Kouchibouguac Lagoon is the more remote, semiprimitive **Côte-à-Fabien.** It lacks showers and some sites require a short walk, but it's more appealing for tenters. The cost is C$14 (US$9) per night. The park also maintains three backcountry sites. **Sipu** is on the Kouchibouguac River and is accessible by canoe or foot; **Petit Large** by foot or bike; **Pointe-à-Maxime** by canoe only. Backcountry sites cost C$10 (US$7) per night for two, including firewood.

BEACHES

The park features some 15 kilometers (9 miles) of sandy beaches, mostly along barrier islands of sandy dunes, delicate grasses and flowers, and nesting plovers and sandpipers. ✪ **Kellys** is the principal beach, and it's one of the best-designed and best-executed recreation areas I've come across in Eastern Canada. At the forest's edge, a short walk from the main parking area, you'll find showers, changing rooms, a snack bar, and some interpretive exhibits. From here, you walk some 540 meters (600 yards) across a winding boardwalk that's plenty fascinating on its own. It crosses a salt marsh, lagoons, and some of the best-preserved dunes in the province.

The long, sandy beach features water that's comfortably warm, with the waves that are usually quite mellow—they lap rather than roar, unless a storm's offshore. Lifeguards oversee a roped-off section of about 90 meters (100 yards); elsewhere, you're on your own. For very young children who still equate waves with certain death, there's supervised swimming on a sandy stretch of the quiet lagoon.

BOATING & BIKING

Ryans—a cluster of buildings between the campground and Kellys Beach—is the place for renting bikes, kayaks, paddleboats, and canoes. Bikes rent for C$4.60 (US$3.05) per hour. Most of the water-sports equipment (including canoes and pedal boats) rent for about C$7 (US$4.65) per hour, with double kayaks at C$12 (US$8) per hour. Canoes may be rented for longer excursions; it's C$29.90 (US$19.95) daily, C$41.75 (US$27.85) for 2 days. Ryans is located on the lagoon, so you can explore up toward the dunes or upstream on the winding river.

The park offers a **Voyageur Canoe Marine Adventure** in summer, with a crew paddling a sizeable canoe from the mainland to offshore sandbars, where the naturalist-guide will help identify the wildlife encountered. Expect to see osprey and bald eagles. The three-hour excursion is C$25 (US$17) adult, C$15 (US$10) for children. Inquire about the trip at the park's information center.

Just outside the park in Saint-Louis-de-Kent visitors can sign up for a 2-hour nature cruise aboard the privately run power yacht **Claire-Fontaine, ☎ 506/876-4212.** Tours include narration about the local ecosystem and wildlife. The price is C$25 (US$17) adult, C$12 (US$8) for children.

HIKING

The hiking and biking trails are as short and undemanding as they are appealing. The one hiking trail that requires slightly more fortitude is the Kouchibouguac River Trail, which runs for some 13 kilometers (8 miles) along the banks of the river.

The Bog Trail is just 1.8 kilometers (1.2 miles) each way, but it opens the door to a wonderfully alien world. The 4,500-year-old bog is a classic domed bog, made of peat from decaying shrubs and other plants. At the bog's edge you'll find a wooden tower ascended by a spiral staircase that affords a panoramic view of this eerie habitat.

The boardwalk crosses to the thickest, middle part of the bog. Where the boardwalk stops, you can feel the bouncy surface of the bog—you're actually standing on a mat of thick vegetation that's floating atop water. Look for the pitcher plant, a carnivorous species that lures flies into its bell-shaped leaves, where downward-pointed hairs prevent them from fleeing. Eventually, the plant's enzymes digest the insect, providing nutrients for growth in this hostile environment.

Callanders Beach and **Cedar Trail** are at the end of a short dirt road. There's an open field with picnic tables, a small protected beach on the lagoon (there are fine views of dunes across the way), and a 1-kilometer (0.6-mile) hiking trail on a boardwalk that passes through a cedar forest, past a salt marsh, and through a mixed forest. This is a good alternative for those who'd prefer to avoid the larger crowds at Kellys Beach.

WHERE TO STAY & DINE

Habitant Motel and Restaurant. Route 134 (RR no. 1, Box 2, Site 30), Richibucto, NB E0A 2M0. ☎ **888/442-7222** or 506/523-4421. Fax 506/523-9155. E-mail: habitant@ nbnet.nb.ca. 29 units. A/C TV TEL. C$89.95 (US$59.95) double. AE, CB, DC, DISC, ER, MC, V. "Small, well-trained pets" allowed.

At about 15 kilometers (9 miles) from the park entrance, Habitant is the best choice for overnighting if you're exploring Kouchibouguac by day. It's a modern, mansard-roofed, Tudor-style complex—well, let's just say "architecturally mystifying"—with a restaurant and small campground on the premises. The rooms are decorated in a contemporary motel style and are very clean. The motel features a distinctive indoor pool, along with a fitness center and sauna.

Dining: The restaurant next door serves three meals a day and is informal, comfortable, and reasonably priced. Seafood dinners are the specialty, including a heaping "fisherman's feast" for C$23 (US$15). (Most main courses are C$8/US$5 to C$15/US$10.) One nice touch: There's a self-serve wine cellar, where wines are sold at liquor-store prices, many under C$20 (US$13).

11 Acadian Peninsula

The Acadian Peninsula is that bulge on the northeast corner of New Brunswick, forming one of the arms of the Baie des Chaleurs (Québec's Gaspé Peninsula forms the other). It's a land of tidy if generally nondescript houses, miles of shoreline (much of it beaches), modern concrete harbors filled with commercial fishing boats, and residents proud of their Acadian heritage. (You'll see everywhere the *stella maris* flag—the French tricolor with a single gold star in the field of blue.)

On a map it looks like much of the coastline would be wild and remote here. It's not. Although a number of picturesque farmhouses dot the route and you'll come upon brilliant meadows of hawkweed and lupine, the coast is more defined by manufactured housing that's been erected on squarish lots between the sea and fast two-lane highways.

Other than the superb Acadian Village historical museum near Caraquet, there are few organized attractions in the region. It's more a place to unwind while walking on a beach, or sitting along harbors while watching fishing boats come and go.

To remind yourself of where you are, every once in a while turn your back on the beach and look over the homes and cultivated fields. You'll see the sharp spires of the boreal forest—spruce and cedar and tamarack—poised as if ready to resume their march to the water's edge if the inhabitants lower their vigilance for just a moment or two.

ESSENTIALS

VISITOR INFORMATION   Each of the areas mentioned below maintains a visitor information center. **Caraquet Tourism Information** is at 51 bd. St-Pierre Est (☎ **506/726-2676**). This office offers convenient access to other activities in the harbor (see below), and there's plenty of parking. Shippagan dispenses information from a wooden lighthouse near the Marine Centre.

GETTING THERE   Route 11 is the main highway serving the Acadian Peninsula.

SHIPPAGAN & MISCOU ISLAND

Both of these destinations require a detour off Route 11 but are worthwhile if you're interested in glimpsing Acadian New Brunswick in the slow lane. As an added bonus, Miscou Island boasts some fine beaches.

Shippagan is a quiet, leafy village that's home to a sizeable crabbing fleet. It's also home to the modern **Aquarium and Marine Centre,** 100 Aquarium St. (☎ **506/336-3013**). The center is on the water near the harbor (prominently posted signs around town will direct you there) and is a good destination if you're the least bit curious about local marine life. You'll learn about the 125 species of native fish hereabouts, many of which are on display. Kids are drawn to the seal tank outside, where trainers prompt the sleek beasts to show off their acrobatic skills. Admission is C$6 (US$4) adults, C$2.50 (US$1.65) children, C$4 (US$2.65) seniors, and C$12 (US$8) families. The center is open from mid-May to early September 10am to 6pm daily; seal feedings are at 11am and 4pm.

Keep driving north on Route 113 and you'll soon cross a low drawbridge to Lamèque Island. If you're traveling through in mid-July, don't be surprised to hear fine baroque music wafting from the Ste-Cecil Church. Since 1975 the island has hosted the **Lamèque International Baroque Music Festival** (☎ 800/320-2276 or 506/344-5846). For about 10 days each summer, talented musicians perform an ambitious series of concerts, held in an architecturally striking, acoustically wonderful church in a small village on the island's north coast. Tickets often sell out well in advance, and are priced at C$20 to C$30 (US$13 to US$20).

North of Lamèque is **Miscou Island,** which for decades was served by a modest ferry. That era ended in the mid-1990s, when a shiny, arched bridge spanned the strait. The bridge made some islanders a bit grumpy, but happily the island still retains a sense of remoteness, especially north of the village of Miscou Centre, where you get into bog territory. The extraordinary view of the islands and ocean from the crest of the bridge serves as some consolation for the breach of isolation.

Drive northward on Route 113 until you run out of road, and you'll come to New Brunswick's oldest lighthouse. **Point Miscou Lighthouse** marks the confluence of the Gulf of St. Lawrence and the Baie des Chaleurs.

The dominant natural feature of Miscou is the bog. The **bog landscape** is as distinctive as that of the Canadian Rockies and the buttes of the desert Southwest. It's flat and green and can stretch for miles. You'll see much of this on northern Miscou Island (some of the bogs have been harvested for peat).

A finely constructed **interpretive nature trail** is on Route 113 north of Miscou Centre. A boardwalk loops through the bog around an open pond. Learn about the orchids and lilies that thrive in the vast and spongy mat of shrubs and roots. Look for the fascinating carnivorous plants (the pitcher plants are relatively easy to spot). The loop takes about 20 minutes, and it's free.

WHERE TO STAY

Miscou Beach Cottage & Camping. Route 113 (Mailing address: 22 Allée Alphonse), Miscou, NB E8T 2A2. ☎ **506/344-1015** or 506/344-8463. 6 cottages. C$60 (US$40) 1-bedroom cottage, C$68 (US$45) 2-bedroom cottage. MC, V. Closed Sept 15–June 15.

Far up Miscou Island are these simple, unpretentious cottages right on the beach. Six cottages sit side by side facing the dunes and the ocean beyond. Small decks front each cottage and invite idleness.

(Beware the voracious mosquito population, which descends at dusk early in the season.) The place has an English caravan park feel, with camp trailers crowded in a field behind the cottages. There's also a no-frills family restaurant on the premises. Not much else goes on here (unless you consider the bare-bones minigolf course), so plan to spend most of your day exploring the long sandy strand out front.

CARAQUET

The historic beach town of Caraquet—widely regarded as the spiritual capital of Acadian New Brunswick—just keeps on going and going, geographically speaking. It's spread thinly along a commercial boulevard parallel to the beach. Caraquet once claimed the honorific "longest village in the world" when it ran to some 22 kilometers (13 miles) long. As a result of its length, Caraquet lacks a well-defined downtown or any sort of urban center of gravity; there's one stoplight, and that's where Boulevard St-Pierre Est changes to Boulevard St-Pierre Ouest. (Most establishments mentioned below are somewhere along this boulevard.)

A good place to start a tour is the **Callefour de la Mer** (51 bd. St-Pierre Est), a modern complex overlooking the man-made harbor. It has a spare, Scandinavian feel to it, and you'll find the tourist information office (see above), a seafood restaurant, a snack bar, a children's playground, and two short strolls that lead to picnic tables on jetties with fine harbor views.

While you're here you can consider your options for viewing the bay. Two-hour boat tours aboard the **île Caramer,** ☎ **506/727-0813,** cost C$15 (US$10) per adult, C$7 (US$5) per child 12 and under. An exhilarating and fun 3-hour whale-watch tour with **Sea of Adventure,** ☎ **506/727-2727,** aboard a high-speed Zodiac costs C$50 (US$33) adult, C$30 (US$20) children 12 and under.

You can also rent a kayak from **Tours Kayaket** (☎ **506/727-6309**) for C$12 (US$8) an hour (C$24/US$16 for a double kayak) and putter around inside the sea wall, or venture out into the bay if conditions are agreeable. For C$35 (US$23) per person, guides will take you on a 3-hour excursion to an island or sandbar; if the wind's ripping, you'll be trailered to a protected river about 10 minutes from downtown.

○ **Village Historique Acadien.** Route 11 (6 miles west of Caraquet). ☎ **506/726-2600.** Admission C$10 (US$7) adult, C$8 (US$5) senior, C$5 (US$3) ages 6–16, C$25 (US$17) family. Daily in summer 10am–6pm (until 5pm in Sept and Oct). Closed mid-Oct to early June.

New Brunswick sometimes seems awash in Acadian museums and historic villages. If you're interested in visiting just one such site, this is the place to hold out for. Some 45 buildings—most of which were dismantled and transported here from other villages on the peninsula—depict life as it was lived in an Acadian settlement between the years 1770 and 1890. The historic buildings are set throughout 458 acres of woodland, marsh, and field. You'll learn all about the exodus and settlement of the Acadians from costumed guides, who are also adept at skills ranging from letterpress printing to blacksmithing. Plan on spending at least 2 to 3 hours exploring the village.

In June 2000, the village will open a major addition, which focuses on a more recent era. Some 26 buildings (all but one are replicas) will be devoted to continuing the saga, showing Acadian life from 1890 to 1939, with a special focus on industry. Among the new buildings will be a traditional hotel, which will house students enrolled in multiday workshops in traditional Acadian arts and crafts.

WHERE TO STAY

Auberge de la Baie. 139 bd. St-Pierre Ouest. ☎ **506/727-3485.** 54 units. A/C TV TEL. C$59–C$97 (US$39–US$65) double. AE, DC, DISC, ER, MC, V.

The Auberge de la Baie is your basic motel that has dressed itself up nicely with a modern lobby and dining room. The rooms are cheerless but adequate (some have cinder-block walls, some have bay views). Particularly inviting is the broad lawn that descends toward the water; stake your claim to a lawn chair and dive into a book. There's a small beach for swimming.

Dining: The oaky, Scandinavian modern-style restaurant is open for all three meals but specializes in seafood dinners. There's salmon with beurre blanc sauce, English-style fish and chips, and the ever-present fried clams with tartar sauce. Entrees range from C$9 to C$15 (US$6 to US$10).

Hotel Paulin. 143 bd. St-Pierre Ouest. ☎ **506/727-9981.** Fax 506/727-3300. 8 units. A/C TV TEL. C$65–C$85 (US$43–US$57) double. MC, V. Closed Nov–May.

This attractive Victorian hotel, built in 1891, has been operated by the Paulin family for the past three generations. It's a three-story red clapboard building with a green-shingled mansard roof, located just off the main boulevard and overlooking the bay. (Some of the charm has been compromised by encroaching buildings nearby.) The lobby puts one immediately in mind of summer relaxation, with royal blue wainscotting, canary yellow walls, and stuffed furniture upholstered in white with blue piping. The rooms were extensively renovated in 1999; six rooms were combined into three suites, and all rooms now have private bathrooms. (The original suite has the only ocean view.) Expect rooms comfortably but sparely furnished with antiques.

Dining: Hotel Paulin's first floor houses a handsome, well-regarded restaurant. Specialties include a delectable crab mousse and a cure for the sweet tooth: brown-sugar pie.

WHERE TO DINE

Caraquet is a good place for seafood, naturally. My preference is still with the Hotel Paulin's restaurant for its charm, but the several inexpensive-to-moderate spots along the main drag all serve fresh seafood nicely if simply prepared.

For a delicious and sophisticated snack, head to **Les Blancs d'Arcadia,** a handsome compound of yellow farm buildings hard against the forest just east of town. The specialties here are cheese and yogurt from the milk of a Swiss breed of goats called Saanen. The goats are raised indoors year-round; you can learn about the goats and the cheese- and yogurt-making process on a tour of the operation, which includes tastings. The 90-minute tour is C$6 (US$4).

There's also a small shop to buy fresh cheeses and milk. I recommend both the peppercorn and the garlic soft cheeses. Les Blancs d'Arcadia, 340-A bd. St-Pierre Est (☎ **506/727-5952**), is en route to Bas Caraquet on Route 145 (watch for the goat sign on the right shortly after you pass the road to St-Simon). Reservations for tours are appreciated.

GRANDE-ANSE

Grande-Anse is a wide-spot-in-the-road village of low, modern homes near bluffs over-looking the bay. The town is lorded over by the stern, stone Saint Jude church. The best view of the village, and a good spot for a picnic, is along the bluffs just below the church. (Look for the sign indicating "quai" 50 yards west of the church.) Here you'll find a small man-made harbor with a fleet of fishing boats, a tiny sand beach, and some grassy bluffs where you can park overlooking the bay.

If you'd prefer picnic tables, head a few miles westward to **Pokeshaw Park.** Just off-shore is a large kettle-shaped island ringed with ragged cliffs that rises from the waves, long ago separated from the cliffs on which you're now standing. An active cormorant rookery thrives among the eerie skeletons of trees, lending the whole affair a somewhat haunted and melancholy air. There's a small picnic shelter for inclement weather. It's open daily 9am–9pm; a small admission fee is charged.

For the full-blown ocean swimming experience, head to **Plage Grande-Anse,** located 2 kilometers (1.2 miles) east of town. This handsome beach has a snack bar near the parking area and is open 10am to 9pm daily. The cost is C$3 (US$2) for adults.

Pope Museum. 184 Acadie St., Grande-Anse. ☎ **506/732-3003.** Admission C$5 (US$3.35) adults, C$2.50 (US$1.65) children, C$3.50 (US$2.35) seniors, C$10 (US$6.65) family. Daily 10am–6pm (tickets sold until 5pm). Closed Sept to mid-June.

Deep vermilion hues and liturgical strains piped into all the rooms mark the modern Pope Museum, founded in 1985—the year after the Pope visited Moncton. The devout will enjoy the portrait gallery featuring portraits of all 264 popes. But all will be fascinated by the intricate model of the Vatican, which occupies much of the cen-tral hall (the top of the dome stands about 6 feet high). Other models of houses of worship include a smaller Florence Cathedral, Bourges Cathedral, Cheops pyramid, and the Great El Hakim Mosque. Head upstairs for displays of various Roman Catholic artifacts and contemporary religious accouterment, including vestments and chalices. Most descriptions are bilingual, but a handful are in French only.

12 Mt. Carleton Provincial Park

New Brunswick isn't all sandy beaches and rushing tides. There's the whole, vast inte-rior, a sprawling land marred by few roads and filled with rolling hills, dense forest, and tenacious blackflies (at least in early summer). This isn't wilderness—most of the land is employed as a vast timber plantation to feed the province's voracious paper and lumber mills. But in 1969, New Brunswick carved out some of the choicest land and set it aside as wilderness park. Mt. Carleton Provincial Park contains 7,052 acres of azure lakes, pure streams, thick boreal forest, and gently rounded mountains, the largest of which afford excellent views. When visiting, look for moose, black bear, coy-otes, bobcat, and more than 100 species of birds. And, of course, blackflies.

ESSENTIALS

GETTING THERE   Mt. Carleton Provincial Park is 43 kilometers (26 miles) east of Saint-Quentin on Route 180. Be aware that Saint-Quentin is the nearest commu-nity for supplies; there are no convenient general stores just outside the park gates. The park is also accessible from Bathurst to the east, but it's a 115-kilometer (69-mile) drive on a road that's mostly paved but gravel in spots. There are no services along the road and frequent logging trucks.

VISITOR INFORMATION   The park's gates are open daily in summer from 7am to 10pm (8am to 8pm in spring and fall). A **small interpretive center** (☎ 506/235-0793), located at the entrance gate, offers background on the park's natural and cultural history. The park is open but unstaffed from mid-October to May.

FEES   The day use fee is C$4 (US$2.65) per car from spring into fall.

CAMPING

Armstrong Brook is the principal destination for visiting campers. It has 88 sites split between the forest near Lake Nictau's shore (no lakeside sites) and an open, grassy field. Campers can avail themselves of hot showers and a bathhouse for washing up. A path leads to the lake's edge; there's a spit of small, flat pebbles that's wonderful for swimming and sunbathing. Camping fees are C$11 (US$7) weekdays, C$14 (US$9) weekends.

Four backcountry sites are located high on the slopes of Mt. Carleton (pre-registration required). The sites, which require a 4-kilometer (2.4-mile) hike, offer views into a rugged valley and a great sense of remoteness. Water is available but should be treated (beavers are nearby). No fires are permitted, so bring a stove. The fee is C$5 (US$3) per night.

Two other remote campsites on the shores of Lake Nictau are accessible by either canoe or a moderate walk. Register in advance; the fee is C$9 (US$6) per night.

HIKING & BIKING

The park has 10 hiking trails that total 68 kilometers (42 miles). The helpful park staff at the gatehouse will be happy to direct you to a hike that suits your experience and mood.

The park's premier hike is to the summit of **Mount Carleton,** the province's highest point at 820 meters (2,697 feet). Although that elevation is not going to impress those who've hiked in the Canadian Rockies, size is relative here, and the views seem endless. A craggy comb of rocks with a 360-degree view of the lower mountains and the sprawling lakes marks the summit. The trailhead is about a 25-minute drive from the gatehouse; allow about 4 hours for a round-trip hike of about 10 kilometers (6 miles).

Overlooking Nictau Lake is **Mount Sagamook,** at an altitude of 777 meters (2,555 feet). It's a steep and demanding hike of about 3 kilometers (1.8 miles) to the summit, where you're rewarded with spectacular views of the northern park.

For the truly gung-ho, there's the ridge walk that connects Sagamook and Carleton via **Mount Head.** The views from high above are unforgettable; you'll need to set up a shuttle with two cars to do the whole ridge in 1 day.

If you've got a mountain bike, bring it. The gravel roads are perfect for exploring. Motor vehicles have been banned from two of the roads, which take you deep into the woods past clear lakes and rushing streams.

5 Prince Edward Island

Prince Edward Island might not be the world's leading manufacturer of relaxation and repose, but it's certainly a major distribution center.

Visitors soon suspect there's something about the richly colored landscape of azure seas and henna-tinged cliffs capped with lush farm fields that triggers an obscure relaxation hormone, resulting in a pleasant ennui. It's hard to conceive that verdant and green PEI and boggy, blustery Newfoundland share a planet, never mind the same gulf.

The north coast is lined with red-sand beaches, washed with the warmish waters of the Gulf of St. Lawrence. Swimming here isn't quite like taking a tepid dip in North Carolina, but it's quite a bit warmer than in Maine or New Hampshire, farther down the Eastern seaboard. Away from the beaches you'll find low, rolling hills blanketed in trees and crops, especially potatoes, for which the island is justly famous. Small farms make up the island's backbone—one-quarter of the island is dedicated to agriculture, with that land cultivated by more than 2,300 individual farms.

The island was first explored in 1534 by Jacques Cartier, who discovered the Mi'kmaq living here. Over the next 2 centuries, dominion over the island bounced between Great Britain and France (who called the island île-St-Jean). Great Britain was awarded the island in 1763 as part of the Treaty of Paris; just over a century later, the first Canadian Confederation was held at Charlottetown and resulted in the creation of Canada in 1867 (PEI didn't join the confederation until 1873). The island is named for Edward Augustus (1767 to 1820), who was the son of George III of England.

The island is compact and its roads are unusually well marked. It's difficult to become disoriented and confused. But do try. I can think of few joys in life as simple and pleasurable as getting lost on some of PEI's back roads.

PEI is steeped in the slower pace of an earlier era; milkmen still make their quiet rounds, and you return soda pop bottles for refilling, not just recycling. Indeed, the population has grown only from 109,000 in 1891 to about 125,000 today. You should take your cue from this comforting cadence and do yourself this favor: schedule 1 or 2 extra days into your vacation, and make absolutely no plans. You will not regret this.

This chapter is divided into the counties that neatly trisect the province. It's easy to remember: they rise in order of royal hierarchy—Prince to Queens to Kings—in the direction of England.

One final note: the island has, somewhat remarkably, managed to retain its bucolic flavor of a century ago, and pockets of kitsch and sprawl are still happily few. But the handwriting is on the wall, especially in the central part of the island. The handwriting reads "Cottage Lots for Sale." Such signs have been springing up in greater number in alfalfa and potato fields, and in coming years more and more of the island is certain to be claimed by subdivisions and shopping plazas.

The sooner you can visit the better.

1 Exploring Prince Edward Island

PEI is Canada's smallest province—just 195 kilometers (about 120 miles) at its greatest length—which keeps the scuttling about down to a minimum and makes it very manageable for day explorations from one or two bases. However, take note: Island roads tend to be slower than you would expect elsewhere, so don't count on speedy travel despite the short distances.

In recent years a number of PEI hotels and attractions have banded together to market some 80 different vacation packages that offer discounts ranging from moderate to generous. There are some good values hidden within. Call ☎ **888/734-7529** or 902/368-4444 to request information on discount packages.

ESSENTIALS

VISITOR INFORMATION   Tourism PEI publishes a comprehensive free guide to island attractions and lodgings that's well worth picking up. The *Visitors Guide* is available at all information centers on the island, or in advance by calling ☎ **888/734-7529** or 902/368-4444. You can also request it by fax (902/629-2428), e-mail (tourpei@gov.pe.ca), or mail (P.O. Box 940, Charlottetown, PEI C1A 7M5). The official PEI Web site is located at www.peiplay.com.

In 1997, PEI opened a splashy new information center in something called **Gateway Village** (☎ **902/368-5465**), just as you arrive on the island via the Confederation Bridge. It's a good spot for gathering brochures and asking last-minute questions. There's also a well laid-out interpretive center featuring nicely designed exhibits about island history and culture. After zipping across the bridge, the exhibits on venturing to the mainland by ice boat in winters past are especially intriguing.

Yet the whole 29-acre Gateway development, which features a number of retail shops selling island products, is a little odd. As the promoters put it, "Gateway Village portrays a turn-of-the-century PEI streetscape encompassing an exposition pavilion, food and retail services, liquor store, visitor information center and the Festivals at Gateway." My suggestion: stop for brochures, maps, and a quick walk through the interpretive center. But then push on. Why not experience the real thing rather than this fussy, faux version?

**WHEN TO GO   **PEI's tourism season is rather brief, running for 6 or 7 weeks from early July to mid-to-late August. Most attractions don't open fully until July and some even close before August is done.

Restaurateurs especially take a lackadaisical approach to open hours during the shoulder months of June and September, and many seem to open according to caprice and whim. This is unfortunate since the weather is often excellent for touring from early June well into September.

Officials and more serious entrepreneurs are striving to convince shops and attractions to maintain more regular hours during the shoulder seasons, but they still have a way to go. If you do plan to visit in June or September, expect to be disappointed when some restaurants and attractions are closed. It may also behoove you to base out of Charlottetown for much of your shoulder-season visit, since the city's restaurants keep year-round hours.

GETTING THERE   If you're coming from the west by car, you'll arrive via the Confederation Bridge, which opened with great fanfare in June 1997.

Sometimes you'll hear it referred to as the "fixed link," a reference to the guarantee Canada made in 1873 to provide a permanent link from the mainland. The dramatic 12.9-kilometer (7.7-mile) bridge is open 24 hours a day and takes about 10 to 12 minutes to cross. Unless you're high up in a van, a truck, or an RV, the views are mostly obstructed by the concrete Jersey barriers that form the guardrails along the sides.

The bridge toll is C$35.50 (US$23.65) round-trip. No fare is paid when you travel to the island; the entire toll is collected when you leave. Credit cards are accepted. Call ☎ 888/437-6565 for more information.

Square One Shuttle (☎ 877-675-3830) offers transportation via seven-person van 4 days weekly between Charlottetown and Saint John, NB; Fredericton, NB; and Halifax, NS.

By Ferry   For those arriving from Cape Breton Island or other points east, **Northumberland Ferries Limited** (☎ 888/249-7245 or 902/566-3838) provides seasonal service between Caribou, NS (just north of Pictou), and Woods Island, PEI. Ferries with a 250-car capacity run from May to mid-December. During peak season (June to mid-October), ferries depart each port approximately every 90 minutes throughout the day, with the last ferry departing at 8pm. The crossing takes about 75 minutes.

No reservations are accepted; it's best to arrive at least an hour before departure to boost your odds of securing a berth on the next boat. Early morning ferries tend to be less crowded. Fares are C$47 (US$31) for a car and all its passengers. Major credit cards are honored. As with the bridge, fares are paid upon exiting the island; the ferry to the island is free.

By Air   The island's main airport is a few miles north of Charlottetown. Commuter flights to Halifax are just a half-hour; direct flights from Toronto are offered summers only. For more information, contact **Air Canada** (☎ 800/776-3000 in the U.S., 800/565-3940 in Eastern Canada) or Canadian Airlines (☎ 800/426-7000 in the U.S., 800/665-1177 in Eastern Canada, or 902/427-5500). (Note that at press time both Air Canada and Canadian Airlines were considering mergers with one another as well as with outside airlines.)

2 The Great Outdoors

Prince Edward Island doesn't have any wilderness or even much wildness to speak of. It's all about cultivated landscapes that have long ago been tamed by farmers. That doesn't mean you can't find outdoor adventure.

Here are some places to start.

BICYCLING   There's perhaps no finer destination in Atlantic Canada for relaxed road biking than Prince Edward Island. The modest size of the island, the gentleness of the hills (the island's high point is just 142m/465 feet), and the loveliness of the landscapes all conspire to provide a memorable biking trip. Although you won't find much rugged mountain biking here, you will find a surfeit of idyllic excursions, especially in the northern and eastern portions of the island. Avoid the Trans-Canada Highway on the south coast and main arterials like Route 2, and you'll find superb biking throughout the secondary road network.

The main off-road bike trail is the ✪ **Confederation Trail.** Eventually, the trail will cover some 350 kilometers (210 miles) along the old path of the ill-fated provincial railway from Tignish to Souris.

At present, about half the trail has been completed, mostly in Prince and Kings Counties; Queens County is still largely under development. The pathway is covered mostly in rolled stonedust, which makes for good travel with a mountain bike or hybrid. Services are slowly developing along the route, with bike rentals and inns cropping up. Ask at the local tourist bureaus for updated information on completed segments. An excellent place to base for exploring the trail is the **Trailside Cafe** (see page 212) in Mount Stewart, where several spurs of the trail converge. The cafe can arrange for return shuttles if you'd prefer one-way cycling.

MacQueen's Island Tours & Bike Shop (☎ **800/969-2822.**), at 430 Queen St. in Charlottetown, organizes bicycle tour packages, with prices including bike rentals, accommodations, route cards, maps, luggage transfers, and emergency road repair service. Five-and 7-night tours are C$899 (US$599) and C$1,199 (US$799), respectively. Rentals are also available at C$25 (US$17) per day, C$100 (US$67) per week. MacQueen's can be reached via e-mail at biketour@macqueens.com, or by calling ☎ 902/368-2453.

For rentals and repairs, you might also try **Smooth Cycle** (☎ **800/310-6550** or 902/566-5530) at 172 Prince St. in Charlottetown. Rentals include helmet and lock and cost C$22 (US$15) per day.

FISHING   For a taste of deep-sea fishing, head to the north coast, where you'll find plenty of outfitters happy to take you out on the big swells. The greatest concentrations of services are at North Rustico and Covehead Bay; see the "Queens County" section, below. Rates are quite reasonable, generally about C$20 (US$13) for 3 hours or so.

Trout fishing holes attract inland anglers, although, as always, the best spots are a matter of local knowledge. A good place to start your inquiries is at Island Rods and Flies, 18 Birch Hill Dr., Charlottetown (☎ **902/566-4157**), which specializes in fly-fishing equipment. Information on required fishing licenses can be had from any visitor information center, or by contacting the **Department of Environmental Resources,** P.O. Box 2000, Charlottetown, PEI C1A 7N8 (☎ **902/368-4683**).

GOLF   PEI's reputation for golf has soared in the last few years. That's due in part to a slew of new and expanded courses—three opened in 1999 alone: Countryview Golf Course, Dundarave Golf Course, and St. Felix Golf and Country Club—and in part because the greens fees haven't followed the same sharply upward trajectory that has afflicted many courses in the United States. As a result, you can golf along the ocean at fees just a fraction of what you'd expect in similarly dramatic settings elsewhere.

One of the best-regarded courses is the **Links at Crowbush Cove** (☎ **902/ 652-2356**). Sand dunes and persistent winds off the gulf add to the challenge at this relatively young (1994) course, which is on the northeastern coast. Another perennial favorite is the **Brudenell River Provincial Golf Course** (☎ **902/652-2342**) near Montague along the eastern shore. In 1999, the course added a second 18-holer, this designed by Michael Hurdzan, who has also created well-regarded courses in Toronto and Vancouver. As part of its expansion, the course also launched the new **Brudenell Golf Academy** (☎ **888/698-4653**) in July 1999. Programs take place on the two golf courses as well as at the 400-yard double-ended driving range, and on the 4 acres of tee decks.

Golf Island PEI publishes a booklet outlining the essentials of the 16 island courses. Request a copy from island information centers or from the provincial tourist information number (☎ **800/463-4734** or 902/368-4444), or write P.O. Box 2653, Charlottetown, PEI C1A 8C3. The information is also available online at www.golfpei.com.

SEA KAYAKING   PEI has 1,260 kilometers (783 miles) of attractive coastline and relatively warm water, making for excellent sea-kayaking.

Paddlers can vary the scene from broad tidal inlets ringed with marsh to rusty-red coastline topped with swaying waves of marran grass. **Outside Expeditions** (☎ **800/207-3899** or 902/963-3366; on the Web, www.getoutside.com) hosts half-day excursions daily at the national park for C$50 (US$33). More ambitious paddlers can sign up for 2- to 7-day trips departing throughout the summer. Excursions are also available from Peake's Wharf in Charlottetown and at Brudenell River Provincial Park in eastern PEI.

SWIMMING   Among PEI's chief attractions are its red sand beaches. You'll find them all around the island, tucked in among dunes and crumbling cliffs. Thanks to the moderating influence of the Gulf of St. Lawrence, the water temperature is more humane here than elsewhere in Atlantic Canada, and it usually doesn't result in unbridled shrieking among bathers. The most popular beaches are at Prince Edward Island National Park along the north coast, but you can easily find other beaches with great swimming.

Among my favorites: Cedar Dunes Provincial Park on the southwest coast, Red Point Provincial Park on the northeast coast, and Panmure Island Provincial Park on the southeast coast.

3 Queens County

This county occupies the center of the province, is home to the island's largest city, and hosts the greatest concentration of traveler services.

The county is neatly cleaved by the Hillsborough River, which is spanned by bridge at Charlottetown. Cavendish on the north shore is the most tourist-oriented part of the entire province; if the phrase "Ripley's Believe It or Not Museum" lacks positive associations for you, you might consider avoiding this area, which has built a vigorous tourist industry around a fictional character, Anne of Green Gables. On the other hand, much of the rest of the county—not including Charlottetown—is quite pastoral and untrammeled.

Two parts of Queens County merit their own sections within this chapter: the capital city of Charlottetown on the south shore, and Prince Edward Island National Park on the north shore. Flip ahead for more detailed information on these destinations.

ESSENTIALS

GETTING THERE   Route 2 is the fastest way to travel east-west through the county, although it lacks charm. Route 6 is the main route along the county's north coast; following the highway involves a number of turns at intersections, so keep a sharp eye on the directional signs.

The **Shuttle** (☎ **902/566-3243**) provides daily service between Charlottetown and several points in Cavendish during the summer season. The rate is C$15 (US$10) round-trip.

VISITOR INFORMATION   The **Cavendish Visitors Centre** (☎ **902/963-2391** summer or 902/566-7050 off-season) is open daily 8am to 10pm June to mid-September and is located just north of the intersection of Route 13 and Route 6.

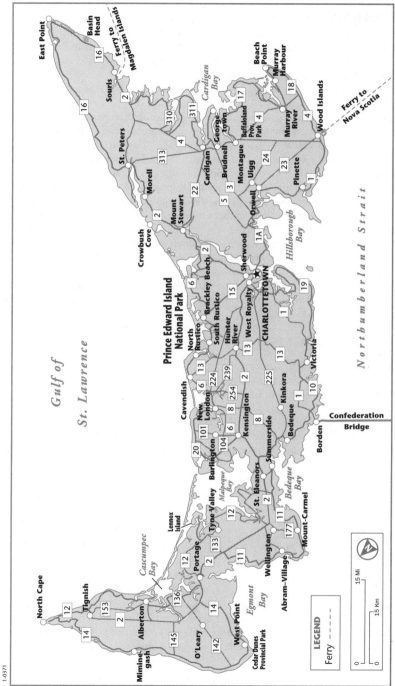

Prince Edward Island

CAVENDISH

Cavendish is the home of the fictional character Anne of Green Gables. If you mentally screen out the tourist traps constructed over the past couple of decades, you'll find the area a bucolic mix of woodlands and fields, rolling hills and sandy dunes—a fine setting for a series of pastoral novels.

However, the tremendous and enduring popularity of the novels has attracted droves of curious tourists, who in turn have attracted droves of entrepreneurs who've constructed new buildings and attractions. The bucolic character of the area has thus become somewhat compromised. There are wax museums and loud amusements, all of which would probably alarm Anne, along with a surfeit of motels and cottage courts. The new developments don't approach the garishness quotient of, say, Niagara Falls, but they're quite unavoidable, especially along Route 6 west of Route 13. Happily, most attractions are set off the road and spread well apart from one another. I wouldn't go so far as to say that the new developments harmonize with the landscape, but the collateral damage has been slight compared to what might have occurred. And the development is rather limited—you need only head east or west of Cavendish on Route 6 for a few miles to be back into the lovely landscapes of rolling farm fields that made the region famous in the first place.

Of the village of Cavendish, you should be aware that there's no there there, to steal from Gertrude Stein. There's no discernible village center; everything is sprawled out along the approach roads. A new commercial development called Avonlea (see below) is seeking to manufacture a new village center, but, well, it's just not quite the same. Those who like their villages quaint and are not terribly interested in the cult of Anne are better off steering for North or South Rustico, among other villages in the area.

EVERYTHING ANNE

All visitors to Prince Edward Island owe it to themselves to read *Anne of Green Gables* at some point. Not that you won't enjoy your stay here without doing this, but if you don't, you might feel a bit out of touch, unable to understand the inside references that seep into many aspects of PEI culture. (Even some gas stations in Cavendish sell Anne dolls.) In fact, Anne has become so omnipresent and popular on the island that a licensing authority was created in 1994 to control the crushing glacier of Anne-related products.

Some background: Lucy Maud Montgomery wrote *Anne of Green Gables* in 1908. It's a fictional account of Anne Shirley, a precocious and bright 11-year-old who's mistakenly sent from Nova Scotia to the farm of the taciturn and dour Matthew and Marilla Cuthbert. (The mistake? The Cuthberts had requested a boy orphan to help with farm chores.) Anne's vivid imagination and outsized vocabulary get her into a series of pickles, from which she generally emerges beloved by everyone who encounters her. It's a bright, bittersweet story, and it went on to huge popular success, spawning a number of sequels.

The story has proven especially enduring in Japan, where it's taught in schools and where the cheeky heroine seems to have boundless appeal. As a result, planeloads of Japanese travelers make the summer pilgrimage to PEI to walk where Anne walked, stroll past the oddly familiar landmarks, and even get married in Anne settings. At any rate, this enduring fascination explains why you'll often see billboards and brochures hereabouts printed with Japanese translations.

Green Gables. Route 6, Cavendish (just west of intersection with Route 13). ☎ **902/672-6350.** Admission: C$2.50 (US$1.65) adult, C$2 (US$1.35) senior, C$1.25 (US85¢) children, and C$6 (US$4) family. Open daily June–Sept; peak season 9am–7pm (until 5pm shoulder seasons).

The best place to start an Anne tour is at Green Gables itself. The house is operated by Parks Canada, which also operates a helpful visitor's center on the site. You can watch a 7-minute video presentation about Montgomery, view a handful of exhibits, and then head out to explore the farm and trails. The farmhouse dates to the mid-19th century and belonged to cousins of Montgomery's grandfather. It was the inspiration for the Cuthbert farm, and it has been furnished according to descriptions in the books.

If you're a diehard Anne fan, you'll delight in the settings where characters ventured, such as the **Haunted Woods** and **Lover's Lane.** But you might need as active an imagination as Anne's to edit out the golf carts puttering through the landscape at the adjacent Green Gables Golf Course, or the busloads of tourists crowding through the house and moving herdlike down the pathways. Come very early or very late in the day to avoid the largest crowds. (*One last note:* Rumors still persist that Green Gables burned down a few years ago. It didn't. These tenacious fictions evidently stem from news reports of a minor fire in 1997.)

Cavendish Cemetery. Intersection of Route 13 and Route 6, Cavendish. Open daily.

This historic cemetery was founded in 1835, but it's best known now as the final resting spot for author Lucy Maud Montgomery. It's not hard to find her gravesite: follow the pavement blocks from the arched entryway, which is across from the Anne Shirley Motel. Montgomery's grave is the one planted with flowers.

Macneill Homestead. Route 6. Cavendish (just east of Route 13 intersection.) ☎ **902/963-2231.** C$2 (US$1.35) adult, C$1 (US65¢ children. July–Aug daily 9am–7pm, June and Sept daily 9am–5pm.

Montgomery lived with her grandparents Alexander and Lucy Macneill from 1876 (when she was just 21 months old) to 1911. Montgomery wrote *Anne of Green Gables,* among other books, while living in their farmhouse. Alas, the building is no longer standing, but visitors can roam the grounds and read interpretive signs about the property's literary history. There's also a small bookshop featuring books by and about Lucy Montgomery. The site will be mainly of interest to true Anne buffs.

Avonlea. Route 6 (across from Rainbow Valley amusement park), Cavendish. ☎ **902/963-3050.** C$5 (US$3.35) adult, C$4 (US$2.65) senior, C$3 (US$2) ages 6–16, C$12 (US$8) family.

This new development of faux historic buildings was opened in the summer of 1999 with the idea of creating the sort of a village center you might find in reading the Anne novels. It's located on a large lot amid amusement parks and motels, and the new buildings have been constructed with an eye to historical accuracy. Several Anne-related buildings and artifacts are located on the site, including the schoolhouse in which Montgomery taught (moved here from Belmont), and a Presbyterian church (moved from Long River), which Montgomery occasionally attended. There's also a variety show, hayrides, staff in period dress, restaurant, several stores (including an art gallery and music shop), and a spot for ice cream and candy.

Anne of Green Gables Museum at Silver Bush. Route 20, Park Corner. ☎ **902/436-7329.** C$2.35 (US$1.55) adults, C75¢ (US50¢) children under 16. Open daily June–Oct 9am–5pm (until 7pm July and Aug).

About 20 kilometers (12 miles) west of Cavendish near the intersection of Route 6 and Route 20 is the Anne of Green Gables Museum at Silver Bush. It's located in the home of Montgomery's aunt and uncle; the author was married here in 1911. For the best view of the "Lake of Shining Waters," take the wagon ride.

Lucy Maud Montgomery Birthplace. Intersection of Route 6 and Route 20, New London. ☎ **902/886-2099.** Admission C$2 (US$1.35) adult, C50¢ (US35¢) ages 6–12. Open daily mid-May to mid-Oct 9am–7pm.

Very near the Anne of Green Gables museum is the Lucy Maud Montgomery Birthplace, where the author was born in 1874. The house is decorated in the Victorian style of the era, and it includes Montgomery mementos like her wedding dress and scrapbook.

Lucy Maud Montgomery Heritage Museum. Route 20, Park Corner. ☎ **902/886-2807.** C$2.50 (US$1.65) adults, children under 12 free. Daily July and Aug 9am–7pm; June and Sept 9am–5pm. Closed Oct 1 to May 31.

This museum is located in the 1879 home of Montgomery's grandfather—perhaps. (Its lineage is a bit unclear.) Attractions include antiques from the family, along with artifacts mentioned in her books. Three times weekly, special day-long events are held, which include readings, picnics by the lake, and the creation of flower-adorned straw hats. (C$80/US$53).

Anne of Green Gables—The Musical. Confederation Arts Centre, Charlottetown. ☎ **800/565-0278** or 902/566-1267. Tickets C$20 to C$36 (US$13 to US$24).

This spritely, professional musical has been playing for years at the downtown arts center, and brings to the stage many of Montgomery's stories and characters.

AMUSING THE KIDS

Cavendish has capitalized on its tourist allure with a handful of "museums" and theme parks to appeal to younger kids. All are located along Route 6 westward from the intersection with Route 13.

The biggest and most elaborate amusement park is **Rainbow Valley** (☎ 902/963-2221). Activities are distributed around 32 acres of forest and field, and they include six water slides, a monorail, swan boats, a maze, and plenty more. The admission fee—C$10 (US$6.65) adults, C$8.50 (US$5.65) children—includes unlimited rides, although waits on water slides can be long on warm days. It's open daily June to early September 9am to 8pm (opens 2 hours later on Sunday).

The smaller, more manageable **Sandspit** (☎ 902/963-2626) has "Indy" go-kart racing, a 60-foot Ferris wheel, a roller coaster, bumper cars, and the like. There's no admission charge to visit the grounds; you can pay as you go (the roller coaster is about C$2/US$1.35) or buy a bracelet that covers all rides. Open daily mid-June to Labor Day.

Rainy-day diversions include Ripley's Believe It or Not! Museum (☎ 902/963-3444) and the **Royal Atlantic Wax Museum** (☎ 902/963-2350), which features a "special Anne of Green Gables scene complete with antique buggy." Both are located near the intersection of Route 6 and Route 13 in Cavendish.

WHERE TO STAY

Cottage courts are to Cavendish what 19th-century inns are to Vermont—they're everywhere, and vary tremendously as to quality. Be aware that many of the cottage courts and motels are more interested in high volume and rapid turnover than personal attention to guests. A number also believe that hanging a straw hat or two on a door allows them to boast of "country charm," when they have anything but.

If you arrive in town without reservations, check the board at the visitor's information center (see above), which lists up-to-the-minute vacancies.

Also, you might ask around among local residents about under-the-table rentals. One August a couple of years back, I rented a handsome three-bedroom Cavendish farmhouse built in 1910 and set in a barley field. It was a lovely 10-minute stroll to the beach down a dirt lane, and the cost was C$100 (US$67) per night. Where did I learn about it? On a scrap of paper tacked to the wall of the local Laundromat.

Cavendish Beach Cottages. Gulf Shore Dr., Cavendish (mailing address: 166 York Lane, Charlottetown, PEI C1A 7W5). ☎ **902/963-2025.** 13 units. TV. C$116–C$160 (US$77–US$107) double. MC, V. Closed early Oct to late May.

Location, location, location. This compound of 13 cottages is located on a grassy rise within the national park, just past the gatehouse into the park. The pine-paneled cottages are available in one, two, or three-bedroom configurations, and all feature ocean views, kitchenettes with microwaves, and outdoor propane barbecue grills. The cottages are a 2-minute walk from the beach. There's also easy access to Gulf Shore Drive, where you'll find some of the island's premier biking.

Green Gables Bungalow Court. Route 6 (Hunter River RR no. 2), Cavendish, PEI C0A 1N0. ☎ **800/965-3334** or 902/892-3542. 40 cottages. TV. C$80–C$115 (US$53–US$77) for up to 4 people. MC, V. Closed mid-Sept to June.

Located next to the Green Gables house, this pleasant cluster of one- and two-bedroom cottages began as a government make-work project promoting tourism in the 1940s. As a result, they're quite sturdily built, and nicely arrayed among lawn and pines. All have kitchens with refrigerators and coffeemakers, and many have outdoor gas grills for an evening barbecue. The linoleum floors and Spartan furnishings take on a certain retro charm after a few hours of settling in. Some cabins were trimmed with cheap sheet paneling, others have the original pine paneling; ask for one with the latter. The beach is about 1 kilometer (0.6 miles) away, and there's a small heated outdoor pool on the premises.

Red Road Country Inn. Route 6, Clinton, PEI C0B 1M0. ☎ **800/249-1344** or 902/886-3154. Fax 902/886-2267. 9 units. C$115–C$175 (US$77–US$117), including full breakfast. MC, V.

Located 20 minutes west of Cavendish, this cream-colored inn sits on 33 acres atop a lovely knoll. Rooms have unobstructed views down a long and rustling hayfield to Harding Creek, which widens and flows into the gulf. (Rowboats are tied up at a dock for guests.) The inn, which doesn't promise much from outside, was built in 1994–95, but adopts a more historic character inside thanks to pine floors, large beams, and the handiwork of the owner, who is also a furniture maker—the guest rooms are each tastefully furnished with his Shaker reproductions and Windsor chairs. A buffet-style breakfast featuring homemade breads is included in the rates; on pleasant days guests like to take their meals to the porch and enjoy the morning sun coming across the gently rounded hills that surround the inn. Televisions are available on request; children over 12 are welcome.

WHERE TO DINE

Cavendish itself offers limited opportunities for creative dining, although it's well stocked with restaurants offering hamburgers, fried clams, and the like. Both places mentioned below require a 10- to 15-minute drive from Cavendish proper, but they're worth it. See also the "Lobster Suppers" box below.

Café on the Clyde. Intersection of Route 224 and Route 258 (6.5km/4 miles south of Route 6 on Route 13), New Glasgow. ☎ **902/964-4304.** Main courses: breakfast and lunch C$2–C$8 (US$1.35–US$5.35), dinner C$9–C$16 (US$6–US$11). AE, DC, JCB, MC, V. Daily in July and Aug 8am–9pm; limited hours June and Sept; closed Oct–May. LIGHT FARE.

This cafe is part of the noted Prince Edward Island Preserve Co, itself a worthwhile stop for the delicious homemade preserves. Light meals are served in the bright and modern dining room just off the preserve showroom. In this popular and often crowded spot, you can order from a menu that has a small but appealing selection; the smoked fish platter and lobster chowder are just the ticket on a drizzly afternoon.

✪ **Herb Garden.** Route 224, Hunter River. ☎ **902/621-0765.** Reservations recommended. Main courses C$15.50–C$19 (US$10–US$13). MC, V. Daily 5–10pm July and August; Thurs–Sun noon–9pm remainder of year. Located on Route 224 between New Glasgow and St. Ann's (2km west of Route 6). REGIONAL/GERMAN.

Set off the road in a quiet landscape of gardens and forest, the Herb Garden is attractive in a sparely decorated, knotty pine kind of way. The restaurant is justly famous on the island for its wholesome, middle-European-inspired cooking. Organically grown ingredients are used (much of it from the five gardens on the property), and all baking is done on the premises. The island-raised lamb is especially good, and other perennials include Wiener schnitzel and scallops in wine sauce. Desserts are outstanding, and include cheesecake and homemade ice cream. Everything here is prepared in small batches, so come early for a better selection—favorites tend to run out before the evening is over. If the weather cooperates, ask for a table on the patio. Watch for the understated sign on Route 224 outside of Hunter River; many harried travelers find the place by speeding past, then making an abrupt U-turn.

NORTH & SOUTH RUSTICO TO BRACKLEY BEACH

A few miles east of Cavendish are the Rusticos, of which there are five: North Rustico, South Rustico, Rusticoville, Rustico Harbor, and Anglo Rustico. The region was settled by Acadians in 1790 and many residents are descendants of the original settlers. North and South Rustico are both attractive villages that have fewer tourist traps and are more amenable to exploring by foot or bike than Cavendish. Although out of the hubbub, they still provide easy access to the national park and Anne-land, with beaches virtually at your doorstep.

North Rustico clusters around a scenic harbor with views out toward Rustico Bay. Plan to park and walk around, perusing the deep-sea fishing opportunities (see below) and peeking in the shops. The village curves around Rustico Bay to end at North Rustico Harbor, a sandspit with fishing wharfs, summer cottages and a couple of informal restaurants (such as the Blue Mussel Cafe, see below). A wood-decked promenade follows the water's edge from the town to the harbor, and is a worthy destination for a quiet afternoon ramble or a picnic. Also here in the bright yellow wharf building is **Outside Expeditions** (☎ 800/207-3899 or 902/963-3366; on the Web, www.getoutside.com), which offers sea kayak excursions of the harbor and surrounding area.

In South Rustico, turn off Route 6 and ascend the low hill overlooking the bay. Here you'll find a handsome cluster of buildings that were home to some of the more prosperous Acadian settlers. Among the structures is the sandstone **Farmer's Bank of Rustico,** established with the help of a visionary local cleric in 1864 to help farmers get ahead of the hand-to-mouth cycle. Renovations have been ongoing for several years; it should be open for tours starting in 2000. Next door is handsome **St. Augustine's Parish Church** (1838) and a **cemetery** beyond. If the church's door is open, head in for a look at this graceful structure.

Brackley Beach is the gateway to the eastern section of the national park, and has the fewest services of all. It's a quiet area with no village center to speak of that will be best appreciated by those who prefer their beach vacations unadulterated.

DEEP-SEA FISHING

PEI's north shore is home to the island's greatest concentration of deep-sea fishing boats. For about C$20 (US$13) per person, you'll get 3 hours out on the seas in search of mackerel, cod, and flounder. Don't worry about lack of prior experience: equipment is supplied; crew members are very helpful; and most will even clean and fillet your catch for you.

In North Rustico, about a half-dozen captains offer fishing trips. Among them are: **Aiden Doiron's Deep Sea Fishing** (☎ 902/963-2442), **Bob's Deep-Sea Fishing** (☎ 902/963-2666), **Bearded Skipper's Deep-Sea Fishing** (☎ 902/963-2334), and **Court Brothers Deep Sea Fishing** (☎ 902/963-2322). A 20-minute drive east of North Rustico, at Covehead Harbor (within the national park), try **Richard's Deep-Sea Fishing** (☎ 902/672-2376) or **Salty Seas Deep-Sea Fishing** (☎ 902/ 672-3246).

SHOPPING

Between Cavendish and Brackley Beach you'll find a number of shops offering unique island crafts and products. Browsing is a good option for a rainy or overcast day that keeps you off the beach.

Cheeselady's Gouda. Route 223, Winsloe North southeast of Oyster Bed Bridge. ☎ **902/368-1506.**

This is a short detour off Route 6, but well worth it. Watch a brief video about the making of gouda cheese, and then get down to business: buying some of the excellent cheeses produced here. If you don't want to stick with the traditional aged cheese, try the flavored varieties, including peppercorn, garlic, and herb. Sizes ranging from a wedge to a wheel are available.

◯ The Dunes Studio Gallery. Route 15, Brackley Beach. ☎ **902/672-2586.**

This architecturally striking, modern gallery on the way to the eastern section of PEI National Park is among the best spots on the island to browse the fine works produced by island artisans and craftspeople. Situated on two open levels, the gallery features pottery, furniture, lamps, woodworking, sculpture, and paintings, along with more accessible crafts including handmade soaps and jewelry. The gallery is also home to an appealing, small cafe, making this a good spot for a lunch and browsing break.

Gaudreau Fine Woodworking. Route 6, South Rustico. ☎ **902/963-2273.**

All woodworking sold here is made on the premises. Items range from elegantly timeless sushi trays to modern wrist rests for computer keyboards crafted from birds-eye maple. Also sold are crafts and paintings from selected island artisans.

Old Forge Pottery and Crafts. Route 6, North Rustico. ☎ **902/963-2878.**

Crafts from several island artisans are featured here, with an especially good selection of the graceful pottery made by Carol Downe, the owner.

Prince Edward Island Preserve Co. Intersection of Route 224 and Route 258 (just off Route 13), New Glasgow. ☎ **902/964-4304.**

PEI Preserve Co. sells accessible luxury. The firm makes a variety of exceptionally tasty preserves at this small factory in a lovely valley. You can sample those that are currently available, and watch the process through a glass window. It's pricey for a jar of jam (C$6.75/US$4.50 at last visit), but that never deters me from stocking up on raspberry and champagne jam and sour cherry marmalade—my two favorites. There's also a cafe on the site. (See "Café on the Clyde" in the Cavendish section, above.)

Seasway Hammock Shop. Churchill Ave., North Rustico. ☎ **902/963-2846.**

The sturdy, attractive hammocks sold at this shop are crafted on the premises by a retired fisherman. They not only look good, they're made to last.

WHERE TO STAY

Barachois Inn. Church Rd., South Rustico (mailing address: P.O. Box 1022, Charlottetown, PEI C1A 7M4). ☎ **902/963-2194.** E-mail: arachoisinn@pei.sympatico.ca. 4 units (1 with private bathroom down hallway). C$125–C$145 (US$83–US$97) double, including full breakfast. MC, V. Closed Nov–March.

The proudly Victorian Barachois Inn was built in 1870, and it is a soothing retreat for road-weary travelers. It's topped with a lovely mansard roof adorned with pedimented dormers, and it boasts a fine garden and historic furnishings throughout. Innkeepers Judy and Gary MacDonald bought the place as derelict property in 1982, and have done an outstanding job bringing it back from the brink, adding modern art along the way to soften the staid Victorian architecture. It's furnished with high-quality period antiques; the two rooms on the third floor are a bit cozier than the spacious second floor suites, but guests feel far away from the world when tucked under the slanted eaves. Room 1 has a canopy bed dating to the 1840s and an unusually large bathroom. Room 3 on the top floor has both a clawfoot tub and a stall shower.

The inn is located amid a cluster of other historic buildings on a gentle rise overlooking Rustico Bay. Factor in some time to just stroll around and enjoy both the village and the inn's tidy garden. Ask about the special occasions package, which includes an Anne of Green Gables–themed carriage ride and picnic lunch.

Shaw's Hotel. Route 15, Brackley Beach C1E 1Z3. ☎ **902/672-2022.** Fax 902/672-3000. E-mail: shaws@auracom.com. 15 units, 20 cottages. TV (cottages only). Inn: C$195–C$255 (US$130–US$170) double, including breakfast and dinner; cottages: C$225–C$350 (US$150–US$233) double. AE, ER, MC, V. Closed Oct–May. Pets allowed in cottages only.

Shaw's is a delightfully old-fashioned compound located down a tree-lined dirt road along a marsh-edged inlet. It's been in the same family since 1860, and even with its regimen of modernization—new in 1999 were a sundeck, a bar, and a dining room addition that accommodates 40 more people—the place still has the feel of a farm-stay vacation in the 19th century. It remains the kind of place where ripply and worn carpeting in the hallways adds to the charm rather than detracts. (One caveat: a new subdivision across the river is starting to encroach on the pastoral environment.)

The hotel's centerpiece is the Victorian farmhouse with its lipstick-red mansard roof. Fifteen guest rooms are located upstairs; they are "boarding-house style," which is to say, small. The cottages vary in size and vintage. None are terribly lavish, but most have the essentials (some with kitchenettes, some just with cube refrigerators). While the new cottages are perfectly fine, the older ones—like my favorite, no. 6 with its dark beadboard and brick fireplace—have a surfeit of creaky, summer home charm. This is still the kind of place where you walk down a sandy lane to get to the beach, and where signs admonish you, "Don't let Chase (the dog) follow you to the beach."

Dining: The spare but handsome main dining room serves breakfast and dinner daily. The dinner menu changes frequently, but typical entrees are filet mignon au poivre, poached halibut with bearnaise, or penne with smoked salmon in a vodka cream sauce. Prices range from C$17 to C$23 (US$11 to US$15). The Lobster Trap Lounge, located in a nearby outbuilding, is open until 1am daily, and it offers more casual fare like chicken pot pie, nachos, and steamed island mussels.

Lobster Suppers

The north shore of Prince Edward Island is home to famous lobster suppers, which are a good bet if you have a craving for one of the succulent local crustaceans. These suppers took root years ago as events held in church basements, in which parishioners would bring a covered hot dish to share and the church would provide a lobster. Everyone would contribute some money, and the church netted a few dollars. Outsiders discovered these good deals, the fame of the dinners spread, and today several establishments offer the bountiful lobster dinners, although few are raising money for charity these days.

Expect a large and impersonal dining experience (Fisherman's Wharf can accommodate 500 diners at a time), especially if you have the misfortune to pull up after a couple of bus tours have unloaded. Lobster is naturally the main feature, although you'll usually find roast beef, ham, or other alternatives. These are typically accompanied by an all-you-can-eat buffet with a button-bursting selection of rolls, salads, chowder, mussels, desserts, and more. The cost? Figure on C$20 to C$30 (US$13 to US$20) per person, depending on the options.

St. Ann's Church Lobster Suppers (☎ 902/621-0635) remains a charitable organization, as it was 3 decades ago when it was the first and only lobster supper on PEI. Located in a modern church hall in the small town of St. Ann, just off Route 224 between Routes 6 and 13, St. Ann's has a full liquor license and the home-cooked food is served at your table (no buffet lines). Lobster dinners are served Monday to Saturday from 4 to 9pm. As befits a church, it's closed on Sundays.

Fisherman's Wharf Lobster Suppers (☎ 902/963-2669) in North Rustico boasts a 60-foot salad bar to go with its lobster; it's open daily from noon to 9pm. And near the PEI Preserve Company in New Glasgow is **New Glasgow Lobster Suppers** (☎ 902/964-2870). Meals include unlimited mussels and chowder; it's on Route 258 (just off Route 13) and is open daily from 4:30 to 8:30pm.

Amenities: You can rent canoes, kayaks, and bikes from an outfitter based on the grounds, and the beach is just a half-kilometer away. Services include baby-sitting, laundry, and secretarial services.

WHERE TO DINE

See also Shaw's Hotel, above, and ✪ **Dalvay-by-the-Sea,** listed under "Prince Edward Island National Park," later in this chapter.

Blue Mussel Café. On the water, North Rustico Harbor. ☎ **902/963-2152.** Reservations not accepted. Main courses, lunch C$4.95–C$10.95 (US$3.30–US$7.30), dinner C$9.95–C$19.95 (US$6.60–US$13.30). AE, MC, V. Open daily 11am–8pm. Closed early fall to early summer. SEAFOOD.

The tiny and trim Blue Mussel Cafe is located at North Rustico Harbor—follow the road northward along the water from North Rustico until you arrive at a cluster of ramshackle fishing buildings. Look for the sign. There's a small indoor seating area and a compact deck with views of the harbor and a tidal marsh. It's not much to look at, but the food makes it worth tracking this place down. "We don't do deep-fried of any kind," says the owner. "No French fries, no fried fish." What you will find are simply prepared meals like grilled salmon, pan-fried scallops, steamed mussels, seafood chowder, and boiled lobster. Lunches include salads, crab rolls, chicken sandwiches, and a complement of seafood items. A budget children's menu features hamburgers, hot dogs, and fish sticks.

Cafe St. Jean. Route 6, Oyster Bed Bridge. ☎ **902/963-3133.** Reservations recommended. Lunch C$7–C$9 (US$5–US$6), dinner C$12–C$25 (US$8–US$17); mostly C$15–C$18/US$10–US$12. Daily 11:30am–9:30pm. Closed Oct to mid-June. Located where Route 6 crosses the Wheatley River, at the southern tip of Rustico Bay. ECLECTIC.

There's a strong emphasis on local and Celtic music at Cafe St. Jean, with original tunes in the background, live music on the deck some evenings, and even CDs and tapes for sale at the cash register. Don't worry—this isn't a ploy to compensate for the quality of the food. Though meals can be inconsistent, the kitchen often scales culinary heights, producing zesty originals. The menu should appeal to most taste buds: There's Cajun salmon with a creole sauce, shrimp with peppercorns, and chateaubriand. Too dressed up? Stick to the fish and chips or one of the excellent cafe salads. The high-backed booths in the restaurant's center can feel a bit confining; angle for a window seat with a view of the Wheatley River.

ORWELL

In southeastern Queens County, the village of Orwell offers a historic detour off speedy Route 1 between Charlottetown and the Wood Islands ferry. Both sites mentioned below are near one another on a side road; there are few landmarks other than simple signs directing you here, so keep a sharp eye out.

The **Orwell Corner Historic Village** (☎ 902/651-8510) is one of the most aesthetically pleasing historic villages in the province. Set on a gentle slope amid a profusion of leafy trees, the village re-creates life in a small agricultural town in the 1890s. You can visit the general store, stop by the blacksmith shop, or wander the lush gardens. If it works out, plan to visit around lunchtime and pick up a picnic from the community hall to enjoy under a shady tree on the grounds. Ask about the lively *ceilidhs* with traditional music, held Wednesday evenings in the community hall (extra charge). The village is one of several sites islandwide managed by the Prince Edward Island Museum and Heritage Foundation. It's open 9am to 5pm daily in July and August (limited hours starting in late May and September through late October). Admission is C$4 (US$2.65), children under 12 free.

A few minutes' drive from the village is the modest, white-shingled **home of Sir Andrew Macphail,** a gifted polymath born here in 1864. Macphail found renown as a medical doctor, pathologist, professor, writer, editor, and agricultural tinkerer. You'll learn about his exceptional career while walking through the house, which includes a handful of exhibits and period furniture. (There's also a restaurant, see below.) But the real allure of the site is a stroll through the 140-acre farm grounds, which are accessible via several trails. It's lush and pastoral, filled with the summer sounds of crickets and songbirds.

Admission to this national historic site (☎ 902/651-2789) is free, with donations happily accepted. It's open daily in summer 10am to 8pm, except on Monday, Tuesday, and Saturday, when it closes at 5pm.

WHERE TO DINE

Sir Andrew Macphail Homestead. Off Route 1, Orwell. ☎ **902/651-2789.** Reservations requested for dinner. Main courses: lunch C$3.50–C$6 (US$2.35–US$4), dinner C$13–C$15 (US$8.65–US$10). V. Mon–Tues 10am–6pm, Wed–Fri 10am–8:30pm, Sat 10am–4pm, Sun 10am–8:30pm. Closed mid-Sept to mid-June. TRADITIONAL.

The simple, sparely decorated restaurant is located in the Macphail homestead (see above) and features a limited menu of classic dishes. Arrive early enough for a leisurely

"The man who farms only for the money .... is a fool, because one who can make money out of farming can make a good deal more out of something else. But for the man who would live a quiet, interesting, reasonable, and useful life there is no other occupation which affords so favorable an opportunity. It demands the exercise of every facility. Every movement of the day is full of surprise, and every effort has its imme- diate reward either in success or failure. For the finest minds it affords an outlet for activity; for the poorest it affords a living without the sordid accompaniment of poverty. And Prince Edward Island presents a field the freest for all who would live this life."

—Sir Andrew Macphail, 1912.

walk through the grounds, then request a table on the sunporch, which is always bright and summery. The menu includes the Macphail haggis, a modern adaptation of the traditional Scottish meal ("There are no sheep stomachs involved," the hostess assured me). Other dishes range from roast lamb to sole almandine, and the menu always includes a vegetarian selection. Lunches feature soups, sandwiches, and salads.

4 Prince Edward Island National Park

Prince Edward Island National Park encompasses a 40-kilometer (24-mile) swath of red-sand beaches, wind-sculpted dunes topped with marran grass, vast salt marshes, and placid inlets. The park is located along the island's sandy north-central coast, which is broached in several spots by broad inlets that connect to harbors. As a result, you can't drive along the entire park's length in one shot. The coastal road is disrupted by inlets, requiring backtracking to drive the entire length. And, actually, there's little point in trying to tour the whole length. It's a better use of your time to pick one spot, then settle in and enjoy your surroundings.

The reddish sand and abstract dunes define the park for many. But also look for woods and meadows nearby, as well as wildlife. You might spot the tracks of red fox, mink, or muskrat. In the marshes and tidal flats, dozens of great blue heron stalk their aquatic prey near sunset. Where beach and dune meet, watch for the piping plover, a small and endangered beach bird.

The national park also oversees the Green Gables house and grounds; see "Cavendish," above.

ESSENTIALS

GETTING THERE   From Charlottetown, Route 15 offers the most direct route to the eastern segments of the park. To head to the Cavendish area, take Route 2 to Hunter River, then head north on Route 13.

VISITOR INFORMATION   Two visitor centers provide information on park des- tinations and activities between June and October. The **Cavendish Visitors Centre** (☎ **902/963-2391** or 902/963-7830) is near the intersection of Routes 6 and 13; it's open daily from 9am to 10pm in the peak summer season (it closes earlier during the shoulder seasons).

The **Brackley Visitors Centre** (☎ **902/672-7474**) is at the intersection of Routes 6 and 15; it's open daily in July and August from 9am to 9pm (9am to 4:30pm in June, September, and October). In the off-season, contact the park administration office (☎ **902/672-6350**) near the Dalvay Hotel.

FEES Between June and September, visitors to the national park must stop at one of the toll houses to pay entry fees. Daily rates in 1997 were C$3 (US$2) adult, C$2 (US$1.35) senior, C$1.50 (US$1) children 6 to 16, C$7 (US$4.65) family. Ask about multiday passes if you plan to visit for more than 3 days.

BEACHES

PEI National Park is nearly synonymous with its beaches. The park is home to two kinds of sandy strands: popular and sometimes crowded beaches with changing rooms, lifeguards, snack bars, and other amenities; and all the other beaches. Where you go depends on your temperament. If it's not a day at the beach without the aroma of other people's coconut tanning oil, head to **Brackley Beach** or **Cavendish Beach.** The latter is within walking distance of the Green Gables house and many other amusements (see "Cavendish," above) and makes a good destination for families.

If you'd just as soon be left alone with the waves, sun, and sand, you'll need to head a bit farther afield, or just keep walking down the beaches until you leave the crowds behind. I won't reveal the best spots here for fear of crowding. But suffice it to say, they're out there.

HIKING & BIKING

Hiking is limited here compared to that at Atlantic Canada's other national parks, but you will find a handful of pleasant strolls. And, of course, there's the beach, which is perfect for long walks.

The park maintains eight trails for a total of 20 kilometers (12 miles). Among the most appealing is the **Homestead Trail,** which departs from the Cavendish campground. The trail offers a 5.5-kilometer (3.3-mile) loop and an 8-kilometer (4.8-mile) loop. The trail skirts wheat fields, woodlands, and estuaries, with frequent views of the distinctively lumpy dunes at the west end of the park. Mountain bikes are allowed on this trail, and it's a busy destination on sunny days. The two short trails at the Green Gables house—**Balsam Hollow** and **Haunted Wood**—are lovely but invariably crowded. Avoid them if you're looking for a relaxing walk in the woods.

Biking along the shoreline roads in the park is sublime. The traffic is light, and it's easy to make frequent stops to explore beaches, woodlands, or the marshy edges of inlets. The two **shoreline drives** within the national park—between Dalvay and Rustico Island, and from Cavendish to North Rustico Harbor—are especially beautiful on a clear evening as sunset edges into twilight. Snack bars are located at Brackley Beach and Covehead Bay.

Your safest bet for bike rentals is in Charlottetown (try **Smooth Cycle,** 172 Prince St., ☎ **800/310-6550** or 902/566-5530), although you can often find rentals closer to the beach. In Brackley Beach, a good option is **Northshore Rentals** (☎ **902/672-2022**), located at Shaw's Hotel.

CAMPING

Prince Edward Island National Park has three campgrounds. Reservations are not accepted, so plan to arrive early in the day for the best selection of sites. Campground fees start at C$17 (US$11) per night (slightly less at Rustico Island), with serviced sites C$23 (US$15). For more information, contact the **Cavendish Visitors Centre** (☎ **902/963-2391** or 902/963-7830).

The most popular (and first to fill) is **Cavendish,** located just off Route 6 west of Green Gables. It has more than 300 sites spread among piney forest and open, sandy bluffs; the sites at the edge of the dunes overlooking the beach are the most popular. The sites aren't especially private or scenic. A limited number of two-way hookups are available for RVs, and the campground has free showers, kitchen shelters, and evening programs.

The **Stanhope** campground lies just across the park road from lovely Stanhope Beach, which is on the eastern segment of the park (enter through Brackley Beach). The road isn't heavily traveled, so you don't feel much removed from the water's edge. Most sites are forested, and you're afforded more privacy here than at Cavendish. Two-way hookups, free showers, and kitchen shelters are offered.

To my mind, the best campground is **Rustico Island.** It's down a dead-end sand-spit, with a number of sites overlooking a placid cove and the rolling countryside beyond. It lacks hookups for RVs, which might explain why sites are usually available here after the other campgrounds fill up. The sites are mostly wooded, very large, and quite private. Supervised swimming is 4 kilometers (2.5 miles) away at Brackley Beach. If you'd rather have quiet than a lifeguard, turn left out the campground gate and walk or bike down the gated dirt road to the pleasant (and often deserted) narrow beach at the mouth of Rustico Bay.

WHERE TO STAY & DINE
Also see listings for "Cavendish" and "North & South Rustico to Brackley Beach," above.

Dalvay-by-the-Sea. Off Route 6, Grand Tracadie (mailing address: P.O. Box 8, Little York, PEI C0A 1P0). ☎ **902/672-2048,** fax (summer only) 902/672-2741. www.aco.ca/dalvay. E-mail: dalvay@isn.net. 34 units. Mid-June to mid-Sept: C$190–C$300 (US$127–US$200) double, including breakfast and dinner (C$20/US$13 less in shoulder seasons). National park entrance fees also charged. 2-night minimum in summer. AE, DC, ER, MC, V. Closed mid-Oct to early June.

This imposing Tudor mansion was built in 1895 by Alexander MacDonald, a partner of John D. Rockefeller. The place is unusually large for a private home, but it's rather intimate for a luxury inn. There are glimpses of the ocean across the road from the upper floors, but the landscaping largely focuses on a beautiful freshwater pond out front. Inside, you'll be taken aback by the extraordinary cedar woodwork in the main entryway, and by the grand stone fireplace. The guest rooms are elegantly appointed and wonderfully solid and quiet; in the evening you'll hear mostly the roar of the sea.

Dining: The Dalvay added a new pavilion-style dining room to the main inn in 1999. Not to worry—it's been constructed in a classic style that blends nicely with the original architecture. The net result has been to add some much-needed seats, along with improved views of the gardens and pond. The well-regarded kitchen features dishes like tea-smoked Atlantic salmon with artichoke salad and crème fraîche. For dessert, try the sticky date pudding with toffee sauce, which was featured in *Gourmet* magazine. For those not on the meal plan, entrees run C$20 to C$25 (US$13 to US$17).

Amenities: The inn is just across the road from one of the park's better beaches; there's also tennis, croquet, lawn bowling, horseshoes, canoeing, bike rentals, a two-hole fairway, and nearby nature trails. An afternoon tea is served from 2 to 4pm.

5 Charlottetown

It's not hard to figure out why early settlers put the province's political and cultural capital where they did: It's on a point of land between two rivers and within a large protected harbor. For ship captains plying the seas, this quiet harbor with ample anchorage and wharf space must have been a welcome sight. Of course, travelers rarely arrive by water these days (unless a cruise ship is in port), but the city's harborside location translates into a lovely setting for one of Atlantic Canada's most graceful and relaxed cities.

Named after Queen Charlotte, consort of King George III, Charlottetown is home to some 40,000 people—nearly one of every three islanders. Within Canada, the city is famous for hosting the 1864 conference that 3 years later led to the creation of the independent Dominion of Canada. For this reason, you're never far from the word "confederation," which graces buildings, malls, and bridges. (In a historic twist, PEI itself actually declined to join the new confederation until 1873.)

Today, the downtown has a brisk and busy feel to it, with a pleasing mix of modern and Victorian commercial buildings, as well as government and cultural centers. Outside the business core, you'll find leafy streets and large, elegant homes dating from various eras, with the most dramatic from the late 19th century. Charlottetown is also blessed with a number of pocket parks, which provide a quiet respite amid the gentle clamor. Charlottetown's only charmless place? The outlying suburbs off Route 2, where you'll find traffic and strip malls of the sort that seem to be proliferating throughout North America.

Charlottetown is centrally located and serves admirably as a base for exploring the rest of the island (only the far western coast is a bit distant for relaxed day tripping). You can be touring Green Gables, relaxing on a north shore beach, or teeing off at Brudenell Provincial Park within 45 minutes of leaving Charlottetown. The capital has the island's best selection of inns and hotels, and a fine assortment of restaurants that ensure you can dine out every night for a week and still be pleasantly surprised. As for scheduling time for exploring the city itself—I'd suggest saving it for a rainy day. And you don't really need much more than a day to take in all the highlights.

ESSENTIALS

GETTING THERE   Both Route 1 (the Trans-Canada Highway) and Route 2 pass through or near Charlottetown. For information on arriving by air, see "Exploring Prince Edward Island" at the beginning of this chapter. **Square One Shuttle** (☎ 877-675-3830) runs seven-person vans 4 days a week between Charlottetown and Saint John, NB; Fredericton, NB; and Halifax, NS.

VISITOR INFORMATION   The city's main Visitor Information Centre (☎ 902/368-4444) is on Water Street (across from 169 Water St. and next to Confederation Landing Park). Look for the brown "?" sign to direct you to a brick building with helpful staffers, an interactive computer kiosk, and an ample supply of brochures. There's also a vacancy board to let you know where rooms are currently available. The center is open daily in July and August 8am to 10pm; in the off-season, 8am to 5pm. There's a second information center at City Hall on Queen Street (☎ 902/566-5548) that's open daily in summer 8am to 5pm.

EXPLORING CHARLOTTETOWN

Charlottetown is a compact city that's easy to reconnoiter once you park your car. Three main areas merit exploration: the waterfront, the downtown area near Province House and the Confederation Court Mall, and parks and residential areas near Victoria Park.

You're best off first heading to the main Visitor Information Centre (see above), and then starting your tour from the waterfront. Parking is generally scarce downtown, but it's relatively abundant near the visitor center, both on the street and in free and paid lots. At the visitor center, be sure to ask for a map and one of the free walking tour brochures, "The First Five Hundred: Heritage and History Walks."

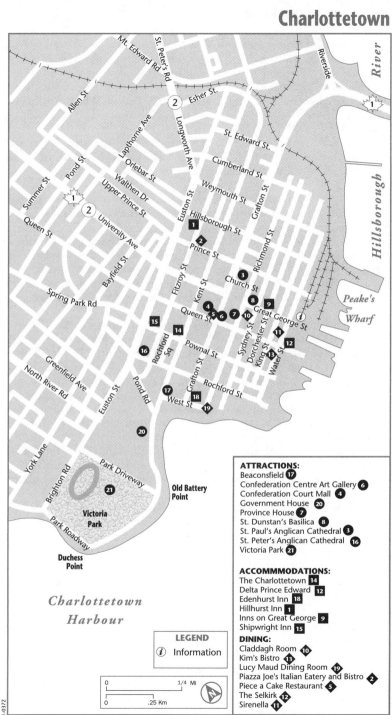

Charlottetown

ATTRACTIONS:
Beaconsfield **17**
Confederation Centre Art Gallery **6**
Confederation Court Mall **4**
Government House **20**
Province House **7**
St. Dunstan's Basilica **8**
St. Paul's Anglican Cathedral **3**
St. Peter's Anglican Cathedral **16**
Victoria Park **21**

ACCOMMMODATIONS:
The Charlottetown **14**
Delta Prince Edward **12**
Edenhurst Inn **18**
Hillhurst Inn **1**
Inns on Great George **9**
Shipwright Inn **15**

DINING:
Claddagh Room **10**
Kim's Bistro **13**
Lucy Maud Dining Room **19**
Piazza Joe's Italian Eatery and Bistro **2**
Piece a Cake Restaurant **5**
The Selkirk **12**
Sirenella **11**

LEGEND
ⓘ Information

0 _____ 1/4 Mi
0 _____ .25 Km

The waterfront has been spruced up in recent years with the addition of **Peake's Wharf,** a collection of touristy boutiques and restaurants that attracts hordes in summer. The complex is attractive and offers good people-watching, but it has a somewhat formulaic "festival marketplace" feel to it and is rather lacking in local character. To see the city from the water, sign up with **Peake's Wharf Boat Cruises** (☎ **902/566-4458**), which offers three tours daily starting at C$12 (US$8), with children under 12 half price.

Next to the wharf is **Confederation Landing Park,** an open, modern park with a boardwalk along the water's edge, lush lawns, and benches nicely situated for indolence. There's also a 220-boat marina, where you can scope out newly arrived pleasure craft.

From Peake's Wharf, you can stroll up **Great George Street.** This is surely one of the most handsome streets in all of Canada, with leafy trees, perfectly scaled Georgian rowhouses, and stately churches.

At the top of Great George Street stop by the **Province House** and **Confederation Arts Center** (see below), then explore the shops and restaurants of downtown Charlottetown. Watch for historical characters: Students dressed in period costume lead free 1-hour walking tours; others portray the Fathers of the Confederation, the politicians who were the key players in the confederation conference. Check with the visitor center for times, or call ☎ **902/629-1864.**

For a pleasant walk affording fine water views, head southwest on Kent Street (just north of the Confederation Mall). At 2 Kent St., you'll see **Beaconsfield** (☎ **902/368-6603**), a mansard-roofed mansion designed in 1877 by locally prominent architect William Harris for a prosperous shipbuilder. The architecture boasts an elegant mix of Georgian symmetry and Victorian exuberance, and the rooms are furnished in high Victorian style. The home, which is part of the Prince Edward Island Museum and Heritage Foundation, hosts lectures and events throughout the year, or you can just stop in and look around. It's open daily in summer 10am to 5pm; admission is C$3.50 (US$2.33), with children under 13 free.

From Beaconsfield, look for the boardwalk that follows the edge of the harbor for 1.5 kilometers (0.9 miles) into **Victoria Park,** which is home to ballfields and grassy picnic areas. The walk along the water has unobstructed views of the harbor and Northumberland Strait beyond.

Along the way look for the 1834 **Government House,** also known as Fanningbank. This sturdy, white-shingled residence with Ionic columns is set back on a broad lawn and is home to the lieutenant governor. It's not open to the public, but you're welcome to explore the grounds. The famous picture of the Fathers of the Confederation (you'll see it most everywhere around town) was taken on the front portico.

✪ **Province House National Historic Site.** 165 Richmond St. ☎ **902/566-7626.** Free admission (donations requested). July–Aug daily 9am–6pm, Sept–June Mon–Fri 9am–5pm.

This neoclassical downtown landmark was built in 1847 in an area set aside by town fathers for colonial administration and church buildings. When it served as a colonial legislature, the massive building rose up from vacant lots of dust and mud; today, as the provincial legislature, it's ringed by handsome trees, an inviting lawn, and a bustling downtown just beyond. This stern and imposing sandstone edifice occupies a special spot in Canadian history as the place where the details of the Confederation were hammered out in 1864. In the early 1980s, the building was restored to appear as it would have looked in that year.

Start your tour by viewing a well-made 17-minute film that documents the process of confederation. Afterwards, wander the halls and view the Legislative Assembly, where legislators have been meeting since 1847. It's surprisingly tiny, but perhaps appropriate given that PEI's legislature has just 27 members, making it the smallest in Canada. Especially impressive is the second-floor Confederation Chamber, where a staffer is usually on hand to explain what took place and to answer that burning question: Why did PEI wait 9 years to join Canada?

Confederation Centre Art Galley and Museum. Queen and Grafton Sts. ☎ **902/628-6142.** C$4 (US$2.65) adult, C$3 (US$2) seniors, C$2 (US$1.35) students, C$10 (US$6.65) family. Summer daily 9am–7pm, off-season Tues–Sat 11am–5pm, Sun 1–5pm.

Part of the Confederation Centre of the Arts (which includes three theaters; see "Charlottetown After Dark," below), this is the largest art gallery in Atlantic Canada. The center is housed in a bland and boxy modern complex of glass and rough sandstone; about the best that can be said of it is that it doesn't detract too much from the stylishly classical Province House next door. (Canadian writer Will Ferguson has referred to the building as "one of the greatest unprosecuted crimes of urban planning in Canadian history.") Inside, however, the gallery is spacious and nicely arranged on two levels, and it features displays from the permanent collection as well as imaginatively curated changing exhibits.

SHOPPING

Charlottetown has a number of shops and boutiques, but few are all that impressive, with some notable exceptions. Better quality and more creative crafts can be found in outposts elsewhere on the island, especially along the north shore.

Seasonal Peake's Wharf on the waterfront has an abundance of shops, most of which are tourist-oriented. This is a good destination if you're in search of a souvenir emblazoned with "Prince Edward Island." You'll also find casual dining, ice cream, and harbor cruises here.

The **Confederation Court Mall** (☎ 902/894-9505) is located downtown across from the Province House. Architecturally, this 90-store mall blends in nicely with its neighbors. Inside, however, the place is less distinctive, and the food courts, escalators, and chain stores (Radio Shack, The Body Shop) might give you a shudder of déjà vu.

Anne of Green Gables Store. 110 Queen St. ☎ **902/368-2663.**

Everything Anne, from dolls to commemorative plates.

The Bookman. 177 Queen St. ☎ **902/892-8872.**

Located across from the mall, this small shop has the city's best selection of used books, with a strong inventory of PEI and Canadian titles.

Cow's. 150 Queen St. ☎ **902/892-6969.**

PEI's answer to Ben & Jerry's. It's as much a clothing store as an ice-cream shop; fans of the premium ice cream scoop up T-shirts and other bovine whimsy. Ice-cream flavors include Wowie Cowie Coffee Toffee Crunch and Cotton Candy Bunny Tails.

The Croft House. Confederation Court Mall. ☎ **902/566-4606.**

Look for tartan and heraldic goods, along with island crafts, Anne souvenirs, and PEI videos.

Great Northern Knitters. 18 Queen St. (in the Prince Edward Hotel). ☎ **902/566-5302.**

This shop off the lobby of the Prince Edward hotel sells a diverse line of unusually well-made sweaters handcrafted on PEI. Every sweater is guaranteed for life.

The Mad Hatter. 100 Kent St. ☎ **902/892-9888.**

Scour the crowded racks for reasonably priced vintage clothes, both funky and formal. There's also candy, candles, wigs, soap, and a selection of new retro clothing.

Paderno Kitchen Store. Confederation Mall. ☎ **902/566-2252.**

Serious amateur cooks trek here to buy the elegant stainless-steel cookware made with heat-conducting pads. These high-quality pots and pans, which come with a 25-year warranty, are made on PEI.

Prince Edward Island Preserve Co. Store. 229 Grafton St. ☎ **800/565-5267.**

If you didn't get to the factory in New Glasgow, stop here to stock up on the fine preserves and other PEI products. (The preserves are priced the same here as at the factory, so you're not saving anything by making a special trip to the source.)

WHERE TO STAY

It's easy to justify splurging on accommodations when in Charlottetown. A number of the fine homes built when the city was at its most prosperous have been converted to inns and bed-and-breakfasts, and most are run by folks who appear to actually enjoy their work.

Two motels are situated within easy walking distance of downtown attractions. The **Islander Motor Lodge,** 146–148 Pownal St. (☎ **902/892-1217**), has 50 rooms a few minutes' walk from Province House. Rates are from C$103 (US$69) double. **Best Western MacLauchlans,** 238 Grafton St. (☎ **800/528-1234** or 902/566-2979), has 148 rooms and 25 suites in two buildings a couple blocks east of the Confederation Court Mall. Rooms and suites range from C$179 to C$259 (US$119 to US$173).

For those traveling on a tight budget, several moderately priced motels are situated along the city's main access roads and across from the airport a few miles from downtown. Two with rooms under C$100 (US$67) are **Royalty Maples Cottages and Motel** (Route 2, ☎ **902/368-1030**) and the **Winfield Motel** (Route 1, ☎ **800/ 267-5525** or 902/566-2675).

EXPENSIVE

Delta Prince Edward. 18 Queen St., Charlottetown, PEI C1A 8B9. ☎ **902/566-2222.** Fax 902/566-2282. 211 units. A/C MINIBAR TV TEL. Peak season C$159–C$319 (US$106–US$213) double; call for off-season rates. AE, DC, DISC, ER, MC, V. Parking C$8 (US$5.35) per day. Pets allowed.

A modern, boxy, 10-story hotel overlooking the harbor, the Prince Edward Hotel is part of the Canadian Pacific chain and has all the amenities expected by business travelers, including coffeemakers, hair dryers, free exercise bikes delivered to your room, and even cordless phones (about half the rooms are cordless). You enter the hotel to a two-story atrium (home to a well-regarded restaurant), then head up to the guest rooms. The better rooms are furnished with reproduction Georgian-style furniture; others have those oak and beige-laminate furnishings that are virtually invisible. The higher rooms have the better views; there's a premium for water views, but the city views are actually nicer (and you can usually glimpse the water, anyway).

Dining: The Selkirk (see below) might be the city's best restaurant, with upscale service and presentation to complement a fine menu. Summers only, a more informal restaurant serves tasty lunches for C$6 to C$12 (US$4 to US$8) on a patio near the harbor.

Amenities: The hotel features an indoor pool and fitness room, a sauna, an outdoor hot tub, afternoon tea, safe-deposit boxes, turndown service, a concierge, room service (to 2am), a shopping arcade, a beauty salon, a business center, and conference rooms. Valet parking, baby-sitting, dry cleaning, and laundry service are also available.

Inns on Great George. 589 Great George St., Charlottetown, PEI C1A 4K3. ☎ **800/ 361-1118** or 902/892-0606. Fax 902/628-2079. www.innsongreatgeorge.com. E-mail: innsongg@atcon.com. 40 units (5 share 2 bathrooms). A/C TV TEL. C$145–C$225 (US$97–US$150) double, including continental breakfast. AE, DC, ER, MC, V. Free parking.

The Inns on Great George opened in 1997 and has since established itself as one of the classiest Charlottetown hostelries. The inn encompasses six striking buildings on and near historic Great George Street. Twenty-four rooms are located in the old (1846) Pavilion Hotel; others are in smaller townhouses and homes nearby. All rooms have been thoroughly updated and refurbished with antiques, down duvets, hair dryers, and early black-and-white prints; all but two rooms are carpeted. The more expensive rooms have fireplaces and Jacuzzis, but many of the others have clawfoot tubs, perfect for soaking in after a day of roaming the city. Room 403 has buttery pine floors, a wonderful tub, and lots of light. Room 308 has a Shaker-style canopy bed, an in-room two-person Jacuzzi, and a gas fireplace. Families or couples traveling together should ask about Room 662, an attractive three-bedroom suite.

Amenities: The inn features a small fitness room. It also has safe-deposit boxes, offers limited room service from an affiliated restaurant, and can arrange for baby-sitting, dry cleaning, and laundry.

✪ **Shipwright Inn.** 51 Fitzroy St., Charlottetown, PEI C1A 1R4. ☎ **902/368-1905.** Fax 902/628-1905. www.isn.net/shipwrightinn. E-mail: shipwright@isn.net. 7 units. A/C TV TEL. C$125–C$250 (US$83–US$167) double, including continental breakfast. AE, DC, ER, MC, V. Free parking.

This understated Victorian home was built by a shipbuilder, and expertly renovated and refurbished. It's decorated with period furniture and with a deft touch—no over-the-top Victoriana here. All rooms have lovely wood floors (some with original ship-planking floors), and three are in a recent addition, which was built with a number of nice touches.

Amenities include hair dryers and down duvets in all rooms, and about half the rooms have Jacuzzis, gas fireplaces, or both. Among the best: the Ward Room, a suite with a private deck; and the Purser's State Room, which shares a lovely deck with another room. Innkeepers Judy and Jordan Hill and their staff are very helpful. The inn is located right in the city, but has a settled, pastoral farmhouse feel to it.

MODERATE

The Charlottetown. Kent and Pownal Sts. (P.O. Box 159), Charlottetown, PEI C1A 7K4. ☎ **902/894-7371.** Fax 902/368-2178. 115 units. A/C TV TEL. C$85–C$235 (US$57–US$157) double. AE, DISC, ER, MC, V. Free parking. Pets accepted.

This 1940s-era hotel—part of the Rodd Hotel chain—is located in a five-story brick building next to a shady park and is just a few minutes' walk to most downtown attractions. The hotel features Georgian flourishes inside and out, and it has been updated and remodeled with a nod to its heritage. The dusky lobby has the feel of a pre-war New York City apartment building, with a vaulted ceiling and echoey composite floors. The rooms, which have opening windows, were tastefully remodeled in the mid-1990s with reproduction-period furniture. Five suites were added in 1999. The hotel will certainly appeal to travelers drawn to the solid construction and under-stated styling of yore, although some of the public areas are growing weary with age and are overdue for remodeling.

Dining/Diversions: The Carvery is open daily for dinner and features hotel favorites like prime rib, jumbo shrimp, Atlantic salmon, and a popular shellfish buffet. Entrees are C$15 to C$20 (US$10 to US$13). Across the lobby, a dinner theater performs nightly in July and August.

Amenities: A low-ceilinged indoor pool is open to guests on the ground floor; there's also a whirlpool, sauna, limited room service, dry cleaning, laundry, and baby-sitting (advance notice required).

Edenhurst Inn. 12 West St., Charlottetown, PEI C1A 3S4. ☎ **902/368-8323.** 7 units. A/C TV TEL. C$115–C$195 (US$77–US$130), including full breakfast. AE, MC, V. No children.

James Eden was a prosperous wine merchant on the island, and in 1897 he built this regal Queen Anne Revival mansion in one of the city's better neighborhoods—looking west toward the sunset over the water. It's three floors tall, and the exterior bustles with turrets, gables, and covered porches. Innkeepers Shayne and Sherri Popwell have done a fine job restoring this historic property to its former splendor, and the rooms are furnished with the appropriate period antiques. When booking, ask about rooms with deluxe touches, such as fireplaces and Jacuzzis.

Hillhurst Inn. 181 Fitzroy St., Charlottetown, PEI C1A 1S3. ☎ **902/894-8004.** 9 units. TV TEL. High season: C$110–C$190 (US$73–US$127); low season: C$85–C$130 (US$57–US$87). Rates include full breakfast. AE, ER, MC, V.

Another fine mansion built in 1897 in another fine neighborhood (3 blocks northeast of Province House), Hillhurst features a raft of nice touches, not the least of which is the extraordinarily detailed woodworking carved by some of the city's shipbuilders. When built, locals called it "the crystal palace" because of its profusion of windows. The rooms are varied in size and style. As is often the case, the third floor rooms require a bit of a hike, and are smaller and more cozy than the rooms on the second floor. The drawbacks? Many of the bathrooms are quite small (often shoehorned into closets), and the furnishings are less historic and creative compared to other comparably priced inns, including Edenhurst and The Shipwright Inn.

WHERE TO DINE

For a late afternoon pick-me-up, try **Beanz,** 38 University Ave. (☎ **902/892-8797**), for its industrial-strength cappuccino. They also sell pastries and offer light lunches.

A locally popular spot for inexpensive meals is **Cedar's Eatery** at 81 University between Fitzroy and Kent (☎ **902/892-7377**). Lebanese dishes are the specialty here, like *yabrak* (stuffed vine leaves) and *kibbee* (ground beef with crushed wheat and spices). There are also sandwiches and burgers. Specials start at C$4.95 (US$3.30), both lunch and dinner.

Claddagh Room. 131 Sydney St. ☎ **902/892-9661.** Reservations helpful. Main courses: lunch C$6–C$10 (US$4–US$7), dinner C$15–C$25 (US$10–US$17). AE, DISC, ER, MC, V. Mon–Fri 11:30am–2pm, Mon–Thurs 5–10pm, Fri and Sat 5–10:30pm, Sun 5–9pm. SEAFOOD.

Despite the Irish name and the Dublin Pub located downstairs, the Claddagh Room isn't the place for corned beef. It's the place for seafood, the house specialty. The seafood chowder is very tasty, as is the bouillabaisse. You can also order lobster from the tank, surf and turf, and a variety of other selections. There's no harbor view, as there is at other seafood places in town, but the preparation and service here are a notch above. Live Irish entertainment is often featured downstairs in the pub during the summer months.

Kim's Bistro. 45 Water St. ☎ **902/894-5149.** Reservations helpful. Main courses, lunch C$6.95–C$12.55 (US$4.65–US$8.35, dinner C$7.55–C$21.95 (US$5.05–US$14.65); entrees mostly C$13–C$15 (US$8.65–US$10). AE, MC, V. Mon–Sat 11am–10pm, Sun 11am–4pm. Closed Oct–May. SEAFOOD/BISTRO.

The small, cheerful restaurant on a side street a short stroll west of downtown opened in 1998, and puts an emphasis on the 18 smoked seafood products made by owner

Kim Dormaar (sold elsewhere as Medallion Smoked Salmon). Lunches include smoked salmon on a bagel, or smoked trout on pumpernickel. The dinner menu offers lighter fare (salmon carpaccio or smoked seafood plate), along with more substantial entrees like island lamb served with a ginger honey sauce, and grilled salmon. On a pleasantly warm summer afternoon, a spot under the maple on the deck out front is one of the best seats in town.

Lucy Maud Dining Room. 4 Sydney St. ☎ **902/894-6868.** Reservations recommended for lunch and dinner June–Sept. Main courses, lunch C$11–C$13 (US$7–US$13), dinner C$18–C$26 (US$12–US$17). Tues–Fri 11:30am–1:30pm, Tues–Sat 5:30–9pm. Closed during school holidays. REGIONAL.

The Lucy Maud Dining Room is located within the Culinary Institute of Canada's campus. The building itself is a bit institutional and charmless, and the 80-seat dining room has much the feel of a hotel restaurant. But plenty of nice touches offset the lack of personality. Among them: custom china and a beautiful view of the bay and Victoria Park from oversized windows. Best of all, diners get to sample some of the best of island cuisine, prepared and served by Institute students eager to please. The lunch and dinner menus change each semester, but typical dinner entrees might include duck breast with a sour cherry sauce, or venison loin with a blueberry peppercorn sauce (the kitchen is noted for its venison). There's always salmon on the menu, and often the curried seafood chowder with fresh tarragon, a local favorite.

Piazza Joe's Italian Eatery and Bistro. 189 Kent St. ☎ **902/894-4291.** Reservations not accepted. Main courses C$8.95–C$15.95 (US$5.95–US$10.65), individual pizzas C$7.95 (US$5.30) and up. AE, MC, V. Mon–Wed 11am–11pm, Thurs–Sat 11am–midnight, Sun 10am–11pm. PIZZA/ITALIAN.

Piazza Joe's, located in a handsome, historic building 1 long block from the Confederation Mall, has gone a bit overboard with the Tuscan-style washed tones and fake ivy climbing fake trellises. But it works in a comic-book kind of way. The place is pleasantly casual and can be loud on weekends, but it offers friendly service, a long menu, and lots of comic-book-type mixed drinks to match the decor. (It's the best spot for a late night meal if you get into town late.) The wood-fired pizza is consistently quite good; take your chances on the rest of the selections, like five-vegetable lasagna or veal ala limone. There's also a bistro menu, with items like burgers, chicken wings, fish and chips, and "nasty nachos." One of the highlights, especially for kids, is the bread bar: You select your own thick slice of homemade bread, lather it with a butter of your choosing (plain, tarragon, garlic, or cheese), and then drop it with tongs on a sizzling grill in the center of the dining room. It's free with any meal.

✪ Piece a Cake Restaurant. 119 Grafton St. (upstairs in the Confederation Court Mall). ☎ **902/894-4585.** Reservations recommended. Main courses: lunch C$7–C$14 (US$5–US$9), dinner C$12–C$20 (US$8–US$13). AE, DC, ER, MC, V. Daily 11am–11pm. Closed Sun Oct–May. ECLECTIC.

This very modern, very handsome restaurant occupies the second floor of a building that's part of the Confederation Court Mall. With hardwood floors, high ceilings, rich custard-colored walls, and window frames suspended whimsically from the ceiling, there's a welcoming, airy grace to the spot. It's the kind of place where friends who don't see each other very often like to get together and relax over a lively meal. The menu is wonderfully far-ranging, and it's hard to imagine someone not finding something appealing—lunches range from a teriyaki salmon wrap to Thai scallop salad to Tuscan grilled chicken sandwiches. Dinners are similarly eclectic and include a range of adventurous pastas. (A personal favorite: "penne on fire," with charred onions, grilled zucchini, toasted pecans, and a tangerine relish.) Other dinner options include

Thai seafood medley, blackened salmon, and pecan-crusted pork loin. Only the unimaginative wine list is a bit of a disappointment. Also ask about the gourmet brown bag lunches—eight choices are offered (C$9.95/US$6.63 to C$13.95/US$9.30 with dessert and beverage), including a lobster salad croissant and a jerk chicken pasta salad.

The Selkirk. In the Delta Prince Edward, 18 Queen St. ☎ **902/566-2222.** Reservations encouraged. Main courses: breakfast C$6–C$9 (US$4–US$6), lunch C$6–C$13 (US$4–US$8.67), dinner C$20–C$28 (US$13–US$19). AE, DC, DISC, ER, MC, V. Daily 6:30am–2pm, 5–11pm. NEW CANADIAN.

Charlottetown's most stylish restaurant is smack in the middle of the lobby of the high-end Prince Edward Hotel. Yet it has a more informal character than many upscale hotel restaurants, with an eclectic mix of chairs and a piano player providing the live soundtrack. The menu is also more ambitious and creative than you'll find elsewhere in the city. The signature appetizer is lobster and prawns served with a three-melon salsa, or you might opt for pheasant confit. Main courses could include sashimi of salmon, oysters, and scallops with a sauce of lime, ginger, and garlic; or a Maritime jambalaya with lobster, mussels, shrimp, scallops, and salmon. Carnivores aren't ignored, with a selection that includes duck breast with a raspberry and green peppercorn vinaigrette, or beef tenderloin with a shiitake ragout. A downside: The lobby location can get clamorous at times, especially when conferees are milling about. Ask for one of the tables under the mezzanine, near the piano.

Sirenella. 83 Water St. ☎ **902/628-2271.** Reservations recommended. Main courses: lunch C$6–C$12 (US$4–US$8), dinner C$9.75–C$24.75 (US$6.50–US$16.50). AE, ER, JCB, MC, V. Mon–Fri 11am–2pm and 5–10pm, Sat–Sun 5–10pm. Closed Sun in winter. ITALIAN.

Sirenella is a locally popular spot that offers good value when the service staff and kitchen are both operating smoothly. Which, alas, is not all the time. When it's missing the mark, expect slipshod service and indifferent meals. When all systems are go, it's another story. You'll understand why the place has diehard fans who swear by its most popular dishes, including the grilled calamari, and ravioli with ricotta, spinach, and prosciutto. Sirenella is tucked on a quiet side street and could be considered either romantically intimate or claustrophobic, depending on your mood.

CHARLOTTETOWN AFTER DARK

A good resource for evening adventure is *Buzz,* a free monthly newspaper that details ongoing and special events around the island with an emphasis on Charlottetown. It's widely available; look at visitor centers or area bars and restaurants.

For high culture, check out the **Confederation Centre of the Arts** (☎ 800/565-0278 or 902/566-1267), where three stages bustle with activity in the warm-weather months. The musical *Anne of Green Gables,* a perennial favorite, is performed here throughout the summer, as are revivals and new shows.

For low culture, head to the **Charlottetown Driving Park** (☎ 902/892-6823), located at Kensington Road on the Hillsborough River at the northeast edge of downtown. Harness racing is slated every few days in afternoons and evenings from June to September; call for the current schedule. Parimutuel betting is offered, and there's a club on the upper level for enjoying snacks and drinks while handicapping the ponies.

The art-house **City Cinema,** 64 King St. (☎ 902/368-3669), has an excellent lineup of domestic and foreign films throughout the year; typically, there's a choice of two films each evening.

Outdoor libations are on tap at **Victoria Row,** on pedestrian-only Richmond Street behind the Confederation Centre. Several restaurants and pubs cluster here and serve meals and drinks on streetside patios; some offer live music. **Kelly's,** 136 Richmond

(☎ **902/628-6569**), has a selection of the island's microbrews. The row is a popular destination for university students and younger locals.

Myron's, 151 Kent St. (☎ **902/892-4375**), features a dance club and cabaret located on two floors with a robust 22,000 square feet of entertainment space. Performers range from country to rock. For live Celtic-flavored music, head for **The Olde Dublin Pub,** 113 Sydney St. (☎ **902/892-6992**). In the strip-mall zone outside of town is the **Lone Star Café & Brewery,** 449 University Ave. (☎ **902/894-7827**). This restaurant and brewpub is part of a popular chain; the beer is quite good, the Tex-Mex food quite forgettable.

6 Kings County

After a visit to Charlottetown and the island's central towns, Kings County comes as a bit of a surprise. It's far more tranquil and uncluttered than Queens County (Anne's reach is much diminished here), and the landscapes feature woodlots alternating with corn, grain, and potato fields. Although much is made of the county's two great commercial centers on the coast—Souris and Montague—it's good to keep in mind that each of these has a population of around 1,500. In some parts of North America, that wouldn't even rate a dot on the map.

Don't arrive here expecting county attractions to go out of their way to amuse and entertain you. You'll have to do that yourself. It's prime biking territory, and walks on the empty beaches are a good tonic if you suffer from a hectic schedule in your non-vacation life. Long drives in the country with occasional stops are likewise relaxing.

If you're headed to southeastern Kings County from Charlottetown, you'll pass Orwell and its historic sites. See the listing above, in Queens County.

ESSENTIALS
GETTING THERE   Several main roads—including Highways 1, 2, 3, and 4—connect eastern PEI with Charlottetown and western points. The ferry to Nova Scotia sails from Woods Island on the south coast. See "Exploring Prince Edward Island" earlier in this chapter for more information.

VISITOR INFORMATION   A large provincial information center (☎ **902/838-0670**) is located in Pooles Corner at the intersections of Route 3 and Route 4 (north of Montague). The center, which is open June to mid-October, also contains well-presented exhibits about local commerce and history, including how to identify local architectural styles.

Another helpful visitor center is located at the old railway depot in Montague on the river. It's open daily in summer.

MURRAY RIVER & MURRAY HARBOUR
It's not especially hard to guess the name of the family that originally settled this area—it seems that "Murray" is appended to every natural landmark of note. These two small and tidy villages offer little drama, but lots of repose. It's hard to imagine a better place to listen to the crickets and the wind in the trees. As you drive, watch for the tight lines of buoys in the coastal waterways: the noted blue mussels are cultivated in mesh bags suspended from ropes attached to these buoys, then shipped worldwide to great acclaim.

EXPLORING THE MURRAYS
Seals are practically as common as crows in this part of PEI. You just have to know where to look. The best way to view these sleek creatures is close-up, from the water.

Visit the island's largest seal colony with **Captain Garry's Seal & Bird Watching Cruises** (☎ 800/496-2494 or 902/962-2494), based in Murray River. You'll travel in enclosed boats (tours offered rain or shine) and see seals, mussel farms, herons, and, with luck, bald eagles. Tours are offered daily in summer; the cost is C$15.50 (US$10.35) adult, C$13.50 (US$9) senior, C$7.50 (US$5) children.

Younger children rarely fail to enjoy **King's Castle Provincial Park** (☎ 902/962-2401), an old-fashioned kiddy wonderland of the sort that was popular in the 1950s and 1960s. This pleasant picnic park, on the shores of the Murray River (there's swimming at a small beach), features life-size storybook characters scattered about field and woodlands. Kids can visit with Goldilocks or the Three Little Pigs, then scamper about the array of playground equipment or get an ice cream at the park's canteen. Open daily 9am to 9pm in summer (closed winter); admission is free. The park is on Route 348 just east of the town of Murray River, on the south bank of the river.

A couple of beaches are worthy of note: A short drive from Murray River along the north bank of the river is remote and peaceful **Poverty Beach.** Dunes back this long strand of eastward-facing beach. You can park at the end of the road and walk along the beach watching for birdlife. Swimming is problematic; the beach is pebbly at low tide, and the currents can sometimes be troublesome. But it's a great getaway: I spent an hour here on a glorious August afternoon and didn't see another soul. North of Poverty Beach is **Panmure Island Provincial Park.** The island is connected to the mainland via a sand-dune isthmus. The contrast between the white sand on the ocean side and the red sand beach on the inside cove is striking. It's a lovely spot, with swimming on the ocean side and views northward to a striking lighthouse.

WHERE TO STAY

Forest and Stream. Route 18, Murray Harbour, PEI C0A 1V0. ☎ **800/227-9943** or 902/962-3537. 3 B&B, 5 cottages (3 1-bedroom, 2 2-bedroom). TV (cottages only). 1-bedroom C$60 (US$40) double, 2-bedroom C$70 (US$47) double (C$10/US$7 per extra person), B&B C$85–C$100 (US$57–US$67) double, including full breakfast. MC, V. Closed Nov–Apr. Small pets allowed in cottages.

These five cottages are located on 20 acres of peaceful woodlands near a narrow lake and the site of an old gristmill. The grounds are shady, lovely, and laced with nature trails; you can also swim in the lake. The cottages, however, are fairly basic, with 1950s-style kitchenettes and linoleum floors, screened-in porches with picnic tables and gas grills outside. The owners constructed a new house on the grounds in 1996, and with it they added three spacious and comfortable guest rooms, each with private bathroom. (It's marketed separately as the Country Charm Bed & Breakfast.) B&B guests can relax in the downstairs common room and, of course, take advantage of the grounds.

Fox River Cottages. Machon Point Rd., Murray Harbour, PEI C0A 1V0. ☎ **902/962-2881.** E-mail: gmachon@auracom.com. 3 units. TV. C$78–C$100 (US$52–US$67) double (C$6/US$4 per additional person), C$600–C$700 (US$400–US$467) double per week ($30/US$20 per additional person). Off-season rates available. V. Closed mid-Oct to mid-May.

These modern two-bedroom cottages with kitchenettes are beautifully situated on 13 acres down a winding dirt road at the edge of a field overlooking the islands of Murray Bay. The cottages are tidy and furnished with televisions and VCRs. The cabins are near one another, but staggered to create a sense of privacy. You can relax on the screened porches, or wander to the river beach and dabble around in the canoe. One unit has a woodstove, and all have electric heat and gas barbecues for evening grilling. If you have a croquet set, by all means bring it.

MONTAGUE

Montague is the region's main commercial hub, but it's a hub in low gear. It's compact and attractive, with a handsome business district on a pair of flanking hills sloping down to a bridge across the Montague River. (A century and a half ago, the town was called Montague Bridge.) Shipbuilding was the economic mainstay in the 19th century; today, it's dairy and tobacco.

EXPLORING THE OUTDOORS

Cruise Manada (☎ **800/986-3444** or 902/838-3444) offers seal- and bird-watching tours daily during peak season aboard restored fishing boats; the cost is C$17 (US$11) adult, C$15 (US$10) senior and student, C$8.50 (US$5.65) children under 12. Trips depart from the marina on the Montague River, just below the visitor center in the old railway depot. Reservations are advised.

Southeast of Montague (en route to Murray River) is the **Buffaloland Provincial Park** (☎ **902/652-2356**), where you'll spot a small herd of buffalo. These were a gift to PEI from the province of Alberta, and they now number about 25. Walk down the 100-yard fenced-in corridor into the paddock and ascend the wooden platform for the best view of the shaggy beasts. Often they're hunkered down at the far end of the meadow, but they sometimes wander near. The park is right off Route 4; watch for signs. Open year-round.

A few minutes north of Buffaloland on Route 4, between Route 216 and Route 317, is the **Harvey Moore Wildlife Management Area** (no phone), a delightful place for a stroll. Named after a revered local naturalist (1916 to 1960) who created this sanctuary in 1949, the park's centerpiece is a 45-minute trail that loops around a pond and through varied ecosystems. A well-written nature guide is available free at the signboard. Watch especially for the waterfowl, with which Moore had an unusually close rapport. Avian visitors include black duck, blue-winged teal, ringneck duck, pintail, and an abundance of Canada geese. Open daylight hours. Free admission.

Brudenell River Provincial Park (☎ **902/652-8966**) is one of the province's better-bred parks, and a great spot to work up an athletic glow on a sunny afternoon. On its 1,500 riverfront acres you'll find two well-regarded golf courses, a golf academy, a full-blown resort (see below), tennis, lawn bowling, a wildflower garden, a playground, a campground, and nature trails. Kids' programs, like Frisbee golf, shoreline scavenger hunts, and crafts workshops, are scheduled daily in summer. You can also rent canoes, kayaks, and jet skis from private operators located within the park. The park is open daily from 9am to 9pm; free admission. Head north of Montague on Route 4, then east on Route 3 to the park signs.

WHERE TO STAY

Brudenell River Resort. Route 3 (P.O. Box 67), Cardigan, PEI C0A 1G0. ☎ **800/565-7633** or 902/652-2332. Fax 902/652-2886. www.rodd-hotels.ca/. 51 units, 82 cabins. TV TEL. Peak season: C$134–C$225 (US$89–US$150) hotel, C$95–C$124 (US$63–US$83) basic cabins; C$154–C$325 (US$103–US$217) deluxe cabins; off-season: C$92–C$150 (US$61–US$100) hotel, C$68–C$89 (US$45–US$59) basic cabins, C$104–C$275 (US$69–US$183) deluxe cabins. AE, DC, ER, MC, V. Closed mid-Oct to mid-May. Pets allowed, C$10 (US$7) per pet per night.

The attractive Brudenell River Resort was built in 1991, and its sleek, open, and vaguely Frank Lloyd Wright–esque design reflects its recent vintage. It's an especially popular destination with golfers—it's set amid two golf courses (one new in 1999) that have been garnering plaudits from serious duffers in recent years. Guests choose between three types of rooms. The hotel proper has 51 well-appointed guest rooms, each with balcony or terrace. The upmarket and new (1999) Echelon Gold Cottages each have two bedrooms, cathedral ceilings, fireplaces, and large-screen TVs. The more basic Countryside Cabins are the best bet for those traveling on a budget; just beware that the detailing isn't of the highest quality, and the units are clustered together a bit oddly, like pavilions left over from some forgotten world exposition.

Dining: The Gordon Dining Room on the first level overlooks the golf course. It's rather cavernous, but the high-backed chairs carve out a sense of intimacy. Breakfast and dinner are served; you'll enjoy what might be described as creative country-club cuisine, with entrees like charbroiled steak, sole in a puff pastry, and pasta primavera. Entrees range from C$14 to C$19 (US$9 to US$13).

Amenities: In addition to the two excellent golf courses (one hosts a Golf Academy offering extensive lessons), the resort has two pools (indoor and out), river swimming, a Jacuzzi, a sauna, two night-lit tennis courts, a health club, jogging and hiking trails, and a children's center. Dry cleaning and baby-sitting are available by request.

Lady Catherine B&B. Route 17, Murray Harbor North (mailing address: RR4, Montague, PEI C0A 1R0). ☎ **800/661-3426.** E-mail: adyc@pei.sympatico.ca. 2 units (multi-bedroom suites available), both with private detached bathroom. C$90 (US$60) double, including full breakfast. AE, MC, V. Pets allowed with advance permission.

Tom Rath has been running this B&B 22 kilometers (14 miles) southeast of Montague for more than a decade, and he's a great resource for local attractions and music. The trim 1907 farmhouse has just two guest rooms (each with private bathroom located across the hall), and an idyllic location amid potato fields with views of the bay and the distant shores of Nova Scotia. It's an informal and relaxing spot, popular with couples, and offers good access to Pamure Island and Poverty Beach (bring your bikes!). Breakfasts are more than filling, and often feature "bilingual French toast" (made with English muffins).

Dining: Rath will prepare a candlelight dinner on request. The seafood dinner is C$75 (US$50) for two; C$50 (US$33) for chicken and pasta.

Rodd Marina Inn & Suites. 1150 Sackville St. (P.O. Box 1540) Montague, PEI C0A 1R0. ☎ **800/865-7633** or 902/838-4075. Fax 902/838-4180. 52 units. A/C TV TEL. C$99–C$124 (US$66–US$83), including continental breakfast. AE, MC, V.

The new Marina Inn was built in 1999, and has the casually modern feel of the sort of mid-sized chain hotel you'd expect to find on a strip at the edge of a mid-sized town. With this difference: it boasts a great location tucked off Montague's main street, right along the Montague River (boat tours available), and smack on a spur of the Confederation Trail. The hotel's rooms are mostly standard sized and equipped with the usual amenities like coffeemakers and hair dryers; I'd request a room on the river side for the view. A dozen "studio-suites" (their term) offer a small sitting area along with microwave, refrigerator, and Jacuzzi.

Amenities: Sundeck, breakfast room, small exercise room.

Where to Dine

Windows on the Water. 106 Sackville St. (corner of Main St.), Montague. ☎ **902/838-2080.** Reservations recommended. Main courses: lunch C$7.50–C$9.25 (US$5–US$6.15), dinner C$10.95–C$19.95 (US$7.30–US$13.30). MC, V. Daily 11:30am–10pm. SEAFOOD.

If you haven't yet dined on PEI mussels, this is the place to let loose. The blue mussels are steamed in a root mirepoix, with sesame, ginger, and garlic. It's a winner. Main courses include sole stuffed with crab and scallop and topped with hollandaise, and the chef's peppered steak—a filet mignon served with sweet peppers, red onion, and mushrooms in a peppercorn sauce. Lunches are lighter, with choices like grilled chicken and mandarin salad, and homemade fish cakes. The appealing and open dining room features pressback chairs and a lively buzz, but if the weather's agreeable, angle for a seat under the canopy on the deck.

SOURIS & NORTHEAST PEI

Some 44 kilometers (26 miles) northeast of Montague is the town of Souris, an active fishing town attractively set on a gentle hill overlooking the harbor. Souris (pronounced *Soo*-ree) is French for "mouse"—so named because early settlers were beset by voracious field mice, which destroyed their crops. The town is the launching point for an excursion to the Magdalen Islands, and it makes a good base for exploring northeastern PEI, which is considered by more urban residents as the island's outback—remote and sparsely populated. You'll also find it somewhat less agricultural and more forested, especially away from the coast, than the rest of the island.

EXPLORING THE AREA

Several good beaches can be found ringing this wedge-shaped peninsula that points like an accusing finger toward Nova Scotia's Cape Breton Island. **Red Point Provincial Park** (☎ 902/357-2463) is 13 kilometers (8 miles) northeast of Souris. It offers a handsome beach and supervised swimming, along with a campground that's popular with families. Another inviting and often empty beach is a short distance northeast at **Basin Head,** which features a "singing sands" beach that allegedly sings (actually, it's more like squeak) when you walk on it. The dunes here are especially appealing. Look also for the nearby **Basin Head Fisheries Museum** (☎ 902/357-7233), a provincially operated museum that offers insight into the life of the inshore fisherman. Admission is C$3.50 (US$2.35), under 12 free. Open daily in peak season 9am to 7pm; closed October through May.

On the north shore is **Campbells Cove Provincial Park** (☎ 902/357-2067). The park features a handsome red-sand beach that extends along a grassy bluff, where a popular campground overlooks the sea. Flanking the campground is agricultural land that's slowly eroding into the gulf; it's a pleasant spot for a long oceanside walk.

At the island's far eastern tip is the aptly named **East Point Lighthouse** (☎ 902/357-2106). You can simply enjoy the dramatic setting or take a tour of the building. Ask for your East Point ribbon while you're here. If you make it to the North Cape Lighthouse on the western shore, you'll receive a Traveller's Award documenting that you've traveled PEI tip-to-tip. Admission to the lighthouse is C$2.50 (US$1.65) adult, C$1 (US65¢) children. Closed September to mid-June.

A spur of the **Confederation Trail** ends in Souris, making this a good spot from which to launch a bike excursion of the area. One suggested day trip would be to link to the main trunk trail, then venture northeast to East Point Lighthouse.

WHERE TO STAY

Ark Inn. Souris RR no. 4, Little Pond, PEI C0A 2B0. ☎ **800/665-2400** or 902/583-2400. Fax 902/583-2176. 15 units. A/C TV TEL. C$150 (US$100) double, including full breakfast. DC, ER, MC, V. Closed early Oct to late May.

Here's a place with huge potential—as yet unrealized when I last visited. The Ark was originally founded in the 1970s on remote Spry Point as a United Nations-funded prototype self-sufficient community affiliated with the New Alchemy Institute—with windmills, solar power, greenhouses, trout ponds, and the like. Oil prices dropped, interest waned, the experiment failed. Enter David Wilmer, owner of Inn at Bay Fortune (see below). He bought the 80-acre property in early 1999, and has undertaken the monumental task of bringing it up to date. (The original design wallowed in the worst of the 1970s-barnboard aesthetic.) The blueprints I saw looked great, and

Wilmer's got a great track record at Bay Fortune, so this property is no doubt worth a look. The location is top-rate—8,000 feet of undeveloped shorefront that invite exploration. A limited-offering dining room is planned for the near future, with possible expansion if everything works out.

✪ **Inn at Bay Fortune.** Route 310 (off Route 2), Bay Fortune, PEI C0A 2B0. ☎ **902/ 687-3745**, off-season 860/296-1348. Fax 902/687-3540. www.innatbayfortune.com. E-mail: innatbayft@auracom.com. 18 units. TEL. Summer C$125–C$250 (US$83.33–US$166.67) double, fall C$105–C$230 (US$70–US$153.33). Rates include full breakfast. DC, ER, MC, V. Closed mid-Oct to late May.

This exceptionally attractive, shingled compound on 46 acres was built by playwright Elmer Harris in 1910 as a summer home, and it quickly became the nucleus for a colony of artists, actors, and writers. (Most recently the home was owned by Canadian actress Colleen Dewhurst, who sold it to current innkeeper David Wilmer in 1988.) Wilmer pulled out the stops in renovating, bringing it back from the brink of decay. In 1998 he added a wing with six new rooms (two with Jacuzzis), including the wonderful North Tower Room 4, with a high ceiling and a balcony overlooking the lodge and bay beyond. (My favorite room remains South Tower Room 4, which requires a schlep up a narrow staircase, but once you're in this high lair it feels a world removed.) The newer rooms are larger than the older ones, but all are quite cozy with a mix of antiques and custom-made furniture. Eight of the rooms have wood-burning fireplaces, and six have propane fireplaces.

Dining: The inn is home to one of PEI's best restaurants; see below.

The Matthew House Inn. 15 Breakwater St. (P.O. Box 151), Souris, PEI C0A 2B0. ☎ **902/687-3461.** Fax 902-687-3461. 6 units. TV TEL. C$145–C$195 (US$14–US$17.33) double, including full breakfast. AE, MC, V. Closed Oct–May. Children over 12 welcome.

Kimberly and Franco Oliveiri came to PEI on vacation from Italy in 1995. They fell in love with the island's grand old homes, and before their holiday had ended they found themselves owners of this fine B&B. ("My husband is very impulsive by nature," says Kimberly.) Located atop a pleasant lawn overlooking the harbor and ferry to the Magdalen Islands, this stately Victorian dates to 1885 and maintains many of the original flourishes inside and out. Eastlake-style furnishings and William Morris touches give the place an architectural richness without seeming too grandmotherly about it. The place will be appreciated by those passionate about historic architecture.

WHERE TO DINE

✪ **Inn at Bay Fortune.** Route 310 (off Route 2), Bay Fortune, PEI C0A 2B0. ☎ **902/ 687-3745**. Reservations strongly recommended. Main courses C$21–C$26 (US$14–US$17.33). AE, MC, V. Daily 5–9pm. Closed mid-Oct to late May. CREATIVE CONTEMPORARY.

To fully appreciate a meal at the Inn at Bay Fortune, arrive early enough to wander the gardens behind the inn. The herbs and edible flowers are a short walk from the kitchen; a little further beyond is the three-acre vegetable garden. This is good introduction to the local products emphasized on the menu. Chef Jeff McCourt worked with founding chef Michael Smith (now at Maple in Halifax) to develop the inn's regional cuisine and its vaunted openness—how many restaurants feature a "Kitchen—Welcome" sign inviting diners to stop in for a visit? The place is wildly successful, with an always-shifting menu that rarely fails to produce a winning meal. For those with a serious interest in cooking, ask about the chef's table (a glass-enclosed booth within the kitchen) and the tasting menus.

An Excursion to the Magdalen Islands

The Magdalen Islands (Îles de la Madeleine), located a 5-hour ferry ride north of PEI, consist of a dozen low, sandy islands, linked to one another by sandspits. About 14,000 people live here, and the islands are dotted with peaceful fishing villages and farming communities. The islands, part of the province of Québec, also boast some 186 miles of beaches, a fact that has not gone unnoticed by urban Québecois in search of leisure. (The island is linked by air and a 2-day ferry from Québec.) It's also famous for its persistent winds, which rake across the Gulf and find little resistance here.

Advance planning is needed for a trip to the islands, since the demand for accommodations often outstrips supply. A free island tourist guide is available by calling ☎ **877/624-4437.** On the Web, head to www.ilesdelamadeleine.com.

Ferry service from Souris to Cap-aux-Meules is provided by the **Coopérative de Transport Maritime (CTMA)** (☎ **902/687-2181** or 418/986-6600, reservations 418/986-3278). The Lucy Maud Montgomery holds 95 cars and 400 passengers. Boats sail daily in summer; the schedule is limited in the off-season, so call for information. One-way rates are C$35 (US$23) adult, C$17.50 (US$11.65) child 5 to 12, C$67 (US$45) automobile.

ST. PETER'S BAY & ENVIRONS

Eastern Kings County attracts few tourists—other than those speeding through en route to East Point. Few commercial services are located here, and it's easy to zip right through without much of a second glance. Yet it's well worth slowing down—the pastoral landscapes are sublime, and the best vistas are found off the paved roads. It's also an area blessed with a number of appealing bike routes, and what may be the island's best golf course. This region has few prominent natural landmarks, with the exception of St. Peter's Bay—a narrow and attractive inlet that twists eastward from the coast. As such, impatient travelers may grow irritated, wishing for more clearly defined destinations. The only cure is to avoid hurrying, take a more desultory path, and welcome the opportunity to get lost.

EXPLORING THE AREA

Follow Route 313 along the north shore of St. Peter's Bay to its tip, and you'll come to the **Greenwich Dunes,** a stunning area of migrating sand dunes capped with grasses. You'll find unique, wind-carved dunes here. This remarkable region was slated for vacation home development up until 1997, when it was acquired by Parks Canada and added as an extension to Prince Edward Island National Park. The park was still in the process of figuring out how to accommodate visitors without harming this unique and fragile ecosystem when I was last on the island. By 2000 the park plans to offer a full interpretive program for visitors.

The town of **Mount Stewart** (on Route 2 just over the county line in Queens County) is located near the confluence of several spurs of the **Confederation Trail,** the island-wide recreation trail that's being carved from an abandoned rail line. The Mount Stewart area is home to some of the better-developed and better-maintained segments of the trail.

The trail's popularity and potential didn't go unnoticed by a father-and-son team, who opened **Trailside Cafe and Inn** (☎ **888/704-6595** or 902/676-3130) and set up a bike rental operation a few years ago. Today, they rent a fleet of some 80 mountain bikes, at rates of C$15 (US$10) half day, C$25 (US$17) full day, C$75 (US$50) for a week. The staff is very helpful with suggestions and directions, and they can arrange for a van shuttle to pick you up at your destination if you'd prefer a one-way trip. Among the most popular trips is the northeast ride toward East Point (67km/40 miles), which takes you over a few low train trestles retrofitted for bikes, and along St. Peter's Bay.

Golf

Hidden away in this quiet part of the island is the **Links at Crowbush Cove** (☎ 800/377-8337 or 902/961-7300), considered by many to be the island's best golf course for both its aesthetics and subtle challenges. (It captured five stars from *Golf Digest*.) The 6,901-yard, par 72 course, built in 1994, is located along the Gulf of St. Lawrence; it has nine water holes and eight that run next to the dunes. (Talk about your sand trap!) The 11th tee tends to be a bottleneck, as golfers are momentarily distracted from their game by the sweeping views up and down the coast. Reserved tee times are available. The course is located west of the village of Morrell; take Route 2 to Route 350 and drive northwest to the course. For more information, call or write P.O. Box 204, Morrell, PEI C0A 1S0.

WHERE TO STAY & DINE

Trailside Cafe & Inn. 61 Main St., Mount Stewart, PEI C0A 1T0. ☎ **888/704-6595** or 902/676-3130. Fax 902/892-7498. Winter: 902/368-1201. E-mail: dbdeacon@isn.net. 4 units. TV. C$65–C$85 (US$43–US$57). AE, DC, ER, MC, V. Closed mid-Oct to June.

The Trailside Cafe is housed in a 1937 grocery store that's been converted to an inn, cafe, and outdoor adventure center (see "Exploring the Area," above, regarding bike rentals). There's nothing fancy here, but the four rooms (each with private bathroom) are comfortable and simply furnished and have nice touches like radiant heat under hardwood floors. Few guests spend much time lingering in their rooms. The clientele consists primarily of bicyclists, who migrate here for its location smack on the Confederation Trail.

Dining: The funky, informal cafe on the first floor is a fine spot for hanging out, especially when there's live music. Dinner and entertainment packages run C$15 to C$30 (US$10 to US$20), and they invariably sell out; reservations are strongly suggested. The cafe serves lunch and dinner from 11am to 9pm daily in summer. The menu is basic, but everything is homemade and tasty. Soups and chowders are perfect for drizzly or blustery days; there's also a smoked salmon plate, lobster rolls, broiled scallops, pizza, and linguine with vegetables. Sandwiches are C$3.50 to C$7.50 (US$2.35 to US$5); dinner entrees are C$8.95 to C$10.95 (US$5.95 to US$7.30).

7 Prince County

Prince County encompasses the western end of PEI and offers a varied mix of lush agricultural land, rugged coastline, and unpopulated sandy beaches. This is Prince Edward Island with calluses. With a few exceptions, the region is a bit more ragged around the edges in a working-farm, working-waterfront kind of way. It typically lacks the pristine-village charm of Kings County or much of Queens County.

Within this unrefined landscape, however, you'll find pockets of considerable charm, such as the village of Victoria on the south coast at the county line, and in Tyne Valley near the north coast, which is reminiscent of a Cotswold hamlet.

In addition, the **Confederation Trail** (☎ 902/853-2181) offers quiet access to the rolling countryside throughout much of northwest Prince County. Several provincial parks here rank among the most inviting on the island.

ESSENTIALS

GETTING THERE   Route 2 is the main highway connecting Prince County with the rest of the island. Feeder roads typically lead from or to Route 2. The Confederation Bridge from the mainland connects to Prince County at Borden Point, southeast of Summerside.

VISITOR INFORMATION   The best source of travel information for the county is **Gateway Village** (☎ 902/368-5465) at the end of the Confederation Bridge. It's open daily year-round.

VICTORIA

The town of Victoria—located a short detour off Route 1 between the Confederation Bridge and Charlottetown—is a tiny and unusually scenic village that's attracted a number of artists, boutique owners, and craftspeople. The village is perfect for strolling—parking is near the wharf and off the streets, keeping the narrow lanes free for foot traffic. Wander the short, shady lanes while admiring the architecture, much of which is in elemental farmhouse style, clad in clapboard or shingle and constructed with sharply creased gables. (Some elaborate Victorians break the mold.) What makes the place so singular is that the village, which was first settled in 1767, has utterly escaped the creeping sprawl that has plagued so many otherwise attractive places. The entire village consists of 4 square blocks, which are surrounded by potato fields and the Northumberland Strait. It's not hard to imagine that the village looked much the same a century ago.

EXPLORING VICTORIA

The **Victoria Seaport Museum** (no phone) is located in a shingled, square lighthouse near the town parking lot. (You can't miss it.) You'll find a rustic local history museum with the usual assortment of artifacts from the past century or so. In summer, it's open daily except Monday from noon to 5pm; admission is by donation.

In the middle of town is the well-regarded **Victoria Playhouse** (☎ 800/925-2025 or 902/658-2025). Built in 1913 as a community hall, the building has a unique raked stage (it drops 7 inches over 21 feet) to create the illusion of space, four beautiful stained-glass lamps, and a proscenium arch (also unusual for a community hall). Plays staged here in summer attract folks out from Charlottetown for the night. It's hard to say what is more enjoyable: the high quality of the acting or the wonderful big-night-out air of a professional play in a small town where nothing else is going on. There's also a Monday-night concert series, with performers offering up everything from traditional folk to Latin jazz. Tickets are C$16 (US$11) adult, C$14 (US$9) seniors and students; discount on matinees.

Among the two dozen or so businesses in the village, the most intriguing are **Island Chocolates** (☎ 902/658-2320), where delicious Belgian-style chocolates are made; and **Weather-Sense** (☎ 902/658-2993), which offers products for weather junkies. You'll also find a quilt maker, a candle maker, a used book store, art galleries, and an antiques shop.

WHERE TO STAY

Orient Hotel. Main St. (mailing address: P.O. Box 162, Charlottetown, PEI C1A 7K4). ☎ **800/565-6743** or 902/658-2503. Fax 902/658-2078. E-mail: orient@pei.sympatico.ca.

6 units. C$85–C$135 (US$57–US$90) double, including full breakfast. AE, MC, V. Closed mid-Oct to mid-May.

The Orient has been a Victoria mainstay for years—a 1926 guide notes that the inn had 20 rooms at C$2.50 per night (of course, then a trip to the bathroom required a walk to the carriage house). The Orient has been modernized in recent years (all rooms now have private bathrooms), but it retains much of its antique charm. The circa-1900 building with its yellow shingles and maroon trim is at the edge of the village overlooking potato fields lurid with purple blooms in late summer. The rooms are painted in warm pastel tones and furnished eclectically with flea-market antiques. Although some of the updating has diminished the charm—such as the velour furniture in the lobby and the industrial carpeting—the place has a friendly low-key demeanor, much like the village itself.

Dining: Mrs. Proffit's Tea Shop on the first floor serves lunch and afternoon tea (open noon to 5pm daily), and has a growing reputation for scones. The light lunches are appropriate to a tea room, and they include tea sandwiches, lobster rolls, and soups and salads. Prices are C$2.95 to C$9.50 (US$1.95 to US$6.35).

WHERE TO DINE

Landmark Café. Main St. ☎ **902/658-2286.** Reservations recommended. Sandwiches around C$5.50 (US$3.65), main courses C$11–C$16 (US$7–US$11). MC, V. Daily 11am–9:30pm. Closed mid-Sept to mid-June. CAFE.

Located across from the Victoria Playhouse, the Landmark Cafe occupies a small, cozy storefront teeming with shelves filled with crockery, pots, jars, and more, some of which is for sale. But the effect is more funky than Ye Olde Quainte, and the limited menu is very inviting. The steamed mussels and vine leaves with feta cheese are a favorite of regulars. Other offerings include salads, lasagna, meat pie, and tarragon-steamed salmon.

SUMMERSIDE

The seaport city of Summerside (pop. 10,000) is western PEI's undisputed commercial center and the island's second-most-populous community. Joseph Green first settled the town in 1785. According to local legend, an acquaintance on the North Shore commented that Green had settled on the island's "summer side." The name stuck.

The town's early prosperity stemmed from shipping and later from fox farms; during World War II a military air base outside of town emerged as an economic mainstay. The town is still recuperating economically from the closure of the base in the late 1980s and is striving to emerge as a tourist destination.

Recent urban development efforts have been aimed at rejuvenating the waterfront, with mixed results. (The busy and wide bypass that separates the waterfront from downtown thwarts most efforts to manufacture charm.) **Spinnakers' Landing,** as the modern waterfront area is dubbed, features a short boardwalk lined with tourist boutiques, restaurants, and boat-tour companies occupying shanty-style buildings. Local performers often are slated for entertainment. Very close by and pretty well overshadowing the landing are an enclosed mall with a large grocery store, the **Harbourfront Jubilee Theatre,** a parking lot, and other out-of-scale developments. Summerside makes for a decent detour or center for resupplying, but it's hard-pressed to compete with other island locales as a traveler's destination.

EXPLORING SUMMERSIDE

For a glimpse of turn-of-the-century Summerside, stop at the contemporary waterfront just long enough to pick up a free walking tour brochure (entitled "Of

Merchant, Fox, and Sail") at the visitor center, then head a few blocks inland to the tree-lined residential streets. A number of very handsome residential buildings are featured along the route, and there's a settled and sedate air to these quiet city blocks. The International Fox Museum (see below) is along the tour route.

College of Piping and Celtic Performing Arts. 619 Water St., Summerside. ☎ 902/436-5377. www.piping.pe.ca. E-mail: college@piping.pe.ca. Concert tickets C$10 (US$7) adult, C$9 (US$6) senior, C$6 (US$4) students. Concerts held Mon–Thurs late June to early Sept.

The College of Piping (as in bagpiping, of course), strives to promote and preserve Celtic culture and arts; it is the only such year-round institution in North America. It's just west of downtown, where you'll find a gift shop on the first floor with what I'd wager is one of the continent's more extensive offerings of bagpipe tapes and CDs (books and other Scottish-related items are also sold). Behind the building is a Quonset-hut–like shelter of fabric and steel that covers a performance space with a capacity of 600 people. Concerts and revues are scheduled frequently throughout the summer at bargain prices. If you have your heart set on hearing some bagpiping, check the lineup carefully. Some nights feature other forms of traditional Celtic music.

International Fox Museum and Hall of Fame. 286 Fitzroy St. ☎ 902/436-2400. Free admission, donations requested. Daily June–Sept 10am–6pm.

Fox farming came to PEI in 1894 and quickly established itself as a profitable endeavor. The industry reached its zenith around Summerside in the early 20th century, when frenzied speculators and buyers were paying as much as C$35,000 for a pair of silver foxes. (By 1913 some 277 fox ranches had been established on PEI.) The museum is located in the historic Holman House (the Victorian cottage built by R. T. Holman, founder of a noted department store chain) and is quaint and appealing. The exhibits are, well, certain to appall animal-rights supporters. Five rooms of displays touch on fashion and furriers, as well as the science of fox farming. You'll learn that pups were raised in cages of just 9 square feet, and see the frightful Rombaugh Mouth Clamp. The ads and photos (including Queen Elizabeth in a silver fox coat) open doors to a lost era.

WHERE TO STAY

Summerside's lodging options were in flux when I traveled here at press time—one of the more established B&Bs had abruptly closed, and some new establishments were just opening. Because they were not yet ready for prime time I can't fully recommend either of these places, but they may be worth checking out.

The Summerside Inn, 98 Summer St. (☎ 902/436-1757) is in an 1891 home that was a shabby boarding house in its most recent incarnation. While architecturally distinctive, some of the rooms still had a rather bleak, boardinghouse feel to them (shag carpeting, darkly painted walls). The innkeepers are renovating bit by bit, so I'm confident improvements will come. Rates are C$65 to C$85 (US$43 to US$57) double, including a continental breakfast.

Across the street is the **Copple Summer Holme,** 92 Summer St. (☎ 902/436-3100), an attractive 125-year-old Georgian-style home with six columns in front. The inn has four guest rooms with private bathrooms, each measuring about 14 by 16 feet, with decor inspired by the four seasons. Two of the rooms can be made into a two-bedroom family suite. Rates are C$81 (US$54) double, including full breakfast.

Another in-town option is the **Loyalist Country Inn,** 195 Harbour Dr. (☎ 902/436-3333), a mid-sized (30-room) modern and fairly charmless hotel that's popular with business travelers. Rates are C$99 to C$169 (US$66 to US$113) for two.

Raspberry Inn. Route 110 (off Route 1A), Lower Freetown, PEI C0B 1L0. ☎ **888/273-2525** or 902/887-2935. E-mail: raspberryinn@pei.sympatico.ca. 3 units. C$75–C$90 (US$50–US$60), including full breakfast. V.

This tidy red farmhouse, circa 1900, is located in the countryside about 10 minutes' drive from Summerside. It's a peaceful retreat, operated by Paul and Susan Marchbank, who work as carpenter and nurse when not hosting guests (the house originally belonged to Paul's grandparents). It's a cozy spot, made all the more so by a lavishly rococo country style (hooked rugs, stuffed bears) throughout. The two upstairs rooms are somewhat small but comfortable; a downstairs parlor and bedroom is converted to a guest room when needed or requested. The Marchbanks offer coffee, tea, and desserts in the evenings to guests returning from dinner out.

WHERE TO DINE

✪ **Seasons in Thyme.** 644 Water St. ☎ **902/888-3463.** www.seasonsinthyme.com. Reservations recommended. Main courses, lunch C$7–C$9 (US$5–US$6); dinner C$17–C$26 (US$11–US$17). AE, DC, ER, MC, V. Mon–Fri 11am–10pm, Sat–Sun 5–10pm. REGIONAL/EUROPEAN.

Chef Stefan Czapalay and his wife Sharlene designed and built this upscale restaurant in 1997 after spending years in Tyne Valley. With its creamy yellow walls, Seasons in Thyme is airy and bright and offers distant views of the bay through arched windows. It's not cozy, but neither is it stuffy, and diners are usually dressed neatly if informally. The focus is on the kitchen (if you're interested, ask about the chef's table) and the innovative meals that emerge from it. The emphasis is on island-raised and grown ingredients, which are spiced up with a riot of robust flavors. Among the menu items: striploin with a brandy-infused peppercorn sauce, and cod poached in apple wine and served with shellfish, corn polenta, and mushrooms. The desserts feature a milk-chocolate paté, and several notable cheesecakes.

TYNE VALLEY

The village of Tyne Valley is just off Malpeque Bay and is one of the most attractive and pastoral areas of western PEI. There's little to do here, but much to admire. Verdant barley and potato fields surround the village of gingerbread homes, and azure inlets encroach here and there; these are the arms of the bay, which is famous for its succulent Malpeque oysters. A former 19th-century shipbuilding center, the village now attracts artisans and others in search of a quiet lifestyle. A handful of good restaurants, inns, and shops caters to visitors.

EXPLORING TYNE VALLEY

Just north of the village on Route 12 is the lovely ✪ **Green Provincial Park** (☎ **902/831-2370**). Once the site of an active shipyard, the 219-acre park is now a lush riverside destination with emerald lawns and leafy trees, and it has the feel of a turn-of-the-century estate. Which, in fact, it was. In the heart of the park is the extravagant gingerbread mansion (1865) once owned by James Yeo, a merchant, shipbuilder, and landowner who in his time was the island's wealthiest and most powerful man.

The historic Yeo House and the Green Park Shipbuilding Museum (☎ **902/831-2206**) are now the park's centerpieces. Managed by the Prince Edward Island Museum and Heritage Foundation, exhibits in two buildings provide a good view of the prosperous life of a shipbuilder and the golden age of PEI shipbuilding. The museum and house are open daily in summer 10am to 5pm. Admission is C$3 (US$2) plus tax adult; children under 12 are free.

Frequent musical and stage performances are held summers at the 125-seat **Brittania Hall Theatre** (☎ 902/831-2191), on Route 178. Prices are reasonable, usually under C$10 (US$7) for both plays and concerts. Call for information on upcoming shows.

When leaving the area, consider taking the highly scenic drive along the bay on Route 12 from Tyne Valley to MacDougall.

WHERE TO STAY

Green Provincial Park (☎ 902/831-2370) may be the most gracious and lovely park on the island, and offers camping on grassy sites overlooking an arm of Malpeque Bay.

Caernarvon in Bayside. Route 12, Bayside, PEI (mailing address: Richmond RR1, C0B 1Y0). ☎ **800/514-9170** or 902/854-3418. www.cottagelink.com/caernarvon. 3 units, 4 cottages. C$100 (US$67) double for B&B (includes breakfast); C$120 (US$80) double for cottage (3-night min); cottages weekly C$665 (US$443) up to 4 people. AE, MC, V.

The sense of quiet and the views over Malpeque Bay across the road are the lure at this attractive, well-maintained cottage compound on 5 acres a few minutes' drive from Tyne Valley. Owners Rusty and Graham Capper have furnished their modern (ca. 1990) knotty pine cottages simply but comfortably. Each has two bedrooms and a sleeping loft, outdoor gas barbecue, cathedral ceiling, and porch with a bay view. This is a good choice if you're looking to get away, but note that it's also popular with families (there's a playground out back) so it may not be the best option for a romantic escape. In the main house the Cappers also offer an attractive three-bedroom suite upstairs, which may be rented by one couple, a family, or friends traveling together, and is priced accordingly.

✪ **Doctor's Inn.** Route 167 (P.O. Box 92), Tyne Valley, PEI C0B 2C0. ☎ **902/831-3057.** www.peisland.com/doctorsinn. 2 units (both share 1 bathroom). C$60 (US$40) double, including breakfast. MC, V. "Well-mannered" pets allowed.

A stay at the Doctor's Inn is a bit like visiting relatives you didn't know you had. Upstairs in this handsome in-town farmhouse are just two guest rooms, which share a bathroom. (Note that you could rent both for less than the cost of a room at some other inns.) There's an upstairs sitting area, and the extensive organic gardens out back to peruse. It's a pleasant retreat, and innkeepers Jean and Paul Offer do a fine job of making guests feel relaxed and at home.

Dining: The Offers serve up one of Atlantic Canada's most memorable dining experiences. They cater to a maximum of six people on any night at a single sitting. You first gather for appetizers and wine in the sitting room, then move to the large oval dining-room table. The extraordinary salads feature produce from the Offer's famous garden (they grow more than two dozen kinds of lettuce), and you'll have a choice of entrees, which are cooked on the woodstove in an old-fashioned kitchen. Look for scallops, arctic char, salmon, veal, or whatever else is fresh. Desserts are fresh-baked and wonderful. Reservations are requested at least 24 hours in advance; dinner is served at 7pm. A four-course meal with wine is C$40 (US$27) per person.

WHERE TO DINE

Also see the "Doctor's Inn," above.

The Shipwright's Café. Route 178, Tyne Valley. ☎ **902/831-3033.** Reservations recommended in summer. C$7.95–C$14.95 (US$5.30–US$9.95); more for lobster. MC, V. Mon–Sat 11am–2pm and 5–8pm, Sun 8:30am–8:30pm. REGIONAL.

This modern, airy, and spacious restaurant is at the edge of the village of Tyne Valley, and shares a building with the local theater. It's elegant yet informal, and you'd be comfortable here in either neat jeans or pre-dinner sport clothes. Expect good service, a modest but useful wine list, and salads with greens from the Offer's organic gardens, just down the street. Justly popular dishes include the local oysters broiled with spinach and cheese, and the seafood chowder, which is rich and loaded with plump mussels.

WESTERN PRINCE COUNTY

PEI's far western coast—from West Point to North Cape—is well suited to a driving tour or exploring more leisurely by bike. You'll find vast agricultural lands and open ocean views, and a more rugged beauty than elsewhere on the island. What you won't find are many tourist services—or even many of the usual services. Even general stores are infrequent, and it's surprisingly hard to find fresh fish or produce, especially given the number of fishmongers and vegetable stands elsewhere in the province. On the other hand, relatively few travelers make it to this far end of the island, lending it a sometimes eerie, sometime exquisite remoteness.

EXPLORING WESTERN PRINCE COUNTY

At the southwest tip of the island is the **Cedar Dunes Provincial Park** (☎ 902/859-8785). Set on 100 oceanside acres, the park features extensive beaches (with life-guard) and views across the strait to New Brunswick and down to the Confederation Bridge. You'll get a good illustration of the shifting sand here: The changing room has been all but engulfed in sand over the past few years.

Edging the beach is the distinctive black-and-white **West Point Lighthouse Museum** (☎ 902/859-3605). Open summers, it features displays about lighthouse history and local lore, including rooms with some of the original furnishings. This is also the headquarters of the PEI Lighthouse Society, so it's a good stop for informa-tion about other island lights. If you're not afraid of heights, scramble up the narrow stairs to the beacon at the top, where you'll be rewarded with sweeping ocean views. Admission is C$2.50 (US$1.65) adult, C$1.50 (US$1) child, C$7 (US$4.65) family. The lighthouse also houses an inn and restaurant (see below).

Inland at the small town of O'Leary, you'll find the **Prince Edward Island Potato Museum** (☎ 902/859-2039), billed as "Canada's Only Potato Museum." I am not making this up. The museum consists of two main exhibit halls. One depicts the his-tory of the cultivated tuber from the ancient Andes to the present. The other features historic potato harvesting equipment. There's also a 12-minute video about PEI pota-toes, in which you'll find the makings of an interesting 3-minute video. Admission is C$2.50 (US$1.65) adult, C$6 (US$4) family. Rates also include admission to the adjacent museums, which include a **community museum** and a restored **little red schoolhouse.** The museums are at 22 Parkview Dr. (watch for signs off Route 142) and are open June to mid-October Monday to Saturday 9am to 5pm, and Sunday 2 to 5pm.

Closer to the northern tip of the island, near Nail Pond, you may still see directional signs (and illustrations on outdated maps) for **Elephant Rock,** a once-huge and striking stone formation grazing at the edge of the sea. Alas, the winter of 1998–99 took its toll, and the trunk was washed away during fierce seas. Some pilgrims still make the trek out here, a few because they've not yet been informed of the loss, some because it's a scenic area, elephant or no. It's yet unclear whether the landowners adja-cent to the formation, who had a good little side business charging a couple dollars for parking, will be able to reposition the formation as something else (Table Rock?) Reports have also surfaced that another elephant rock may be aborning up the coast as the erosion continues apace. Ask around locally for an update.

North Cape is a blustery, dramatic point where the seas swirl around from north and west, mixing off the point. You can take pictures of the **lighthouse** (1866), walk along the low, crumbling cliffs, and then visit the small **Interpretive Centre and Aquarium** (☎ **902/882-2991**) for a bit more information about local marine life and history. (Above the center is the **Wind & Reef Restaurant,** which offers seafood with a view of the sea.) Admission to the center is C$2 (US$1.35) adult, C$1 (US65¢) seniors and children; it's open late May to mid-October.

And all those strange towering devices next to the center? That's the **Atlantic Wind Test Site,** where an array of traditional and state-of-the-art windmills are being refined to better harness the winds. You can admire the eerie sound they make in the cape's persistent breeze, but the site itself is closed to the public. Guides at the center can answer any questions you might have.

WHERE TO STAY & DINE

The provincial park **campgrounds** at both **Cedar Dunes** (☎ **902/859-8785**) and **Mill River** (☎ **902/859-8786**) are very attractive. Mill River has more of a country-club feel, surrounded by acres of grass, tall trees, and a handsome golf course. Cedar Dunes, next to the West Point Lighthouse and at the edge of encroaching dunes, is open and grassy; a short boardwalk across the dunes delivers you to the beach. Cost of the campgrounds is C$15 (US$10) unserviced or C$17 (US$11) with electric.

West Point Lighthouse. RR no. 2, West Point, PEI C0B 1V0. ☎ **800/764-6854** or 902/859-3605. Fax 902/859-3117. 9 units. C$85–C$130 (US$57–US$87) double, off-season rates till June 19 and after Sept 9. AE, MC, V. Closed Oct–May.

Two of the nine guest rooms at the West Point Lighthouse are actually in the light-house itself—something quite unique. One room, Keepers Quarters, faces landward and has a low ceiling, but hold out for the Tower Room, with a 13-foot ceiling, an extravagant canopy bed, and unrivaled views. (Book well in advance.) The other guest rooms are in a newer addition and are the size of cozy motel rooms, but they are nicely decorated with quilts and full bathrooms. The best of these is Room 9, a corner room with a wonderful breeze and great views.

Dining: The first-floor restaurant is a popular destination for day-trippers who venture here for the beach and seafood. Breakfast (not included in room rates) is under C$5 (US$3), lunch is mostly under C$10 (US$7), and dinners range widely from C$10 to C$26 (US$7 to US$17). Expect traditional dinner entrees like fisherman's platter, seafood fettuccine, chicken breast, and steak and scallops.

6 Newfoundland & Labrador

If you have but one atom of adventure in you, you'll know it after a few minutes poring over a map of Newfoundland and Labrador. Your electrons begin to pulse madly. Your heart races. All those isolated harbors! All those miles of remote lakes! And those extraordinary names that dot the map: Jerry's Nose, Snook's Arm, Leading Tickles, Heart's Delight, Happy Adventure, Chapel Island, St. Bride's, Mistaken Point, Misery Hill, Breakheart Point, Cape Pine, Shuffle Board.

Newfoundland and Labrador might be the Eastern seaboard's last best place. (These two distinct geographic areas are administered as one province, so sometimes the phrase "Newfoundland and Labrador" refers to a single place, sometimes to two places.) Wild, windswept, and isolated, the province often reveals a powerful paradox. Although the landscape is rocky and raw—at times it looks as if the glaciers had receded only a year or two ago—the residents often display a genuine warmth that makes visitors feel right at home. Tourists only recently started arriving here in any number, and long-time residents more often than not like to chat, offer advice, and hear your impressions of their home. Travelers who are usually reluctant to ask questions of locals for fear of embarrassment usually drop their hesitation after an encounter or two.

An excursion to The Rock—as the island of Newfoundland is commonly called—is magical in many ways. Not only in the extraordinary northern landscape and the gracious people, but also in the rich history that catches many first-time visitors off guard. This is where European civilization made landfall in the New World—by both the Vikings and the later fishermen and settlers in the wake of John Cabot's arrival here in 1497—and you'll find traces of that rich legacy at almost every turn. Although other parts of North America might claim an equally historic lineage, there are few places in the New World where one feels as if not a whole lot has transpired since the first settlers sailed into the harbor some centuries ago. History isn't buried here; it's right on the surface.

One last note: There's some to-and-fro among travelers about how to accent "Newfoundland." Correctly done, there's a little bit of emphasis on the final syllable, but it's subtle. Here's a trick. Recite this bit of doggerel: "You just won't understand, 'Til you've been to Newfoundland." Now drop everything but the last word.

1   Exploring Newfoundland & Labrador

Don't let the maps of the Atlantic Provinces fool you. Newfoundland (and sometimes Labrador) is commonly published as an inset map alongside Nova Scotia, Prince Edward Island, and New Brunswick. **Carefully note the scale.** Whereas an inch might equal 30 kilometers in Nova Scotia, it may be 60 or 70 kilometers in Newfoundland. The amount of time to travel anywhere on the island goes up accordingly. The island has about the same land mass as Pennsylvania, but that's misleading because the island is twisted and pulled as if made of taffy, and thus it seems bigger when you're traveling from one end to another. One example: that peninsula that extends northward along the west coast? It takes about 8 or 9 hours to drive from Port aux Basques (where the ferry from Nova Scotia docks) to the tip at St. Anthony's.

A couple of weeks is enough for a bare-bones tour of the whole island, although you'll be frustrated by all that gets left out. You're better off selecting a few regions and focusing on those.

For those arriving by ferry: If you've got less than a week, you should probably come and go via Port aux Basques and focus on Gros Morne National Park, which is commonly the highlight of a stay here, especially for outdoor-oriented travelers. If you're planning on at least 2 weeks, you should consider arriving and leaving the island at opposite ports (see below), completing a traverse of the island.

For those arriving by air: St. John's is well situated for exploring the wonderful Avalon Peninsula, and the intriguing Bonavista Peninsula isn't too distant. If you have your heart set on venturing to Gros Morne or beyond, plan to spend a couple of weeks, or be prepared for some hours behind the wheel. It's about 7 to 8 hours straight driving from St. John's to the national park. The best option in this case would be to fly in to St. John's, and depart via Deer Lake.

ESSENTIALS

WEATHER & TIME   The weather in Newfoundland might charitably be called "mercurial." You might very well experience all four seasons during a 1-week trip to the island—from relatively warm and sunny days (the average high temperature in summer is about 70°F/21°C) to the downright frigid (it often dips into the range of 40°F/4°C or lower on summer evenings). If you have a rain suit, bring it. When the rain pairs up with the high winds, the results can be, well, less than comforting.

Note that Newfoundland keeps its own clock, and "Newfoundland time" is a *half-* hour ahead of Atlantic time.

VISITOR INFORMATION   Visitor information centers aren't as numerous or well organized in Newfoundland as they are in Nova Scotia or Prince Edward Island, where almost every small community has a place to load up on brochures and ask questions. In Newfoundland, you're better off stocking up on maps and information either in St. John's or just after you disembark from the ferries, where excellent centers are maintained.

The *Newfoundland and Labrador Travel Guide,* published by the province's department of tourism, is hefty and helpful, with listings of all attractions and accommodations. Request a free copy before arriving by calling ☎ **800/563-6353** or 709/729-2830. You can also request it by fax (709/729-1965), e-mail (info@tourism.gov.nf.ca), or mail (P.O. Box 8730, St. John's, NF A1B 4K2). The guide is available on the ferries and at the province's information centers.

Newfoundland is better wired than you might expect when it comes to the Internet, and many residents and businesses maintain Web sites. A quirky site at which to launch an Internet exploration of the island is www.bigkahoona.com.

GETTING THERE **Air transportation** to Newfoundland is typically through Gander or St. John's, although scheduled flights are also available to Deer Lake and St. Anthony's. Flights originate in Montréal, Toronto, Halifax, and London, England. Airlines serving the island include **Air Canada/Air Nova** (☎ 800/422-6232 in Canada, 800/776-3000 in the United States), **Canadian Airlines** (☎ 800/426-7000), **Air Labrador** (☎ 800/563-3042 within Newfoundland, or 709/896-3387), and **Interprovincial Airlines** (☎ 800/563-2800 within Newfoundland, 709/576-1666 elsewhere). Flight time from Toronto to St. John's is about 3 hours. (Note that at press time both Air Canada and Canadian Airlines were considering mergers with one another as well as with outside airlines.)

Marine Atlantic (☎ 800/341-7981; www.marine-atlantic.ca) operates a year-round **ferry service** from North Sydney, Nova Scotia to Port aux Basques, with as many as three sailings each way daily during the peak summer season. The crossing is about 5 hours; one-way fares are C$20 (US$13) adult, plus C$62 (US$41) automobile. A seasonal ferry (summers only) also connects North Sydney with Argentia on the southwest tip of the Avalon Peninsula. This crossing is offered three times weekly in summer and takes 14 to 15 hours. The one-way fare is C$55 (US$37) adult, C$124 (US$83) car. On both ferries, children 5 to 12 years old are half-price (children under 5 free). Reserved reclining seats, sleeping berths, and private cabins are available.

Seasonal ferries also connect Lewisporte, Newfoundland, with Goose Bay, Labrador. The trip is about 38 hours. Fares are C$97 (US$65) adult, C$160 (US$107) car. Call ☎ 800/563-6353 for information and reservations.

For all ferries, advance reservations are strongly advised during the peak travel season. As many as 100 cars have been backed up at Port aux Basques awaiting the next berth off the island. The reservation policy is quite fair: When you reserve over the phone with a credit card, you pay a C$25 (US$17) deposit. You can cancel or change your reservations up to 48 hours before departure for a full refund of your deposit. The balance is due at the terminal; you're required to check in at least 1 hour before sailing to hold your reservation. The terminals all have snack bars, rest rooms with free showers, television lounges, and up-to-date facilities.

GETTING AROUND Newfoundland has no rail service, but several bus lines connect the major ports and cities. **DRL Coachlines** (☎ 709/738-8090) has one bus daily from Port aux Basques to St. John's. The trip takes 13 hours, and one-way fare is C$90 (US$60).

To explore the countryside, you'll need a car. Major rental companies with fleets in Newfoundland include **Avis** (☎ 800/879-2847), **Budget** (☎ 800/268-8900), **Hertz** (☎ 800/263-0600), **Thrifty** (☎ 800/367-2277), **Tilden** (☎ 800/387-4747), **Enterprise** (☎ 800/325-8007), and **Rent-A-Wreck** (☎ 800/337-0116).

Sock away some extra cash for gasoline when traveling the island. The price of fuel on Newfoundland tends to be a bit higher than in other Atlantic provinces.

2 The Great Outdoors

BIKING Bike touring in Newfoundland is for the hearty. It's not that the hills are necessarily brutal (although many are). But the weather can be downright demoralizing. Expect more than a handful of blustery days, complete with horizontal rains that seem to swirl around from every direction. The happiest bike tourists seem to be those who allow themselves frequent stays in motels or inns, where they can find hot showers and places to dry their gear. **Aspenwood Hike and Bike Tours,** P.O. Box 622, Springdale, NF A1C 5K8 (☎ 709/673-4255), arranges mountain biking trips

Cape Chidley

Ungava Bay

Hebron

QUEBEC

Nain

Davis Inlet

LABRADOR

Hopedale

Makkovik

Lobstick Lake

502

Michikamau Lake

Lake Melville

Rigolet

Cartwright

Esker

501

500

Churchill River

520

Labrador City

500

Mud Lake

Happy Valley–Goose Bay

Wabush

389

Mealy Mountains

Kenamu River

510

Battle Harbour

Pinware

Red Bay

L'Anse-Amour

L'Anse-au-Loup

St. Anthony

Blanc-Sablon

St. Barbe

430

Englee

Harrington Harbour

Gros Morne National Park

Sept-îles

Baie Verte

Twillingate

Terra Nova National Park

Anticosti Island

Lewisporte

330

Corner Brook

1

Gander

Bonavista

Deer Lake

235

Stephenville

Grand Falls

230

Gulf of St. Lawrence

NEWFOUNDLAND

80

St. John's

480

360

70

10

Channel-Port aux Basques

Grand Bank

210

Argentia

Havre–Aubert

100

Prince Edward Island

St-Pierre

90

NEW BRUNSWICK

Summerside

Charlottetown

Fredericton

Moncton

North Sydney

Saint John

NOVA SCOTIA

Halifax

Yarmouth

Atlantic Ocean

Atlantic Ocean

0   150 Mi
0   150 Km

LEGEND
Ferry - - - - -

1-0373

in and around central Newfoundland; **Freewheeling Adventures,** RR no. 1, Hubbards, NS B0J 1T0 (☎ **902/857-3600**), runs van-supported trips based in hotels and B&Bs.

BIRD WATCHING   If you're from a temperate climate, bird watching doesn't get much more interesting or exotic than in Newfoundland and Labrador. Seabirds typically attract the most attention, and eastern Newfoundland and the Avalon Peninsula are especially rich in bird life. Just south of St. John's is the **Witless Bay Ecological Reserve,** where several islands host the largest colony of breeding puffins and kittiwakes in the western Atlantic. On the southern Avalon Peninsula, **Cape St. Mary's** features a remarkable sea stack just yards from easily accessible cliffs that's home to a cacophonous colony of northern gannets. (See sections on the Avalon Peninsula later in this chapter.)

CAMPING   In addition to the two national parks, Newfoundland maintains a number of provincial parks open for car camping. (About a dozen of these were "privatized" in 1997 and are now run as commercial enterprises, although many still appear on maps as provincial parks.) These are listed in the provincial travel guide, as are most privately run campgrounds.

   If you're properly equipped, you might want to take part in a traditional activity in Newfoundland called "gravel-pit camping." Basically, that means pulling over to the side of the road (typically in a gravel pit) and spending the night away from organized campgrounds. You'll see gravel-pit campers all over the island, often in beautiful and dramatic spots overlooking coves or ponds. Although there's no law guaranteeing public access as there is in some Scandinavian countries, it's a hallowed tradition, and as long as you don't pitch your tent or park your RV in someone's driveway, you usually won't be hassled.

CANOEING   A glance at a map shows that rivers and lakes abound in Newfoundland and Labrador. Canoe trips can range from placid puttering around a pond near St. John's to world-class descents of Labrador rivers hundreds of miles long. The Department of Tourism produces a free brochure outlining several canoe trips; call ☎ **800/563-6353.** A popular guide—*Canyons, Coves and Coastal Waters*—is sold in bookstores around the province, or it can be ordered by mail from **Newfoundland Canoeing Association,** P.O. Box 5961, St. John's, NF A1C 5X4.

   Several outfitters offer guided canoe trips, both on the island and the mainland. Among them: **Newfoundland and Labrador Ecotour Adventures,** 8 Virginia Place, St. John's, NF A1A 3G6 (☎ **709/579-8055**); and **X-plore Newfoundland,** P.O. Box 63, Corner Brook, NF A2H 6C3 (☎ **709/634-2237**).

FISHING   Newfoundland and Labrador are legendary among serious anglers, especially those stalking the cagey Atlantic salmon, which can weigh up to 18 kilograms (40 lb.). Other prized species include landlocked salmon, lake trout, brook trout, and northern pike. More than 100 fishing-guide services on the island and mainland can provide everything from simple advice to complete packages that include bush-plane transportation, lodging, and personal guides. One fishing license is needed for Atlantic salmon, one for other fish, so be sure to read the current *Newfoundland & Labrador Hunting and Fishing Guide* closely for current regulations. It's available at most visitor centers, or by calling ☎ **800/563-6353** or 709/576-2830. To request it by mail, write the **Department of Tourism, Culture & Recreation,** P.O. Box 8730, St. John's, NF A1B 4K2.

HIKING & WALKING   Newfoundland has an abundance of trails, but you'll have to work a bit harder to find them here than in the provinces to the south. The most obvious hiking trails tend to be centered around national parks and historic sites, where they are often fairly short—good for a half-day's hike, rarely more. But Newfoundland has hundreds of trails, many along the coast leading to abandoned communities. Some places are finally realizing the recreational potential for these trails, and are now publishing maps and brochures directing you to them. The **Bonavista Peninsula** and the **Eastport Peninsula,** both on Newfoundland's east coast, are two areas that are attracting attention for world-class trails that were all but overlooked until recently.

The best-maintained trails are at **Gros Morne National Park,** which has around 100 kilometers (60 miles) of trails. In addition to these, there's also off-track hiking on the dramatic Long Range for backpackers equipped to set out for a couple of days. Ask at the park visitor center for more information.

More adventurous hikers will find enjoyment by just pulling over and setting off across one of the island's vast and intriguing bogs, following a compass heading out and back. These areas are spongy, but you'll rarely sink through the peat. Waterproof shoes will increase your enjoyment, and the phrase "bogged down" will be rather more evocative for you in the future.

SEA KAYAKING   With all its protected bays and inlets, Newfoundland is ideal for exploring by sea kayak. But there's a catch: The frigid water. There's a reason you'll see icebergs offshore, and it's called the Labrador Current. You'll need to be well prepared in the event you end up in the drink, because you won't have a lot of time for a rescue before the cold gets you in its grip. Experts traveling with their own gear can pick and choose their destinations. I would suggest that the area northeast of Terra Nova National Park, with its archipelago centering around St. Brendan's Island, would hold up well under close scrutiny.

Novices should stick to guided tours. **Eastern Edge Outfitters** (☎ 709/782-7465) offers a variety of tours, mostly on the Avalon Peninsula. Rates range from C$100 (US$67) for a 1-day tour to C$1,200 (US$800) for an 11-day tour, which includes all equipment and meals.

Mike Henley of **Sea Kayaking Adventures,** ☎ 709/726-9283, is based in St. John's and leads paddling tours at Witless Bay, Cape Broyle, and Conception Bay, with prices starting at C$35 (US$23) for a 2-hour sunset paddle. Extended tours and customized trips may be arranged.

At **Terra Nova National Park,** 2-hour sea kayak tours leave from the Marine Interpretation Centre and explore protected Newman's Cove. (See the "Terra Nova National Park" section later in this chapter.)

3 Southwestern Newfoundland

For most travelers arriving by ferry, this region is the first introduction to The Rock. And it's like starting the symphony without a prelude, jumping right to the crescendo. There's instant drama in the brawny, verdant Long Range Mountains that run parallel to the Trans-Canada Highway en route to Corner Brook. There are also the towering seaside cliffs of the Port au Port Peninsula, and intriguing coastal villages that await exploration. You might also be surprised that winds can blow with such intensity hereabouts, yet not attract any comment from the locals.

PORT AUX BASQUES

Port aux Basques is a major gateway for travelers arriving in Newfoundland, with ferries connecting to Nova Scotia year-round. It's a good way station for those arriving late on a ferry or departing early in the morning. Otherwise, it can easily be viewed in a couple of hours when either coming or going.

This appealing harborside village is situated on treeless emerald hills that define the terrain around the harbor. "Downtown" consists of brightly colored, boxy homes set on the hills around a compact commercial zone. A narrow boardwalk snakes along the water's edge and links the ferry terminal and the town; it's worth the walk if you've got an hour or two to kill before your ferry, especially at sunset, which brings out the supple contours of the surrounding hills. At the edge of town are a tiny mall and newer residential neighborhoods. The town also has a one-screen movie theater and a few family-style restaurants.

ESSENTIALS

GETTING THERE   Port aux Basques is commonly reached via ferry from Nova Scotia. See "Exploring Newfoundland & Labrador," above, for ferry information. The Trans-Canada Highway (Route 1) links the major communities of southwestern Canada. Port aux Basques is 905 kilometers (543 miles) from St. John's via the Trans-Canada Highway.

VISITOR INFORMATION   In Port aux Basques, the **Provincial Interpretation and Information Centre** (☎ 709/695-2262) is located on the Trans-Canada Highway about 2 miles from the ferry terminal. You can't miss it, it's the modern, ecclesiastical-looking building on the right. Inside are displays to orient you regarding the island's regions, and racks aflutter with great forests of brochures. From mid-May to the end of October the center is open daily from 6am to 11pm.

EXPLORING PORT AUX BASQUES

The **Gulf Museum,** 118 Main St. (☎ 709/695-3408), across from the Town Hall, has a quirky assortment of artifacts related to local history. The museum's centerpiece is a Portuguese astrolabe dating from 1628, which was recovered from local waters in 1981. Also intriguing is a display about the *Caribou,* a ferry torpedoed by a German U-boat in 1942 with a loss of 137 lives. The museum is open daily from 9am to 7pm; admission is C$2 (US$1.35) adult, C$1 (US65¢) children, C$5 (US$3.35) family.

On the way out of town you'll pass the **Port aux Basques Railway Heritage Center,** Route 1 (☎ 709/956-2170), dedicated to the memory of the *Newfie Bullet,* the much-maligned, much-reminisced-about passenger train that ran between Port aux Basques and St. John's from 1898 to 1969. (The highway across the island opened in 1966, dooming the train.) The train required 27 hours to make the trip (at an average speed of 48km/30 miles per hour), and during a tour of several restored rail cars you'll learn how the train made the run through deep snows of winter, how the passengers slept at night (very cozily, it turns out), and life aboard the mail car and caboose. Tours last just 15 minutes and cost C$2 (US$1.35) adult, C$1 (US65¢) children, C$5 (US$3.35) family.

Departing from the edge of Railway Heritage Center is the **T'Railway,** a coast-to-coast pathway being converted from the old train line. It's used by pedestrians, bikers, and ATVers, and in this stretch it runs through marsh and along the ocean to Cheeseman Park (see below) and beyond. It's a good spot to get your mountain bike limbered up for further adventures.

J. T. Cheeseman Provincial Park (☎ 709/695-7222) is 15 kilometers (9 miles) west of town on Route 1 (confusingly, you follow Route 1 East out of town). Much of the park lies along sandy dunes, which are home to the piping plover, an endangered species. An observation platform offers a view of the plover's habitat; bring

Map Legend:
- **Ferry** - - - -
- —— Coastal Freight and Passenger Service

binoculars and patience (they're present here from early May to mid-August). The park has 102 campsites, along with a section of the T'Railway, which is good for walking or mountain biking.

WHERE TO STAY

About a half-dozen hotels and B&Bs offer no-frills shelter to travelers at Port aux Basques. The two largest are **Hotel Port aux Basques,** Route 1 (☎ **709/695-2171**), and **St. Christopher's Hotel,** Caribou Road (☎ **800/563-4779**). Both might be described as "budget modern," with clean, basic rooms in architecturally undistinguished buildings. I'd give St. Christopher's the edge since it's located on a high bluff with views of the town and the harbor. Both have around 50 rooms and charge around C$60 (US$40) for a double.

WHERE TO DINE

Dining opportunities are limited. Both hotels mentioned above have dining rooms, serving basic, filling meals. A 10-minute walk from the ferry terminal on the boardwalk is the **Harbour Restaurant,** 121 Caribou Rd., ☎ **709/695-3238,** a family-style restaurant that serves budget-friendly meals (entrees C$4.95/US$3.30 to C$13.95/US$9.30, with most under C$10/US$6.65). Expect fried fish, fried chicken, fish cakes, sandwiches, and the like. Most tables have good views of the harbor.

CORNER BROOK

With a population of about 35,000, Corner Brook is Newfoundland's second-largest city. Like St. John's, it's also dramatically sited—in this case, on the banks of the glimmering Humber River, which winds down through verdant mountains from beyond Deer Lake, then turns the corner to flow into Humber Arm. The hills on the south shore of the Humber are nearly as tall as those in Gros Morne National Park, making a great backdrop for the town, which has gradually expanded up the shoulders of the hills.

Corner Brook is a young city with a long history. The area was first explored and charted in 1767 by Capt. James Cook, who spent 23 days mapping the islands at the mouth of the bay. But it wasn't until early in this century that the city started to take its present shape. Copper mines and the railroad brought in workers; in the early 1920s the paper mill, which still dominates downtown, was constructed. By 1945 it was the largest paper mill in the world.

The city has grown beyond its stature as a mill town, and has a more vibrant feel than other spots anchored by heavy industry. This is no doubt aided in large part by the energy from two institutions of higher learning: Sir Wilfred Grenfell College of Memorial University of Newfoundland, and the College of the North Atlantic. You'll also find well-developed services and suppliers, including grocery stores, banks, hotels, and restaurants. This is your last chance to stock up and indulge if you're headed to Gros Morne—from here on out, you'll be dependent on small grocery stores and mom-and-pop restaurants.

ESSENTIALS

GETTING THERE   Corner Brook is on the Trans-Canada Highway 218 kilometers (135 miles) north of Port aux Basque. Air access is via the **Deer Lake Regional Airport** (☎ **709/635-3601**).

VISITOR INFORMATION   The **Corner Brook Tourist Chalet** (☎ **709/639-9792**) is up the hill, just off the Trans-Canada Highway at the intersection of West Valley Road and Confederation Drive (near the Best Western Mamateek). It's open daily in summer.

EXPLORING CORNER BROOK

Downtown Corner Brook looks promising on your approach—it's located on the hill-flanked Humber Arm, a well-protected ocean inlet and famed salmon fishing area. With the residential areas stacked neatly on the hills around the commercial center in the valley, it's got great topographical interest.

Alas, downtown is likely to disappoint sightseers. Simplifying somewhat (quite a bit, actually), the city center consists of a large paper mill and two small malls. The enclosed malls offer basic goods but little charm. The mill offers an interesting olfactory experience when the wind is right.

It's still worth the detour: tree-lined **West Street** is fun to explore, where you'll find coffee shops, restaurants, and pharmacies. The **Corner Brook Museum and Archive,** 2 West St., (☎ **709/634-2518**), is housed in a solid 1920s-era building that once was home to customs offices, the court, and the post and telegraph offices. A visit here offers a quick way to learn just how young the city really is (grainy black and white photos show empty hills surrounding the paper mill as late as the 1920s), and how civilized it has become. An assortment of locally significant artifacts (a prominent doctor's desk, ship models) rounds out the collection. The museum is open daily 10am to 8pm; admission is C$2 (US$1.35) adult, C$1 (US65¢) youth.

Nearby, at Glynmill Inn, you can follow a connector trail to the **Corner Brook Stream Trail,** which runs through the heart of the city. The trail is being developed along the 12-mile length of the stream (formerly the city's water supply), but for now it offers access to a narrow and pleasantly green sanctuary within the city. From Glynmill Inn you'll round a man-made pond; from here you can head upstream to Margaret Bowater Park (a locally popular spot with swimming pool and playground), or downstream toward Main Street and City Hall.

The Newfoundland Emporium, 7 Broadway (☎ **709/634-9376**), is a traditional downtown stop for travelers. It's an eclectic shop with a mix of antiques, crafts, books, and—in the owner's words—"flotsam and jetsam." It's the city's best destination for souvenirs.

OUTDOOR PURSUITS

For outdoor enthusiasts, Corner Brook makes an excellent base for exploring outlying mountains and waters.

Mountain bikers should plan a stop by **T&T Professional Bicycle,** 166A Humber Rd. (☎ **709/634-6799**). These guys know their business; ask for suggestions on where to go, and for the free map of backcountry bike routes. Didn't bring your bike? You can also rent one here.

Some of the region's best **hiking** is found along Route 450 toward Bottle Cove (see "A Road Trip from Corner Brook," below). But other hikes will get you quickly up into the hills around Corner Brook. At Marble Mountain ski area (head east on the Trans-Canada Highway), you can park at the ski lodge parking lot and follow a 1.0-kilometer/0.6-mile trail up to **Steady Brook Falls,** which is especially impressive after a summer rain. More extensive hikes are outlined in "Corner Brook Hiking Guide and Map," available free at the visitor's information center.

Anglers in search of the noted Atlantic salmon that spawn in the Humber have a wide selection of outfitters who provide an all-inclusive **fishing** experience; one price covers transportation from the airport, accommodations, meals, and a guide. Try the **Strawberry Hill Resort** in Little Rapids (☎ **709/634-0066**), or **Upper Humber Tours** in Deer Lake (☎ **709/635-5351**). Other outfitters are listed in the province's "Hunting and Fishing Guide," available at provincial information centers or in advance by calling ☎ **800/563-6353.**

Atlantic Canada has just one **downhill ski area** that I'd classify as a destination resort, and that's **Marble Mountain,** just a 10-minute drive from Corner Brook. You can eye the steep hills just north of the city. With a location near the Gulf of St. Lawrence and in the path of persistent northwest winds, it gets plenty of powder dumps in the winter, and the 1,600-foot vertical drop is respectable. Many skiers take advantage of packages that include airfare, lodging, lift tickets, and a rental car; ask for a brochure by calling ☎ **709/637-7616** or pointing your browser at www.marble-mountain.com.

WHERE TO STAY

Corner Brook is home to several convenient chain motels. Among others, you'll find the **Best Western Mamateek Inn,** 64 Maple Valley Rd. (☎ **800/563-8600** or 709/639-8901) near the tourist information booth, and the **Holiday Inn,** 47 West St. (☎ **709/634-5381**), which is within walking distance of the city's best restaurant (see below). Rooms start at C$89 (US$59) for a double at either place.

Camping is offered on the north banks of the Humber at **Prince Edward Park,** ☎ **709/637-1580,** with 68 sites spread along a bluff from which you can often spot osprey and bald eagles. Both fully serviced (C$16/US$11) and unserviced sites

(C$12/US$8) are available. Exit the Trans-Canada Highway at Marble Mountain and follow Route 440 until you see the signs. It's about 10 minutes' drive from downtown.

Glynmill Inn. 1 Cobb Lane (near West St.), Corner Brook, NF A2H 6E6. ☎ **800/563-4400** (in Canada) or 709/634-5181. Fax 709/634-5106. 81 units (including 23 suites). A/C TV TEL. C$79–C$155 (US$53–US$103) double. AE, DC, ER, MC, V.

This Tudor inn is set in a quiet parklike setting an easy stroll to the services and shops of West Street. Built in 1924 (and extensively renovated in 1994), the four-story hotel has a surfeit of charm and appealing detailing. The rooms are tastefully decorated with colonial reproductions; the popular Tudor Suite has a private Jacuzzi. You'll get far more character here than at the chain motels in town, and for about the same price.

Dining: The inn's two dining rooms are quite popular among local diners, with steaks being especially popular. The setting can feel a bit institutional (they do a rousing business with conventions and banquets), but the food is quite good. Dinner entrees run from C$12 to C$21 (US$8 to US$14).

WHERE TO DINE

✪ Thirteen West. 13 West St. ☎ **709/634-1300.** Reservations recommended on weekends. Main courses, lunch C$8–C$14 (US$5.35–US$9.35), dinner C$15.50–C$26.50 (US$10.35–US$17.65). AE, DC, ER, MC, V. Mon–Fri 11:30am–2:30pm and 5:30–9:30pm (until 10:30pm Fri), Sat 5:30–10:30pm, Sun 5:30–9:30pm. GLOBAL.

Western Newfoundland's best restaurant can easily compete with the better restaurants of St. John's in both the quality of the food and the casual but professional attitude. Tucked along shady West Street in an unobtrusive building (there's a patio fronting the street for the rare balmy night), the kitchen does an outstanding job preparing top-notch meals, and the staff knows how to make good service seem easy. At lunchtime look for offerings like grilled chicken breast wrap and baked scallop crepes with bacon and leeks. In the evening, you'll find a menu with items such as grilled salmon with a dill pesto, grilled chicken breast with a curry rub, and a steak with shrimp combo prepared with Asian spices. Don't leave without sampling at least one of the delightful desserts, which include standards like creme caramel and profiteroles, along with more inventive selections like sautéed bananas with a rum pecan caramel sauce and vanilla ice cream.

A ROAD TRIP FROM CORNER BROOK

One of western Newfoundland's most scenic drives is between Corner Brook and Bottle Cove, driving west on Route 450, also known as **Captain Cook's Trail.** It takes about 45 minutes to an hour to drive to the end of the road at Bottle Cove if you don't make any stops. But you should. The region stands up well to a leisurely excursion.

The road is winding and dramatic, running between the looming Blow Me Down Mountains and the dark and dappled waters of Humber Arm. Near Lark Harbor is **Blow Me Down Provincial Park** (☎ 709/681-2430), a fine destination for a hike and a picnic. Start off with the half-mile hike to the lookout tower. Along the way you can view the Governor's Staircase, a unique rock formation some 450 million years old. Continue along the up-and-down trail for 3.5 kilometers (2.1 miles) one-way to Tortoise Point, with its exceptional views of the Bay of Islands. The park is open daylight hours and there's no admission charged.

On the way back to Corner Brook is the **Blow Me Down Nature Trail** (west of the village of Frenchman's Cove, about 500 meters west of the bridge over the brook). This is an especially appealing walk on a warm day, since this easy 1-kilometer (0.6-mile) trail leads to great swimming holes in Blow Me Down Brook. Bring towels!

DEER LAKE

Deer Lake is an unassuming crossroads town near the head of the Humber River where travelers coming from the south either continue on the Trans-Canada Highway toward St. John's, or veer northwest to Gros Morne National Park, some 71 kilometers (43 miles) distant. Deer Lake is the gateway for those coming by air directly to western Newfoundland. There's little to detain a visitor here; it's a good spot to buy gas, peruse the brochures at the provincial information center, then push on.

Deer Lake is located 50 kilometers (30 miles) north of Corner Brook on the Trans-Canada Highway. **Deer Lake Regional Airport** (☎ 709/635-3601) serves western Newfoundland with scheduled flights both within the island and to Halifax. Car rentals are available.

EXPLORING DEER LAKE

Lucky is the traveler who arrives here during the short **strawberry** season (mid- to late July some years; early August in others). If you're here at the right time, do yourself a favor and stop at one of the several seasonal roadside stands for a pint or two. They're plump, they're cheap, and they're sinfully sweet and flavorful—nothing at all like the tasteless commercial berries that invade grocery stores in the United States and elsewhere.

The **Newfoundland Insectarium** (☎ 709/635-4545) opened in 1999 on Route 440 one-half kilometer from the Trans-Canada Highway. Funded privately and operated as a for-profit venture, the insectarium will appeal to impressionable children and anyone fascinated with bugs. It's housed in a retrofitted dairy farm framed in red cedar, with most of the exhibits on a spacious second floor. These include more than 4,000 mounted actual insects (no faux bugs are displayed here), and 28 terrariums with live insects, including tiger beetles, American cockroaches, and honeybees. A walking trail and bug-themed gift shop (chocolate-coated crickets!) round out the experience. It's open daily in summers 9am to 9pm; mid-September to mid-June it's open Tuesday to Friday 9am to 5pm, weekends 10am to 5pm. Admission is C$6 (US$4) adult, C$5 (US$3.35) seniors, C$4 (US$2.65) children 5 to 14, C$20 (US$13) families (parents and schoolchildren).

WHERE TO STAY & DINE

Deer Lake Motel. Route 1, Deer Lake, NF A0K 2E0. ☎ **800/563-2144** in Newfoundland, 709/635-2108. 56 units. A/C TV TEL. C$65–C$83 (US$43–US$55) double, C$110 (US$73) suite. AE, DC, ER, MC, V.

This serviceable motel is located right on the Trans-Canada Highway, and its clean, basic rooms come with coffeemakers. On the premises are also a coffee shop, lounge, and restaurant. It's a good place to lay your head if you're arriving late en route to Gros Morne or points north or east; otherwise, there's little call to remain overnight in Deer Lake.

4 Gros Morne National Park

"Gros Morne" translates roughly from the French as "big gloomy," and if you arrive on a day when ghostly bits of fog blow across the road and scud clouds hover in the glacial valleys, you'll get a pretty good idea how this area got its name. Even on brilliantly sunny days there's something about the stark mountains, lonely fjords cut off from the ocean, and miles of tangled spruce forest that can trigger mild melancholia.

Gros Morne National Park is one of Canada's true treasures, and few who visit here fail to come away awed. In fact, it's been officially designated as one of the world's treasures. In 1987, the park was declared a **UNESCO World Heritage Site,** which in large part reflected the importance of an area called the **Tablelands.** This geological quirk formed eons ago, when a portion of the earth's mantle broke loose during the continental drift and was forced to the surface, creating an eerie, rust-colored tableau. (See the sidebar below for more information.)

The park is divided into two sections, north and south, riven by the multi-armed Bonne Bay (locally pronounced like "Bombay"). Alas, a ferry connecting the two areas has not operated for years, so exploring both sections by car requires backtracking. The park's visitor center and most tourist services are found in the village of Rocky Harbour in the north section. But you'd be shortchanging yourself to miss a detour through the dramatic southern section, a place that looks to have had a rough birth, geologically speaking.

The dramatic terrain throughout the park is of a scale large enough to be appreciated if you prefer to tour by car. But to really get a sense of the place, plan to get out often on foot, by bike, or in a boat. Excellent hikes and awe-inspiring boat rides take you right into the heart of the park's wild character. To do the park justice, plan on spending at least 3 days here. A week would not be too much if you're an ardent hiker.

If you'd prefer to let someone else do the planning for you, contact **Gros Morne Adventure Guides** (☎ 709/458-2722), which organizes guided sea kayaking and hiking excursions around the park.

ESSENTIALS

GETTING THERE   From the Trans-Canada Highway in Deer Lake, turn west on Route 430 (the Viking Trail). This runs through the northern section of the park; it's 71 kilometers (44 miles) from Deer Lake to Rocky Harbour. For the southern section, turn left (south) on Route 431 in Wiltondale; from the turn, it's 28 kilometers (17 miles) to Woody Point.

VISITOR INFORMATION   The main national park **visitor information center** (☎ 709/458-2066) is just south of Rocky Harbour on Route 430. It's open daily from 9am to 10pm. The center features exhibits on park geology and wildlife; there's also a short film about the park that's picturesque but not terribly informative. Interactive media kiosks are exceptionally well-done; you can view video clips depicting highlights of all hiking trails and other attractions simply by touching a video screen. The center is also the place to stock up on field guides, as well as to request backcountry camping permits.

Across the bay just outside of Woody Point on Route 431 en route to Trout River is the brand-new (to open in 2000) **Discovery Centre.** At press time, no phone number, admission price, or other information was available, but the new building promises to be an enlightening stop, with plans calling for interactive exhibits, a fossil room, and a multimedia theater to help make sense of the Gros Morne landscape. More information is available at the visitor center.

FEES   All visitors must obtain a permit for any activity within the park. Daily fees are C$3.25 (US$2.15) adult, C$2.50 (US$1.65) senior, C$1.75 (US$1.15) child 6 to 18, and C$6.50 (US$4.35) family. Four-day passes are available for the price of 3 days.

GROS MORNE'S SOUTHERN SECTION

The road through the southern section dead-ends at Trout River, and accordingly it seems to discourage convenience-minded visitors who prefer loops and through-routes. That's too bad, because the south contains some of the park's most dramatic terrain. Granted, you can glimpse the rust-colored Tablelands from north of Bonne

Bay near Rocky Harbour, thereby saving the 50-kilometer (30-mile) detour. But without actually walking through the desolate landscape, you miss much of the impact. The south also contains several lost-in-time fishing villages that predate the park's creation in 1973, and a new Discovery Centre (see above) with exhibits about the park's natural history.

The region's scenic centerpiece is **Trout River Pond,** a landlocked fjord some 15 kilometers (9 miles) long. You can hike along the north shore to get a great view of the Narrows, where cliffs nearly pinch the pond in two. For a more relaxed view, sign up for a boat tour, which surrounds you with breathtaking panoramic views. ✪ **Tableland Boat Tours** (☎ **709/451-2101**) offers excursions aboard a 40-passenger tour boat. Two-and-a-half-hour trips are offered daily at 10am, 1pm, and 4pm in July and August (1pm only in June and September). The cost is C$25 (US$17) adult, C$9.25 (US$6.15) children ages 6 to 16. Tickets are sold at a gift shop between the village of Trout River and the pond; watch for signs.

HIKES & WALKS

For a superb panorama encompassing ocean and mountains, watch for the **Lookout Trail** just outside of Woody Point en route to Trout River. This steep trail is about 5 kilometers (3 miles) round-trip.

The **Tablelands Trail** departs from barren Trout River gulch and follows an old gravel road up to Winterhouse Brook Canyon. You can bushwhack along the rocky river a bit farther upstream, or turn back. It's about 2 kilometers (1.2 miles) each way, depending on how adventurous you feel. This is a good trail to get a feel for the unique ecology of the Tablelands. Look for the signboards that explain the geology at the trailhead, and at the roadside pull-off on your left before reaching the trailhead.

Experienced hikers looking for a challenge should seek out the ✪ **Green Gardens Trail.** There are two trailheads to this loop; I'd recommend the second one (closer to Trout River). You'll start by trekking through a rolling, infertile landscape, and then the plunge begins as you descend down, down, down wooden steps and a steep trail toward the sea. The landscape grows more lush by the moment, and soon you'll be walking through extraordinary coastal meadows on crumbling bluffs high above the surf.

The trail follows the shore northward for about 4 or 5 kilometers, and it's one of the most picturesque coastal trails I've hiked anywhere in the world. In July, the irises and a whole symphony of other wildflowers are blooming wildly. The entire loop is about 16 kilometers (9.6 miles) and is rugged and very hilly; allow about 5 or 6 hours. An abbreviated version involves walking clockwise on the loop to the shore's edge, then retracing one's steps back uphill. That's about 9 kilometers (5.4 miles).

CAMPING

The two **drive-in campsites** in the southern section—**Trout River Pond** and **Lomond**—both offer showers and nearby hiking trails. Of the two, Trout River Pond is more dramatic, located on a plateau overlooking the pond; a short stroll brings you to the pond's edge with wonderful views up the fjord. Lomond is near the site of an old lumber town and is popular with anglers. Camping is C$15.25 (US$10.15) per site.

Three exceptional **backcountry campsites** are located along the Green Garden Trail (registration required at the park Visitors Centre; C$10 (US$7) per night). The northernmost site is near the coast in a ravine where Wallace Brook meets the ocean. The two southern sites are on grassy bluffs above pebble beaches, and both have outstanding coastal views.

Journey to the Center of the Earth

If you see folks walking around the Tablelands looking twitchy and excited, they're probably amateur geologists. The Tablelands are one of the world's great geological celebrities, and a popular destination among pilgrims who love the study of rock.

To the uninitiated, the Tablelands area—south of Woody Point and the south arm of Bonne Bay—will seem rather bleak and barren. From a distance, the muscular hills rise up all rounded and rust-colored, devoid of trees or even that pale green furze that seems to blanket all other hills. Up close, you discover just how barren they are—little plant life seems to have established a toehold.

There's a reason for that. Some 570 million years ago, this rock was part of the earth's mantle, that part of the earth just under the crust. Riding on continental plates, two land masses collided forcefully hereabouts, and a piece of the mantle was driven up and over the crust, rather than being forced under, as is usually the case. Years of erosion followed, and what's left is a rare glimpse of the earth's skeleton. The rock is so laced with magnesium that few plants can live here, giving it a barrenness that seems more appropriate for a desert landscape in the American Southwest than the rainy mountains of Newfoundland.

WHERE TO STAY

Victorian Manor. Main St. (P.O. Box 165), Woody Point, NF A0K 1P0. ☎ **709/453-2485.** www.grosmorne.com/victorianmanor. 7 units, including 3 B&B (2 with shared bathroom), 3 efficiency units, and 1 guest house. C$50–C$70 (US$33–US$47) double, C$125 (US$83) guest house. Rates include continental breakfast. AE, MC, V.

This 1920 home is one of the most impressive in the village, but that doesn't mean it's extravagant. It's more solid than flamboyant, set in a residential neighborhood near the town center and a few minutes' walk to the harbor. The attractive guest house has its own whirlpool. If that's booked, ask for one of the efficiencies, which cost about the same as the rooms but afford much greater convenience, especially considering the slim dining choices in town.

WHERE TO DINE

Seaside Restaurant. Main St., Trout River. ☎ **709/451-3461.** Main courses C$9–C$19 (US$6–US$13). MC, V. Daily noon–9pm. Closed Oct–June. SEAFOOD.

The Seaside has been a Trout River institution for years, and it's clearly a notch above the tired fare you often find in tiny coastal villages. The restaurant is nicely polished without being swank, and it features magnificent harbor views. The pan-fried cod is superb, as are a number of other seafood dishes. (Sandwiches and burgers are at hand for those who don't care for seafood.) Desserts are quite good, such as the partridgeberry parfait, but the service can be slow when the place fills up.

GROS MORNE'S NORTHERN SECTION

Gros Morne's northern section flanks Route 430 for some 75 kilometers (45 miles) between Wiltondale and St. Paul's. The road winds through the abrupt, forested hills south of Rocky Harbour; beyond these, the road levels out, following a broad coastal plain covered mostly with bog and tuckamore. East of the plain rises the extraordinarily dramatic monoliths of the Long Range. This section contains the park's visitor center as well as the park's one must-see attraction: **Western Brook Pond.**

The hardscrabble fishing village of **Rocky Harbour** is your best bet for tourist services, including motels, B&Bs, Laundromats, and small grocery stores. One caveat, however: Rocky Harbour and the surrounding area lack a well-lit, well-stocked grocery store of the sort one might expect near a national park of international importance. What you'll find are modest-sized grocery stores—the sorts of places where you'll want to check the dates on bread and milk very carefully.

EXPLORING THE NORTHERN SECTION

If you have time for only one activity in Gros Morne—and heaven forbid that's the case—make it the boat trip up ✪ **Western Brook Pond.** The trip begins with a 20-minute drive north of Rocky Harbour. Park at the Western Brook Pond trailhead, then set off on an easy 45-minute hike across the northern coastal plain, with interpretive signs explaining the wildlife and bog ecology you'll see along the way. (Keep an eye out for moose.) Always ahead, the mighty monoliths of the Long Range rise high above, inviting and mystical, more like a 19th-century scene from the Rockies than the Atlantic seaboard.

You'll soon arrive at the pond's edge, where there's a small collection of outbuildings near a wharf, where the tour boats dock. Once aboard one of the vessels (there are two), you'll set off into the maw of the mountains, winding between the sheer rock faces that define this landlocked fjord. The spiel on the boat is recorded, but even that unfortunate bit of cheese fails to detract from the grandeur of the scene. You'll learn about the glacial geology and the remarkable quality of the water, which is considered among the purest in the world. Bring lots of film and a wide-angle lens. The trip lasts about 2½ hours. The cost is C$30 (US$20) adults, C$14 (US$9) students (6 to 16; must be accompanied by an adult), children under 6 free when with parents. For reservations, contact the Ocean View Motel (☎ **709/458-2730**) in Rocky Harbour.

If rain or heavy fog puts a damper on outdoor activities, there's a modern indoor pool at the **Recreation Complex,** ☎ **709/458-2350,** on Route 430 high above Rocky Harbour. The view of Bonne Bay from the outdoor terrace is great, and the pool is inviting. This is also a good spot for a shower if you're staying at the park's one showerless campground. Tickets good for a 1-hour swim cost C$3 (US$2) for adults, C$2 (US$1.35) for children.

If you're looking for diversion that requires minimal physical effort, both the **SS Ethie** shipwreck and **Broom Point** (both near Western Brook Pond) are worth stopping for. The coastal steamer *Ethie* met its fate during a storm in 1919; all passengers were saved, including an infant shuttled to shore in a mailbag. The wreck has long been prominent in song and story, but the years have taken their toll on the rusting scrap. The hull is all but gone, leaving only the massive boiler and some other stray parts. But the cobbles nearby are beautiful.

Broom Point is an easy stroll out to a picturesque and rocky peninsula, where active fishing operations take place. The views from the point are outstanding; don't miss the superb sand beach down a side trail to your left as you walk toward the point.

HIKES & WALKS   The summit of **Gros Morne Mountain** is the Mt. Everest of this national park—at 2,644 feet it's the highest peak in the park, and the most demanding. What makes it especially challenging isn't so much the height or the length (about 16km/10 miles round-trip). It's the terrain. You expend considerable energy scrambling over loose scree on the upper reaches. But the views of the bay and beyond to the Gulf of St. Lawrence are well worth it if the weather cooperates. Allow about 7 or 8 hours for the whole excursion, and bring plenty of water and food. Pick up a trail brochure at the information center. (If you're traveling with a pet, note that this is the one trail on which dogs aren't allowed.)

Even if you're not planning on signing up for the **Western Brook Pond** boat tour (reconsider!), you owe yourself a walk up to the pond's wharf and possibly beyond. The 45-minute one-way trek from the parking lot north of Sally's Cove follows well-trod trail and boardwalk through bog and boreal forest. When you arrive at the wharf, the view to the mouth of the fjord will take your breath away. A very well executed outdoor exhibit explains how glaciers shaped the landscape in front of you.

Two spur trails continue on either side of the pond for a short distance. The **Snug Harbour Trail,** which follows the northern shore to a primitive campsite (registration required), is especially appealing. After crossing a seasonal bridge at the pond outlet, you'll pass through scrubby woods before emerging on a long and wonderful sand and pebble beach; this is a great destination for a relaxed afternoon picnic and requisite nap. The hike all the way to Snug Harbour is about 8 kilometers (4.8 miles) one-way.

Three easy but enjoyable strolls depart from the Berry Hill Campground just north of Rocky Harbour. **Berry Hill Pond** is a perfect place for walking off your meal in the evening; it's a loop just 2 kilometers (1.2 miles) long. The equally short (1.5km/ 1-mile) round-trip hike up **Berry Hill** is a saunter except for a demanding set of steps at the end; a short loop trail around the summit affords excellent views. Departing from the same parking area is the somewhat more demanding **Baker Brook Falls Trail.** This level trail runs 10 kilometers (6 miles) round-trip, ending at a wooden platform overlooking tumultuous, wild cascades. The trail crosses large amounts of bog on boardwalks.

CAMPING   The northern section has three campgrounds open to car campers. The main campground is **Berry Hill,** which is just north of Rocky Harbour. There are 146 drive-in sites, plus six walk-in sites on the shores of the pond itself. It's just 10 minutes' drive from the visitor center, where evening activities and presentations are held.

Shallow Bay has 50 campsites and is near the park's northern border and an appealing 4-kilometer (2.5-mile) sand beach. Both of these campgrounds have showers and flush toilets.

Green Point is an intimate, popular campground with just 18 sites divided between two areas. The upper area is more open and has views of the gulf; the lower area is set amid evergreen and offers more privacy and shelter from the wind. Green Point has pit toilets and no showers. In mid-summer, the northern section campgrounds tend to fill up readily; it's best to arrive soon after the 2pm checkout time to secure a site. Rates at Berry Hill and Shallow Bay are C$15.25 (US$10.15) per site (C$11/US$7.35 for Green Point). Reservations are very helpful during peak season; call ☎ **800/ 563-6353.**

BACKPACKING   Backcountry camping is available only at **Snug Harbour** on Western Brook Pond. This requires an 8-kilometer (5-mile) hike from the road. Register for a site at the visitor center; the cost is C$10 (US$7).

For an unforgettable but exceedingly demanding adventure, inquire at the center about the backpack trips along the **Long Range** and the **North Rim.** On both of these, you strike out cross-country, bushwhacking through the high subarctic terrain. These traverses require 2 or 3 nights to complete. You also need to be in good physical condition and well versed in a range of backcountry skills, including proficiency with map and compass. A brief pretrip orientation at the visitor center is mandatory, as is the rental of a small (pager-sized) locator beacon to help pinpoint your location should you become disoriented. A one-time backcountry fee of C$35 (US$23) per person is charged (including locator rental) for these trips.

WHERE TO STAY

Rocky Harbour has more tourist services than any other village in or around the park, but it still has trouble handling the influx of travelers in July and August. Two or three bus tours can pretty well fill up the town. One B&B owner told me she turned away 20 people seeking a room one night in July. It's an unwise traveler who arrives without a reservation.

The largest motel in town is the **Ocean View Motel** (☎ 709/458-2730), located on the harbor. It has 44 basic rooms (some have small balconies with bay views), but everything feels a bit chintzy, from the carpeting to the walls to the furnishings. The motel is popular with bus tours, and it often fills up early in the day. Rooms are C$65 to C$70 (US$43 to US$47) double in season.

Gros Morne Cabins. P.O. Box 151, Rocky Harbour, NF A0K 4N0. ☎ **709/458-2020** or 709/458-2369. 22 units. TV. C$75 (US$50) 1-bedroom; C$99 (US$66) 2-bedroom. Price is for 2; C$5 (US$3) per extra person. Open year-round; call for off-season rates. AE, DC, MC, V. Pets allowed.

My favorite thing about the Gros Morne Cabins? Pulling up and seeing the long lines of freshly laundered sheets billowing in the sea breeze, like a Christo installation. The trim and tidy log cabins are clustered tightly along a grassy rise overlooking Rocky Harbour, and all have outstanding views toward the Lobster Cove Head Lighthouse. Inside they're new and clean, more antiseptically modern than quaintly worn. Each cabin is equipped with a kitchenette, and gas barbecues are scattered about the property. The complex also includes a store and a Laundromat. There's a pizza place just across the street for relaxed sunset dining at your own picnic table.

Sugar Hill Inn. P.O. Box 100, Norris Point, NF A0K 3V0. ☎ **709/458-2147.** Fax 709/458-2166. www.sugarhillinn.nf.ca. E-mail: info@sugarhillinn.nf.ca. 6 units, 1 cottage. TV TEL. C$76–C$172 (US$51–US$115) double. AE, MC, V. Closed mid-Oct to mid-Jan.

This appealing green-shingled inn opened in 1991 on the road between Rocky Harbour and Norris Point. The six rooms are quite comfortable, although some guests have found them a bit condo-like and sterile. Nice touches abound, like hardwood floors in all rooms, plenty of natural wood trim, well-selected furnishings, and a shared sauna and hot tub in a cedar-lined room. The upstairs sitting room is spacious and bright, with a fireplace and modern furnishings; it's a good spot to swap local adventure ideas with other guests.

Dining: The inn's dining room serves breakfast and dinner daily (note that breakfast isn't included in the room rates). Dinners are usually C$28–C$30 (US$19 to US$20) for a three-course meal, and focus on seafood.

Wildflower Inn. Main St. North, Rocky Harbour, NF A0K 4N0. ☎ **888/811-7378** or 709/458-3000. 7 units (3 with private bathroom; 4 share 2 bathrooms). C$49–C$64 (US$33–US$43) double, including continental breakfast. MC, V.

This circa 1930s home near the village center was modernized and updated before its opening as a B&B in 1997, giving it a casual country look inside. The rooms are tastefully appointed if a bit small, although two newly added rooms have private baths and are a bit larger. The neighborhood isn't especially scenic (there's an auto repair shop across the way), but the house is very peaceful, the innkeepers are exceptionally friendly, and this is a great choice for those seeking reasonably priced lodging with a comfortable, homey feel.

WHERE TO DINE

Fisherman's Landing. Main St., Rocky Harbour. ☎ **709/458-2060.** Sandwiches C$3.50–C$7.50 (US$2.35–US$5), main courses C$7–C$15 (US$4.65–US$10). MC, V. Summer 6am–11pm; limited hours off-season. SEAFOOD.

With its industrial carpeting and generic chain-restaurant chairs and tables, Fisherman's Landing is lacking in homespun character. But it does offer efficient service and dependable meals, with specialties like fish and chips, cod tongues, and squid rings. For breakfast, there's the traditional Newfie fisherman's breakfast of a mug of tea, served with homemade bread and molasses. Meals are quite reasonably priced, and you can get in and out faster than at most other joints. There's also a glimpse of the harbor from a few tables, provided that not too many RVs park out front.

5 The Great Northern Peninsula

On a map, the Great Northern Peninsula looks like a stout cudgel threatening the shores of Labrador. If Newfoundland can even be said to have a beaten track, rest assured that the peninsula is well off it. It's not as mountainous or starkly dramatic as Gros Morne, but the road unspools for kilometer after kilometer through tuckamore and evergreen forest, along restless coast and the base of geologically striking hills. There are few services, and even fewer organized diversions. But it has early history in spades, a handful of fishing villages clustering along the rocky coast, and some of the most unspoiled terrain anywhere. The road is in good repair, with the chief hazard being a stray moose or caribou. In the spring the infrequent polar bear might wander through a village, often hungry after a long trip south on ice floes.

How nice is it? On one camping vacation I drove down a rocky road one evening to make dinner and watch the sun sink over the Labrador hills across the straits. I came upon a waterfall that tumbled into a magical cobblestone cove, where driftwood was piled chest-high for firewood. A beautiful grassy plateau—perfect for a tent—overlooked the sea. I had recently stocked up on food, and I had a milk crate full of books I wanted to read.

To make a long story short, it was 3 days before I was finally able to extricate myself from this idyllic spot. And this might be the place I recall most fondly when I think back on travels in Newfoundland.

ESSENTIALS

GETTING THERE   Route 430, which is also called the Viking Trail, runs from Deer Lake (at the Trans-Canada Highway) to St. Anthony, a 433-kilometer (260-mile) jaunt. Scheduled flights on **Air Labrador** (☎ 800/563-3042 within Newfoundland, 709/896-3387 elsewhere) and **Interprovincial Airlines** (☎ 800/563-2800 within Newfoundland, 709/576-1666 elsewhere) stop at St. Anthony, where rental cars are available. The airport is on Route 430 approximately 30 kilometers (18 miles) west of St. Anthony.

VISITOR INFORMATION   For information about the Great Northern Peninsula and the Viking Trail, contact the **Viking Trail Tourism Association,** P.O. Box 430, St. Anthony, NF A0K 4S0, ☎ 709/454-8888. Visitor centers are located at St. Anthony (☎ 709/454-4010) and Hawkes Bay (☎ 709/248-5344).

PORT AU CHOIX

A visit to Port au Choix (pronounced port-a-*shwaw*) requires a 13-kilometer (8-mile) detour off the Viking Trail, out to a knobby peninsula that's home to a sizeable fishing fleet. The windswept lands overlooking the sea are low, predominantly flat, and lush with grasses. Simple homes speckle the landscape; most are of recent vintage.

The town's chief attraction is the historic site (see below). But be sure to visit the archaeological excavations at **Philip's Garden.** (Ask for directions at the historic site's visitor center.) Getting here requires a 20-minute hike over low coastal cliffs of fissured slabs splashed with rust-orange lichens. And although there's little here other than a placard or two to mark the site of the millenniums-old native settlement, it doesn't take much to imagine an ancient community taking root here. If you hunker down behind a rock to find solace from the howling winds, look carefully in the grass for the unusually tasty wild strawberries, which are no bigger than blueberries.

Port au Choix National Historic Site. Point Riche Rd., Port au Choix. ☎ **709/861-3522.** Admission C$2.50 (US$1.65) adult, C$2 (US$1.35) senior, C$1.50 (US$1) children (6 to 16), C$6 (US$4) family. Daily mid-June to mid-Sept 9am–8pm.

Back in 1967 a local businessman began digging the foundation for a new movie theater in town. He came upon some bones. A lot of bones. In fact, what he stumbled upon turned out to be a remarkable burying ground for what are now called the Maritime Archaic Indians.

This group of hunters populated parts of Atlantic Canada starting 7,500 years ago, predating the Inuit, who only arrived around 4,000 years ago. These early natives relied chiefly on the sea, and among artifacts recovered here are slate spears and antler harpoon tips, which featured an ingenious toggle that extended after being thrust into flesh. One of the enduring historical mysteries is the disappearance of the Maritime Archaic Indians from the province about 3,500 years ago; to this day no one can explain their sudden departure.

You'll learn about this fascinating historic episode at the modern visitor center. From here, staffers will be able to direct you to various nearby sites, including the original burial ground, now surrounded by village homes. (Don't miss Philip's Garden; see above.) You can also visit the nearby lighthouse, scenically located on a blustery point thrusting into the Gulf of St. Lawrence.

L'ANSE AUX MEADOWS

Newfoundland's northernmost tip is not only exceptionally remote and dramatic, but is also one of the most historically significant spots in the world. A Viking encampment dating from a.d. 1,000 was discovered here in 1960, and it has been thoroughly documented by archaeologists in the decades since. An unusually well-conceived and well-managed national historic site (see below) probes this earliest chapter in European expansion, and an afternoon spent here piques the imagination.

Another fine way to fire up your fantasies is to sign up for a tour on the *Viking Saga,* a replica of one of the early ships. Based in Noddy Bay (about 1.5km/1 mile south of L'Anse aux Meadows), this handsome *knaar* (a type of work boat) was built after extensive study of a Viking ship recovered from the bottom of a fjord near Roskilde, Denmark. This boat has been upgraded to meet current safety standards (this includes the addition of an engine), but it's prohibited from carrying passengers under sail. You'll get a good sense of life aboard these compact boats as you motor along the remote coast, and you might see whales and icebergs in the bargain.

Two-hour tours are offered four times daily from June to mid-September. The fare is C$26 (US$17) adult, C$13 (US$9) children 5 to 12, under 5 free. Call for reservations at ☎ **709/623-2100.**

One other note: the year 2000 marks the millennial anniversary of the Viking settlement, and a number of activities are slated to commemorate this historic linking of old world and new. If you're traveling in summer 2000, expect more crowds than usual. It might also behoove you to book a room well in advance.

☉ L'Anse aux Meadows National Historic Site. Route 436, L'Anse aux Meadows. ☎ **709/623-2608.** Admission C$5 (US$3.35) adult, C$4.25 (US$2.85) senior, C$2.75 (US$1.85) child 6–16, C$10 (US$6.65) family. Daily 9am–8pm in peak season; 9:30am–4:30pm in shoulder season. Closed mid-Oct to early June.

In the late 1950s a pair of determined archaeologists named Helge Ingstad and Anne Stine Ingstad pored over 13th-century Norse sagas searching for clues about where the Vikings might have landed on the shores of North America. With just a few scraps of description, the Ingstads began cruising the coastlines of Newfoundland and Labrador, asking locals about unusual hummocks and mounds.

At L'Anse aux Meadows, they struck gold. In a remote cove noted for its low, grassy hills, they found the remains of an ancient Norse encampment that included three large halls, along with a forge where nails were made from locally mined pig iron. As many as 100 people lived here for a time, including some women. The Vikings abandoned the settlement after a few years to return to Greenland and Denmark, thus ending the first experiment in the colonization of North America by Europeans. It's telling that no graves have ever been discovered here.

Start your visit by viewing the recovered artifacts in the visitor center and watching the half-hour video about the site's discovery. Then I suggest signing up for one of the free guided tours of the site. The guides offer considerably more information than the simple markers around the grounds. Near the original encampment are several re-created sod-and-timber buildings, depicting how life was lived 1,000 years ago. These are tended by costumed interpreters, who have a wonderful knack of staying in character without making you feel like a dork when you ask them questions. If you time it right, you might be rewarded with a bit of flatbread cooked old-style over an open fire.

ST. ANTHONY

The seaport town of St. Anthony—named by explorer Jacques Cartier in 1534—was first visited by 16th-century French and Basque fishermen. Today, with its 3,200 residents, St. Anthony is the northern peninsula's largest town, and its undisputed commercial center. It's a good place to restock on basic supplies or secure a motel room for day trips to L'Anse aux Meadows, about 50 kilometers (30 miles) north of town.

Be sure to visit **Fishing Point Park,** at the end of a dirt road at the mouth of the harbor. With propitious timing and some luck, you'll be able to view icebergs and whales from the rugged, rocky bluffs. A series of short trails and wooden platforms makes life easy for the casual explorer.

In the evening, there's live entertainment at the **Great Viking Feast at Leifsburdur** (☎ **709/454-3431**). In a replica sod hut, up to 85 diners can feast on local fare like Jigg's dinner (boiled meat and potatoes), moose stew, cod tongues, and baked cod, while being amused by a crew of Vikings. The show is staged daily at 7:30pm from July through early September (reservations required), and costs C$32 (US$21), which includes dinner.

Grenfell House Museum and Interpretation Centre. West St., St. Anthony (across from the hospital). ☎ **709/454-4010.** Admission C$5 (US$3.35) adult, C$4.25 (US$2.85 senior, C$2.25 (US$1.50) children 6–16, $10 (US$6.65) family. Daily May–Sept 9am–8pm (until 5pm in Sept).

Dr. Wilfred Grenfell is more or less the patron saint of St. Anthony. A devout Christian, Grenfell was born in England and as a young man became active in providing medical care to North Sea fishermen. In 1892, he visited Newfoundland and Labrador. Appalled by the conditions, he founded the first hospital; he was to spend much of the rest of his life ministering to residents of remote outports and agitating for better services from the government. In 1912, he established the International Grenfell Association, which established hospitals and nursing homes throughout the region. Grenfell was restless in trying to improve the lot of the northland's residents, and to improve the delivery of medicines and services. One example: In 1909 he experimented using reindeer rather than sled dogs for winter travel, having observed that the dogs had the unfortunate habit of savaging the driver if he fell helpless in deep snow.

An interpretive center features two floors of exhibits that nicely fill visitors in on the Grenfell's history. There's also a 14-minute video that's worth watching. Afterwards, you can tour the handsome house the grateful town built for Grenfell and his devoted wife, Anne, in 1910. It's furnished with numerous artifacts and interesting exhibits about Grenfell's life and works. You'll also learn about Grenfell cloth, a versatile fabric made of Egyptian cotton and invented in 1922 specifically to withstand the rigors of severe winter travel. (Garments made of Grenfell cloth are available at Grenfell Handicrafts, ☎ **709/454-3576,** in the interpretation center.)

WHERE TO STAY & DINE

The Lightkeepers. Fishing Point Park. ☎ **709/454-4900.** Reservations not accepted. Main courses C$8–C$22 (US$5–US$15). AE, MC, V. Daily 11am–10pm. Closed Oct–May. SEAFOOD.

Located at scenic Fishing Point Park, this cafe is housed in a simple but handsome white building with fire-engine red trim overlooking the ocean. Inside, it's sparely decorated and flooded with natural light. The proprietors have placed binoculars on windowsills for you to scope out the whales and icebergs while awaiting your meal. The daily specials are fresh and tasty. Perennial favorites include cod tongue, butter-fried cod, and seafood chowder. The truly famished can order the Commissioner's Feast, which includes samples of "all the seafood in the house" plus lobster or crab (C$89/US$59 for two with lobster, C$69/US$46 with crab).

✪ Tickle Inn at Cape Onion. RR no. 1, Cape Onion, NF A0K 4J0. ☎ **709/452-4321** (June–Sept) or 709/739-5503 (Oct–May). E-mail: adams.tickle@nf.sympatico.ca. 4 units (all share 2 bathrooms). C$50–C$65 (US$33–US$43) double. Rates include deluxe continental breakfast. MC, V. Closed Oct–May.

If you're seeking that end-of-the-world flavor, you'll be more than a little content here. Set on a remote cove at the end of a road near Newfoundland's northernmost point (you can see Labrador across the straits), the Tickle Inn occupies a solid fisherman's home built around 1890 by the great-grandfather of the current innkeeper, David Adams. (He's a retired school counselor from St. John's.) After lapsing into decrepitude, the home was expertly restored in 1990, and it has recaptured much of the charm of a Victorian outport home. The guest rooms are small but comfortable, and they share two bathrooms. Before dinner, guests often gather in the parlor and enjoy snacks and complimentary cocktails. One of the highlights of a stay here is exploring the small but superb network of hiking trails maintained by Adams, which ascend open bluffs to painfully beautiful views of the Labrador Straits. The inn is about a 40-minute drive from L'Anse aux Meadows.

Dining: Meals are served family-style at 7:30pm each evening. (Your only other option for a meal is to drive a considerable distance to the nearest restaurant.) The food here is excellent, featuring local cuisine. You might have Cape Onion soup with a touch of Newman's port, or the "Polaris paella," with squid, scallops, and shrimp. Time your visit for berry season and you can expect such delights as the northern berry flan for dessert.

6 Central Newfoundland

Spruce. Larch. Spruce. Bog. Spruce. Lake. Spruce. Bog.

You get the idea. This 350-kilometer (215-mile) stretch of the Trans-Canada Highway is long and, if you're in a grumpy mood, awfully tedious. Travelers crossing the interior typically spend more of their time cursing slow-moving RVs and wishing for passing lanes than admiring the scenery. The vast forest is certainly monumental, and along the way you'll crest some hills and take in panoramic views of lakes or ocean inlets that finger their way down from the north. You can also detour to some appealing fishing villages on the north coast. These notwithstanding, Newfoundland's interior is widely regarded as an area you pass through, linking more inviting areas, not one in which you linger. If you've been saving a book-on-tape in the trunk, this is the time to rummage around and get it out.

Grand Falls-Windsor and Gander are both regional service centers, and offer reasonable destinations to stretch your legs at one of the attractions, gas up, get a bite to eat, perhaps spend a night if evening is encroaching. But neither offers much as destinations for travelers, with the exception of hunters, fishermen, canoeists, and backpackers who might choose to employ the towns as bases from which to explore the woody, boggy, lake-filled interior. The area around Twillingate is a distinct exception—it's well worth the northward detour off the Trans-Canada, and could easily occupy a traveler who enjoys low-key, off-the-beaten-path destinations.

GRAND FALLS-WINDSOR

The settlement of Grand Falls dates back to 1903, when British tycoons Lord Northcliffe and Lord Rothermere grew concerned that a restless Germany might disrupt the supply of newsprint from the Continent. They liked what they found at Grand Falls, where the Exploits River rushed over cascades amid a seemingly endless supply of timber. An ambitious paper mill was constructed on the banks of the river; it cost C$7.5 million to build and employed 15,000 mill and woods workers when it was finally completed in 1909. The mill took root and expanded over the decades. Today, it's a major regional employer owned and operated by Abitibi-Price.

The once-independent towns of Grand Falls and Windsor were joined as a single municipality in 1991, resulting in the ungainly name. It's also a bit cumbersome to get from one town to the other since the Trans-Canada Highway neatly bisects the two. There's really little need to venture to Windsor, however; focus your attention on Grand Falls, which is south of the highway.

The **visitor information center** (☎ 709/489-6332) is just off the Trans-Canada Highway on the west side of town. It's well-marked from the highway.

EXPLORING GRAND FALLS-WINDSOR

You'll find a worthwhile detour to the **Salmonid Interpretation Centre** (☎ 709/489-7350), across the river from the mill. Finding the place is a bit of a trick; you should stop at the visitor information center on the Trans-Canada Highway west of town and ask for a map, which the staff will happily supply.

The interpretation center is more intriguing than you might think. Not only will you get a good view of the rocky gorge through which the river tumbles lustily, but you also will be able to watch the Atlantic salmon laboring their way up the fish ladder, which opened in 1992. A series of concrete pools linked by short waterfalls leads to a main holding tank, where the fish are counted before a final gate is opened and they continue their upstream journey.

Inside the exhibit center you can descend to an observation area below ground and see the impatient salmon through aquariumlike walls. The fish are surprisingly majestic, though the exhibits themselves are scattered and a bit dull. The staff is happy to answer your questions. If you're passing through town around lunch or dinner, the cozy restaurant, located at the interpretation center, offers basic, reasonably priced meals.

The center is open mid-June through mid-September daily from 8am to dusk. Admission is C$3 (US$2) adult, C$2 (US$1.35) seniors and children.

Back across the river in Grand Falls is the **Mary March Museum,** 22 St. Catherine St., ☎ 709/292-4522. It honors a Beothuk Indian who was captured in 1819 at Red Indian Lake; she died of tuberculosis after a year in captivity. The museum covers Newfoundland's 5,000-year history of inhabitation, from the early Maritime Archaic Indians on through the Paleo-Eskimo, Beothuk, Mi'kmaq, and, eventually, Europeans. Intriguing artifacts such as ancient stone gouges and the geometrically incised game pieces and pendants of the Beothuk are displayed. The museum also offers a perspective on the local pulp and paper industry, and the coming of the railway. Hours are May 1 to late October daily from 9am to 5pm. Admission is C$2.50 (US$1.65) adult, C$2 (US$1.35) students and seniors, under 18 free.

The area around Grand Falls-Windsor is great for backcountry exploring, although you need guidance owing to the extensive logging operations to feed the mill. **Red Indian Adventures** (☎ 709/486-0892) is located 19 kilometers (11 miles) west of Grand Falls-Windsor in Aspen Brook, right off the Trans-Canada Highway. Proprietors Paul and Joy Rose offer a full range of excursions and classes, ranging from whitewater kayak courses (the rapids on the Exploits River are vigorous and challenging) to daylong sea kayaking trips in Notre Dame Bay. Rates for day tours are C$75 to C$95 (US$50 to US$63) per person.

WHERE TO STAY & DINE

Camping is close to town at **Beothuk Park** (☎ 709/489-9832), just a few minutes' drive west of the visitor information center. The park backs on to a sizeable lake; the campsites are mostly quite private. The fee is C$11 (US$7) per night.

The **Mount Peyton Hotel** (☎ 800/563-4894 or 709/489-2251) is the town's largest hotel and motel (take your pick: the seasonal motel is on the north side of the Trans-Canada Highway, the year-round hotel on the south). It has 102 hotel rooms and 48 motel and housekeeping units; some rooms are air-conditioned. I prefer the slower pace of the Robin Hood (below); the Mount Peyton can be noisy with highway sounds, and is often bustling with meetings or conference attendees. Doubles run C$72 to C$90 (US$48 to US$60).

Hotel Robin Hood. 78 Lincoln Rd., Grand Falls-Windsor, NF A2A 1N2. ☎ **709/489-5324.** Fax 709/489-6191. E-mail: robin.hood@nf.sympatico.ca. 14 units. A/C TV TEL. C$70–C$75 (US$47–US$50) double. AE, DC, ER, MC, V.

This modern, basic, comfortable hotel is in a quiet area between the residential and commercial neighborhoods of Grand Falls. The building was constructed in 1997 and has been well maintained; all the rooms are larger than standard-issue motel rooms. (Those on the second floor are slightly bigger than those on the first.) It's the closest hotel to the salmon interpretation center.

Dining: With its beadboard wainscotting, Friar Tuck's is more pleasantly intimate than one might expect from a hotel restaurant. The restaurant is open for dinner and lunch; the menu includes traditional favorites along the lines of fish and chips, lamb chops, fresh salmon, and pepper steak (dinner entrees run C$10.95 to C$15.95 (US$7.30 to US$10.65).

TWILLINGATE

North and South Twillingate Islands are a photographer's dream. You'll find a bit of everything here—historic fishing harbors, gently rolling forested ridges, jagged cliffs washed by the surf, and open rocky barrens that roll down to the sea. There's also a good chance of spotting whales and icebergs—a good many of the Greenland icebergs seem to drift into Notre Dame bay to the west of Twillingate, where they can be spotted in late spring and early summer.

Twillingate was named by early French fishermen, who noted a striking resemblance between the rocky cliffs of this region and the stone shores of their hometown of Toulinguet, near Brest, France. The spelling was subsequently Anglicized. The region around Twillingate is actually an archipelago linked by a series of causeways, and the drive northward on Route 340 from Boyd's Cove is extremely picturesque, with views of inlets and harbors cropping up between the low, green, forested hills. Twillingate (pop. 5,000) itself is a surprisingly active commercial center, with a number of bustling stores lining the road down to the old harbor. It's been connected to the mainland by causeway since 1972.

The communities around Twillingate have shown more entrepreneurial drive in offering services for travelers than you typically find in Newfoundland's villages. A number of homes have been converted to B&Bs, and the route on to the two Twillingate Islands is lined with homemade billboards touting boat tours, B&Bs, and restaurants.

ESSENTIALS

GETTING THERE—Twillingate is 142 kilometers (88 miles) northeast of Grand Falls-Windsor. Coming from the west, turn north on Route 340 approximately 50 kilometers (31 miles) east of Grand Falls-Windsor. From the east, head north on Route 330 at Gander, then take Route 331 to connect with Route 340 at Boyd's Cove. Gander to Twillingate is 102 kilometers (63 miles).

VISITOR INFORMATION—The regional **visitor information center** (☎ **709/628-7454**) is located on Route 340 in Newville. It's open late June to early September, Monday to Friday 8:30am to 8:30pm, and weekends 8:30am to 6:30pm.

EXPLORING TWILLINGATE

As you reach Twillingate's harbor on Route 340 you'll arrive at a "T" intersection at Main St. You can go right or left; both directions merit exploration.

Turning left leads to Long Point and the region's most prominent lighthouse. Along the way you'll pass The **Twillingate Museum and Crafts Shop** (☎ **709/884-2825,** off-season 709/884-2571) housed in a 1914 white clapboard building that was formerly the rectory for St. Peter's Anglican Church. Inside the handsome home you'll find displays of goods that might have been found in this outport community late in the 19th century, including hooked rugs, cranberry glass, dolls, and fashions. There's also a display of local artifacts from the Maritime Indian culture, and a display about Georgina Stirling, a soprano from town who was once the toast of European opera houses, performing as Madame Toulinguet (she's buried at St. Peter's).

The museum also houses an inviting gift shop, with handknit sweaters, jams, and a selection of local history books. It's open daily from mid-June to mid-September 9am to 8pm. Admission is C$1 (US65¢) adult, C50¢ (US35¢) children.

Continuing on, the road to Long Point passes through small communities before entering undeveloped barrens riven with coves and cliffs. You'll soon pass **Seabreeze Municipal Park** (C$2/US$1.35 admission in summer), with picnic tables and dramatic hiking trails along the cliffs. The rusted equipment in the meadows are from a short-lived copper mine, which operated here between 1908 and 1917. The area is not only unusually beautiful; it's also of interest to geologists owing to the ancient lava flows exposed in the cliff faces.

A few minutes' drive beyond the park is the **Long Point Lighthouse,** Twillingate's one must-see destination. The red-and-white milk-bottle-shaped lighthouse, built in 1876, isn't open to the public, but you can park along the cliffs and enjoy the sweeping views from these high headlands. (Photographer's curse: Antennae and microwave towers share the headland with the light.) Whales and icebergs are often spotted from here.

On the other side of the parking lot is the **Long Point Interpretive Center** (☎ **709/884-5755**), owned and operated by Suzanne Carter and Garry Troake. Inside you'll find a well-stocked gift shop and tea room serving local specialties (occasionally including seal flipper), and downstairs is a free display on local natural history. It's open May to mid-October 9am to 9pm daily.

Turning right at Twillingate's main intersection takes you on a winding road through clustered homes along the harbor's edge. In 2 kilometers (1.2 miles) you'll come to **Weil Winery** (☎ **709/884-2707**), which has produced Notre Dame fruit wines since 1998. Among the varieties available here are dogberry, partridgeberry, blueberry, and rhubarb wines. You're probably thinking Kool-Aid, but some of the wines are far drier than you might imagine. You can learn about the process and pick up a few bottles at the retail store.

Continue along the road until you reach the CAUTION: ONE LANE TRAFFIC sign. Park here and continue on by foot to find some wonderful **hiking trails.** The lane leads to a summer cottage and private property, but foot traffic is permitted. To the left is a broad cobblestone beach; to the right are rocky, open hills and headlands laced by a network of informal hiking trails (look for cairns) that lead to oceanside cliffs and spectacular views. In mid- to late summer, bring containers so you can return with a bountiful crop of the raspberries and blueberries that grow in such profusion here. These berries are also among the plumpest and sweetest I've found on the island. None of the trails are over long or demanding; allow about 2 hours or so.

WHERE TO STAY

Camping is available in season at **Dildo Run Provincial Park** (☎ **709/629-3350**) on Route 340 in Virgin Arm, about 20 minutes south of Twillingate. The park has 55 sites, many along the water. A nicely maintained hiking trail winds along the remote coastline to Black Head, a hike of about an hour. Rates are C$11 (US$7) per night.

Iceberg Spotting

Twillingate is famous for the number of icebergs that float into area, then often run aground, providing a theatrical backdrop. That's not to say you'll be guaranteed icebergs if you arrive in mid-summer. Some years are good for sighting icebergs; some are not. Numerous factors conspire to determine when and if icebergs will show up; these range from the thickness of sea ice to the direction of ocean currents to the summer temperature in the Arctic the previous year, when glaciers in Greenland calved to produce the icebergs.

If icebergs are in the area, you should be able to spot them from the Long Point lighthouse—or any of the other headlands or bays around Twillingate. (As anyone who's seen *Titanic* knows, icebergs tend not to be subtle or elusive.) Your best bet is to arrive in June or July, although I saw a solitary iceberg in the distance on my last trip here in mid-August.

Speaking of *Titanic,* you can get closer view of icebergs via boat tour, two of which are offered from Twillingate harbor. **Twillingate Island Boat Tours** (☎ **800/611-2374** or 709/884-2242) has been operating since 1985, and offers iceberg and whale-watching tours from the Iceberg Shop, painted with colorful murals of icebergs. (Turn right on Main Street when you enter Twillingate.) Also offering tours is **Twillingate Adventure Tours** (☎ **888/447-8687** or 709/884-5999), with a 40-passenger vessel. Tours typically run about C$25 to C$30 (US$17 to US$20) per adult; children's fares are half-price.

One of Atlantic Canada's most dramatically sited campgrounds is at **Seabreeze Municipal Park** near the Long Point Lighthouse. It offers primitive camping (no showers or washrooms), with sites that are grassy and perched at the edge of soaring cliffs. The sunsets can't be beat, and the price is a deal at C$4 (US$3) per night.

Anchor Inn Motel. Main St. (P.O. Box 550), Twillingate, NF A0G 4M0. ☎ **709/884-2777.** Fax 709/884-2326. 22 units. TV TEL. C$68–C$70 (US$45–US$47) double. AE, MC, V.

The Anchor Inn is a well-maintained, relatively modern (1973) hotel just off the harbor. It was extensively updated in 1995, and has been kept up nicely since. Don't expect fancy: It's boxy and bland with beige siding, and the rooms are standard motel units with durable furniture. The better deals by far are the efficiency units in a separate building on a rise above the motel. They cost only C$2 more, and are larger and have small kitchens (you can buy fresh seafood in town and cook it yourself). Ask for a room with a harbor view. If you can't snag a room with a kitchen, there's a restaurant on the premises.

Harbour Lights Inn. 189 Main St. (P.O. Box 729), Twillingate, NF A0G 4M0. ☎ **709/884-2763.** Fax 709/884-2701. 9 units. TV. C$60–C$75 (US$40–US$50) double. MC, V.

This attractive home on a hill and across the road from the harbor was built in the 19th century for a British customs collector. It's been thoroughly updated with vinyl siding and some furniture that was imported from the suburbs, circa 1978. Guest rooms are located on the upper two floors. The best are the higher-priced nos. 4 and 5, which have burnished pine floors, in-room Jacuzzis, and wonderful views of the harbor. They're worth the extra few dollars.

WHERE TO DINE

Options for dinner out are limited in Twillingate, despite the growing influx of travelers. The **Anchor Inn Motel** dining room (see above) and **R&J Restaurant** (Main St., ☎ 709/884-2212) remain the local favorites. Both serve family fare; at R&J you'll find burgers, sandwiches, pizza, fried chicken, and the like.

Another option is **Marg's Kitchen** (☎ 709/884-2292), housed in the Beach Rock Bed & Breakfast in scenic Little Harbor, a few minutes' drive from Twillingate. Margaret Pardy serves a limited number of seafood dinners here to non-guests (reservations required), which include her homemade relishes and preserves. Meals run C$15 to C$20 (US$10 to US$13).

GANDER

Gander, pop. 13,000, has historic resonance for aviation buffs. In the 1930s, when the island was still a British colony, the British Air Ministry developed a new airfield here. As the nearest fog-free spot to England, Gander was envisioned as a key link in transcontinental air traffic. World War II erupted less than a decade later, and the air base took on an outsized importance as a staging area and refueling depot for troops and supplies heading overseas. After the war, the airstrip became a familiar sight to a generation of groggy tourists headed to Europe, since planes had to stop here to refuel before or after the leap across the Atlantic.

The Boeing 707—which *could* leap the Atlantic from New York to Europe in a single bound—diminished Gander's importance, and today the air field is a shadow of its former self. The airport still exists and still gets a fair amount of commercial traffic (especially when St. John's is fogged in), but Gander's Trans-Canada Highway is now a more familiar sight to motorists refueling before continuing their way east or west.

The **visitor information center** (☎ 709/256-7110) is well marked on the south side of the Trans-Canada Highway (next to the Aviation Museum and across from the Albatross Motel) as you drive through town.

EXPLORING GANDER

The Trans-Canada Highway skirts the southern edge of the downtown, which isn't really worth a detour. The town was developed after the advent of the automobile, and as a result you'll find a handful of cheerless shopping plazas and fast-food joints. It's mostly a good place to stock up on supplies if you're headed for Twillingate or Terra Nova National Park. I will admit, however, that I saw something in Gander I'd never seen before. On an otherwise quiet Sunday, an evangelical rock group had set up on one of the covered shopping plaza walkways, facing a parking lot. They played for two dozen or so appreciative listeners, who sat in their cars facing the band, parked covered-wagon-style in a large semicircle.

A handful of hotels, restaurants, and gas stations are on the Trans-Canada Highway. You'll also find the **North Atlantic Aviation Museum** (☎ 709/256-2923), which is identified by the butt-end of a plane jutting out of the hangarlike building. A couple of historic planes can be viewed on the grounds, including a very handsome firefighting plane. With its emphasis on aviation arcana, the museum itself will be of interest chiefly to confirmed airplane addicts. It's open 9am to 9pm daily in summer; fall through spring it's open Monday to Friday 8:30am to 4:30pm. The cost is C$3 (US$2) adult, C$2 (US$1.35) seniors and children 6 to 16.

Just east of town, look for a sign directing you to the **Silent Witness Memorial.** This memorial marks the site where a plane carrying members of the U.S. 101st

---

The Crusade for Confederation

You'll constantly stumble across the name Joseph Smallwood when traveling in Newfoundland, much the way you hear of Simon Bolivar in Venezuela or Abe Lincoln in Illinois. Smallwood was a diminutive, fedora-wearing politician from Gambo who was driven by the belief that Newfoundland should join the Canadian confederation. Most of Canada confederated in 1867, but with its strong sense of uniqueness, Newfoundland resisted until 1949.

You can learn about Smallwood's successful crusade in his hometown of Gambo, between Gander and Terra Nova National Park. A minute's detour off the Trans-Canada Highway brings you to the **Smallwood Interpretive Center** (☎ 709/674-4222), which opened in 1999 in a former riverside sporting club. As you enter the center you'll see a life-sized figure of Smallwood in his den, complete with items donated by the family. Turn left into the main exhibit, and you'll learn all about "Joey's" crusade to bring the island into the confederation, as well as his prodigious post-confederation activities. The center is open daily from June through August 10am to 6pm; limited hours in the off-season. Admission is C$3 (US$2) adult, C$2 (US$1.35) students and seniors, under 12 free.

Within the center is a small cafe decorated with all the provincial flags, which offers sandwiches, tarts, and other light fare. It makes a good lunch stop.

Airborne mysteriously went down shortly after takeoff in 1985. The plane was returning from a peacekeeping mission in the Middle East; all 259 on board were killed, marking it as the worst aviation disaster on Canadian soil. The memorial is especially bittersweet since the view of Gander Lake from the crash site is breathtaking.

WHERE TO STAY & DINE

Two largish hotels right on the Trans-Canada Highway offer the best accommodations in town, although neither will win personality awards. The **Albatross Motel** (☎ 800/563-4900 in Canada or 709/256-3956) has 103 modern rooms and a ground-floor restaurant and cocktail lounge. Prices range from C$66 to C$115 (US$44 to US$77). Nearby is the **Hotel Gander** (☎ 800/563-2988 in Canada, or 709/256-3931) with 154 rooms, an aviation theme, a small indoor pool, modest fitness facilities, and a chain-hotel-style restaurant that offers many traditional Newfoundland specialties. Room rates are C$72 to C$119 (US$48 to US$79). Both are popular with bus tours, conference planners, and wedding parties. Another option is **Sinbad's Motel,** Bennett Drive (☎ 800/568-8330 or 709/651-2678), a 66-room motel off the highway that has an above-average dining room. Rates are C$66 to C$115 (US$44 to US$77).

7 Terra Nova National Park

You may have heard other travelers rave about Gros Morne National Park as you discussed your impending trip to Newfoundland. At the same time, you might have heard a deafening silence that fell upon the island's other national park, Terra Nova, on the island's eastern shore.

There's a reason for that. Words like "dramatic" and "grandeur" don't get tossed around here much. This is an exceedingly pleasant spot with lots of boreal forest and coastal landscape, along with a surplus of low, rolling hills. Within its boundaries forest and shoreline are preserved for wildlife and recreation, and make for excellent exploration. But the terra, however nova, isn't likely to take your breath away. (With one possible exception: the cliffy hills at the mouth of Newman Sound.) More than likely, a visit here will leave you soothed and relaxed, your nerves unjangled.

Activities and facilities at Terra Nova have mostly been designed with families in mind. There's always something going on, from playing with starfish at the interpretation center to games and movies at the main campground. The park has a junior naturalist program, many of the hikes are just the right duration for younger kids, and there's a fine (and relatively warm) swimming area at Sandy Pond.

If your goal is to put some distance between yourself and the noisy masses, plan to head into the backcountry. A number of campsites are accessible by foot, canoe, or ferry. Out here, you'll be able to scout for bald eagles and shooting stars in silence.

ESSENTIALS

GETTING THERE   Terra Nova is located on the Trans-Canada Highway. It's about 240 kilometers (144 miles) from St. John's, and 630 kilometers (378 miles) from Port aux Basques.

VISITOR INFORMATION   Visitor information is available at the **Marine Interpretation Centre** (☎ 709/533-2801) at the Saltons Day-Use Area, about 5 kilometers (3 miles) north of the Newman Sound Campground. It's open daily from June to mid-October from 9am to 9pm (limited hours after Labor Day).

FEES   A park entry fee is required of all visitors, even those just overnighting at a park campground. Fees are adult C$3.25 (US$2.15) per day; seniors C$2.50 (US$1.65); children 6 to 16 C$1.75 (US$1.15); family C$6.50 (US$4.35). Four-day passes are available in all categories for the price of 3 days. Fees may be paid at the Marine Interpretation Centre.

EXPLORING THE PARK

A trip to the park should begin with a visit to the spiffy, modern **Marine Interpretation Centre** (see above). It's located on a scenic part of the sound, encased in verdant hills, and from here the sound looks suspiciously like a lake. Oceangoing sailboats tied up at the wharf will suggest otherwise, however.

The center has a handful of exhibits focusing on local marine life, and many are geared toward kids. There's a touch tank where you can scoop up starfish and other aquatic denizens, and informative displays on life underwater. Especially nifty is an underwater video monitor that allows you to check out the action under the adjacent wharf with a joystick and zoom controls. There's also a Wet Lab, where you can conduct your own experiments under the guidance of a park naturalist. The center is free with your paid park admission. You'll also find a snack bar and gift shop here.

While here, check with the ranger on duty for all your options in exploring the park. They're good at pointing you in the right direction, whether your interests are soft adventure or going *mano a mano* with nature in the backcountry.

HIKING & BOATING

The park has 80 kilometers (48 miles) of maintained **hiking trails.** Many of these are fairly easy treks of an hour or so through undemanding woodlands. The booklet you'll receive when you pay your entrance fee offers descriptions of the various treks. Among the more popular is the 4.5-kilometer (2.7-mile) **Coastal Trail,** which runs between Newman Sound Campground and the Marine Interpretation Centre. You get great views of the sound, and en route you pass the wonderfully named Pissing Mare Falls.

The most demanding is the **Outport Trail,** a 50-kilometer (30-mile) loop currently under development that winds in and around the south shore of Newman Sound past abandoned settlements. It's possible to overnight at two backcountry sites. The whole trip typically takes 3 days, with the going often slowed by bogs and rough, wet trail sections.

Maps and advice on hiking options are available at the Marine Interpretation Centre.

For **canoeing,** head to either Sandy Pond or Southwest Arm. Canoes are available for rent at Sandy Pond by the hour or day. You can cobble together a very attractive 10-kilometer (6-mile) one-way trip from Sandy Pond by paddling to Beachy Pond (this requires a 400-meter/440-yard portage), then continuing onward to Dunphy's Pond.

The park also lends itself quite nicely to **sea kayaking.** If you've brought your own boat, ask for route suggestions at the information center. (Overnight trips to Minchin and South Broad coves are good options, as are day trips to Swale Island.) If you're a paddling novice, sign up with **Terra Nova Adventure Tours** (☎ 709/256-8687), located at the Marine Interpretation Centre. The crew leads guided tours of the sound three times daily, when you're likely to spot eagles and maybe even a whale. The tours last between 2 and 3 hours and cost C$45 (US$30) per adult, C$35 (US$23) youth. Reservations aren't required, but are often helpful.

For a more passive view from the water, consider a tour with **Ocean Watch Tours** (☎ 709/533-6024), which sails in a converted fishing boat four times daily from the wharf at the Marine Interpretation Centre. You're all but certain to see bald eagles and old outports, and, with some luck, whales and icebergs. Tours are C$25 (US$17; 2 hours) and C$30 (US$20; 3 hours).

CAMPING

Terra Nova's main campground is at **Newman Sound.** It has 417 campsites (mostly of the gravel-pad variety) set in and around spruce forest and sheep laurel clearings. Amenities include free showers, limited electrical hookups, grocery store and snack bar, evening programs, Laundromat, and hiking trails. Be aware that the campground can be quite noisy and bustling in peak season. Fees are C$12 to C$17 (US$8 to US$11).

At the park's northern border is the somewhat more rustic **Malady Head** camping area. This is the better destination for those looking for quiet. It has 153 campsites, along with showers and access to a popular hiking trail. If you want your own campfire, head here; at Newman Sound fires are restricted to community fire pits. The fee is C$12 (US$8) per site.

The park also maintains five **backcountry campsites.** Between four and eight parties can camp at each site, and all but Beachy Pond allow open fires. Dunphy's Island is accessible by canoe only and involves a 400-meter portage; on the shore across from the island site is another site, which is also accessible via a 5-kilometer (3-mile) footpath.

For a more coastal backcountry experience, head for either **Minchin Cove** or **South Broad Cove.** Both can be reached via demanding hikes (14.5km/6.7 miles and 17km/10 miles, respectively) on the **Outport Trail,** which departs from Newman Sound Campground (see above). You can also arrange to be dropped off by boat, then picked up later; ask at the visitor center for details. Backcountry campers need to register in advance and pay a fee of C$8 (US$5) per site.

WHERE TO STAY & DINE

Campgrounds are the only option within the park itself. At the north end of the park, the town of Eastport (see "Nearby Excursions," below) is 16 kilometers from the Trans-Canada Highway on Route 310, and offers several places to stay overnight. Try **Laurel Cottage Bed & Breakfast,** 41 Bank Rd., Eastport, NF A0G 1Z0 (☎ **888/677-3138** or 709/677-3138), with three bedrooms in a 1926 bungalow tucked off the main road with ocean views. Rooms are C$52 to C$65 (US$35 to US$43). Right on a sandy beach is **Seaview Cottages,** 325 Beach Rd., Eastport, NF A0G 1Z0 (☎ **709/677-2271**), with 23 basic cottages and a small indoor heated pool. Rates are C$45 to C$55 (US$30 to US$37).

At the southern edge of the park:

Terra Nova Park Lodge. Route 1, Port Blandford, NF A0C 2G0. ☎ **709/543-2525.** Fax 709/543-2201. www.terranovagolf.com. E-mail: info@terranovagolf.com. 82 units (including 5 suites). A/C TV TEL. C$95–C$200 (US$63–US$133) double. AE, DC, DISC, MC, V.

This modern three-story resort is a short drive off Route 1 about 2 kilometers (1.2 miles) south of the park's southern entrance. Most notably, it's adjacent to the well-regarded, 6,500-yard Twin River Golf Course, one of Atlantic Canada's more scenic and better regarded links. The hotel isn't lavish and lacks a certain personality. It feels rather inexpensively built (pray that you don't have heavy-footed children staying overhead), and it features bland, cookie-cutter rooms. On the other hand, it's clean, comfortable, and well located for a golfing holiday or exploring the park. It's a popular spot with families, since kids can roam the grounds, splash around the pool, and congregate at the downstairs video games.

Dining: The Clode Sound Dining Room is open daily for all three meals. It offers standard resort fare with an emphasis on chicken and beef with some seafood; dinners include fried cod, filet mignon, pork chops and applesauce, and surf and turf. Dinner entrees are priced from C$9.95 to C$20.95 (US$6.65 to US$13.95). Mulligan's Pub is downstairs.

Amenities: Golf-related facilities include a pro shop, driving range, mini-golf, and gift shop. There's also a heated outdoor pool, a fitness room, a sauna, a Jacuzzi, two tennis courts, a game room, and free laundry.

NEARBY EXCURSIONS

Route 310 runs along the northern edge of Terra Nova National Park, and winds along inlets and hillsides to the Eastport peninsula. Around the town of Eastport are a number of fine sandy **beaches** both hidden in coves and laid out in long strands edging the road. Notable beaches are located along Route 310 between Eastport and Salvage, and in the aptly named village of **Sandy Cove** (follow signs to the right when you enter Eastport).

Across from the Sandy Cove beach is the start of **The Old Trails.** The main trail winds along a wooded ridge and past remote ponds approximately 9 kilometers (5 miles) to the village of Salvage. The trail is still under development and hiking may be a bit rugged. Bring lunch, sturdy hiking boots, and a compass, and plan to make an adventure of it. Brochures with general trail descriptions are available at the **Eastport Peninsula Heritage Society** (☎ **709/677-2032**), and often at area visitor information centers.

From Eastport, continue on toward the picturesque fishing village of **Salvage,** about 10km (6 miles) along. The drive follows along the water with the periodic detour up into the hills. The village itself is tucked in and around several coves, and everywhere great slabs of rock protrude from the earth, lending a sort of cinematic drama. More about the region's history can be found at the **Salvage Fisherman's Museum,** set on a low hill overlooking the harbor (☎ **709/677-2414**). It's housed in the oldest building in the area—an 1860 home that's now filled with displays on the whys and hows of fishing. Open daily in summer; admission is C$1 (US65¢) adult, C25¢ (US15¢) children under 12.

A longer excursion is a ferry trip that winds through a beautiful archipelago to remote **St. Brendan's Island.** From Burnside, just north of Eastport, the ferries run five times daily in summer, with round-trip fares of C$5.50 (US$3.65) for a passenger, C$16.50 (US$11) for a car and passenger. (Pay when leaving the island.) The island is home to several small communities located along some 9 kilometers (5.5 miles) of unpaved road, but St. Brendan's offers little in the way of services for travelers—just a few general stores, and no restaurants or overnight accommodations. There are no services—or even buildings, for that matter—at the island's ferry landing. This makes a good destination for adventurous mountain bikers; otherwise you might consider just taking the ferry out and back as a low-budget boat tour. The islands between Burnside and St. Brendan's are uninhabited, wild, and beautiful; I spotted three bald eagles perched along the shore during the 45-minute crossing.

8 The Bonavista Peninsula

The Bonavista Peninsula juts northeast into the sea from just south of Terra Nova National Park. It's a worthy side trip for travelers fascinated by the island's past. You'll find a historic village, a wonderfully curated historic site, and one of the province's most intriguing lighthouses. It's also a good spot to see whales, puffins, and icebergs.

Along the south shore of the peninsula is **Trinity,** an impeccably maintained old village. (It's the only village in Newfoundland where the historic society has say over what can and can't be built.) Some long-time visitors grouse that it's becoming overly popular and a bit dandified with too many B&Bs and traffic restrictions. That might be. But there's still a palpable sense of tradition to this profoundly historic spot. And anyway, it's the region's only destination to find good shelter and a decent meal.

From Trinity it's about 40 kilometers (24 miles) out to the tip of the peninsula. Somewhere along the route, which isn't always picturesque, you'll wonder whether it's worth it. Yes, it is. Keep going. Plan to spend at least a couple of hours exploring the dramatic, ocean-carved point and the fine fishing village of **Bonavista** with its three excellent historic properties.

Note that there's little in the way of interesting accommodations or restaurants this far out, so it's better to plan this as a day trip (perhaps from Trinity) rather than an overnight. That state of affairs is likely to change with the popular new national historic site in Bonavista luring more travelers. At press time there was talk of a new hotel being built, but nothing had yet materialized.

ESSENTIALS

GETTING THERE   Depending on the direction you're coming from, the Bonavista Peninsula can be reached from the Trans-Canada Highway via Route 233, Route 230, or Route 230A. Route 230 runs all the way to the tip of the cape; Route 235 forms a partial loop back and offers some splendid water views along the way. The round-trip from Clarenville to the tip is approximately 240 kilometers (144 miles).

VISITOR INFORMATION   The **Southern Bonavista Bay Tourist Chalet** (☎ **709/545-2130**) is on Route 230 just west of the intersection with Route 235. It's open daily 8:30am to 8:30pm in summer.

TRINITY

The tiny coastal hamlet of Trinity, with a year-round population of just 200, once had more residents than St. John's. For more than 3 centuries, from its first visit by Portuguese fishermen in the 1500s until well into the 19th century, Trinity benefitted from a long and steady tenure as a hub for traders, primarily from England, who supplied the booming fishing economy of Trinity Bay and eastern Newfoundland.

Technological advances (including the railroad) doomed Trinity's merchant class, and the town lapsed into an extended economic slumber. But even today, you can see lingering traces of the town's former affluence, from the attractive flourishes in much of the architecture to the rows of white picket fences all around the village.

In recent years the provincial government and concerned individuals have taken a keen interest in preserving Trinity, and it's clearly benefiting from a revival in which many homes have been preserved, and a good number made over as bed-and-breakfasts. Several buildings are open to the public as provincial historic sites, two others as local historical museums. Most are open mid-June through early October, then shuttered the remainder of the year. Allow about 3 hours to wander about and explore.

Days on which the popular historic pageant is held (see "Tours & Shows," below) bring a flood tide of visitors to Trinity, making parking and rooms scarce, and meals sometimes difficult to obtain. The village is also well worth seeing on non-pageant days, when a great quiet settles in.

Start your voyage into the past at the **Trinity Interpretation Center** (☎ 709/464-2042) at the Tibbs House, open 10am to 5:30pm daily. (It's a bit tricky to find, since signs don't seem to be a priority. Follow the one-way road around the village and continue straight past the parish hall. Look on the left for the pale green home with the prominent gable.) Here you can pick up a walking-tour map and get oriented with a handful of history exhibits.

Several ticket options exist; if you want to visit just one or two places, individual tickets are C$2 (US$1.35) or C$2.50 (US$1.65). For a full day, the better bet is the C$5.50 (US$3.65) ticket, which admits you to six buildings. Most maintain the same hours as the interpretation center.

A minute's walk away is the brick **Lester-Garland Premises,** where you can learn about the traders and their times. This handsome Georgian-style building is a convincing replica (built in 1997) of one of the earlier structures, built in 1819. The original was occupied until 1847, when it was abandoned and began to deteriorate. It was torn down (much to the horror of local historians) in the 1960s, but parts of the building hardware, including some doors and windows, were salvaged and warehoused until the rebuilding.

Next door is the **Ryan Building,** where a succession of the town's most prominent merchants kept shop. The grassy lots between these buildings and the water were once filled with warehouses, none of which survived. The new Rising Tide theater, built in 1999, approximates one of the warehouses; a good imagination is helpful in envisioning the others.

A short walk away, just past the parish house, is the **Hiscock House,** a handsome home where Emma Hiscock raised her children and kept a shop after the untimely death of her husband in a boating accident at age 39. The home has been restored to appear as it might have been in 1910, and helpful guides fill in the details.

The Trinity Museum on Church Road (☎ 709/464-3720) contains a selection of everyday artifacts that one might have seen in Trinity a century or more ago; the nearby **Green Family Forge Blacksmith Museum** will leave you well informed about one of the essential local industries.

TOURS & SHOWS

An entertaining way to learn about the village's history is through the **Trinity Pageant** (☎ **888/464-1100** or 709/464-3232). On Wednesdays, Saturdays, and Sundays at 2pm, actors lead a peripatetic audience through the streets, acting out episodes from Trinity's past. Tickets are C$6 (US$4), children under 12 free. In the evenings, the innovative **Rising Tide Theatre** (same phone as the pageant) offers a number of performances throughout the summer, most depicting island episodes or themes. In the past the cast staged their shows at impromptu venues around town (upstairs at the parish hall, in a field at the water's edge, on the front porch of a B&B, and the like). In 2000 they opened a 255-seat theater in a newly constructed building architecturally styled after a historic waterfront warehouse. The performances are top-rate, and well worth the money (C$12/US$8 to C$20/US$13).

Also recommended is the 2-hour historical **walking tour** of Trinity led daily at 10am by Kevin Toope (☎ **709/464-3723**). Toope's family has been in the area for generations, and Kevin (a schoolteacher in St. John's most of the year) has put together an informed and entertaining tour of the village he knows so well. After a tutored loop around the winding streets, you'll come away with lots of fascinating facts and bits of color that help bring the town to life. One example: what happened to the family of one of the town's merchant princes, who owned practically everything and treated his employees with contempt? Historians have traced only one descendent: a derelict in London.

OUTDOOR PURSUITS

A trail system on the Bonavista Peninsula is being created through woodlands and over headlands. The **Discovery Trail Tourism Association** (☎ **709/466-3845**) has been working with other groups to develop and promote hiking trails on the Bonavista peninsula. A trail guide was recently in the works, and may be available by the time you read this; call or ask locally about its availability.

A superb hike is found 15 minutes' drive south of Trinity outside the fishing village of New Bonaventure. The ✪ **Kerley's Harbor Trail** departs from the end of the parking area adjacent to St. Johns Anglican Church (make the first right as you enter New Bonaventure and drive uphill to the end of the road). The 2-kilometer (1.2-mile) trail—a grassy lane that winds over rolling hills and past a pristine pond—requires about 35 minutes, and ends at the abandoned outport of Kerley's Harbor. This well protected cove is flanked with rocky hills and open meadows that are dotted with fallen homes. Along the waters are remnants of fishing stages. It's as melancholy as it is beautiful.

WHERE TO STAY

All properties mentioned below are in the heart of Trinity's historic area. Reservations are essential during the peak summer season, especially on Wednesdays, Saturdays, and Sundays when the pageant is scheduled. Those who come unprepared risk a drive to Clarenville to find a room.

Lockston Path Provincial Park (☎ **709/464-3553**) is a 15-minute drive from Trinity in Port Rexton. The park has 56 unserviced campsites, along with a modern comfort station with free hot showers. Sites are C$11 (US$7).

Bishop White Manor. Gallavan's Lane, Trinity, NF A0C 2S0. ☎ **709/464-3299**, off-season 709/464-3327. Fax 709/464-2104. wwww.trinityexperience.nf.ca. 9 units. C$70–C$80 (US$47–US$53) double, including full breakfast. MC, V. Closed mid-Oct to mid-May.

This historic house with early woodwork and tin ceilings was home to Newfoundland's first native-born bishop, and is convenient to just about everything in Trinity.

It's more serviceable than elegant, and the small rooms are very small. The extra cost for a larger room is worth it, especially if it's a rainy day. There's limited common space on the first floor, although the rear deck is a nice spot to unwind if the weather's sunny.

✪ Campbell House. High St., Trinity, Trinity Bay, NF A0C 2S0. ☎ **877/464-7700** or 709/464-3377. www.campbellhouse.nf.ca. 4 units. TEL. C$95 (US$63) double in main house, C$225 (US$150) 2-bedroom suites (up to 4 people), including full breakfast. AE, DC, ER, MC, V. Closed mid-Oct to late May.

This handsome 1840 home and two nearby cottages are set amid lovely gardens on a twisting lane overlooking Fisher Cove. Two rooms are on the second floor of the main house, and these have a nice historic flair, even to the point that they'll require some stooping under beams if you're over 5-feet-10-inches tall. Two rooms are located in a lovely and simple pine-paneled Gover House just beyond the gardens, and they feature an adjacent waterfront deck and a full kitchen on the first floor. Innkeeper Tineke Gow recently added a third property on Fisher Cove—the Kelly House, dating from the 1940s. The cottages are rented to just one party at a time, who can use one, two, or three bedrooms (priced accordingly). Gow is a great source of information on local adventures. Reserve well in advance for July and August, when the inn only rarely has a free room.

Hangashore Bed & Breakfast. 1 Ash's Lane, Trinity, Trinity Bay, NF A0C 2S0. ☎ **709/464-3807** or 709/754-7324 in the off-season. 3 units (all share 2 bathrooms). C$55–C$75 (US$37–US$50) double, including full breakfast. AE, MC, V. Closed Nov–May. Pets allowed.

The Hangashore is owned by the same folks who run the always-cordial Monkstown Manor in St. John's, and is a place for travelers happy to trade space for conviviality. The rooms in this historic 1860 home are cozy (read: tiny), just as they would have been in, well, 1860. But they're utterly uncluttered in a modern Scandinavian sort of way, and painted with bold, welcoming colors. There's a parlor with television and telephone downstairs, and relaxed breakfasts are served around a pine picnic-style table in a cheerful ground-floor room.

Village Inn. Taverner's Path (P.O. Box 10), Trinity, Trinity Bay, NF A0C 2S0. ☎ **709/464-3269.** Fax 709/464-3700. www.oceancontact.com. E-mail: beamish@nf.sympatico.ca. 8 units. C$52–C$72 (US$35–US$48) double. MC, V. Open by advance arrangement from Nov–Apr. "Small, well-behaved pets" allowed.

The eight rooms in this handsome old inn, located on what passes for a busy street in Trinity (busy with pedestrians, that is), has a pleasantly lived-in feel, with eclectic but leaning-toward-Victorian furniture, and the small dining room feels as if it hasn't changed a whit in 75 years. Innkeepers Christine and Peter Beamish do a fine job of making guests feel at home; they also run **Ocean Contact,** a whale-watch operation that uses a 26-foot rigid-hull inflatable. Ask about tour availability when you book your room.

WHERE TO DINE

Eriksen Premises. West St. ☎ **709/464-3698.** Reservations advisable during peak season. Main courses, lunch C$4.95–C$6.95 (US$3.30–US$4.65), dinner C$9.95–C$18.95 (US$6.65–US$12.65). MC, V. Daily 8am–9:30pm. Closed Nov to mid-May. TRADITIONAL.

Despite some inelegant touches (like butter served in those pesky plastic tubs with the peel-off tops), this is Trinity's best restaurant, and it offers good value. The restaurant shares the first floor of a B&B with a gift shop, and has a homey feel with oak floors, beadboard ceiling, and Victorian accents. (There's also dining on an outside deck, which is especially inviting at lunchtime.) The meals are mostly traditional: cod tongue, broiled halibut, scallops, liver and onion, and chicken. The service and food quality are consistently a notch above the expected. Desserts, like the cheesecake with fresh berry toppings, are especially good.

Village Inn. Taverner's Path. ☎ **709/464-3269.** Main courses C$7–C$17 (US$5–US$11). MC, V. Daily 8am–9pm. TRADITIONAL/VEGETARIAN.

The pleasantly old-fashioned dining room at the Village Inn (see "Where to Stay," above) has a good reputation for its vegetarian meals (something of a rarity in Newfoundland), with options including a lentil shepherd's pie and a rice and nut casserole. But those looking for comfort food are also well-served here, with options like meat loaf, fried cod, liver and onions, and a ham plate. This is country cooking at its finest; everything is made from scratch, from soups to dessert.

BONAVISTA

Bonavista is a 45-minute drive from Trinity, and is a strongly recommended day trip for those spending a night or two in the area.

If you're approaching Bonavista on Route 230, I'd suggest it's worth your while to detour on Route 238 through **Elliston.** This is a pretty coastal village and worth the few extra kilometers. More to the point, this route brings you into the town of Bonavista via a scenic road across high upland barrens. You'll get great views of the whitewashed town with the expansive bay beyond as you crest the hill. This bay is noted for its icebergs, which can linger late into summer. This road provides a grand vantage point to scan the horizon for icebergs and "bergy bits" before you head down to sea level.

EXPLORING THE TOWN

The ✪ **Ryan Premises National Historic Site** (☎ **709/468-1600**) opened in 1997 with Queen Elizabeth herself presiding over the ceremonies. Located in downtown Bonavista, the new site is a very photogenic grouping of white clapboard buildings at the harbor's edge. For more than a century, this was the town's most prominent saltfish complex, where fishermen sold their catch and bought all the sundry goods needed to keep an outport functioning. Michael Ryan opened for business here in 1857; his heirs kept the business going until 1978. (One elderly resident recalled that you could "get everything from a baby's fart to a clap of thunder" from the Ryans.) The spiffy complex today features an art gallery, local history museum, gift shop, handcrafted furniture store, and what may be the most rare and extraordinary of all: a truly fascinating exhibit on the role of the codfish industry in Newfoundland's history. An hour or two here will greatly abet you in making sense of the rest of your visit to the island.

The property is open daily from mid-June to mid-October from 10am to 6pm. Admission is C$3 (US$2) adult, C$2.25 (US$1.50) seniors, C$1.50 (US$1) youth, and C$6.50 (US$4) family.

On the far side of the harbor, and across from a field of magnificent irises, is the beautiful **Mockbeggar Property** (☎ **709/729-2460**). Named after an English seaport that shared characteristics with Bonavista, the home was occupied by prominent Newfoundland politician F. Gordon Bradley. It's been restored to how it appeared when Bradley moved here in 1940, and it features much of the original furniture. With a few telltale exceptions (note the wonderful 1940s-era carpet in the formal dining room), it shows a strong Victorian influence. The house is managed as a provincial historic site, and admission is C$2.50 (US$1.65) adult, children under 12 free (also includes admission to Cape Bonavista Lighthouse, see below). It's open daily in summer from 10am to 5:30pm.

A replica of the ***Mathew,*** ☎ **709/468-1493,** the ship John Cabot sailed when he first landed in Newfoundland in 1497, opened at Bonavista's harbor in 2000. This compact ship is an exacting replica, based on plans of the original ship. (Don't confuse this ship with the other *Mathew* replica, which crossed the Atlantic and sailed around Newfoundland in 1997.) An interpretive center and occasional performances staged wharfside provide context for your tour aboard the ship, which is designed as a floating museum. Because it's an exact copy, and looks roughly as it did 500 years ago, the ship doesn't have an engine or any modern safety devices, and thus isn't allowed to leave the dock for passenger cruises. It will stay tied up along the dock in summer, and stored in an architecturally striking white clapboard boathouse in the off-season.

The ship is open from mid-June to early September, daily from 10am to 6pm. At press time, tours were C$2 (US$1.35) adult, C$1 (US65¢) children and seniors, but rates were subject to change.

JUST NORTH OF TOWN

The extraordinary ✪ **Cape Bonavista Lighthouse** is located 6 kilometers (3.6 miles) north of town on a rugged point. Built in 1843, the lighthouse is fundamentally a stone tower around which a red-and-white wood-frame house has been constructed. The keepers' quarters (the lightkeeper and his assistant both lived here) has been restored to the year 1870. You can clamber up the narrow stairs to the light itself and inspect the ingenious clockwork mechanism that kept six lanterns revolving all night long between 1895 and 1962. (With some help—it took 15 minutes to wind the counterweight by hand, a job that had to be performed every 2 hours.) This light served mariners until 3 decades ago, when its role was usurped by an inelegant steel tower and beacon. Open daily in summer 10:30am to 5:30pm; admission is C$2.50 (US$1.67) adult, free under 12 (also includes admission to Mockbeggar Property, see above).

Below the lighthouse on a rocky promontory cleft from the mainland is a lively puffin colony. Dozens of these stumpy, colorful birds hop around the grassy knob and take flight into the sea winds. They're easily seen from just below the lighthouse; bring binoculars for a clearer view. Red-footed common murres dive for fish below, and whales are often sighted just offshore. This is the only place I've ever had whales and puffins in sight through my binoculars at the same time. (And there was a beautiful iceberg just off to my left.)

Also nearby is a statue of John Cabot. Although no one can prove it, long-standing tradition holds that Cape Bonavista was the first land spotted by the Italian explorer (who was working for the English) in 1497. The statue is located in handsome Landfall Municipal Park, next to the lighthouse, where you'll find picnic tables and an exceptional example of a quiggly fence.

En route to the lighthouse you'll pass a turnoff to Dungeons Provincial Park. It's 2 kilometers (1.2 miles) down a gravel road through coastal cow, goat, and sheep pastures. Park and follow the short trail to a punchbowl-like cavity some 50 yards across. Relentless waves carved two tunnels under the pasture, and eventually the grassy roof collapsed, leaving this gaping hole flushed by the surf. Admission is free.

9 The Baccalieu Trail

The Baccalieu Trail forms a loop around the long, narrow, and unnamed peninsula that separates Conception Bay from Trinity Bay. It doesn't have the distinguished 18th-century pedigree of neighboring Bonavista Peninsula, which was the region's mercantile center in the early days. But I think the history here is actually more intriguing in a quirky kind of way. Episodes here feature the mysterious Amelia Earhart, the cranky Rockwell Kent, and the pioneers of both the Arctic exploration and transatlantic communication.

Be aware that the drive isn't uninterruptedly picturesque. It's notably unscenic for a long stretch south of Carbonear on the Conception Bay side. But elsewhere you will come upon vistas that will leave you absolutely speechless.

ESSENTIALS

GETTING THERE   The Baccalieu Trail is composed of Routes 80, 70, and 60. The entire detour to Bay de Verde and back from the Trans-Canada is about 260 kilometers (156 miles).

VISITOR INFORMATION   The **Provincial Interpretive and Information Center** (☎ 709/759-8514) is on the Trans-Canada Highway just west of Route 80 in Whitbourne. It's open daily in season from 8:30am to 8:30pm.

DILDO

The picturesque fishing town of Dildo consists of homes clustered along a hilly harbor's edge and a forested prominence rising near the outer point. (It's about 12 kilometers north of the Trans-Canada Highway on Route 80.) While fishing has ground to a near-halt since the cod moratorium, cultural tourism has picked up some of the slack, with visitors trekking here to view traces of the once-thriving Indian culture. A highlight is a visit to an island in the mouth of the harbor, which was occupied at various times by Beothuk, Dorset Eskimo, and more modern Indians.

A good place to start a tour is the **Dildo Interpretive Centre** (☎ 709/582-3339), on the harbor as you come into town. (Look for the giant squid made of fiberglass in the parking lot, an actual-size model of one caught locally in 1933.) The center opened in 1997 and features displays of some of the nearly 6,000 Eskimo artifacts recovered by archaeologists on the island, including harpoon endblades, knives, soapstone bowls and lamps, and scrapers. The center also features a touch tank with crabs and starfish for kids, and exhibits on the more recent lumbering and fishing industries of the region. The center is open daily (summers only) 10am to 5pm; admission is C$2 (US$1.35) adult, C$1 (US65¢) children.

A trip to see the excavations on Dildo Island, just a few minutes' boat ride away, may be arranged through **Dildo Island Boat Tours,** ☎ 709/582-2687, which offers 2- to 3-hour excursions that include a picnic lunch on a beach. Archaeologists are still actively excavating the island's most promising sites, and it's a good opportunity to talk with them about the finds. It's also a beautiful island, and an afternoon spent exploring here is an afternoon well spent. Advance reservations are required; the cost is C$25 (US$17) per person.

Oh, yes .... the town's name. You may be wondering. The generally accepted theory is that it was named by early Spanish sailors for a person or place in Spain. Other theories: it may be from a local Indian word meaning "still waters," or, less tenably, from the chorus of an old ballad. Nobody really knows.

HEART'S CONTENT

Heart's Content was named either after an early ship that visited here, or because of the vaguely heart-shaped harbor. In any event, this is a pleasing coastal village that claims a prominent footnote in the annals of telecommunications. In 1858 the **first trans-atlantic telegraph cable** was brought ashore, connecting England with Newfoundland and beyond to the United States; Queen Victoria and U.S. President James Buchanan exchanged messages. After 27 days and 732 messages the cable mysteriously failed, and another cable, this one to Heart's Content, was installed in 1866. This was to blossom as a vital link between the New and the Old World. It also provided employment for 300 people in this little village and brought a measure of culture and prosperity. In the late 1800s some 1,200 people lived here; since the 1950s, the population has hovered around 600.

You can still see rusted and frayed cables jutting from an embankment near the center of town. The brick cable station with its distinctive gingerbread trim is just across the road. At the **Cable Station Historic Site** (☎ **709/583-2160**), you can see the impressively bulky antique equipment and learn more about how involved this historic enterprise really was. (Side note: The displays and exhibits were installed in the 1970s, and will be of special interest to those who enjoy period pieces dating from the era of Abba and platform shoes.) Open daily June through August 10:30am to 6pm; admission is C$2.50 (US$1.65) adult, children under 12 free.

At the rocky point at the mouth on the north side of the harbor is a relatively modern barber-pole-striped **lighthouse** set amid impressive, rounded rocks that seem to heave up from the earth. Wonderful views of Trinity Bay can be had from here; it's a good spot for a picnic.

BACCALIEU ISLAND

Cliff-girded **Baccalieu Island,** about 3.5 kilometers (2 miles) off the peninsula's tip, is 5 kilometers (3 miles) long and has a rich history as a fishing center and location of an important lighthouse. Today, it's better known for the vast colonies of seabirds, 11 species of which breed here. These include puffins, northern fulmar, common murre, and northern gannet. The island is also home to thick-billed murre and razorbills, and a staggering three-million-plus Leach's storm petrels. Alas, boat tours to the island haven't been offered on a regular basis in a couple of years. Committed birders might be able to drum up a local fisherman or other boat owner who'd be willing to go out; ask at the provincial information center in Whitbourne for suggestions.

The village of **Bay de Verde** at the northern tip of the peninsula is worth an excursion even if you're not trying to visit the island. A road now reaches this remote fishing village, but it still very much has the feel of an outport untouched by modern trends. It's dominated by trim, old-fashioned houses on rocky terraces overlooking the harbor.

HARBOUR GRACE

Harbour Grace is a historic town that sprawls along a waterfront with views out to Conception Bay. It's not a picture-perfect town—there's plenty of charmless modern architecture mixed among the historic—but you'll get a good sense of the region's rich history with an hour's poking around.

Near the Harbour Grace Visitor Center at the south end of town are two modest memorials to transportation before the roads. *The Spirit of Harbour Grace,* a DC-3 airplane from Labrador Air, is mounted in a graceful banked turn, like a trout rising to take a fly. Just offshore and slightly out of kilter is the **SS Kyle,** a handsome coastal steamer that lies aground and listing to port. The *Kyle* was one of the last of the wood- and coal-burning coastal steamers. Launched in 1913, it plied Newfoundland's waters until 1967, when a northeaster blew her from her moorings and she came to rest on a mussel bed. A paint job in 1997 made her somewhat more festive.

Harbour Grace occupies a prominent niche in the history of **early 20th-century aviation.** A cluster of pioneer pilots used the town airfield as a jumping-off point for crossings of the Atlantic. Indeed, Newfoundland was abuzz with daring pilots during aviation's pioneer days. The first nonstop crossing of the Atlantic was by J. Alcock and A. W. Brown, who flew from Newfoundland to Ireland in 1919, 8 years before Charles

Lindbergh left New York to become the first solo pilot to cross the Atlantic. In 1928, Amelia Earhart flew to Wales from Newfoundland, and 4 years later she became the first woman to solo the transatlantic trip, taking off from Harbour Grace.

You can revisit this rich history at the **Harbour Grace Airfield,** the first aerodrome in Newfoundland. It's a stunningly beautiful and pristine spot on a hillside overlooking the harbor and the town—it appears not to have changed a bit since Earhart took off for Europe more than a half-century ago. You can scramble atop the monolith at the north end of the airfield to get a sweeping view out into Conception Bay, with the lush, grassy airstrip stretching out below.

Find the airfield by driving 1 mile north of the information center on Route 70, then turning left. The paved road soon stops; you don't. Continue 1.5 kilometers (0.9 mile) from Route 70, and turn right on another dirt road. Continue 1.6 kilometers (1 mile), passing the end of the airstrip, and then turn right and drive to the top of the low hill. There's a small plaque commemorating the early fliers.

More local history is on view at the **Conception Bay Museum** (☎ **709/596-1309**) on Water Street. Located on a low bluff overlooking the harbor and distant sea stacks, the museum occupies a three-story brick and granite building that was a customs station when built in 1870. Inside you'll find artifacts and costumed guides, who offer walking tours of the town's **Heritage District** by appointment. The museum is open daily in summer 10am to 4pm (closed daily from 1 to 1:30pm for lunch). Admission is C$2.50 (US$1.65) adult, C$1.50 (US$1) seniors, C$1 (US65¢) children.

Boat tours of the harbor are offered by the **Great Easton,** (☎ **709/596-2172**), a firm named after the master pirate Peter Easton. The 26-foot fiberglass motorboat accommodates up to 12 passengers, and during a two-hour tour you'll get a close-up view of the SS *Kyle,* and learn some of the rich folklore that's taken root in and around Conception Bay. It's best to book ahead.

WHERE TO STAY & DINE

There are a couple of motels along the Baccalieu Trail, especially on the southern stretches of Route 70. Carbonear has two basic, serviceable motels: **Fong's Motel** (☎ **709/596-5114**) and **Carbonear Motel** (☎ **709/596-5662**). Rooms at both run around C$55 to C$65 (US$37 to US$43).

NaGeira House. 7 Musgrave St. Carbonear, NF A1Y 1A4. ☎ **800/600-7757,** or 709/753-7540. Fax 709/754-4990. www.nageirahouse.com. E-mail: nageirahouse@nfld.com. 4 units. C$89–C$129 (US$59–US$86) double, includes full breakfast (discounts in off-season). MC, V.

The NaGeira House is named after an Irish princess, who was kidnapped in the 17th century and was spirited away to Carbonear, where she lived out her life. The inn opened in 1999 in a wonderful old gabled home, and the innkeepers have a good eye for detail, from the down duvets and quality linens, to the delicious breakfasts. The rooms vary widely as to size, from very small for the least expensive, to a spacious master suite with in-room Jacuzzi and fireplace. If you opt for the smallest room, you'll still have access to the comfortable common room.

Rothesay House Inn. 34 Water St., Harbour Grace, NF A0A 2M0. ☎ **709/596-2268,** off-season 709/786-0186. Fax 709/786-7570. www.rothesay.com. E-mail: rothesay@nf.sympatico.ca. 4 units. C$55–C$75 (US$37–US$50), including a full breakfast. AE, MC, V.

The Queen Anne-style Rothesay House dates to 1910, and sits on a low rise looking across the street to the harbor beyond. It's well situated for exploring Harbour Grace and the Baccalieu Trail, and has four comfortable guest rooms, each with private bath.

Dining: The inn's popular restaurant is open for three meals daily. The menu changes with the availability of goods, and tends to have a number of selections for carnivores—a nice break from the more common emphasis on seafood islandwide. The menu might include pork loin chops with an apple and cream sauce, chateaubriand, or orange basil chicken. (Of course, there's also salmon or cod.) A three-course meal is C$22 (US$15).

BRIGUS

The trim and tidy harbor-front village of Brigus is clustered with wood-frame homes and narrow lanes that extend out from the picturesque harbor. Brigus is remembered by some art historians as the town that gave the boot to iconoclastic American artist Rockwell Kent, who lived here, briefly, in 1914 and 1915. World War I was on, and Kent was suspected of "pro-German activities." His crime? Singing songs in Pennsylvania Dutch. Kent eventually returned to Newfoundland in 1968 as a guest of the premier and forgave the province and the people.

Near the harbor, look for the **"Brigus Tunnel,"** built in the summer of 1860 by Capt. Abraham Bartlett, whose deepwater dock was on one side of a low, rocky ridge but whose warehouses were on the other. He resolved the problem by hiring a Cornish miner to create a pathway. Although the dock and warehouses are gone, and local teens have adorned the tunnel with graffiti, you can still stroll through and be rewarded with a fine view of the harbor.

If you're in town come evening, the **Baccalieu Players** stage various shows and dinner cabarets, and host comedy nights at various venues in Brigus and beyond. For information, ask at any shop locally, or call ☎ **709/528-4817.**

Brigus Museum. 4 Magistrates Hill. ☎ **709/528-3391.** Admission C$1 (US67¢) adult, C50¢ (US33¢) children. Daily 11am–6pm mid-June to early Sept.

This is one of the finest small museums in the province. Local history is the focus of this replica of an 1820 stone barn, which has been nicely curated with a limited but well-chosen selection of artifacts. These include a beautiful plate hand-painted by Rockwell Kent during his short and controversial residency here.

Hawthorne Cottage National Historic Site. Village Center, Brigus. ☎ **709/528-4004.** Admission C$2.50 (US$1.65) adult, C$2 (US$1.35) senior, C$1.50 (US$1) children (6 to 16), C$6 (US$4) family. Daily 10am–8pm in summer; 10am–6pm off-season.

This elaborate gingerbread cottage on a lovely landscaped yard in the town center was home to Capt. Bob Bartlett, who was among the support crew accompanying Robert E. Peary on his successful trip to the North Pole in 1909. (Bartlett has been lauded as the "greatest ice navigator of the century.") The cottage was originally built in 1830, was moved here from 10 kilometers (6 miles) away in 1833, and is now furnished much as it might have been by the local gentry at the turn of the century.

10 St. John's

St. John's is a world apart from the rest of Newfoundland. The island's small outports and long roads through spruce and bog are imbued with a deep melancholy. St. John's, on the other hand, is vibrant and bustling. Coming into the city after traveling the hinterlands is like stepping from Kansas into Oz—the landscape suddenly seems to burst with color and life.

This attractive port city of just over 100,000 residents crowds the steep hills around a deep harbor. Like Halifax, Nova Scotia, and Saint John, New Brunswick, St. John's also serves as a magnet for youth culture in the province, and the clubs and restaurants tend to have a more cosmopolitan feel and sharper edge.

St. John's harbor is impressive, protected from the open seas by stony hills and accessible only through a pinched gap called The Narrows, a rocky defile of the sort you'd expect to see Atlas straddle. The Narrows is at the north end of the harbor and hidden from view from much of downtown, so first-time visitors may think they've stumbled upon a small lake—albeit one with tankers and other ocean-going ships.

This is very much a working harbor, the hub of much of the province's commerce. As such, don't expect quaint. Across the way are charmless oil-tank farms, along with off-loading facilities for tankers. A major containership wharf occupies the head of the harbor. Along the water's edge on Harbour Street downtown, you'll usually find hulking ships tied up; pedestrians are welcome to stroll and gawk, but wholesale commerce is the focus here, not boutiques.

If you can arrange it, come to St. John's after you've explored the more remote parts of Newfoundland. At that point—after a couple of weeks or even a few days of sketchy restaurant food and lackluster motel rooms—you'll *really* appreciate the city's urban attitude, the good choice of hotels and motels, and the varied cuisine of city restaurants.

ESSENTIALS

GETTING THERE   St. John's is located 131 kilometers (79 miles) from the ferry at Argentia, 905 kilometers (543 miles) from Port aux Basques. **St. John's International Airport** offers flights to Halifax, Montréal, Ottawa, Toronto, and London, England. See "Getting There" at the beginning of this chapter for ferry and airline information. The airport is 6 kilometers (4 miles) from downtown; taxis from the airport to downtown hotels are approximately C$12 (US$8) for one traveler, C$2 (US$1.35) for each additional traveler.

VISITOR INFORMATION   In summer, visitor information can be obtained at the **Tourist Information Rail Car** (☎ 709/576-8514) on Harbour Drive, along the waterfront. It's open daily in summer 9am to 5pm. Off-season, look for information at City Hall (☎ 709/576-8106) on New Gower Street. The e-mail address is tourism@city.st-johns.nf.ca.

GETTING AROUND   Metrobus serves much of the city. At press time, fares were C$1.50 (US$1) for a single trip. Route information is available at the visitor information center or by calling ☎ 709/722-9400.

Taxis are plentiful around St. John's, and charge an initial fee of C$2 (US$1.35) plus C$2 (US$1.35) each additional mile. One of the larger and more dependable outfits in the city is **Bugden Taxi** (☎ 709/726-4400).

ORIENTATION   St. John's is built on the side of a steep hill, and the downtown is oriented along three streets—**Harbour, Water,** and **Duckworth**—that run parallel to the water's edge. These are relatively level, each following the hill's contours, one above the other. Cross streets that link these run the gamut from moderately challenging inclines to clutch-smoking vertical. Duckworth and Water Streets contain the bulk of the downtown's shops and restaurants.

Outside of downtown, St. John's is an amalgam of confusing roads that run at peculiar angles to one another and that suddenly change names as if on a whim. You can try to navigate with a map, but it's just as easy to keep an eye on a landmark—like Signal Hill—and head your car in the general direction you want to go. The city's small enough that you'll never get too lost and you'll eventually end up on the main ring road, which goes by various names, including Columbus Drive, Confederation Parkway, and Prince Philip Drive.

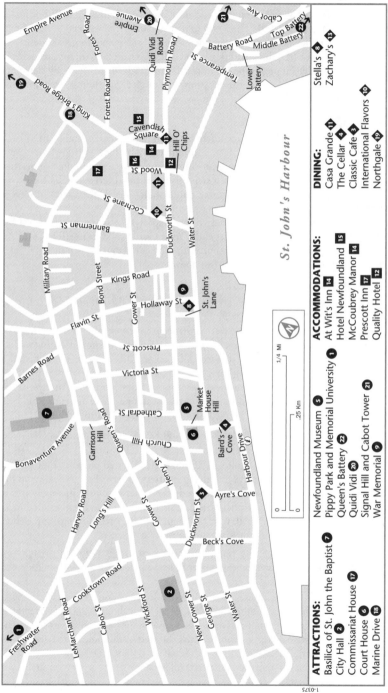

St. John's

St. John's Harbour

ATTRACTIONS:
Basilica of St. John the Baptist **7**
City Hall **2**
Commissariat House **17**
Court House **6**
Marine Drive **18**
Newfoundland Museum **5**
Pippy Park and Memorial University **1**
Queen's Battery **22**
Quidi Vidi **20**
Signal Hill and Cabot Tower **21**
War Memorial **9**

ACCOMMODATIONS:
At Wit's Inn **14**
Hotel Newfoundland **15**
McCoubrey Manor **14**
Prescott Inn **17**
Quality Hotel **12**

DINING:
Casa Grande **11**
The Cellar **4**
Classic Cafe **3**
International Flavors **10**
Northgale **12**
Stella's **8**
Zachary's **13**

Empire Avenue
Forest Road
Empire Avenue
Quidi Vidi Road
Plymouth Road
Temperance St.
Battery Road
Top Battery
Middle Battery
Lower Battery
Cabot Ave.
King's Bridge Road
Forest Road
Cavendish Square
Hill O' Chips
Wood St.
Cochrane St.
Bannerman St.
Military Road
Bond Street
Kings Road
Duckworth St.
Water St.
St. John's Lane
Gower St.
Hollaway St.
Flavin St.
Prescott St.
Barnes Road
Victoria St.
Cathedral St.
Market House Hill
Church Hill
Baird's Cove
Harbour Drive
Queen's Road
Garrison Hill
Henry St.
Bonaventure Avenue
Ayre's Cove
Duckworth St.
Beck's Cove
Harvey Road
Long's Hill
Gower St.
Cookstown Road
LeMarchant Road
Cabot St.
Wickford St.
New Gower St.
George St.
Water St.
Freshwater Road

1/4 Mi
.25 Km

1-0375

SPECIAL EVENTS   The annual **Newfoundland and Labrador Folk Festival** celebrates its 25th year in 2001. The 3-day festival is held over a weekend in early August, and includes performers from all over the province, who gather to play at Bannerman Park in downtown St. John's. (Bring a lawn chair.) Even after all these years tickets are still very affordable (at press time it cost just C\$5 (US\$3) for an afternoon slate of performers, C\$7 (US\$5) for the evening). Contact St. John's tourism office (☎ 709/576-8514) for more information.

EXPLORING ST. JOHN'S

Parking is rarely a problem in downtown St. John's. Bring loonies and quarters to feed the meters. Once you park, you can continue easily by foot; the downtown area is compact enough. In my experience St. John's drivers are uncommonly respectful of pedestrians. If you so much as take a step off the curb—or even let a look cross your face suggesting you just might, at some point, want to cross the street—drivers will slow to a halt and wave you across.

The city produces a free, informative and helpful 40-page pocket-sized brochure, entitled **"Exploring the City of Legends: Your Guide to Walking Tours and Auto Tours of St. John's."** It's a good resource for launching your visit to the city. Ask for it at the tourist information rail car (see above).

DOWNTOWN ATTRACTIONS

Anglican Cathedral of St. John the Baptist. Church St. ☎ **709/726-5677.** Free tours June 15–Sept 30, Mon–Sat 10am–5pm, Sun 10am–5pm.

This impressive hillside cathedral was constructed in stages from 1843 to 1885, with additional rebuilding following the great fire of 1892. Designed in high Gothic Revival style by noted English architect Sir George Gilbert Scott, the cathedral has very fine stained glass, lavish oak carvings, and blue-stone walls from nearby quarries. (The sandstone of the arches and bays was shipped from Scotland.) After you admire the historically significant architecture and the small one-room museum, stop by the crypt, where sweets and tea are served Monday to Friday 2:30 to 4:30pm.

Commissariat House. King's Bridge Rd. ☎ **709/729-6730.** Free admission. Mid-June to mid-Oct daily 10am–5:30pm.

This stellar Georgian house, built in 1821, has served varied purposes over the years. Originally constructed as offices and living quarters to serve Fort William and other military installations, the home subsequently served as a rectory, nursing home, and children's hospital. Now a provincial historic site, the home has been restored to look as it would have looked in 1830, with the English china, fine paintings, and elaborate furnishings that would befit an Assistant Commissary General.

Newfoundland Museum. 285 Duckworth St. ☎ **709/729-2329.** C\$3 (US\$2) adult, C\$2.50 (US\$1.65) seniors and students, under 18 free. Summer 9:30am–4:45pm daily; closed Mon off-season.

This compact downtown museum offers a good introduction to the natural and cultural history of the island. On the first floor you'll learn about the flora and fauna, and find out that the moose is not native to Newfoundland. The second floor concentrates on the various native cultures, from Beothuk through Inuit (look for the delicate carvings of bear heads). The more sparsely exhibited third floor suggests how 19th-century life was lived in Newfoundland's outports. Allow about an hour for a leisurely tour.

✪ **Signal Hill.** Atop Signal Hill at the entrance to St. John's harbor. ☎ **709/772-5367.** Free admission to grounds; admission to interpretive center C\$2.50 (US\$1.65) adult, C\$2 (US\$1.35) senior, C\$1.50 (US\$1) children (6 to 16), C\$6 (US\$4) family. Open daylight hours.

You'll come for the history but stay for the views. Signal Hill is St. John's most visible and most visit-worthy attraction. The rugged, barren hill is the city's preeminent landmark, rising up over the entrance to the harbor and topped by a craggy castle with a flag fluttering high overhead—the signal of the name. The layers of history here are rich and complex—flags have flown atop this hill since 1704, and over the centuries a succession of military fortifications occupied these strategic slopes, as did three different hospitals. The "castle" (called Cabot Tower) dates to 1897, built in honor of Queen Victoria's Diamond Jubilee and the 400th anniversary of John Cabot's arrival in the new world. The hill also secured a spot in history in 1901, when Nobel laureate Guglielmo Marconi received the first wireless transatlantic broadcast—three short dots indicating the letter "S" in Morse code, sent from Cornwall, England—on an antennae raised 400 feet on a kite in powerful winds.

A good place to start a tour is at the interpretive center, where you'll get a good briefing about the hill's history. Four days a week, military drills and cannon firings take place in the field next to the center (Wednesday and Thursday at 7pm, Saturday and Sunday at 3 and 7pm). From here, you can follow serpentine trails up the hill to the Cabot Tower, where you'll be rewarded with breathtaking views of the Narrows and the open ocean beyond. (Cape Spear can be seen in the distance to the south.) Look for icebergs in the early summer and whales any time. Interpretive placards, scattered about the summit, feature engaging photos from various epochs.

Exploring Farther Afield

Quidi Vidi (pronounced "kitty vitty") is a tiny harbor village that sets new standards for the term "quaint." The village is tucked in a narrow, rocky defile behind Signal Hill, where a narrow ocean inlet provides access to the sea. It's photogenic in the extreme, and a wonderful spot to investigate by foot or bike (it's rather more difficult by car). The village consists mostly of compact homes, including the oldest home in St. John's, with very few shops. Visit here while you can; in late 1999, following rancorous local debate, development plans were approved for the addition of modern housing in the area. To get to Quidi Vidi, follow Signal Hill Road to Quidi Vidi Road; turn right onto Forest Road.

From here you can easily connect to **Quidi Vidi Lake,** where **St. John's Regatta** is held the first Wednesday in August, as it has been since 1826. Look for the trail leading to the lake from near the entrance to Quidi Vidi, or ask locally.

Art Gallery of Newfoundland and Labrador. Allandale Rd. and Prince Philip Dr. ☎ **709/737-8209.** Free admission. Tues–Sun noon–5pm, Fri 7–10pm.

Located on the campus of the Memorial University of Newfoundland, the four galleries of the art museum are housed in an architecturally undistinguished modern building with two levels. Permanent and rotating exhibits mostly showcase Newfoundland talent, but the occasional touring show highlights other Canadian artists. Consult the local newspaper to see what's currently on display.

Memorial University Botanical Garden at Oxen Pond. Mt. Scio Rd. ☎ **709/737-8590.** Admission C$2 (US$1.35) adult, C$1 (US65¢) seniors and children (5–17). Open May–Nov daily 10am–5pm. Take Thorburn Rd. past Avalon Mall, turn right on Mt. Scio Rd.

An abundant selection of northern plants makes this garden well worth seeking out (it's tucked over a wooded ridge on the city's western edge, behind Pippy Park). The main plots are arranged in gracious "theme gardens," including a cottage garden, a rock garden, and a peat garden. Among the most interesting is the Newfoundland Heritage Garden, with examples of 70 types of perennials traditionally found in island gardens. The floral displays aren't as ostentatious or exuberant as you'll find in other public gardens in Atlantic Canada (the gardens of Halifax and Annapolis Royal come to mind), but they will be of great interest to amateur horticulturists curious about boreal plants. Behind the gardens are winding hiking trails leading down to marshy Oxen Pond.

Fluvarium. Pippy Park, off Allandale Rd. ☎ **709/754-3474.** Admission C$4 (US$2.65) adults, C$3.25 (US$2.15) seniors and students, C$2.25 (US$1.50) children. Summer daily 10am–6pm; limited hours and days in the off-season. Guided tours on the half-hour; feeding time 4pm.

This low, octagonal structure at the edge of Long Pond (near the University) actually descends three stories into the earth. The second level features exhibits on river ecology, including life in the riffles (that's where trout spawn) and in shallow pools, which are rich with nutrients. On the lowest level you'll find yourself looking up into a deep pool that's located alongside the building. Watch for brown trout swimming lazily by.

Institute for Marine Dynamics. Kerwin Place, on the campus of Memorial University. ☎ **709/772-4366.** Tours are free, but reservations are required. Offered May–Aug, Mon–Fri 9am–4:30pm.

This is an oddly fascinating research facility. Work done here included engineering studies for the Hibernia oil platform (a 60-story-high drilling rig located offshore southeast of Newfoundland) and the Confederation Bridge to Prince Edward Island. On the tour you'll see three remarkable tanks, in which models of ships (as much as 12 feet long) and other marine structures are put through their paces. The world's longest ice tank is located here (a huge pool in a hangar-sized freezer), and you'll see the 200-meter (600-foot) towing tank, with wavemakers and a retractable beach. Children must be 10 years or older; reservations required.

OUTDOOR PURSUITS

Pippy Park (☎ 709/737-3655) is on the city's hilly western side adjacent to the university and contains 3,350 acres of developed recreation land and quiet trails. The popular park is home to the city campground and Fluvarium (see above), as well as miniature golf, picnic sites, and playgrounds.

For bike rentals, head downtown to **Canary Cycles,** 294 Water St. (☎ 709/579-5972) where Joe Planchant offers several different types of bikes, with rates around C$20 (US$13) per day, extra for lock and helmets.

The **Grand Concourse** (☎ 709/737-1077) is an ambitious project to link much of St. John's with pedestrian pathways. Although about 40 kilometers (25 miles) have been completed, much is still under development and segments can end with disconcerting abruptness. Two inviting existing segments include the loop around Quidi Vidi Lake, and the Rennie's River Trail between Pippy Park and Quidi Vidi Lake. Bikes are not permitted on the trails. Ask at the information centers for current trail status and map availability.

To see the city from the water, head to the harbor. The traditional fishing schooner *J&B* (☎ 709/753-7245) was built in Trinity and holds 40 passengers. The 2-hour tours depart from Pier 6 and usually offer a glimpse of whales and a dose of traditional Newfoundland music; the cost is C$20 (US$13) adults, C$16 (US$11) seniors, and C$10 (US$7) ages 6 to 16.

One highly recommended hike is the ✪ **North Head Trail,** which runs from Signal Hill to an improbable cluster of small buildings between rock face and water called The Battery. You should be reasonably fit and unafraid of heights; allow about 2 hours, assuming departure and return from near the Hotel Newfoundland.

On foot, follow Duckworth Street between the hotel and Devon House, then bear right on Battery Road. Stay on the main branch (a few smaller branches may confuse you) as it narrows then rises and falls while skirting a rock face to the Outer Battery. The former fishermen's homes at the Battery are literally inches from the road and not much farther from the water, and most have drop-dead views of the Narrows and the city skyline. There's a whimsical, storybook character to the place, and the real estate is now much sought after by city residents.

At the end of the Battery you'll cross right over someone's front porch (it's OK), and then the North Head Trail begins in earnest. It runs along the Narrows, past old gun emplacements, up and down heroic sets of steps, and along some narrow ledges (chains are bolted to rock as handrails for a little extra security in one spot). The trail then ascends an open headland before looping back and starting the final ascent up Signal Hill. After some time exploring here and soaking up the view, you can walk on the paved road back down Signal Hill to Duckworth Street.

SHOPPING

A number of downtown shops tout "traditional Newfoundland" crafts and souvenirs, and the offerings range from high-quality goods to tourist-oriented schlock.

The Bird House and Binocular Shop. 166 Duckworth St. ☎ **709/726-2473.**

This is a recommended stop for both serious and aspiring birders. The shop has a selection of field guides, binoculars, and spotting scopes, along with backyard bird supplies. Binoculars are also available for rent. The shop distributes a free brochure with a checklist of local species and suggested birding areas around St. John's.

David Ariss Fine Art. 179 Water St. ☎ **877/211-1511** or 709/579-4941.

David Ariss offers both contemporary and traditional art from some of Newfoundland's most respected artists, with a strong representation of Inuit art. There's another Ariss gallery in Halifax if you miss this one.

✪ **Devon House Craft Center.** 59 Duckworth St. ☎ **709/753-2749.**

The nonprofit Devon House (operated by the Newfoundland and Labrador Crafts Development Association) displays the works of more than 150 of the province's artisans in an attractive old house across from the Hotel Newfoundland. There's also a gallery of current crafts and design.

Downhomer Shoppe and Gallery. 303 Water St. ☎ **888/588-6353** or 709/726-2135.

The best destination for your basic Newfoundland souvenirs—T-shirts, coffee mugs, postcards, dolls in tartans, etc.

Fred's CDs and Tapes. 198 Duckworth St. ☎ **709/753-9191.**

There's a great selection of Newfoundland music here, and a knowledgeable sales staff. You can sample many of the CDs on headphone before you buy.

Newfoundland Bookstore. 100 Water St. ☎ **709/722-5830.**

A selection of books about Newfoundland (as well as those by Newfoundlanders) are offered at this cozy Water Street shop.

Newfoundland Weavery. 177 Water St. ☎ **709/753-0496.**

The weavery started as a weaving supply store in 1972, and has since expanded to become a showcase for local arts and crafts, including pottery, oilskin coats, and pewter work.

O'Brien's Music Store. 278 Water St. ☎ **709/753-8135.**

A popular hangout for local musicians looking for equipment, O'Brien's also carries an excellent selection of local tapes and CDs, and the staff is very knowledgeable in all things musical. Music can also be ordered by mail or via the store's Web site at www.obriens.nf.ca.

EXCURSIONS FROM ST. JOHN'S

Some 11 kilometers (7 miles) southeast of downtown is North America's most easterly point, home to dramatic **Cape Spear National Historic Site** (☎ 709/772-5367). Here you'll find a picturesque lighthouse dating back to 1836, and underground passages from abandoned World War II gun batteries. A visitor center will orient you; leave plenty of time to walk the hiking trails and scout for whales surfacing out to sea. Admission to the lighthouse, which has been restored to its 1839 appearance, is C$2.50 (US$1.65) adults, C$2 (US$1.35) seniors, C$1.50 (US$1) ages 6 to 16, and C$6 (US$4) family. The lighthouse is closed mid-October to mid-May, but the grounds are open year-round.

Just 14 kilometers (8.7 miles) west of St. John's is Portugal Cove, from which frequent **ferries** (☎ 709/895-6391) depart for **Bell Island.** This is a handsome and historic island, with abrupt cliffs edging the eastern shore. The island was a thriving community early in this century; an iron mine employed hundreds from 1895 to 1966, after which it no longer made economic sense to scratch ore out of the earth. The island remains honeycombed with impressive mine shafts, many extending far out under the sea.

The **No. 2 Mine** (☎ 709/488-2880), has been maintained as a museum of sorts, where visitors can relive the life of a miner, who made his way through the perpetual underground night with a carbide lantern. During a 40-minute tour you'll descend by foot 650 feet underground, to where flooding now makes the mine shaft impassable. The mine actually descends 1,700 feet into the earth, and is 2 to 3 miles long. Tours are offered frequently daily in summer; rates are C$5 (US$3) adult, C$3 (US$2) for children under 12.

While on Bell Island, ask locals about the **Grebe's Nest,** a rocky point marked by an offshore sea stack. (I didn't see grebes—or any other interesting seabird life, for that matter—while I was here.) But scramble down to the shore, head south along the water, and you can make your way though a man-made tunnel about 50 meters long, which leads to a secluded beach on the other side surrounded by towering, crumbling cliffs. Kids love the mystery and remoteness of this place.

WHERE TO STAY

Campers should head to municipal **Pippy Park Campground** (☎ 709/737-3669), just a couple miles from downtown off Allandale Road. The campground has 184 sites, most with full hookups, and a sociable tenting area. Rates range from about C$14 (US$9) for an unserviced site to C$20 (US$13) for a fully serviced site. It often books up in summer, so it's wise to call ahead for reservations.

EXPENSIVE

Delta Newfoundland. 120 New Gower St., St. John's, NF A1C 6K4. ☎ **800/563-3838** or 709/739-6404. Fax 709/570-1622. 285 units. A/C MINIBAR TV TEL. C$99–C$185 (US$66–US$123) double. AE, DC, DISC, ER, MC, V. Pets allowed with advance permission.

The sleek and modern Delta Newfoundland, built in 1987, is located downtown near City Hall and caters largely to businesspeople. It lacks the views and the ineffable sense of class that you'll find at the Hotel Newfoundland, but it has nice touches like ship models in the lobby and a handsome pool table as the centerpiece of the lounge. It also is well located for prowling the city, and features a number of amenities that choosy travelers will appreciate, like hair dryers and coffeemakers in all rooms.

Dining: The attractive restaurant off the lobby offers breakfast, lunch, and dinner daily. The dinner menu is continental with a Mediterranean touch, and features dishes like seafood casserole, shrimp brochettes, and beef in various incarnations. Dinner entrees are priced from C$14 to C$24 (US$9 to US$16).

Amenities: Indoor pool, fitness room, sauna, Jacuzzi, squash courts, children's program, safe-deposit boxes, limited room service, concierge, free newspaper, valet parking (fee), baby-sitting, dry cleaning, and laundry.

✪ **Hotel Newfoundland.** Cavendish Square (P.O. Box 5637), St. John's, NF A1C 5W8. ☎ 800/441-1414 or 709/726-4980. Fax 709/726-2025. 301 units. A/C MINIBAR TV TEL. Weekends C$110–C$190 (US$73–US$127) double, midweek C$129–C$252 (US$86–US$168) double. AE, DC, DISC, MC, V. Pets C$20 (US$13) extra per night.

The Hotel Newfoundland was built in 1982 in a starkly modern style, but it boasts a refined sensibility and attention to detail that's reminiscent of a lost era. What I like most about the hotel is how the designers and architects hid their best surprises. The lobby has one of the best views of the Narrows in the city, but you have to wander around to find it. It's a wonderful effect, and one that's used nicely throughout. (This helps compensate for the somewhat generic, conference-hotel feel of much of the decor.) The rooms themselves are standard sized and are nothing remarkable, although all have coffeemakers and bathrobes. About half have harbor views.

Dining: The hotel's lobby is home to three establishments. The rather formal **Cabot Club** ranks among the best restaurants in the city, and is known for tableside Caesar salads, caribou soup, and entrees like traditional pan-fried cod and halibut with a saffron truffle butter. Dinner entrees are C$22.50 (US$15) to C$39.75 (US$26.50). The colorful Mediterranean-inspired **Bonavista Cafe,** newly built in 1999, is lighter on the wallet, with lunch offerings such as burgers and generous sandwiches (C$6/US$4 to C$8.50/US$6), and dinners like Greek lamb chops, vegetable fettuccine, and poached salmon (C$10/US$7 to C$19/US$13). **The Narrows** lounge is the spot for a nightcap.

Amenities: Indoor pool, fitness room (with computerized golf course simulator), Jacuzzi, sauna, business center, beauty salon, art gallery, concierge, 24-hour room service, safe-deposit boxes, baby-sitting, dry cleaning, and laundry.

Winterholme. 79 Rennies Mill Rd., St. John's, NF A1C 3R1. ☎ **800/599-7829** or 709/739-7979. Fax 709/753-9411. E-mail: winterholme@nf.sympatico.ca. 11 units. TV TEL. C$99–C$179 (US$66–US$119). AE, DC, ER, MC, V.

This stout, handsome Victorian mansion was built in 1905 and is as architecturally distinctive a place as you'll find in Newfoundland, with prominent turrets, bowfront windows, bold pediments, elaborate molded plaster ceilings, and woodwork extravagant enough to stop you in your tracks. (The oak woodwork was actually carved in England and shipped here for installation.) Room 7 is one of the most lavish I've seen; the former billiards room features a fireplace and two-person Jacuzzi, along with a plasterwork ceiling and a supple leather wing chair. Room 1 is oval-shaped and occupies one of the turrets; it also has a Jacuzzi. The attic rooms are less extraordinary, but still appealing with their odd angles and nice touches. The mansion is located a 10-minute walk from downtown.

MODERATE

✪ **At Wit's Inn.** 3 Gower St. St. John's, NF A1C 1M9. ☎ **877/739-7420** or 709/739-7420. Fax 709/576-3641. E-mail: sleepongower@roadrunner.nf.net. 4 units. TV. C$79–C$99 (US$53–US$66) double, includes breakfast. AE, MC, V.

Forgive the innkeepers their pun. This lovely century-old home was wonderfully restored and opened as an inn in 1999 by a former Toronto restaurateur. It will appeal to anyone who loathes the "kountry klutter" found in establishments striving too hard for a personality. Decorated with sure eye for bold color and simple style, this is a welcoming urban oasis just around the corner from the Hotel Newfoundland. The rooms are not all that spacious, but neither are they too small, and each is nicely furnished with down duvets and VCRs. (The largest room is on the top floor, requiring a bit of a hike.) The beautifully refinished floors and elaborately carved banister are notable, as are many of the old fixtures (like the servant's intercom) that have been left in place. A full breakfast is served in the first floor dining room, wine and cheese are offered in the late afternoon, and there's a butler's pantry for snacking in between times. At Wit's Inn offers luxury touches at a relatively affordable price.

McCoubrey Manor. 8 Ordnance St., St. John's, NF A1C 3K7. ☎ **888/753-7577** or 709/722-7577. Fax 709/579-7577. www.wordplay.com/mccoubrey. E-mail: mccmanor@ nfld.com. 6 units. TV TEL. C$89–C$129 (US$59–US$86) double, including continental breakfast. AE, DC, MC, V.

McCoubrey Manor offers the convenient location of the Hotel Newfoundland (it's just across the street), but with Victorian charm and a more casual B&B atmosphere. The adjoining 1904 town houses are decorated in what might be called a "contemporary Victorian" style and are quite inviting. Upstairs rooms have private double Jacuzzis; Room 1 is brightest, and faces the street. Room 2 has a sunken Jacuzzi, an oak mantled fireplace, and lustrous trim of British Columbia fir. Just around the corner are two spacious two-bedroom apartments with full kitchens. What they lack in elegance they make up for in space; families take note. There's also a washer and dryer on the premises for guests (C$10 (US$7) extra to use it). Kids older than toddler age are welcome.

Prescott Inn. 19 Military Rd. (P.O. Box 204), St. John's, NF A1C 2C3. ☎ **709/753-7733.** Fax 709/753-6036. E-mail: jpeters@nfld.com. 16 units (7 share 3 bathrooms), plus 7 units at the Battery with kitchen and private bathrooms. TV TEL. C$50–C$105 (US$33–US$70) double, including full breakfast. AE, DC, MC, V. Pets allowed.

The Prescott Inn is composed of an unusually attractive grouping of wood-frame town houses painted a vibrant lavender-blue. Some of the historical detailing has been restored inside, but mostly the homes have been modernized. Some rooms have carpeting; others have hardwood floors. All are furnished with eclectic antiques that rise above flea-market quality but aren't quite collectibles. The lower-priced rooms share washrooms and are among the city's better bargains. All guests are welcome to relax on the shared balcony that runs along the back of the building. Room 3 might be the best of the bunch, and it is the only guest room with a private Jacuzzi. If you want a room with one of the best views in the city, ask about the Battery, a scenic village-like neighborhood perched precariously over the harbor a short drive away. The Battery units all have private baths and kitchens.

Quality Hotel. 2 Hill O'Chips, St. John's, NF A1C 6B1. ☎ **800/228-5151** or 709/754-7788. 162 units. A/C TV TEL. C$90–C$130 (US$60–US$87). AE, DC, DISC, ER, MC, V.

Courteous service and a great downtown location are among the merits of this modern chain hotel, situated just down the hill from the Hotel Newfoundland. The rooms are standard-sized but comfortable and clean; they're set apart mainly by their views—ask for one overlooking the Narrows. You can walk to downtown restaurants and attractions within a few minutes. The Battery and Signal Hill are a pleasant hike in the other direction. There's free covered parking beneath the hotel, and a better-than-average restaurant serving three meals daily on the premises.

INEXPENSIVE

Monkstown Manor. 51 Monkstown Rd., St. John's, NF A1C 3T4. ☎ **888/754-7377** or 709/754-7324. Fax 709/722-8557. www.pigeoninlet.nfnet.com. E-mail: krussel@ pigeoninlet.nfnet.com. 4 units (all share 2 bathrooms) plus 2 housekeeping units (private bathrooms). C$65–C$75 (US$43–US$50) double, including continental breakfast. AE, MC, V. Street parking. Pets allowed in housekeeping units.

A stay here is like a visit with old college friends. This narrow Victorian home, a short drive or moderate walk from downtown, is run with an infectious congeniality; at times it feels more like a dormitory than an inn. More likely than not people will be playing music on the ground floor or chatting at length about bands they saw the night before. (The owners are very musical, and they run a production company that specializes in Newfoundland folk music.) The rooms in the main house have buttery wooden floors and funky decorating; the units with small kitchens are a couple doors away. The two shared baths in the main house have Jacuzzis, so at times you might have to wait your turn.

WHERE TO DINE

Budget travelers should wander up the city's hillside to the intersection of LaMarchant and Freshwater Streets. Within a 2-block radius, you'll find numerous options for cheap eats at both eat-in and take-out establishments. A local favorite is **Ches's Fish and Chips,** 8 Freshwater Rd. (☎ 709/722-4083), which has been serving up pleasingly unhealthy portions of fried food, chicken wings, and burgers at this location since 1958. Ches's will also deliver; call ☎ 709/726-3434.

For the strongest coffee in town, head to **HavaJava** at 216 Water St. (☎ 709/753-5282).

EXPENSIVE

The Cellar. Baird's Cove (near waterfront, just downhill from Supreme Court building). ☎ **709/579-8900.** Reservations encouraged. Main courses: lunch C$8–C$15 (US$5–US$10), dinner C$15–C$29 (US$10–US$19). AE, DC, DISC, ER, MC, V. Mon–Fri 11:30am–2:30pm and 5:30–9:30pm (until 10:30pm Fri), Sat 5:30–10:30pm, Sun 5:30–9:30pm. ECLECTIC.

The classy interior is a surprise here—the restaurant is located on a nondescript street and through a nondescript entrance. Inside, it's intimate and warm, not unlike an upper-crust gentleman's club. The kitchen has been turning out fine meals for some time now, developing a reputation for creativity and consistency. The menu is constantly in play, but look for reliable standbys like the delicious gravlax, and the homemade bread and pastas. Fish is prepared especially well, and some cuts are paired with innovative flavors like ginger and pear butter. Lunches are the better bargain, featuring tasty offerings like baked brie in phyllo with red currant and pineapple chutney, or scallop crepes with bacon, leeks, and Swiss cheese.

✪ **Northgale.** 8 Kenna's Hill. ☎ **709/753-2425.** Reservations suggested. Main courses: lunch C$9–C$18 (US6–US$12), dinner C$18–C$29 (US$12–US$19). AE, ER, MC, V. Mon–Fri 11:30am–2pm, daily 5:30–10pm. Drive north on King's Bridge Rd. to Kenna's Hill. HAUTE NEWFOUNDLAND.

The Northgale was known for years as the Stone House restaurant before undergoing a recent ownership and name change. Longtime fans fretted, but ultimately most were pleased that the creative menu and even some of attentive waitstaff have remained unchanged, and the restaurant continues to serve up some of the best meals in Newfoundland. The focus is on local fare, with dishes like wild game and seafood prominent on the menu. You might start with cod au gratin or onion soup with cognac and camembert croutons, but leave room for the generous main courses, such as lamb with garlic sauce, grilled salmon with dill sauce, or Labrador partridge with partridge-berries. Caribou and moose appear as specialties from time to time, when high-quality meat is available. The setting is wonderful, in an 1834 stone house with walls 3 feet thick. Quidi Vidi Lake is a short walk away, offering a perfect spot for a postprandial stroll.

MODERATE

Casa Grande. 108 Duckworth. ☎ **709/753-6108.** Reservations helpful. Main courses: lunch C$7–C$8.95 (US$5–US$6), dinner C$10–C$16 (US$7–US$11). AE, DC, ER, MC, V. Mon–Fri 11:30am–2:30pm and 5–10pm (until 11pm Fri), Sat 5–11pm, Sun 5–9pm. MEXICAN.

If you've developed Mexican-food withdrawal after all those outport meals of fried fish, plan to satisfy your cravings here—you won't find better Mexican food in Newfoundland, and you'd be hard-pressed to find better elsewhere in Atlantic Canada. Seating is on two floors of a narrow storefront just down the hill from the Hotel Newfoundland. Angle for the front room of the upper level, where you'll get views of the harbor. It's often crowded and the service can be irksome; but come prepared for a wait and you'll get excellent value for your money. All the dishes are well prepared; the chile relleno has developed something of a cult following.

Classic Café. 364 Duckworth. ☎ **709/722-4083.** Reservations not necessary. Main courses, breakfast, and lunch C$4–C$11 (US$3–US$7), dinner C$8–C$17 (US$5–US$11). DC, ER, MC, V. Daily 24 hours. CANADIAN.

This come-as-you-are spot is appropriately named—it's truly classic St. John's, and everyone seems to drop in here at one time or another. There's a quiet, more sedate dining room upstairs in this 1894 hillside home. But the real action is in the crowded street-level bistro. Breakfast is served 24 hours a day—but don't expect a limp croissant and tea. Macho breakfasts (for example, a sirloin with eggs, toast, home fries, and baked beans) appeal to a mixed group, from burly longshoremen to hungover musicians. Non-breakfast entrees in the evening are equally generous and often surprisingly good.

Stella's. 106 Water St. ☎ **709/753-9625.** Reservations suggested. Main courses: lunch C$4–C$9 (US$3–US$6), dinner C$11–C$14 (US$7–US$9). MC, V. Tues–Fri noon–3pm, Wed 6–9pm, Thurs–Fri 6–10pm, Sat noon–10pm. NATURAL/WHOLE FOODS.

This is *the* destination for those pining away for an oversized plate of fresh greens after too much time in the canned-vegetable hinterlands. The cozy restaurant on Water Street is often hectic and the service can be strained, but the food is consistently impressive. Among your choices: pan-fried cod, chicken burrito, curried scallops, Thai veggie stir-fry, and Oriental almond tofu. There's no soda, but a good selection of wonderful homemade concoctions, including a milk shake and "bogwater"—a mix of carrot, ginger, and celery juices—will quench your thirst. The partridgeberry milk shake is also a winner.

Zachary's. 71 Duckworth (across from Hotel Newfoundland). ☎ **709/579-8050.** Reservations encouraged. Main courses: breakfast C$3.29–C$7.49 (US$2.19–US$4.99), lunch C$5.49–C$8.99 (US$3.66–US$5.99), dinner C$8.99–C$19.99 (US$5.99–US$13.33). AE, ER, MC, V. Daily 8am–10pm. TRADITIONAL.

This informal spot with wood-slat booths offers a slew of Newfoundland favorites, like fish cakes, fried bologna, and toutons—and that's just for breakfast. Dinners emphasize seafood—entrees include grilled salmon, seafood fettuccine, and pan-fried cod—but you'll also find steaks and chicken. Desserts are all homemade; especially tempting are the cheesecake, carrot cake, and date squares. You'll find more inventive spots for dinner, but you probably won't do better for reliable quality if you're on a tight budget. Breakfasts are outstanding and are served all day.

INEXPENSIVE

International Flavors. 124 Duckworth St. ☎ **709/738-4636.** Reservations not necessary. Dinner plates C$6.89 (US$4.59). V. Mon–Sat 11am–5:30pm (often later). Closed Sunday. INDIAN.

This is my favorite cheap meal in St. John's. This storefront restaurant has just five tables, and all the dinners are priced at C$6.89 (US$4.59), which includes a decent mound of food. You'll usually have a choice of four or so dishes. Smart money gets the basic curry. Also recommended is the very satisfying mango milk shake.

ST. JOHN'S AFTER DARK

The nightlife in St. John's is extraordinarily vibrant, and you'd be doing yourself an injustice if you didn't spend at least one evening on a pub crawl.

The first stop for a little local music and cordial imbibing should be **George Street,** which runs for several blocks near New Gower and Water Streets, close to City Hall. Every St. John's resident confidently asserts that George Street is home to more bars per square foot than anywhere else on the planet. I have been unable to track down a global authority that verifies pubs-per-square-foot, but a walk down the street did little to rebut their claims.

George Street is packed with energetic pubs and lounges, some fueled by beer, others by testosterone, still more by lively Celtic fiddling. The best strategy for selecting a pub is a slow ramble around 10pm or later, vectoring in to spots with appealing music wafting from the door. At places with live music, cover charges are universally very nominal and rarely top C$5 (US$3).

To get started: If you're looking for good local folk music, arrive early to get seats at the **Blarney Stone** (George Street, ☎ 709/754-1798), which puts on few airs and features wonderful Newfoundland and Irish folk music. **Trapper John's** (2 George St., ☎ 709/579-9630) is also known for outstanding provincial folk music, but it tries a bit harder for that Ye Olde Newfoundland character. This is a traditional "screeching in" spot for visitors (this involves cheap Newfoundland rum and some embarrassment).

For blues, there's the lively **Fat Cat** (5 George St., ☎ 709/722-6409). For a more upscale spot with lower decibel levels, try **Christian's Bar** (23 George St., ☎ 709/753-9100), which offers the nonalcoholic option of specialty coffees.

If George Street's beery atmosphere reminds you of those nights in college you'd just as soon forget, a few blocks away are two pubs tucked down tiny alleys known for their genial public-house atmospheres. The **Duke of Duckworth** (325 Duckworth St., ☎ 709/739-6344) specializes in draft beers and pub lunches. **The Ship Inn** (265 Duckworth St., ☎ 709/753-3870) is a St. John's mainstay, featuring a variety of local musical acts that seem to complement rather than overwhelm the pub's cozy atmosphere.

11 The Southern Avalon Peninsula

The Avalon Peninsula—or just "The Avalon," as it's commonly called—is home to some of Newfoundland's most memorable and dramatic scenery, including high coastal cliffs and endless bogs. More good news: It's also relatively compact and manageable, and it can be viewed on long day trips from St. John's, or in a couple of days of scenic poking around. It's a good destination for anyone who's short on time, yet wants to get a taste of the wild. The area is especially notable for its bird colonies, as well as its herd of wild caribou. The bad news? It's out in the sea where cold and warm currents collide, resulting in legendary fogs and blustery, moist weather. Bring a rain suit and come prepared for bone-numbing dampness.

While snooping about, also listen for the distinctive Irish-influenced brogue of the residents. You'll find no more vivid testimony to the settlement of the region by Irish pioneers.

ESSENTIALS

GETTING THERE   Several well-marked, well-maintained highways follow the coast of the southern Avalon Peninsula; few roads cross the damp and spongy interior. A map is essential.

VISITOR INFORMATION   Your best bet is to stop in the St. John's tourist bureaus (see above) or at the well-marked tourist bureau just up the hill from the Argentia ferry before you begin your travels. Witless Bay has a tourist information booth at the edge of the cobblestone beach and is stocked with a handful of brochures. It's open irregularly.

WITLESS BAY ECOLOGICAL RESERVE

The Witless Bay area, about 35 kilometers (21 miles) south of St. John's, makes an easy day trip from the city, or can serve as a launching point for an exploration of the Avalon Peninsula. The main attraction here is the ✪ **Witless Bay Ecological Reserve** (☎ 709/729-2424), comprising four islands and the waters around them, and located a short boat ride offshore. Literally millions of seabirds nest and fish here, and it's a spectacle even if you're not a bird watcher.

On the islands you'll find the **largest puffin colony in the western Atlantic Ocean,** with some 60,000 puffins burrowing into the grassy slopes above the cliffs, and awkwardly launching themselves from the high rocks. The tour boats are able to edge right along the shores, about 20 or 25 feet away, allowing puffin watching on even foggy days. Also on the islands is North America's second-largest murre colony

While the islands are publicly owned and managed, access is via privately operated tour boat, several of which you'll find headquartered along Route 10 in Bay Bulls and Bauline East. It's worth shopping around since prices can vary considerably.

Bay Bulls is the closest town to St. John's, and is home to three of the more popular tours: **Mullowney's,** ☎ 877/783-3467; **O'Brien's,** ☎ 877/639-4253; and **Gatherall's,** ☎ 800/419-4253. Two-and-a-half hour tours from here range between C$32 (US$21) and C$39 (US$26) per adult.

Captain Murphy's Seabird & Whale Tours (☎ 709/334-2002) is based in Witless Bay, a bit further south, and offers several trips daily; tours last 2 to 2½ hours and cost C$30 (US$20) per adult, C$20 (US$13) teens, and C$15 (US$10) children.

Budget travelers would do well to continue further south to Bauline East, where the 30-foot *Molly Bawn* (☎ 709/334-2621) offers 1¼-hour tours in search of puffins, whales, and icebergs. Tours depart every hour and a half during peak season; the cost is C$15 (US$10) adult, C$10 (US$7) children under 12.

A quieter and more intimate way to explore the area is to sign up for a 3-hour tour with **Bay Bulls Sea Kayaking Tours** (☎ 709/334-3394). You'll kayak along the bay's shores, visit sea caves and small beaches, and possibly spot puffins and whales visiting the bay. The price is C$45 (US$30) per person.

LAMANCHE PROVINCIAL PARK

LaManche means "the sleeve" in French, and the area is so named because of the long, narrow cove found here. This well-protected site was settled in 1840. Around 50 people still occupied homes on the steep hillsides flanking the cove as late as 1966, when a powerful storm all but destroyed the village. The occupants resettled elsewhere, leaving the remote village to be reclaimed by the elements.

Hikers can today follow a 30-minute pathway to the village's coveside site, which is both melancholy and beautiful. Stone and concrete foundations can be found amid the grass and weeds. Towering gray-black cliffs rise above the cove, where a river gorge meets the sea. It's a perfect place for an afternoon of nothing.

The park is well marked on Route 10, about 53 kilometers (32 miles) south of St. John's. Admission is free. The hike to the cove departs from the campground's fire exit road.

FERRYLAND

Historic Ferryland is among the most picturesque of the Avalon villages, set at the foot of rocky hills on a harbor protected by a series of abrupt islands at its mouth.

Ferryland was among the first permanent settlements in Newfoundland. In 1621, the **Colony of Avalon** was established here by Sir George Calvert, First Baron of Baltimore (he was also behind the settlement of Baltimore, Maryland). Calvert sunk the equivalent of C$4 million into the colony, which featured luxe touches like cobblestone roads, slate roofs, and fine ceramics and glassware from Europe. So up-to-date was the colony that privies featured drains leading to the shore just below the high tide mark, making these the first flush toilets in North America. (Or so the locals insist.) Later the Dutch, and then the French, sacked the colony during ongoing squabbles over territory, and eventually it was abandoned.

Recent excavations have revealed much about life here nearly 4 centuries ago. Visit the **Colony of Avalon Interpretation Centre** (☎ **877/326-5669** or 709/432-3200) with its numerous glass-topped drawers filled with engrossing artifacts, and then ask for a tour of the six archaeological sites currently being excavated (the tour is included in the cost of admission). Other interpretive exhibits include a reproduction of a 17th-century kitchen, and three gardens of the sort you might have overseen had you lived 400 years ago. After your tour, take a walk to the lighthouse at the point (about 1 hour round-trip), where you can scan for whales and icebergs. Ask for directions at the museum.

The site is open daily mid-June to mid-October; admission is C$3 (US$2) adult, C$2.50 (US$1.65) seniors, C$2 (US$1.35) students, and C$6 (US$4) family.

WHERE TO STAY & DINE

The Downs Inn. Route 10, Ferryland, NF A0A 2H0. ☎ **709/432-2808.** Fax 709/432-2659. E-mail: acostello@nf.sympatico.ca. 4 units (2 share 1 bathroom). C$55 (US$37) double. V.

This attractive building overlooking the harbor served as a convent between 1914 and 1986, when it was converted to an inn. The furnishings reflect its heritage as an institution rather than a historic building—there's dated carpeting and old linoleum, and the furniture is uninspired. (Much of the religious statuary was left in place—a nice touch.) Ask for one of the two front rooms, where you can watch for whales from your windows.

Dining: The front parlor has been converted to a tea room, where you can order a nice pot of tea and a light snack, like carrot cake or a rhubarb tart. Some sandwiches are available. Innkeeper Aidan Costello also operates **Southern Shore Eco Adventures** and can create custom tour packages for kayaking, hiking, or whale watching.

AVALON WILDERNESS RESERVE

Where there's bog, there's caribou. Or at least that's true in the southern part of the peninsula, which is home to the island's largest caribou herd, numbering some 13,000.

You'll see signs warning you to watch for caribou along the roadway; the landscape hereabout is so misty and primeval, though, that you might feel you should also watch for druids in robes with tall walking staffs.

The caribou roam freely throughout the 1,700-square-kilometer reserve, so it's largely a matter of happenstance to find them. Your best bet is to scan the high upland barrens along Route 10 between Trepassey and Peter's River (an area that's actually out of the reserve). Check with the **Provincial Parks Division** (☎ 709/729-2421) in St. John's for more information.

On Route 90 between St. Catherines and Hollyrood is the **Salmonier Nature Park** (☎ 709/729-6974), where you're certain to see caribou—along with other wildlife— if you can't find the herd on the reserve. This intriguing and well-designed park is fundamentally a 2½-kilometer nature trail, almost entirely on boardwalk, which tracks through bog and forest, and along streams and ponds. Along the route are more than a dozen unobtrusive pens, in which orphaned or injured wildlife can be observed. (It's the only such facility in the province.) Among the animals represented: arctic fox, snowy owl, moose, bald eagle, mink, otter, beaver, and lynx. It's located 11 kilometers (6.8 miles) south of the Trans-Canada Highway; admission is free. Gates are open in summer daily 10am to 5pm, and all visitors must depart by 6pm. Closed mid-October to June 1.

WHERE TO STAY & DINE

Trelawny Retreat Home. Route 91, Colinet, NF A0B 1M0. ☎ **709/521-2498,** off-season 709/596-6272. 4 units. C$65 (US$43) double, including full breakfast. V.

This tidy guest house overlooks one of the inlets to St. Mary's Bay. It's smack in the tiny village of Colinet, west of the wilderness reserve and well-situated for exploring the Avalon Peninsula. (Colinet is about an hour from St. John's, and 40 minutes from Cape St. Mary's.) It's built around an older home, but guests stay in a new, bright addition in the rear. The public rooms are spacious and elegantly furnished with an eclectic mix of antiques, including Victorian, Asian, and art nouveau. The guest rooms vary in size and one has its bathroom down the hall; the rooms upstairs have twin beds.

Trepassey Motel and Restaurant. Route 10, Trepassey, NF A0A 4B0. ☎ **709/438-2934.** Fax 709/438-2179. 10 units. TV. C$59 (US$39) double. MC, V.

Trepassey is an unvarnished fishing village of 1,200 south of the reserve and near Newfoundland's southernmost tip. The 10 rooms are clean and basic, arrayed along a single hallway that connects to the restaurant. The specialty is cod tongues, but you can find a variety of other basic dishes like pork chops, turkey, and roast beef. Most everything is under C$12 (US$8). At breakfast, try a partridgeberry muffin.

CAPE ST. MARY'S

The Cape St. Mary's Ecological Reserve ranks high on my list of favorite places on Newfoundland. Granted, it's off the beaten track—some 100 kilometers (60 miles) from the Trans-Canada Highway—but it's worth every kilometer. A couple of notes about the surrounding area: the terrain in this southwest part of the Avalon is unique—mostly open barrens covering low, rolling hills. At times along Route 92 between North Harbour and St. Bride's, even a moderately persuasive person might convince you that you were in Oklahoma.

Also, the 46-kilometer (28.5-mile) drive along Route 100 between St. Brides and Placentia is like a mini-Cabot Trail, the noted Cape Breton drive. The road climbs to open headlands, then swoops down to river valleys and through small villages. At every turn another extraordinary view of Placentia Bay unfolds. If you're arriving via

Argentia ferry, the drive south is a suburban introduction to Newfoundland. Save your favorite tape or CD for the ride (Wagner's "March of the Valkyries" would not be a bad choice), and play it loud.

❍ Cape St. Mary's Ecological Reserve. Off Route 100 (5km/3 miles east of St. Bride's). ☎ **709/729-2424.** Trail to bird island is free; admission to interpretive center C$3 (US$2) adult, C$1 (US65¢) child, C$7 (US$5) family. Guided tours C$5 (US$3); includes admission to center). Mon, Wed, Fri 9am–7:30pm; Tues, Thurs, Sat 8am–7pm; Sun 9am–7pm. Closed Nov 1–April 30.

Cape St. Mary's is home to some 5,500 pairs of northern gannets—big, noisy, beautiful, graceful white birds with cappuccino-colored heads and black wing-tips. While they can be seen wintering off the coast of Florida and elsewhere to the south, they're seldom seen in such cacophonous number as here. Most are nesting literally on top of one another on a compact, 100-meter (300-foot) sea stack. At any given moment hundreds are flying above, around and below you, which is all the more impressive given their nearly 2-meter (6-foot) wingspan.

You needn't take a boat ride to see this colony. Start your visit at the visitor center, which offers a quick and intriguing introduction to the indigenous bird life. Then walk 15 minutes along a grassy cliff-top pathway—through harebell, iris, and dandelion—until you arrive at an unfenced cliff just a couple dozen yards from the sea stack (it's close enough to be impressive even in a dense fog). Also nesting on and around the island are 10,000 pairs of murre, 10,000 kittiwakes, and 100 razorbills. Note that the viewing area is not fenced, and peering down at the surging surf and hundreds of birds on the wing *below* is not recommended for acrophobes. Guided tours are offered twice daily (small extra charge), and are well worthwhile.

WHERE TO STAY & DINE

Atlantica Inn and Restaurant. Route 100, St. Bride's, NFG A0B 2Z0. ☎ **709/337-2860.** 5 units. TV TEL. C$40 (US$27) double. AE, ER, MC, V.

The Atlantic won't win points for charm—it's a basic, aluminum-sided box among some of the newer houses in the village. But it offers great value at the price, and the five rooms are well maintained and comfortable, if a bit small. The attached restaurant is by and large the only game in town, offering three inexpensive meals daily (dinner entrees are C$7/US$5 to C$13/US$9).

Bird Island Resort. Route 100, St. Bride's, NF A0B 2Z0. ☎ **709/337-2450.** Fax 709/337-2903. 20 units. TV. C$49–C$69 (US$33–US$46) double. AE, ER, MC, V.

This modern, unaffected motel is located behind Manning's food market, where you'll stop to ask for a room. It's the preferred spot in town, and offers some unexpected amenities, like a laundry room open to guests, a tiny fitness room, and a minigolf course (all rooms come with clubs and balls). The rooms vary in size. The double efficiency units feature a separate sitting room, and several of the rooms have kitchenettes, which come in handy given the dearth of restaurants in town. The rooms that get snapped up first are 1 through 5, and with good reason: they all have kitchenettes (some have two bedrooms) and all face the ocean, with great views (assuming the fog hasn't moved in).

PLACENTIA & ARGENTIA

Placentia was settled by the Spanish in 1662 along a cove that proved perfect as a summer fishing base. Although the town has grown and modernized, it remains small, and it requires little effort to imagine the place centuries ago, when the Spanish and better-equipped Basque fishermen grappled for fish and drying space during the short season.

It's especially easy to let your imagination go when viewing the town from **Castle Hill National Historic Park** (☎ 709/227-2401), just outside of town. This prominent hill overlooking the harbor was fortified variously by the French and English in the 17th and 18th centuries. The visitor center is expertly done, with historic maps and dioramas showing how the hilltop fortress once looked. Afterward, stroll to the summit to explore the fort's ruins and to take in the expansive views of town and sea. This is a great first stop if you're just arriving via ferry. You'll get historical background about European settlement, and learn plenty about the historical importance of the cod fisheries.

The site is open year-round; in summer, hours are daily 8am to 8pm. The grounds are free; viewing the exhibits in the visitor center costs C$2.50 (US$1.65) adult, C$2 (US$1.35) senior, C$1.50 (US$1) ages 6 to 16, C$6 (US$4) family.

The town of **Argentia,** a former military base, is on the far side of Castle Hill from Placentia. The **visitor information center** (☎ 709/227-5272) on Route 100 has an informative exhibit on how a historic fishing village was displaced by the base during World War II. An instant city of some 26,000 people occupied the land, which was used by U.S. forces until 1994. In the annals of the war, the region is remembered mostly for one significant event: U.S. President Franklin D. Roosevelt and British Prime Minister Winston Churchill met on a ship just offshore as part of the Atlantic Conference, in which they hammered out their goals for the end of the war. A monument commemorating this historic meeting is located at **Ship Harbor,** about 24 kilometers (15 miles) north of Dunville, which is east of Argentia.

The sprawling former military base is mostly shuttered and melancholy these days, the buildings lonely against the scrappy hills and with only a few souls to enjoy the heartbreakingly beautiful views of Placentia Sound. As part of the conversion to civilian use, the base authority recently established the **Backland Trail** (☎ 709/227-5502), which ascends wooded hills and passes bunkers, lookouts, and old radar sites. Ask for information on the trail at the visitor information center; the road to the trailhead departs from Route 100 just downhill from the center, which is open daily in summer 9am to 7pm (opens at 6am to greet the incoming ferry traffic 3 days per week).

12 Labrador

Labrador may be far removed and remote, but it has long played an outsized role in the collective consciousness of the region. For several centuries, this deeply indented coastline was noted for its robust fisheries, and itinerant fleets plied the waters both inshore and offshore, harvesting what the sea had to offer. The empty, melancholy landscape of rolling hills along the coasts and inland serves much the same function that the American West frontier played in the United States—it's both a land of opportunity stemming from the natural resources (primarily mining these days), and it's a place where outdoorspeople have historically tested their mettle in a harsh environment, stalking big game and big salmon.

Although sparsely settled, people have been part of the landscape for centuries. The Innu (American Indian) culture in Labrador goes back 8,000 years, and the Inuit (Eskimo) culture 4,000 years. The Vikings sighted Labrador in 986 but didn't come ashore until 1010. Traces of the Vikings remain in the shape of "fairy holes"—deep, cylindrical holes in the rocks, angled away from the sea, where they are thought to have tied their boats.

The 16th century brought Basque whalers, as many as 2,000 of them, and they returned to Europe with 20,000 barrels of whale oil in what might be one of the globe's first oil booms. It has been said that the whale oil of Newfoundland and Labrador was as valuable to the Europeans as the gold of South America. Vestiges of a whaling station remain on Saddle Island, off the coast of Red Bay on the Labrador Straits.

Next came the British and French fishermen, fur traders, and merchants, who first came here in summers to fish, hunt, and trade, and then established permanent settlements in the 1700s. Many of the Europeans married Innu and Inuit women, but conflicts between Inuit whalers and the European settlers along the south coast prompted the Inuit communities to move to the far north, where they remain today.

Only about 30,000 people live in Labrador: 13,000 in western Labrador, 8,000 in Happy Valley-Goose Bay, with the remaining residents spread along the coast. Approximately four-fifths of those born here will remain here, with strong ties to family and neighbors. These close-knit communities typically welcome visitors warmly.

Many visitors come here for the sportfishing of brook trout, Atlantic salmon, arctic char, lake trout, white fish, and northern pike. Others come for wilderness adventure, hiking, and camping under the undulating northern lights. Still others are simply curious about a remote part of the world.

Labrador has three basic destinations, if your definition of destination includes places to stay overnight and eat. (If you come with tent and supplies, the whole, howling landmass is your destination.) **Labrador West,** including Labrador City and Wabush, is reached by train from Sept-îles, Québec (pronounced "Set-*teel*") and via Route 389, also from Québec. **Central Labrador** includes the commercial and industrial hub centered around Happy Valley-Goose Bay. The **Labrador Straits,** easily accessible from the island of Newfoundland via ferry, offer small fishing villages and glimpses of the rich history at several sites.

The most scenic route to Labrador—and the only way to visit some of the outports—is by the coastal ferry along "Iceberg Alley." The Marine Atlantic ferry that serves the coast offers cabin accommodations as well as facilities for day passengers—and it's the only means of transportation along much of the Atlantic coast of Labrador. See "Getting There" under "Exploring Newfoundland & Labrador" at the beginning of this chapter for more information.

SPECIAL-INTEREST/ADVENTURE TOURS   Those considering a trip to Labrador would do well to consider a packaged adventure tour. The rough terrain, limited transportation, and paucity of visitor services enhances the appeal of letting someone familiar with the land do the planning.

Labrador is considered a world-class destination among anglers. Nearly 50 fishing camps are scattered throughout the region, and many can arrange floatplane access. The **Provincial Tourism Authority** (☎ 800/563-6353 or 709/944-7788) can provide a list of outfitters.

Several outfitters cater to the adventure traveler, and can arrange trips that match your interests and abilities. Larry Bradley and his **Break Away Adventures** offers several adventure travel packages. These range from a 14-day all-inclusive hiking expedition in northern Labrador (C$3,000/US$2,000), to a 5-day fly and hike expedition southeast of town (approximately C$1,500/US$1,000), and canoe excursions of 1 to 3 days or more. If you're planning your own trip, Bradley is a good person to speak with for ideas and suggestions. Well in advance of your trip, contact Break Away Adventures, P.O. Box 612, Stn. B, Happy Valley-Goose Bay, Labrador A0P 1E0, ☎ 709/ 896-9343, e-mail: lbradley@cancom.net.

THE LABRADOR STRAITS

The Labrador Straits are the easiest part of Labrador to explore from Newfoundland. The southeast corner of Labrador is served by ferries shuttling between St. Barbe, Newfoundland, and Blanc Sablon, Québec. (Blanc Sablon is on the Québec-Labrador border.) From Blanc Sablon, you can travel on the one and only road, which runs 80 kilometers (48 miles) northward, dead-ending at Red Bay. (Plans call for extending this road in the future, but it may be another decade.)

Ferries are timed such that you can cross over in the morning, drive to Red Bay, and still be back for the later ferry to Newfoundland. Such a hasty trip isn't recommended, however. Better to spend a night, when you'll have a chance to meet the people, who offer the most compelling reason to visit.

The **M/S _Northern Princess_** (☎ 709/931-2309 or 418/461-2056) runs from May 1 until ice season, usually sometime in early January. The crossing takes about 1 hour and 45 minutes, and reservations are encouraged in summer (half the ferry can be reserved; the other half is first-come, first-served). One-way fares are C$9 (US$6) adult, C$4.75 (US$3.15) children, C$18.50 (US$12.35) automobile.

The terrain along the Labrador Straits is rugged, and the colors muted except for a vibrant stretch of green along the Pinware River. The few small houses are clustered close together; during the winter it's nice to have neighbors so nearby. Homes are often brightened up with "yard art"—replicas of windmills, wells, and churches.

In summer, icebergs float by the coast, and whales breach and spout offshore. The landscape is covered with cotton grass, clover, partridgeberries, bakeapples, fireweed, buttercups, and bog laurel. The fog rolls in frequently; it will either stay a while or roll right back out again. The capelin come and go as well. The tiny migrating fish crash-land on the shore by the thousands during a week in late June or early July. Local residents crowd the beach to scoop up the fish and take them home for an easy supper.

The **Visitor Information Centre** (☎ 709/931-2013) in the small, restored **St. Andrews Church** in L'Anse au Clair, the first town after the ferry, is open from June to September. The tourist association has developed several footpaths and trails in the area, so be sure to ask about them; also ask about the "fairy holes." If you come in mid-August, plan to attend the annual **Bakeapple Festival,** celebrating the berry that stars in the desserts of Newfoundland and Labrador.

EXPLORING THE LABRADOR STRAITS

Drive the "slow road" that connects the villages of the Labrador Straits. Traveling southwest to northeast, here is some of what you'll find along the way.

In L'Anse au Clair, **Moore's Handicrafts,** 8 Country Rd., just off Route 510 (☎ 709/931-2022), sells handmade summer and winter coats, traditional cassocks, moccasins, knitted items, handmade jewelry, and other crafts, as well as homemade jams. They also do traditional embroidery on Labrador cassocks and coats, and if you stop on the way north and choose your design, they'll finish it by the time you return to the ferry—even the same day. Prices are quite reasonable. The shop is open daily in season 8am to 10pm.

The **Labrador Straits Crafts and Museum** (☎ 709/931-2067) is just outside **L'Anse-Amour** (pop. 25), 19 kilometers (12 miles) from L'Anse au Clair. Two exhibit rooms focus mainly on the role of women in the history of the Labrador coast. Also you see photographs of the pilots who flew the first nonstop east-to-west transatlantic flight; they flew off course in April 1928 and landed on Greely Island, off the Labrador-Québec coast. The museum is open daily mid-July through mid-September; admission is C$2 (US$1.35) per adult.

The **Point Amour Lighthouse** (1858), at the western entrance to the Strait of Belle Isle, is the tallest lighthouse in the Atlantic provinces and the second tallest in all of Canada. The walls of the slightly tapered, circular tower are 6½ feet thick at the base. You'll have to climb 122 steps for the view. The dioptric lens was imported from Europe for the princely sum of C$10,000. The lighthouse, which kept watch for submarines during World War II, is still in use and was maintained by a resident lightkeeper right up until 1995. It's open to the public June to mid-October from 10am to 5:30pm (☎ **709/927-5825**); the fee is C$2.50 (US$1.65), children under 12 free. The lighthouse is a 3.3-kilometer (2-mile) drive from the main road.

After you pass the fishing settlements of **L'Anse au Loup** ("Wolf's Cove") and **West St. Modeste,** the road follows the scenic Pinware River, where the trees become noticeably taller. Along this stretch of road, you'll see glacial erratics—those odd boulders deposited by the melting ice cap. **Pinware Provincial Park,** 43 kilometers (26 miles) from L'Anse au Clair, has a picnic area, hiking trails, and 15 campsites. The 50-mile-long Pinware River is known for salmon fishing.

The highway ends in Red Bay. The **Red Bay National Historic Site Visitor Centre** (☎ **709/920-2197**) showcases artifacts from the late 1500s, when Basque whalers came in number to hunt the right and bowhead whales. Starting in 1977, excavations turned up whaling implements, pottery, glassware, and even partially preserved seamen's clothing. From here you can also arrange tours of **Saddle Island,** the home of Basque whaling stations in the 16th century. Transportation to archaeological sites on the island is available in summer Monday through Saturday from 9am to 4pm. You can also opt to view Saddle Island from the observation level on the third floor. Admission is C$5 (US$3) adult, C$3.75 (US$2.50) senior, C$2.75 (US$1.85) ages 6 to 16, C$10 (US$7) family. The site is open 9am to 6:30pm during the mid-summer months, 10am to 6pm during the early summer and fall. Closed mid-October to mid-June.

WHERE TO STAY

Beachside Hospitality Home. 9 Lodge Rd., L'Anse au Clair, Labrador, A0K 3K0. ☎ **800/563-8999** or 709/931-2662. 6 units (all with shared bathroom). C$38–C$45 (US$25–US$30) double. MC, V.

A stay here offers an excellent opportunity to meet a local family and learn firsthand about life in this region of Labrador. Three bedrooms have a separate entrance, and all share two full baths. There is a whirlpool bath, and guests have access to a telephone. Home-cooked meals are available by arrangement, or you can cook for yourself in the kitchen or outdoors on the grill.

Grenfell Louie A. Hall. 3 Willow Ave. (P.O. Box 137), Forteau, Labrador, A0K 2P0. ☎ **709/931-2916.** 5 units (all share 2 bathrooms). C$45 (US$30) double. V.

History buffs love the Grenfell Hall—it was built in 1946 by the International Grenfell Association as a nursing station, and there's plenty of reading material about the coast's early days. The rooms are furnished with basic, contemporary-country furniture, and there's a common room with TV, VCR, and fireplace. The innkeepers can arrange to transport you to and from the ferry. (If you're just curious about the place, you're invited to stop in for C$3/US$2 per person or C$5/US$3 per couple.) Meals are available by advance arrangement, and usually feature seafood (typically cod or salmon) along with homemade bread, preserves, and dessert; the cost is C$15 to C$20 (US$10 to US$13) for the three-course meal.

Lighthouse Cove B&B. L'Anse-Amour, Labrador A0K 3J0. ☎ **709/927-5690.** 3 units share 2½ bathrooms. C$40 (US$27) double, including continental breakfast. MC, V.

Hosts Cecil and Rita Davis have lived in this simple home, overlooking rocks, water, and beach, for more than 4 decades, so they can tell you much about the region. A light breakfast is included in the room rate; full breakfast and seafood supper are available on request, with dinners costing C$12 (US$8) extra. From the house you can walk along a footpath to Point Amour Lighthouse.

Northern Light Inn. L'Anse au Clair, Labrador, A0K 3K0. ☎ **800/563-3188** (from Atlantic Canada) or 709/931-2332. Fax 709/931-2708. 59 units (includes 5 suites and 5 housekeeping units). TV TEL. C$70–C$120 (US$47–US$80) double. AE, DC, ER, MC, V.

The largest and most modern hotel in the region (it added 28 rooms in 1998), the Northern Light Inn offers comfortable, well-maintained rooms, a gift shop, a friendly staff, and a dining room. The restaurant, open from 8am to 11pm, serves soups, sandwiches, baskets of scallops, fried chicken, and pizza from C$2 to C$9 (US$1 to US$6). In the adjacent Basque Dining Room, seafood is the specialty, with prices ranging from C$2 to C$5 (US$1 to US$3) for appetizers and C$11 to C$14 (US$7 to US$9) for main courses. The coffee shop doubles as a lounge in the evening.

WHERE TO DINE

Seaview Restaurant. 35 Main St., Forteau. ☎ **709/931-2840.** Most items C$2–C$13 (US$1.35–US$8.65). AE, MC, V. Summer daily 9am–11:30pm; rest of year Mon–Sat 9am–11:30pm, Sun noon–10pm. HOME COOKING.

This family-style restaurant in Forteau, 8 miles northeast of L'Anse au Clair, offers eat-in or take-out meals. Seafood dishes are the specialty; the seafood basket is particularly popular. There's an adjacent grocery store and bakery, where you can buy homemade bread, peanut-butter cookies, and much more. The same management has 8 basic motel rooms, with television and telephone jacks (C$65/US$43 double).

LABRADOR WEST

The most affluent and industrialized part of Labrador, Labrador West lies on the Québec border and is home to the twin towns of **Wabush** and **Labrador City,** 7 kilometers (4 miles) apart. The two towns share many attractions, activities, and services. This region offers top-notch cross-country skiing and has hosted two World Cup events. Labrador West is also home to the largest open-pit iron ore mine in North America, which produces almost half of Canada's ore. Exhibits on local history are open for view at the **Height of Land Heritage Centre,** 1750 Bartlett Dr., ☎ **709/944-2284,** which is in the city's first bank and post office; it's open daily and is free.

Labrador City or Wabush make a good base for hiking, canoeing, and birding trips. Ask for directions to **Crystal Falls,** where a half-mile hike takes you to the falls and a view over the city. You can also play 18 holes at the **Tamarack Golf Course,** or go windsurfing, scuba diving, or sailing on one of the many surrounding lakes. And, in the winter, go cross-country skiing at **Meniheck Nordic Ski Club** (☎ **709/944-6339**), a complete ski center with 40 kilometers (24 miles) of groomed trails for all skill levels.

The annual **Labrador 400 Sled Dog Race,** held here in March, draws about 25 teams from Canada and the United States, who match skills on 400 miles of challenging terrain.

Labrador City is the terminus of the **Québec North Shore and Labrador Railway** (the QNS&L), which departs from Sept-Îles, Québec, and is the only passenger train service in the entire province of Newfoundland and Labrador. The 8- to 10-hour trip covers 260 miles, across 19 bridges, through 11 tunnels, along riverbanks, through forests, and past rapids, mountains, and waterfalls, and finally through subarctic vegetation. In summer a highlight is the **vintage dome car** (1958) with sofa seats that was once part of the Wabash Cannonball (☎ **418/968-7805** in Québec; 709/944-8205 in Newfoundland and Labrador).

For more information about activities in the area, contact **Labrador West Tourism Development Corporation** (☎ **709/282-3337**).

CENTRAL LABRADOR

From the North West River and Mud Lake to the Mealy Mountains, a visit to the interior of Labrador will bring you deep into a land of lakes, rivers, and spruce forests, where the horizon looks the same in every direction. Many believe that the Lake Melville area is "Markland, the land of forests" in the Viking sagas.

Outdoor activities include berry picking from August to the first snowfall of November, excellent sportfishing, canoeing the famed **Churchill River,** kayaking the rapid-filled **Kenamou River,** and snowmobiling. Look for the *Them Days* quarterly magazine (☎ **709/896-8531**), which chronicles the stories and memories of Labrador's people, published in Happy Valley-Goose Bay and sold virtually everywhere.

Three displays of local history are exhibited at the local mall, the **Northern Lights Building** (☎ **709/896-5939**) at 170 Hamilton River Rd. You'll see examples of regional animals in the displays, including black bear, wolf, fox, lynx, otter, beaver, bald eagle, loon, duck and the Canada goose. Also here are the **Military Museum** (uniforms, weapons, and other items from the Royal Newfoundland Regiment), and the **Newfie Bullet Model Railway** ("one of the largest collection of O Gauge Lionel toy trains on the east coast of Canada"). Admission to all exhibits is free; the building is open year-round.

In 1997, Labrador's first provincial museum was built in Happy Valley-Goose Bay. The **Labrador Interpretation Center,** Hillview Drive (☎ **709/896-0214**), is home to displays of some of Labrador's finest art.

To take a little bit of Labrador home with you, stop by **Labrador Crafts and Supplies,** 367 Hamilton River Rd. (☎ **709/896-8400**), in Happy Valley-Goose Bay. The largest crafts store in Labrador, it sells Innu tea dolls, grasswork, soapstone carvings, labradorite jewelry, hooked rugs, and parkas.

WHERE TO STAY

Convenient to the airport, TransLab Highway, and marine dock, the full-service **Labrador Inn** (☎ **800/563-2763** or 709/896-3351) has 74 rooms; doubles are C$75 to C$94 (US$50 to US$63), and a suite is C$150 (US$100). The restaurant serves traditional Canadian cuisine with some local dishes, including game meats and seafood.

THE NORTH COAST

In 1771, Moravian missionaries began to arrive on Labrador's North Coast, bringing with them prefabricated buildings from Germany, some of which are still standing. The **Hopedale Mission National Historic Site** (☎ **709/933-3777**) was built in 1782 and is the oldest wood-frame building east of Québec. It's located in the village of Hopedale, accessible via the ferry from Happy Valley-Goose Bay to Nain. Tours are by advance appointment only. In Nain, the **Piulimatsivik-Nain Museum** displays a fine collection of Moravian mission and Inuit artifacts housed in one of the mission buildings. The free museum is open by appointment year-round (☎ **709/922-2842**).

The Inuit live along the North Coast, largely in Makkovik, Rigolet, Hopedale, and Nain. They continue to fish, hunt, and carry on many aspects of their traditional culture. Skilled outdoor enthusiasts love the North Coast for hiking, sea kayaking, camping, and climbing in the Torngat Mountains.

Unless you have your own cruising boat or airplane, about the only way to explore the coast is aboard the ***Northern Ranger,*** a working supply vessel operated by provincial ferry services. The excursion from St. Anthony, Newfoundland, to Nain, Labrador—with numerous stops at tiny ports of call along the way—takes 12 days round-trip. The cabins are cozy but all have views; you'll eat your meals in the ship's cafeteria with the crew and local passengers. It's a unique way to experience what's arguably the last frontier left on the Atlantic seaboard.

Cruises start after ice-out in early July and run through October. They're not cheap. With a standard cabin the fare is C$2,700 (US$1,800) per person, or C$3,000 (US$2,000) for a deluxe cabin. That includes all meals and tours at various stops. Information requests and reservations are handled through the main Newfoundland provincial tourism number, ☎ **800/563-6353.**

Index

FROMMER'S® COMPLETE TRAVEL GUIDES

Frommer's® Dollar-a-Day Guides

Australia from $50 a Day
California from $60 a Day
Caribbean from $70 a Day
England from $70 a Day
Europe from $60 a Day
Florida from $60 a Day

Hawaii from $70 a Day
Ireland from $50 a Day
Israel from $45 a Day
Italy from $70 a Day
London from $85 a Day
New York from $80 a Day

New Zealand from $50 a Day
Paris from $85 a Day
San Francisco from $60 a Day
Washington, D.C.,
   from $60 a Day

Frommer's® Portable Guides

Acapulco, Ixtapa &
   Zihuatanejo
Alaska Cruises & Ports of Call
Bahamas
Baja & Los Cabos
Berlin
California Wine Country
Charleston & Savannah
Chicago

Dublin
Hawaii: The Big Island
Las Vegas
London
Maine Coast
Maui
New Orleans
New York City
Paris

Puerto Vallarta, Manzanillo
   & Guadalajara
San Diego
San Francisco
Sydney
Tampa & St. Petersburg
Venice
Washington, D.C.

Frommer's® National Park Guides

Family Vacations in the
   National Parks
Grand Canyon

National Parks of the
   American West
Rocky Mountain

Yellowstone & Grand Teton
Yosemite & Sequoia/
   Kings Canyon
Zion & Bryce Canyon

Frommer's® Great Outdoor Guides

New England
Northern California

Southern California & Baja
Washington & Oregon

Frommer's® Memorable Walks

Chicago
London

New York
Paris

San Francisco
Washington D.C.

Frommer's® Irreverent Guides

Amsterdam
Boston
Chicago
Las Vegas

London
Los Angeles
Manhattan

New Orleans
Paris
San Francisco

Seattle & Portland
Vancouver
Walt Disney World
Washington, D.C.

Frommer's® Best-Loved Driving Tours

America
Britain
California

Florida
France
Germany

Ireland
Italy
New England

Scotland
Spain
Western Europe

THE UNOFFICIAL GUIDES®

SPECIAL-INTEREST TITLES